Detroit Monographs in Musicology/Studies in Music, No. 54

Editor
Susan Parisi
University of Illinois

Joseph Misliweczek

Josef Mysliveček, "Il Boemo"

The Man and His Music

By Daniel E. Freeman

Harmonie Park Press Sterling Heights, Michigan 2009

Cover and frontispiece:

Josef Mysliveček

Engraving by Anton Niederhofer from Frantisek Martin Pelcl's *Abbildungen böhmischen und mährischen Gelehrter und Künstler*, vol. 4 (Prague, 1782)

Printed and bound in the United States of America
Published by
Harmonie Park Press
Liberty Professional Center
35675 Mound Road
Sterling Heights, Michigan 48310-4727
www.harmonieparkpress.com

Publications Director, Elaine Gorzelski
Editor, Susan Parisi
Cover design, Mitchell Groters
Book design and Typographer, Colleen McRorie

Library of Congress Cataloging-in-Publication Data

Freeman, Daniel E.
Josef Mysliveček, "Il boemo": the man and his music / by Daniel E. Freeman.
p. cm. — (Detroit monographs in musicology/studies in music ; no. 54)
Includes bibliographical references and index.
ISBN 0-89990-148-4 (978-0-89990-148-0 : alk. paper)
1. Mysliveček, Josef, 1737-1781. 2. Composers—Czech Republic—Biography. 3. Music—Czech Republic—18th century—History and criticism. I. Title.

ML410.M99F74 2009
780.92—dc22
[B]

2009022828

For Ruth Lillian Brummond
and in memory of
Michael Ross Anderson

Contents

Illustrations

Figures

Music Examples

Examples

Examples

Examples

Acknowledgments

The author gratefully acknowledges the assistance of the American Council of Learned Societies and the International Research and Exchanges Board (IREX) in providing the travel funding that enabled the examination of Mysliveček documents and related holdings in various European libraries and archives, in particular the extensive collections in Prague. Any expression of thanks to IREX should also include recognition of the generosity of three agencies of the United States government that help to subsidize the IREX research grants: the United States Information Agency, the United States Department of State, and the National Endowment for the Humanities. In applying for funding I was gratified to have the support of three distinguished music scholars—Michael Beckerman, Robert L. Marshall, and John Walter Hill—and I wish to record here my deep appreciation for their help.

Many dedicated scholars and librarians aided the successful completion of this volume. Among the musicologists who provided valuable information and shared ideas with me, I would like especially to single out Christian Moritz-Bauer, Karl Böhmer, Harrison James Wignall, James A. Ackerman, and Anelide Nascimbene. I am also grateful for insights and bibliographical tips received from Stanislav Bohadlo, John A. Rice, Robert Münster, Wolf-Dieter Seiffert, and Bathia Churgin, as well as for some excellent suggestions on writing style from Herbert Kellman and Martin Anderson. The encouragement of all of these individuals was a valued source of strength to me during the preparation of the manuscript. A number of research institutions critical to the subject matter at hand extended very helpful service to me, especially the library of the Ajuda Palace in Lisbon, the České Muzeum Hudby in Prague, and the music department of the Bibliothèque Nationale de France, whose director, Catherine Massip, kindly supplied me with detailed documentation that made it possible to resolve several difficult problems regarding source materials. No less helpful was the staff of the RISM central office in Frankfurt-am-Main, in particular Christiane Albrecht. For assistance with two special topics, I am indebted to Gabriella McIntyre and Leo van de Pas. For her meticulous attention to the editing of the manuscript, I could have found no more sympathetic collaborator than Susan Parisi of Harmonie Park Press. The volume also benefited from the excellent work of typographer Colleen McRorie, whom I here thank, as I do also Mitchell Groters, who designed the cover. And I express profound thanks to Elaine Gorzelski, president of the Press, for her support of the project over many months.

The preparation of this volume coincided with many difficult episodes in my life, thus I wish to offer my heartfelt appreciation to friends who made the worst times much more bearable, especially those who made me laugh when I needed to most, and those who have offered steadfast encouragement in support of this research. These friends are L. Joseph LeBeau, John and Judie Lucchesi, Joan Gacki, Margaret Hanegraaf, Krista Feeney, Jean London, Connie Suchta, Carole Nimlos, Mary-Louise Clary, Johan Dirks, Inge Schwochau, Elizabeth Buschor, Mary McDiarmid, Scot Pearson, and Remigijus Klyvis. Finally, special thanks are in order for Bohumil and Helena Socha, who offered me warm hospitality and excellent lodging in Prague whenever I needed it.

Daniel E. Freeman

Minneapolis, March 2009

Josef Mysliveček, "Il Boemo"

The Man and His Music

Introduction

In the period of Mozart's youth, the most prolific composer of Italian *opera seria* and one of the most important symphonists was Josef Mysliveček (1737–81), an extraordinary Czech musician. His name, however, rarely earns more than passing mention in surveys of the history of opera and orchestral music. What is more, although he was regarded for several years both by Leopold and Wolfgang Mozart as an intimate friend, there has been little appraisal of Mysliveček's intriguing relationship with the Mozart family or of the use of his music as models for Wolfgang's compositions. Thus there is some irony in the fact that incidents from Mysliveček's adventurous life have provided enough material to sustain an opera[1] and several literary treatments,[2] not to mention multiple biographies,[3] including one published in the Soviet Union in 1964 under the dramatic title *Resurrection from the Dead*.[4]

Mysliveček's obscurity of course is not total. In the Czech Republic his music is well known even to ordinary music-lovers, even though his life in the West for the most part remains "forgotten history" (to use the title attached to the Czech translation of the above-mentioned biography[5]). Only a few peripheral details tend to be remembered by westerners, for example, the apocryphal nickname "il divino Boemo," Mysliveček's reputation for sexual promiscuity, and the loss of his nose after a botched operation to alleviate the effects of venereal disease. Still, the high quality of Mysliveček's music inevitably surprises western audiences offered the rare chance to sample it.

National biases have played an unfortunate role in creating this state of affairs. Had Mysliveček been born in Germany the modern-day revival of his reputation and works would likely have fared much better, as with his almost exact contemporary Johann Christian Bach. Bach's outlook and

---

[1] *Il divino Boemo* by Stanislav Suda (completed 1912, first performed 1927).

[2] Among these are the romanetto *Il divino Boemo* by Jakub Arbes (1884), which introduced Mysliveček's nickname "Il divino Boemo," and two novels: Carl von Pidoll, *Boemo divino* (Munich: Paul Hugendubel, 1943, also published as *Liebling der Götter* [Zurich: Stauffecher-Verlag, 1958]); and Soňa Špálová-Ramešová, *Il divino Boemo* (Prague: Nakladatelství lidova demokracie, 1958). A BBC radio play by Graham Fawcett, "Mozart's Bohemian Friend," first broadcast on 24 July 1988, is the only fictional treatment of Mysliveček's life that has appeared yet in English.

[3] The biographies and other principal monographs will be discussed below.

[4] Marietta Shaginian, *Voskreshenie iz mertvykh: povest' ob odnom issledovanii* (Resurrection from the Dead: The Story of an Investigation) (Moscow: Khudozhestvennaya literatura, 1964). It was a notable success; though largely unnoticed in the western musicological community, at least four editions were published before the collapse of the Soviet Union in 1991. Marietta Sergeevna Shaginian (1888–1982), winner of both the Stalin and Lenin prizes, authored seventy-nine books, including many novels, short stories, and travelogues. Shaginian's interest in Mysliveček was all the more remarkable considering that she was not a professional musicologist.

[5] See below note 12.

abilities were very similar to Mysliveček's but he was born in Leipzig, the son of the universally celebrated Johann Sebastian Bach, rather than in Prague, the son of a Czech-speaking miller. Thus there is today a larger body of musicological research on J. C. Bach and generally broader promotion of his compositions to the musical public. Mysliveček's Czech heritage, in contrast, has become a pronounced disability. Ironically, in his own day Mysliveček was regarded by some as a German: the Irish tenor Michael Kelly, for example, identified Mysliveček as a German in his *Reminiscences* (1826), as did Charles Burney in volume 4 of his *General History of Music* (1789).

The reason for this confusion was that at the time of Mysliveček's birth in 1737, Bohemia had been ruled by the Austrian Habsburgs for over two centuries and most Europeans considered Bohemia to be a part of Germany.[6] Its cultural life was dominated by the tastes of a German-speaking nobility and intelligentsia. The Czech language was looked upon as suitable only for the lower classes. In western Europe, Czech did not even have a name of its own—Burney, for one, referred to it only as "Sclavonian dialect."[7] By the late nineteenth and early twentieth centuries, this situation had of course changed: by then Czech nationalism had long reclaimed the language, and no one would have confused a person named Mysliveček for a German.

Mysliveček thus came to be regarded as a Czech, unlike Christoph Gluck, who was just as Czech as Mysliveček but is still generally thought of as German. Other eighteenth-century Bohemian composers with German-sounding surnames (such as Stamitz and Gassmann) have also been embraced by German and Austrian scholars as co-nationals. In the twentieth century, when national political sympathies frequently made their presence felt in music scholarship, there was almost nobody available to champion Mysliveček outside of his native country except Paul Nettl, who was himself of Bohemian birth. In a seminal article of 1940 on eighteenth-century Czech musical culture, Nettl ascribed nationalist—if not national socialist—motives to contemporary German scholars who ignored or disparaged the contributions of eighteenth-century Czech composers.[8] After the Second World War, traditions of music scholarship that burgeoned in North America and were firmly based on German teaching unwittingly maintained the biases Nettl condemned.

During the period of Communist rule in Czechoslovakia (1948–89), Eastern European scholars who wished to reach out to the West faced almost insurmountable obstacles. Contacts with foreigners were discouraged, international travel was severely restricted, and it was very difficult to obtain research materials from foreign sources. These factors tended to restrict the scope of research Czech scholars undertook and their ability to disseminate their ideas abroad. For many westerners, a lack of familiarity with the Czech language became the biggest impediment to exploring Czech musicological literature and subjects.[9]

---

[6] See, for example, Thomas Nugent, *The Grand Tour* (2nd ed., London, 1756), a guidebook for English travelers to the Continent. After enumerating the regions of Germany, Nugent remarks (2:5): "to these circles modern geographers add Bohemia, Silesia, and Moravia."

[7] *Dr. Burney's Musical Tours in Europe*, 2: *An Eighteenth-Century Musical Tour in Central Europe and the Netherlands*, ed. Percy A. Scholes (London: Oxford University Press, 1959), 134. Besides other clues, his use of the phrase "Sclavonian dialect" is an indication that Burney consulted Nugent, *The Grand Tour*, 2:15. Variations of this phrase go back as least as far as Edward Brown's *A Brief Account of Some Travels in Divers Parts of Europe* (London, 1685), 164: "the common language of Bohemia is a dialect of the Sclavonian." The article "Bohème" in the *Encyclopédie* of Diderot and d'Alembert (1751) reports the native language to be "une dialecte de l'Esclavon" (2:294). In Germany in the eighteenth century, the Czech language was referred to as "böhmisch."

[8] Paul Nettl, "The Czechs in Eighteenth-Century Music," *Music & Letters* 21 (1940): 362–70. Nettl was discreet about identifying the offending parties, although he did mention the influence of national socialist groups.

[9] Other composers born in Bohemia in the eighteenth century who have been robbed of their proper reputations include Pavel Vranický, Antonín Vranický, Václav Pichl, and Antonín Rejcha (Reicha).

Certain aspects of Mysliveček's musical career have also contributed to his current obscurity. He would be much better known today had he been active in London or Paris, for example, or spent a significant amount of time in Vienna, rather than spending most of his career in Italy. It is a pity that Burney never witnessed one of Mysliveček's operatic productions (he surely would have left some quotable impression) and perhaps unfortunate, too, that Mysliveček's reputation as a composer of opera derives from unreformed[10] serious operas of a type generally held in low esteem today by non-specialists. If he had been able to make good on his promise to obtain an operatic commission for Mozart at the Teatro San Carlo in Naples, he might even now be looked upon as a hero. And if Mozart's first Milanese opera had been *Nitteti*, as originally planned, and not *Mitridate, re di Ponto*, Mozart's interest in Mysliveček's opera *Nitteti* would probably have been recognized long ago.

* * * *

In the Czech Republic (and former Czechoslovakia) there has been a great deal of research on Mysliveček, particularly since the Second World War. A landmark biography of Mysliveček by Jaroslav Čeleda (1890–1974), based on his meticulous examination of Prague civic records during the 1920s and 1930s, was published in 1946. It made possible a more accurate chronology of Mysliveček's childhood and early manhood than could be found in any of the biographical resources produced up to that time.[11] In 1965 Marietta Shaginian's Russian biography was translated into Czech.[12] Another biography, by Rudolf Pečman, was published in 1981,[13] followed by a richly illustrated documentary collection by Stanislav Bohadlo, *Josef Mysliveček v dopisech* (Josef Mysliveček in Letters) in 1989.[14] Outside the former Czechoslavakia, a biography in Italian, by Dario della Porta, appeared in 1981.[15] All these works brought to light important new information and insights about Mysliveček, but by and large were difficult to obtain outside of the countries in which they were printed. Unfortunately the Italian biography, linguistically accessible to most western scholars, contains the most factual errors.

Until the publication of the *New Grove Dictionary of Opera* in 1992, most English speaking readers had little choice but to rely on the biographical notice by David DiChiera prepared for the *New Grove*

---

[10] The relationship of Mysliveček's operatic works to the reform movement of the 1760s and 1770s associated with Gluck is examined in chapter 7.

[11] Jaroslav Čeleda, *Josef Mysliveček: tvůrce pražského nářečí hudebního rokoka tereziánského* (Josef Mysliveček: Founder of the Prague Dialect of Theresian Musical Rococo) (Prague: Josef Svoboda, 1946). Many of the discoveries had been summarized earlier in his "Il Boemo divino Venatorini," *Hudba a Škola* 4 (1931–32): 65–67, 96–97, 118–21, 151–54. It took until the 1990s for some of Čeleda's most important findings to find their way into western musicological literature. A few biographical documents were brought to light earlier in the twentieth century by Alois Hnilička and presented in his "Josef Mysliveček," *Zvon* 9 (1909): 260–63, 279–81, 291–95. Hnilička also produced a biographical sketch of Mysliveček for his *Portréty starých českých mistrů hudebních* (Portraits of the Early Masters of Czech Music) (Prague: Fr. Borový, 1922), 57–63.

[12] Marietta Shaginian (Šagiňanová), *Zapomenutá historie* (Forgotten History), trans. Anna Nováková (Prague: Mladá Fronta, 1965).

[13] Rudolf Pečman, *Josef Mysliveček* (Prague: Editio Supraphon, 1981). It closely paraphrases Čeleda's text in its early chapters. Pečman is incorrect (p. 7) in stating that most of the documents consulted by Čeleda were destroyed during the last days of World War II, when parts of Prague, including the Town Hall in the Old City, were damaged by German occupiers. Almost all of the materials are still preserved in the Archiv Hlavního Města Prahy.

[14] Stanislav Bohadlo, *Josef Mysliveček v dopisech* (Josef Mysliveček in Letters) (Brno: Opus Musicum, 1989). Most of the information in this study appeared in a series of articles in *Opus musicum* in 1987 and 1988.

[15] Dario della Porta, *Josef Mysliveček: profilo biografico-critico* (Rome: Il Bagatto, 1981).

Dictionary of Music and Musicians,[16] a text based on his earlier article for *Die Musik in Geschichte und Gegenwart*.[17] Both versions repeat the accumulated myths of two centuries without an attempt to collate the sources of Mysliveček's music. By 2001 the present author's biographical entry for Mysliveček in the second edition of the *New Grove* dictionary offered a more accurate overview of Mysliveček's biography and musical output,[18] as did also the biographical notice by Christian Moritz-Bauer in the new edition of *MGG* (2004).[19] But by necessity these dictionary articles could not correct all of the questionable information that had circulated about Mysliveček for decades—speculation reported as fact, spurious love affairs, operatic productions that never took place, etc.

In recent years several initiatives concerned with the dissemination of Mysliveček's compositions have been launched. Some of these projects are continuing, others remain only half-finished. They include attempts to produce thematic catalogs (one has been published),[20] plans to record all of Mysliveček's symphonies,[21] and an undertaking to publish the librettos of Mysliveček's operas.[22] Newer projects are detailed in the main text of this work.

* * * *

Mysliveček's iconography provides a sampling of the difficulties that frustrate investigations into Mysliveček's life and music. At present, only one putative portrait of Mysliveček is accessible, an engraving by Anton Niederhofer (see frontispiece). The engraving was published with František Martin Pelcl's posthumous biographical sketch of Mysliveček (Prague, 1782)[23] and another version of it was appended to a manuscript of excerpts from Mysliveček's opera *Il gran Tamerlano*.[24] Since the Niederfhofer engraving was produced in Prague after Mysliveček's death, it is not clear whether it actually depicts Mysliveček or his identical twin brother, who was still working in Prague as a miller at the time and would have readily been available as a reasonable substitute for the intended subject. A certain roughness in the face bespeaks the persona of a manual laborer.

---

16 *The New Grove Dictionary of Music and Musicians* (hereafter, cited as *New Grove*) (London: Macmillan, 1980), 15:6–8.

17 *Die Musik in Geschichte und Gegenwart* (hereafter, cited as *MGG*) (Kassel: Bärenreiter, 1961), 9: cols. 1238–41.

18 *New Grove*, 2nd ed. (2001), 17:582–85.

19 *MGG* (2004), Personenteil, 12: cols. 263–69.

20 The first thematic catalog, begun by the Czech scholar and musician Jan Pohl (1861–1914), is believed to be preserved somewhere in the České Muzeum Hudby in Prague (shelf number V B 84), but cannot now be located by its staff. Ramona Matthews's effort to catalog Mysliveček's instrumental works as part of a dissertation project at the University of Maryland in the 1970s was abandoned and passed on to Angela Evans. Together with Robert Dearling, Evans eventually produced *Josef Mysliveček (1737–1781): A Thematic Catalogue of His Instrumental and Orchestral Works* (Munich: Katzbichler, 1999). For further information on this catalog and correction of catalog entries, see Catalog 1 below. A thematic catalog of vocal works by Stanislav Bohadlo, with assistance from Christian Moritz-Bauer (announced in Bohadlo's *Josef Mysliveček v dopisech*, p. 154), remains incomplete, but is available in draft copy at this website: www.jmc.cz/stan/myslivecek.

21 This project, announced in Pečman, *Josef Mysliveček*, 259, yielded some Supraphon recordings from the the early 1980s: see Part 4 below.

22 This project is mentioned in Bohadlo, 8–9.

23 František Martin Pelcl, "Joseph Misliweczek: ein Tonkünstler," in *Abbildungen böhmischen und mährischen Gelehrter und Künstler* (Prague, 1782), 4:189–92 (reproduced in Appendix 1 below).

24 Bibliothèque Nationale de France, Département de la Musique, Ms. 2367.

FIG. I.1 Josef Mysliveček.
Pastel drawing attributed to Georg Friedrich Schmidt

Confusion also surrounds the source of a pastel drawing of a more refined gentleman identified by Jaroslav Čeleda as Mysliveček and reproduced as the frontispiece in Čeleda's 1946 biography (fig. I.1). Čeleda attributed the drawing to the German artist Georg Friedrich Schmidt (1712–75), but offered only a caption with the artist's name and the indication "Mnichov" (Munich) by way of explanation for its origins. Marietta Shaginian, whose main interest was in analyzing the drawing for character traits, visited Čeleda in Prague in the 1950s and discussed the Schmidt portrait with him, but did not report whether she saw an original or a reproduction.[25] Among a number of publications, Shaginian's and Rudolf Pečman's biographies reproduce this pastel without comment as to its origins or what happened to it. Its fate and present location are unknown. The two chief bibliographical resources concerning Schmidt's artistic oeuvre do not mention the drawing.[26] Regarding the origins

[25] *Zapomenutá historie*, 74.

[26] See especially Joseph Eduard Wessely, *Georg Friedrich Schmidt: Verzeichnis seiner Stiche und Radirungen* (Hamburg, 1887); and Paul Dehnert, "Georg Friedrich Schmidt, der Hofkupferstecher des Königs," *Jahrbuch Preussischer Kulturbesitz* 16 (1980): 321–39. There is no entry for Schmidt in *The Dictionary of Art* (London: Macmillan, 1996).

of the drawing, it is impossible to place Schmidt and Mysliveček in the same location: except for activity in Paris between 1736 and 1744 and St. Petersburg between 1757 and 1762, Schmidt lived virtually his entire life in Berlin, whereas Mysliveček is not known to have visited any of these cities. Mysliveček was resident in Munich in 1777 and 1778, but Schmidt had by then died. How could they have met? An unsubstantiated legend that Mysliveček visited Munich in 1773 hardly provides a reliable answer.

The present study may not be able to resolve this particular Mysliveček puzzle, but it will endeavor to realize a more complete "resurrection from the dead" for Mysliveček than was possible sixty years ago when the Čeleda study was published, or even forty or twenty-five years ago, when the Shaginian and later the Pečman and Della Porta monographs appeared. The gains of research in the last decades make possible the integration of more recently discovered documentation with what was previously known about Mysliveček's life and a more accurate collation of musical sources than was heretofore available. The chapters that follow sift and systematize this data. In so doing they attempt to paint a fresh picture of the man and his music, one that casts light also on his milieu and on his compositional strengths. Josef Mysliveček enjoyed a pivotal role in the European musical world of the late 1760s and 1770s. As will be seen, the fictionalized embellishment added over the years to make his story more piquant was unnecessary—the truth about Josef Mysliveček is interesting enough.

Part 1

A BIOGRAPHY OF JOSEF MYSLIVEČEK

1

"A NOBLE IMPULSE": THE EARLY YEARS IN PRAGUE

Josef Mysliveček's origins can be traced to a family of millers who prospered in the city and environs of Prague in the seventeenth century. The family name, roughly equivalent to the English "Hunter," is not uncommon in the Bohemian lands, and Jaroslav Čeleda identified several branches in the Prague area.[1] The standard spelling of the name in modern Czech literature reflects an orthography that entered common usage in the nineteenth century. In Mysliveček's day, written Czech tended to avoid diacritical markings and in many respects resembled Polish—thus the spelling Misliweczek (without the characteristic *háček*) is common. Most of the surviving documents signed by Mysliveček were drawn up in Italy, where he consistently adopted the partly Italianized spelling Misliwecek (also without a *háček*). More completely Italianized spellings such as Mislivecek and Mislivvecek are also found in Italian documents, just as Misliwetschek is occasionally found in German language sources. Outside of Italy, it is common to encounter "y's" substituted for one or both "i's" in spellings such as Myssliwetschek and Mislyweczek. Mysliveček's twin brother, Jáchym, spelled the name Myslyweczek. Many of the clumsy spellings found in non-Bohemian sources appear to be the result of bewilderment as to how such a name could possibly be rendered in letters. One of the odder variants comes from the *Reminiscences* of the Irish tenor Michael Kelly, who spelled the name Metzlevisic.[2]

Mysliveček's grandfather, Pavel (Paul) Mysliveček (ca. 1653–1703), lived in Horní Šárka (Upper Šárka) to the northwest of Prague.[3] Pavel's name is first recorded in connection with his marriage to Josef's grandmother, the widow Ludmila Málková (ca. 1657–1720),[4] on 18 September 1688 at the parish church of St. Roch on the grounds of the Praemonstratensian Strahov Monastery, then the westernmost religious institution within the Prague city limits.[5] Ludmila had previously been married to another miller, one Jan Málek. Together, Mysliveček's grandparents operated Oak

---

[1] Jaroslav Čeleda, *Josef Mysliveček: tvůrce pražského nářečí hudebního rokoka tereziánského* (Josef Mysliveček: Founder of the Prague Dialect of Theresian Musical Rococo) (Prague: Josef Svoboda, 1946) (hereafter, cited as Čeleda), 13–22.

[2] Michael Kelly, *Reminiscences*, ed. Roger Fiske (London: Oxford University Press, 1975), 22.

[3] Pavel Mysliveček's dates can be established from St. Roch burial records in Strahov Monastery (Čeleda, 22–23). His age at his death, 15 December 1703, is recorded as "*circa* 50."

[4] Ludmila Myslivečková's dates can also be established from St. Roch burial records. She was sixty-three when she died 16 April 1720 (Čeleda, 24).

[5] St. Roch marriage records, 1660–1757 in Archiv Hlavního Města Prahy, *Liber copulatorum Premonstratensium in Monto Sion vulgo Strahof*, 1:74; transcribed in Čeleda, 21 and 280.

Mill (Dubový mlýn) in Horní Šárka.[6] At the time of their marriage, Šárka was a rural area nearly empty of residents; as late as 1771, only thirty-one houses were recorded there. Oak Mill (still marked in maps of Prague) originally belonged to the Strahov Monastery, but the Myslivečeks were able to purchase it from the monastery in 1696,[7] after which it became the core of the family's property holdings.

In all, ten children belonging to Pavel and Ludmila were born at Oak Mill and raised alongside three children of Jan Málek.[8] The composer's father Matěj (Matthias), the seventh child of Pavel and Ludmila, was baptized on 21 February 1697 at St. Roch.[9] All of the couple's surviving children were minors at the time of their father's death in 1703. In order to help support her family, Ludmila Mysliečková married another miller, Jiří Fořt, and operated Oak Mill with him until her death in 1720.[10] When Ludmila's estate was settled in 1721, Oak Mill was bequeathed to Matěj Mysliveček to the exclusion of his older brothers, who had already left their mother's household at the time of her death.[11]

Matěj Mysliveček was a man of considerable ambition and application who amassed a fortune in the milling business. While retaining ownership of Oak Mill, he followed the example of his older brother Norbert (1695–1743), the most successful of his many siblings, and moved to Prague. Matěj's residence in the Old City of Prague is recorded in 1726,[12] though it took him several years to establish himself there. At first, he worked in a mill in Šárka owned by the Strahov Monastery, then sometime in the early months of 1728 he became tenant of Sova Mills (Sovové mlýny) on Kampa Island off the west bank of the Vltava (Moldau) River (fig. 1.1).[13] After the move to Prague, Matěj prospered and was able to acquire farm land, livestock, and vineyards in the countryside near Prague, and, in the 1730s, the ownership of Sova Mills (fig. 1.2).[14] By the time of his marriage in 1735, he was one of the most respected members of the millers' guild in Prague.

Matěj Mysliveček chose as his wife Anna Terezie Červenková (1706–67), a resident of the Old City in the parish of St. Giles (Jiljí) on the east bank of the Vltava near Prague Bridge (now Charles Bridge), at that time the only bridge over the Vltava River. Besides the names of her parents, Gregor and Magdalena, the only information that survives from Anna Terezie's early life is the date of

---

6 Ibid., 20–24. The area is now part of the district Nebušice. Horní Šárka, Dolní Šárka (Lower Šárka), and Tichá Šárka (Quiet Šárka) were annexed into greater Prague in the early twentieth century. See Jaroslav Janáček, ed., *Dějiny Prahy* (The History of Prague) (Prague: Nakladatelství politické literatury, 1964), 672, 746–47. On the expansion of greater Prague in the nineteenth and twentieth centuries, see also *Baedeker's Prague*, 2nd ed. (New York: Prentice Hall, 1991), 20–28.

7 Čeleda, 52.

8 Ibid., 24.

9 A documentary biography of Matěj Mysliveček is in ibid., 52–108; baptismal record (Archiv Hlavního Města Prahy, *Liber Parochialis Eccl. S. Rochi*, 1:314), transcribed on pp. 29 and 281.

10 Čeleda, 23–24.

11 Ibid., 49–51.

12 Until 1784, Prague was divided into three districts considered cities in their own right: Old City on the east bank of the Vltava River, New City (to the south and east of the Old City wall), and Lesser Side (Malá Strana) on the west bank of the Vltava. On the hill overlooking Malá Strana was the castle district (Hradčany), a special administrative area. One often finds references to the three cities of Prague in documents from the eighteenth century. Their boundaries are still commonly marked in maps of Prague.

13 The name derives from the mills' one-time owner, Václav Sova. Their general location is indicated today by a street on Kampa Island called U Sovových mlýnů.

14 See Čeleda, 64–65, for an enumeration of these acquisitions. A survey map dated 3 July 1745 (Archiv Hlavního Města Prahy, I 135, 571/34a) specifies Matěj Mysliveček's properties on the Vltava and Sazava rivers (fig. 1.2). It includes what appears to be a crude portrait of Matěj, whose name is written in the lower right as Matieg Myslyweczek.

FIG. 1.1 ***Prague. West bank of the Vltava (Moldau) River and Kampa Island. Engraving by Joseph Gregory based on a drawing of Ludwig Kohl (1794). The water wheels correspond to the location of the Sova Mills***

Courtesy of the Archiv Hlavního Města Prahy

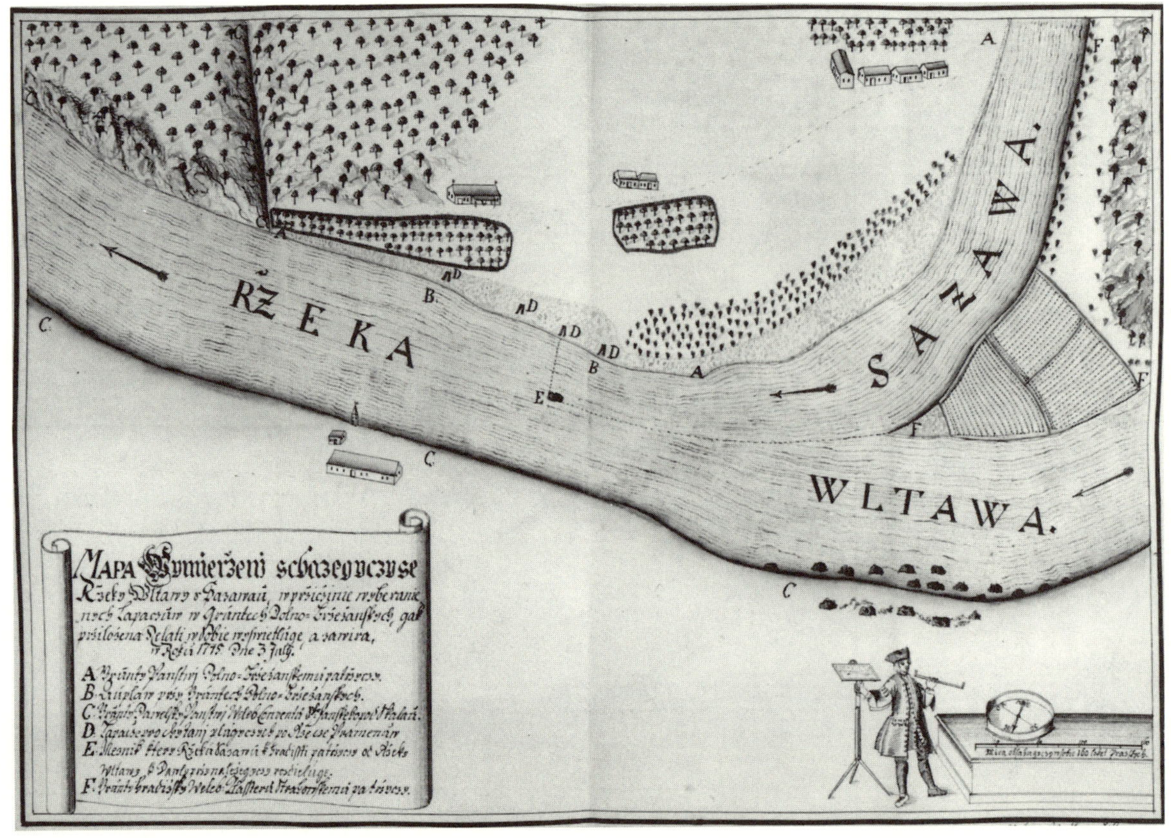

FIG. 1.2 Mysliveček family land on the banks of the Vltava and Sazava rivers. From a survey map, 1745 (detail); see above note 14. The figure at the bottom is likely a representation of Mysliveček's father Matěj

Courtesy of the Archiv Hlavního Města Prahy

her baptism at St. Giles (6 September 1706).[15] Her marriage took place at the same church on 10 August 1735.[16]

After nineteen months of marriage, Matěj and Anna Terezie produced the child who would one day make such a name for himself in European musical society. The date that has come down, 9 March 1737, can be traced only to a short biographical sketch about Josef Mysliveček prepared in 1782, the year following his death, by the Czech historian and journalist František Martin Pelcl (1734–1801).[17] It is believed that Pelcl had access to Mysliveček's relatives, in particular his twin brother, Jáchym, who was still working as a miller in Prague in the early 1780s. According to Pelcl, Josef's birth occurred within an hour of his younger twin brother, whom he identified inexplicably as Franz.

While Pelcl specified Prague as Mysliveček's birthplace,[18] Ernst Ludwig Gerber indicated a "village near Prague,"[19] probably relying on a remark in the German edition of Charles Burney's travels through Germany and the Low Countries which reported that Mysliveček was brought up in a village school.[20] Several later lexicographers accepted Gerber's phrase or supplied a specific location, most commonly Horní Šárka.[21] On balance, Prague is more believable. Not only would Pelcl have had access to information from the family, but it is known that Matěj Mysliveček was a resident of Sova Mills on Kampa Island throughout his early years of marriage. In addition, Charles-Ferdinand University matriculation records from 1753 identify Josef Mysliveček as a "Bohemian from Prague."[22] Designations of this type referred to a student's place of birth, not his residence; Christoph Gluck, who entered the University in 1731, for example, was recorded as "Gluck

---

[15] A documentary biography of Anna Terezie Červenková is in Čeleda, 109–27. The baptismal record names her parents (Archiv Hlavního Města Prahy, JIL N 2, p. 506; transcribed in Čeleda, 66 and 281).

[16] Marriage record (Archiv Hlavního Města Prahy, JIL O 3, p. 44; transcribed in Čeleda, 29–30, 65–66, 281). In the document, but not mentioned by Čeleda, is information about a commemoration of the ceremony at Strahov Monastery (identified by its traditional alternative name, Mt. Sion).

[17] František Martin Pelcl, "Joseph Misliweczek: ein Tonkünstler" (hereafter, cited as Pelcl), in *Abbildungen böhmischen und mährischen Gelehrter und Künstler* (Prague, 1782), 189–92; Mysliveček's biography appears alongside that of Danish astronomer (and sometime Prague resident) Tycho Brahe, who, like Mysliveček, went through much of his life without a nose. A transcription and a translation of Pelcl's biography of Mysliveček are in Appendix 1 below.

[18] Two lines of authority on the birthplace have existed since the late eighteenth century. The Czech line, descended from Pelcl, is older than the German line descended from Gerber. Reference works that follow the Czech line in their entries for Mysliveček include Gottfried Johann Dlabacž (Jan Bohumír Dlabač), *Allgemeine historisches Künstler-Lexikon für Böhmen and zum Theil auch für Mähren und Schlesien* (Prague, 1815; reprint, New York and Hildesheim: Georg Olms, 1973); Constant von Wurzbach, *Biographisches Lexikon des Kaiserthums Oesterreich* (Vienna, 1856–91; reprint, New York: Johnson Reprint, 1966), see 18 (1868): 362–65; *Československý hudební slovník* (The Czechoslovak Music Dictionary) (Prague: Státní hudební vydavatelství, 1963–65); *New Grove Opera* (1992); *The New Grove Dictionary of Music and Musicians* (hereafter, cited as *New Grove*), ed. 2001; and *Die Musik in Geschichte und Gegenwart* (hereafter, cited as *MGG*), ed. 2004.

[19] Ernst Ludwig Gerber, *Historisch-Biographisches Lexikon der Tonkünstler* (Leipzig, 1790–91; reprint, Graz: Akademische Druck und Verlagsanstalt, 1977).

[20] Charles Burney, *Tagebuch einer musikalischen Reise* (Hamburg, 1773; reprint, Kassel: Bärenreiter, 1969), 1:8. See also *Dr. Burney's Musical Tours in Europe*, 2:135; and Charles Burney, *The Present State of Music in Germany, the Netherlands, and United Provinces* (London, 1773), 2:15.

[21] See, for example, François-Joseph Fétis, *Biographie universelle des musiciens*, 2nd ed. (Paris, 1866–70); Robert Eitner, *Biographisches Quellen-Lexikon der Musik und Musikgelehrten* (Leipzig: Breitkopf & Härtel, 1902); Carlo Schmidl, *Dizionario universale dei musicisti* (Milan: Sonzogno, 1938); *Enciclopedia dello spettacolo* (Rome: Le Maschere, 1954–66); *MGG*, ed. 1961; and *New Grove*, ed. 1980. The last two specifically indicate Horní Šárka as the village near Prague. Strangely, the *Enciclopedia dello spettacolo* indicates the Prague district of Nusle as Mysliveček's birthplace.

[22] See p. 21, below.

Christopherus Palatinus Erspachensis" (a Palatine from Erasbach), even though he had lived almost all of his life to that time in Bohemia, including the last three or four years in Prague.[23]

Jaroslav Čeleda located baptismal records for dozens of Mysliveček relatives, but nothing for Josef, his brother Jáchym, or his sister Maria Anna (born in 1740 or 1741). When Matěj Mysliveček married in St. Giles Church in 1735, he identified himself as a parishioner at St. Nicholas (Mikuláš) in Malá Strana, which was dedicated at that time to St. Wenceslas (Václav). According to records in the Archiv Hlavního Města Prahy, Sova Mills (č.p. 503-III)[24] was in the jurisdiction of this church.[25] Although Čeleda was certain that Josef was born at Sova Mills, no baptismal records for any children of Matěj Mysliveček are preserved from St. Nicholas Church.[26] Closer to Sova Mills was the church of Virgin Mary under the Chain (Kostel Panny Marie pod Řetězem), but its baptismal records, which were combined with those of the church of Virgin Mary Victorious (Kostel Panny Marie Vítězné) between the years 1720 and 1784, also reveal nothing.[27] The same is true of many other churches throughout the region.[28] That the Mysliveček children were not baptized seems a remote possibility; they may have been baptized at home.

An inventory of the estate of Matěj Mysliveček (fig. 1.3), prepared shortly after his death on 1 January 1749,[29] records, besides his real estate, personal possessions, and debts, the names and ages of his three children in descending order of age: Jozeff (age 12), Joachim (age 12), and Maria Anna (age 8). This inventory, the earliest document that mentions Josef Mysliveček, was commissioned on 8 February and completed 18 March 1749. An age of twelve years for Josef Mysliveček on the later date agrees with Pelcl's indication of Josef's birthdate as 9 March 1737. Placement of Josef's name before his brother Jáchym's likely signifies that Josef was the first-born. His later duties as executor of his father's estate and status as principal beneficiary would also bespeak this position.

There is little to report about Mysliveček's childhood save some anecdotes recorded by Pelcl.[30] It can be said that Mysliveček had a comfortable family life, in large part because of his father's continued acquisition of real estate, including, in 1740, Blue Ship House (*dům U modrého šifu*) in the Old City (č.p. 464-I).[31] For the remainder of his youth, Mysliveček lived in this handsome town house, whose exterior has been beautifully restored in recent years. About the same time that his father bought Blue Ship House, he vacated Sova Mills and began to operate another mill, Kutil Mill, on the east bank of the Vltava River next to Prague Bridge (fig. 1.4).[32] At first, Matěj was the

---

[23] Daniel Heartz, "Coming of Age in Bohemia: The Musical Apprenticeships of Benda and Gluck," *Journal of Musicology* 6 (1988): 522.

[24] The abbreviation "č.p." stands for descriptive number (*číslo popisné*). During the reign of Maria Theresa č.p. numbers were assigned to every structure in Prague. Even today they offer a better way of identifying the old buildings than the ever-changing street numbers. In the historic districts, typically, both numbers are still found on the structures. The Roman numeral identifies the "city" in which an address is located (I for Old City, II for New City, III for Malá Strana).

[25] Čeleda (p. 141) believed incorrectly that Sova Mills fell under the jurisdiction of Kostel Panny Marie Vítězné.

[26] St. Nicholas Church baptismal records are in Archiv Hlavního Města Prahy, MIK N 8.

[27] Archiv Hlavního Města Prahy, PMŘ N 2 O 2.

[28] Čeleda, 140–43. These would include two other churches closely associated with the Mysliveček family, St. Giles in the Old City and St. Roch in Strahov Monastery, whose records Čeleda also examined.

[29] Archiv Hlavního Města Prahy, 1186: *Liber inventarium ab A. 1748*, ff. 42–48.

[30] Pelcl, 189; Appendix 1 below. Apparently even their father had a difficult time telling the twins apart.

[31] Čeleda, 72–81. The street number of Blue Ship House has changed several times over the centuries. It is presently no. 8 on Melantrichova Street. Before the introduction of house numbers, dwellings were customarily identified by decorative signs posted on their fronts. Blue Ship House was named for a sign of this type.

[32] Ibid., 79.

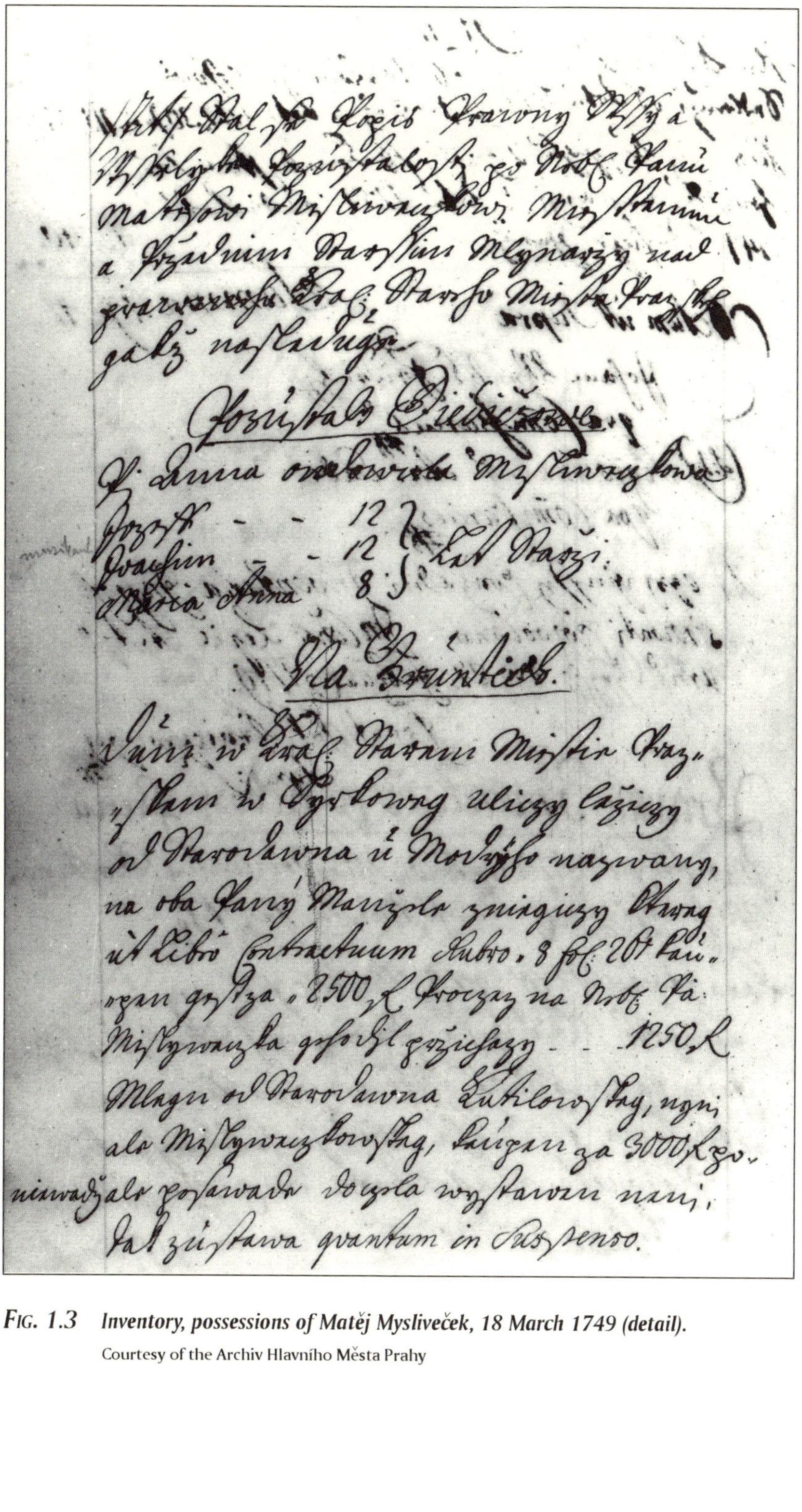

FIG. 1.3 ***Inventory, possessions of Matěj Mysliveček, 18 March 1749 (detail).***

Courtesy of the Archiv Hlavního Města Prahy

Fig. 1.4 ***Prague Bridge (now known as Charles Bridge) across the Vltava River.***
From Friedrich Bernhard Werner,* Delineatio et repraesentatio notabilissimorum prospectuum Pragae *(Augsburg, ca. 1740). The water wheels at the lower right correspond to the location of Kutil Mill

Courtesy of the Print Collection, Miriam and Ira D. Wallach Division of Arts, Prints, and Photographs, The New York Public Library, Astor, Lenox, and Tilden Foundations

tenant of Kutil Mill (named after a family that once owned it), but in 1747 he bought it outright.[33] A commemorative plaque has been erected on the southwest corner of the modern-day Smetana Museum to mark the spot where it was once located. In 1742, 1743, and 1747 Matěj purchased further real estate in the countryside.[34]

As prosperous as they were, the family would not have been insulated completely from the military conflicts that afflicted Prague during Mysliveček's childhood and young adulthood, first the War of the Austrian Succession (1740–48)[35] and then the Seven Years' War (1756–63). Each was fought over the efforts of Frederick the Great of Prussia to wrest control of the province of Silesia (an ancient possession of the crown of Bohemia)[36] from its rightful ruler, the Empress Maria Theresa. Prague was captured by Bavarian forces allied with Prussia at the end of November 1741 and, for most of the next year, was occupied by French troops also allied with Prussia.[37] Residents endured a curfew and onerous exactions of many types, as Austrian forces surrounded the city and the French soldiers were cut off from sources of food. Restoration of Austrian control in the city came in the middle of December 1742 with reprisals by Empress Maria Theresa against suspected collaborators and accusations of disloyalty against Bohemians generally.[38] In September 1744 the Austrians abandoned Prague and for two months the city was again occupied by the Prussians. During the military campaigns of the Seven Years' War Prague was not occupied by foreign troops but was heavily bombarded by the Prussians in May and June 1757. Although the city's principal architectural treasures were preserved, a large number of houses were destroyed.[39]

Mysliveček and his brother would have started their schooling about the time of the Prussian occupation in 1744, perhaps at the Dominican normal school in the Old City attached to St. Giles Church, near Blue Ship House. Their attendance is presumed there until 1747.[40] According to Pelcl, Mysliveček's father had the twins also study music at this time.[41] Charles Burney, when he toured

---

[33] Ibid., 91–93.

[34] Ibid., 86, 88, 90.

[35] Matthew Smith Anderson, *The War of the Austrian Succession, 1740–1748* (London and New York: Longman, 1995), esp. 87, 112–13, 134; and Reed Browning, *The War of the Austrian Succession* (New York: St. Martin's Press, 1995), esp. 75–79, 107–27, 181–85. See also Janáček, *Dějiny Prahy*, 389–99; Čeleda, 83–90; Jan Vlk et al., *Dějiny Prahy* (The History of Prague) (Prague: Paseka, 1997), 1:439–57; and Peter Demetz, *Prague in Black and Gold: Scenes from the Life of a European City* (New York: Hill and Wang, 1997), 291–94.

[36] For an overview in English of the history of Bohemia, see Robert William Seton-Watson, *A History of the Czechs and Slovaks* (London: Hutchinson, 1943; reprint, Hamden, CT: Archon Books, 1965). More recent discussion of the place of Bohemia in European politics is in Piotr Wandycz, *The Price of Freedom: A History of East Central Europe from the Middle Ages to the Present* (London: Routledge, 1992), and in Lonnie R. Johnson, *Central Europe: Enemies, Neighbors, Friends* (New York and Oxford: Oxford University Press, 1996). For the political situation in the eighteenth century, see Robert J. Kerner, *Bohemia in the Eighteenth Century* (New York: Macmillan, 1932; reprint, Orono, ME: Academic International, 1969); for conditions affecting the peasants, see William E. Wright, *Serf, Seigneur, and Sovereign: Agrarian Reform in 18th-Century Bohemia* (Minneapolis: University of Minnesota Press, 1966).

[37] Struggle for the recapture of Prague was anticipated in summer 1742. As Voltaire said, "all Europe had its eyes on Prague": see François-Marie Arouet Voltaire, *Histoire de la guerre de 1741*, ed. Jacques Maurens (Paris: Garnier Frères, 1971), 33, quoted in Browning, *War of the Austrian Succession*, 120. In fact, the French simply evacuated Prague in December 1742 without a fight.

[38] The majority of Bohemian nobles swore allegiance to Elector Charles Albert of Bavaria (instead of Maria Theresa, the legitimate queen of Bohemia) after his invasion of the country in 1741: see Kerner, *Bohemia*, 30. The electors of the Holy Roman Empire raised Charles Albert, not Maria Theresa's husband, Francis of Lorraine, to the imperial dignity in the election of 1742 held to select a replacement for her father, Charles VI. She acquired the imperial dignity in 1745, when Charles Albert (as Emperor Charles VII) died suddenly and her husband was elected emperor.

[39] Janáček, *Dějiny Prahy*, 397–99; Vlk et al., *Dějiny Prahy*, 447–51; Čeleda, 120–23.

[40] Čeleda, 152–57.

[41] Pelcl, 189; Appendix 1.

the region in 1772, mentioned the sophisticated music training available to boys and girls throughout Bohemia and Moravia,[42] though he reported that the Prague elementary schools did not have such instruction. Since at least one elementary school mandated music instruction,[43] it is difficult to accept his statement as accurate. Burney specifically recounted that Mysliveček was brought up at a village school, not in Prague,[44] information that may have come from Josef Seger, Mysliveček's composition teacher in the early 1760s with whom Burney conversed extensively. But it is doubful that Matěj Mysliveček would have sent his sons to the countryside as boarders when they could receive music lessons in the Prague parish in which the family resided. Josef Mysliveček and his brother were probably taught by musicians attached to St. Giles—the choirmasters Ildephons Hancke or Antonín Rames or the organist Karel Zikmund[45]—or perhaps by Felix Benda, the distinguished choirmaster of St. Michael's Church, who lived on Michalská Street only a short distance from Blue Ship House.[46]

According to Pelcl, Mysliveček went on to study philosophy under Jesuit tutelage.[47] At present, only Mysliveček's enrollment in the philosophy faculty at Charles-Ferdinand University in Prague can be verified. Since a gymnasium education was normally a prerequisite for entrance to university, Čeleda seems on firm ground in specifying the Jesuit Gymnasium (college) in the Clementinum as the site of the Mysliveček twins' pre-university training. His hyphothesis that they attended it between the years 1747 and 1753 was based on the standard ages for matriculating students, but is certainly incorrect, since both were known to have been students at Charles-Ferdinand University by early 1753 (see below).[48] Practical music-making was highly regarded at the Jesuit Gymnasium, and proficiency in music was required of every entering student, including the ability to sing and play at least one instrument.[49] In view of his expertise on the violin attested to in later documents, the violin was probably the instrument that Josef Mysliveček played best.

If Josef Mysliveček's attendance at the Jesuit Gymnasium can be presumed between 1747 and 1752, his study at the gymnasium would have coincided with a period of crisis within his family occasioned by the death of his father on New Year's Day of 1749.[50] Matěj's death brought hardship to his family, because he died intestate. Although an inventory of his possessions ordered by a probate court in February of 1749 revealed considerable wealth,[51] his estate was tied up in judicial

---

[42] *The Present State of Music*, 2:4; *Dr. Burney's Musical Tours*, 2:131–32; *Tagebuch*, 3:2. For music instruction in Bohemian schools, see also Barbara Ann Renton, "The Musical Culture of Eighteenth-Century Bohemia, with Special Emphasis on the Music Inventories of Osek and the Knights of the Cross" (Ph.D. diss., City University of New York, 1990), 18–23, 77–93. A description of the educational system in Bohemia is in Kerner, *Bohemia*, 344–52.

[43] St. Martin's: see Čeleda, 154–55.

[44] *The Present State of Music*, 2:15; *Dr. Burney's Musical Tours*, 2:135; *Tagebuch*, 3:8.

[45] Čeleda (152–57) identifies the three likely candidates.

[46] Ibid., 156. No documents substantiate these plausible hypotheses, though they have been reported as fact in reference works; see especially *Československý hudební slovník* and *New Grove*, ed. 1980.

[47] Pelcl, 189; Appendix 1. Post-elementary education in Bohemia was under the supervision of the Jesuits from the 1620s until the suppression of the order by Emperor Joseph II in 1774; see Kerner, *Bohemia*, 344–52.

[48] Čeleda, 157–69.

[49] Renton, "Musical Culture," 84; and Emil Trolda, "Jesuité a hudba" (The Jesuits and Music), *Cyril* 66 (1940): 53–57, 73–78; and 67 (1941): 2–10, 42–46, 53, 63, 106–08.

[50] Death date in list of deceased members of Prague millers' guild; transcribed in Čeleda, 103–04; St. Giles burial record, 3 January 1749 (Archiv Hlavního Města Prahy, JIL Z 2; transcribed in Čeleda, 106 and 281).

[51] This inventory, completed 18 March 1749 (*Liber inventariorum ab A.1748*, ff. 42–48, Archiv Hlavního Města Prahy, 1186) lists assets of various kinds at over 9,000 gulden, debts of 6,431 gulden owed to him, and his own debts of 2,650 gulden, 9 kreutzer.

proceedings until 1767.[52]

Virtually the only assets that Matěj's survivors could draw upon immediately were a roof over their heads (Blue Ship House) and a means to earn a living in the family mills.[53] The administration of the Mysliveček lands and mills was an enormous burden for Mysliveček's mother, who was forced to take out loans.[54] She returned her family to a stable footing by remarrying on 6 June 1752, taking as her second husband the miller Jan Čermák (d. 1772), in St. Giles Church, where she had married Matěj Mysliveček seventeen years before.[55] Čermák moved into Blue Ship House and assisted in the operation of Kutil Mill. Nothing is known of his earlier life or his relationship with his three stepchildren. The marriage appears to have produced no issue.

After his appearance in the inventory of his father's estate, the next surviving documents associated with Josef Mysliveček mention him first as a university student, then as an apprentice miller.[56] The precise dates of his attendance at Charles-Ferdinand University (now Charles University) cannot be verified, since the 1753 roster of students is the earliest roster that survives, but it likely records the results of his first year of coursework. In March 1753, when he was sixteen, Mysliveček dropped out. The reason for his withdrawal is notated next to his name: "D. Josephus Missliweczek Bohemus Pragensis/Nihil profecit in logica, in Martie vale dixit eodem anno" (Josef Mysliveček, a Bohemian from Prague, having made no progress in logic, said goodbye in March of this same year).[57] Josef's twin was a little more successful as a university student,[58] but he followed his brother into the millers' profession that May, also without graduating.

On 4 April 1753 the Mysliveček twins applied to begin apprenticeships as millers, and for the next eight years the records of the Prague millers' guild provide information about their activities.[59]

---

[52] For the final distribution of his estate, see chapter 2.

[53] By decree, Matěj's widow was permitted the use of all her husband's real estate during probate proceedings (Čeleda, 116).

[54] A loan of 500 gulden was taken out on 2 February 1749, and on 27 July, 500 gulden more (ibid., 110–13).

[55] Ibid., 119, 281. Even this step did not completely relieve her of the necessity of borrowing money: Čeleda (124) found record of a loan of 2,000 gulden from Countess Eleonore von Neuberg in 1764.

[56] Marietta Shaginian discovered the list of students from 1753: see Marietta Shaginian (Šagiňanová), *Zapomenutá historie* (Forgotten History), trans. Anna Nováková (hereafter, cited as Shaginian) (Prague: Mlada Fronta, 1965), 78–79, though she reported in error that it recorded Josef's enrollment at Jesuit Gymnasium. Charles University is the oldest university in central Europe. Founded by Holy Roman Emperor Charles IV in 1348, it was renamed Charles-Ferdinand University in honor of Holy Roman Emperor Ferdinand II after the defeat of the Bohemian Estates at White Mountain in 1620. The name was retained until 1882.

[57] The matriculation records of the philosophy faculty for 1753–1882 are in Archiv Univerzity Karlovy, Prague. The attendance of the Mysliveček twins (carton no. 117, no. 354) bears the legend: "Nomina Philosophorum Vetero Prague, qui tum anno 1752 vigente in 53, cum 53 et 54 Lectiones Philosophices exercerunt. Professore P. Ignatio Frantz S. Jesu."

[58] "D. Joachimus Missliweczek Boh:Pragensis/Exiguum testimonium abtulit ex Humanibus sed etiam exigue in alteribus profecit. Factus Molitor in logica, Mense Majo." The first sentence indicates "a little evidence" of success in humanities, "but also scant progress in the other disciplines." Rudolf Pečman, in *Josef Mysliveček* (Prague: Supraphon, 1981) (hereafter, cited as Pečman), 25, took this to mean that Jáchym was performing satisfactorily. The second sentence is more problematic. Shaginian (79) reported incorrectly that the word "logica" is illegible. Pečman did not examine the document himself and thought that this was an illegible place name. Neither claim is true. A possible explanation for "Factus Molitor in logica, Mense Majo" is that "in logica" was added after the name of each student with a blank space left before it to record the degree of proficiency when the information became available. In Jáchym's case, rather unusual information was recorded: "Factus Molitor, Mense Majo" (became a miller in the month of May). The phrase "in logica" was extraneous in this context.

[59] See *Manuale Panuw Pržiseznjch Starssych Mlynaržuw Zemskych w Kralowstwy wssych Tržech Kral: Miest. Prazskych* (records of the Prague millers' guild, 1742–76, in Archiv Hlavního Města Prahy, 3032). Their request to enter apprenticeship (4 April 1753) is recorded on f. 32v, and their acceptance (4 May 1753) on f. 33v; transcribed in Čeleda, 175 (latter document entries reversed: Josef's name appears first).

Coming so soon after his departure from university, Josef's application hints at a quick decision reached about a career choice prompted by his academic failure. His mother and stepfather may have insisted on this course of action,[60] and Jáchym may have come under similar pressure. The twins' three-year apprenticeship as millers began on 4 May 1753, one month after their application was submitted. Neither Josef nor Jáchym was apprenticed to their stepfather, following the usual custom of the guild. Instead, Josef was apprenticed to a family acquaintance, Václav Klika, and Jáchym to one Antonín Šouša. Klika then operated Sova Mills, where the twins were likely born. According to Pelcl,[61] the twins also began studies about this time with the distinguished engineer, architect, and painter Johann Ferdinand Schorr (1686–1777),[62] who apparently taught them hydraulics and other mathematical subjects, studies stipulated by the guild as necessary for the training of millers in connection with their civic responsibilities regarding the maintenance of waterways.[63]

The Mysliveček twins completed their apprenticeship in 1756,[64] but waited until 30 August 1758 to apply for admission to the Prague millers' guild as journeyman millers. Their request was granted the same day.[65] To achieve the rank of master miller, the regulations of the guild required certifiable knowledge of hydraulics, specifically the ability to construct a hydraulic model.[66] Both completed their projects successfully, and on 26 October 1761 were admitted into the Prague guild as master millers.[67]

By his mid-twenties, Mysliveček had received no instruction in composition and had diligently worked in the family milling operations. Then, in the early 1760s, he changed his plans radically and pursued ever after the life of a composer and violin virtuoso. The process by which he came to follow what Pelcl referred to as this "noble impulse"[68] is little understood. Pelcl implies that the death of Mysliveček's father somehow released him from a moral obligation to work in the family trade or help support his family members.[69] But his father had died in 1749 (and his stepfather would die only in 1772). A more likely catalyst for his taking up music as a profession was the resumption in Prague in 1760 of Italian *opera seria* productions, the genre in which Josef Mysliveček would one day excel so brilliantly.[70]

---

[60] Pelcl claimed (p. 190) that Josef's apprenticeship was instigated by his father (who had died four years earlier), perhaps confusing his father with his stepfather.

[61] Ibid.; Appendix 1.

[62] For a short biography of Schorr, see Čeleda, 171–73.

[63] These requirements are detailed in ibid., 182–83.

[64] The completion of the three-year apprenticeship is recorded in *Manuale*, f. 59 (31 March 1756); transcribed in Čeleda, 179.

[65] See *Manuale*, f. 70v; transcribed in Čeleda, 181.

[66] Ibid., 182–83.

[67] Their application for admittance to the rank of master miller is recorded in the *Manuale*, ff. 92–92v (21 January 1761); transcribed freely in Čeleda, 184. Their acceptance is recorded in the *Manuale*, f. 101 (26 October 1761); transcribed in Čeleda, 186.

[68] Pelcl, 190; Appendix 1.

[69] Ibid.

[70] For a nearly complete list of Italian operatic performances in Prague in the eighteenth century, see Pravoslav Kneidl, "Libreta italské opery v Praze v 18. století" (Librettos of Italian Opera in Prague in the Eighteenth Century), *Strahovská knihovna* 1 (1966): 97–131; 2 (1967): 115–88; 3 (1968): 190–201; and 4 (1969): 186–215. See also the listings (in some respects more complete and accurate) in Claudio Sartori, *I libretti italiani a stampa dalla origine al 1800* (Cuneo: Bertola and Locatelli, 1990–94), first appendix volume, 143–46.

Regular performances of Italian opera had been introduced in Prague later than in the other principal cities of the Holy Roman Empire—only in 1724 when the Sporck Theater was founded.[71] A little over a decade later, financial mismanagement under the Venetian impresario Antonio Denzio compounded by a lack of support from the aristocracy and low attendance at productions led to the disbanding of his company. In 1737 a new theater, the Divadlo v Kotcích, literally "theater in the stalls" (in German, Kotzentheater),[72] was constructed in a market area of the Old City known as the "Kotce" (stalls).[73] In librettos, the Divadlo v Kotcích was identified semi-officially as the new theater or royal theater (i.e., of the kingdom of Bohemia). Operatic performances, typically the productions of traveling impresarios and their companies, were presented there between 1738 and 1782.

In Prague, productions tended to be infrequent because of the reliance on itinerant impresarios. The intermittent fighting during the two wars was equally disruptive for opera. During the French occupation in 1742, the Divadlo v Kotcích was used as a storehouse for provisions, and there were no operatic performances there at all in 1740–43 and 1745. During the Seven Years' War, the theater also closed for long periods. A single comic opera, Domenico Fischietti's *La ritornata di Londra*, is known to have been performed in 1757, the year of the Prussian bombardment. No serious operas appear to have been staged anywhere in the city from 1755 through 1759.

The arrival in Prague of the impresario Joseph Kurz (Bernardon) ushered in a revival of *opera seria* productions beginning with the carnival season of 1760;[74] Kurz was succeeded by the impresario Gaetano Molinari in 1762, and he by Giuseppe Bustelli in 1764. The popularity of serious opera continued in Prague without interruption until the 1770s. During the 1780s, most operas in the city were performed either in the Thun Palace in Malá Strana, or, after 1783, in the newly built Estates' Theater, the venue for the premiere of Mozart's *Don Giovanni* (1787).[75] By then there were fewer productions of *opera seria* in both theaters, a change to be expected in light of the preferences of later eighteenth-century audiences for comic opera and *dramma giocoso*.

Mysliveček was sixteen or seventeen years old and apprenticed to the miller Václav Klika in 1754 when the last verifiable performances of *opera seria* took place in Prague before the outbreak of the Seven Years' War.[76] It is difficult to imagine that he received encouragement from his family

---

[71] For the early history of Italian operatic performances in Prague and the history of the Sporck Theater, see Daniel E. Freeman, *The Opera Theater of Count Franz Anton von Sporck in Prague* (Stuyvesant, NY: Pendragon Press, 1992).

[72] The unavoidable association in modern times for anyone proficient in German: the "vomit theater."

[73] A collection of essays devoted to the history of this theater is Václav Štěpán and Jan Pömerl, eds., *Divadlo v Kotcích* (Prague: Panorama, 1992). An older study, Oskar Teuber, *Geschichte des Prager Theaters*, 3 vols. (Prague, 1883–88), remains a useful resource.

[74] Carnival season fell between Christmas and Ash Wednesday. Theaters all over Europe were generally prohibited from mounting opera and almost all theatrical entertainments during Lent. In Italy, frequently, a new opera would go into production on St. Stephen's Day (26 December), as soon after Christmas as possible. Since the date of Ash Wednesday varied, the number of carnival operas could vary depending on the length of the season and the initial reception of the operas.

[75] This theater was built by Count Franz Anton von Nostic-Rieneck (1725–94) between 1781 and 1783, and was intended to promote works in German on the model of the Hoftheater in Vienna. Soon after its opening, it became the most prestigious venue in Prague for theatrical entertainments of many types in German, Italian, and Czech, besides balls and concerts. The theater is sometimes referred to as the Nostic Theater, but was generally known in the 1780s and 1790s as the National Theater (of the kingdom of Bohemia). In 1798, it was purchased by the Bohemian Estates, the origin of its modern name, the Estates' Theater. On the early operation of the theater, see Teuber, *Geschichte*, 2:46–91.

[76] Kneidl, "Libreta," part 2, pp. 132–34; and Sartori, *I libretti*. Operas presented that year included Francesco Zoppis's *Siroe*, Antonio Duni's *Demetrio*, and the anonymous pastiche *Tigrane*. Otakar Kamper reported performances of an anonymous *Artaserse* and an anonymous *Tamerlano* in 1754, but his indication of librettos for these cannot be verified: see Otakar Kamper, *Hudební Praha v XVIII. věku* (Musical Prague in the Eighteenth Century) (Prague: Melantrich, 1935), 245.

to attend opera performances. But in 1760, at age twenty-three, he would have been more independent and much more likely to have developed musical tastes receptive to an appreciation of Italian serious opera.

In pursuing his career as a musician, it is clear that Mysliveček was as ambitious in his own way as his father had been in his life. Whereas his father prized material possessions, to quote Pelcl, Mysliveček "preferred fame and honors to any amount of wealth."[77] To achieve this in the 1760s, a composer almost had to be involved with the production of Italian *opera seria*. It was then the most prestigious and glamorous musical genre, the one associated with the grandest social gatherings and patronized by some of the most notable dignitaries in Europe. For composers, regardless of their talents in other areas, the pinnacle of recognition and financial success in the profession could generally be achieved only through success in the leading opera theaters.

Josef Mysliveček must have realized this sometime in the early 1760s. Whether the "noble impulse" toward study of music was from the beginning geared toward a career as an opera composer, it must have become his goal very soon or he would not have left for Italy. The first obstacle he faced was a lack of training in composition. Pelcl mentions that he first turned to Franz Habermann,[78] choirmaster at the monastic Cajetans' Church (Kostel Panny Marie u Kajetánů) and the monastic church of the Maltese Order (Kostel Panny Marie pod Řetězem), who as a young man had traveled extensively and held musical posts in France, Italy, and Spain. A master of church music, Habermann was renowned for his skill in contrapuntal writing. His experience in composing dramatic music (several oratorios and at least one *opéra comique*) may also have influenced Mysliveček's decision to approach him. But Pelcl reported that his pace of instruction was too slow, and so Mysliveček turned instead to Josef Seger, organist at the Týn Church (Kostel Panny Marie před Týnem) and the Crucifers' Church of St. Francis Serafin in the Old City.[79] Seger confirmed to Charles Burney that Mysliveček had been his student.[80] Unlike Habermann, Seger never left the Bohemian lands and, as far as is known, had no experience with dramatic music. He mainly composed works for organ, especially preludes, toccatas, and fugues, the sort of thing Mysliveček showed no interest in cultivating later in his life. But from Seger, Mysliveček apparently received excellent grounding in compositional technique.

Pelcl claimed that Mysliveček composed symphonies within half a year of instruction,[81] and there does survive a C major symphony dated 1762 in one of the music collections of the Waldstein family that may well represent the fruits of Mysliveček's studies with Habermann and Seger. It constitutes Mysliveček's earliest known work.[82] Whether it was once part of a cycle of six early symphonies mentioned by Pelcl is not clear. Pelcl reported that the symphonies of this cycle were intended to evoke the first six months of the year, furthermore that they were performed in a theater with greater success than the composer expected and were published anonymously to see

[77] Pelcl, 192; Appendix 1.

[78] Ibid., 190; Appendix 1.

[79] Ibid.

[80] *The Present State of Music*, 2:15; *Dr. Burney's Musical Tours*, 2:135; *Tagebuch*, 3:8.

[81] Pelcl, 190; Appendix 1.

[82] See Catalog 1, p. 281, below. The music collection of the Waldstein estate of Doksy, presently housed in the České Muzeum Hudby in Prague, is described in Milada Rutová, "Valdštejnská hudební sbírka v Doksech" (The Waldstein Music Collection in Doksy) (Ph.D. diss., Charles University, 1971). A summary of this work is in *Sborník Národního Muzea v Praze*, series A 38 (1974): 173–227.

whether they would find favor among connoisseurs.[83] Unfortunately, these claims are impossible to verify. No sources of Mysliveček symphonies have ever been found that match works to months of the year. As far as Pelcl's claims for publication are concerned, no secular instrumental music of any type is known to have been published in Prague during this period.[84] Typically, composers there had their compositions published in Nuremberg, Augsburg, or Vienna.[85] That a publishing house would accept the financial risk of publication just to see how a composer's work would take among connoisseurs seems highly unlikely. Mysliveček's Op. 1 symphonies were published in Nuremberg by Johann Ulrich Haffner about 1763, but not anonymously. In using the German word *herausgegeben*, Pelcl may have meant that the symphonies circulated in manuscript in Prague, not literally that they were published. Whether or not remnants of the evocative symphonies referred to by him survive, or ever existed, the early Mysliveček symphonies that are extant were extraordinary accomplishments for a composer only beginning to write music.

Pelcl's parenthetical remark that the symphonies were performed in a theater may shed light on how Mysliveček began his association with his most important early patron, Count Vincenz von Waldstein (1731–97), first cousin once removed of Count Ferdinand von Waldstein (1762–1823), the friend of Beethoven who was the dedicatee of his Piano Sonata in C Major, op. 53.[86] Vincenz von Waldstein assisted other Bohemian musicians in obtaining training in Italy, including Antonín Kammel, later a professional acquaintance of Mysliveček. Čeleda surmised that Mysliveček's early symphonies would have been performed in Count Waldstein's palace in Malá Strana,[87] which in 1762 Waldstein had redecorated to make it suitable for performances by the Molinari opera company.[88] Mysliveček's symphonies would have provided a fine complement.

The existence of the symphony of 1762 provides excellent evidence to suggest that Mysliveček's decision to pursue a musical career probably came sometime at the end of 1761 or the beginning of 1762. He took his training as a miller seriously enough to see his way through to becoming a master miller in October of 1761, but by the end of the next year had begun to produce musical works (purportedly after six months' training in composition). Pelcl remarked that Mysliveček's success as a composer in Prague prompted him to seek training in Italy.[89] Indeed this would have been an essential move if he had ambitions to establish himself as a composer of opera. There was no point in his remaining in Prague, since only works by foreigners, especially Italians, saw performances there in the early 1760s, a reflection of a prevailing attitude that native Bohemian

---

[83] Pelcl, 190; Appendix 1.

[84] A sampling of the sorts of musical collections published in Prague in the eighteenth century is in Jiří Sehnal, "Pobělohorská doba (1620–1740)" (The Post-White Mountain Period), in *Hudba v českých dějinách* (Music in Czech History), 2nd ed. (Prague: Editio Supraphon, 1989), 211–12. The catalogs of published music in RISM report no symphonic prints from eighteenth-century Prague.

[85] Giovanni Maria Rutini, for example, produced three sets of keyboard sonatas while resident in Prague in the late 1740s and 1750s, all published by Haffner in Nuremberg. See William S. Newman, *The Sonata in the Classic Era*, 3rd ed. (New York: W. W. Norton, 1983), 204–05.

[86] For information on the Waldstein family, see Wurzbach, *Biographisches Lexikon*, 52:207–42. Another relative, Count Ferdinand's brother Joseph Karl Emanuel von Waldstein (1755–1814), employed the aged Casanova as librarian at his castle of Duchcov.

[87] Čeleda, 210.

[88] Application to mount operatic productions in the palace was made on 18 September 1762 in consideration of 1,000 gulden spent on redecoration. Permission to begin productions was granted 13 November 1762; on 31 October 1767 application was made to permit the Bustelli company to perform there in consideration of a further 2,500 gulden spent on redecoration. Copies are in the Waldstein family archives, estate of Mnichovo Hradiště (Rodinný Archiv Valdštejnů, Dokeská manipulace I-6/A17).

[89] Pelcl, 190; Appendix 1.

composers were inferior. A series of Gluck operas had been performed in Prague in the early 1750s (*Ezio* and *Ipermestra* in 1750 and *Issipile* in 1752), but only because Gluck was then a member of the traveling company of Giovanni Battista Locatelli. For a Bohemian composer to achieve an international reputation there was no alternative to emigration, and Mysliveček may well have found inspiration from talented co-nationals. Gluck had left the same post Seger held (organist at Týn Church) to seek opportun-ities outside Bohemia, as had dozens of other musicians extending back decades, including Florian Leopold Gassmann, a native of Most (Brüx), who had gone off to Venice while still a boy. In Gassmann's case, after he established himself in opera there (his first work, a *Merope* of 1757), he was summoned, in 1763, to the imperial court in Vienna, where he became a successful composer of comic operas.

Charles Burney, when he visited Bohemia in 1772, had no troubling identifying reasons for the mass emigration of talented Czech musicians. In particular he noted a lack of patronage within the country[90] due to the habit of Bohemian nobles to reside for long periods in the imperial capital of Vienna. In the early and mid-eighteenth century the nobility in Bohemia by and large had little identification with the native population. Many of the prominent families were of foreign origin and owed their lands and titles to their ancestors' loyal service to the Habsburgs during the Thirty Years' War, when many Protestant Czech noble families had been exiled and their lands confiscated. Some Czech families, such as the famous Kinskýs and Lobkovices, had retained their positions within the country, but only because they had shared with the newcomers an unquestioned loyalty to the Habsburg emperors. In Vienna, the Bohemian nobles were among the most trusted of imperial advisors, and they did much to enrich musical life there through their patronage of musicians from all parts of the Habsburg domains. But in Bohemia, few nobles fostered native Czech culture of any type.

Burney might well have noted the disadvantages presented by the absence of a royal or viceregal court. Even though the Habsburg emperors had held the title king of Bohemia since 1526, they never maintained a permanent court in Prague during the eighteenth century. Such a court would have sponsored operatic performances and provided opportunities for composers. Without one, the population base in the city was not sufficient to support a rich musical culture comparable to the music cultures of London, Paris, or Venice. In the first half of the century Prague struggled to maintain a population of about 40,000 persons, only a fraction of the populations of these cities. And of the cities that belonged to the Hapsburg rulers in the mid-eighteenth century, Prague was only fourth in population, after Vienna, Milan, and Brussels.[91]

In Burney's view, the excellent musical training in the Bohemian elementary schools was largely wasted, for there was little use for the musical skills learned there except in recreational music-making and congregational singing. Many of the most gifted instrumentalists found employment outside the country, especially in Germany,[92] which was preferable to the usual predicament of instrumentalists remaining in Bohemian noble households; most of them had grown up on a nobleman's estate and had to double as his servant and his musician.[93] Only churches and an occasional aristocratic or ecclesiastical patron could provide composers with steady employment. If character traits revealed

[90] *The Present State of Music*, 2:10–12; *Dr. Burney's Musical Tours*, 2:133–34; *Tagebuch*, 3:5–6.

[91] For population statistics for Prague and major cities in the eighteenth century, see Vlk et al., *Dějiny Prahy*, 462–64.

[92] This phenomenon is substantially documented in Sterling E. Murray, "Bohemian Musicians in South German 'Hofkapellen' during the Late Eighteenth Century," *Hudební věda* 3 (1978): 153–73.

[93] See Renton, "Musical Culture," 141–67.

in later documents about Mysliveček can be taken as an indication, he was temperamentally unsuited for the mundane duties required in the typical church post of choirmaster (*regens chori*).

Had Mysliveček wanted to become a Kapellmeister (i.e., the head of a secular musical establishment), it is unlikely that he could have obtained such a post in Bohemia of the 1760s. The noble families had been forced to curtail their households considerably in the wake of the wars of the mid-eighteenth century and were inclined to employ only their own retainers as musicians. In the 1760s there was not a single eminent Kapellmeister in the entire kingdom of Bohemia. All the leading composers in Prague at this time were choirmasters: besides Seger and Habermann, also František Xaver Brixi, choirmaster of St. Vitus Cathedral, and Franz Joseph Oehlschlägel, choirmaster at Strahov Monastery. Had Mysliveček obtained service as a choirmaster or Kapellmeister, the position would probably not have satisfied him. Composing opera for public theaters in Italy offered the sort of independence that Mysliveček seems to have craved.[94]

The imperative of seeking foreign musical training must have been obvious to Mysliveček. Still, the question of financing a journey would have been troublesome for almost anyone. Mysliveček's father had left a handsome estate at the time of his death in 1749 but Josef Mysliveček had no access to the proceeds. In the early 1760s, the distribution of the inheritance had still not been settled, and he had only his own resources and powers of persuasion on which to rely. At this stage, the dynamic and charming personality revealed in the Mozart family correspondence[95] must have proved to be as important as Mysliveček's musical talents, for he seems already to have been able to manipulate wealthy patrons into helping him. This ability would never fail him almost to the end of his days. He had the interest and support of Count Vincenz von Waldstein, and he probably received assistance from Count Franz Joseph von Pachta or Count Johann Joseph von Pachta, one of whom Mysliveček recommended to Mozart as a valuable professional contact in 1777.[96] Another source of patronage may have been the Vratislav (Wratislaw) family. Countess Maria Antonia von Vratislav (1739–1816), daughter of one of the most distinguished members of the Kinský family, figures as the dedicatee of Mysliveček's Op. 1 symphonies.[97] Mysliveček's twin brother, Jáchym, assisted him financially as well.[98]

Mysliveček's departure for Italy was recorded by Pelcl as 5 November 1763,[99] a date likely correct or nearly correct in the absence of any documents placing Mysliveček in Bohemia after

---

[94] He would later describe himself to Leopold Mozart as a "viaggatore" (wanderer): see chapter 4, p. 80.

[95] See chapters 3 and 4.

[96] The Count Pachta mentioned in Mozart's letter to his father, 11 October 1777 has traditionally been identified as Count Johann Joseph Philipp von Pachta, whose date of death is frequently given as 1822. His name has been confused with Count Johann Joseph von Pachta (1723–1822), a general by profession, who later became an acquaintance of Mozart and whose nephew was Count Johann Joseph Philipp (1754–1834) (information from Count Percival von Pachta-Rayhofen). Count Franz Joseph von Pachta (1710–99) was a prominent statesman in Bohemia and brother of Count Johann Joseph. A sign of his generosity towards musicians can be gauged from the dedication to him of these operatic productions in Prague: the anonymous *Adelaide* (1744), Hasse's *Semiramide riconosciuta* (1746 and 1760), the anonymous *Artaserse* (1760), and Domenico Fischietti's *Il signor dottore* (1762). See Kneidl, "Libreta," part 2; and Sartori, *I libretti*.

[97] She was the youngest child of Count Franz Ferdinand von Kinský (1678–1741), whose activities are described in Wurzbach, *Biographisches Lexikon*, 11:288–89. Her husband, Count Franz de Paula Adam von Vratislav (1732–88), was dedicatee of an anonymous *Arianna e Teseo* opera produced in Prague in the early 1760s. According to a libretto listed in Sartori, a *Nitteti* with music by Count Johann von Čejka (Czeyka) was performed at an unidentified venue in Prague in spring of 1768 with an all-noble cast that included the countess as a singer.

[98] See Mysliveček to Count Vincenz von Waldstein, 3 October 1765, quoted in chapter 2, pp. 32–33.

[99] Pelcl, 191; Appendix 1.

September of 1763.[100] Departure in early November of 1763 would have assured travel on roads clear of snow in the North and his arrival in Venice with time to spare before the start of the carnival operatic season of 1764. Before he left, however, he was solicited by the *Bürgermeister* and town council of Mladá Boleslav (Jungbunzlau), a small town to the northwest of Prague, to resolve a dispute about water rights among the communities on the river Jizera.[101] They wrote to Mysliveček in Prague on 3 September 1763 after the town's miller, Johann Georg Hübner, had suggested that a member of the millers' guild in Prague be brought in to settle the dispute. Their choice was Josef Mysliveček. His response, prepared on 7 September 1763, constitutes the earliest known document written in his own hand. The communication between the parties serves as a reminder that German, not Czech, was the ordinary language of government and the educated segments of Bohemian society throughout the eighteenth century.[102]

> I have just received the gracious letter you sent to me on the third of this month and can assure you that I would be delighted to demonstrate my modest skill at your pleasure, provided that I were a duly-sworn miller in this realm (as your letter indicates). Since this dispute unquestionably requires one [i.e., a duly-sworn miller], I am not able to resolve it, but hope for your kind favor and remain your well-born and obliging servant
>
> Josef Misliwetzek
>
> Prague 9 September 1763

Since, as he stated, Mysliveček was not a duly-sworn miller in the kingdom of Bohemia, a certain Franz Xaver Liskowetz (Liskovec) offered to adjudicate the dispute in a letter dated the same day.[103] The matter was later settled on 9 July 1764 by Mysliveček's stepfather, Jan Čermák, and another miller associated with the Mysliveček family, Jan Výkysalý.[104] The revelation that Josef Mysliveček was no longer a member of the millers' guild in the autumn of 1763 could offer no better confirmation of his determination by this time to abandon manual labor as a means of making a living and seek his fortune as a musician outside his native land.

---

[100] See below. The significance of this event may be gauged from the fact that the only specific dates supplied by Pelcl are Mysliveček's birth, death, and departure for Italy.

[101] The correspondence was discovered in the municipal records of Mladá Boleslav in 1950 and first published in a Czech translation: see Josef Sýkora, "Nález dopisu Josef Mysliveček" (The Discovery of a Letter of Josef Mysliveček), *Bertramka* 3 (1951): 7–8.

[102] Okresní Archív in Mladá Boleslav, Registratura Oeconomicum, III-6, kart. no. 16; transcribed with Czech translation in Stanislav Bohadlo, *Josef Mysliveček v dopisech* (Josef Mysliveček in Letters) (hereafter, cited as Bohadlo) (Brno: Opus Musicum, 1989), 16–17, with the request that Mysliveček serve as an adjudicator. The text of his response is in Appendix 2 below.

[103] See Bohadlo, 19–20, for a transcription of Liskowetz's letter to the town fathers of Mladá Boleslav.

[104] Čeleda, 175, 257.

2

IL BOEMO ITALIANIZZATO: LIFE, 1763–68

The independence Mysliveček enjoyed at the start of his period of study in Italy would have been the envy of many northern musicians. Gluck, for example, was able to come to Italy only after joining the household of Prince Antonio Maria Melzi in Vienna in 1737. Prince Melzi returned to Milan that same year with his household, providing Gluck with the break that made it possible for him to launch his career as a composer of opera in Italy about five years later. Václav Pichl benefited from a similar experience. Pichl left Vienna in 1777 to join the household of the Archduke Ferdinand, then governor of Lombardy in Milan, and flourished in Italy for about twenty years. Mysliveček, on the other hand, never had to rely on regular musical employment. Throughout his life he shunned the responsibilities of institutional servitude, preferring to wander about at will. Precisely how he financed his early travels will probably never be documented fully, but whatever combination of earnings, savings, loans, or gifts he had at his disposal allowed him to live more or less wherever he wished in Italy.

Since Mysliveček was in Italy to learn to compose *opere serie*, it could have made sense for him to have sought training in Naples, site of the Teatro San Carlo, the most prestigious venue in Europe for this type of entertainment.[1] Neapolitan-trained composers dominated operatic composition in Italy then, and the city of Naples, famed for its conservatories, did not want for excellent teachers. Within a decade Mysliveček's own career would revolve principally around Naples. He had more operas performed at the Teatro San Carlo than in any other location, and, judging by the directions his compositional style took following each of his returns to Naples, he found artistic renewal in the city.

Nonetheless, Mysliveček chose Venice as his base of operations when he first arrived in Italy. Venice may have lost its leadership as a center for the production of Italian opera after the 1720s, but it remained a major operatic center in the 1760s, and it could boast a larger number of theaters than any other Italian city. Mysliveček might also have been swayed by the beauty of the city, its relative nearness to Bohemia, and its place as the principal source of repertory and singers for the opera impresarios of Prague. Between 1724 and 1735, the Sporck Theater had virtually been an

[1] For contemporary opinions on the prestige of the Teatro San Carlo and Neapolitan musical traditions in general, see Michael Robinson, *Naples and Neapolitan Opera* (Oxford: Clarendon Press, 1972), 1–35. Mozart seems to have agreed with the conventional wisdom: of the prospect of composing an opera for Naples, he told his father (11 October 1777), "certainly it is a real distinction to have written operas in Italy, especially for Naples"; see Emily Anderson, ed., *The Letters of Mozart and His Family*, 3rd ed. (London: Macmillan, 1985), 304 (hereafter, cited as Anderson); Wilhelm A. Bauer and Otto E. Deutsch, eds., *Mozart: Briefe und Aufzeichnungen*, (Kassel: Bärenreiter, 1962), 2:44 (hereafter, cited as Bauer and Deutsch).

operatic satellite of Venice,[2] and, from 1738 to 1782, the impresarios who put on productions in the Divadlo v Kotcích also relied heavily on their connections in Venice to acquire singers and repertory. When *opera seria* productions returned to Prague in the early 1760s after a long absence, the music of the Venetian Baldassare Galuppi was most often heard.[3] The only work by a major Neapolitan composer presented in Prague during this time was Nicolò Jommelli's *Ifigenia* (autumn, 1762). In the area of comic opera, the population was more receptive to Neapolitans: in Mysliveček's day, the minor Neapolitan composer Domenico Fischietti even resided in Prague.[4] Still, all the Fischietti comic operas performed in Prague except one (*La donna di governo*, 1763) were originally staged in Venice.

Another consideration for Mysliveček could have been the itinerary of the impresario Joseph Kurz, whose last *opera seria* productions in Prague took place during the carnival season in 1763. Kurz then traveled to Venice, where he is recorded as a librettist and impresario at the Teatro San Cassiano during the 1763–64 operatic season.[5] Among the star singers at the Cassiano that season was Antonia Maria Girelli Aguilar,[6] who had been the most important interpreter of serious operatic roles in Prague in the early 1760s.[7] It is possible that Mysliveček intended to follow Kurz to Venice and to use him as a contact.

Pelcl was certain that the instruction in composition Mysliveček received in Venice came from Giovanni Battista Pescetti, a venerable composer of opera who was then second organist at St. Mark's.[8] Mysliveček might have heard a sampling of Pescetti's music in a production of *Ezio* mounted in Prague in the autumn of 1760, though it seems unlikely that this production alone would have prompted him to approach Pescetti. Mysliveček probably also weighed other considerations, such as Pescetti's reputation, his willingness to teach him, and the amount of remuneration he expected.

Pescetti could not have transmitted the most recent trends in operatic composition from his own experience. His heyday as a composer of opera had been in the 1720s and 1730s. The *Ezio* staged in Prague in 1760 had originally been performed in Venice in 1747. Very little of Pescetti's

---

[2] Freeman, *Opera Theater*.

[3] Galuppi was very popular in Prague throughout the mid-eighteenth century. In the early 1760s, there were productions of his *Alessandro nell'Indie* (1760), *Demofoonte* (1760), *Antigona* (1762), *Solimano* (1764), and *Ipermestra* (1764), and of his comic operas *Le nozze* (1760 and 1764), *Il filosofo di compagna* (1762), *Gli tre amanti ridicoli* (1763), and *L'amante di tutte* (1763). The repertory of the Divadlo v Kotcích is listed in Kneidl, "Libreta," part 2:115–87; and Sartori, *I libretti*, first appendix volume.

[4] Fischietti was in the Molinari company that performed in Prague in 1762–64 and in the Bustelli company that followed until 1765, when he became Kapellmeister at the court of Dresden. His music was known in Prague as early as 1756, when his opera *Lo speziale* was given during carnival (Kneidl, part 2:134), followed by *La ritornata di Londra* in 1757. Productions of the following comic and serious operas are also recorded: *Il mercato di Malmantile* (1760), *Il signor dottore* (1762), *Zenobia* (1762), *Olimpiade* (1763), *La donna di governo* (1763), *Alessandro nell'Indie* (1764), *Vologeso re de' Parti* (1764), and *Nitteti* (1765).

[5] Kurz produced operas in Prague between autumn of 1760 and carnival of 1763 (Kneidl, "Libreta," part 2:141–45). In autumn 1763 he is recorded as impresario and author of the scenario of *La morte di Dimone* at the Teatro San Cassiano, and he produced three works there during carnival in 1764. For chronological listings of the repertory of the Venetian opera houses, see Sartori, *I libretti*, first appendix volume, 191–207; and Taddeo Wiel, *I teatri veneziani* (Venice, 1898; reprint, Leipzig: Breitkopf & Härtel, 1978). Listings up to 1769 are also in Irene Alm, *Catalog of Venetian Librettos at the University of California, Los Angeles* (Berkeley, Los Angeles, and Oxford: University of California Press, 1993).

[6] She is recorded in Ferdinando Bertoni's *Achille in Sciro* and Antonio Gaetano Pampani's *Demofoonte* (both during carnival in 1764).

[7] She appeared in Prague in Galuppi's *Le nozze* (unknown season, 1760), Giuseppe Scarlatti's *Adriano in Siria* (unknown season, 1760), Giuseppe Carcani's *Olimpiade* (spring, 1760), George Christoph Wagenseil's *Demetrio* (autumn, 1760), and Antonio Mazzoni's *Didone abbandonata* (carnival, 1761), then returned to Prague in 1764–65 to appear in another series of productions.

[8] Pelcl, 191; Appendix 1.

operatic music survives (nothing of his *Ezio*, for example), though there is a complete score of his last opera, *Zenobia* (Padua, 1762), in the collection of the Ajuda Palace in Lisbon. It is a commonplace and conservative work in all respects. Pescetti may not have been a significant model for any of Mysliveček's early vocal compositions, perhaps with the exception of the dramatic cantata *Il Parnaso confuso*, but he would have been more than competent to assist Mysliveček in mastering the modes of musical expression associated with Italian opera. Specifically, Pelcl attributed to Pescetti instruction in the setting of recitative, an undertaking that hardly required the talents of the most imaginative composers of the day.

Mysliveček possessed an outgoing personality that led him continually to seek new acquaintances, professional contacts, and patrons. It is easy to imagine him in Italy composing music for prominent music-lovers and providing entertainment (especially violin playing) in much the same way that the Mozart family found so lucrative. He also accepted students, but whether he was engaged in teaching on a regular basis or only occasionally cannot be ascertained.[9] The informal sort of musical employment in which he was involved typically left no record of payments. No surviving documents confirm Mysliveček's whereabouts during 1764, but the documentary record resumes the next year in connection with his ties to Count Vincenz von Waldstein.

Illuminating information about Mysliveček's relationship with Count Waldstein is revealed in correspondence originally discovered by Eva Mikanová.[10] The count had dealings with both Josef and his twin brother, Jáchym, who was employed by the Waldstein family for several months in 1763 to assist in the transport of timber down the Elbe River to Dresden.[11] Correspondence addressed to Count Waldstein from 1765 and 1766 mainly concerns the affairs of one of Waldstein's household musicians, Joseph Benedikt Obermayer, who studied composition and violin with Mysliveček in Italy. Mysliveček wrote from Florence to Count Waldstein in Waldsteinruhe (Valdštejnsko) on 1 April 1765 to report on Obermayer's progress:[12]

> I have learned from a letter of my brother how anxious you are to have Joseph Obermair return to your household, therefore I will not fail to send him back by the end of May or sooner with my most obedient expression of gratitude. As far as he is concerned, I can assure you that he plays the violin properly, and I have proceeded as diligently as possible in teaching him composition. He has asked me, since he is so near Rome, whether I could provide him with funds to travel there in order to give him something to do and more to hear.

---

[9] Only three of his students are known by name: the Bohemian Joseph Benedikt Obermayer (see below); the German composer and theorist Georg Joseph Vogler (the Abbé Vogler; see chapter 3); and the Englishman James Hugh Smith Barry (see chapter 5).

[10] Eva Mikanová, "Neznamá mozartská bohemika" (Unknown Bohemian Mozartiana), *Hudební rozhledy* 41 (1988): 181–85; and her chapter "Obermayerův učitel v Itálii" (Obermayer's Teacher in Italy) in Bohadlo, 21–43.

[11] Mikanová, "Obermayerův učitel," 22. The documents confirming this connection were once housed in the Státní Oblastní Archiv Praha, pracoviště Mnichovo Hradiště (Prague State Provincial Archive, workplace for Mnichovo Hradiště), but have been returned to the Waldstein estate of Mnichovo Hradiště (Münchengrätz) to the northeast of Prague. Those concerning Jáchym Mysliveček are in the Ústřední Správa Valdštejnských Velkostatků (central administration of the Waldstein estates), stará manipulace VI-II-14, VIII-14-4 to VIII-14-8; učetní přílohy, kart. 1123; and hlavní pokladna 1761–64, kart. 1105. The timber trade was one of the most lucrative business interests of the Waldstein family, famed for its commercial activities. Another of its operations is described in Herman Freudenberger, *The Waldstein Woolen Mill: Noble Entrepreneurship in Eighteenth-Century Bohemia* (Boston: Baker Library, 1963).

[12] The original letter, previously in the Státní Oblastní Archiv Praha, is in the Mnichovo Hradiště Estate, Rodinný Archiv Valdštejnů (Waldstein family archives), III-21/28b, along with other surviving letters from the Mysliveček twins to Count Waldstein; transcriptions and facsimiles are in Mikanová, "Obermayerův učitel," 26–43. The text is in Appendix 2 below.

> I will be traveling quite soon to Venice, and since we will be coming together, your excellency would render me a great favor in sending traveling expenses addressed to Venice as compensation in so far as it is well known that the Italian air quickly empties the purse, and with many fine phrases one is there relieved of one's money. Otherwise you can be certain that I have spared no effort to have him serve your excellency properly and to please you. [Obermayer] will also bring back some of his compositions. And for the future, I hope forevermore to warrant your boundless graciousness and affection and remain the unworthy servant of your excellency and grace
>
> Joseph Misliwecek

Probably Mysliveček's spending habits (and not the "Italian air") were responsible for emptying his purse so quickly. From Florence, on 13 April, he wrote another letter about Obermayer to Count Waldstein, this one not explicit about financial matters:[13]

> Your grace will pardon me for taking the liberty to inconvenience you with the present letter, but in order to fulfill my most obligatory duty with the sufficiency I am driven to perform, I could not possibly neglect the one [Obermayer] your excellency entrusted to me; he also exhibits a great appetite for service to your excellency, which you will recognize well, because he was able to further his musical vocation due to your grace; for my part, because of his good behavior during the whole time, I recommend him to your protection. As you will see, he is well qualified in violin playing as well as in composition, and much more indeed is to be hoped from him; I send this in recognition of your boundless grace and high affection and remain your excellency and grace's most unworthy servant
>
> Joseph Misliwecek

Jáchym also wrote to Count Waldstein. On 18 April 1765, from Prague, he echoed his brother's remark about the excellent progress made by Obermayer and he mentioned his brother's need to be reimbursed for his expenses.[14] In another letter, dated 10 May 1765, Jáchym repeated the request.[15] Apparently, Josef Mysliveček feared that his own letters might not reach the count. The letter writing campaign did not produce a completely satisfactory result, since Josef found it necessary to petition Count Waldstein again after Obermayer had returned to the Waldstein household, as his letter from Venice, 3 October 1765, makes clear:[16]

> I hope that the present unworthy letter will find you in good health, and that Joseph Obermayer has arrived safely. There is a bill here for 30 ducats needed to reimburse me for the costs of his journey, yet I have been waiting over a month for the travel money. Thus I quite obediently request that a draft be made for the 30 ducats to be paid to me. If you would be gracious enough

[13] The text is in Appendix 2 below.

[14] Ibid.

[15] Ibid.

[16] Ibid.

to send me somewhat more in order to lessen my expenses, I would be delighted, for my brother up to now has very poorly looked after me as far as money is concerned. I kiss in deepest humility the hem of your and your excellency countess's garments and strive to be your excellency and grace's unworthy servant

Joseph Misliwecek

Five weeks later, the money had apparently not yet been disbursed. Mysliveček's letter to Count Waldstein is addressed from Venice on 13 November 1765:[17]

> I hope that Monsieur Josef Obrmeir has arrived to serve you, and in addition I advise you, that the banker here has given it to be understood that the draft for 30 zecchini to be sent to me has been postponed. This appears impossible to me. Thus I submissively request that I be informed when to expect it, for Obrmeir will be able to confirm for what purpose this money was advanced to him. I await a positive report kissing the hem of your garments and considering myself your excellency and grace's most unworthy servant
>
> Joseph Misliwecek

Mysliveček's final letter to Count Waldstein about Obermayer, written from Venice on 12 February 1766, was a rather clumsy attempt at damage control. It appears that Obermayer had not corroborated Mysliveček's image of himself as someone who selflessly attended to his student's needs. In fact, from what Mysliveček writes, Obermayer seems to have caused Count Waldstein to have canceled altogether the disbursement of the payment referred to in Mysliveček's letter of 13 November 1765:[18]

> I inform you with the present letter that I have duly received your letter of 29 November, and with it the accounting of Obrmeir. The latter, however, has caused me great heartbreak, for he has told your excellency falsehoods (for which I have never given him any cause). In so far as he has committed this misdeed (I do not know the reason), I must try to offer my side of the story, however briefly told. I certify that Obrmeir, whom I had perform in Florence at the residence of the Marchese [Carlo] Riccardi,[19] tried to play a bad trick by wanting to sit on the wagon like a hussar and go into the service of the marchese. Upon hearing this, I would in no way permit a person to whom I had been entrusted by your grace to go through with such an ungrateful act and did everything possible to prevent it. Indeed, I thought that it would be best to deter him as soon as possible, since the first attempt had not been successful. In order to prove that I am a loyal servant of the illustrious house of Waldstein, I have sent strong corroboration in the form of an affidavit from our landlord in Florence, attached here, in which he says that although

---

[17] Ibid.

[18] Ibid.

[19] Marchese Carlo Riccardi was a scion of a distinguished Florentine family (his given name is revealed in the testimonial of Tommaso Mancini transcribed in note 20 below). On the family and its principal residence, the Palazzo Medici Riccardi, see Marcello Vannucci, *Le grandi famiglie di Firenze* (Rome: Newton Compton, 1993), 373–80.

> [Obermayer] said that I treated him like a servant, he himself strongly maintains that he ate and slept with me, saw to my laundry and clothing the whole time in the most inexpensive way I know, and that I never gave him money (which I once had) for entertainment. Now that I have accurately described his character, and because I am here in Venice to tell the story, I feel that I must inform you that he tried to obtain employment in various locations in order not to return to your excellency, which showed to me great ingratitude both to your excellency and to me for what I have done for him. I have also come to realize in the letter sent to me, that whereas I set aside my needs in order for him to return, I made no pretense to recover anything except the travel money, which I know well your grace will grant to me undeservedly at last. I request this from your high and bountiful grace hoping to remain until death your excellency and grace's unworthy true servant
>
> Joseph Misliwecek

With his letter Mysliveček included an undated testimonial from Tommaso Mancini, the landlord who looked after Mysliveček and Obermayer when they stayed in Florence together:[20]

> At the request of Signor Giuseppe Mislivecek I provide here true testimony that Giuseppe Obomeir against the will of said Signor Mislivecek wanted to go into the service of the Marchese Carlo Riccardi, and that said Mislivecek would not permit such a thing, because he said it would have been an act of ingratitude to his benefactor. I also attest that had said Signor Mislivecek not taken action most insistently, the result would have been that the count would never have seen Obomeir again. This I affirm.
>
> Tommaso Mancini

Mysliveček's elaborate attempt to turn Count Waldstein against Obermayer did nothing to help Mysliveček obtain the funds he sought. In fact, there exists a much later letter to Count Waldstein that concerns Mysliveček's debts from the time he taught Obermayer. On 22 May 1785, a certain Gnümitz wrote to the count requesting that one of Mysliveček's creditors in Venice from the 1760s, a tailor named Huttner then living in Prague, be paid for the clothing that had been ordered for Obermayer on Mysliveček's credit.[21] Receipts in the possession of the tailor confirm that Mysliveček had spent the sums he claimed to meet Obermayer's requirements for clothing. As far as is known, Count Waldstein took no responsibility for retiring that debt.

This record of correspondence reveals unflattering character traits in most of the participants. As regards Mysliveček, patterns of behavior are disclosed that will be encountered later in this narrative, in particular his unabashed attitude about asking patrons for money. Although he did back down from his demand for gratuities in addition to the travel funds he provided for Obermayer, he did so only after he realized how seriously his integrity had been compromised in the eyes of Count Waldstein. There is evidence, too, that Mysliveček expected his brother, Jáchym, to subsidize his self-indulgent lifestyle. In sum, the letters reinforce the image of Mysliveček as a manipulative

[20] The text is in Appendix 2.

[21] Rodinný Archiv Valdštejnů, III-21/28a; transcribed in Bohadlo, 146 (facsimile, 148–49). The text is in Appendix 2.

(but charming) ne'er-do-well that is revealed in the Mozart correspondence. Mysliveček's attempt to lash back at Obermayer with the report of disloyalty corroborated by his Florentine landlord strikes one as desperate, if not petty; the purpose could only have been to see Obermayer disciplined by Count Waldstein. Although the landlord Mancini confirmed Mysliveček's account of Obermayer's wish to leave Waldstein's service, he did not back up Mysliveček's claim that he never treated Obermayer as a servant. For his part, Count Waldstein refused to reimburse Mysliveček for expenses incurred legitimately to train and assist his household musician. The only admirable behavior documented in this series of letters is the loyalty of Jáchym Mysliveček, who seems to have felt that his older twin was entitled to a certain fraternal deference. But however the count viewed the behavior of his two protégés neither seems to have earned his permanent disapproval. Obermayer continued in his service for decades, and Mysliveček felt comfortable enough in 1773 to hint at a gratuity from Count Waldstein in return for the dedication to him of a set of string quintets.[22]

The financial problems Mysliveček complained of eventually forced him to take extraordinary measures to continue his residence in Italy. On 1 November 1766, Josef Mysliveček negotiated a promissory note for 1000 gulden at 5% interest from Strahov Monastery in Prague on the collateral of Oak Mill, which he expected to inherit.[23] Correspondence about the loan was handled through the Austrian embassy in Venice, which had been headed since 1764 by Count Giacomo Durazzo, the former director of music and theater at the imperial court in Vienna who had been a supportive patron to Gluck. The loan agreement was signed at the embassy by a proxy representing Mysliveček. The loan was never repaid. After ten years of delinquency, Strahov Monastery repossessed Oak Mill and sold it to satisfy Mysliveček's debt.[24]

If, as Pelcl claimed, Mysliveček prized "fame and honors" more than "any amount of wealth,"[25] his efforts to raise money to stay in Italy would have been worth the trouble. He quickly acquired a reputation as an excellent composer of both vocal and instrumental music. While the precise output and chronology of Mysliveček's early instrumental works from Italy are difficult to determine, they certainly comprised string quintets, string quartets, and string trios.[26] Some of these compositions are advertised in the Breitkopf catalog in 1767, the first of many such listings.[27] The regular inclusion of Mysliveček's works in Breitkopf catalogs was a sure sign of his growing reputation and of the widespread dissemination of his instrumental music. But success as a composer of dramatic music was more important to Mysliveček, and for opera at least there is a somewhat firmer chronology of his works.

---

[22] This letter, Rodinný Archiv Valdštejnů, III-21/28, is translated and discussed in chapter 3.

[23] Čeleda, 228–29. The particulars of the loan are detailed in *Kniha Weszñicze Nebussicz (Nowy Registra Gruntowny neb Purgkrechtny)*, 5439, ff. 140-41, 174-75, Archiv Hlavního Města Prahy. Mysliveček's note was signed by proxy Johann Ernst Götzer at the Austrian Embassy in Venice, 1 November 1766. Čeleda mistakenly reported the loan as 2000 gulden, not 1000.

[24] According to *Kniha Weszñicze Nebussicz*, 5439, ff. 176v–82v, Strahov Monastery sold Oak Mill to one Jan Tuskaný after a complaint lodged in 1776 revealed that 1500 gulden were still owed from Mysliveček's loan. The amount was calculated as a principal of 1000 gulden, plus ten years' simple interest at 5%. See also Čeleda, 245–46, 272.

[25] Pelcl, 192; Appendix 1.

[26] Dates for Mysliveček's instrumental works are given in Catalog 1 below. His early instrumental works in Italy probably included the String Trios, op. 1, published in Paris ca. 1768; the String Quintets, op. 2, published in Paris and Lyon perhaps in 1767 or 1768; and the String Quartets, op. 3, published in Paris and Lyon perhaps in 1768 or 1769, besides a number of symphonies and overtures.

[27] Barry S. Brook, ed., *The Breitkopf Thematic Catalogue: The Six Parts and Sixteen Supplements, 1762–1787* (New York: Dover, 1966). The first music of Mysliveček to appear was a set of six string trios (most now lost). Sixteen other sets (or individual works) were subsequently listed up to the 1782/84 supplement. See Catalog 1 below for complete information.

In 1766, about two-and-a-half years after his arrival in Venice, Mysliveček's opera *Semiramide* was performed during the summer fair in Bergamo (fig. 2.1).[28] The unique surviving exemplar of the libretto for that production, housed in the Biblioteca Civica Angelo Mai in Bergamo, attributes the music to "Giuseppe Mislivecek detto il Boemo" (fig. 2.2), the first recorded use of the nickname Pelcl claimed was coined because Mysliveček's name was too difficult for Italians to pronounce.[29] Various reference works have asserted that the Italian equivalent of Mysliveček's surname, "Venatorini," was also in common use,[30] but it in fact was almost unheard of.[31] In the libretto for his first Italian opera, Mysliveček is already referred to as "celebre" ("famous") only four years after beginning his career as a composer.

It is clear that Mysliveček, as a non-Italian newcomer, found it easier to get a work performed at this provincial operatic center than in one of the major houses. The accomplishment was impressive, nonetheless; as mentioned earlier, Gluck did not see one of his operas produced in Italy until about five years after his arrival in the country. Mysliveček's connections in Venice may have assisted him in getting *Semiramide* performed (Bergamo was one of the westernmost territories controlled by the Venetian Republic in the 1760s). Operatic culture in Bergamo was heavily dependent on repertory and personnel from the Venetian theaters. Staging opera in Bergamo had earlier been a precarious undertaking; it had been performed only in the open air, in temporary wooden structures, or occasionally in the houses of nobles.[32] After 1760, a group of nobles sponsored a small theater, formerly a salon in the Bergamo citadel, and it was there that Mysliveček's first operatic production was accommodated. The extent of Mysliveček's participation in that production is not known. He almost certainly had some say in the selection of the singers, two of whom had recently appeared in Prague. The interpreter of the title role was Caterina Galli, a singer recorded in librettos from the Divadlo v Kotcích for the two seasons 1760–61 and 1761–62,[33] and another singer was Antonio Pini, recorded as one of the principal singers at the Divadlo v Kotcích in the 1763–64 season.[34] In the autumn of 1763, shortly before his departure for Venice, Mysliveček might have heard Pini in Prague.

Mysliveček's *Semiramide* of 1766 is unquestionably a remarkable musical achievement. For a standard of comparison, one may point to Paisiello's first serious opera, *Lucio Papirio dittatore*, performed at the Teatro San Carlo in Naples in 1767 when Paisiello was only a little younger than Mysliveček (Mysliveček turned twenty-nine in 1766, Paisiello was twenty-five in 1767). With all of the advantages of Paisiello's conservatory training and immersion in Neapolitan operatic culture,

---

[28] Sartori, *I libretti*, 5:177; and Appendix vol. 1:8. Sartori transcribed the libretto's date of publication incorrectly as 1765, a mistake that became the basis for misdated citations in several reference works in the 1990s, including *New Grove Opera*.

[29] Pelcl, 191; Appendix 1.

[30] The earliest authority for this claim is Gerber, *Historische-Biographisches Lexikon*. From Gerber, it found its way into Fétis, *Biographie universelle*; Wurzbach, *Biographisches Lexikon*, Schmidl, *Enciclopedia dello spettacolo*; *MGG*, ed. 1961, *Československý hudební slovník*; and *New Grove*, ed. 1980.

[31] The only important source from Mysliveček's lifetime that gives his name as Venatorini is the so-called *Quartbuch* catalog: see p. 277 below.

[32] For a brief description of opera in Bergamo, see Luigi Pelandi, "Teatri scomparsi: il Teatro di Cittadella ed il Teatro Cerri nel Palazzo della Ragione," *Rivista di Bergamo* 3, no. 7 (1952): 12–18.

[33] She is recorded in librettos for Wagenseil's *Demetrio* (autumn, 1760), Galuppi's *Alessandro nell'Indie* (autumn, 1760), Pescetti's *Ezio* (autumn, 1760), Antonio Mazzoni's *Didone abbandonata* (carnival, 1761), Hasse's *Solimano* (carnival, 1761), the anonymous *Artaserse* and *La clemenza di Tito* (autumn, 1761), Andrea Bernasconi's *Baiazet* (carnival, 1762), and the anonymous *Arianna e Teseo* (carnival, 1762).

[34] He is recorded in the anonymous *Demofoonte* and *Demetrio* (autumn, 1763) and Domenico Fischietti's *Alessandro nell'Indie* (carnival, 1764).

SEMIRAMIDE

DRAMMA PER MUSICA

DEL SIGNOR ABATE

PIETRO METESTASIO

POETA CESAREO

NEL TEATRO DI FIERA

DI BERGAMO

DEDICATO

A SUA ECCELL. LA NOB. DONNA

LA SIGNORA MARCHESA

CATTERINA

MARTINENGO.

IN BERGAMO, MDCCLXVI.

PER FRANCESCO TRAINA.

Con Licenza de' Superiori.

FIG. 2.1 Title page of the libretto for Mysliveček's Semiramide *(Bergamo, 1766)*

Courtesy of the Biblioteca Civica Angelo Mai, Bergamo

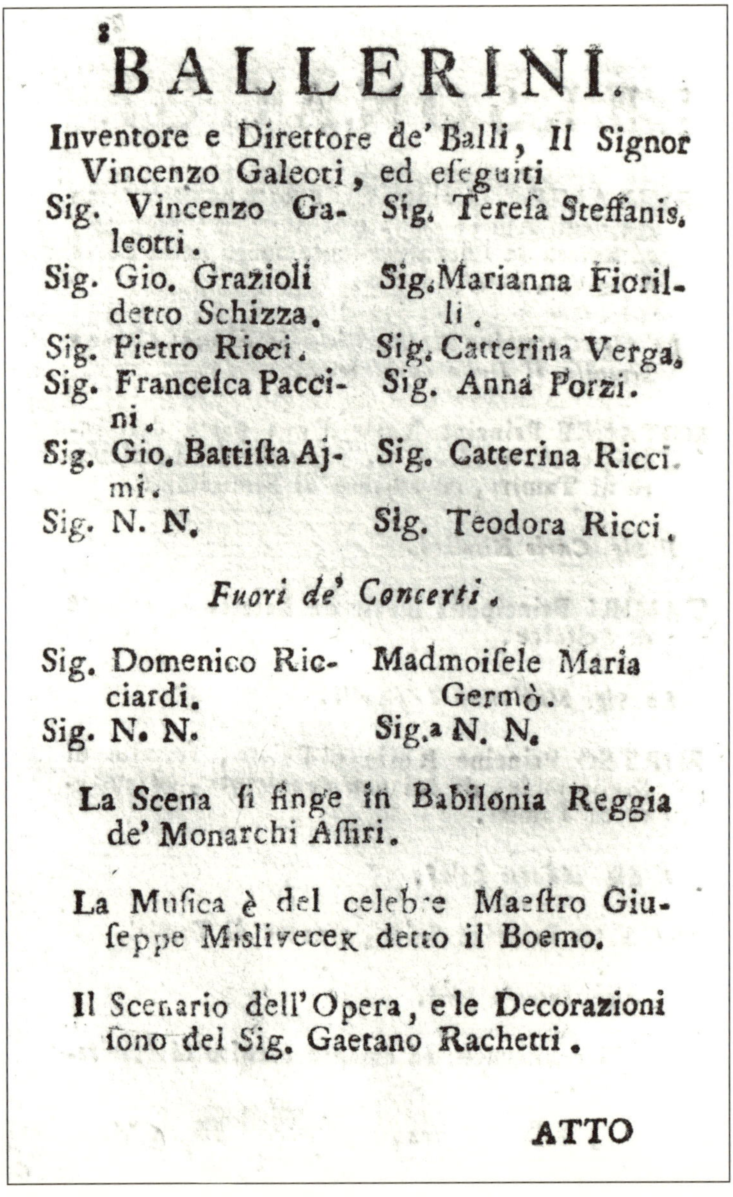

8

BALLERINI.

Inventore e Direttore de' Balli, Il Signor Vincenzo Galeoti, ed eſeguiti

Sig. Vincenzo Galeotti.	Sig. Tereſa Steffanis.
Sig. Gio. Grazioli detto Schizza.	Sig. Marianna Fiorilli.
Sig. Pietro Ricci.	Sig. Catterina Verga.
Sig. Franceſca Paccini.	Sig. Anna Porzi.
Sig. Gio. Battiſta Ajmi.	Sig. Catterina Ricci.
Sig. N. N.	Sig. Teodora Ricci.

Fuori de' Concerti.

Sig. Domenico Ricciardi.	Madmoiſele Maria Germò.
Sig. N. N.	Sig.a N. N.

La Scena ſi finge in Babilonia Reggia de' Monarchi Aſſiri.

La Muſica è del celebre Maeſtro Giuſeppe Mislivecek detto il Boemo.

Il Scenario dell'Opera, e le Decorazioni ſono del Sig. Gaetano Rachetti.

ATTO

Fig. 2.2 Partial cast list from the libretto for Semiramide *(Bergamo, 1766)*

Courtesy of the Biblioteca Civica Angelo Mai, Bergamo

his first serious opera is vastly inferior to Mysliveček's first opera in terms of melodic inventiveness, musical cohesion, and textural richness.

Mysliveček was able to get a great deal of mileage out of the music he composed for *Semiramide*. According to a surviving libretto, it was performed again in Alessandria at the Teatro Guasco in October of 1766 with Caterina Galli and Antonio Pini repeating their roles. Judging by an annotation in a score in the České Muzeum Hudby in Prague, it may also have been repeated in Alessandria in 1767.[35] When Mysliveček returned to Bohemia in 1768, *Semiramide* was performed in Prague,[36] and it may have been revived there in 1769 as well.[37] But the most enduring use for the music in *Semiramide* was as re-texted sacred arias that were copied in ecclesiastical institutions throughout Bohemia for decades.

There is a good possibility that *Semiramide* is the work that Pelcl meant when he wrote that Mysliveček's first opera was performed in Parma.[38] Pelcl's remark has puzzled researchers since no connection between Mysliveček or his music and the court of Parma has been documented in existing studies.[39] That did not prevent later embellishment of Pelcl's account, to the point of introducing a name and date for the opera supposedly given at Parma (a *Medea* in the carnival of 1764).[40] There have also been assertions of a love affair between Mysliveček and one of the leading singers in Parma in the mid-1760s, Lucrezia Aguiari.[41] No evidence has ever been uncovered to support this claim.

Marietta Shaginian advanced a specious theory that the work referred to by Pelcl was the small-scale dramatic cantata *Il Parnaso confuso*, and that it was performed as part of a wedding celebration at the court of Parma,[42] a theory expanded on by Rudolf Pečman, who considered *Il Parnaso confuso* to be Mysliveček's first opera and dated it "with the greatest probability" from 1765.[43] The

---

[35] Ms. XXXVII-D-343. This collection of parts includes the attribution, "Semiramide, in Alessandria 1767 nella fiera d'ottobre, musica del Sig. Giuseppe Misliweczek, detto il maestro Boemo, adesso in Praga l'anno 1769." No libretto survives to contradict this claim in favor of another work. Some scepticism may be justified since the sponsors of the theater in Alessandria where *Semiramide* was performed (the Solerio family) had the theater shut down shortly after Mysliveček's production closed in 1766. They were uncomfortable with the criticism leveled by clergy and disapproving townspeople who regarded the sponsorship of a theater an unbecoming activity for respectable nobility. See Andrea Tafuri, *La vita musicale di Alessandria, 1729–1968* (Alessandria: Ferrari-Occella, 1968), 54. The Teatro Guasco was eventually replaced by a civic theater. No opera productions there can be documented from librettos until 1768 (Sartori, *I libretti*).

[36] A libretto for a production during autumn in 1768 is in the Universitní Knihovna of the Národní Knihovna České Republiky in Prague.

[37] See note 35 above. No libretto survives for any other *opera seria* in Prague for carnival in 1769.

[38] Pelcl., 191; Appendix 1.

[39] The most important of these studies are Paolo Emilio Ferrari, *Spettacoli drammatico-musicali e coreografici in Parma dal 1628 al 1883* (Parma, 1884); and Nestore Pelicelli, "Musicisti in Parma nel sec. XVIII," *Note d'archivio per la storia musicale* 11 (1934): 20–57, 48–81; and 12 (1935): 27–42, 82–92.

[40] 1764 is first found in the entry for Mysliveček in Schmidl, *Dizionario universale dei musicisti*, 2:153, although Fétis hinted at it (*Biographie universelle des musiciens*, 2nd ed., 6:271). The title *Medea* was supplied by Ulisse Prota-Giurleo for the *Enciclopedia dello spettacolo*, 7, col. 990. Prota-Giurleo also added the name of a librettist (Friedrich Wilhelm Gotter) and a season of performance (carnival). The librettist's name apparently derives from a production of *Medea* with music by Jiří Antonín Benda that was performed in Leipzig in 1775. Prota-Giurleo probably did not realize that Gotter was only seventeen years old in 1764. The claims were repeated in *MGG*, ed. 1961, and *New Grove*, ed. 1980.

[41] The first mention of this myth is in *Grove's Dictionary of Music and Musicians*, 5th ed., ed. Eric Blom (London: Macmillan, 1954), 5:1047. Although completely unsubstantiated, it was accepted in Shaginian's biography, Pečman's biography, the Bohadlo collection of letters, and the entries for Mysliveček in *MGG*, ed. 1961, and *New Grove*, ed. 1980.

[42] Shaginian, 202–13.

[43] Rudolf Pečman, *Josef Mysliveček* (Prague: Editio Supraphon, 1981) (hereafter, cited as Pečman), 82–95; and Pečman, "Il Parnaso confuso—první Myslivečkova opera" (Il Parnaso confuso—the First Mysliveček Opera), *Opus musicum* 7 (1975): 136–43.

text of *Il Parnaso confuso* was written by Pietro Metastasio for the marriage of Archduke Joseph (later Holy Roman Emperor Joseph II) to the Bavarian princess Maria Josepha, an event that took place 23 January 1765. It is known that a performance of *Il Parnaso confuso* with music by Gluck took place earlier that month at Schönbrunn Palace in Vienna. Rudolf Pečman conjectured that Joseph's sister, Archduchess Maria Amalia, who performed the role of Apollo in the Gluck setting, brought the text to Parma, where she later reigned as duchess. He further believed that Maria Amalia celebrated her own wedding with Mysliveček's setting.

Regrettably, Pečman's dating of the marriage celebrations of Maria Amalia to Duke Ferdinand of Parma is mistaken. Archduchess Maria Amalia was married to Duke Ferdinand of Parma by proxy in Vienna on 27 June 1769 and in person at Colorno on 18 July 1769.[44] No connection between Maria Amalia and the court of Parma existed in 1765. It should be emphasized nonetheless that an early date of composition for *Il Parnaso confuso* (the music survives in undated manuscripts in Prague and Rome) is corroborated by stylistic features, especially the choice of aria forms. Mysliveček lived in a period of rapid evolution of aria forms. None of his other dramatic works employs such a high proportion of strict *da capo* arias as this work does, a sure sign that it was composed no later than 1767.[45] That the score of *Il Parnaso confuso* somehow made it to the Cistercian monastery of Osek[46] and that some of its arias were disseminated in Bohemian ecclesiastical institutions are also hints that the music was completed by 1768 and that, along with his other early dramatic works, Mysliveček could have brought it back to Bohemia when he returned that year. The setting may have been a preparatory work that he composed in 1765 or 1766 to gain experience with vocal composition before he attempted a full-scale opera. There is no particular reason to believe that Mysliveček's *Il Parnaso confuso* was composed for Parma.

More reliable confirmation of a connection with the court of Parma comes from a score of *Semiramide* in the library of the Ajuda Palace in Lisbon that is part of the vast collection of opera scores assembled by King José I of Portugal (*r.* 1750–77) through agents in Italy. The king sought to have all works performed at the major operatic centers in Italy copied and added to his library.[47] Operas performed in minor centers in Italy, such as Bergamo and Alessandria, ordinarily were not copied for his court. The score of *Semiramide*, which is dated 1766 without an indication of the venue of performance, matches the binding and scribal hand of other scores in the Ajuda Palace Library that were copied at the court of Parma in the 1760s.[48] Whether or not Mysliveček's *Semiramide* was performed in its entirety, used as a source of arias, or simply was part of the collection of scores at Parma, the above evidence suggests that there must have been some contact between Mysliveček and the court of Parma.

---

[44] *Burke's Royal Families of the World*, 1: *Europe & Latin America* (London: Burke's Peerage, 1977), 338.

[45] Three of the work's six arias are in strict *da capo* form. In the much more extensive *Semiramide*, the same number of arias are in strict *da capo* form ("Talor se il vento fremi" from act 1, scene 14; "Voi, che le mie vicende" from act 2, scene 3; and "Ciel mi vuole appresso" from act 3, scene 1). In Mysliveček's second opera, *Bellerofonte* (1767), only one aria comes close to being cast in strict *da capo* form—"Già cinto sembrami" from act 2, scene 1, in which the *dal segno* repeat begins in the middle of the opening ritornello.

[46] See Catalog 2 below.

[47] For operatic culture surrounding the court of Portugal, see Marita P. McClymonds, *Niccolò Jommelli: The Last Years, 1769–1774* (Ann Arbor: UMI Research Press, 1980), 19–58.

[48] The binding and the scribal hand resemble those in the score for Tommaso Traetta's *Feste d'Imeneo*, for example, performed at the court of Parma in 1760. The Ajuda Library manuscripts are cataloged in Marianna Amélia Machado Santos, *Biblioteca da Ajuda: catálogo de música manuscrita* (Lisbon: Biblioteca da Ajuda, 1959).

According to Pelcl, the success of Mysliveček's first opera (whatever he thought it was) brought Mysliveček to the attention of the Neapolitan ambassador to Parma, who invited Mysliveček to compose an opera for performance at the royal court in Naples.[49] In comparing the musical quality of the two works, *Semiramide* would have been much more likely to elicit such a reaction than would *Il Parnaso confuso*. The identity of the ambassador is more difficult to say. The Kingdom of the Two Sicilies maintained no regular diplomatic relations with the duchy of Parma in the 1760s; the only ambassadorial exchanges between the two courts were *ad hoc* delegations that delivered felicitations on the marriages of King Ferdinand IV of the Kingdom of the Two Sicilies in 1768 and Duke Ferdinand of Parma in 1769.[50]

It is possible that an ambassador in one of the other states Mysliveček visited brought him to the attention of the Neapolitan court—for example, Count Giuseppe Finocchietti di Faulon, ambassador from the court of Naples to the Republic of Venice throughout this period, or, in view of Mysliveček's known residence in Florence from time to time, Marchese Luigi Viviani, the long-serving ambassador from Naples to the grand duchy of Tuscany. Viviani was a friend and frequent correspondent of Marchese Bernardo Tanucci, who was the most powerful member of the regency council that governed Naples and Sicily during the minority of King Ferdinand IV (1759–67) and later, between 1767 and 1774, served as prime minister of the realm.[51] Viviani could have provided Mysliveček with the powerful connection at the royal court that would in all probability have been necessary to arrange an operatic production with music by a non-Italian with little experience.[52]

However Mysliveček's commission was arranged, his engagement to compose an opera for the 1767 carnival season in Naples was confirmed by 14 October 1766. In a letter from Naples to the Bolognese composer Giovanni Battista Martini, the German tenor Ignaz Wierl parenthetically made the following observations:[53]

> Here there is nothing new [to report]; the first opera at the Real Teatro di San Carlo finished last month; the next, written by Signor Maestro Piccinni, will be presented on 4 November and the last of the upcoming carnival season, it is believed, will be written by a certain Signor Misliwecek of Bohemian nationality —that is all I can say regarding theatrical matters.

This, it seems, is how Mysliveček's name was first introduced to Padre Martini, later one of his closest professional acquaintances and most valued supporters.

To understand Wierl's remarks fully, a short digression on the scheduling of operatic entertainments at the Teatro San Carlo is warranted. In Venice, singers were usually engaged by theaters for

---

[49] Pelcl, 191; Appendix 1.

[50] Otto Friedrich Winter, ed., *Repertorium der diplomatischen Vertreter aller Lände* (Graz and Cologne: Hermann Böhlaus, 1965), 3:300 and 425.

[51] A useful resource in English is Harold Acton, *The Bourbons of Naples (1734–1825)* (London: Methuen, 1956).

[52] Pečman advances the theory that Count Durazzo, imperial ambassador in Venice, was responsible for Mysliveček's first operatic commission in Naples, supposing a friendship between Durazzo and Tanucci and a sea-voyage to Naples arranged under Durazzo's auspices (Pečman, 110–11). No documentary evidence is given to support this scenario.

[53] The bulk of Padre Martini's correspondence is summarized in Anne Schnoebelen, *Padre Martini's Collection of Letters in the Civico Museo Bibliografico in Bologna: An Annotated Index* (hereafter, cited as Schnoebelen) (New York: Pendragon Press, 1979). This letter, I.1.167 (Schnoebelen, no. 5637), is transcribed in full in Bohadlo, 48. The text is in Appendix 2 below.

the autumn season, and they usually remained at the same theater through the following carnival season or spring. Elsewhere (in Turin, for example) only the carnival season saw performances of *opere serie*. In Naples, by contrast, singers of *opere serie* were engaged for an operatic season that began on 30 May and lasted through the carnival season of the following year. At the Teatro San Carlo, operatic productions generally commemorated the birthdays or name-days of the Spanish and Neapolitan royal families. The king of Spain, Charles III, had been the highly respected king of the Kingdom of the Two Sicilies between 1735 and 1759. While Charles's son, Ferdinand IV, ruled Naples and Sicily between 1759 and 1825, Charles III remained influential in shaping the political policies of the Kingdom of the Two Sicilies until his death in 1788. His watchful eye is reflected in the importance accorded his birthday and name-day in arranging the operatic season at the San Carlo. 4 November, Charles's name-day (the feast of St. Charles Borromeo), and 20 January, his birthday, were always commemorated with new operatic productions. The name-day of King Ferdinand IV, 30 May (the feast of St. Ferdinand III of Castile and Leon) marked the beginning of the opera season, and his birthday (12 January) was incorporated into the carnival celebrations. Celebratory cantatas were sometimes performed on Ferdinand IV's birthday, but new operas were not presented until Charles III's birthday (20 January). When Archduchess Maria Carolina arrived from Vienna to marry Ferdinand IV in 1768, another important day—her birthday of 13 August—was added to the round of operatic entertainments at the Teatro San Carlo. Her presence in Naples also enhanced the importance of 4 November, which was celebrated as her name-day along with that of her father-in-law.

Using this chronological framework, it is possible to identify the first opera of the 1766–67 season that was referred to by Wierl: Giuseppe Scolari's *Antigono*, first performed on 30 May 1766.[54] The Piccinni opera mentioned in the Wierl letter was *Il Cid*, first performed for the name-day of the king of Spain on 4 November 1766. Wierl made no mention of the first opera of the carnival season of 1767 (Antonio Sacchini's *Lucio Vero*, first performed on 27 December 1766), but the last opera of the carnival season was Mysliveček's *Bellerofonte*, performed with overwhelming success on 20 January 1767.

Mysliveček's first Neapolitan opera was composed under circumstances quite different from those that had attended the productions of *Semiramide* only a few months earlier. Whereas the Bergamo and Alessandria productions of *Semiramide* were dedicated to obscure local nobility (Marchesa Caterina Martinengo and the Count of Autremont, respectively), the production of *Bellerofonte* was prepared for a crowned head of state. The cast included Anton Raaff and Caterina Gabrielli, two of the most famous operatic stars of the day. From this time until his death, Mysliveček's new productions would almost always feature at least one performer of comparable stature with vocal writing of commensurate difficulty. Raaff became a close friend, whom Mysliveček shared with the Mozart family. Gabrielli, reputedly, became Mysliveček's lover, though there is no more foundation to this claim than to the reports of his affair with Lucrezia Aguiari.[55] Somewhat better documented is a compliment from Gabrielli that Mysliveček wrote better for her voice than any other composer, but even this statement is suspect.[56]

---

[54] The Teatro San Carlo repertory is listed in Sartori, *I libretti*; and in Felice Filippis and Raffaele Arnese, *Cronache del Teatro di S. Carlo* (Naples: Edizioni Politica Popolare, 1961–63).

[55] The earliest mention of an affair with Gabrielli is in *Grove Dictionary*, 5th ed. (5:1047). It was repeated in many works, including *MGG*, ed. 1961; the Shaginian biography; *New Grove*, ed. 1980; the Pečman biography; and the Bohadlo collection of documents.

[56] The source of the anecdote appears to be Carl Friedrich Cramer's *Magazin der Musik* (Hamburg, 1783; reprint, Hildesheim: Georg Olms, 1971), 1:166. Of Gabrielli's appearing in Mysliveček's *Armida* in Milan in 1780, Cramer reported, "man sagt, dass sie sich alle

Some details about the circumstances of the production of *Bellerofonte* on 20 January 1767 can be gleaned from documents once housed in the Archivio di Stato in Naples that were thought to have been destroyed during World War II. In an article primarily about legal action taken against Mysliveček in Naples in 1774,[57] Ulisse Prota-Giurleo revealed that the libretto to *Bellerofonte* was proposed to the king by the impresario of the San Carlo, Giovanni Tedeschi (Amadori), on 23 December 1766, and that the *Giunta dal canto* (a committee that oversaw operatic productions at court) found the libretto had been set successfully for other court theaters and that excellent reports had come in about Mysliveček's abilities as composer of both vocal and instrumental music.

In less than a month, Mysliveček wrote the entire opera, as well as a cantata to honor the birthday of the king of Spain on 20 January 1767. There is no question of the importance *Bellerofonte* had in establishing Mysliveček's reputation. It was clearly memorable to Pelcl, since it is the only opera he mentioned by name in his biographical sketch of Mysliveček. The Italian audience, he claimed, was astonished at the quality of the music, written as it was by a Czech.[58] To their credit, the Neapolitans had never had difficulty accepting northerners who composed in the operatic styles they enjoyed. From this time until his death in 1781, more works by Mysliveček were presented at the San Carlo than works by any other composer.

In the wake of Mysliveček's success in Naples, new opportunities to expand his reputation were not long in coming. *Bellerofonte* was repeated in Siena in the spring of 1767 to celebrate the entrance into the city of the new rulers of the grand duchy of Tuscany, Archduke Leopold of Austria (later Holy Roman Emperor Leopold II) and his wife, Maria Luisa of Bourbon, a sister of King Ferdinand IV of Naples. It was she who, putatively, denigrated Mozart's opera *La clemenza di Tito* (calling it "una porcheria tedesca") when it was performed in Prague in 1791 for her coronation as queen of Bohemia. Mysliveček's *Bellerofonte* doubtless pleased this couple more and may have laid the foundation for his later commissions in Florence. For their part, the Neapolitans were delighted with *Bellerofonte* and they brought Mysliveček back almost immediately to compose another opera, this time for the name-day of the king of Spain on 4 November 1767. The result, *Farnace*, was one of the last and one of the best settings of a venerable libretto by Antonio Maria Lucchini.

Mysliveček's second opera for Naples was followed very soon by a commission to compose a setting of Metastasio's *Il trionfo di Clelia* for the carnival season in Turin in 1768, with Caterina Gabrielli in the title role. Besides establishing his reputation in Turin, this production brought Mysliveček into contact with Abbé Quirino Gasparini, the local composer who later was instrumental in bringing Mysliveček into contact with Padre Martini. It is clear from surviving payment records from *Il trionfo di Clelia* that Mysliveček was paid at a level commensurate with his status as a newcomer of growing reputation. The opera premiered on 26 December 1767.[59]

---

ihre Arien ausdrücklich dazu von Misliwizeck habe schreiben lassen; und doch hatte es wenig gefehlt, dass sie nicht einen Abend wäre ausgepfiffen worden" (it is said that she [previously] had all of her arias written expressly for her by Mysliveček, a policy that failed so little for her, that she had not been hissed at even a single evening). A variant appeared in Fétis, *Biographie universelle*, 2nd ed., 6:272: "La célèbre cantatrice Gabrielli aimait beaucoup à chanter les airs du musicien de la Bohème, et disait qu'aucun compositeur n'écrivait aussi bien pour sa voix" (the renowned singer Gabrielli very much loved to sing the arias of this Bohemian musician, and she said that no other composer wrote as well for her voice). From Fétis, the remark was paraphrased in *MGG*, ed. 1961 and *New Grove*, ed. 1980.

[57] See Appendix 1.

[58] Pelcl, 191; Appendix 1.

[59] Marie-Thérèse Bouquet, *Storia del Teatro Regio di Torino* (Turin: Cassa di Risparmio, 1976), 1:320–21; Margaret Ruth Butler, *Operatic Reform at Turin's Teatro Regio: Aspects of Production and Stylistic Change in the 1760s* (Lucca: Libreria Musicale Italiana, 2001), 294. Using

Early in 1768 Mysliveček seems to have cut short his stay in Turin and to have returned to Bohemia for a few months to attend to family matters, including the final settlement of his father's estate. As a result of judicial decrees of 21 March and 12 October 1767[60] (fig. 2.3), Mysliveček fell upon a small fortune in real estate, all of which he eventually lost. Specifically, Mysliveček inherited Oak Mill in Horní Šárka and all its surrounding fields and vineyards, the whole estate valued at 7,000 gulden.[61] In 1776, to satisfy a debt of 1000 gulden owed to Strahov Monastery, it was sold.[62] Kutil Mill in the Old City of Prague went to his brother, Jáchym, who lived there until his death in 1788. Mysliveček's mother received ownership of Blue Ship House in the Old City and was to be paid 1,000 gulden by each of her sons from their shares of Matěj's estate. It is doubtful that she received any of this money, as she died a short time later (11 December 1767) and was buried in St. Giles. Her second husband, Jan Čermák, new owner of Blue Ship House, followed her to the grave on 30 March 1772.[63] As executor of the estate, Josef was directed to pay 1,500 gulden to his sister Maria Anna, an obscure figure about whom virtually nothing is known except that she was a nun who took the name Sister Bernarda.[64] The money due her was to be paid to her convent, but, apparently, was never paid.[65]

For somebody with Mysliveček's lifestyle, the settlement of the estate was worse than inheriting nothing: he received no liquid assets, yet was to make cash payments to his female relatives based on the value of the land he possessed. His response seems to have been to ignore the judicial decrees concerning his financial obligations and neglect the management of the mill in Horní Šárka entirely.

Jaroslav Čeleda believed that Mysliveček was back in Prague by February 1768.[66] It is logical to assume that he returned to Prague to attend to matters related to the death of his mother and settlement of his father's estate, but it is clear that he also sought to reestablish his reputation as a composer in his native city. To assist in this effort, he apparently brought back with him scores for all principal dramatic works he had composed in Italy up to that time: the dramatic cantata *Il Parnaso confuso* and the operas *Semiramide*, *Bellerofonte*, *Farnace*, and *Il trionfo di Clelia*. Arias from these works form the basis of the vast dissemination of Mysliveček vocal works in Bohemian ecclesiastical

---

the monetary values of *lire*, *soldi*, and *denari* of the original documents, it is recorded that Mysliveček was paid L.1,136 to prepare the music for *Il trionfo di Clelia*. Antonio Sacchini was paid only L.946.13.4 in the 1765–66 season for his *Alessandro nell'Indie*, whereas J. C. Bach, at a similar stage in his career in the 1760–61 season, received L.1,230.13.4 for his *Artaserse*. Also in the early stages of his career, Giovanni Paisiello was paid L.1,230.13.4 for his *Annibale in Torino* in the 1770–71 season. An established master of *opera seria* in the 1764–65 season, Francesco de Majo, received L.1,662.10 for his *Motezuma*. The least well-paid composers in Turin tended to be local figures such as Quirino Gasparini and Ignazio Celoniat. The former received only L.700 for his *Mitridate* in the 1766–67 season, while the latter received even less (L.600) for his *Ecuba* in the 1768–69 season. In contrast, Caterina Gabrielli commanded L.8,500 to sing in Mysliveček's opera.

[60] Čeleda, 230–33. Archiv Hlavního Města Prahy, I 135, documents nos. 443/1–5. 443/1 is a decree dated 19 November 1765 ordering an audit of the value of the mill buildings once owned by Matěj Mysliveček. 443/2 is a report dated 30 January 1766 detailing their worth. 443/3 is an undated document suggesting a formula for division of the estate among the living heirs. 443/4, dated 8 May 1767, is a formal proposal to divide the estate. 443/5 is a contract dated 12 October 1767 that confirms the acceptance of the proposal by Josef Mysliveček, Jáchym Mysliveček, and their mother Anna Čermáková. Josef's participation in these proceedings was through proxy.

[61] Čeleda, 232–37. The division of the estate is recorded in Archiv Hlavního Města Prahy, *Liber contractuum*, 4621, ff. 98–100v.

[62] See p. 35 above.

[63] Čeleda, 125–26, 143–44. Blue Ship House was sold outside the Mysliveček family after Jan Čermák died in 1772.

[64] Ibid., 271–73, contains a summary of all the available information about her.

[65] Ibid., 271–72.

[66] Ibid., 237–38.

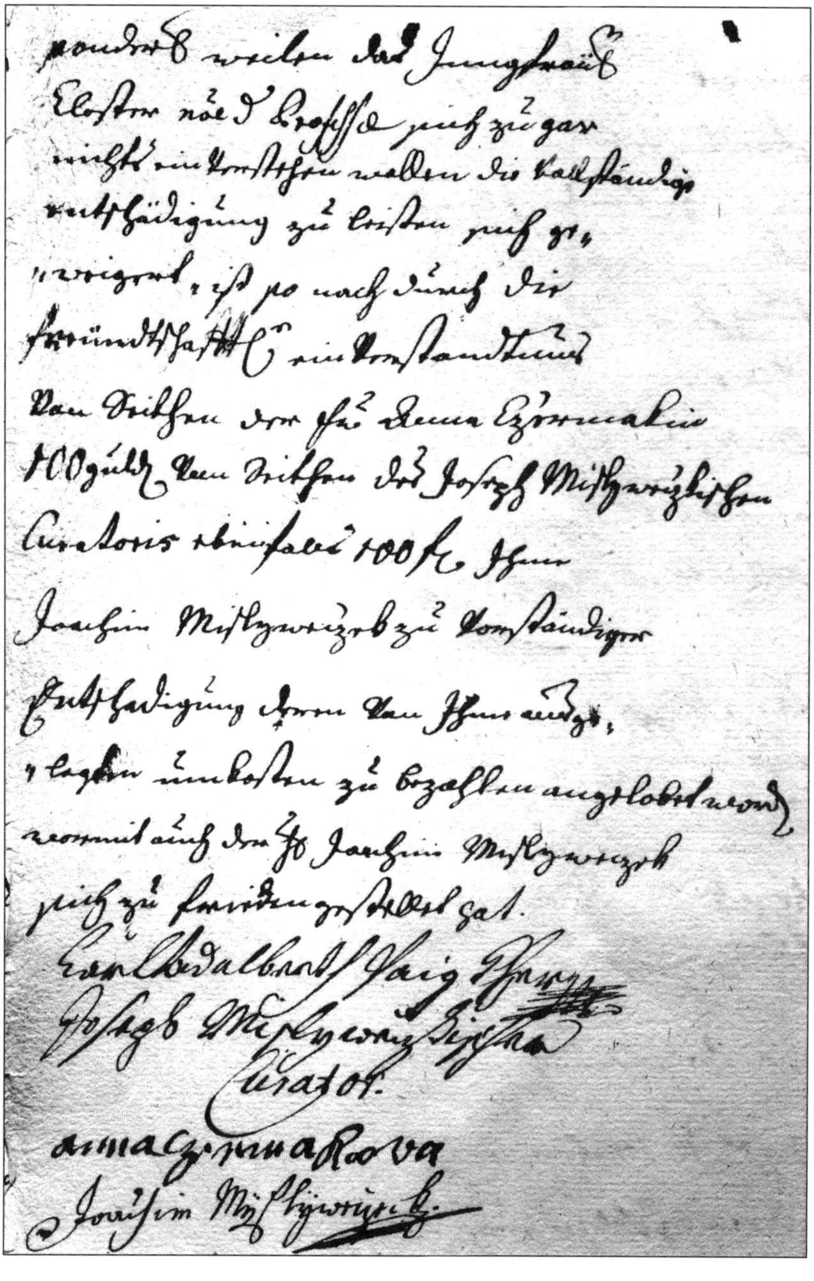

Fig. 2.3 ***Contract recording assent of Mysliveček family members to estate settlement, 12 October 1767. Signature "Joseph Mislyweczek infra Curator" was added by proxy***

Courtesy of the Archiv Hlavního Města Prahy

institutions: dozens and dozens of Mysliveček aria manuscripts survive from all parts of Bohemia, typically with sacred Latin words substituted for the original Italian; favorite arias were copied by personnel in Bohemian and Moravian churches and monasteries well into the nineteenth century. *Semiramide*, *Bellerofonte*, and *Farnace* were all mounted in Prague in 1768, an amazing occurrence. Among native Bohemian composers, only Gluck had previously seen full-scale productions of his operas in Prague, and in the later eighteenth century the only other composer to duplicate the feat was Jan Antonín Koželuh.[67] The fact that Mysliveček's nationality was carefully noted in two of the librettos for the Prague productions is confirmation of the novelty of such an achievement.[68]

While all surviving librettos for the Prague production of *Bellerofonte* indicate that the opera was performed during carnival in 1767, this period is unlikely: Mysliveček was in Naples for the premiere of *Bellerofonte* on 20 January 1767. It would have been difficult for his music to the opera to have reached Prague in time to mount a carnival production there in the same year. The cast list in the Prague librettos for *Bellerofonte* records singers engaged for the 1767–68 season at the Divadlo v Kotcích, not for the 1766–67 season.[69] Furthermore, some of the singers listed in the *Bellerofonte* librettos are recorded as singing elsewhere during the Prague carnival operatic season of 1767.[70] It thus appears likely that *Bellerofonte* was actually performed in Prague sometime during the carnival of 1768, at about the time of Mysliveček's return to the city. From the libretto it can be established that productions of *Semiramide* and *Farnace* took place in autumn and December of 1768, respectively.

Following the performances of *Bellerofonte*, *Farnace*, and *Semiramide* in 1768, no more Mysliveček operas were heard in Prague until the twentieth century—a reason to suspect that Mysliveček never went back there. Nonetheless, fresh examples of Mysliveček's dramatic music continued to arrive in Prague from Italy in the form of oratorios. These were usually performed at the magnificent church of St. Francis Serafin (sometimes referred to as Knights' or Crucifers' Church) in the Old City,[71] a church associated with the obscure Bohemian religious order, the Military Order of the Knights of the Cross with the Red Star. For the first of these productions, much fuss was made in the Prague newspaper *Der Unsichtbare* about Mysliveček's Italian successes.[72]

---

[67] Koželuh's operas *Alessandro nell'Indie* and *Demofoonte* were performed in 1769 and 1771, respectively.

[68] The German portion of the bilingual libretto for *Farnace* (performed December, 1768) attributes the music in the following manner: "Die Musik ist eine sinnreiche Erfindung des berühmten Herrn Josef Misliwezek sonst der Böhm genannt. Dessen Geschicklichkeit und Kunst Italian selbst (wo diese Kunst am meisten blühet!) bewunderet" (The music is the ingenious invention of the famous Mr. Josef Misliwezek, otherwise called the Bohemian. Whose skill and art Italy itself [where this art most blossoms] admires). The libretto for *Bellerofonte* specifically indicates Mysliveček as a native of Prague.

[69] As in Venice, it was customary in Prague to engage singers for an operatic season beginning in the autumn and continuing through the following carnival and spring seasons. The cast of *Bellerofonte* in Prague included Antonio Prati, Angela Calori, Emanuelle Cornacchia, Marianna Ottini, Stella Lodi, and Giovanni Delpini. This cast list matches the one printed for the anonymous *Arianna e Teseo* performed in autumn, 1767. In contrast, the cast for Pietro Guglielmi's *Tamerlano* (carnival, 1767) included Piero de Mezzo, Cecilia Buini, and Gertrude Celini in addition to Calori, Cornacchia, and Delpini, who remained for the 1767–68 season.

[70] Antonio Prati is recorded in Parma for appearances in an *Ipermestra* and a *Tigrane* during carnival in 1767, whereas Stella Lodi appeared in Vienna in Piccinni's *Le contadine bizzarre* during the same carnival season.

[71] The first Mysliveček oratorio performed there was *Tobia* in 1770, followed by *Adamo ed Eva* in 1771, *La passione* in 1773, *La liberazione d'Israel* in 1775, and *Isacco figura del redentore* in 1778: see Catalog 2 below. In addition, *La passione* was reprised in 1782.

[72] The following announcement (including some laudatory doggerel) recorded the production of *Tobia* in 1770 (*Der Unsichtbare*, issue no. 8, dated 28 April 1770, pp. 71–72): "Unter denen verschiedenen geistlichen Singspielen, die gegen das Ende der Charwoche in einigen Kirchen unsere Stadt alljährlich aufgeführet zu werden pflegen, hat sich dasjenige gewiss ausnehmend hervorgethan, welches unsern in Wälschland so berühmten Herrn Misliweczek zum Verfasser hat, and wir für heuer den grossmüthigen Freygebigkeit eines von unseren verehrungswürdigen Grossen zu danken haben. Wie prächtig liess, in Liedern und Chören,/ der Böhme da sein

Mysliveček's return to Prague provided him with a glorious personal triumph, but he did not remain there long to savor it. Ostensibly newly wealthy (but actually critically short of ready cash), he embarked once again for Italy.

Vaterland/ Italiens erlauchte Tonkunst Hören!/ Horcht! Kenner: Mraw!/ und Süssig spannt,/ Zu sanften Solo's schon die Seiten/ Der Stimme, die zum Herzen singt,/ Die Zaubertriller abzustreiten;/ Und Fialens Hautbois dringt/ Durchs Ohr ins Innerste Seele,/ Die ganz vor lauter Lust erklingt,/ und, dass der Luft die Ewigkeit nicht fehle,/ Die Rührung, so sie fühlt, zu Jesu Grabe bringt."

The record of Prague newspapers is spotty for the eighteenth century. A survey of information about music making reported in the principal surviving issues is in Jiří Berkovec, ed., *Musikalia v pražském periodickém tisku 18. století* (Musicalia in Prague Periodical Literature of the Eighteenth Century) (Prague: Státní Knihovna ČSR, 1989).

3

"FAME AND HONORS": LIFE, 1768–76

Mysliveček's return to Italy in 1768 initiated a period of particular accomplishment that lasted approximately eight years. In that time he composed most of his greatest compositions, attracted attention for his work in many parts of Europe, and became the friend and confidant of distinguished musical figures, among them Wolfgang and Leopold Mozart. Mysliveček's dynamic personality (as Wolfgang Mozart described it, "full of fire, spirit, and life"[1]) assisted him in his quest for recognition, though his financial irresponsibility and other discreditable behavior led to some unfortunate consequences.

It is not known exactly how long Mysliveček remained in Bohemia in the early months of 1768, although he must have returned by the summer, when the documentary record of his movements picks up again in connection with his residence in Padua. Upon his return from Bohemia, Mysliveček may have continued to use Venice as a base of operations for his expanding career, but he also began to spend time in nearby Padua, maintaining ties there from at least the summer of 1768 until 1774. The presence of Giuseppe Tartini in Padua could have been an attraction since Mysliveček was also a gifted violinist,[2] but probably more compelling to him were opportunities for patronage from academies and the Basilica del Santo.[3] The first record of Mysliveček's presence in Padua comes from an account of a cantata performance at the Accademia Ricovrati in honor of Marino Cavalli, the leader of the Accademia Delian, on 30 August 1768.[4]

The potential for continued patronage in Padua was very high, owing in particular to Marchese Giuseppe Ximenes of Aragon (1718–84), a Florentine who had resided in Padua since 1762 and who in 1768 began an informal academy that promoted native composers, such as Giuseppe and Antonio Calegari, and notable foreigners, such as Mysliveček, Johann Gottlieb Naumann,[5] and Mozart. Also

---

[1] The characterization is Mozart's: see his letter to his father, 11 October 1777, in Anderson, 302–06; Bauer and Deutsch, 2:43–46.

[2] The careers of Tartini and cellist Antonio Vandini, who often performed together in Padua, point to interesting musical connections between Prague and Padua in the eighteenth century. Both Tartini and Vandini had resided in Prague in the 1720s. Seger still remembered them in 1772; see Burney, *The Present State of Music*, 2:13; *Musical Tours*, 2:134; *Tagebuch*, 3:7.

[3] An earlier Bohemian émigré in Padua, Bohuslav Černohorský, had been organist at the Basilica del Santo (1715–20 and 1731–41). On patronage in Padua, see *Storia della musica al Santo di Padova*, ed. Sergio Durante and Pierluigi Pietrobelli (Vicenza: Neri Pozza, 1990) and *Mozart, Padova e la Betulia liberata: Committenza, interpretazione e fortuna delle azioni sacre metastasiane nel '700*, ed. Paolo Pinamonti (Florence: Olschki, 1991).

[4] This performance is described in Elisa Grossato, "Le accademie musicali a Padova (1766–1790)," in *Mozart, Padova*, ed. Pinamonti, 203. In some earlier literature (for example, *New Grove*, ed. 1980), the performance date is given as 1763.

[5] During periods of activity in Italy (1757–64, 1765–68, and 1772–74), Naumann, a Saxon affiliated with the Dresden Court from 1764, established himself as a composer of vocal music in the serious style.

staying in Padua in this period was the composer Giovanni Battista Ferrandini, a pensioner and agent of Elector Maximilian III Joseph of Bavaria. Working on behalf of the elector, Ferrandini identified composers who could be commissioned to compose operas for the carnival season in Munich. Mysliveček eventually received an operatic commission from the court at Munich, as did Tommaso Traetta, Antonio Sacchini, and Pietro Pompeo Sales after they had visited Padua.[6]

In terms of compositional output, Mysliveček's oratorios remain the most significant legacy of his association with Padua. Although he composed oratorios only from 1769 to 1776, he was indisputably one of the leading masters of the genre in his day. All of Mysliveček's early oratorios were written for performance in Padua: *Tobia* (1769), *I pellegrini al sepolcro* (1770), *Betulia liberata* (1771), and the mysterious *Giuseppe riconosciuto* (perhaps early 1770s).[7]

As stimulating as the time he spent in Padua must have been, Mysliveček would never have confined himself to one city year after year. On the contrary, he seems to have tried to satisfy the demand for his works captured in Pelcl's remark that "all of Italy" wished to hear Mysliveček's "extraordinary style of expression."[8] He had already established his reputation in Naples (1767), and had seen his *Il trionfo di Clelia* produced successfully in Turin (carnival, 1768). In 1769 he achieved even more success in Venice with his setting of Metastasio's *Demofoonte* staged at the Teatro San Benedetto. According to Pelcl, the opera was so popular that sonnets were written in Mysliveček's honor and Venetian nobles "stood in line as Mysliveček left the theater" to render him "public expressions of esteem." Lack of independent confirmation, of course, makes Pelcl's account somewhat suspicious; his assertion that Italians "were convinced for the first time that their own great *maestri* could be surpassed by a musician from this side of the Alps" is also difficult to accept.[9]

As in most cities where Mysliveček had occasion to stay, Florence in 1769 offered Mysliveček plenty of opportunity for patronage. His first commissioned opera there, a setting of Metastasio's *Ipermestra*, premiered at the Pergola Theater on 27 March 1769. His friend Anton Raaff sang Danao and Elisabetta Teiber had the title role. The production met with predictable success.[10] Grand Duke Leopold of Tuscany (*r.* 1765–90), former archduke of Austria, had encountered Mysliveček's music two years earlier in Siena, where he saw *Bellerofonte* play. Since the beginning of his reign Leopold had been eager to have new *opere serie* of high quality mounted at the Pergola Theater. Earlier, for a long period the Pergola had mainly staged pastiches and revivals of operas originally produced elsewhere.[11] During a surprise visit to Florence, Leopold's brother, Holy Roman Emperor

---

[6] I am grateful to Karl Böhmer for bringing these connections to my attention. On Ferrandini, see Paolo Cattelan, "Giovanni Ferandini, musicista 'padovano'," in *Mozart, Padova*, ed. Pinamonti, 217–44. Sales, a Brescian, was mainly active in Germany after 1756. The Florentine Sacchini was one of the most successful conservative *opera seria* composers of the 1760s and 1770s. Traetta, trained in Naples, is best known today for the "reformed" operas he composed in the late 1750s and early 1760s for the court of Parma.

[7] The surviving score and librettos for these performances are listed in Paolo Cattelan, "L' 'Accademia' nei dintorni del Santo (1768–1785)," in *Storia della musica*, ed. Durante and Pietrobelli, 234–37. An extant libretto to *Giuseppe riconosciuto* records Mysliveček's setting of the text for Padua. A score attributed to him in the card catalog of the Capella Antoniana in Padua is the work of Johann Adolf Hasse.

[8] Pelcl, 191; Appendix 1 below.

[9] Ibid. Pelcl is incorrect that this performance took place in 1768 (he said one year after the Neapolitan production of *Bellerofonte*). He must also not have been aware of the earlier successes in Italy of Handel, Hasse, Gluck, and J. C. Bach, among other northerners.

[10] Robert Lamar Weaver and Norma Wright Weaver, *A Chronology of Music in the Florentine Theater, 1751–1800* (Warren, MI: Harmonie Park Press, 1993), 259–60. The dancing and scenery appear to have been as much responsible for the success of the production with the public as Mysliveček's music.

[11] These developments are described in the introduction to ibid.

Joseph II, attended two performances of *Ipermestra* (on the nights of 15 and 29 April 1769).[12] It is not known whether he and Mysliveček met or whether his attendance may have been one of the factors that induced Mysliveček to travel to Vienna in 1772. Also in Florence in these years were Marchese Eugène de Ligneville, director of music at the court of Tuscany, and the English nobleman George Nassau Clavering, the third Earl Cowper (1738–89), who lived in Florence during most of his adulthood.[13] Mysliveček's friendship with Lord Cowper is manifested in Mysliveček's dedication of two sets of published symphonies to him.[14]

The year 1770 saw the initiation of Mysliveček's friendship with Padre Giovanni Battista Martini and Mysliveček's first encounters with Leopold and Wolfgang Mozart. Their correspondence provides the most important record of Mysliveček's activities in the 1770s besides the travels that can be established from performance dates of dramatic works. There can be little doubt that one of the most important reasons Mysliveček sought to cultivate Padre Martini was to gain admittance to the Accademia Filarmonica in Bologna. His friendship with the Mozarts, by contrast, seems to have been motivated less by self-interest, for at this time their personal connections worked much more for the enrichment of Wolfgang than for Mysliveček. Between 1770 and 1778 Mysliveček's activites and personality are mentioned, and sometimes commented on at length, in twenty-eight surviving letters of the Mozart family—but even this considerable record represents only a portion of the personal contact and correspondence they must have shared.

At the start of the year 1770 Mysliveček found himself without an opera commision at carnival time for the first time in four years. But he did have a project ready for the spring, a setting of Metastasio's *La Nitteti* for performance in Bologna. Desiring to meet Padre Martini in Bologna, Mysliveček solicited letters of introduction from Anton Raaff and from Abbé Quirino Gasparini, then the *maestro di capella* at the court of Turin. Gasparini and Mysliveček had likely encountered one another in the winter of 1767–68 when Mysliveček's *Il trionfo di Clelia* played at the Teatro Regio in Turin. On 27 February 1770, Gasparini wrote to Padre Martini about several matters, one his recommendation of Mysliveček:[15]

> Signor Giuseppe Myslivecech, called il Boemo, who will have to come to Bologna to compose the opera for this spring, writes to me from Venice urgently to introduce him to you, most reverend father. I will be anxious to do this, for he is an honest man who fervently hopes to make the acquaintance of your most esteemed person. He was the one who composed the praiseworthy first opera for [the carnival season in] Turin [two years ago].

---

[12] Ibid., 260.

[13] On Lord Cowper, see Elizabeth Gibson, "Earl Cowper in Florence and His Correspondence with the Italian Opera in London," *Music and Letters* 68 (1987): 235–52; and John Ingamells, comp., *A Dictionary of British and Irish Travellers in Italy, 1701–1800* (New Haven and London: Yale University Press, 1997), 245–47. Lord Cowper was related to ruling families in several countries (see below note 33). Elector Palatine Karl Theodor, patron of the Mannheim orchestra, with whom he corresponded frequently, was a distant cousin. I am grateful to Christian Moritz-Bauer for bringing this connection to my attention.

[14] See Catalog 1 below.

[15] Bologna, Civico Museo Bibliografico Musicale, I.21.60; summary in Schnoebelen, no. 2211; facsimile and transciption in Bohadlo, 50–52; transcription in Anelide Nascimbene, "Mysliveček e i Mozart a Bologna: Documenti, cronaca e critica," in Giacomo Fornari, ed., *Mozart: Gli orientamenti della critica moderna* (Lucca: Libreria Musicale Italiana, 1994), 7. The portion of text concerning Mysliveček is in Appendix 2 below.

This may provide evidence that Mysliveček continued to use Venice as his principal residence in Italy when he had no operatic commission to attract him elsewhere. Perhaps in response to a fresh request from Mysliveček, Gasparini wrote again to Padre Martini from Turin a few days later (3 March 1770). This short letter was devoted entirely to recommending Mysliveček:[16]

> Most reverend father maestro, most esteemed sir,
>
> Signor Giuseppe Mislivecechi, called il Boemo, who composed an opera for the royal theater in Turin two years ago in a praiseworthy manner, and is obliged to compose an opera for Bologna this spring, most earnestly desires to make the acquaintance of your worthy person, and I would like to present him to you in this letter with all my heart. He is a most honest man, diligent in his work, and thus I do not despair of your willingness to receive him. On this occasion I am happy to render humble respects, and with full esteem consider myself to be your reverend father's most humble, devoted, and obliging true servant
>
> Quirino Gasparini
>
> Turin 3 March 1770

Anton Raaff also obliged Mysliveček, though not in a timely manner, as his letter to Martini of 5 May 1770 from Bonn demonstrates:[17]

> Most reverend and venerable father maestro,
>
> It has been almost a year now since I have been making plans to write to you, father maestro, in order to renew my old true service to you, but my intentions up to now have been ineffective. You, father maestro, know the reason why there is no need to write further about it. A wolf can change its coat, but not its nature; I am growing old, but will always be remiss in writing. My dear friend Mislivecek wrote to me a while back that he would be traveling to Bologna to compose an opera and requested me to write to you, father maestro, and recommend him to you as well as to Signor Cavaliere Don Carlo.[18] I was very much inclined to do so, but I did not succeed in conquering this carrion of sluggishness. I made plans to do it one day after another, but nothing came of them. Now finally a compulsion (albeit belated) has come to me, which I regard as better than never; I suppose that my friend will have made the acquaintance of father maestro without my recommendation, and it will be known that he is skilled in his craft and as esteemed by all as he is by this truly honorable German; the reception of his opera by this time will be decided, I hope to his advantage, because it is the nature of theatrical works that nobody, I believe, if he is capable, will ever compromise a good result.

---

[16] Bologna, Civico Museo Bibliografico Musicale, I.21.61; Schnoebelen, no. 2212; facsimile and transcription in Bohadlo, 60; transcription in Nascimbene, "Mysliveček," 7–8. The text is in Appendix 2 below.

[17] Bologna, Civico Museo Bibliografico Musicale, I.4.100; Schnoebelen, no. 4253; transcription in Bohadlo, 62; Nascimbene, "Mysliveček," 9–10; and Pierluigi Petrobelli, "The Italian Years of Anton Raaf," in *Mozart-Jahrbuch 1973/74* (Salzburg: Internationale Stiftung Mozarteum, 1975): 259. The portion concerning Mysliveček is in Appendix 2 below.

[18] The reference is to Carlo Broschi (the castrato Farinelli), who had been living in retirement near Bologna since 1762.

Raaff was almost certainly correct that Mysliveček by this time had met Padre Martini.

It is not certain when Mysliveček arrived in Bologna, but he was definitely there by the end of March, as is confirmed in the *Reisenotizen* of Leopold and Wolfgang Mozart of 24–29 March 1770.[19] The Mozarts were staying at the Pellegrino Inn, which, as Leopold told his wife in a letter of 24 March 1770, was the best in Bologna.[20] Although neither Mysliveček nor his opera is mentioned by name in their surviving correspondence from these weeks, Leopold's letter of 27 March to his wife discusses preparations for Mysliveček's *La Nitteti*. The singer intended for the role of Beroe was Caterina Gabrielli, but she had not come up from Palermo (a considerable disappointment to the Bolognese) and had been replaced by Clementina Spagnuoli, whom the Mozarts reported meeting.[21] Even without Gabrielli, the production met with success. It was reported as being very pleasing to Grand Duke Leopold, who heard it when he passed through Bologna in June 1770. For his benefit, it was brought into production a second time.[22]

Mysliveček remained in Bologna for some months, as can be established from the Mozart correspondence. After their triumphant tour through central and southern Italy during the spring and summer of 1770, Wolfgang and Leopold Mozart returned to Bologna on 20 July. On 4 August, Leopold mentioned to his wife that Mysliveček had come to see him during the last few days. This is the first appearance of Mysliveček's name in surviving Mozart family correspondence.[23] Mysliveček had received a contract to compose an opera for Milan for carnival in 1772 (it would be *Il gran Tamerlano*, one of his greatest operatic successes). Generally, Leopold identified new acquaintances with whom his wife was not familiar, but here he spoke of Mysliveček in a matter-of-fact way that presumes either the existence of lost correspondence explaining who Mysliveček was or some knowledge of him predating the Mozarts' first trip to Italy. Further evidence for this supposition comes from Leopold's letter to his wife of 27 October. The Mozarts had arrived in Milan on 18 October 1770 to begin preparations for the production of Wolfgang's *Mitridate*:[24]

> When we were in Bologna, Herr Misliwetschek visited us very often and we constantly went to see him. He often mentioned Johannes Hagenauer and, of course, Herr Cröner. He was writing an oratorio for Padua, which he has probably finished by now.[25] Then he is going to Bohemia. He is an honest fellow and we became intimate friends.

This brief mention of Mysliveček is full of puzzles. There is no record that he traveled to Bohemia shortly after this time, and what he would have had to say about Johannes Hagenauer, a son of

---

[19] Bauer and Deutsch, 1:330.

[20] Anderson, 120; Bauer and Deutsch, 1:326.

[21] Ibid., 123; ibid., 1:328. In Anderson, the singer Leopold Mozart calls "La Spagnoletta" is identified incorrectly as Giuseppa Useda. Spagnuoli was then at the Pellegrino Inn where Mysliveček and the Mozarts were (ibid., 1:330).

[22] A letter of Count Gian Luca Pallavicini, 13 June 1770, discovered by Nascimbene in the Archivio di Stato in Bologna, discusses the need to revive *Nitteti* for the expected visit of the grand duke on 18 June. See Nascimbene, "Mysliveček," 15–16; the article includes details about the production based on documentation in the Pallavicini Archive. Also see *Notizie del mondo*, 30 June 1770 (no. 52, p. 430), quoted in Bohadlo, 56, which confirms that Mysliveček had the opportunity to meet Leopold in Bologna at this time.

[23] Anderson, 152; Bauer and Deutsch, 1:377.

[24] Ibid., 167; ibid., 1:398–99.

[25] The oratorio referred to could be *I pellegrini al sepolcro*, *Giuseppe riconosciuto*, or *Betulia liberata*.

the Mozarts' landlord in Salzburg, is completely unclear. The identity of Herr Cröner has never been established.

Mysliveček could have made a visit or visits to Salzburg at some point during the 1760s on his way to or back from Venice. (Salzburg lies almost directly between Prague and Venice and was the only major cultural center between those cities.) In view of Mysliveček's outgoing personality and obvious fondness for "society," it is tenable that he made friends in Salzburg during his travels, including acquaintances of the Mozarts, and that the latter left Leopold and Wolfgang Mozart with some impression of Mysliveček. Unless he made more trips from Prague than are now known, Mysliveček and the Mozarts could not have met each other in Salzburg. When Mysliveček first traveled from Prague to Venice (November-December, 1763), the Mozarts were in Paris, and in 1768 when he returned to the North, they were not in Salzburg but were residing in Vienna (from September 1767 through November 1768, except for a side-trip to Moravia in late 1767 to protect Wolfgang and Nannerl from an outbreak of smallpox in Vienna). Until March 1770, Mysliveček probably never met any member of the Mozart family.[26]

An addendum Wolfgang Mozart attached to his father's letter of 22 December 1770 hints at a connection between Mysliveček and Salzburg. In it Mozart asked his sister to find out whether a certain symphony of Mysliveček's was in Salzburg; if not, Wolfgang wanted to bring a copy with him (fig. 3.1).[27] It is extremely rare in the Mozart correspondence to find incipits of music that are not by Wolfgang. In the postscript Wolfgang included an incipit for the Mysliveček symphony (actually, the overture to *Demofoonte* of 1769), which he had probably picked up in Bologna earlier that year. If Mysliveček had made visits to Salzburg, this could explain why Wolfgang's query was posed the way it was: a certain Mysliveček symphony could be in Salzburg if Mysliveček had earlier established contact with musicians there and had brought or sent the symphony or various symphonies to Salzburg.

There can be no doubt that Wolfgang Mozart came to know a good deal of Mysliveček's music at this time besides the overture to *Demofoonte* of 1769. One exposure came about from Wolfgang's preoccupation with the composition of his first opera, *Mitridate re di Ponto*, for performance in Milan in December 1770. Completing that work appears to have led him to study Mysliveček's *La Nitteti* carefully,[28] and to have borrowed a number of musical ideas from it and to have borrowed other ideas from Gasparini's setting of *Mitridate*.[29] That Mozart would be interested in Mysliveček's *La Nitteti* should not be surprising since the original commission Mozart received had in fact been for a *La Nitteti* opera. The Milanese commissioners later settled on *Mitridate* and it was that text that Mozart eventually set.[30]

Mysliveček departed Bologna near the end of the year (the exact date is not known) and returned to the Pergola Theater in Florence, where his *Motezuma* was mounted with considerable success in 1771 as the second opera of the carnival season.[31] He remained in Florence during Lent

---

[26] Leopold Mozart's letter of 9 January 1773 mentions that Mysliveček had not yet met Maria Anna Mozart, who did not accompany her husband and son on any of their trips to Italy: see p. 61, below.

[27] The full letter is in Anderson, 176; Bauer and Deutsch, 1:411.

[28] See chapter 11.

[29] Luigi Ferdinando Tagliavini, "Quirino Gasparini and Mozart," in William W. Austin, ed., *New Looks at Italian Opera: Essays in Honor of Donald J. Grout* (Ithaca: Cornell University Press, 1968), 151–71.

[30] On Mozart's use of *Nitteti* as a partial model for *Mitridate*, see Harrison James Wignall, "Mozart, Guglielmo d'Ettore, and the Composition of *Mitridate*" (Ph.D. diss., Brandeis University, 1995), especially 1:173–210; see also chapter 11 below.

[31] Weaver and Weaver, *A Chronology*, 278–79.

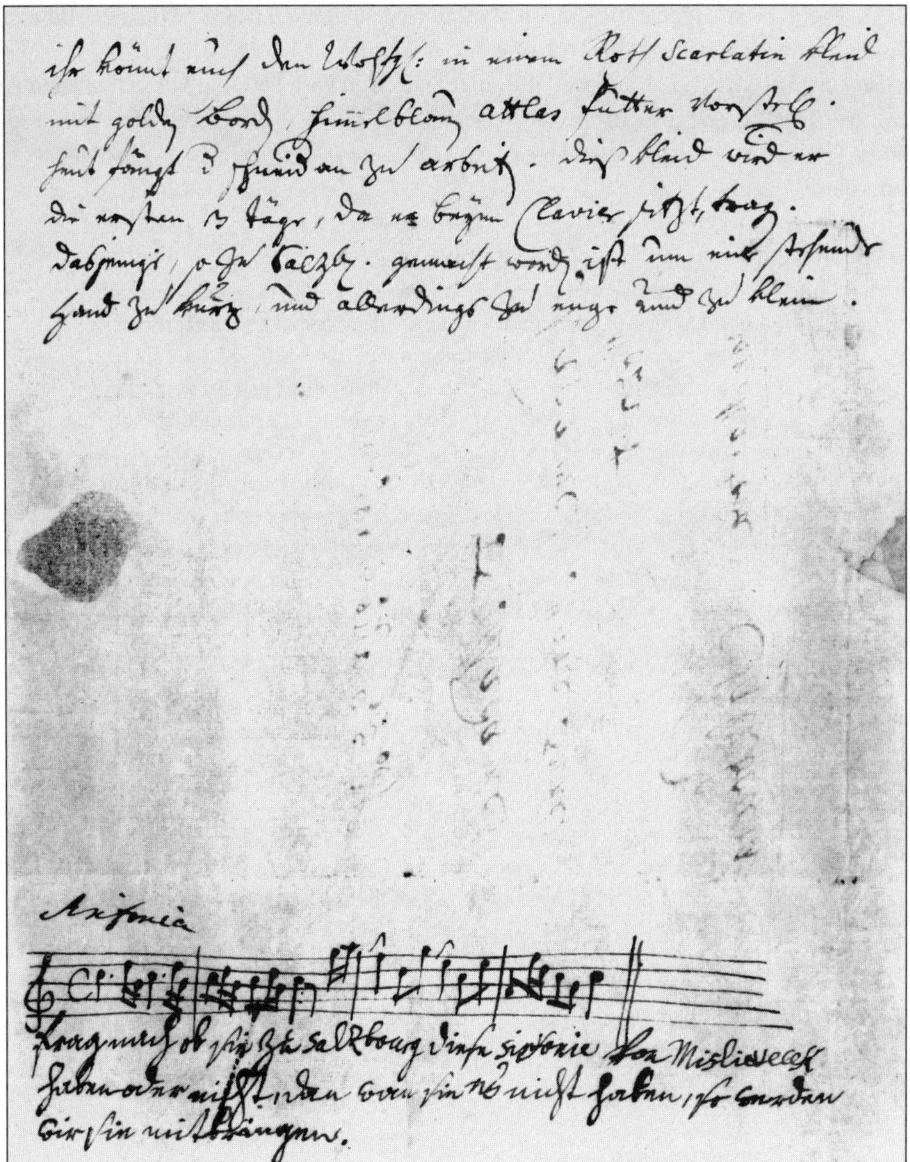

Fig. 3.1 Conclusion of Leopold Mozart's letter from Milan, 22 December 1770 and postscript (at bottom of page) in W. A. Mozart's handwriting with incipit of Mysliveček's overture to Demofoonte *(1769)*

Courtesy of the Music Division, Library of Congress

to see his new oratorio *Adamo ed Eva* performed at the Accademia degli Ingegnosi on 24 March 1771. Mysliveček would repeat the pattern of producing an opera for carnival followed by an oratorio for the Lenten season in Milan the next year and in Munich in 1777.

Early in 1771 Mysliveček adopted the custom (shared with Leopold Mozart) of sending Padre Martini New Year's greetings. The letter he sent on 26 January, three days after the premiere of *Motezuma*, reveals that he was on good terms with Giovanni Marco Rutini and with Marchese Eugène de Ligneville:[32]

> Most venerable and esteemed sir, father maestro,
>
> I beg your pardon for not fulfilling earlier my duty in sending greetings for a most happy new year full of every prosperity, according to the appropriate vows. The reason is my theatrical activities which, thanks to God, were successful to the extent that I have reason to be grateful to the gracious public here. Up to now I have not been able to extend to you most esteemed greetings from the Marchese Ligneville and Maestro Rutini. How delighted I am to bring from them the most excellent greetings to you. I hope to have the high honor of coming before you in Bologna at the latest at the start of Lent. In the meanwhile I ask to retain for myself your strongest protection, and kissing your hand I grant myself the honor of calling myself forever the most humble, most devoted, and most obsequious servant of the most virtuous father maestro
>
> Giuseppe Misliwecek

Also from about this time is confirmation of the good opinion Lord Cowper held of Mysliveček, in a letter he sent to Padre Martini that is believed to date from 1771:[33]

> I find myself unexpectedly favored by you, most reverend father, with the first two volumes of your famous work on the history of music. From the natural inclination that I have for works about the art of music, which was mentioned to you by Maestro Mislivecech, I send to you sentiments of gratitude that I hope will nourish from your gentleness the desire to correspond further: in the meanwhile I take the present occasion with your leave to consider myself in a position to acquire the right to declare myself the most devoted and obliging servant of you, most reverend father
>
> De Nassau Cowper

Shortly after leaving Florence, Mysliveček must have felt that the time was right to press for admission to the Accademia Filarmonica in Bologna, an honor that the much younger Wolfgang Mozart had attained on 10 October 1770. As of 1770, only thirteen non-Italian musicians, only four of whom were composers, had been admitted to the Accademia Filarmonica since its formation in

---

[32] Bologna, Civico Museo Bibliografico Musicale, I.4.57; Schnoebelen, no. 3329; facsimile and transcription in Bohadlo, 64; transcription in Nascimbene, "Mysliveček," 18; facsimile in Shaginian, 235. The text is in Appendix 2 below.

[33] Bologna, Civico Museo Bibliografico Musicale, I.18.30; Schnoebelen, no. 3521; transcription in Bohadlo, 72. In closing Lord Cowper drew attention to his descent from the house of Nassau, a connection that made him a relation of ruling families in Great Britain, the Netherlands, and Prussia, besides a host of nobility in Protestant central Europe. The text is in Appendix 2 below.

1666.[34] Something of a vogue for foreign membership had ensued after the admission of Marchese Ligneville in 1756, the first non-Italian admitted since 1731. The membership of Grétry followed in 1765, Naumann in 1768, and Mozart in 1770. During the period 1765–85, Padre Martini's international outlook created a sort of window of opportunity for non-Italians, but, almost as soon as he died in 1784, this window was closed. As the names of entrants such as Marchese Ligneville, the Barons Nesselrode (1769) and Chambrier (1771), and Count Karl von Colloredo[35] (1771), seem to bear out, wealth and exalted social station aided non-Italians to secure admission. Payment of an entrance fee was expected. That Mysliveček paid the fee is alluded to in a letter from Antonio Bianchi to Padre Martini of 7 December 1771; in it Bianchi expressed hope that he would be able to gain admittance for the reduced fee incurred by the two recent Slavic entrants, Mysliveček and Signor Massimo (Maxim Berezovsky).[36]

Mysliveček applied for admission on 15 May 1771 and was admitted upon the acceptance of the contrapuntal exercise he presented, the motet "Veni sponsa Christi"—the only conservative *alla breve* liturgical composition that survives from his pen.[37] Ever after, Mysliveček proudly attached the title "accademico filarmonico" to his name at every appropriate opportunity.[38] Admitted the same day was Maxim Berezovsky, the first Russian known to have composed an Italian opera (a *Demofoonte* performed in Livorno and Florence in 1773).[39] The only other Slavic musicians admitted to the Accademia Filarmonica in the eighteenth century were a similar pair in the 1780s: one Czech, Václav Pichl in 1783, and one Russian, Yevstigney Fomin in 1785.

Preparations for the production of Mysliveček's *Il gran Tamerlano* in Milan during the winter of 1771–72 brought him again into contact with Leopold and Wolfgang Mozart. They were in Italy to see Wolfgang's opera *Ascanio in Alba* performed in Milan (on 17 October 1771). Mysliveček arrived a few weeks too late to witness the success enjoyed by the younger Mozart there. In a letter of 23 or 24 November 1771, Leopold reported to his wife that "Herr Misliwetschek, who arrived yesterday and is writing the first opera [for the forthcoming carnival season in Milan], was with us today"[40]—an indication that the Mozarts had been among the first acquaintances Mysliveček had called on. Since Leopold and Wolfgang Mozart remained in Milan until 15 December 1771, they likely had further visits with Mysliveček.

---

[34] Laura Callegari Hill, *L'Accademia Filarmonica di Bologna, 1666–1800: Statuti, indici degli aggregati e catalogo degli esperimenti d'esame nell'archivio, con un'introduzione storica* (Bologna: A.M.I.S., 1991), especially table, pp. 261–91.

[35] Count Karl (b. 1718–d. Venice 1786), an uncle of Archbishop Hieronymus von Colloredo of Salzburg, listed his residence as Vienna in the records of the Accademia Filarmonica. See Wurzbach, *Biographisches Lexikon*, 2:418.

[36] Bologna, Civico Museo Bibliografico, H.86.101; Schnoebelen., no. 744; facsimile and transcription in Bohadlo, 74–75. After thanking Padre Martini for assisting him in preparing a sample composition, Bianchi wrote "Se avrò la sorte d'esserci admesso, l'avverto di farlo con la minor spesa, cioè come fecero il Signor Maestro Misliwecek, et il Signor Massimo." (If I have the good fortune to be admitted, I give you notice that it will be done with the lesser expense incurred by Signor Maestro Mysliveček and Signor Massimo).

[37] His application is in the Accademia Filarmonica Archives; transcription in Bohadlo, 66, and Nascimbene, "Mysliveček," 23; facsimile in Shaginian, 252–53 (certification of admittance on p. 256; see also Nascimbene, 22–25). An excerpt from Mysliveček's test composition, in facsimile, is in Shaginian, 254–55; an incipit is in Callegari Hill, *L'Accademia Filarmonica*, 140. See also Osvaldo Gambassi, *L'Accademia Filarmonica di Bologna: Fondazione, statuti, e aggregazion* (Florence: Olschki, 1992), 115 and 445.

[38] Its first recorded use was in the libretto for his next opera, *Il gran Tamerlano* of 1772.

[39] Berezovsky's travels in Italy were subsidized by the imperial court of Russia and he was among the foreigners who entered the Accademia Filarmonica only after a period of study with Martini or his assistant Stanislao Mattei. In many ways Berezovsky was a Russian counterpart to Mysliveček, especially as regards their mutual interest in Italian serious opera and their adventurous lives (his was also the subject of fictional embellishment). In the Shaginian biography there is a huge digression on Berezovsky (pp. 249–58).

[40] Anderson, 206; Bauer and Deutsch, 1:451.

The production of Mysliveček's *Il gran Tamerlano* was one in a series of events marking the new political structure in the duchy of Milan that brought Empress Maria Theresa's son Archduke Ferdinand to rule as a replacement for a governor who was not a member of the imperial family.[41] In this period the Regio-Ducal Teatro was magnificently refurbished and, in autumn 1771, operas of Hasse (*Ruggiero*) and Mozart (*Ascanio in Alba*) were performed there in celebration of Ferdinand's nuptials, followed in 1772 by Mysliveček's *Il gran Tamerlano* as the first carnival opera. *Il gran Tamerlano* was one of the most frequently performed operas of its era in Milan, enjoying forty-seven performances during the carnival season of 1772.[42] Only in carnival seasons so short as not to permit production of two works were there more performances of a single opera. Even at that, only three other works had longer runs, Mysliveček's *Armida* (1780) and two others whose performance occurred under special conditions.[43] *Il gran Tamerlano* was so successful that during Lent that year the Regio-Ducal Theater remained open for performances of Mysliveček's oratorio *Adamo ed Eva*,[44] though the customary suspension of gambling remained in effect. Without the attraction of gambling, the idea of operatic performances in Lent did not take hold, the beauties of Mysliveček's music notwithstanding.[45]

In the midst of this artistic triumph, Mysliveček sent Padre Martini New Year's greetings on 7 January. The letter mentions Giuseppe Cicognani, a member of the cast of *Il gran Tamerlano* who had appeared in Mysliveček's *Ipermestra* in Florence in 1769:[46]

> Most venerable and esteemed sir, father maestro,
>
> In order to carry out my most humble duty, I grant myself the honor of wishing you a most happy new year full of every prosperity according to the appropriate vows. Thanks to God my opera has achieved universal approval to the extent that I could not have asked for more. But since I did not receive the music left with you, most reverend father, after the arrival of Cicognani, I request that the book of six symphonies be consigned to Signor Don Marchi[47] and that you hold on to the two scores [of *Nitteti* and *Motezuma*] until I return. In the meanwhile I ask to be allowed to continue to consider myself favored to have the high honor of calling myself always the most humble and devoted servant of your most reverend father
>
> Giuseppe Misliwecek

Cicognani was from Cesena (near Bologna) and had been in Bologna when Mysliveček first met the Mozarts.[48] The symphonies referred to are likely the set of six Mysliveček had recently composed

[41] The implications for operatic music are discussed in Kathleen Kuzmick Hansell, "Opera and Ballet at the Regio Ducal Teatro of Milan, 1771–1776: A Musical and Social History" (Ph.D. diss., University of California-Berkeley, 1980).

[42] Ibid., 191–92: a notice in *Gazzetta di Milano*, 1 January 1772, reported the "particular approbation" of Archduke Ferdinand, his wife, and the large audience in attendance.

[43] Ibid., 188, 192.

[44] Franco Piperno, "Drammi sacri in teatro (1750–1820)," in *Mozart, Padova*, ed. Pinamonti, 289–316.

[45] Hansell, "Opera and Ballet," 192–94.

[46] Bologna, Civico Museo Bibliografico Musicale, I.4.58; Schnoebelen, no. 3330; facsimile and transcription in Bohadlo, 74, 82; transcription in Nascimbene, "Mysliveček," 18; facsimile in Shaginian, 233. The text is in Appendix 2 below.

[47] The identity of this person has not been resolved. Bohadlo (p. 77) suggests the singer Luigi Marchesi (1755–1829). As he was only sixteen years old at the time, the hypothesis seems highly unlikely.

[48] Anderson, 123; Bauer and Deutsch, 1:328, 330.

in Florence (to be published by William Napier in London with dedication to Lord Cowper). Mysliveček wrote again to Padre Martini on 17 January:[49]

> Most venerable and esteemed father maestro,
>
> I hope that you, reverend father, will have received another letter of mine in which I requested to have Signor Don Marchi send the six symphonies and the scores of *Nitteti* and *Motezuma*. Now therefore because of the great haste that I wish to have them, you will have the goodness to consign to Signor Marchi the six symphonies and the said scores, which he will solicitously take the trouble to send to me. I ask to remain under your strong protection, and consider myself always your reverend father's most humble, devoted servant
>
> Giuseppe Misliwecek

It is unknown whether Mysliveček returned to Bologna at this time or received the music that he appears (from his letter) to have been so anxious to retrieve.

Haydn's early biographer Georg August Griesinger left a rare record of Mysliveček's estimation of the work of two contemporary composers in an anecdote that must derive from Mysliveček's stay in Milan in 1771–72:[50]

> The author was told by a very reliable source that the violinist Mysliveček, a Bohemian by birth, had heard some quartets performed during his stay in Milan; and when they told him that the composer was Johann Baptista Sammartini, then a man of seventy, he had cried out in utter astonishment, "At last I know Haydn's precursor, and the model on which he patterned himself!" It seemed to me worthwhile to investigate this statement more closely, since I had never heard Haydn's originality doubted, especially in his quartets. So I inquired of Haydn whether he had known Sammartini's works in his youth, and what he thought of that composer. Haydn told me that he had in fact heard Sammartini's music, but he had never valued it, "for Sammartini was a scribbler." He laughed heartily when I produced Mysliveček's supposed discovery and said that he recognized only Emanuel Bach as his prototype.

It is difficult to know what to make of this amusing little story. In its favor, one can point to its accurate chronology: the details of Mysliveček's peregrinations were unlikely to have been at Griesinger's fingertips, but he did report correctly that Mysliveček was in Milan when Sammartini was about seventy years old.

---

[49] Bologna, Civico Museo Bibliografico Musicale, I.4.59; Schnoebelen, no. 3331; facsimile and transcription in Bohadlo, 76, 78; transcription also in Nascimbene, "Mysliveček," 19; facsimile in Shaginian, 234. The text is in Appendix 2 below.

[50] Georg August Griesinger, *Biographische Notizien über Joseph Haydn* (Leipzig, 1810; reprint, Leipzig: VEB Deutscher Verlag für Musik, 1979), 14–15. The translation is from H. C. Robbins Landon, *Haydn: Chronicle and Works*, 1: *The Early Years, 1732–1765* (Bloomington and London: Indiana University Press, 1980), 61. Haydn's opinion of Sammartini as a scribbler ("ein Schmierer") is lacking in the transcription in Anna Cattoretti, "Giovanni Battista Sammartini: Cronologia della vita, testimonianze e giudizi dei suoi contemporanei," in *Giovanni Battista Sammartini and His Musical Environment*, ed. Anna Cattoretti, Studi sulla storia della musica in Lombardia, 4 (Turnhout: Brepols, 2004), 644–45.

The subject of Mysliveček's traveling back to the North had been broached in Leopold Mozart's letter of 27 October 1770, which states that Mysliveček was expected to return to Bohemia as soon as he had finished an oratorio for Padua. The trip Mysliveček finally made in 1772 can be firmly documented only for Vienna, but he may also have visited other cities. Since the seventeenth century, composers of Italian opera, after establishing their reputations in Italy, had been attracted to northern destinations by rulers and impresarios eager to advertise their sponsorship of the finest possible operatic productions. The most common stopping places in Mysliveček's day were London, Paris, and St. Petersburg. It was to these cities that Antonio Sacchini, Niccolò Piccinni, Giovanni Paisiello, Pietro Guglielmi, and Baldassare Galuppi had traveled after receiving invitations from such sponsors. As far as is known, Mysliveček did not respond to any summons, but he may have been encouraged by the success of his *Il gran Tamerlano* in Milan to seek opportunities of his own making north of the Alps.

The potential for patronage in Vienna was considerable for Mysliveček, who after all was a subject of the Habsburg rulers and had had personal contact with three of Empress Maria Theresa's sons: Emperor Joseph II, who had attended performances of *Ipermestra* in Florence in 1769; Leopold, the grand duke of Tuscany; and Archduke Ferdinand, the ruler of Lombardy. Mysliveček certainly knew Count Durazzo, the imperial ambassador in Venice who had formerly been director of music and theater at the imperial court, and from his days in Prague in the early 1760s, he likely also knew the incumbent director in Vienna in 1764, the Bohemian Count Johann Wenzel von Sporck.[51]

Mysliveček's residence in Vienna in September 1772 is confirmed by Charles Burney. After giving a long list of musicians present in the city that month, Burney adds: "To these celebrated names, may be added . . . Misliwiceck, a Bohemian, just returned from Italy, where he has established a great reputation by his operas as well as his instrumental music."[52] Mysliveček seems to have made some attempt to build up a reputation as a violinist (being careful to bring concertos with him),[53] but it is not known what attention he might have attracted. No operatic productions resulted from the visit.

Čeleda believed that Mysliveček's excursion out of Italy in 1772 brought him to Prague for the last time, perhaps to settle some affairs associated with the death of his stepfather on 20 March or to visit his relations.[54] It is even possible that family matters were the principal reason for Mysliveček's trip to the North and the visit to Vienna a mere sidelight. Nonetheless, no confirmation of a visit to Prague at this time has been uncovered. The lack of evidence that any more Mysliveček operas were produced in Prague, or that a new wave of vocal music from Italy led to a fresh dissemination of arias among Bohemian ecclesiastical institutions, tends to render the hypothesis less presumable.

By autumn 1772 Mysliveček had returned to Italy. After his overwhelming success the previous carnival season, staying in Milan must have seemed a sensible alternative, and it was there that he again met Wolfgang and Leopold Mozart. They arrived in Milan on 4 November (their third trip to Italy) for the planned production of Wolfgang's *Lucio Silla* during carnival in 1773. On 7 November Wolfgang reported to his mother that "Mysliveček is still here."[55] After the successful production of

---

[51] On Count Sporck's role in fostering and regulating opera productions in Prague in the early 1760s, see Čeleda, 218–20.

[52] *The Present State of Music*, 1:364–65; *Dr. Burney's Musical Tours*, 2:124–25; *Tagebuch*, 2:271.

[53] Chappell White, *From Vivaldi to Viotti: A History of the Early Classical Violin Concerto* (Philadelphia: Gordon and Breach, 1992), 184. There is a good possibility the violin concertos now in the Gesellschaft der Musikfreunde in Vienna (see Catalog 1) were for this purpose.

[54] Čeleda, 243–44. The death of Jan Čermák led to the sale of Blue Ship House. It was purchased by the widow Anna Maria Süssmayer, a relative of Mozart's pupil Franz Xaver Süssmayer, in 1773.

[55] Anderson, 214; Bauer and Deutsch, 1:458.

Lucio Silla, Leopold sent greetings from Mysliveček to his wife (letter of 9 January 1773),[56] mentioning that Mysliveček longed to meet her, and on 16 January 1773 told her that Mysliveček "kisses Nannerl's hand."[57] On 23 January Wolfgang sent greetings from Mysliveček to his sister. This is the last letter of the Mozarts from Italy that mentions him.[58]

Wolfgang and Leopold returned to Salzburg on 13 March 1773. Lack of surviving correspondence from the Mozart household over the next four years makes it difficult to judge the extent Mysliveček tried to keep in touch with them, but there is evidence that he maintained contact. In Leopold's letter to his wife from Vienna (8 September 1773), Wolfgang reported writing out a short note to his mother on top of the bass part of a Mysliveček violin concerto (fig. 3.2).[59] On 18 September 1773, in another of Leopold's letters from Vienna, there is reference to a letter from Mysliveček in Naples.[60] Considering the depth of feeling about Mysliveček revealed in Wolfgang Mozart's later correspondence from 1777, as well as Leopold Mozart's knowledge of Mysliveček's personal affairs, there is no reason to doubt a continuous exchange of correspondence between the Mozarts and Mysliveček throughout the period 1773–77.

The Mozart correspondence from Italy in the early months of 1773 also speaks against Fétis's assertion that Mysliveček composed an opera *Erifile* for Munich in 1773.[61] Operatic premieres in this era almost always required the presence of the composer, who would have been needed to work with the singers. Yet the Mozart letters confirm that Mysliveček was in Italy during carnival season in 1773 (the only time of year *opere serie* were generally given in Munich in the 1770s). Even more convincing evidence again Fétis's claim comes from the *Unger Journal* (a chronicle of events in Munich compiled by a courtier from Dresden), the primary authority documenting operatic performances at the Bavarian court between 1769 and 1775. For 1773, only performances of Gluck's *Orfeo* and Tozzi's *Zenobia* are recorded.[62]

From spring 1773 to spring 1775 Mysliveček embarked on the most concentrated period of operatic composition of his lifetime, one that led to success after success throughout Italy. A signal honor came to him in May 1773, when his opera *Demetrio* was performed to celebrate the opening of a new theater in Pavia,[63] an event that received special mention from Pelcl.[64] In the late summer

---

[56] Ibid., 224; ibid., 1:473–74.

[57] Ibid., 225; ibid., 1:475.

[58] Ibid., 227; ibid., 1:477.

[59] Ibid., 243; ibid., 1:497.

[60] Ibid., 246; ibid., 1:502.

[61] Fétis, *Biographie universelle des musiciens*, 6:271. An anecdote about the failure of *Erifile* was repeated in *New Grove*, ed. 1980: ". . . cet ouvrage ne répondit pas à ce qu'on attendait du compositeur: lui-même avoua qu'il s'était point senti en verve en l'écrivant, et qu'il n'était inspiré que sous le ciel de l'Italie; semblable en cela à Winckelmann et à Thorwaldsen, qui, après de longs séjours à Rome, n'ont pu vivre sous le climat du Nord qui les avait vus naître" (this work did not measure up to what was expected of the composer; he himself acknowledged that he was not enthused about writing it, and that he was only inspired under Italian skies, similar in this respect to Winckelmann and Thorvaldsen, who were no longer able to live in their native northern climes after long stays in Rome). Johann Joachim Winckelmann (1717–68) was the notable archaeologist and art historian; Bertil Thorvaldsen (1768–1844) was a prominent sculptor of Danish birth.

[62] I am grateful to Karl Böhmer for bringing this resource to my attention. The musical events recorded in the *Unger Journal* are transcribed in Eduard Joseph Weiss, "Andrea Bernasconi als Opernkomponist" (Ph.D. diss., University of Munich, 1923).

[63] The most complete appraisal is in Anelide Nascimbene, "'Il Demetrio' di Josef Mysliveček," in *Gli affetti convenienti all'idee: Studi sulla musica vocale italiana*, ed. Maria Caraci Vela (Naples: Edizioni Scientifiche Italiane, 1993), 203–39.

[64] Pelcl, 192; Appendix 1 below.

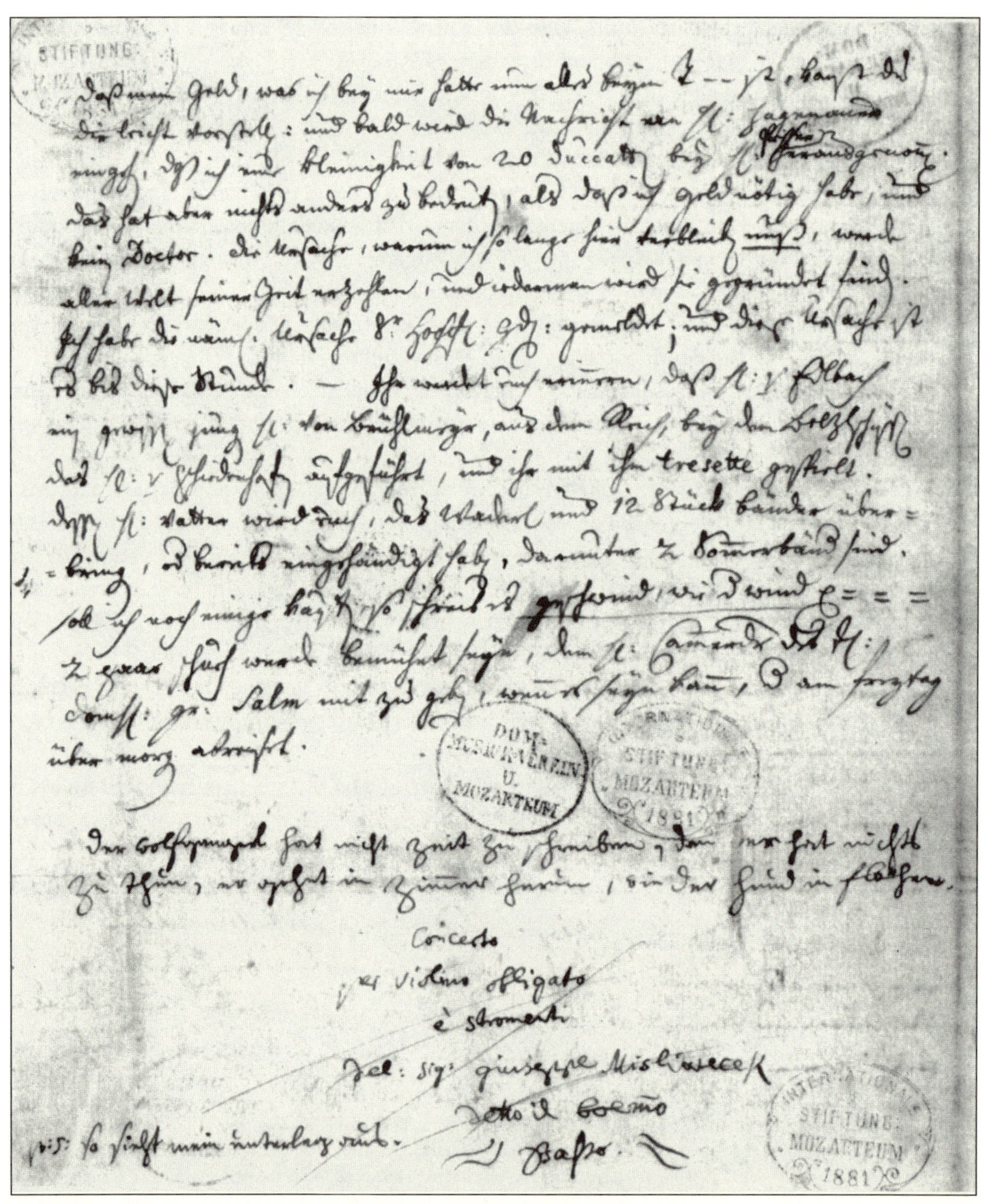

Der Wolfgangerl hat nicht Zeit zu schreiben, denn er hat nichts zu thun, er geht im Zimmer herum, wie der Hund in flöhen.

Concerto
per violino obligato
e stromenti
del: sig: giuseppe Misliwecek
detto il boemo
Basso.

p:s: so sieht mein unterlage aus.

FIG. 3.2 **Conclusion of Leopold Mozart's letter from Vienna, 8 September 1773. W. A. Mozart's postscript (bottom of page) includes a transcription of the title page of the bass part of a Mysliveček violin concerto**

Courtesy of the Mozarteum, Salzburg

of the same year, Mysliveček renewed his contacts with the Teatro San Carlo in Naples, this time producing a *Romolo ed Ersilia* to honor the birthday of Queen Maria Carolina on 13 August.

Mysliveček's return to Naples in 1773 is the subject of an anecdote recorded by Ulisse Prota-Giurleo.[65] Although Mysliveček's contract with the court of Naples obliged him to present himself by 15 June, he could not be traced until 23 July, having been delayed at the border for lack of a passport. His return may also have been delayed or disrupted by a serious carriage accident.[66] To have something ready for the queen's birthday, the impresario of the Teatro San Carlo, Gaetano Santoro, proposed parceling out the three acts of *Romolo ed Ersilia* among three resident composers—Niccolò Piccinni, Giovanni Paisiello, and Giacomo Insanguine—and making Mysliveček liable for their fees. Pasquale Cafaro, *primo maestro* of the Neapolitan royal chapel, would have supervised the production. When asked his opinion, he stated that he believed Mysliveček could do the work in a week, if necessary. The impresario's fears proved groundless: Mysliveček arrived and fulfilled his commission brilliantly in time for the production on 13 August. *Romolo ed Ersilia* was so successful that Mysliveček was immediately contracted to return for the queen's birthday the next year.

Mysliveček's last known communication with his old patron Count Vincenz von Waldstein dates from the time of this visit to Naples. On 14 September he wrote to Count Waldstein shortly after *Romolo ed Ersilia* went into production about some quintets he may have intended to dedicate to him:[67]

> Excellency!
>
> I know that your innate goodness will exceed my lack of merit in the ardour that I take to inquire about the precious health of everyone in your excellency's family. In recognition of the boundless thanks received from your excellency for my most negligible merit I hope that you will have the grace to permit me to present before your feet six quintets which have had a great success all over Italy. I have the intention of having them printed in London to put them at the disposal of the public and of critics. With the most profound respect I will dedicate them humbly to your excellency with your illustrious name at the front. I hope to attain all the perfection that my devilish pen lacks in opera. In hopes of being able to send them off, I ask that you could graciously send me the titles which should appear in the dedication of the print. In expectation of these I request in the meanwhile to continue under your bountiful protection. At the feet of your excellency, I am your most humble devoted obsequious servant
>
> Giuseppe Misliwecek
>
> P.S. This carnival I will write the first opera at Turin and the second at Venice. My most secure address is in Milan at the residence of Signor Francesco Weiskopf, postmaster in Milan.

---

[65] Appendix 1 below.

[66] A carriage accident is reported in Burney, *Tagebuch*, in the index to volume 2, next to Mysliveček's name: "Ist diese Jahr (1773) auf einer Reise nach Neapel, wo er eine von seinen Opern aufführen sollte, umgeworfen, und unglücklicherweise zu Tode gekommen!" (this year [1773] his carriage upset on a trip to Naples, where one of his operas was to be performed, and he unfortunately has died!). Mysliveček later told Mozart that the illness for which he sought surgical treatment in Munich in 1777 was bone cancer caused by a carriage accident, not venereal disease, as implied in Leopold Mozart's letters (see chapter 4 below).

[67] The original is in Mnichovo Hradiště, collection Rodinný Archiv Valdštejnů, dokeská manipulace, III-21/28; facsimile and transcription in Bohadlo, 92–96; facsimile in Milada Rutová, "Valdštejnská hudební sbírka v Doksech," *Sborník Národního Muzea v Praze*, series A, vol. 28 (1974), 230–31. The text is in Appendix 2 below.

The quintets referred to are probably those preserved in the Estense Library in Modena.[68] No London print of them has come to light, and it seems unlikely that the project came to fruition.

One of Mysliveček's boasts that did come to pass was his completion of two operas for carnival season in 1774, *Antigona* in Turin and *La clemenza di Tito* in Venice. No information is available concerning *Antigona*'s reception, but *La clemenza di Tito* appears to have been one of Mysliveček's rare operatic failures. That carnival season was one of only two (the other was 1780) when Mysliveček, whether out of vanity or financial necessity, took on the dangerous challenge of providing new works that needed to be ready for performance at nearly the same time in two different operatic centers. Demand for his work was something he clearly wished to draw attention to in his letter to Count Waldstein. Mysliveček's hurried pace resulted in his composing music for *La clemenza di Tito* of lower quality than he usually produced. To make matters worse, a serious fire in the Teatro San Benedetto on the evening of 5–6 February 1774 destroyed the sets and forced the opera to be withdrawn.[69]

More pleasant to report from Mysliveček's stay in Venice during the early months of 1774 is the beginning of his association with the theorist Georg Joseph Vogler. The latter's biographer Karl Emil von Schafhäutl claimed that Abbé Vogler met Mysliveček in Venice in 1774 at the same time he met Johann Adolf Hasse and his wife, singer Faustina Bordoni.[70] Whereas Hasse gave Vogler instruction in setting aria texts, Mysliveček taught him how to set recitative, just as Pescetti had taught Mysliveček the same skill in the city ten years earlier. Regrettably, no impression of Mysliveček is recorded in Vogler's extant writings.

In June 1774, Mysliveček's *Atide* was staged in Padua, the last production of one of his dramatic works there. Mysliveček was then very ill. According to Wolfgang Mozart's later letter to his father (11 October 1777), written after Wolfgang had visited Mysliveček in a Munich hospital, "When his illness was at its worst he composed an opera for Padua."[71] It is unknown how long Mysliveček had been suffering from the illness, believed to be syphilis on the evidence of various letters of Leopold and Wolfgang Mozart, but there is little doubt that Mysliveček composed for at least the last seven years of his life in a state of constant pain.[72]

Mysliveček return to Naples later in the summer was rewarded with a series of successful productions at the Teatro San Carlo. Documents discovered by Lucio Tufano in the Archivio di Stato in Naples contribute much new information about the opportunities created at this time both by Mysliveček's proven talent as an opera composer and the failure of J. C. Bach to fulfill planned

---

[68] See Catalog 1.

[69] An account of the fire is in the Florentine journal *Notizie del mondo* (19 February 1774 issue, pp. 116–17).

[70] Karl Emil von Schafhäutl, *Abt Georg Joseph Vogler: sein Leben, Charakter und musikalisches System* (Augsburg, 1888), 7–8, and in the *Allgemeine Musikalische Zeitung* 13 (1878), col. 26. I am grateful to Christian Moritz-Bauer for bringing this connection to my attention. Vogler was traveling in Italy in the party of Elector Palatine Karl Theodor. Record of his studies with Mysliveček might be found in *Roemisches Reiss-Tags-Buch*, Sign. Cod. germ. 1980, of the Bayerische Staatsbibliothek, Munich, a journal of the elector's journey (information from Christian Moritz-Bauer).

[71] Anderson, 306; Bauer and Deutsch, 2:46.

[72] Although Mysliveček rarely followed the common practice of re-using musical numbers from past operas, the *sinfonia* to *Atide* was borrowed from *Antigona*, and four of the arias and the final chorus were borrowed from other works: "Prence che affanno" (act 2, scene 3) and "Quel traditore intendo" (act 2, scene 5) were from *Romolo ed Ersilia* (act 1, scene 5 and 8, respectively); "Sento nell'alma mia" (act 2, scene 2) was from *Il gran Tamerlano* (act 1, scene 10); "Da quei vezzosi" (act 2, scene 1) represents a re-texting of "Tradito ed oppresso" from *Il gran Tamerlano* (act 1, scene 13); and the final chorus, "Numi, che in ciel regnate," appears to be a parody of the final chorus of *Romolo ed Ersilia*, "Numi, che intenti siete." Mysliveček's illness may explain the use of borrowing to help complete the music for the *Atide* production.

commissions.[73] As mentioned earlier, an invitation to compose an opera for the birthday of Queen Maria Carolina of Naples of 13 August 1774 resulted from the success of Mysliveček's opera *Romolo ed Ersilia* of 1773. It can now be established that the management of the San Carlo originally decided by spring of 1774 that the libretto to be set for the queen's birthday opera that year would be Metastasio's *L'eroe cinese*—on account of its brevity ("per la sua brevità").[74] It is not known when *Artaserse* was substituted for *L'eroe cinese*, but the setting of *Artaserse* that Mysliveček eventually did produce for the queen's birthday was so well received that he was immediately commissioned to compose an opera (his first setting of Metastasio's *Ezio*) for the nameday of the king of Naples on 30 May 1775.[75]

Extra work for the Teatro San Carlo resulted from the unreliability of Johann Christian Bach. As of April 1774, the San Carlo expected to obtain from Bach new settings of Metastasio's *Demofoonte* for the birthday of the king of Spain on 4 November 1774 and *Antigono* for the birthday of the king of Naples on 20 January 1775, but he backed out of these commitments by September 1774.[76] As part of finding replacement settings, the management of the San Carlo solicited Mysliveček's opinion about whether it would be better to revive a 1758 setting of *Demofoonte* by Hasse for the birthday of the king of Spain or a version of Gluck's *Orfeo* with additions by J. C. Bach. Mysliveček strongly recommended *Orfeo* in a communication drawn up on 8 September 1774:[77]

> In fulfillment of the most revered commands, I have examined the opera *Demofoonte* by the celebrated maestro Signor Hasse, called Il Sassone, and the drama by Signor Cavaliere Kluck, and find that *Demofoonte*, notwithstanding its great mastery, could not be produced without substantial alteration for present-day audiences; *Orfeo*, however, being an extraordinary new spectacle well suited for Their Royal Majesties, I find a better choice for performance, and almost certain to earn success from the discerning public here.

Mysliveček conducted the *Orfeo* production himself on 4 November 1774 and was asked to supply additions of his own to supplement those already provided by J. C. Bach.[78] After rejecting the Hasse setting of *Demofoonte* as well as plans to use Gaetano Latilla as a replacement composer for J. C. Bach, the San Carlo had Mysliveček produce a new *Demofoonte* setting for the birthday of the king of Naples on 20 January 1775 that was particularly successful.[79]

From this period there is a remarkable account of a financial maneuver that went awry for Mysliveček, who was perpetually short of funds. Apparently, he refused to repay the full loan a merchant had advanced him, claiming that he had been mistreated by the merchant.[80] To fight the

---

[73] See Lucio Tufano, "Josef Mysliveček e l'escuzione napoletana dell'*Orfeo* di Gluck (1774)," *Hudební věda* 43 (2006): 257–79.

[74] Ibid., 260.

[75] Ibid., 265. On the reception of *Artaserse*, see also Bohadlo, 89.

[76] Tufano, "Josef Mysliveček," 260–64.

[77] Ibid., 267; text in Appendix 2 below. The note was originally transcribed by Alessandro Ademollo in a series of articles devoted to Gluck in Italy that appeared in the journal *Fanfulla della domenica* in 1890. The original document no longer survives.

[78] See chapter 7. The music for this production, preserved in the Conservatorio di Musica S. Pietro a Majella in Naples, is available in Ernest Warburton, ed., *The Collected Works of Johann Christian Bach*, vol. 11 (New York and London: Garland, 1987). It is almost certain that the music untraceable either to Gluck or Bach originated from Mysliveček.

[79] The *Notizie del mondo* of 31 January 1775 reported that it received "un'applacuso straordinario": see Bohadlo, 97.

[80] For the documentation, uncovered by Ulisse Prota-Giurleo, see Appendix 1.

expected legal action against him (imprisonment for debt), he appealed to the imperial court's ambassador in Naples through Count Johann Joseph von Vlček (Wilczek), a fellow Bohemian. When policemen arrived to arrest Mysliveček at his lodgings (12 September 1774), he presented a patent of protection from Count Vlček (prepared 30 August). The case moved to the imperial court where the Neapolitan ambassador in Vienna, Giuseppe Bologna, Marchese della Sambuca, consulted with Count Wenzel Anton von Kaunitz, the Habsburg foreign minister. Mysliveček's patent of protection was upheld and it was his creditor who found himself in prison (for usury). The matter was settled definitively when Mysliveček paid the merchant a reduced amount. The episode forms an illuminating sidelight to Mysliveček's career with its demonstration of his intrepid, resourceful nature and ability to manipulate powerful friends on his behalf. There were few eighteenth-century composers whose personal affairs took up the time of statesmen as eminent as Kaunitz.

The only surviving letter from Mysliveček himself during his stay in Naples in 1774–75 is to Padre Martini (12 May 1775), written for the purpose of introducing flautist Johann Baptist Wendling. It must have been presented to Martini by Wendling.[81]

> Most illustrious and reverend father!
>
> The bearer of this letter is the renowned Monsieur Wendling, flute virtuoso in the service of his highness the Elector Palatine, who is traveling in the company of a knight from the same court. He would take satisfaction and pleasure in paying his respects to you, thus you will forgive me, if I beg you to receive him with your usual innate goodness. Concerning myself, I can tell you that once I have finished the opera [*Ezio*], I will leave [Naples] to have the honor soon to pay my own respects. In the meanwhile I kiss your hands begging to retain your strongest patronage. And give me the honor of declaring myself forever the most devoted and obsequious servant of your most reverend lordship
>
> Giuseppe Misliwecek

How Mysliveček came to known Wendling, who worked for the Elector Palatine Karl Theodor in Mannheim, is not known,[82] but his association with a flautist bolsters the presumed authenticity of Mysliveček's Flute Concerto in D Major. Other than this, the only available documentation of Mysliveček's activities in Naples in 1774 and 1775 derives from favorable reports of his operatic productions. The last, *Ezio*, was attended by the British ambassador in Naples, Sir William Hamilton, and by Archduke Maximilian Franz of Austria, the youngest surviving son of Maria Theresa, who as elector of Cologne (1784– 1801) was a patron of the Beethoven family.[83]

---

[81] Bologna, Civico Museo Bibliografico Musicale, I.4.60; Schnoebelen, no. 3332; transcription and facsimile in Bohadlo, 102–04; transcription in Nascimbene, "Mysliveček," 19; facsimile in Shaginian, 237. The text is in Appendix 2 below.

[82] Connections cultivated by Mysliveček's patron Lord Cowper, a distant cousin of Karl Theodor (see note 13 above) might have provided the opportunity when Karl Theodor traveled to Italy in 1773–74.

[83] The *Notizie del mondo* (4 July 1775) recorded their attendance in the company of the king and queen of Naples on 21 June 1775: see Bohadlo, 98. Sir William Hamilton, British ambassador to the Kingdom of the Two Sicilies between 1764 and 1800, and his first wife, Lady Catherine, were music lovers who enjoyed unusually close personal relations with the Neapolitan royal family. Wolfgang and Leopold Mozart met them during a visit to Naples in May, 1770. See Leopold's letters to his wife of 19 and 26 May (Anderson, pp. 135, 139); see also Ingamells, comp., *A Dictionary of British and Irish Travellers*, 453–60.

Mysliveček is next traceable to Florence, where he exceeded his earlier success in opera and oratorio. The premiere of his last oratorio, *Isacco figura del redentore*, took place at the Casino dei Nobili in Florence on 10 March 1776 under the sponsorship of Lord Cowper by musicians in his employ.[84] The oratorio was repeated on 13 March at a gathering of the Accademia degli Armonici, a group of music-lovers headed by Lord Cowper.[85] Probably the only reason Mysliveček had *Isacco* produced at this time was because he was stranded in Florence due to ill health.[86] He was to have traveled to Munich at the end of 1775, but was too weak to make the journey.[87]

In the autumn, Mysliveček had the pleasure of witnessing an even greater success with his *Adriano in Siria* at the Cocomero Theater (first performance, 8 September).[88] Giovanni Ansani, one of the finest tenors of the day, was the outstanding singer. Ansani's future wife, singer Giuseppa Maccherini, was withdrawn from the production after having been recommended to Mysliveček by Padre Martini. Mysliveček felt so uneasy about this that he wrote to Martini on 25 August 1776 to explain what had happened:[89]

> Most venerable and esteemed sir, father maestro!
>
> I am very much aware of the honor that your lordship deigned to grant me in recommending Signora Giuseppa Maccherini. And I certainly would not be remiss in my duty to serve this lady with all my feeble strength when she had such a powerful recommendation [as yours], which for me would invariably have the force of law. But this lady's indisposition and the bad behavior of the impresarios has made it absolutely impossible for her to sing in the production. I am truly very sorry in this case not to be able to follow your most revered directions. In the meanwhile I ask you to continue your strongest patronage on my behalf and grant me the enviable honor of declaring myself forever the most humble, most devoted, and most obsequious servant of your most reverend lordship
>
> Giuseppe Misliwecek

One year before he bragged to Wolfgang Mozart about his ability to influence the selection of singers to be utilized in his productions,[90] Mysliveček had to back out of an important sponsorship. Maccherini's preparations for the role of Emirena were not wasted, however; within a year she appeared in two other productions of *Adriano in Siria*, probably both using at least some of Mysliveček's music.[91] For his part, Mysliveček was able to make good on Padre Martini's recommendation at a

---

[84] Weaver and Weaver, *A Chronology*, 352.

[85] Ibid.

[86] Ibid. A notice in the *Gazzetta di Toscana* (9 March 1776) about *Isacco figura del redentore* offers this reason for Mysliveček's detainment in Florence: "alcune indispozioni di salute."

[87] See chapter 4.

[88] Concerning the circumstances of this performance, see Weaver and Weaver, *A Chronology*, 361–63.

[89] Österreichische Nationalbibliothek (Handschriften- und Inkunabelsammlung, VII. 83); transcription and facsimile in Bohadlo, 101–02; transcription in Nascimbene, "Mysliveček," 20; facsimile in Shaginian, 237. The text is in Appendix 2 below.

[90] See chapter 4.

[91] For the singing career of Giuseppa Maccherini Ansani, see Sartori, *I libretti*, appendix vol. 2:382–83 (roles recorded between 1766 and 1791). Padre Martini may have recommended her for the Florence production of *Adriano in Siria* because of her appearance as

slightly later time, specifically when he made her *prima donna* at the Teatro San Carlo in for productions of his operas *La Calliroe* and *L'olimpiade* in 1778. Maccherini's replacement in the role of Emirena in the Florentine *Adriano*, Clementina Chiavacci, was notably successful. The notice in *Gazzetta di Toscana* was ecstatic in its praise and reported that almost all of the arias in the production had to be repeated.[92]

Ill or not, Mysliveček had not lost his touch, but his successes in Florence in 1776 brought to an end a long period of brilliant compositional activity in Italy. That kind of intense work could be revived only partially during the last four years of his life. What would come to dominate the time remaining to him was constant pain caused by chronic illness, the resulting restriction of his movements, and the dismal effects of a lifetime of profligacy.

Emirena in an anonymous production of *Adriano in Siria* in Genoa during carnival in 1776. She and Giovanni Ansani appeared in a production of *Adriano in Siria* in Livorno during carnival in 1777. The surviving libretto bears no indication of who contributed music, but there is a very strong possibility that at least some of Mysliveček's music was used for that production, coming as it did so soon after the Mysliveček *Adriano* in Florence in which they prepared the same roles of Osroa and Emirena that they sang in Livorno (see also Catalog 2 below). In spring 1777, Maccherini appeared again as Emirena in another production of *Adriano*, this time in Pavia. The libretto for the Pavia production attributes all the music to Mysliveček and gives her name as Giuseppa Maccherini Anzani, an indication that she married Giovanni Ansani sometime in the early months of 1777.

[92] Weaver and Weaver, *A Chronology*, 362. Similarly positive were reports of the opera published in the *Gazzetta universale*: see Bohadlo, 99.

4

IL BOEMO TRADITORE: A TRIP TO MUNICH AND THE BREAK WITH THE MOZARTS, 1776–78

In view of his failure to establish himself in northern Europe in 1772, the invitation Mysliveček received from the court of Munich to compose an opera for the carnival season of 1777 must have been particularly gratifying. He had been commissioned to compose music for the carnival season in Munich in 1776, but serious illness had prevented him from leaving Florence at the end of 1775. For a substitute opera in 1776, the electoral court composer Joseph Willibald Michl was called upon to set Metastasio's *Il trionfo di Clelia* at short notice with the help of the court Kapellmeister Andrea Bernasconi, who composed the recitatives.[1]

The text chosen for Mysliveček's carnival opera of 1777 was Metastasio's *Ezio*, which Mysliveček had set for the court of Naples less than two years before. Earlier research had assumed that he revised his Naples *Ezio* for Munich, but Karl Böhmer has demonstrated that Mysliveček's *Ezio* for Munich was actually a completely different setting and that it utilizies only a few scattered motives from his earlier version.[2] Mysliveček had little choice in the matter since the commission required that new arias be composed for all the singers who had been contracted. The elector of Bavaria, Maximilian III Joseph, was very particular about the selection of singers. In order to satisfy his usual preference for castratos, the elector saw to it that an established male soprano, Tommaso Consoli, was engaged along with Luigi Marchesi, another major figure in the early stages of his career. However, no care was taken to balance these singers with a female singer of the stature of Anna de Amicis-Buonsollazzi, who had graced the Naples production, and the result was a cast much less distinguished than the one that had been assembled for the Naples *Ezio*. Although not apparent at the time, Mysliveček's Munich *Ezio* marked the end of an era in operatic production at the electoral court. After Maximilian III Joseph died in December 1777, the Bavarian lands fell to the Elector Palatine, Karl Theodor, who favored more French-influenced operatic styles. The production of

---

[1] Much new information about Mysliveček's activities in Munich is in Robert Münster, "'Die hiesige ongnierte Lebensart gefallet allen . . .': Nachrichten zum Münchner Musikleben der Jahre 1771 bis 1779 aus den Briefen Joseph Franz von Seinsheims an seinem Bruder Adam Friedrich von Seinsheim," in *Mozarts Idomeneo und die Musik in München zur Zeit Karl Theodors*, ed. Theodor Göllner and Stephan Hörner (Munich: Bayerische Akademie der Wissenschaften, 2001), 237–51. Count Joseph Franz von Seinsheim was a Bavarian minister of state, his brother Adam Friedrich was prince-bishop of Würzburg and Bamberg. Their correspondence (preserved in the private collection of Schloss Sünching in Bavaria) contains fascinating information about musical life in Munich. Joseph Franz's letter of 27 December 1775 (transcribed in Münster, "Die hiesige," 244), mentions replacing Mysliveček (identified as "Mislowiek"), who was "dangerously" ill in Florence, with Michl and Bernasconi.

[2] Karl Böhmer, *W. A. Mozart's Idomeneo und die Tradition der Karnevalsoper in München*, Mainzer Studien zur Musikwissenschaft no. 39 (Tutzing: Hans Schneider, 1999), 75–92; and Böhmer, "Josef Mysliveček: Ezio," *Concerto* 13 (July/August 1996): 42–43.

Mozart's *Idomeneo* in carnival of 1781 was a typical manifestation of the new direction Karl Theodor mandated for the electoral court opera.

Many details about the Munich *Ezio* production are recorded in surviving correspondence from the Bavarian Seinsheim family and the elector of Bavaria. On 21 December 1776 Count Franz Joseph von Seinsheim, struggling a bit with Mysliveček's name, wrote to his brother Adam Friedrich with some news about the preparations for Mysliveček's opera:[3]

> The grand opera to be given here should be very beautiful. The famous Bohemian composer Wickelseck (or whatever his name is) wrote the music, the libretto is Metastasio's *Ezio*, and there also should be quite lovely sets and dancing to be seen. The composer is here at present. Otherwise he resides mainly in Italy, especially in Florence.

A subsequent letter (4 January 1777) mentions the dress rehearsal:[4]

> The dress rehearsal of the new opera took place today, and it will be performed for the first time next Monday. The music will be much praised, and the ballets should be especially beautiful and magnificent as well owing to the diverse array of costumes and the lovely sets, which cost much more than the opera itself.

The first performance, on 10 January 1777, was not an unqualified success, partly because one of the singers (probably Rosa Manservisi) had lost her voice:[5]

> Yesterday the opera was performed for the first time. The music was expected to be artful, but many believed they had should have heard better music that delighted the ear more, considering that the composer, even though a Bohemian, is one of the most famous in Italy. The female singer had a strong catarrh and much of the time lost her voice. It is thought that she has suffered damage to her lungs and has no hope of regaining her former voice. But the two castratos [Consoli and Marchesi] were excellent, and old Panzachi [Domenico de Panzacchi] also distinguished himself, especially as an actor.

In a letter of 22 January, Count Seinsheim reported that the production had become quite successful with the public even though Manservisi was still not well.[6] Seven days later he attributed its success more to the dancing and sets than to the music.[7]

[3] As cited in Münster, "Die hiesige," 246; text in Appendix 2 below.

[4] Transcription in Münster, "Die hiesige," 246; text in Appendix 2 below.

[5] Letter of Count Seinsheim, 11 January 1777; transcription in Münster, "Die hiesige"; text in Appendix 2 below. In another part of this letter, Count Seinsheim indicated that Emperor Joseph II (who was in Munich, traveling incognito as "Count Falkenstein") was to attend a performance on 13 January.

[6] Ibid., letter of 22 January 1777.

[7] Ibid., letter of 25 January 1777. The beauty of the sets and costumes (not to mention the singing of Marchesi, Consoli, and Panzacchi) was also reported in the *Gazzetta universale* of Florence, 4 February 1777; transcription in Bohadlo, 105.

The elector of Bavaria communicated his reactions to his sister Maria Antonia Walpurgis (1724–80), the dowager electress of Saxony and a gifted composer in her own right. On 23 January, confining his remarks to the singing of Tommaso Consoli in the role of Valentiniano III and Rosa Manservisi in the role of Onoria, the elector noted his approval of Consoli and his displeasure with Manservisi, and he contradicted the good reports his sister had apparently heard about Manservisi's singing.[8] Then on 2 February, he mentioned that Manservisi's singing had improved, and he went on to single out Luigi Marchesi for his performance.[9] However, Count Seinsheim, writing three days later, did not sing Marchesi's praises, but instead expressed his hope that the tenor Ludwig Aloysius Costa, a member of Count Adam Friedrich's household, would replace Marchesi, since Marchesi was then having trouble getting through his arias.[10] Five days later the opera closed.[11]

Apparently more favorably received than *Ezio* was a Lenten production of Mysliveček's oratorio *Isacco figura del redentore*, which was probably performed as a sacred opera in the electoral court theater.[12] It had been assumed that Mysliveček's oratorio was first performed in Munich during the autumn of 1777, based on Wolfgang Mozart's comment in his letter of 11 October 1777[13] that "all Munich" was talking about it. But evidence in the Seinsheim correspondence confirms that *Isacco* actually received its Munich premiere on 21 February 1777—which means that at the time Mozart wrote his letter, all Munich was *still* talking about it. It is not known where Mozart heard the title *Abramo ed Isacco*; in the Seinsheim correspondence Mysliveček's work is referred to by its original title *Isacco figura del redentore*:[14]

> Yesterday a beautiful oratorio was given in the old theater [i.e., the Salvatortheater] with music by Misslowez (or whatever his name is), a Bohemian who composed the opera [just given]. The singers are mainly the ones who sang in the opera, except for the bass [perhaps Gaetano Ravanni], who is very good, the famous tenor [Giovanni] Valesi, and a singer from Weilheim who has a very beautiful voice. The subject was *Isacco figura del redentore*. Very

[8] The correspondence between Maximilian III Joseph and his sister is preserved in the Sächsisches Hauptstaatsarchiv in Dresden. Excerpts concerning the Munich *Ezio* are transcribed in Eduard Weiss, "Andrea Bernasconi als Opernkomponist" (Ph.D. diss., University of Munich, 1923), 89–90. The key passage from the letter of 23 January 1777 reads: "Consoli chante bien et ce fait honeur; on Voue à mal informé que la Rosa etoit tant bien servi, la premiere aire est mauvaise, la seconde trop forte pour elle, et ce n'est que la troisieme qui est un espece de rondeaux, qu'elle execute come il faut, et qui est pour sa voix" (Consoli sings well and does himself honor. You were informed incorrectly that Rosa Manservisi sings as well as he does. Her first aria is bad, the second one is too difficult for her and it is only the third one, a *rondeau* that she sings as it should be and is suitable for her voice). Manservisi's three arias were "Quanto mai felici siete" (act 1, scene 7), "Finchè per te mi palpita" (act 2, scene 8), and "Peni tu per un'ingrata" (act 3, scene 1). In fact, the first of these, not the third, is cast in *rondeau* form. Manservisi was probably the singer who lost her voice according to Count Seinsheim and disrupted the production (see note 5 above).

[9] Ibid., 90. The key passage reads, "L'opera va toujours mieux, la feme c'est beaucoup remise; Marchesi y fait un merveille l'impertinent, mais ne l'est acteur rien moin, quand il quite son role" (The opera is always going better, and the female singer has much recovered; Marchesi performs marvelously in his role, no less as an actor than as a singer).

[10] Letter of 5 February; see Münster, "Die hiesige," 247.

[11] Ibid., letters of 8 and 12 February 1777.

[12] See chapter 7.

[13] Anderson, 302–06; Bauer and Deutsch, 2:43–46.

[14] Letter of 22 February 1777; transcription in Münster, "Die hiesige," 247–48; text in Appendix 2 below. The identity of the singer from Weilheim is unknown. A letter of 8 March 1777 reports that Clemens Wenzeslaus, elector of Trier, attended a performance of the oratorio, which he enjoyed very much, especially the singing of Marchesi.

> many people attended, indeed the subscription was suspended, which yielded Count Seeau [intendant of dramatic performances at the electoral court] much profit. The singers, especially Marchesi as Isaac and Valesi as Abraham, sang incomparably well. This oratorio was better received than the last opera [Mysliveček's *Ezio*].

The sudden death of Elector Maximilian III Joseph on 30 December 1777 led to the cancellation of Mysliveček's cantata *Enea negl'Elisi*, scheduled to be one of the operatic entertainments during carnival in 1778.[15] The cantata's title is known from the Mozart correspondence,[16] although the score bears a different title, *Il tempio d'eternità.*[17] It has been postulated that Mysliveček's oratorio *La passione* may also have been performed in Munich sometime during his stay there.[18] The elector's death was the principal news Mysliveček relayed from Munich on 6 January 1778 in the last of the New Year's greetings he is known to have sent Padre Martini:[19]

> Most reverend and esteemed Padre Martini!
>
> In order to carry out my most humble duty, I have the honor of sending most happy New Year's greetings to your most reverend lordship, full of every prosperity according to the appropriate vows and desires. Other than this, I relate to you the unhappy news that on 30 December last, his highness the elector of Bavaria died at the age of 51 years from illness. His successor will be the Elector Palatine, who is already here and, it is said, will remain. It gave me great pleasure that Maestro Ottani achieved unusual applause with his opera at Naples.[20] This is the usual result of being able to boast oneself the student of such a great and famous maestro as your most reverend lordship. I am commissioned for two operas in Naples for the upcoming season this year [*Calliroe* and *L'olimpiade*]. If the poor state of my health permits it, I will have the good fortune this spring to pay my respects to your most reverend lordship in Bologna. In the meanwhile I beg to continue under your valuable

---

[15] While there is confusion in the dating of the surviving librettos from the Munich *Ezio*, and while Elector Maximilian III Joseph sometimes had operas repeated during the carnival season after their first performance, it is doubtful that *Ezio* was reprised in 1778. In Sartori, *I libretti*, the dates of the two extant Munich *Ezio* exemplars are given as 1778, not 1777, but all other documentation indicates a performance only in 1777. Moreover, one singer listed in the librettos, Angela Galliani, is also recorded in a libretto for Felice Alessandri's *Creso*, an opera that was performed in Mantua during carnival in 1778.

[16] According to Franz Michael Rudhart (*Geschichte der Oper am Hofe zu München*, [Freising, 1865], 165), the opera ready for presentation during carnival in 1778 was Carlo Monza's *Attilio Regolo*. Preparations for this work, which were to include a performance of the cantata *Enea negl'Elisi*, are mentioned in Leopold Mozart's letter to his son, 13 November 1777; see Anderson, 365; Bauer and Deutsch, 2:113.

[17] The score was once housed with other dispersed items in the collection of Electress Maria Anna of Bavaria; see Gertraut Haberkamp and Robert Münster, *Die ehemaligen Musikhandschriftsammlungen der Königlichen Hofkapelle und der Kurfürstin Maria Anna in München*, Kataloge Bayerischer Musiksammlungen no. 9 (Munich: Henle, 1982). The entry for this work appeared on Bl. 35r; see Catalog 2 below.

[18] Münster, "Die hiesige," 247, note 43. The basis of this speculation is the existence of a score of the oratorio (in Frankfurt-am-Main, Stadt- und Universitätsbibliothek, Musik- und Theaterabteilung, Manskopfisches Museum) that was copied in Munich by the electoral court copyist Sixtus Hirsvogel.

[19] Österreichische Nationalbibliothek, Vienna, Handschriften- und Inkunabelsammlung, 7/83–2; transcription in Bohadlo, 140; text in Appendix 2 below.

[20] A reference to the opera *Catone in Utica* by Bernardo Ottani, performed at the Teatro San Carlo on 4 November 1777. Ottani had been one of Martini's most successful students.

> protection with the most profound respect of your reverend lordship's most humble, devoted, and obsequious servant
>
> Giuseppe Mysliwecek

Although the new elector, Karl Theodor, was an enthusiastic patron of music (he brought the famous Mannheim orchestra with him to Munich), Mysliveček appears not to have been interested in waiting around to see if his talents might be desired for the court musical establishment. As he told Padre Martini, he had operatic commisions to fulfill in Naples. Clearly he had decided to look elsewhere for opportunities even before Maximilian III Joseph's death—the only thing delaying Mysliveček in Munich was illness.

While the centerpiece of Mysliveček's stay in any location was always dramatic vocal music, much more had occupied his time in Munich than music-making at the electoral court. The months he spent there were among the most productive of his career and led to the composition of some of his most imaginative instrumental music. He probably wrote his wind octets in Munich, as well as keyboard music, concertos, string quartets, symphonies, and even a German melodrama, *Theodorich und Elisa*. Ill as he was, he was able to take full advantage of the stimulating musical environment.

No less remarkable than his output of musical compositions was his last personal encounter with Wolfgang Amadeus Mozart. The most revealing accounts currently known of Mysliveček's activities in this period and of his failing health are to be found in the Mozart family correspondence from 1777 and 1778. Wolfgang Mozart had occasion to see Mysliveček in the autumn of 1777, when Wolfgang and his mother were in Germany in search of musical employment more satisfactory than the position he held at the archiepiscopal court in Salzburg. One of his first stops was Munich, where he hoped to find a post in the elector's musical establishment. On 1 October 1777, Leopold Mozart wrote from Salzburg to his son in Munich about an unexpected letter he had received from Mysliveček that offered Wolfgang the prospect of an operatic commission at the Teatro San Carlo in Naples for carnival in 1779. There seems little question that Mysliveček was already well aware of Wolfgang's professional frustrations in Salzburg, or he would not have approached Leopold about the matter. Leopold transcribed the bulk of Mysliveček's letter:[21]

> Yesterday I received quite unexpectedly a letter from Misliwetcek. I will copy it out for you in its entirety:
>
> "Some posts ago I received the news from Naples that owing to several important commitments the authorities have had to engage a certain Maestro Valentini for the carnival opera.[22] Nevertheless they will undertake to pay 100 cigliati to your son for an opera for the next year. The impresario Don Gaetano Santoro would like you to write to him saying that you will refuse to

[21] Anderson, 287–88; Bauer and Deutsch, 2:25–26. The translations used here are based on Anderson's texts with minor alterations. As in all his correspondence with the Mozarts, Mysliveček wrote in Italian.

[22] The identity of Maestro Valentini cannot be established with certainty. The two operatic composers active in Mysliveček's day who bear that surname, Giovanni Valentini and Michelangelo Valentini, both seem unlikely candidates. The opera actually performed for carnival in 1778 was Ignazio Platania's *Bellerofonte*, a work likely modeled on Mysliveček's own setting of eleven years earlier. It is possible that Platania's name was garbled by Mysliveček or Leopold Mozart (or both) and came out "Valentini" in this letter. Much the same happened with the name of Giuseppa Maccherini (Ansani), who appears as "Marchiani" in a letter of Wolfgang Mozart (11 October 1777; see p. 76 below).

allow your son to come for less than 100 cigliati, but stating that for this sum he will compose whatever opera is allotted to him. Indeed I am much tormented by those impresarios who insist on my writing two operas next year; and at the moment I am awaiting the contract. I will have the worst of the bargain, but no matter. I am well known in Naples and have written six operas. So I know that they will want me to write the first and probably the third. For more safety I always advise the carnival opera [i.e., the "fourth" opera of a Neapolitan season]. Heaven knows whether I will be able to go to Naples, but as they wish it, I will accept the contract. If I cannot go, I will return it. I will inform you in due course what operas have been allotted to me. Then you may write to Don Gaetano Santoro about the fee and the opera itself, or send me your letter which I will forward to him. Meanwhile, a thousand greetings to your whole most esteemed family, and I have the honor, etc., etc."

You see from this letter that I cannot answer it at once, because I still have to wait to hear from him what operas he is going to compose. Moreover, he does not seem to have the faintest idea that you are in Munich. So I am waiting for a letter from you, which I hope to receive tomorrow morning, and then I shall be able to make a decision; for one must be guided by circumstances. The journey to Naples is too far and too expensive, especially if you decide to go beyond Munich. Our subject is now quite a different one; and should you have the good fortune, which is hardly likely, to get an appointment in Munich, you could not run away the first year. But in that case you could draft the letter to Santoro to the effect that the offer brings you honor and insures a contract for an opera in Naples for some other year, when it would be more convenient and practicable. If in the meantime Herr Misliwetcek hears or has heard that you are in Munich, your excuse, if you do not wish to see him, will have to be that your Mamma forbids you to do so and that other people have persuaded you, and so forth. It is indeed a pity. But, if he is sensible, he will appreciate the point and will not nourish a grievance against a mother. Even if he does manage to reach Naples, what sort of figure will the poor fellow, who is now without a nose, cut in the theater? But this happened through his own fault. Where does the blame lie, but on himself and on the horrible life he has led? What a disgrace he is before the whole world! Everybody must fly from him and loathe him. It is indeed a real calamity that he has brought on himself.

It is obvious that Mysliveček was very proud of the manner in which he was being courted by the Neapolitan impresario, and he did compose the first and third operas of the 1778–79 season: *Calliroe* for the name-day of the king of Naples on 30 May and *L'olimpiade* for the name-day of the king of Spain on 4 November.[23] Having to compose two operas would seem to be the reason behind Mysliveček's complaint that he would get "the worst of the bargain." Apparently he had told the Neapolitan *Giunta dal canto* that the fee for only one opera would barely cover his traveling expenses

[23] The second opera, Ignazio Platania's *Il re pastore*, was performed for the birthday of the queen of Naples on 13 August; the fourth, or carnival opera, was Vicente Martín y Soler's *Ifigenia in Aulide*, performed in honor of the birthday of the king of Spain on 20 January 1779.

from Munich to Naples, and the *Giunta* had then offered him two operas in order to make the prospect more attractive.[24]

As regards Mysliveček's relations with the Mozart family, Leopold's letter clearly suggests he had either maintained close contacts with Mysliveček over the years or was keen to collect gossip about him. Indeed, Leopold seems to have relished the chance to repeat the gossip he had heard. Here are the first references both to Mysliveček's nose being burned off and the unmistakable implication that Mysliveček was suffering from venereal disease. It is astounding to what degree Leopold felt he could take Mysliveček's feelings for granted. He seems to have believed that Mysliveček should meekly accept social ostracism as punishment for his sexual misconduct and gladly assist his son even in the face of a social snub. He clearly felt that Wolfgang would have been perfectly within his rights not to see him in Munich at all as a gesture of condemnation, especially if his mother concurred. Leopold would learn in short order how fundamentally he misjudged the attitude of both his son and his wife towards Mysliveček's sufferings. Leopold may have disapproved of what he believed to be Mysliveček's moral failings, but he was only too happy to use their friendship to advance his son's musical career. On 6 October 1777 he scolded Wolfgang for not sending some report of an encounter with Mysliveček:[25]

> You say nothing about Missliwetcek [in your letter of 3 October], as though he were not in Munich. How then am I to reply to his letter? I suppose that he will have heard you are there.

Wolfgang's response, a huge section of a letter written to his father from Munich on 11 October 1777, stands without parallel in the entire Mozart correspondence. No other composer is ever rendered such a detailed and sympathetic consideration of his personal affairs, and few incidents in Mozart's whole life led to such an outpouring of emotion in writing. Since Mysliveček was recovering from an operation, Mozart visited him in the Ducal Hospital (Herzogsspital), the best private hospital in Munich, which was ordinarily reserved for retainers of the electoral household. Mysliveček had somehow managed to receive treatment there.[26] Mozart writes about Mysliveček:[27]

> Why have I said nothing so far about Misliwececk? Because it was a relief not to have to think of him for a while. For whenever he was mentioned, I was obliged to hear how highly he has been praising me and what a good and true friend of mine he is! At the same time I felt pity and sympathy for him. People described his appearance to me, and I was nearly distracted. Was I to know that Misliwetcek, so good a friend of mine, was in a town, even in a corner of the world where I was and was I not to see him, to speak to him? Impossible! So I resolved to go and see him. But on the previous day I went to the governor of the Ducal Hospital and asked him whether he could not arrange for me to talk to Misliwetcek in the garden, since, although everyone,

---

[24] See the document transcribed by Ulisse Prota-Giurleo in Appendix 1, p. 386, below.

[25] Anderson, 297; Bauer and Deutsch, 2:36–37.

[26] A description of the Ducal Hospital, famed for its adjacent gardens, is in Ludwig Hollweck, ed., *In München Anno 1782* (Munich: Süddeutscher Verlag 1970), 79.

[27] Anderson, 302–06; Bauer and Deutsch, 2:43–46.

even the doctors, had assured me that there was no longer any danger of infection, I did not want to go to his room, as it was very small and smelled rather strongly. The governor said that I was perfectly right and told me that he usually took a walk in the garden between eleven and twelve, and that if I did not find him there, I was to ask whether he would not come down. I went therefore on the following day with Herr von Hamm, Secretary of War (about whom I will have something to say later on),[28] and with Mamma to the hospital. Mamma went into the church and we walked into the garden. [Mysliveček] was not there, so we sent him a message. I saw him coming across the garden toward us and recognized him at once by his walk. I should say here that he had already sent me his compliments through Herr Heller, the cellist,[29] and had begged me to be so kind as to visit him before my departure. When he came up to me, we shook hands in the most friendly fashion. "You see," he said, "how unfortunate I am!" These words and his appearance, which Papa already knows about, as it has been described to him, so wrung my heart that all I could say half sobbing was, "With my whole heart I pity you." "My dear friend", he said, for he saw that I was moved and began at once to speak more cheerfully, "do tell me what you are doing. I was told that you were here, but I could hardly believe it. Was it possible that Mozart was in Munich and had not visited me all this time?" I replied, "Indeed I must beg your forgiveness. I have had so many calls to pay. I have so many true friends here." "I am sure that you have very true friends here, but none as true as I, that I can assure you." He asked me whether I had not heard from Papa about a letter—"Yes," I interrupted, "he wrote to me (I was so distracted and trembled so in every limb that I could hardly speak), but not in detail." He then told me that Signor Gaetano Santoro, the Naples impresario, had been obliged owing to obligations and patronage to give the carnival opera this season to a certain Maestro Valentini, but that next year he would have three to distribute, one of which would be at his disposal. "Since I have already composed six times for Naples, I have not the slightest objection to taking on the less important opera and giving you the better one, I mean, the one for carnival. God knows whether I will be able to travel. If I cannot, then I will just return the contract. The cast for next year is excellent; they are all singers whom I have recommended. My credit in Naples, you see, is so high that when I say, 'Engage this man', they engage him at once." The primo uomo is Marchesi,[30] whom he praises very highly and so does the whole of Munich. Then there is Marchiani,[31] a good prima donna, and further, a tenor [Giovanni Ansani], whose name I have forgotten, but who, as he says, is the best tenor in Italy. "I implore you," he urged, "to go to Italy. There one is really esteemed and

[28] Joseph von Hamm Edler von Sonnenfels (1728–95), Bavarian minister of war. Wolfgang and his mother had the idea of sending Hamm's daughter to Salzburg to study music with Leopold, a project that never materialized.

[29] Gaudenz Heller, a Bohemian cellist in the employ of the Bavarian court.

[30] The male soprano Luigi Marchesi had appeared earlier in the year in *Ezio* and *Isacco figura del redentore* at the electoral court. Before then, his experience in serious opera was limited to subsidiary roles in three works performed in Milan and Venice in 1775. The appearances Mysliveček made possible for him in Naples in 1778–79 established him permanently as a star.

[31] Giuseppa Maccherini, after 1777 wife of the tenor Giovanni Ansani, with whom she had appeared in Florence in 1776 in Mysliveček's *Adriano in Siria* (see chapter 3 above).

valued." And I am sure he is right. When I think it over carefully, I have to admit that in no country have I received so many honors, nowhere have I been so esteemed as in Italy; and certainly it is a real distinction to have written operas in Italy, especially for Naples. He told me that he would draft a letter to Santoro for me, and that I was to come to him tomorrow and copy it. But I could not possibly bring myself to go to his room; and yet if I wanted to copy it, I should have to do so, for I could not write in the garden. So I promised him to call without fail. But on the following day I wrote to him in Italian saying, *quite frankly*, that it was impossible for me to come to him, that I had eaten nothing and had only slept for three hours, and in the morning felt like a man who had lost his reason, that he was continually before my eyes, and so forth—all statements which are as true as that the sun can shine. He sent me the following reply:

"You feel my suffering too keenly. I am grateful for your good heart. If you go to Prague, I will give you a letter for Count Pachta.[32] Do not take my misfortune so much to heart. My illness began as the result of a carriage accident and then I fell into the hands of ignorant physicians. Patience, God's will be done."

He has sent me the following draft of a letter to Santoro:

"The longing I have had for a considerable time to serve your illustrious person and that most worthy public of Naples by appearing with my humble works in your royal theater, is the reason why (disregarding the long and expensive journey) I agree and am willing to compose an opera next year for the royal theater for 100 cigliati. But, if possible, I should like to have the contract for the last one, I mean, the carnival opera, because my interests will not allow me to accept a commission before that time. I trust that you will be so gracious as to agree and that when you have received the royal approval, you will send the written contract to Maestro Misliwecek, through whom I will safely receive it. Meanwhile, longing to make the acquaintance of such a distinguished person, I have the honor to assure you that I am ever, etc."

Misliwetcek also showed me some letters in which my name was frequently mentioned. I am told that he was quite astonished when people here talked about Beecke[33] or other clavier-players of the same kind, and has always exclaimed, "Make no mistake. No one can play like Mozart. In Italy, where the greatest masters are to be found, they talk of no one but Mozart. When he is mentioned, everyone is silent." I can now write the letter to Naples when I choose, but the sooner the better. First, however, I would like to have the opinion of that very wise court Kapellmeister, Herr von Mozart!

I have an inexpressible longing to write another opera. It is a long way to go, it is true, but it would be a long time before I should have to write it. Many things may happen before then. But I think that I ought to accept it. If in the meantime I fail to secure an appointment, oh well, then I can fall

[32] Either Count Johann Joseph von Pachta (1723–1822) or Count Franz Joseph von Pachta (1710–99); more likely the former, a dilettante musician who later became the dedicatee of Mozart's six *German Dances*, K509. On the Pachta family, see chapter 1, note 96.

[33] Ignaz von Beecke was adjutant and music director to Prince Kraft Ernst von Öttingen-Wallerstein, then resident in Munich.

> back on Italy. I will still have my certain 100 ducats at the carnival and once I have composed for Naples, I will be in demand everywhere. Moreover, as Papa is well aware, there are also *opere buffe* here and there in the spring, summer and autumn, which one can write for practice and something to do. I would not make very much, it is true, but, all the same, it would be some-thing; and they would bring me more honor and credit than if I were to give a hundred concerts in Germany. And I am happier when I have something to compose, for that, after all, is my sole delight and passion. And if I secure an appointment or if I have hopes of settling down somewhere, then the contract will be an excellent recommendation, will give me prestige and much more value. But all this is only talk—talk out of the fullness of my heart. If Papa can prove conclusively that I am wrong, well, then I will acquiesce, although unwillingly. For I have only to hear an opera discussed, I have only to sit in a theater, hear the orchestra tuning their instruments—oh, I am quite beside myself at once.
>
> Tomorrow Mamma and I are taking leave of Misliwetcek in the garden. For only the other day, when he heard me say that I had to fetch my mother in the church, he said, "If only I were not such a sight, I would very much like to meet the mother of such a great virtuoso." I implore you, my dearest Papa, to reply to Misliwecek. Write to him as often as you have time. You can give him no greater pleasure, for the man is completely deserted, and often no one goes to see him for a whole week. "I assure you," he said, "it seems very strange that so few people come to see me. In Italy I had company every day." If it were not for his face, he would be completely the same, full of fire, spirit, and life, a little thin, of course, but otherwise the same excellent fellow. All Munich is talking about his oratorio *Abramo ed Isacco*, which he produced here. He has now finished, except for a few arias, a cantata or serenata for Lent.[34] When his illness was at its worst he composed an opera for Padua.[35] But nothing can help him. Even here it is said that the doctors and surgeons maimed him. He has a fearful cancer of the bone. The surgeon Caco, that ass, burned his nose. Imagine what agony he must have suffered. Herr Heller has just been to see him. When I wrote that letter to him yesterday, I sent him the serenata which I composed in Salzburg for Archduke Maximilian [*Il re pastore* of 1775]; and [Heller] gave it to him with the letter.

Perhaps the most remarkable aspect of this long passage is the concern Mozart expressed for Mysliveček's physical condition. Although there is reason to believe that Mysliveček had been involved in a serious carriage accident while traveling to Naples in 1773,[36] the explanation he offered in 1777 to account for his illness—bone cancer precipitated by a carriage accident—seems out of the question. The references to bone degeneration and surgery for facial disfigurement point unmistakably to symptoms of tertiary syphilis, which destroys the septum. The letter is also revealing in personal details relevant both to Mysliveček (his distinctive gait and charismatic personality, "full of fire, spirit, and life") and to Mozart (especially his reputation as a virtuoso keyboard performer and his

[34] Presumably this would be *Enea negl'Elisi*, a cantata mentioned in a letter of Leopold Mozart of 13 November 1777 as ready for the elector of Bavaria.

[35] *Atide*, performed in June of 1774.

[36] See p. 63 above.

penchant for theatrical composition). For his part, Mysliveček could not have been more sympathetic to Wolfgang Mozart's professional frustrations or more supportive in encouraging him to travel to Italy and Prague, as various others had also encouraged Mozart to do. The elector of Bavaria had faulted Mozart for not having enough experience in Italy,[37] whereas his friends the Dušeks had enthusiastically recommended Prague to him through his father.[38] Mysliveček tried to supply Mozart with solid connections to pursue musical opportunities in both locations. He offered to write a recommendation to one of the Counts Pachta and he drafted a letter for Mozart to copy and send to the impresario Santoro in Naples.

Not only Wolfgang but also his mother fell under Mysliveček's spell. Her impression of Mysliveček is striking for its tenderness. Very little of Maria Anna Mozart's personality is revealed in the extant family correspondence, but these remarks by her, included in Wolfgang's long letter of 11 October 1777 to Leopold, offer some idea of the qualities that her son and husband treasured in her:[39]

> Today we were with Misliwetcek, Wolfgang and I, from eleven until half past twelve. He is indeed to be pitied. I talked to him as if I had known him all my life. He is a true friend to Wolfgang and has said the kindest things about him everywhere. Everybody has told us so.

In the continuation of this letter, Wolfgang mentioned that he and his mother were to leave the next day for Augsburg.[40] The Mozart family's connections with Mysliveček did not cease after their departure from Munich, however. On the contrary, the promise of a commission for Wolfgang in Naples seems never to have been far from the thoughts of Leopold or Wolfgang for months. For Wolfgang, the afterglow of the affectionate meeting with Mysliveček in Munich lasted an equally long time. During this trying period, Mysliveček must have seemed like a savior to the Mozart family, since he appeared to offer Wolfgang a way out of his difficulties in finding suitable employment and composition projects worthy of his talents.

Leopold's anxiety over the Naples commission comes through in a letter to his son dated 12 October 1777. In typical fashion, he was ready with copious advice about how to handle the new opportunity, but he also responded less insensitively toward Mysliveček's plight than before. In the face of a united family front, he apparently backed down from his earlier criticism, though he still made reference to the sordid nature of Mysliveček's illness, declaring that it was something to discuss at a later time:[41]

> What you write about the opera in Naples *I myself thought of long ago.* Did Herr Missliwetcek give you Don Santoro's address? You may now send him the letter from Augsburg or enclose it to me; it does not matter, provided it is

---

[37] In a letter to his father of 29 September 1777, Mozart reported a conversation between Prince Zeil and Elector Maximilian III Joseph in which the latter indicated Mozart had to make a name for himself in Italy before his court would be willing to hire him (the remark may have been a pretext).

[38] Leopold told Wolfgang in a letter of 28 September 1777 that he had approached František Dušek, a keyboard player and music teacher in Prague, and his wife Josefa, for whom Mozart had written the *scena* "Ah, lo previdi," K272, in Salzburg in August of 1777, about Mozart visiting Prague.

[39] Anderson, 306; Bauer and Deutsch, 2:47.

[40] Ibid., 308; ibid., 2:49.

[41] Ibid., 310–11; ibid., 2:51–52.

> written clearly and intelligibly. If you do not have his address, then you must send me the letter. I will correspond with Misliwetcek and set things going; but everything depends on the address. Meanwhile what could I have written to Missliwetcek when I did not know whether you had seen him or not? Moreover, I could not send you my opinion upon the matter, as I did not know what might lie behind it. For I was convinced that Missliwetcek knew that you were in Munich, since you both arrived there on the 22nd and he did not write to me until the 28th. About the whole history of his illness I will write more fully some other time. He is indeed to be pitied! Only too well do I understand your fright and your terror, when you saw him. I should have felt exactly the same. You know how tender-hearted I am!

Leopold wrote to his son again on 15 October 1777 from Salzburg with further news of Mysliveček:[42]

> I will write by the next post to Venice and see whether you cannot secure the opera for Ascension [i.e., May of 1778].[43] Missliwetcek has informed me with the greatest delight that, although he never expected it, he had the pleasure of seeing both you and Mamma, "who," he writes, "is truly a charming lady, worthy of Signor Mozart." He tells me that he has now sent twelve symphonies and six quintets with oboe obbligato to the archbishop and he asks me to arrange for their performance and to endeavor to make the archbishop remember him for his earlier music and this present contribution: "Endeavor to remind the prince in my interest of my earlier music and the compositions that I am now sending him. I am a wanderer," and so forth. He adds at the end: "I will send some keyboard sonatas to your daughter." I will be very curious to hear what will happen about the Naples contract that we are hoping to obtain, while in the meantime we must try to secure the contract for Ascension. You must think ahead and aim at getting on. Should you obtain a good appointment in Mannheim or in some other center, this will not prevent you from undertaking a journey to Italy, for every great lord, who really loves music, regards it as a personal honor if someone in his service makes a reputation for himself.

Mysliveček seized the opportunity to benefit from his relationship with the Mozart family by cultivating the archbishop of Salzburg through Leopold. With Mysliveček's cooperation needed to secure a Naples opera commission for Wolfgang, Leopold was drawn into Mysliveček's machinations to secure commissions for himself. The Mysliveček works alluded to in Leopold's letter cannot be established precisely. But good possibilities come to mind: the quintets with oboe obbligato sent to the archbishop are almost certainly the six quintets for oboe or flute plus string quartet offered for sale in the Breitkopf catalog of 1782/84.[44] The identity of the twelve symphonies is not as easy to determine. One possibility is that the ten symphonies and overtures preserved in the Pfarrkirche

---

[42] Ibid., 320–21; ibid., 2:60.

[43] This project, to be arranged through the impresario of the Teatro San Benedetto, Michele Dall'Agata, was no more successful than the project for Naples that Mysliveček was to arrange. As far as is known, Dall'Agata did not reply to Leopold's inquiries.

[44] See Catalog 1 below. All the quintets survive, either completely or in fragmentary form.

collection from Weyarn, a Bavarian collection bearing the date 1778, are a remnant of this set.[45] They could be left over from the set sent to Salzburg. At present it is almost impossible to surmise what music by Mysliveček had earlier been enjoyed by the archbishop. Considering the wording of Mozart's postscript to his father's letter of 20 December 1770, however, it is conceivable that Mysliveček's symphonies were known in Salzburg as early as the 1760s.

It appears that Wolfgang wanted to collaborate with his father in the effort to obtain the Naples commission. He replied to Leopold on 16 October from Augsburg:[46]

> I will probably send off to Misliwecek today the letter for Gaetano Santoro, as we arranged. He has already given me the address. I beg you to write soon to poor Misliwecek, because I know that your letter will certainly cheer him up.

On 20 October 1777 Leopold attempted to mollify his son's concerns for Mysliveček with the almost impatient remark, "I have told you that I wrote to Missliwetcek."[47] Ten days later, on 30 October, he reported to Wolfgang the reply he had just received in a letter that reveals the extent to which Leopold was now acting as Mysliveček's agent in obtaining patronage from the archbishop of Salzburg:[48]

> This very moment, at half past eleven in the morning, I have received four letters—one from your little cousin,[49] one from Herr Stein,[50] one from Herr von Hamm, and the fourth from Misliwetcek. . . . Herr Misliwetcek sent me six short keyboard pieces for Nannerl, and his letter, in fair copy, is a polite and concise reminder about the music which he sent some time ago to the archbishop. So I will now show this letter to the countess.[51] *I had advised him to adopt these tactics*. If the countess refuses to deal with the matter, then I shall take it up with the chief steward. I would like Misliwecek to be paid decently. The letter is drafted quite clearly; he mentions that the copying and binding of both batches of musical scores cost him about ten ducats.

The six short keyboard pieces sent to Nannerl are undoubtedly the *Six Easy Divertimentos* published in London in 1777, which consist of single-movement sonatas, all but one of them cast in rondo form.[52] One of these works figures in a portion of Leopold's letter to Wolfgang of 2 November 1777:[53]

---

[45] Mss. 625–634; see Part 4 below. Six of these works (Symphonies 42–47) are also preserved as a set in the University Library of the Národní Knihovna České Republiky in Prague.

[46] Anderson, 326; Bauer and Deutsch, 2:66.

[47] Ibid., 333; ibid., 2:74.

[48] Ibid., 345; ibid., 2:90–91.

[49] Maria Anna Thekla Mozart, the "Bäsle," a cousin of Wolfgang with whom he was briefly infatuated.

[50] Johann Andreas Stein, the organ builder and keyboard maker from Augsburg.

[51] Countess Antonia Lodron, sister of the archbishop of Salzburg.

[52] There are only two collections of keyboard music by Mysliveček, the *Easy Divertimentos* (London, 1777) and the *Easy Lessons* (Edinburgh, 1784). The six *Easy Lessons* are all cast in two movements. Mozart's use of musical ideas from Mysliveček's keyboard sonatas is discussed in Daniel E. Freeman, "Josef Mysliveček and Mozart's Piano Sonatas K. 309 (284b) and 311 (284c)," in *Mozart-Jahrbuch 1995* (Kassel: Bärenreiter, 1995): 95–109.

[53] Anderson, 353; Bauer and Deutsch, 2:98.

> The countess tried to get me to allow Nannerl to pay her a visit in order that she could play the keyboard rondo that Missliwecek has sent her. The object of my visit was in fact mainly on account of Missliwecek's letter. She assured me that by the last post the archbishop had sent to him in Munich a draft for twenty-five or thirty ducats. She invited me several times to visit her more often and she ended by asking me to send you her greetings.

On 6 November Leopold wrote again to Wolfgang instructing him to make connections through Mysliveček with Anton Raaff, with whom Mysliveček had remained on good terms:[54]

> I am anxious to hear whether you gain the favor of Herr Raaff, to whom I send my humble greetings. He has always been praised to me as a very honest Christian. I wrote to Misliwecek and asked him to write to Raaff about you.

Wolfgang responded to his father's mention of Mysliveček's sonatas on 13 November 1777, praising their qualities highly. Among other things, this letter demonstrates Mozart's desire to see what Mysliveček was composing whenever they came into contact:[55]

> I know what Misliwetceck's sonatas are like, for I played them in Munich. They are quite easy and pleasing to the ear. I should advise my sister, to whom I send my most humble greetings, to play them with plenty of expression, taste and fire, and to learn them by heart. For they are sonatas which are bound to please everyone, which are easy to memorize and very effective when played with the proper precision.

On the same day, still mindful of the promised commission for Naples, Leopold wrote a letter to Wolfgang that reveals his first scepticism about the outcome:[56]

> I think that I have told you that Missliwetcek wrote a fair-copy letter to me (as I asked him to, in order that I might show it to the person in question), in which he urged me to find out whether the music he sent both some years ago and again recently had been delivered to the archbishop. As a result, he was sent a draft for twenty-five ducats. He now informs me that he received it on November 8th and that on his doctor's advice he will remain a while longer in Munich for the benefit of his health, which is improving, and so that he may be able to travel more safely. He adds that he is going to present to the elector a cantata (*Enea negl'Elisi*) which, he feels sure, will be performed together with Monza's opera,[57] as the elector has ordered the score to be copied immediately. He tells me further, that, as I requested, he has written to Signor

[54] Ibid., 360–61; ibid., 2:107.

[55] Ibid., 370–71; ibid., 2:120–21.

[56] Ibid., 364–65; ibid., 2:113.

[57] This would be *Attilio Regolo* by the Milanese composer Carlo Monza. The death of Elector Maximilian (30 December 1777) led to the cancellation of the opera and the cantata; see Rudhart, *Geschichte der Opera*, 165.

> Raaff, that he has received his own contract for the operas for May 30th and November 4th and that he is now waiting for the contract for you, which, however, cannot arrive for another month. As soon as he receives it, he will forward it to me in Salzburg. To tell the truth I am really not counting on this contract, for you know what excuses these Italians make and what tangles of wires there are at Naples. I heard today that the archbishop commissioned Brunetti[58] yesterday to write to Missliwetcek and order some *concertoni*, which may or may not be included in the twenty-five ducats.

Eventually six *concertoni* were sent to the archbishop (see Leopold Mozart's letter of 13 April 1778 below).[59] The thread of reports about this commission picks up in a letter of 12 January 1778, in which Leopold described once again Mysliveček's attempts to seek income from the archbishop of Salzburg. Leopold's impatience with Mysliveček is obvious:[60]

> Misliwetcek has written to say that at the prince's request he composed two *concertoni*, which he sent to Brunetti, but has had no reply. I have written to tell him that he will get nothing for them, as they were probably included in the former payment, but that he ought to go on reminding Brunetti until the latter gets tired of paying the six kreuzer fee and sets things going . . .

Leopold's irritation with Mysliveček is even more pronounced in his letter of 26 January:[61]

> Misliwetcek wrote again the other day to say that he was hoping to receive shortly your contract from Naples. But I regard it as an excuse, for he only makes an announcement like this when he wants me to do something for him.

In a letter of 16 February 1778, as part of a lengthy diatribe in which Leopold contrasted Wolfgang's character as an adult with the idealized image he had about his childhood persona, Leopold criticized his son for failing to see through the faults of flatterers:[62]

> . . . it is just your good heart that prevents you from detecting any shortcomings in a person who showers praises on you, has a great opinion of you and flatters you to the skies, and who makes you give him all your confidence and affection . . .

---

[58] Antonio Brunetti, *Konzertmeister* at the court of Salzburg from 1777.

[59] Three survive: the three concertos for two clarinets, two horns and bassoon listed in Catalog 1. That six were completed can be surmised from a catalog of music offered for sale in 1799: *Verzeichniss alter und neuer sowohl geschriebener als gestochener Musikalien, welche in der Kunst- und Musikalienhandlung des Johann Traeg, zu Wien, in der Singerstrasse Nr. 957 zu haben sind* (Vienna: Johann Traeg, 1799); see fascimile in Alexander Weinmann, ed.,*Johann Traeg: die Musikalienverzeichisse von 1799 und 1804 (Handschriften und Sortiment)*, Beiträge zur Geschichte des Alt-Wiener Musikverlages, series 2, no. 17, vol. 1 (Vienna: Universal Edition, 1973). On p. 53 under "double concertos" is listed for sale, in manuscript, a set six concertos by Mysliveček for 2 clarinets, 2 horns and bassoon with string accompaniment. I am grateful to Christian Moritz-Bauer for bringing this information to my attention.

[60] Anderson, 445–46; Bauer and Deutsch, 2:223–24.

[61] Ibid., 453; ibid., 2:241.

[62] Ibid., 483; ibid., 2:283–84.

Although Mysliveček is never mentioned explicitly, Leopold must have had him in mind.

Wolfgang's affection for Mysliveček had by now been seriously eroded as well. On 22 February, he wrote his father from Mannheim, bringing up Mysliveček in a most surprising manner that went to the heart of the uneasy relations between father and son and to Leopold's attempts to control and manipulate Wolfgang's actions. As a means of defending himself against Leopold's accusations of improper appearances with the daughters of Wolfgang's friend Fridolin Weber, Wolfgang contrasted himself with Antonio Brunetti and Josef Mysliveček:[63]

> There are people who think that no one can love a poor girl without having evil designs; and that charming word *maîtresse*, in German "whore," is really much too charming!—I am no Brunetti and no Misliwetcek! I am a Mozart, and a young and clean-minded Mozart.

On 13 April 1778, clearly feeling used and mistreated, Leopold reported again of Mysliveček's behavior in an unflattering light. Obviously, Mysliveček finally felt well enough to make plans to leave Munich in order to prepare the opera required for the name day of the king of Naples on 30 May. Leopold writes:[64]

> Well, we have had no letter from you today. The postman did call—and brought one from Missliwetcek, who writes to say that instead of the twenty-five or thirty ducats he was expecting for the six *concertoni*, which he rewrote at the archbishop's orders, he has only received enough to meet the expenses of the journey, and that he is leaving Munich on Maundy Thursday [16 April] and so forth. In every single letter (and he has written very often asking for my assistance) he has made some excuse about the contract for Naples, which he is expecting to receive, he says, by every post. Thus he now informs me that: "So far I have not received the contract from Naples, but I hope to settle the affair on my arrival. I am leaving for Naples on Maundy Thursday. Meanwhile I must ask a favor of you (otherwise he would not have written to me), and that is to send me Bach's six concertos, etc.[65] Herr Hamm has asked me to do him this kindness. They (he and his daughter) do not dare write to you themselves, etc." That I can well believe. For Herr Hamm was *so polite* as to send me no reply whatever to my letter of six months ago, in which I asked only 200 gulden a year for his daughter's *full board and lodging, including her instruction*. So Missliwecek had to ask on his behalf for the concertos. Well, he can wait for them and I will write and tell Missliwetcek the reason.

It is likely that Mysliveček knew as early as the end of 1777 that Wolfgang's commission for Naples would not be forthcoming; in the early months of 1778 he nevertheless continued to dangle it as a possibility in order to manipulate Leopold Mozart.

---

[63] Ibid., 487; ibid., 2:290. A specific incident of sexual misconduct by Brunetti would have been in Mozart's mind: as *Konzertmeister* at the court of Salzburg, he sired a child out of wedlock by Judith Lipps, the sister-in-law of Michael Haydn, whom Brunetti then married in 1778.

[64] Ibid., 527; ibid., 2:339.

[65] It is reasonably certain that the Bach referred to here is J. C. Bach, but the set of concertos is not clear—perhaps Op. 13 (1777).

The last mention of Mysliveček in Wolfgang Mozart's extant correspondence is in his letter of 7 August 1778 from Paris to his friend the Abbé Bullinger in Salzburg. By this time, Wolfgang was thoroughly disillusioned with his former friend and even lowered himself to ridiculing Mysliveček's facial disfigurement with a jibe that was meant to illustrate the mediocrity of the musical establishment at the court of Salzburg:[66]

> . . . content yourself with this one, that Salzburg is no place for my talent. In the first place, professional musicians there are not held in much consideration; and, secondly, one hears nothing, there is no theater, no opera; and even if they really wanted one, who is there to sing? For the last five or six years the Salzburg orchestra has always been rich in what is useless and superfluous, and absolutely destitute of what is indispensable; and such is the case at the present moment. Those cruel French are the cause of the orchestra having no Kapellmeister.[67] I feel assured, therefore, that quiet and order are now reigning there! That, of course, is the result of not making provision in time. Half a dozen Kapellmeisters should always be held in readiness, so that if one drops out, one can be instantly substituted. But where, at present, can they get one? Yet the danger is pressing! It will not do to allow order, peace and intelligence to gain the upper hand in the orchestra, or the mischief will spread further and in the long run become irremediable. Are there really no ancient periwigs with asses' ears, no lousy heads available, who could restore the concern to its former disabled condition? I will certainly do my best in the matter. Tomorrow I intend to hire a carriage for the day and drive round to all the hospitals and infirmaries and see if I cannot find some Kapellmeister for them. Why were they so careless as to let Misliwetceck give them the slip?—and he was so near, too! He would have been a fat morsel for them. It would not be easy to get someone like him and someone moreover who has just been discharged from the Duke Clemens Conservatory.[68] He would have been the man to terrify the whole court orchestra by his presence.

Shrewd as he was, Leopold had been bamboozled by Mysliveček, along with Wolfgang, and there was no mistaking it. The final word on Mysliveček's relationship with the Mozart family comes from Leopold's letter of 13 August 1778. In it Leopold took the opportunity to draw attention to his devotion and self-sacrifice toward Wolfgang by pointing out how much money he had spent on correspondence with Mysliveček in a futile attempt to arrange the Naples opera commission. He also used Mysliveček as an example of one of Wolfgang's professed friends who was actually faithless and self-serving:[69]

---

[66] Anderson, 594–95; Bauer and Deutsch, 2:439.

[67] Ferdinando Bertoni was offered the post of *Kapellmeister* by the archbishop of Salzburg, but declined it to travel to Paris and London instead.

[68] A pun on the name of the Ducal Hospital in Munich where Mysliveček convalesced.

[69] Anderson, 598; Bauer and Deutsch, 2:443–44.

> Experience (which you can only gain through misfortune) has quite convinced me that there is no true friend—using the word *in its fullest sense*—but a father. Even children are not *in the same degree* friends towards their own parents. Just reflect—think things out and face facts—and you will find enough examples in the world to persuade you of the truth of my dictum. It is for this reason too that God found it necessary to lay down the commandment that children should honor their parents, and even to add a punishment, whereas he did not think it necessary to enjoin upon parents any such commandment. Missliwecek's letters have cost me a fortune and they all say that your contract for Naples is ready, fixed, and absolutely certain. After I had helped him to obtain thirty-seven ducats, he left Munich before Easter, and I have not had a line from him since then.

Josef Mysliveček, who cultivated the Mozarts in 1777–78 as long as he dared, found his relationship with them definitively terminated by the spring of 1778. He then resumed his earlier way of living in Italy, traveling from one operatic center to another in search of sustenance and acclaim.

5

IL BOEMO MORTALE: FINAL DECLINE, 1778–81

Continued professional success must have provided Mysliveček at least some compensation for the distressing personal problems that plagued the last three years of his life: neither his musical inspiration nor his ability to attract fresh opportunities was much impaired until nearly the end of his struggles. The two opera commissions he completed for Naples in 1778 (mentioned in the Mozart correspondence) were well received. According to one newspaper account,[1] the performance of *Calliroe* that took place on 30 May 1778 in honor of the name day of the king of Naples was a considerable success, featuring as it did an impressive array of singers reputedly recommended by Mysliveček, among them Luigi Marchesi, Giovanni Ansani, and Giuseppa Maccherini Ansani. The second opera, *L'olimpiade*, one of the finest musical settings produced of the popular libretto of Metastasio, also received an enthusiastic reception when it was performed on 4 November 1778 for the name day of the king of Spain.[2] In his *Reminiscences* of 1826, the Irish tenor Michael Kelly recalled that it had been the first opera he saw in Naples in the late 1770s. Nearly five decades after the event, he remembered both the production and the principal singers:[3]

> At San Carlo's are performed grand serious operas (the other three theaters are for the opera buffa), the first I saw there was Metastasio's *Olimpiade*, the music by Metzlevisic, a German of great musical celebrity. I thought it very fine, and the performance exquisite.
>
> The celebrated Marchesi, the first soprano, performed the part of Megacle; his expression, feeling, and execution in the beautiful aria, "Se cerca se dice l'amico dov'è," were beyond all praise. Ansani, then the finest tenor voice in Europe, was there; and Macherini, his wife, was the principal female singer; she had a very sweet voice, but small, and of limited compass; the Neapolitans call her "La cantante con la parucca," from her being shaved during illness, previous to her engagement;[4] but they like her in spite of her wig!

---

[1] The *Gazzetta universale*, 9 June 1778 (quoted in Bohadlo, 129) praises Luigi Marchesi, Giovanni Ansani, Giuseppa Maccherini Ansani, and Pietro Muschietti, and singles out Marchesi for his "most perfect" acting abilities and "most beautiful" voice.

[2] *Gazzetta di Napoli*, 10 November 1778; transcription by Ulisse Prota-Giurleo, "L'Abate Galiani messo in imbarazzo da un musicista boemo," *Nostro tempo* (December 1957); translation in Appendix 1 below.

[3] Kelly, *Reminiscences*, ed. Fiske, 22. His attendance at *L'olimpiade* belies his own chronology of his visit to Italy. Kelly claimed he left Ireland 1 May 1779 (p. 10), but probably departed in May 1778.

[4] The illness alluded to prevented Giuseppa Maccherini Ansani from appearing in Mysliveček's *Adriano in Siria* in Florence in 1776. See chapter 3 above.

Interesting commentary about *L'olimpiade* can also be found in the 1784 compilation of Carl Friedrich Cramer's *Magazin der Musik*.[5] In a section devoted mainly to the disappointing appearance of Luigi Marchesi in Francesco Bianchi's *L'olimpiade* as performed in Milan during carnival in 1782, Cramer included a footnote about other *L'olimpiade* settings that singled out Marchesi's appearance in the Mysliveček setting at the Teatro San Carlo in Naples four years earlier. Cramer made note of the masterly music Mysliveček wrote for the same aria that Kelly remembered:[6]

> This excellent drama was also set by the renowned maestro Misliwicek and performed at the royal theater of San Carlo in Naples in 1778. The famous aria "Se cerca, se dice" and especially the second section "Che abisso di pene, lasciare il suo bene," elicited wonderment to the point of delirium. Misliwicek's composition of this aria is truly a masterpiece of the most beautiful, most meaningful vocal style, featuring a completely new, very intricate accompaniment. The composition surpasses in very many places those of Sacchini and Pergolesi. What would Rousseau, who in his dictionary expressed himself in such vivid terms about Pergolesi's composition of this aria, have said about this, if he had heard it set by Misliwicek and sung by Marchesi?

Cramer's admiration of "Se cerca, se dice" was echoed by Ernst Ludwig Gerber, who became an authority for many later dictionary entries on Mysliveček.[7]

Mysliveček's final year of unmitigated success in the opera houses of Italy was 1779, when he was able to savor favorable notices both in Venice and Naples one last time. In Venice, his *La Circe* was staged at the Teatro San Benedetto during the Ascension season,[8] and it seems to have redeemed his standing with the Venetian public after the failure of *La clemenza di Tito* five years earlier. Unfortunately, only a few stray arias survive of the music for *La Circe*.[9] Mysliveček's last opera for Naples was his second setting of the *Demetrio* libretto of Metastasio. It was performed for the birthday of the queen of Naples on 13 August 1779, just after an eruption of Mt. Vesuvius. Michael Kelly described the volcano's discharge vividly,[10] but said nothing about the opera production. From the comments that are recorded, it would appear that Mysliveček's *Demetrio* received a rather mild reception in Naples. The notices about the production are positive, but considering the way that Italian newspapers tended to inflate favorable reactions to operatic productions, the bland commentary reported about this one is probably an indication only of a respectable success.[11]

---

[5] Carl Friedrich Cramer, *Magazin der Musik* (Hamburg, 1784; reprint, Hildesheim: Georg Olms, 1971), 2:563.

[6] Ibid.; text in Appendix 2 below. On p. 72 of the same volume, an anonymous correspondent from Rome advanced the opinion that the finest settings of "Se cerca, se dice" produced were written by Mysliveček and Sarti.

[7] Ernst Ludwig Gerber, *Historisch-Biographisches Lexikon der Tonkünstler*, part 1, col. 953. The principal imitator was Fétis.

[8] *Gazzetta universale*, 25 May 1779; see Bohadlo, 132. Bohadlo traced Mysliveček's residence in Venice to an inn in the San Luca district at this time from a list of foreigners registered with the authorities (Venice, Archivio di Stato, Inquisitori di Stato, Forestieri 1779, busta 760: entry of 18 April 1779).

[9] See Part 4.

[10] Kelly, *Reminiscences*, ed. Fiske, 27–29.

[11] The *Gazzetta universale*, 24 August 1779, notes the opera encountered "general applause"; transcription in Bohadlo, 133–34. See also the *Gazzetta di Napoli*, 17 August 1779; transcription in Prota-Giurleo, "L'Abate Galiani"; translation in Appendix 1 below.

There is no reason why contemporary observers need have doubted that Mysliveček's run of luck in the opera theaters could have continued indefinitely, but the carnival season of 1780 brought disappointments to Mysliveček in Milan and in Rome that have traditionally been regarded as the death knell for his career as a composer. According to Pelcl,[12] Mysliveček came to Milan at the invitation of Archduke Ferdinand of Austria, governor of Lombardy, to compose an opera for the newly built Teatro alla Scala (opened in 1778 as a replacement for the Regio-Ducal Teatro, which had burned to the ground 25 February 1776). The result was *Armida*, a work that incorporates elements from French serious opera in a way that brought Mysliveček closer to an ideal of reform opera than any of his earlier dramas. Although a distinguished cast had been assembled, including two of Mysliveček's most favored stars, Luigi Marchesi and Caterina Gabrielli, *Armida* initially failed, to the extent that some of Mysliveček's music had to be replaced. Judging from the music that survives from *Armida*, a possible explanation for the unsatisfactory reception of the opera is a certain lack of polish and a certain lack of virtuoso passage-work in some of the arias, the likely result of Mysliveček over-extending himself after agreeing to compose music for two different operas during the same carnival season (a situation that had also occurred in carnival of 1774).

An exceptional amount of contemporary commentary survives about the production of *Armida* in Milan, mainly due to a series of mishaps that marred it. Beginning 4 January 1780, the *Gazzetta universale* reported on the irregularities of the production almost like a saga:[13]

> Milan, 29 December . . . On Sunday *Armida* went into production in the Regio-Ducal Teatro della Scala. This drama was translated from the French of Quinault, set to music by Signor Maestro Giuseppe Misliwecek, called *Il Boemo*, and the ballets were produced by Signor Angiolini, one of them *Achille in Sciro*, the other *Annetta e Lubino*. The principal interpreters of the opera, Signora Caterina Gabrielli and the incomparable soprano Luigi Marchesi, earned for themselves the greatest acclaim, but the spectacle as a whole did not glean the applause hoped for (indeed, the sponsoring nobles spared no expense for it). On the following Monday the opera buffa *Lo sposo disperato*, set to music by Signor Anfossi, went into production at the Teatro della Canobiana, but this work shared the same fate as the serious opera.

The private life of Caterina Gabrielli proved a considerable interference. At the beginning of the new year she gave birth at the age of forty-nine:[14]

> [Milan] 5 January 1780. The famous virtuosa Gabrielli was happily delivered in the last few days of a baby girl, and baptismal rites were performed on Sunday in the parish church of Saints Nazzario and Celso. The sponsors were Count Ferdinando Gardines della Cerra, Grande of Spain of the first class, and Princess Buttera of Naples. In their places stood the merchant Carlo Castelli and Signora Butteroni. In lieu of gifts being presented, a donation in the amount of one hundred lire was paid to the poor.

---

[12] Pelcl, 192; Appendix 1 below.

[13] Transcription in Bohadlo, 134–35; text in Appendix 2 below.

[14] Transcription in Shaginian, 347, note 145; text in Appendix 2 below. The identity of the baby's father is unknown.

Gabrielli's lying-in, mentioned in the 12 January issue of the *Gazzetta universale*, affected her performance and led to some changes in the opera:[15] "Signora Gabrielli has gone a week without singing, and for tomorrow evening has prepared some new arias with music by Signor Sarti."[16] As reported in the *Gazzetta universale*, the three new arias were better received than the original arias Mysliveček had composed:[17]

> Milan, 19 January. The grand opera *Armida*, presently performed in the new theater [La Scala], has now found universal applause. Signora Caterina Gabrielli appeared last Sunday evening with three new arias. It is said that she sang them with such strength and mastery that they were heard at the pinnacle of their capability. Also the incomparable Signor Marchesi and Signor Adembergh[18] augmented the fine quality of the spectacle.

With its new music, *Armida* achieved an enviable degree of success, and it soon became one of the most frequently performed operas of its day in Milan.[19] Further irregularities plagued the production nonetheless. In a letter to his brother of 2 February 1780, the Milanese literatus Pietro Verri[20] mentioned an evening in which Gabrielli had informed the management of the theater that she was out of voice—meaning that she was willing to sing the recitatives for her role, but not necessarily the arias. Apparently the production director had neglected to forewarn the audience of her indisposition and, when she left the stage without singing the expected aria after a recitative, there were angry outcries from the house.[21] Gabrielli was then advised to sing her duet with Luigi Marchesi.[22] The audience listened attentively to Marchesi, but jeered Gabrielli. The crueliest insult that resounded in the theater, Verri reported, was the word "old" (*vecchia*), but as far as he was concerned both Gabrielli's figure and her voice were as fine as they had ever been.

A different type of disruption occurred at La Scala on 30 January 1780, when a piece of plaster fell from an architrave beneath one of the boxes and hit a musician.[23] The female singer on stage

---

[15] "La Sig. Gabrielli è stata per una settimana senza cantare, e per domani a sera ha preparate dell'arie nuove, musica del Sig. Sarti" (quoted in Bohadlo, 135).

[16] Giuseppe Sarti was in Milan, having been appointed *maestro di capella* at Milan Cathedral in the previous year. The identity of the substitute arias is unknown. They may have been borrowed from earlier works or newly composed for Gabrielli.

[17] Transcription in Bohadlo,135; text in Appendix 2 below. Following the scene numbers of the only surviving complete score (in the Ajuda Palace, Lisbon), Gabrielli's original arias, sung in the title role, were "So, che amor lusinga" (act 1, scene 3), "Cedo l'armi, il cor s'arrende" (act 1, scene 11), "Se il mio duolo" (act 2, scene 7), and "Idol mio serena i rai e consola" (act 3, scene 4). The latter two are undistinguished and lacking in technical brilliance, thus the ones most likely marked for replacement.

[18] Valentin Adamberger, the German tenor best known for his interpretation of Belmonte in the original production of Mozart's *Die Entführung aus dem Serail* (1782).

[19] Hansell, "Opera and Ballet," 188 and 192.

[20] The letter's contents are discussed in John A. Rice, "Sense, Sensibility, and Opera Seria: An Epistolary Debate," *Studi musicali* 15 (1986): 109; the original text is in Giovanni Seregni, ed., *Carteggio di Pietro e Alessandro Verri* (Milan: Giuffrè, 1940), 11:21–23. Pietro Verri (1728–97) was one of the most prominent intellectuals in late eighteenth-century Italy, best known abroad as an economist.

[21] It may be reasonable to assume this incident occurred with her first aria, "So, che amor lusinga"; perhaps an aria of Sarti had replaced it by the time of Verri's letter.

[22] The duet was "È felice la mia sorte," the last number in act 2, which was never replaced by another composer's work.

[23] The date of this incident can be established from the *Gazzetta enciclopedica di Milano*, parte civile-politica, 1 (1780): 26. Its account is more detailed than Verri's: the plaster fell just after the conclusion of the second ballet (i.e., the beginning of act 3).

(unnamed by Verri) cried out and ran offstage,[24] while the orchestra dispersed in disarray. Someone shouted "fire" and audience members fled toward the single exit. Soldiers with bayonets tried to prevent them from leaving. Some people were hurt in the scuffle that ensued, but nobody died.[25] The performance continued to the end of the opera, though the audience members and performers were apparently thoroughly traumatized.[26]

Another incident involving Caterina Gabrielli cannot be dated precisely, but allegedly took place during a performance one evening during January of 1780.[27] After she concluded the aria that ended act 1 of the opera,[28] Gabrielli was applauded and there were calls for her to repeat the aria. She refused. Dancers came on stage to perform the ballet between the first and second acts, but the audience members continued to demonstrate. Gabrielli finally returned to the stage, but by then it was too late: the audience had lost patience with her and greeted her with jeers. She then left the stage without singing.

For his part, Luigi Marchesi had no trouble earning the affection of the Milanese audience from the start,[29] even though he found it necessary to substitute some of Mysliveček's music as well. The failure of *Armida* was so well known and so long remembered that it was described in Cramer's *Magazin der Musik* in 1783 and 1784, in both instances as part of detailing the careers of its principal stars, Caterina Gabrielli and Luigi Marchesi. The brief mention of *Armida* in Cramer's 1783 volume, of greater interest for Gabrielli, has been excerpted earlier in this study.[30] A much more detailed account appeared in the 1784 volume in the course of describing Marchesi's singing career:[31]

> Twice he sang the principal role in the theater at Milan, both times during carnival. The first opera was given in 1780, the second in 1782.[32] In the first year, he caused half-mad delirium (*fece fanatismo*); the second year he did not please the audience much in the first opera, perhaps due to his obstinacy, but he did please in the second. Because of the shortness of the carnival season in the first year, only a single opera was given, namely *Armida* by the Bohemian composer Herr Misliwicek. The music fell through, and the singers found it necessary to substitute arias by other composers according to their discretion. Marchesi inserted a rondò in the second act, "Mia speranza, io pur vorrei," which had been set for him by the incomparable *Domkapellmeister*

[24] If the *Gazzetta enciclopedica di Milano* is correct that the disruption occurred at the beginning of act 3, the singer on stage would have been Caterina Lorenzini performing with the chorus as an "amante fortunata."

[25] Seregni, ed., *Carteggio*, 22.

[26] *Gazzetta enciclopedica di Milano*.

[27] Seregni, *Carteggio*, 21, note 1, mentions that this story (apparently from unidentified eighteenth-century correspondence in the Archivio Visconti di Saliceto) was passed on to him by a friend.

[28] Mysliveček's aria in this position was "Cedo l'armi il cor," perhaps replaced by this time with an aria by Sarti.

[29] The *Gazzetta enciclopedica di Milano*, p. 7, recording the first performance as 26 December 1779, reported Marchesi "shone" in the aria "Ah, disponi la mia sorte" (act 2, scene 4, in the Ajuda Palace, Lisbon, score) as well as in his duet with Gabrielli in the same act, "È felice la mia sorte," but was silent about Gabrielli's singing. The review was probably written in early January 1780, since an aria by Sarti was substituted for "Ah, disponi la mia sorte" no later than the middle of January.

[30] See chapter 2, note 56, above.

[31] See *Magazin der Musik* 2 (1784): 560–62; text in Appendix 2 below.

[32] In carnival season in 1782, Marchesi appeared in Milan in Felice Alessandri's *Ezio* and Francesco Bianchi's *L'olimpiade*.

> Sarti in another opera for Florence the previous autumn,[33] as well as a minuet, "Se piangi, e peni," in the third act by Kapellmeister Bianchi from Cremona.[34] In these pieces he excited extraordinary enthusiasm, particularly with the rondò; but he nonetheless achieved no less acclaim from the bravura aria that remained from Misliwicek's composition.[35]

On 19 February 1780 Pietro Verri wrote to his brother with his own report of Marchesi's abilities,[36] and an even more worshipful encomium survives in a letter of 15 January 1780 from the poet Francesco Zaccheroli to the Marchese Francesco Albergati Capacelli.[37] By then, Mysliveček's aria "Ah, disponi di mia sorte" had already been substituted by Giuseppe Sarti's rondò "Mia speranza, io pur vorrei," and Zaccheroli could not say enough in praise both of Marchesi's singing and Sarti's music.

Mysliveček did not tarry long enough in Milan to witness the full disaster of *Armida*. Instead he traveled on to Rome, where he had little better luck with his opera *Medonte*, which went into production at the Teatro Argentina on 26 January. Cramer compared its reception to the hostile reception that Jommelli's opera *Achille in Sciro* had received in Rome during carnival in 1771.[38] According to Cramer, Jommelli had been so distraught by the viciousness of the crowd that he had never visited Rome again (indeed he did not). Cramer reported that Mysliveček's commission from the Teatro Argentina had been arranged to please Archduke Ferdinand in Milan, but *Medonte* failed miserably: "all of Rome was of the opinion that there had never been such dreadful music."[39] A notice in the *Gazzetta universale* (1 February 1780) is more positive, recording a "most successful reception" and singling out the singing of Tommaso Consoli.[40] The rondò that Consoli sang in the role of Arsace, "Luci belle, se piangete," became one of the most widely disseminated of all of Mysliveček's vocal pieces.[41]

---

[33] Sarti's *Achille in Sciro*, performed at the Pergola Theater, Florence (autumn 1779). The rondò "Mia speranza, io pur vorrei" would have replaced Mysliveček's aria "Ah, disponi di mia sorte."

[34] This selection, from Francesco Bianchi's *Castore e Polluce* (also performed at the Pergola Theater in autumn 1779), replaced the aria "Il caro mio bene" (act 3, scene 1 in the Lisbon score), which is presently Mysliveček's best-known composition in the form of an arrangement for voice and piano attributed to Mozart with the text "Ridente la calma," K153/210a.

[35] This would have been "Più non vi sento in seno" from act 1, scene 9, an aria borrowed from Mysliveček's *Demetrio* of 1779 (in act 2, scene 9, with the text "Non so frenare il pianto").

[36] Seregni, ed., *Carteggio*, 27–28; near-complete transcription and discussion of contents in Rice, "Sense, Sensibility," 114.

[37] The letter includes descriptions of the audience and theater. Transcription in *Opere drammatiche complete e scelte prose di Francesco Albergati Capacelli* (Bologna, 1827), 5:358–63; German translation in *Magazin der Musik* 2 (1784): 572–78; excerpts in Rice, "Sense, Sensibility," 110–12.

[38] *Magazin der Musik* 2 (1784): 50–51, an account from a *Tagebuch eines Reisenden* believed to be by the writer Johann Wilhelm von Archenholtz (1741–1812). The circumstances of the production are detailed in McClymonds, *Nicolò Jommelli*, 93–94. *Achille in Sciro* was composed hurriedly when Jommelli was desperately short of money and had difficulty meeting contractual obligations.

[39] *Magazin der Musik* 2 (1784): 51–52; text in Appendix 2 below. It has also been reported that performances were suspended because the Roman nobility objected to a popular uprising portrayed in the first act, though no documentation has been published to support this claim; see Della Porta, *Josef Mysliveček*, 25 and 33.

[40] Quoted in Bohadlo, 136. An announcement in the Roman newspaper *Diario ordinario* of 29 January 1780 (quoted in Mario Rinaldi, *Due secoli di musica al Teatro Argentina* [Florence: Olschki, 1978], 228–29), offers no information about the opera's reception, which is a bad sign: generally, if Italian newspapers had nothing good to say about an operatic production, nothing was said at all.

[41] "Luci belle se piangete" survives in twenty manuscript copies (see Catalog 2). As late as 1817 it was advertised for sale in Hofmeister's catalog of music in Germany; see [Carl Friedrich Whistling] and Friedrich Hofmeister, *Handbuch der musikalischen Litteratur* (Leipzig, 1817; reprint, New York: Garland, 1975).

Although there has been a widespread assumption in the existing literature about Mysliveček that the failure of *Armida* and *Medonte* essentially ended his operatic career, he was able to enjoy one one last success before his death with *Antigono*, performed in Rome at the Teatro Alibert (or Teatro delle Dame). Only a few stray vocal pieces from this opera are extant, but one of them, the rondò "Ho perduto il mio tesoro," became so popular that it eventually saw publication as far afield as Philadelphia.[42] Although the popes permitted operatic productions in Rome only during the carnival season for most of the eighteenth century, Pope Pius VI issued a decree in 1780 that allowed opera theaters to mount productions between spring and autumn.[43] The opportunity suddenly presented to Mysliveček compensated him for the failure of *Medonte.* The *Gazzetta universale* of Florence featured two notices about *Antigono*, the first an announcement on 1 April of its preparations (it went into production on 5 April),[44] the second, on 15 April, a report about its reception:[45]

> Rome, 8 April. On Wednesday evening the Teatro Alibert opened with great magnificence with a production of *Antigono* with all new music by Signor Giuseppe Misliwecek. This work was very favorably received, especially the overture, the rondò of Santorini,[46] an aria of Ansani,[47] and the scene of Berenice.[48] The ballets were produced by Signor Onorato Viganò, who saw fit to repeat one of those seen in the past carnival. Their highnesses the national nobility arranged for this spectacle a great concourse of persons of all classes. For this occasion Monsignor Spinelli, governor of Rome, had copious refreshments, sweets, etc. served . . .

By taking advantage of a musical environment conducive to the performance of sacred works, Mysliveček was able to revive his reputation as a composer of oratorios in Rome during the last year of his life, though not by composing new works. Rather, he arranged performances of his oratorios *Isacco* and *La passione* at the church of Santa Maria della Vallicella. Both oratorios continued to be performed frequently into the 1790s.[49]

---

[42] See Part 4.

[43] Maria Grazia Pastura, "Legislazione pontificia sui teatri e spettacoli a Roma," in Bianca Maria Antolini, et al., eds., *La musica a Roma attraverso le fonti d'archivio: Atti del Convegno internazionale Roma 4–7 giugno 1992* (Lucca: Libreria Musicale Italiana, 1994), 174. The pope's motivation is unknown. Eventually, the audience base could not be maintained when operas were performed the greater part of the year, and it became unprofitable to stage productions outside of carnival season. Pius VI responded in 1787, allowing one theater at a time to remain open between spring and autumn.

[44] Bohadlo, 137.

[45] Transcription in ibid., 138; text in Appendix 2 below.

[46] Undoubtedly "Ho perduto il mio tesoro" from act 2, sung by Pietro Benedetti in the role of Demetrio.

[47] This must be one of the arias "Tu m'involasti un regno" (act 1, sc. 8) or "Di che ricuso il trono" (act 3, sc. 1). Giovanni Ansani's other vocal piece in the title role, "Se mai senti, amato bene" (act 2, scene 9) has a rondò text, not an aria text. The music for none of these vocal pieces survives.

[48] Undoubtedly a reference to Berenice's scene in act 2, scene 11 (the finale), which features the aria "Non partir bell'idol mio," originally sung by Giuseppe Benigni. (In Rome, only male singers were allowed on stage at this time.) The music survives in the collection formerly housed in the Staatliche Hochschule für Musik in Munich; see Catalog 2 below.

[49] Joyce L. Johnson, *Roman Oratorio, 1770–1800: The Repertory at Santa Maria Vallicella* (Ann Arbor: UMI Research Press, 1987), 151–54. There were nine performances of *Isacco figura del redentore* and seven performances of *La passione* at Santa Maria Vallicella between 1779 and 1791; see Catalog 2 below. Both were performed in late November of 1780 within a few weeks of Mysliveček's death.

Tragically, the exposure Mysliveček received in Rome during the last few months of his life offered him little respite from poverty and illness. Although reports have circulated since the second half of the nineteenth century that he lived in luxury in a villa in the Piazza del Popolo in Rome during his final days,[50] in actuality, he subsisted in squalor in lodgings off the Strada del Corso. It is known that in the months before his death he was forced to take out eight loans from the Monte della Pietà Bank (which lent money to the poor without interest), the first on 12 April 1780 in the midst of the successful production of his opera *Antigono*.[51] There is reason to believe that he continued to write at least some music, for example the wind quintets dedicated to Prince Abbondio Rezzonico, a nephew of Pope Clement XIII, of which an autograph score survives (see fig. 5.1), but no new opportunities for dramatic productions presented themselves after the spring of 1780.

No inkling of Mysliveček's thoughts at the time of his death has been preserved, only the record of his burial in the church of San Lorenzo in Lucina in Rome on 4 February 1781.[52] There is no confirmation that Mysliveček died on the same day that he was buried, although 4 February 1781 has been accepted as the date of his death ever since his passing was first announced in the *Gazzetta universale* of Florence (notice transcribed below). Eleven days after his death, on 15 February 1781, an inventory of his possessions (fig. 5.2) was prepared by a notary at the request of Giuseppe Raimondi Monaldini, a representative of František Cardinal Hrzán, ambassador from the court of Vienna to the Holy See.[53] Mysliveček's belongings had been collected by the wife of the innkeeper who had been his landlord, and these were stored in a sealed trunk bearing the arms of Cardinal Hrzán, a fellow Bohemian. Hrzán was perhaps the last of the many powerful personages on whom Mysliveček had relied for assistance. The inventory specified some clothing, a steel sword with its sheath, the receipts for loans from the Monte della Pietà Bank, and a bundle of personal papers, including some unidentified music. Although he was nearly destitute, he had held on to possessions he would have needed most to make an appearance at a court or fashionable residence—for example, his sword, a coat with satin buttons, a pair of velvet breeches, and some silk shirts and stockings, all of which could have been pawned or sold. No furniture or musical instruments were found remaining to him.

Four days following, the son of a Roman jeweler presented a claim on Mysliveček's estate that is described in an addendum to the inventory of Mysliveček's possessions. It seems that Mysliveček had pawned a gold watch, which the jeweler's family was permitted to keep. This is the only extant

---

[50] Čeleda, 245; Shaginian, 311–13. The myth first appeared in František Ladislav Rieger, "Josef Mysliveček," *Dalibor* 3 (1860): 97–98, 105–06, 114, and it is mentioned in Josef Srb-Debrnov, *Dějiny hudby v Čechách a na Moravě* (The History of Music in Bohemia and Moravia) (Prague, 1891), 77. Although Mysliveček was impoverished at the time of his death, there is no basis for the claim in the *Grove Dictionary* (ed. 1954) that he died "naked in a shed."

[51] The source of this information is the inventory of Mysliveček's possessions prepared 15 February 1781 (see note 53). Receipts for eight loans, dated 12 April, 9 September, 30 September, and 29 November 1780 and 19 January, 20 January, 23 January, and 1 February 1781, amounting in total to 109 *scudi*, were found among his belongings. There is no record that any portion was paid back.

[52] An entry in the burial records of San Lorenzo in Lucina (Archivio del Vicariato) confirms the day of Mysliveček's burial. Transcription in Josef Srb-Debrnov, "Hudba v Čechách ve věku 17. A 18tém" (Music in Bohemia in the Seventeenth and Eighteenth Centuries), *Dalibor* 5 (1883): 421–23; Alois Hnilička, "Josef Mysliveček," 260–63, 279–81, 291–95; the chapter on Mysliveček in Hnilička, *Portréty starých českých mistrů hudebních*; and Čeleda, 248; facsimile in Bohadlo, 9. The entry (p. 277) reads: "Sig. D. Giuseppe Misliwecek, an. 65 da Praga, morì all'improviso, dimorante agli 8. Cantoni, e fu in questa chiesa sepolto" (Signor Josef Mysliveček, aged 65 years from Prague, died suddenly, a resident of the Otto Cantoni, and was buried in this church). Undoubtedly the indication "sacerdote" was actually intended to refer to Abbé Martin Absolon, another native of Prague whose name is found in the list of deceased immediately after Mysliveček. The age of sixty-five years probably refers to Absolon as well.

[53] Rome, Archivio Storico Capitolino, Archivio Urbano, Sezione 42, vol. 196, ff. 89–92.

Fɪɢ. 5.1 ***Mysliveček, Wind Quintet in D Major, movement 1, beginning. Autograph score (Rome, ca. 1780)***

Courtesy of the Bischöfliche Priesterseminar und Santini–Sammlung, Münster

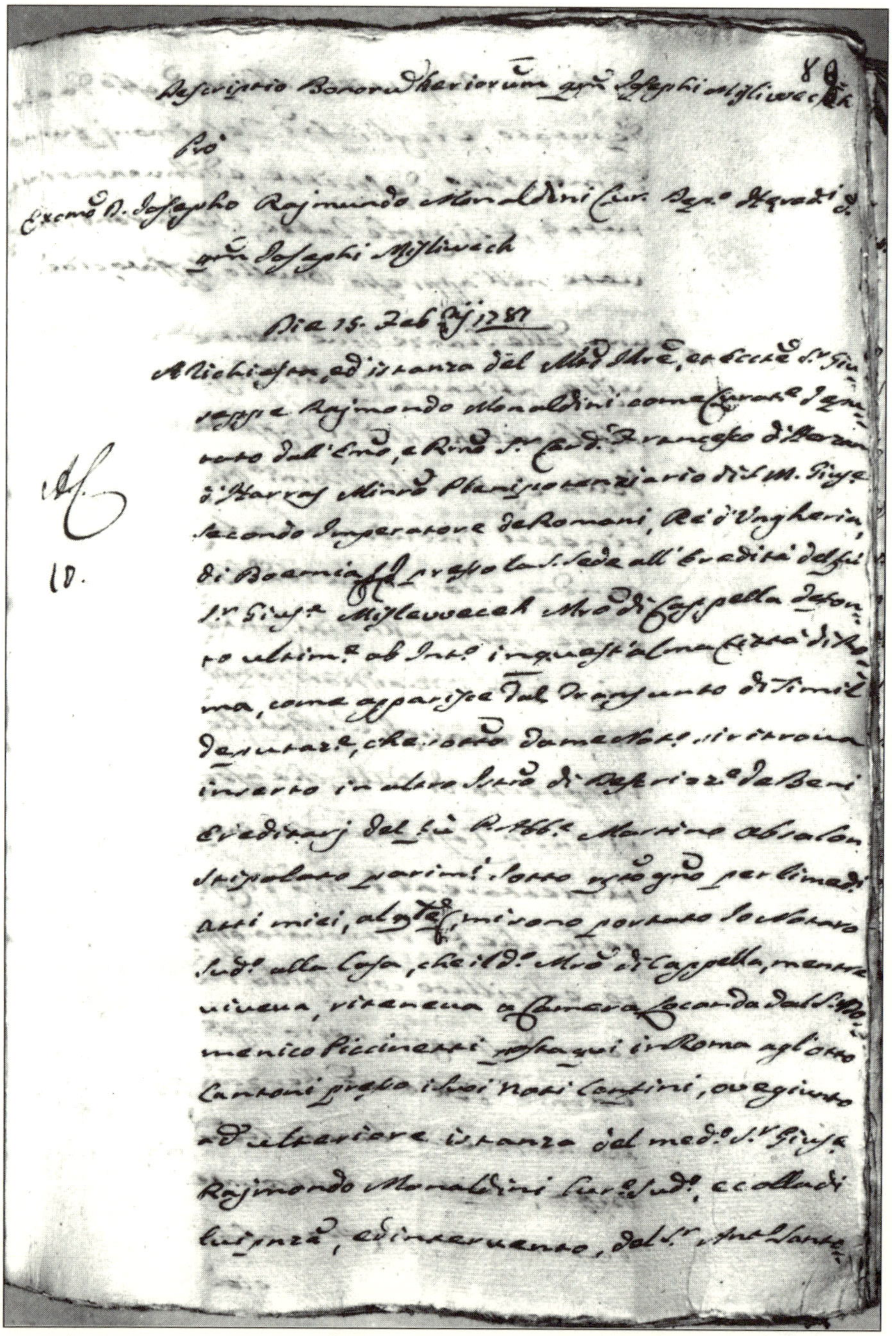

Fig. 5.2 ***Inventory of Mysliveček's possessions (Rome, 15 February 1781), first page***

Courtesy of the Archivio Storico Capitolino, Rome

record of what once could have amounted to a small fortune in baubles presented to Mysliveček by wealthy patrons appreciative of his musical talents and personal charm.[54] Whatever became of Mysliveček's other possessions is unknown; perhaps the trunk was sent back to Bohemia to Mysliveček's twin.

Mysliveček's death was reported mistakenly in northern Europe as early as 1773 in the German edition of Burney's travels through Germany and the Low Countries,[55] and some confusion about his death persisted long after the event actually occurred. He was listed as still living in Forkel's *Musikalischer Almanach* for the years 1783 and 1784, the correct date of his death not appearing until the 1789 issue.[56] Farther south, an accurate announcement appeared almost immediately. On 17 February 1781, a brief obituary appeared in the *Gazzetta universale* that provides information about the circumstances of Mysliveček's burial:[57]

> Rome, 10 February. After a long and painful illness, the famous *maestro di cappella* Signor Giuseppe Misliwecek, called il Boemo because of his birth in Prague, passed away last Sunday on the fourth of this month. This excellent professor had visited almost all of the courts of Europe, where his abilities received loud applause, and he won the friendship of the greatest music lovers. One of his students, an English gentleman, assumed the expenses of his funeral, which took place in the church of San Lorenzo in Lucina, where he was honorably buried.

It is gratifying to observe that Mysliveček was not completely without supporters at the time of his death. For many decades, the only clue to the identity of the "English gentleman" who paid Mysliveček's funeral expenses came from the Pelcl biography, which offered only the surname "Barry."[58] Twentieth-century scholars added the title "Sir" and the Christian name Edward to the family name.[59] It appears virtually certain that the mystery of the man's identity has now been resolved by Christian Moritz-Bauer, who found a record of one James Hugh Smith Barry (1746–1801), an English collector of art and antiquities in Italy during the 1770s and early 1780s.[60] He can be traced with certainty to Florence in 1775 and 1776, when Mysliveček was resident there, and also to Rome in 1780, at the time of Mysliveček's final illness and death. Consistent with the report of Mysliveček's death in the *Gazzetta universale*, this Barry, as son of the Honorable John Smith Barry of Belmont Hall, Cheshire, and Fota Island, Cork, was a "gentleman," not a "nobleman," as assumed

---

[54] Pelcl claimed there had once been many such gifts; see Appendix 1 below.

[55] See chapter 3, note 66 above.

[56] See Johann Nicolaus Forkel, *Musikalischer Almanach für Deutschland auf das Jahr 1783* (Hamburg, 1782; reprint, Hildesheim and New York: Georg Olms, 1974), 52–53; idem, *Musikalischer Almanach für Deutschland auf das Jahr 1784* (Hamburg, 1783; reprint, Hildesheim and New York: Georg Olms, 1974), 103; and idem, *Musikalischer Almanach für Deutschland auf das Jahr 1789* (Hamburg, 1788; reprint, Hildesheim and New York: Georg Olms, 1974), 104.

[57] Transcription in Bohadlo, 7; text in Appendix 2 below.

[58] Pelcl, 192; see Appendix 1 below.

[59] Barry was first referred to as a "Sir" in Prota-Giurleo, "L'Abate Galiani," 192; see Appendix 1 below. David DiChiera then supplied the Christian name Edward for his articles on Mysliveček in *MGG* (ed. 1961) and *New Grove* (ed. 1980). DiChiera has informed me that he has no recollection as to how the name Edward was arrived at.

[60] On Smith, see *A Dictionary of British and Irish Travellers in Italy*, comp. Ingamells, 56–57. Moritz-Bauer's findings have been incorporated into the biographical notice he prepared on Mysliveček for *MGG* (ed. 2004).

in many musicological sources.[61] There is no trace of a memorial in marble erected by Barry to Mysliveček in the church of San Lorenzo in Lucina, as Pelcl claimed,[62] but latter-day admirers did erect a commemorative marble plaque in the church sometime in the early 1990s.[63]

On 28 February 1781, the *Wiener-Zeitung* published a notice of Mysliveček's death, essentially a German translation of the obituary in the *Gazzetta universale*.[64] A few weeks later Wolfgang Mozart took up residence in Vienna (on 16 March 1781). He must have heard of Mysliveček's demise at some point, but no reaction is recorded. A response similar to that accorded the news of J. C. Bach's death the following year would have aided Mysliveček's posthumous reputation enormously,[65] but by the early 1780s could not have been reasonably expected in light of the betrayal of Mozart's trust at the time of Mysliveček's stay in Munich in 1777 and 1778.

Working as he did in a musical culture that depended on the constant production of new works to sustain the interest of music lovers, Mysliveček's death meant there would be little potential for the expansion of his reputation. There were some new productions of his oratorios and the "dramatic cantata" *Il Parnaso confuso* into the 1790s,[66] but there were no new productions of any of his operas, even though some of Mysliveček's arias did find their way into pastiches for a few years after his death. Publication of Mysliveček's instrumental music nearly ceased,[67] and only a few arias continued to be disseminated in published form. However a surprisingly large amount of Mysliveček's music was advertised for sale in the 1799 catalog of the Viennese publisher Johann Traeg.[68] The last of Mysliveček's music to be in circulation outside of ecclesiastical institutions in the Bohemian lands was advertised for sale in Hofmeister's catalog in 1817.[69]

---

[61] Barry's status as a "gentleman" would make him ineligible for the title "Sir," which can be held only by knights and hereditary baronets in the British nobility.

[62] Pelcl, 192; see Appendix 1 below.

[63] The plaque includes this inscription in Czech and Italian along with Mysliveček's dates of birth and death: "V této bazilice byl pohřben český skladatel Josef Mysliveček, řečený Il Boemo, přitel Mozartův"/"In questa basilica è stato sepolto il compositore ceco Giuseppe Misliwecek, detto Il Boemo, amico di Mozart" (In this basilica was buried the Czech composer Josef Mysliveček, called Il Boemo, a friend of Mozart). I am grateful to James Ackerman for providing me with a transcription.

[64] Czech translations in Hnilička, 280, and Čeleda, 248; text in Appendix 2 below. The *Wiener-Zeitung* provides the earliest identification of James Hugh Smith Barry as a "nobleman" (Edelmann), the designation adopted by Pelcl (see Appendix 1).

[65] When Wolfgang informed his father that J. C. Bach had died, he wrote, "What a loss to the musical world!" (letter from Vienna, 10 April 1782, in Anderson, 800).

[66] See Catalog 2 for a listing of all known eighteenth-century productions of Mysliveček's dramatic music.

[67] See Catalog 1 below.

[68] That catalog listed for sale a symphony in D major, six concertos for two clarinets, two horns, and bassoons with string accompaniment, six string quintets, twelve string quartets, three violin sonatas, and various vocal arias (see pp. 16, 53, 55, 65, 99, 213, and 303). The most likely candidate for the symphony would be the widely-disseminated overture to *Il gran Tamerlano* (1772), which matches the instrumentation specified (oboes, horns, and strings); it is extant in a manuscript in Vienna (see Catalog 1). The string quintets were probably the ones published ca. 1767 by Venier and Castaud as Op. 1, which were more widely circulated in the eighteenth century than the second set from the early 1770s. The twelve string quartets were probably his last two published sets (brought out by André in Offenbach in 1778 and Hummel in Berlin in 1781). The Traeg catalog is specific in indicating the three violin sonatas as works for violin plus bass, not accompanied sonatas with a written-out keyboard part. Five such sonatas survive, three in a single manuscript in Genoa (see Catalog 1). It will never be possible to determine which vocal pieces were available from Traeg, but it would be odd if "Luci belle, se piangete" were not one of them. See Weinmann, ed., *Johann Traeg: Die Musikalienverzeichnisse von 1799 und 1804*, vol. 1.

[69] This would include the scene and rondò "Luci belle, se piangete" from *Medonte*, two sets of string quartets, and a set of string trios (see Catalogs 1 and 2).

* * * *

After his death, the realm in which Josef Mysliveček's name was remembered best (as with so many defunct musicians) was that of music scholarship. František Pelcl's short biography appeared in 1782 and became the basis for dictionary entries on Mysliveček for over two hundred years. Mysliveček's eminence in the eighteenth century earned him a place in Gerber's monumental biographical dictionaries,[70] and he appeared in Dlabač's equivalent dictionary for Bohemia and Moravia as well.[71] The summaries of Mysliveček's life that are found in these works were based on Pelcl's biography and their appearance marked the effective end of attempts by lexicographers to examine primary source materials until the twentieth century.

Although Charles Burney had very little to do with Mysliveček during his lifetime, he recognized Mysliveček's talents in the fourth volume of his *General History of Music* (1789). After praising the accomplishments of Handel, Hasse, Graun, and Gluck as composers of Italian opera, Burney observed: "After these, the German composers whose works have been performed in Italy, and equally admired with those of the best masters of that country, may be enumerated John Christian Bach, Gasman, and Misliwecek."[72] In 1786, Carl Friedrich Cramer listed Mysliveček among the greatest composers of vocal music of his day.[73] A fuller summation of Mysliveček's achievements is found in a collection of music criticism by Christian Daniel Schubart published in 1806 as *Ideen zu einer Ästhetik der Tonkunst*, where in a special section devoted to biographical sketches of famous musicians (probably dating from ca. 1784), he offered his readers this notice:[74]

> Mysliveček, a Bohemian and very famous composer. He spent most of his time in Italy and wrote grand operas, which achieved great success in Florence, Turin, and Genoa. His vocal style is simple and penetrating, his arias and cavatinas are rich in original motives, his recitatives profound, and his choruses strong and uplifting. To a high degree, he understood the art of using accompanimental instruments in a way that did not hinder the vocal line. His chamber works also were sought after and performed as masterpieces in all European orchestras. This excellent artist died in Florence in 1722 at the age of thirty-eight years. Because he was productive, the world possesses a rich store of his masterworks.

The date of death supplied must have been a typographical error (probably meant to be 1782).

As with so many masters of "early music," the nineteenth-century musical world exhibited scant interest in Mysliveček. Nonetheless, his birthday, 9 March, was occasionally noted and matched to the issue date of certain nineteenth-century periodicals.[75] At least once, even the premiere of

---

[70] Gerber, *Historisch-Biographisches Lexikon der Tonkünstler*; and Gerber, *Neues Historisch-Biographisches Lexikon der Tonkünstler* (Leipzig, 1812–14; reprint, Graz: Akademische Druck- u. Verlagsanstalt, 1966).

[71] Dlabacž, *Allegemeines historisches Künstler-Lexikon*.

[72] Burney, *A General History of Music*, 4:583.

[73] *Magazin der Musik* 2 (1786):1081. The other composers cited were Anfossi, Salieri, Sacchini, Sarti, Ottani, Fischietti, Cimarosa, Traetta, Gazzaniga, Paisiello, Caruso, and de Majo.

[74] Christian Daniel Schubart, *Ideen zu einer Ästhetik der Tonkunst* (Vienna, 1806; reprint, Hildesheim: Georg Olms, 1969), 229; text in Appendix 2 below.

[75] *Der Österreichische Zuschauer* 30 (1838): 300; *Allgemeine Wiener Musik-Zeitung* 2 (1842): 124; and *Bohemia* 31, no. 69 (1858): 509.

one of his operas was commemorated this way (*Ezio* of 1775), an extraordinary occurrence, given that its music was never heard.[76] From the time of the publication of Gerber's biographical dictionary in the early 1790s, Mysliveček has always held a place in the principal biographical dictionaries on music. In the nineteenth century, he was also accorded entries in general biographical dictionaries,[77] including a substantial notice in Wurzbach's dictionary of notable citizens of the Habsburg lands.[78]

In the nineteenth century, misinformation about Mysliveček began to accrue in reference works produced outside the Bohemian lands. The worst offender was Fétis, who introduced many dubious details,[79] including reports that Mysliveček was employed as a church musician in Prague; that his first set of symphonies was composed in 1760; that he was called to Parma in 1764; that he was in a state of profound misery when he met Mozart in 1770; that the Englishman Barry subsidized him for years; that he composed an *Erifile* for Munich in 1773; and that *Erifile* failed because he was inspired only under Italian skies. The most serious unsubstantiated claims introduced in the Mysliveček literature in the twentieth century followed the publication of the *Grove Dictionary* in 1954. In particular, claims that Mysliveček had love affairs with the singers Lucrezia Aguiari and Caterina Gabrielli began to be repeated widely without skepticism. In fact, there is no record of the names of any persons with whom Mysliveček may have been romantically involved. As regards his failure to marry, Mysliveček's need for freedom seems to have extended into his personal life as well.

Certain Czech music scholars began to seek out the documentary record of Mysliveček's life in the late nineteenth and early twentieth centuries.[80] Josef Srb-Debrnov and an architect friend in Rome tried to locate the marble monument supposedly erected in Mysliveček's honor by the Englishman Barry; no monument was found, but the record of Mysliveček's death in San Lorenzo in Lucina emerged.[81] It was about this time also that Mysliveček started to become known as "Il divino Boemo" as a result of the title of the romanetto by the Czech author Jakub Arbes published in 1884.[82] No reference work claimed this as Mysliveček's nickname, however, until the publication of the fifth edition of the *Grove Dictionary* in 1954. *The New Grove Dictionary* of 1980 added the further embellishment that it was specifically Neapolitans who began to call him "Il divino Boemo." Other fictionalized treatments of Mysliveček's life followed the Arbes story, including an opera by Stanislav Suda, *Il divino Boemo*, which was first performed in Plzeň in 1927.[83]

---

[76] *Neue Wiener Musik-Zeitung* 6 (1857): 134 (issue of 13 August 1857).

[77] See, for example, *Oesterreichische National-Encyklopädie*, 3 (Vienna, 1835), 690–91; *Allgemeine Deutsche Biographie*, 22 (Munich, 1885; reprint, Berlin: Duncker & Humblot, 1970), 11–12; and *Nouvelle biographie générale*, 37 (Paris, 1866), col. 97. For the Czech lands, there were also entries in *Riegerův Slovník naučný* and *Ottův Slovník naučný*.

[78] Wurzbach, *Biographisches Lexikon*, 18 (1868): 362–65.

[79] Fétis, *Biographie universelle*, 2nd ed., 6:271–72.

[80] The most prominent publications would be Srb-Debrnov, "Hudba v Čechách"; Kateřina Emingerová, "Český skladatel - příznivec Mozartův" (A Czech Composer - Well-Wisher of Mozart), *Zvon* 8 (1908): 598–99; Hnilička, "Josef Mysliveček" and the chapter on Mysliveček in Hnilička, *Portréty starých českých mistrů hudebních*; Viktor Joss, "Mysliweczek," *Der Auftakt* 7 (1927): 94–95; Kateřina Emingerová, "Klavírní skladby Jos. Myslivečka" (The Keyboard Compositions of Josef Mysliveček), *Česká hudba* 24 (1930-31): 102–04; Jaroslav Čeleda, "Il Boemo divino Venatorini" and "Houslové skladby Josefa Myslivečka" (The Violin Compositions of Josef Mysliveček), *Česká hudba* 36 (1932-33): 238–40.

[81] Srb-Debrnov, "Hudba v Čechách," 422.

[82] See the Introduction, note 2.

[83] The most complete listing of fictionalized treatments of Mysliveček's life is found in Rudolf Pečman, *Josef Mysliveček und sein Opernepilog* (Brno: Universita J. E. Purkyně, 1970), 188. Among the works included are plays, novels, and stories, both in German and in Czech.

The Czech efforts to create interest in Mysliveček's music yielded some successes before World War II. A few Mozart scholars produced studies of him,[84] and the first pieces of his music to be printed since the late eighteenth century were published.[85] Performances of Mysliveček's operas started up again in the 1930s, undoubtedly inspired by the example of German revivals of operas by Handel and other pre-Romantic composers. In 1931, *Motezuma* was given in Prague, followed in 1937 by the Naples *Ezio* of 1775 to celebrate the bicentennial of the composer's birth.[86] In 1961, a burst of revivals facilitated by the state-subsidized musical culture of socialist-era Czechoslovakia was signaled by a performance of *Medonte* in Opava, a production made possible by Marietta Shaginian's donation of a copy of a score of the opera preserved in St. Petersburg. In 1967, a musicological conference was organized in Brno around a performance of *Il gran Tamerlano*, and concert performances of *Ipermestra*, the second *Demofoonte*, and the oratorio *Tobia* were produced there in 1970–72. *Il gran Tamerlano* was later produced in Prague in 1977 and in Reggio Emilia in 1979, the second of these performances providing another occasion for a musicological conference. Scattered productions of operas and oratorios in several parts of Europe have continued since then, among them a number of performances of the oratorio *Isacco figura del redentore*, the most recent in Paris in 2003. The oratorio *La passione* was performed for the first time since the eighteenth century in Cologne in 2004, then in Caen in 2007. Operatic revivals have included a production of *Romolo ed Ersilia* in Turin in 1996 and *Antigona* at Schloss Rheinsberg and Prague in 2006.

The Supraphon release of *Isacco figura del redentore* as *Abramo ed Isacco* in the early 1970s led to the recording of many more Mysliveček works, and publication of Mysliveček's music has continued steadily since a large body of works were prepared for publication by Emil Hradecký in the mid-1950s.[87] Incredible as it may seem, the 1990s actually saw the emergence of a Mysliveček imitator as a composer.[88]

In spite of all of the publication and recording activity during the last several decades, Mysliveček's music remains more or less unknown to western musicologists for reasons explained in the introduction to this work. As difficult as it has been to establish accurate information concerning his biography, detailed discussion of his musical style is even harder to come by. The remainder of this volume will address the latter deficiency by presenting an appraisal of Myslivecek's output of music compositions and a special consideration of his musical relationship to Wolfgang Amadeus Mozart.

---

[84] See especially Marc Pincherle, "Un oublié: Il divino Boemo," in *Feuillets d'histoire de violon* (Paris: Leguoix, 1927), 103–09; Georges de Saint-Foix, "Un ami de Mozart: Joseph Mysliweczek," *Revue musicale* 9 (March 1928): 124–28; Saint-Foix, "Mozart, d'après Mysliweczek," *Musique* 2 (1929): 840–43; Paul Nettl, "Mozart und Mysliveček," *Prager Rundschau* 7 (1937): 114–24; and Nettl, *Mozart in Böhmen* (Prague: Karlin, Neumann, 1938), which includes a chapter entitled "Mozart und Myslivetschek."

[85] Hugo Riemann edited a Mysliveček Trio in B-flat (Breitkopf & Härtel, 1904) and a set of *duetti notturni* were published ca. 1901; see Catalogs 1 and 2.

[86] A survey of productions of dramatic works by Mysliveček up to 1980 is in Pečman, 246–47.

[87] See Catalog 1.

[88] The composer Kevin Franz Josef Harris considers his *Concert Aria*, op. 31, an imitation of the style of Mysliveček's *Bellerofonte*.

Part 2

THE MUSIC OF JOSEF MYSLIVEČEK

6

"AN EXTRAORDINARY STYLE OF EXPRESSION"

František Martin Pelcl used the phrase "an extraordinary style of expression" to evoke the excellence of Josef Mysliveček's musical works,[1] a pleasing judgment that slightly overstates the composer's talent: using the strictest standards of comparison, it is clear that the quality of his writing falls below the level of the mature Haydn and Mozart. Imaginative as he was, Mysliveček did not create compositions that have become concert favorites or standard repertory items up to the present day. In his best work he produced very fine music, though not of the utmost inspiration. The composer most similar to him in terms of ability and outlook was Johann Christian Bach, his near-exact contemporary. Like Mysliveček, J. C. Bach was a master of Italian *opera seria* and Italianate instrumental styles, but avoided comic opera entirely. Among Mysliveček's rivals in the opera theaters of Italy, Mysliveček's music is perhaps closest in style to that of Antonio Sacchini, a composer who was able to match the melodic and textural richness of Mysliveček's dramatic writing.

Considered as a representative of Czech musical culture of the eighteenth century, Mysliveček's place is unquestionably distinguished, even taking into account the difficulty in categorizing musicians born in the kingdom of Bohemia properly as "Czech" (with its connotation of Slavic ethnic heritage) or simply "Bohemian" (a designation that can include persons of German, Jewish, or mixed ethnic heritage). Since Mysliveček was a descendant of Christian Slavs whose native language was Czech, his status as a "Czech composer" cannot be disputed. As such, the case can be made that he was the most gifted "Czech" composer of the eighteenth century. One might consider Jan Dismas Zelenka a talent of similar brilliance in the first half of the eighteenth century, but Mysliveček's versatility could not be matched either by Zelenka or by any of the leading Czechs or Bohemians active in the second half of the eighteenth century, among them František Benda, Jiří Benda, Johann Stamitz, František Xaver Richter, Josef Antonín Štěpán/Steffan, František Xaver Dušek, Florian Gassmann, František Xaver Brixi, Jan Křtitel Vaňhal, Václav Pichl, František Antonín Rössler/Rossetti, Leopold Koželuh, Pavel Vranický, Antonín Vranický, and Jan Ladislav Dusík. Some of these individuals, Pavel Vranický in particular, were capable of equaling or exceeding the quality of Mysliveček's music in individual works, but none was able to demonstrate a similar level of mastery in such a large number of musical genres.

A comparison with Gluck invites special discussion, since his ethnicity has been the subject of some confusion. Gluck is best described as a Czech and not a German or Bohemian of German ancestry, as many scholars believed in the twentieth century. The research of Daniel Heartz has

[1] Pelcl, 191; transcription and translation in Appendix 1.

revived long-forgotten and highly convincing evidence that Gluck's true native language was Czech and that he was actually descended from Czechs, not Germans.[2] The standardized modern spelling of his surname relates properly to the Czech "kluk" ("boy"), rather than to the German "Glück" ("luck" or "fortune").[3] Gluck was born in what is now German territory because of his father's movements in the service of the Lobkovic family, who owned land in Bavaria, but he returned to Bohemian soil as a child and acquired his education among Czech people. The early nineteenth-century lexicographer Jan Bohumír Dlabač did not hesitate to embraced Gluck as a fellow countryman, nor did Mozart's first biographer, the Praguer František Xaver Němeček.[4] Nonetheless, the efforts of German musicologists to portray Gluck as a German have been so successful that even many latter-day Czechs music scholars have considered him to be non-Czech. He was excluded from the biographical entries in the *Československý hudební slovník* in the 1960s, and more recently, his Czech identity has been denied by at least one scholar called upon to evaluate the question.[5] Like Mysliveček, Gluck was able to achieve remarkable success outside his native land through the composition of operas. He exceeded Mysliveček by far in the degree to which he was able to attract attention from music critics, glean honors from European rulers, and leave an imprint on the history of opera. Still, his abilities as a composer of instrumental music were severely limited. Mysliveček, with a much more varied and interesting output of musical works, was clearly a better-rounded composer.

No matter who is most deserving of the appellation "greatest Czech composer of the eighteenth century," it is a distinction that does not have quite the same meaning as it would for a composer of the nineteenth or twentieth centuries. For an eighteenth-century composer, the phrase is tied only to territorial origins, not to a strongly-felt national musical identity. Music critics in the eighteenth century did not recognize a Czech or Bohemian heritage of art music any more than geographers recognized a Czech homeland. Observers such as Charles Burney took care to describe the unique character of musical culture in the Bohemian lands and its unusual production of talented musicians, but nobody felt it necessary to describe a Czech style of composition in the way that Germany, France, and Italy were each acknowledged to have many talented musicians as well as distinguished traditions of composition. If anything, Czech (or "Bohemian") musicians were considered to be a special category of German musicians. It is true that certain musical styles and genres were cultivated in different ways than in the rest of Europe, but Bohemians for the most part adopted the prevailing styles of their day and cultivated genres that had originated elsewhere in Europe.[6] No composers who remained in the Bohemian lands contributed any important stylistic trends that were widely imitated outside their homeland.

The weakness of art music traditions originating in the Bohemian lands is important to remember in evaluating Mysliveček's orientation as a composer. For a musician, the whole point of leaving one's homeland was to gain employment and recognition in foreign centers. Mysliveček was a

---

[2] See Daniel Heartz, "Coming of Age in Bohemia: The Musical Apprenticeships of Benda and Gluck," *Journal of Musicology* 6 (1988): 510–26.

[3] In an appraisal of Gluck's opera *Orfeo* prepared for the management of the Teatro San Carlo in Naples in 1774, Mysliveček himself spelled the name "Kluck," following Czech usage (see Appendix 2).

[4] See *W. A. Mozart's Leben nach Originalquellen beschrieben von Franz Niemetschek*, ed. Ernst Rychnovsky (Prague: Taussig, 1905), 22. Němeček's biography of Mozart was originally published in 1798.

[5] See Jiří Vysloužil, "Das Musikland Böhmen im Zeitalter der Klassik," in *Untersuchungen zu Musikbeziehungen zwischen Mannheim, Böhmen und Mähren im spaten 18. und fruhen 19. Jahrhundert*, ed. Christine Heyter-Rauland and Christoph-Hellmut Mahling (Mainz: Schott, 1993), 13–14.

[6] For a Czech perspective on this question, see also ibid., 14–15.

"careerist"; the road to fame he sought involved assimilating the musical language of the regions in which he worked, just as Zelenka, the Bendas, Gluck, and others had done before him. This should be kept in mind in the face of a tendency of some Czech style critics to claim Czech folk music as a stylistic resource in Mysliveček's music. For many, this has been more or less an article of faith, and it has led to some unfortunate results in practice.[7] Almost any passage in Mysliveček's music that is rhythmically lively and simple in texture has the potential to be labeled folk-like, but a question that needs to be addressed by advocates of this view is what possible incentive Mysliveček could have felt to invoke such a gesture. For eighteenth-century audiences in Italy, the folk idioms of a distant people would hardly have had the quaint, charming, or delightfully exotic qualities that would have made them attractive under the right circumstances to nineteenth- or twentieth-century audiences. Rather, the folk elements would more likely have sounded crude, vulgar, or strange. It is conceivable that Mysliveček at times could not keep out some stylistic influences from the ethnic heritage of his native land, even after many years' absence, but the notion that he consistently introduced ethnic gestures into his compositions is best relegated to the realm of wishful thinking. Mysliveček composed in an internationalist classic style that offered few means to identify the nationality of a composer from the sound of the music. The genre on which he pinned his greatest hopes and concentrated his greatest energies—Italian *opera seria*—was the least susceptible of all to influence from the less-elevated musical traditions of the day. The point to be made is not that the use of Czech national music as a stylistic resource in Mysliveček's music is unimaginable, only that it was never an important part of his musical language.

Although Mysliveček's career was rather short (less than twenty years), his music makes for interesting study not only for its intrinsic merit, but also for its appearance at a critical juncture in the history of music, namely, at the outset of what is now recognized as a "high classic" style around the year 1770. Along with the music of better-known composers such as Haydn, Boccherini, and J. C. Bach, Mysliveček's music underwent a marked increase in quality and sophistication as European art music emerged from the aesthetic limitations of early classicism. A sense of increased maturity and assurance is quite palpable generally in compositions created after about 1770, and it extends even to such details as the greater care taken to indicate dynamic and articulation markings in musical scores. Mysliveček was a master of the new textural subtleties, melodic types, and expressive capabilities that were ushered in at this time. The results in his works are comparable or superior in quality to any music composed by J. C. Bach or Boccherini, but in comparison to the mature works of Haydn and Mozart, Mysliveček's writing usually does suffer for its short-windedness, limited developmental range, and less distinctive melodic materials.

Perhaps the most important consideration that helps one to understand the nature of Mysliveček's compositional output is his association with an Italian version of musical classicism that has not yet received full recognition. Attention has frequently been accorded the leading Italian composers active during the earliest phases of classicism in the 1730s and 1740s, but studies devoted to the later phases of the 1750s and 1760s tend to concentrate on German composers. Italian musical culture had scarcely lost its prestige in these later decades, however, either in vocal or

---

[7] A particularly questionable assertion is found in Pečman, 235, in which the opening of the overture to the opera *Medonte* is claimed to have a folk-like flavor. Indeed the whole opera is claimed to incorporate folk elements, which Pečman even surmised might have led to its failure. In face, the opening of the overture to *Medonte* is based on a "hammer-stroke" motive that was a stock figure used to open concertos and symphonies at least since the early eighteenth century.

instrumental music, and just a few examples are needed here to emphasize the relative strength of Italian musical traditions in comparison to German ones. Italian symphonies and keyboard sonatas, for example, were published and copied down in northern Europe throughout the middle years of the eighteenth century, whereas it is inconceivable that sets of German keyboard sonatas would have been published in Italy in the same era: Italians were essentially indifferent to German instrumental music until the late eighteenth century. Even more revealing is the popularity of Italian opera in the German lands. In Italy of the late eighteenth century, a production of an opera composed by a German and sung in German would have been impossible to imagine, yet in many German centers, the opposite anomaly (the production of operas by Italian composers sung in Italian) was normal.

Patterns of musical emigration also have much to say about the relative prestige of Italian and German musical traditions. Northerners such as J. C. Bach, Gluck, and Mysliveček immigrated to Italy as mere students eager to master Italianate modes of musical expression, whereas composers such as Jommelli, Piccinni, Paisiello, Cimarosa, and Galuppi were offered lucrative professional opportunities in northern Europe because various patrons there wanted to advertise their appreciation of Italian music. In the 1760s, Italy was a net exporter of musical style and Germany was a net importer; that is the basic distinction that sums up the relative strength of the two countries' musical institutions in the period when Mysliveček emerged as a notable composer. It is no wonder that Mysliveček, who had the freedom and resources to study music wherever he wished in Europe, instinctively chose Italian training as the most desirable.

Italian traditions do provide some interesting contrast to German ones in these years, in general exhibiting traits that belie Charles Rosen's puzzling characterization of early classic style as "mannerist," in writing about the music of C. P. E. Bach and Haydn between about 1755 and 1775.[8] Though hesitant to use "so abused" a word, Rosen sees "mannerism" as the best characterization of an approach to composition in this period that was "highly individualistic" in the absence of an "integrated" style of expression. Careful consideration of the circumstances under which C. P. E. Bach and Haydn worked, however, would suggest that the eccentricities to be observed in their music in the 1760s and 1770s might not be simply another manifestation of a broadly practiced "mannerism." Both were employed in isolated and peripheral musical centers (Berlin, Hamburg, Eszterháza), environments that seem to have led their creative energies into rather unique and extraordinary directions. C. P. E. Bach's music, in particular, was not germane in shaping the course of the principal stylistic developments of his day. Nothing else could be expected of a composer who did not leave Germany, composed no operas, and wrote only a minimal number of symphonies. C. P. E. Bach was revered among keyboard players in Germany for his position as a composer of keyboard sonatas, but the fact is that keyboard music did not count for very much.[9] Success with the sophisticated, public-oriented musical genres, especially symphony and *opera seria*, was what gained attention from the European musical world. Many writers of the last hundred years would have been wise to take note of Carl Friedrich Abel's observations in this regard.[10] Musical style was

---

[8] See *The Classical Style: Mozart, Haydn, and Beethoven*, rev. ed. (New York: W. W. Norton, 1997; original ed., 1971), 47–48.

[9] Johann Adolf Scheibe (*Critischer musicus*, 1740), remarked that sonatas were of much less consequence than symphonies, concertos, and overtures, and Johann Wilhelm Hässler, in his autobiography (1786), that "mere keyboard sonatas I shall not be writing so much any more, since I am urged on all sides to [compose] more important works"; quoted in William S. Newman, *The Sonata in the Classic Era*, 3rd ed. (New York: W. W. Norton, 1983), 37.

[10] Carl Friedrich Abel observed that "If Sebastian Bach and his admirable son Emanuel, instead of being music directors in commercial cities, had been fortunately employed to compose for the stage and public of great capitals, such as Naples, Paris, or London, and

actually about as "integrated" during the early classic period as at any time in the history of music, to the point where it is difficult, if not impossible, to single out composers who were individually responsible for shaping the principal trends. There was a tendency among composers to adopt similar techniques more or less simultaneously, almost as if there were "something in the air" that compelled them.

Although classicism in music was more internationalist in orientation than baroque music had been, national stylistic identities did endure to some extent. In comparison to German music of the 1760s and 1770s, Italian music was gracious, melodious, and diatonic, still evocative of a "natural" homophonic style based on vocal idioms that had arisen in the 1730s in reaction to the "artifice" of the baroque. In Italy there was no radical experimentation among the leading masters of vocal or instrumental music and no period in the late eighteenth century when minor-key works were in vogue, as they were in Germany at times during the 1760s and 1770s. Among all of Mysliveček's instrumental compositions, only five works employ a minor mode for the principal key. As an exponent of Italian musical traditions somewhat enriched by northern harmonic and textural traits, Mysliveček exhibited a near comprehensive mastery of the leading classic genres. The only glaring omission was his total lack of interest in comic opera. It could be said that the time his Italian rivals in the theater spent writing comic operas, Mysliveček spent writing instrumental music. Italians who specialized in instrumental music generally were not (or did not aspire to be) successful as composers of vocal music. Many, such as Giovanni Battista Sammartini, Giuseppe Tartini, Giovanni Benedetto Platti, and Giovanni Marco Rutini, cultivated vocal music little, if at all, and those who made their names principally from opera but also wrote instrumental music, such as Baldassare Galuppi, generally produced only inferior instrumental works. In the 1760s and 1770s, Mysliveček stood out among them, demonstrating an ability to compose some of the best *opere serie* of his day as well as some of the best symphonies, concertos, and chamber music.

* * * *

It is only to be expected that distinctive traits of rhythm, texture, and phrasing permeate Mysliveček's works in many genres. All of the stylistic procedures he favored are found commonly among the leading composers of the 1760s and 1770s, but Mysliveček cultivated certain of these procedures to a degree not seen in the work of most of his contemporaries. One of the musical elements that Mysliveček liked to manipulate most was syncopation, both in melody and accompaniment; there is hardly a composition by him that does not indulge his love of it in one way or another. A hallmark of the rhythmic profile of his melodic phrases is a syncopated pattern that rose to prominence in the early classic period (its basic form: ex. 6.1). Such patterns could be embellished by dividing the note values into halves or quarters (ex. 6.2) and interrupting the flow of the phrases with rests (ex. 6.3). When used with an anacrusis (or "pick-up"), the patterns are suited to the natural rhythms and cadences of Italian declamation;[11] without a pick-up, they are compatible with the natural

---

for performers of the first class . . . they would have extended their fame, and been indisputably the greatest musicians of the eighteenth century"; quoted in Hans T. David and Arthur Mendel, eds., *The Bach Reader* (New York: W. W. Norton, 1966), 262.

[11] Further discussion of the character of these rhythmic patterns is in Daniel E. Freeman, "The Earliest Italian Keyboard Concertos," *Journal of Musicology* 4 (1985–86): 139–41.

EXAMPLE 6.1. A basic syncopated rhythmic pattern found frequently in the music of Josef Mysliveček.

EXAMPLE 6.2. Mysliveček, Trio for Flute, Violin, and Bass in G Major (Flute Trio 2), first movement, meas. 1–4.

EXAMPLE 6.3. Mysliveček, Symphony in A Major (Symphony 27), second movement, meas. 1–8 (horns, oboes tacent).

cadences of Czech speech, which features short, sharp accents on the first syllable of most words.[12] The term "Lombardian rhythm" is often used to designate the latter type of syncopoation. A favorite variant, often seen in symphonic style and overture style, features two thirty-second notes followed by a dotted eighth note (ex. 6.4).[13] Mysliveček's penchant for such rhythms may have been inspired by an instinctive affinity for his native language, but their prevalence in Italian music of the early classic period makes it difficult to assert that this connection was a motivating factor. As an indication of how closely such rhythmic patterns were identified with Italian style, it is instructive to note that J. C. Bach used them frequently when he worked in Italy, but largely discarded them once he moved to England. The music of the Bohemian composer Antonín Kammel, who studied in Italy, contains many of the same syncopated rhythmic patterns so beloved by Mysliveček, whereas they are not nearly so prominent in the music of Vaňhal, Gassmann, or Dušek. Mysliveček used endless variations of simple syncopated patterns as the basis of the rhythms for his melodies.

Mysliveček's accompanimental patterns exhibit a great deal of experimentation with syncopation as well. In particular, his symphonies and operatic arias often feature passages with a driving

Example 6.4. Mysliveček, Overture to *Motezuma* (Overture 11), first movement, meas. 1–9 (horns, oboes omitted).

---

[12] On the use of Czech speech patterns in music and the musical character of Czech folk music, see Karl Michael Komma, *Das böhmische Musikantentum* (Kassel: Johann Philipp Hinnenthal-Verlag, 1960).

[13] The same rhythmic figure is prominent in the overture to Antonio Sacchini's overture *San Filipo* (1765), included in *The Symphony, 1720–1840*, ed. Barry S. Brook (New York and London: Garland, 1985), series A (Italy), 3:103–16.

syncopated drone in one of the middle or upper voices (ex. 6.5). He also introduced "interlocking" accompaniments that combine downbeats in the bass and offbeats in the middle or upper voices (ex. 6.6 is a conventional use; ex. 6.7 is a more imaginative treatment), configurations that go to the heart of the new textural sophistication cultivated in the late 1760s and early 1770s.[14]

Composers of the earlier periods of classic style, as part of their quest for simplicity and "naturalness," tended to employ rather spare textures that were "treble dominated." Most of the rhythmic interest centered on the top voice, which was frequently enlivened with generous sprinklings of grace notes and alternations between duplets and triplets. The lower voices tended to be neutralized, often moving in near-endless streams of eight notes (or equivalent note values, depending on the meter and tempo), an accompanimental style often referred to as "drum bass." In the four-part writing of symphonies and string quartets and the string accompaniments in concertos and arias, the textures were frequently simplified by doubling the first and second violins or doubling the viola and bass part at the unison or octave. Often, too, the first and second violins could move in simple parallel thirds and sixths. The result was textures in two or three parts even when a four-part string ensemble was present. A basic two-part texture is typical of Haydn's early symphonies, for example.

EXAMPLE 6.5. Mysliveček, Symphony in F Major, op. 1, no. 4 (Symphony 5), third movement, meas. 1–13 (horns, oboes omitted). Edited from Ms. V B 56 of the České Muzeum Hudby with permission.

[14] For more on this subject, though no discussion of Mysliveček, see Eric Weimer, *Opera Seria and the Evolution of Classical Style, 1755–1772* (Ann Arbor: UMI Research Press, 1984).

Example 6.6. Mysliveček, Aria "Se cerca, se dice" from *L'olimpiade*, meas. 1–6 (horns, oboes tacent).

Example 6.7. Mysliveček, Aria "Splende così talora" from *Il Bellerofonte*, meas. 125–43 (horns, oboes tacent 125–41, omitted 142–43).

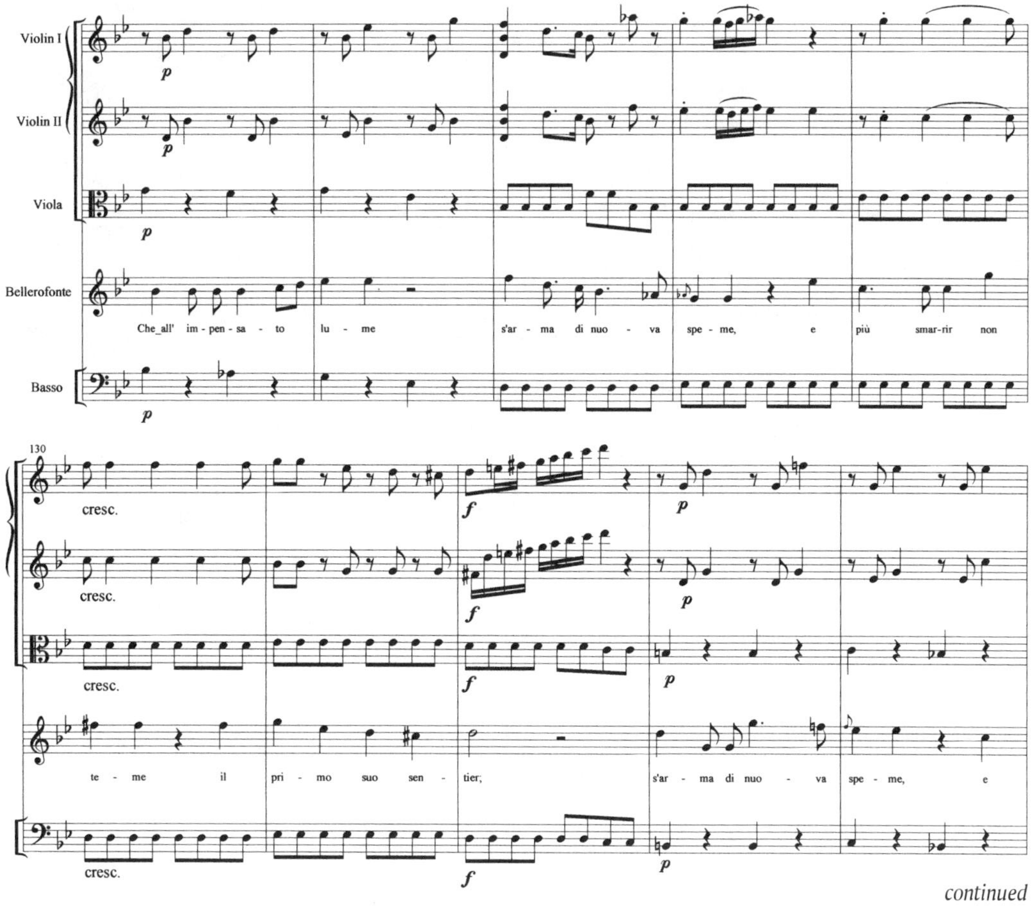

Violin I
Violin II
Viola
Bellerofonte
Basso
p
Che_all' im - pen - sa - to lu - me s'ar - ma di nuo - va spe - me, e più smar-rir non

130
cresc.
f
p
te - me il pri - mo suo sen - tier; s'ar - ma di nuo - va spe - me, e

continued

Example 6.7—*continued*

By the late 1760s, more sophisticated textural procedures were cultivated alongside the older ones, especially "layered" textures of at least two distinct rhythmic patterns in the accompaniment. The middle voices frequently contained the greatest rhythmic animation (ex. 6.8, a typical configuration by Mysliveček). Layered textures are often found in their most sustained form in slow movements; in fast movements the patterns tend to shift quickly.

Streams of eighth notes in the bass ("drum bass") may be described as an old-fashioned accompanimental technique in the 1770s, but Mysliveček never tired of them completely. He also had a fondness for a kind of accompaniment that will be referred to here as the "pumping bass," a figure built around a stationary bass note (ex. 6.9). Mysliveček used these patterns to help drive the musical momentum in his compositions forward, the "pumping bass" especially for sections requiring an extra measure of excitement or emotional intensity.

The greatest interest of Mysliveček's textural treatment lies in the way that the patterns were continually in flux, the most interesting ends achieved when the textural shifts do not coincide with the phrasing of the main melodic line. Mysliveček's constant transformation of textural configurations was allied to his ability to present a seemingly inexhaustible array of melodic ideas that

EXAMPLE 6.8. Mysliveček, String Quartet/Symphony in E-flat Major (String Quartet 9/Symphony 32), second movement, meas. 1–6. Edited from Ms. V B 72 of the České Muzeum Hudby with permission.

EXAMPLE 6.9. Mysliveček, Rondò "Luci belle, se piangete" from *Medonte*, after an arrangement for voice and piano published in the *Musikaliskt tidsfördrif*, Stockholm, 1794, meas. 97–106.

complement the ever-changing arrangements of voices. In the 1760s and 1770s, these shifts in texture and melodic style could be very fast-paced. By the 1780s, composers had learned to lay out their compositions on broader lines.

Another kind of subtlety that can be found in Mysliveček's music is related to a phenomenon referred to by Charles Rosen as "classical counterpoint," a concept of dubious validity that has gained limited currency nonetheless.[15] In the simpler style of the early classic period, there was never much doubt within a phrase about which voice carried the melody and which voices were

[15] See Rosen, *The Classical Style*, 45–94; Weimer, *Opera Seria*, 116–17.

accompanimental, but in the years around 1770, more flexible approaches to the idea of accompanimental and melodic function came to prominence. A single melodic phrase might begin in one voice and finish in another; just what the melody consists of might not be clear; several voices may participate in the presentation. In example 6.10, what voice is it that carries the melody? Surely it is a composite distributed over the violin parts.

EXAMPLE 6.10. Mysliveček, Symphony in F Major, op. 1, no. 4 (Symphony 5), second movement, meas. 1–10 (horns, oboes tacent). Edited from Ms. V B 56 of the České Muzeum Hudby with permission.

In example 6.11, a portion of the opening ritornello of an aria from the opera *Bellerofonte* of 1767, it is possible to see the clever manner in which melody lines could be handed off from one voice to another. At the start of measure 14 the obbligato horn part supplies harmonic support, but at measure 20 the harmonic tone is transformed into a melodic tone and, by the time the phrase finishes at measure 24, the phrase has taken on a completely new character. For a few measures after that, the horn is the principal melody instrument, but before the second phrase finishes in measure 34, the horn disappears without completing a phrase in its own part. The violins acquire a melodic function again in measure 26 in dialogue with the horn, then take over the melody completely in measure 29. The confusion about which instruments carry the melodic line (and at what point) makes this passage so interesting. The symmetry of the design is also noteworthy: the violins start out as the melodic instruments, then yield to the horn, and in the second phrase the horn is preeminent at first but cedes its melodic function back to the violins in stages. During the course of twenty-one measures and two phrases, there are no less than six textural configurations among the instruments, including unisons.

It is this type of sophistication in manipulating melody, texture, and phrasing that helps define the transition from an "early classic" style to a "high classic" style in the years around 1770. The exchange of melodic and accompanimental function between voices within a phrase, as seen in example 6.11, is a clear instance of the technique, and it is this that Charles Rosen designates "classical counterpoint." He considers it a "revolutionary" device of which he has found no examples prior to Haydn's Op. 33 string quartets of 1781, though he adds that "it would not be surprising if

EXAMPLE 6.11. Mysliveček, Aria "Palesar vorrei col pianto" from *Il Bellerofonte*, meas. 13–34.

continued

Example 6.11—*continued*

one turned up."[16] Here, indeed, we see the technique in a composition of Mysliveček dating from not later than 1767. It would be best, however, not to attach undue importance to its use here: it is actually just one of many new ways of fashioning textures and phrasing that can already be found in music of the 1760s.

[16] Rosen, p. 117.

Whether it is appropriate to designate this technique a type of "counterpoint" is another question. If counterpoint in its traditional definition refers to two or more melodies sung or played simultaneously, then this absence of simultaneous entities that are all clearly melodic would suggest that "counterpoint" is a misnomer. A greater problem with the term is that it preempts the proper identification of the wide variety of genuine contrapuntal procedures found in the works of Mysliveček's generation.

Example 6.12 provides an excellent illustration of Mysliveček's treatment in the 1760s. The point of imitation at the beginning is prompted in part by archaic genre traditions (string trios of the 1760s still bear traces of procedures used in the old baroque trio sonatas), but the bass line is more typical of the drum bass accompaniments of the early classic period rather than continuo basses of the baroque period. Counterpoint disappears for a short time, but re-appears in measure 16. The tremolo in the second violin part sets up a type of layered texture typical of the 1760s that would be totally incompatible with baroque style. Habitually, the motives used by

Example 6.12. Mysliveček, String Trio in A Major, op. 1, no. 2 (String Trio 8), first movement, meas. 1–27.

continued

EXAMPLE 6.12—*continued*

Mysliveček as the basis of his contrapuntal excursions are much more light-hearted (*galant*) than those typical in baroque music. His points of imitation can be as ingenious as those of any Italian composer of baroque chamber music but, enlivened with rhythmic animation in accompanying parts, they achieve what in the 1760s was a fully modern sound. This style of counterpoint is the true "classical counterpoint."

Mysliveček's techniques of organizing phrases are generally typical of his day. The ideal of neatly balanced phrasing with antecedent-consequence structures seems to have been instinctive and generally served him well. He excelled in connecting phrases made up of disparate motives and textures (as in ex. 6.13), unlike many less talented composers whose works can suffer from repetition, awkward breaks in musical continuity, and a lack of unifying elements. Mysliveček almost always avoided these common foibles and additionally had a knack for phrase extension—the technique of prolonging the anticipation of a cadential close by avoiding the resolution of cadential preparations (ex. 6.13). The sudden lurch downward in measure 9, accompanied by a sudden change in texture and exchange of melodic function between the violins, creates a highly effective and rather witty means to withhold the expected cadence in the tonic key and keep the listener wondering about the direction the composition is taking.

EXAMPLE 6.13. Mysliveček, String Quartet in E-flat Major, op. 3, no. 5 (String Quartet 5), first movement, meas. 1–13.

A composer's approach to sonata form is a topic of perpetual interest, and it has particular importance in the work of Italianate composers whose compositions were even more dominated by straightforward binary forms and sonata forms than the compositions of northern composers. Especially in the 1760s, it is normal for all three movements of Mysliveček's typical three-movement instrumental cycles to be cast in some species of binary form or sonata form. Variations, minuets with trios, and rondos were not common until later. Whether or not it is proper to make judgments about a composer's "progressiveness" or "backwardness" based on his handling of binary forms and sonata forms, it is clear that procedures seen in the 1760s and 1770s were more flexible than in the last two decades of the eighteenth century, and they do require some explanation to help understand the options available to a composer of Mysliveček's generation.

The most important phenomenon related to binary form and sonata form during Mysliveček's career as a composer was the effective abandonment of "rhyming" versions of these forms in preference to "rounded" versions. In the simplest terms, the rhyming scheme is recognizable when only the latter portion of the exposition is recapitulated at the end of a movement, a procedure inherited from typical binary forms of the late baroque period. The major key version is diagrammed in brief here:

General thematic areas:	|:	A	B	:||:	(unstable)	B	:|
Key areas:		I	V		(unstable)	I	

In the rounded form, the more modern type in the 1760s, a full recapitulation of the entire exposition occurs; it is the basis of sonata form:

General thematic areas:	|:	A	B	:||:	(unstable)	A	B	:|
		"exposition"			"development"	"recapitulation"		
Key areas:		I	V		(unstable)	I	I	

The preponderance of rhyming schemes can help to date a work. Except in very compact movements, it was generally only the oldest composers, such as C. P. E. Bach, who continued to use rhyming schemes into the late 1770s.

Two key points about Mysliveček's treatment of sonata form bear mention. One is the frequent absence of repeat signs in his music. Although this is consistent with Italian orientation, Mysliveček left off repeat signs in his overtures, symphonies, and chamber works to a degree rarely seen in his day. It made sense in opera overtures to suppress repeats so that introductions to the dramatic works would not be overly long, but the lack of repeats in Mysliveček's instrumental movements frequently leaves the listener longing to hear the lovely ideas one more time.

The other key point to be made about Mysliveček's treatment of sonata form concerns the way in which sonata-form events are well articulated and systematically applied, even in some of his earliest compositions from the early and mid-1760s. It is tempting to speculate that the regularity of his approach was a legacy of the technical studies he was required to pursue as part of his training to become a master miller. Mysliveček's handling of the exposition of sonata form offers the best illustrations of his treatment. The melodic events of the exposition, a descendant of the first repeated section of baroque binary dance forms, were formalized earlier and more rigidly than the other portions of sonata form ever were. In fact, the general proportions and character of the exposition were more or less settled upon by the 1760s even before the rounded binary scheme had definitively replaced the rhyming schemes inherited from the baroque.

The first event of a standard exposition is an opening phrase or complex of phrases to introduce the tonic key and present an easily recognizable thematic reference point, the "first theme," as it is generally known. Mysliveček almost always offers the listener a clear cadence in the tonic key to mark off the first theme, after which there is typically a textural "jolt" accompanied by techniques such as increased rhythmic activity, a sudden change in dynamic level, and a new melodic style. The effect of the jolt is to inform the listener in a slightly unsettling way that the music is now embarking on an excursion to a new key area by means of a musical section referred to in modern times as a "bridge" or "transition." Example 6.14, from his Symphony in F Major (No. 28), shows a well-articulated first theme with a jolt at measure 9 to signal the beginning of a modulation to the new key. A clear first theme marked off with a cadence in the tonic is not found by any means as consistently in the works of most of Mysliveček's contemporaries, including Haydn and the young Mozart.

"Second themes" have the reputation of being soft, sweet, and lyric in nature, a characterization applicable to Mysliveček's works. Their appearance was usually dramatized by a momentary cessation of musical activity, as in measure 32 of the Overture to *L'Ipermestra* (ex. 6.15). For Mysliveček, "second themes" were also a place to indulge special effects, such as imitative counterpoint, or, in symphonic music, wind solos. They are usually incorporated into a complex of several themes or phrases that emphasize stable harmonies and clear-cut phrasing to create another recognizable harmonic and thematic reference point, and they almost always occupy the longest section in the exposition.

The "close," the last musical event of the exposition, offers a rousing flourish to confirm the modulation to the dominant and usually features *forte* dynamics, repetitions of cadence patterns, and repetitions of dominant-tonic harmonic progressions. In Mysliveček's work, its conclusion is frequently signaled by a standard dotted-note figure, as in the final measure of the third movement of the String Quintet in E Major, op. 2, no. 2 (ex. 6.16), a figure sometimes over-used in Mysliveček's instrumental music. He did not employ extended codas in his sonata forms, nor were they common in the work of most composers until the 1780s.

EXAMPLE 6.14. Mysliveček, Symphony in F Major (Symphony 28), first movement, meas. 1–17 (horns, oboes omitted).

EXAMPLE 6.15. Mysliveček, Overture to *L'Ipermestra* (Overture 7), first movement, meas. 30–41. Edited from Ms. V B 61 of the České Muzeum Hudby with permission.

In the 1760s and 1770s, the more archaic way to begin the development section was simply to repeat the opening motive of the exposition in the dominant key. Mysliveček was an exponent of the more modern (and less mechanical) procedure of beginning the development in a surprising, unpredictable way with a motive selected from the interior of the exposition. He is among the composers who did not lavish a great deal of attention on development sections. His tend to be brief, often hardly more than re-transitions from the exposition to the recapitulation. Especially in movements without repeat signs, his overall forms approach sonata form without development. If the level of sophistication seen in the development sections of Haydn or Mozart in the 1770s is sought, then Mysliveček must be considered wanting.

Composers in the earlier decades of the eighteenth century who used rhyming binary schemes tended to bring back only the second half or so of the first repeated section as a recapitulation in order to create the pleasing sense of harmonic resolution needed to bring a movement to a close. Even in the 1760s many composers, including Mysliveček, sometimes brought back only a portion—

EXAMPLE 6.16. Mysliveček, String Quintet in E Major, op. 2, no. 2 (String Quintet 2), third movement, meas. 29–39.

typically, the portion beginning with the transition to the second theme—in the recapitulation. As a rule, the less complete the recapitulation, the more extensive the development section. Mysliveček's opera overtures tend to have more complete recapitulations in the 1760s than his works in other genres, but by the 1770s all sonata forms in Mysliveček's writing featured a full recapitulation including the first theme of the exposition and most or all of the rest of the thematic material heard in the first repeated section. Mysliveček, like other composers of the 1770s, never felt obliged in the recapitulation to bring back the themes of the exposition in the same order (although he and others usually did).

No preliminary overview of Mysliveček's compositional style would be complete without drawing attention to the excellence of his slow movements. Slow movements by most composers who worked in the 1760s and 1770s frequently strike modern listeners as mere interim diversion; often the listener can hardly wait for them to end in order to hear something more interesting or exciting. On the whole, Mysliveček's slow movements offer more in the way of expressive power and memorable melodic ideas than those of other composers of his generation. Among Mysliveček's instrumental compositions, his slow movements often turn out to be the most satisfying portions.

7

TALES OF LONG AGO AND FAR AWAY: MYSLIVEČEK'S OPERAS

For all his skill as a composer of instrumental music, Josef Mysliveček concentrated his greatest energies on vocal music in serious style, a strategy that offered him the best potential to earn a living outside of an aristocratic or ecclesiastical establishment. Whether uncomfortable with comic style or simply uninterested in it, he neglected it completely in favor of three outlets for the expression of serious vocal style in Italian: opera, oratorio, and cantata. All three types of compositions were constructed more or less from the same musical building blocks—principally arias and recitatives—but typically differed in length, subject matter, performance context, and performing resources. By far the most prestigious was opera, thus it is fitting that a consideration of Mysliveček's contributions to individual musical genres begins with an evaluation of his operatic output.

Josef Mysliveček completed twenty-six serious operas in Italian between 1766 and 1780, a larger number than any other composer in Europe during the same period. As a northerner, Mysliveček was remarkable for his ability to penetrate the ranks of a select group of musicians who were mainly responsible for composing the serious operas performed in Italian theaters of the day. Generally only a few composers attracted commissions on a regular basis from theaters throughout Italy. Examples from the 1760s and 1770s include Francesco de Majo, Pasquale Anfossi, Pietro Guglielmi, Giovanni Paisiello, Giuseppe Sarti, Antonio Sacchini, Niccolò Piccinni, Tommaso Traetta, and Domenico Cimarosa. Other composers, such as Carlo Monza in Milan, Ignazio Celoniat in Turin, Ferdinando Bertoni in Venice, and Giacomo Insanguine in Naples, generally wrote operas only for theaters in their native regions. Other northerners who were able to draw attention to themselves in Italy for a time, such as J. C. Bach, Florian Gassmann, and Joseph Schuster, did not remain there long enough to establish a record of productions comparable to Mysliveček's.

Twenty-four of Mysliveček's operas survive in the form of complete or near-complete scores (see Catalog 2). The music for the other two, *La Circe* of 1779 and *Antigono* of 1780, is lost except for a few excerpts. The collection of Italian opera scores assembled by King José I of Portugal, now preserved in the Ajuda Palace in Lisbon, provides—ironically—a more complete record of Mysliveček's production of operas than any archive in Italy. King José (r. 1750–77) commissioned copies of the scores used for operatic productions at all the principal theaters of Italy, thereby providing his court with an unparalleled sampling of the latest Italian styles. Since scores continued to be copied for the court even after his death, the entire period of Mysliveček's operatic activity is well represented in the Ajuda collection: eighteen works in all, including the only known score of *La clemenza di Tito* and a valuable copy of his first opera, *Semiramide* of 1766.[1] Two other important repositories of Mysliveček's operatic scores are the libraries of the Conservatorio di Musica S. Pietro a Majella in Naples and the Conservatorio di Musica Luigi Cherubini in Florence. The České Muzeum Hudby in Prague surpasses all other archives for its collection of individual operatic arias by Mysliveček, most of them with sacred Latin texts substituted for the original Italian. Sizeable accumulations of Mysliveček's arias are also found in the Monumento Nazionale di Montecassino, the library of the Conservatorio di Musica S. Pietro a Majella in Naples, the Santini-Bibliothek in Münster, and the music department of the Bibliothèque Nationale in Paris.

Although the stream of new commissions that Mysliveček obtained year after year attests to an enduring demand for his music, none of his individual operas ever succeeded in attracting widespread attention in Italy. The anomaly is not difficult to explain. It was the nature of operatic culture in Mysliveček's day that serious operas were carefully fitted to the musical and scenic resources assembled for a single operatic run. What was generally in demand was a composer's style of writing, not any specific work by him. The culture of comic opera, in contrast, depended heavily on the production of favorite works enjoyed time and time again. Occasionally a serious opera did emerge with sufficient appeal to attract audiences throughout Italy for a period of years (examples would be J. C. Bach's *Catone in Utica* during the 1760s and Giuseppe Sarti's *Medonte* during the 1770s), but this was not common. Mysliveček's *Semiramide*, *Bellerofonte*, *Adriano in Siria*, and *La Calliroe* may be considered his most successful operas if the number of revivals is taken as an indication (see Catalog 2). Still, these works were revived only in provincial operatic centers. No Mysliveček opera ever saw a revival at one of the great Italian houses.

The near complete lack of operatic music by Mysliveček in modern or facsimile editions remains a disappointment.[2] Aside from the numerous editions of Mozart's arrangement of the aria "Il caro mio bene," originally written for Mysliveček's *Armida*, all that is currently available is one aria from *Bellerofonte*, two arias from *Ezio* of 1775, and one aria each from *Motezuma*, *Atide*, and *Artaserse* that happened to be borrowed in the Munich version of the oratorio *Isacco figura del redentore* (see Catalog 2).[3] Mysliveček was neglected by the editors of the facsimile series *Italian Opera, 1640–1770*, but some of his music likely appears in a facsimile edition of the score for a production of Gluck's *Orfeo* performed in Naples in 1774.[4] In that score, in addition to alterations known to have been made by J. C. Bach for a production of Gluck's *Orfeo* in London in 1770, there are unidentified additions consistent with Mysliveček's style. It is reasonable to suppose that Mysliveček, who led the orchestra for the production, composed their music.[5]

---

[1] See Mariana Amélia Machado Santos, *Biblioteca da Ajuda: Catálogo de Música Manuscrita* (Lisbon: Biblioteca da Ajuda, 1959). In spite of the large number of Mysliveček operas scores available to the court of Portugal, there is no evidence that any of them were ever produced there.

[2] A modern edition of Mysliveček's *Motezuma*, ed. Daniel E. Freeman, is forthcoming in the series *Monuments of Tuscan Music* (Louisville: Musica Toscana).

[3] The borrowed arias are found in James Ackerman, ed., *Josef Mysliveček: Isacco figura del redentore* (Madison: A-R Editions, 2000). One other aria from *Ezio* of 1775, "Questa è la bella face," is scheduled to appear in a collection of Italian arias in the *Monuments of Tuscan Music* series published by Musica Toscana.

[4] A facsimile edition of the music for this production, based on the score preserved in the library of the Conservatorio di Musica S. Pietro a Majella, is in volume 11 of *The Collected Works of Johann Christian Bach, 1735–1782*, ed. Ernest Warburton (New York and London: Garland, 1987).

[5] See Lucio Tufano, "Josef Mysliveček e l'esecuzione napoletana dell'*Orfeo* di Gluck (1774)," *Hudební věda* 43 (2006): 257–79. The unidentified passages include the recitative for act 1, scene 1, and act 2, scenes 1 and 2; the accompanied recitatives for act 1,

ITALIAN *OPERA SERIA* CONVENTIONS

In order to give the reader some idea of what to expect from a Mysliveček opera, it may be helpful to outline the general features of serious Italian opera of his day, familiar as many of these are to scholars and connoisseurs alike. Perhaps the most important consideration for an understanding of the place of this operatic genre in European musical culture is the high prestige associated with its productions, performers, and composers. The various vocal and instrumental genres cultivated by composers of Mysliveček's day can be divided into classes almost as rigid as the social strata that characterized eighteenth-century European society. There were "low" genres and "high" genres similar to distinctions of social class, each of which carried with it an array of stylistic characteristics that composers generally respected while leaving themselves some room for individuality and the adoption of recent style developments.[6] Once a choice of genre was made, the working-out of a composition was in many respects predetermined, decision after decision having been mandated by a genre tradition. In the eighteenth century, a sense that these traditions should be carefully maintained was strong, and it can be correlated to attitudes concerning the importance of order and hierarchy in society, politics, and religion. To a large degree, the history of western art music since the eighteenth century has been shaped by the gradual weakening of genre traditions as social and political attitudes prizing freedom, equality, and individuality became more widespread. In earlier periods, the more "elevated" the genre, the more sophisticated the compositional techniques expended on it. It was generally only composers who possessed an all-encompassing mastery of technique, such as Bach and Mozart, who would lavish attention on "low" genres (at the risk of being accused of over-complexity). The attention justifiably accorded the music of these masters has tended to obscure generic "class" distinctions for the average listener, but they are frequently evident in the works of less-gifted composers of the eighteenth century.

Indisputably the highest (most "aristocratic") musical genre in Europe of Mysliveček's day, vocal or instrumental, was Italian serious opera (*opera seria*). It graced the grandest social events, incurred the most expensive production costs, and demanded the best-paid performers. No other national operatic traditions could approach the prestige of Italian *opera seria*. The singers who appeared in it were considered to be the best in Europe. If they were engaged for anything else, it would be in other serious works, such as oratorios and cantatas, almost never the "low" genre of comic opera. Many began their careers singing in comic operas, but the leading singers ceased to appear in them once established in serious opera.[7] The most successful composers of Italian serious opera were generally the wealthiest and most respected in Europe.

Considering the poor reputation of eighteenth-century Italian *opera seria* in modern times, Mysliveček's lack of interest in comic opera is regrettable, even though it is understandable within

---

scene 7, and act 2, scene 3; the arioso "Il silenzio, la pace" (act 1, scene 7); the choruses "Sciolto ognun dal terreo" (act 1, scene 6) and "Chiari fonti, ermi ritiri" (act 2, scene 5); and the arias "La legge accetto, oh Dei" (act 1, scene 5), "Se quel dolor" (act 1, scene 7), "Uno sposo così fido" (act 2, scene 1), and "Spieghi alle belle" (act 2, scene 2). For another detailed discussion of this production, see Michael Robinson, "The 1774 S. Carlo Version of Gluck's *Orfeo*," *Chigiana* 29–30 (1972–73): 395–413.

[6] Explicit confirmation that eighteenth-century music criticism was capable of grouping musical genres in a hierarchy analogous to distinctions of social class is in Cramer, *Magazin der Musik* 1, part 2, 889–90.

[7] Even a singer as young as Giacomo David, a leading tenor who appeared in Mysliveček's *Medonte* in 1780, made virtually no appearances in comic operas after the very beginning of his career in 1770–71, despite the declining popularity of serious opera in the 1780s and 1790s and the demand for tenor voices in comic works and "mixed" works that included scenes in both comic and serious style.

the context of Mysliveček's background and professional goals. The internationalist style of Italian serious opera did not present the obstacles of setting regional dialects or devising subtle means to enhance comic action with music. Other northerners who sought prominence in the composition of Italian serious opera, for example J. C. Bach (who also wrote no comic operas), seem to have found these obstacles similarly daunting and hardly worth the trouble, either from the standpoint of prestige or financial gain. There is interesting testimony about this matter from Mozart, who in a letter to his father of 11 October 1777 offered his opinion that the composition of comic opera was something that one did for "practice" or just "something to do."[8] The rewards of cultivating comic styles were generally left to the Italians themselves.

For eighteenth-century audiences, *opera seria* could be a thrilling spectacle, but what a modern listener can expect from a typical Mysliveček *opera seria* is governed to a large extent by genre traditions that now seem hopelessly outdated, among them the monotonous alternation of recitatives and arias, the suspension of dramatic action mandated by the performance of lengthy arias, and the use of male sopranos for heroic roles. The plots and characterizations strike most spectators today as impossibly stilted. Conservative composers in the 1760s and 1770s were nonetheless quite comfortable with the conventions that had been handed down to them. Working as he did in Italy, Mysliveček's operas exhibit the same aversion to radical Gluckian "reform" elements that was shared by most Italian composers of his day. Many of these traits were, after all, French in orientation, thus foreign. Whatever "reform" trends did become popular enough to be widely accepted he soon came to terms with. In view of Mysliveček's firm endorsement of plans to stage Gluck's *Orfeo* in Naples in 1774 (see chapter 3), there is justification to speculate that his conservative approach to opera did not originate from any strong personal convictions at all, but rather from the wishes of the theater impresarios who commissioned his works and the singers who appeared in them.

Some of the most basic expectations one could form about a typical Mysliveček opera would be determined by traditions associated with librettos, especially those of Pietro Metastasio, the author of the texts for sixteen of Mysliveček's twenty-six operas, most of them originally set to music in the 1720s and 1730s. In spite of the dominance of Metastasio's texts, it would be rash to regard him as a personal favorite of Mysliveček, since it is largely unknown what hand Mysliveček took in choosing the texts he set. It was customary in Mysliveček's day for the management of the theater, not the composer, to select either a pre-existent libretto or commission a new one.[9] In provincial centers, arrangements were perhaps more flexible. It is possible that Mysliveček may have taken some part in the choice of texts he set to music from time to time, but it is unlikely that he ever collaborated closely with any poet. The general procedure of the leading opera theaters was for the management simply to present a composer with a text and expect him to set it effectively according to the abilities of singers who had been engaged by the theater.

The popularity of Metastasio's librettos was waning in Mysliveček's day, but they were still set frequently and provided something of a defining standard. The overall dramatic presentation would be put forward in three acts. In the first half of the eighteenth century, when Metastasio wrote most of his best-known dramas, the three acts of serious operas in Italian were roughly equal

[8] For the letter, see Anderson, 302–06; Bauer and Deutsch, 2:43–46.

[9] The selection of the librettos for *Bellerofonte* and *Romolo ed Ersilia* by the Neapolitan *Giunta dal canto* are described in Prota-Giurleo, "L'Abate Galiani" (see Appendix 1). Further documentation concerning the selection of libretto texts by the management of the Teatro San Carlo during the years 1773–75 is in Tufano, "Josef Mysliveček."

in length, but as the century wore on, the third acts were customarily abbreviated. It is presumed that they became increasingly shorter in order to make the length of an evening's entertainment less wearing for the audience as the arias became ever longer and more elaborate and opera-goers started to find the conventions of the style ever more tiresome. Whatever the explanation, it would not have been surprising to encounter only half or less the number of arias in the third act as the number of arias in the first or second acts. In order to accommodate a short third act, preexistent librettos by Metastasio and others were frequently cut.

The dramatic setting of an *opera seria* in Mysliveček's day was almost always long ago or far away, a convention descended from the birth of opera in the 1590s. (Eighteenth-century comic opera, in contrast, was the opera of the "here and now.") There was never any attempt to recreate authentically the cultures of the ancient and exotic places portrayed in *opera seria*. Rather, librettists conjured up escapist, other-worldly settings that depicted idealized societies populated by virtuous, valorous individuals.

Metastasian story types were typically spun around the lives of genuine historical figures who once lived in southern Europe, North Africa, and the Near or Middle East. In selecting subject matter, the European Dark Ages marked a general chronological boundary that ordinarily was not breached. Gioacchino Pizzi's popular libretto *Il gran Cidde*, based on the life of the Spanish hero who made war against the Muslims in the eleventh century, is an example of a rather late setting for Mysliveček's day. Other examples are the *Armida* operas based on Torquato Tasso's *Gerusalemme liberata*, which are set at the time of the Crusades. Some librettists took advantage of the chronological flexibility permitted when locations were very distant from Europe. The farther away the scenario, the less need there was to maintain an ancient time frame. Thus Agostino Piovene's *Il gran Tamerlano* could be based on a character from central Asia of ca. 1400, Timur the Lame. Also far afield was Vittorio Amedeo Cigna-Santi's *Motezuma*, a story based on the Spanish conquest of Mexico in the early sixteenth century. A time as recent as this was permissible, since the opera libretto did satisfy one of the two compulsory requirements (great geographical distance or chronological distance from the spectators).

Besides historical settings, classical myths were also tapped for operatic subject matter. Following traditions that also extend back to the earliest operas, the librettists of the French *tragédies lyriques* favored Greek myths, and in Italy of the 1760s and 1770s they appear most typically in Franco-Italian operatic fusions. Examples of Mysliveček operas based on Greek myths include *Bellerofonte* of 1767, *Atide* of 1774, and *La Circe* of 1779. Stories built around mythological characters do not differ in any essential way from those built around historical characters, except that mythological characters could embody qualities of immortality and eternal youth, and through tricks of stagecraft it was possible for spectators to enjoy simulated demonstrations of the characters' supernatural powers.

The literary genre to which most Metastasian librettos belong is the *melodramma a lieto fine* ("music drama with happy ending"). The stories center on emotional conflicts faced by royal or aristocratic families, whose members maintain exemplary moral behavior and fulfill conventional sex roles (at least by the end of the opera). The main source of dramatic conflict in Italian *opera seria* is usually some sort of difficulty that keeps lovers or spouses separated or distressed until a miraculous solution presents itself near the end of the third act. Perhaps insufficiently recognized by modern critics is the overriding significance of the resolution of love intrigues into happy marriages. Whatever social or political commentary can be read into eighteenth-century operatic librettos, there can be no doubt that the importance of marriage as the only valid goal of amorous attraction was their core message, whether the action was serious or comic.

Centered as it was on the love-making of royal and aristocratic persons, *opera seria* developed its own discourse of "courtly love" that audiences today can find pretentious and artificial. In an age when most royal marriages were arranged, librettists came up with fanciful pretexts to explain how the royalty of adversarial nations could somehow come into close enough proximity to enable members of the competing ruling families to fall in love and resolve outstanding political differences. The most common pretext was the captivity of a principal character after his or her nation's defeat in battle, very much an aspect of the other-worldly nature of Italian serious opera. In Europe in the eighteenth century, royal personages had very limited opportunity to interact face-to-face with the royalty of other nations, and it was unheard of for rulers (much less their daughters) to be taken captive after unsuccessful battles in the way that happens so frequently in eighteenth-century librettos.[10]

Metastasio's librettos were famous for the moral dilemmas posed for the main characters. Sometimes they are forced to choose between conflicting virtues, sometimes between virtue and legitimate self-interest. In *L'olimpiade*, for example, a conflict is set up which puts friendship and carnal love in opposition, whereas in *Artaserse* friendship and filial devotion clash. If there is discreditable or dubious behavior among the principal characters (usually no more than one is allowed to be evil), moral rehabilitation is the preferred technique of bringing about a happy resolution to all discord. In serious librettos from the late seventeenth and early eighteenth centuries, evil characters were more frequently killed off. But no matter how wickedness is extinguished in an eighteenth-century serious opera, no characters left on the stage by the end of the drama are permitted to be morally corrupt. Virtue always triumphs.

The characters in a Metastasian drama typically number about a half dozen, their relationships bound up with strata of love intrigues institutionalized by customs involving the employment of singers, who were divided into tiers based on their reputations, salaries, and the number and difficulty of their arias. There is a first tier of characters, sung by the *primo uomo* (a castrato) and *prima donna*, and often a second tier, sung by the *second'uomo* and *seconda donna*. All are royal or aristocratic, but the characters of the second tier are generally slightly lower in rank than those of the first tier. A *prima donna* might be a queen, whereas a *seconda donna* would more likely be a princess or a lady at court. Two happy marriages are usually necessary to resolve the love intrigues of both tiers. The cast is customarily filled out with parents or confidants not directly involved in the love intrigues who offer advice and emotional support to the principals.

An advantage of Metastasian drama was the flexibility it offered impresarios in the way of production costs. Staging could be as grand or as spare as circumstances dictated; few of the demands for spectacle common to French serious opera were needed to put on an Italian serious opera successfully—the only essential element was dazzling vocal artistry. Elaborate stage machinery was rarely obligatory, and costumes and sets could be simple or lavish. Traditions of French serious opera demanded that ballet be integrated into the body of the drama, whereas Italian traditions left open the possibility of ballet between the acts if a theater was capable of arranging it. Productions of Mysliveček's operas in the leading theaters of Italy often included ballets between the acts, but

[10] One incident that did come close to approximating common scenarios in eighteenth-century Italian opera occurred shortly after the Battle of Blenheim in 1704 during the War of the Spanish Succession. Elector Maximilian II Emanuel of Bavaria, an ally of the defeated French, was separated from his two sons, both of whom were captured by the Austrians and held in captivity until 1715. The elder of the two brothers, later Elector Charles Albert of Bavaria, married the archduchess Maria Amalia, daughter of his former captor Holy Roman Emperor Joseph I, in 1722.

Rudolf Pečman is incorrect in claiming this an indication of "reform" thinking on Mysliveček's part.[11] Aside from the fact that ballet actually integrated into the main drama (not merely ballet present as *entr'actes*) is the true sign of the adoption of Gluckian "reforms," it was the impresario or the management of a theater that decided whether or not ballet was to be included. The music for any ballets would not have been written by Mysliveček in any case; that was the responsibility of the ballet masters (whose contributions are recorded in many librettos). Mysliveček is not known to have composed any dance music for his operas.

MYSLIVEČEK'S OPERAS

Mysliveček's operas are best evaluated within a chronological framework of three distinct periods of creative activity. The first period encompasses the operas he composed up to *Demetrio* of 1773, including a significant advance in technique that resulted from his first commission from the Teatro San Carlo in Naples in 1767. A second period extends from Mysliveček's return to Naples in the summer of 1773 to his setting of *Ezio* for Munich in 1777. The last period, initiated by another return to Naples in 1778, comprises his last seven operas. Arguably the most important defining characteristic of each period has to do with the choice of formal schemes for the vocal set pieces. Mysliveček's first period was dominated by the dal-segno aria, the second by sonata-form amalgamations, and the third by slow-fast arias and rondò. In the third period, the slow-fast vocal pieces were not by any means the most numerous of the aria types present, but they appear to have been accorded the greatest attention from the composer as a means to leave the most striking impression possible on audiences.

SEMIRAMIDE (1766)

Mysliveček's first opera, *Semiramide*, represents a special preparatory phase in the composer's first period of writing. A setting of a venerable Metastasian libretto, its story is based on the life of opera's most famous warrior queen of antiquity, Semiramis of Babylonia,[12] who is reunited at the end of the drama with a long-lost husband (the latter a fictitious addition). The limited resources available to Mysliveček in Bergamo, where this opera was first performed, mandated a relatively simple musical setting, but *Semiramide* nonetheless exemplifies many basic principles that underlie his entire production of operas, in particular the primacy of arias as the center of musical interest. Mysliveček was above all a master of the lengthy, elaborate arias referred to uneasily by some as "vocal symphonies," just the sort of musical numbers that admirers of operatic "reform" find so objectionable.

---

[11] Perhaps the most succinct presentation of this view is found in Rudolf Pečman, "Josef Mysliveček als Reformator der Neapolitanischen Oper seria," in Eitelfriedrich Thom and Frieder Zschoch, eds., *Der Einfluss der italienischen Musik in der ersten Hälfte des 18. Jahrhunderts*, (Michaelstein & Blankenburg: Kultur- und Forschungsstätte Michaelstein, 1988), 18–22.

[12] For an appraisal of the use of warrior queens as operatic characters in the seventeenth and eighteenth centuries (including special attention to Semiramis), see Daniel E. Freeman, "*La guerriera amante*: Representations of Amazons and Warrior Queens in Venetian Baroque Opera," *Musical Quarterly* 80 (1996): 431–60.

Before examining some of the musical techniques used to create *Semiramide*, it will be helpful to underscore the existence of a unique resource available to composers in Mysliveček's day who set Metastasian texts: a large repertory of recent operas on the same texts. Metastasio's librettos were set dozens of times over, and it is clear that Mysliveček knew at least some of the earlier settings of the librettos he set. In the case of *Semiramide*, it seems possible to identify an immediate model in a setting by Tommaso Traetta produced at the Teatro San Cassiano in Venice during carnival of 1765 (at a time when Mysliveček was likely resident in the city). The shared appearance in both composers' operas of choruses at the beginning of act 2, a duet at the end of act 2, and a terzetto at the end of act 3 (none of whose texts are found in the original libretto of 1729) almost certainly points to Mysliveček's reliance on Traetta's setting. It also seems unlikely that the complicated sectional structure of "Saper bramate tutto il mio core" (act 2, scene 4 in both versions) would be so similar had Mysliveček not made reference to the older composer's work. Traetta is most famous for the "reformed" operatic works he composed at the court of Parma in the late 1750s and early 1760s. His rather restrained style of writing would have served as a useful point of departure for the music Mysliveček needed to supply for the less-gifted singing personnel available in Bergamo.

AN EXAMPLE OF DAL-SEGNO FORM: THE ARIA "NON SÒ, SE PIÙ T'ACCENDI"

To help illustrate the methods used by Mysliveček to set operatic arias throughout his early periods of activity in Italy, it will be useful to analyze at some length the first aria in *Semiramide*, "Non sò, se più t'accendi," from act 1, scene 3, sung originally by Caterina Galli in the title role. Opening arias from the 1760s and 1770s generally offer a good sample of the kind of writing that would dominate an entire work. Compared to arias written for Italian theaters able to engage the most skilled singers and instrumentalists, the opening aria of *Semiramide* is conventional in formal treatment, modest in proportions, and restricted in virtuosity.

One of the most basic decisions that had to be made about the setting of an operatic text was the choice of overall form. Mysliveček worked in an era when aria forms were evolving rapidly and composers throughout Europe were seeking alternatives to the strict da-capo (or "ABA") structures that had dominated Italian opera since the 1690s. The most significant development of the 1760s in terms of form was the widespread abandonment of the full repeats of the A section after the B section was heard. As arias became ever longer, abbreviated repeats became almost a necessity, otherwise the arias would have lasted about as long as contemporary symphonies, an interval of time that was impractical both vocally and dramatically. Instead of starting the repeat at the beginning of the A section, the starting point was brought up ever further into the interior of the A section. Only half (or less) of the A section was repeated in the works of fashionable composers of the mid-1760s. The point of return was specified in scores by a sign (*segno*) that took the form of an elaborate decorated "S," hence the common name for the aria forms with abbreviated returns: dal-segno arias.

In the period of Mysliveček's first known exposure to opera during the early 1760s, the strict da-capo aria was still preeminent in Italy. Pescetti's *Zenobia* (Padua, 1761), the last opera written by Mysliveček's teacher in Venice, contains fourteen arias in the traditional strict da-capo form out of eighteen arias total; only one aria exhibits the most modern form of the dal-segno aria by starting the return at about the mid-point of the A section (in the other three arias, the repeat begins at earlier points). Many younger composers in Italy were almost equally conservative. Antonio Sacchini's *Andromaca*, performed in Naples at the Teatro San Carlo on 30 May 1761, includes twelve strict da-capo arias, and Francesco de Majo's *Artaserse*, performed in Venice during carnival of 1762, shows a similar preponderance of them. Exponents of "reform" opera, such as Traetta, tended to drop the full repeats earlier than other composers. Traetta's *Feste d'Imeneo*, performed in 1760 at the court of Parma, for example, contains no strict da-capo arias at all. There were still six strict da-capo arias in Traetta's *Semiramide* of 1765 (and three in Mysliveček's version), but by about 1767, they essentially disappeared from the operatic stages of Italy after seven decades of intensive cultivation. Their structure had created a suitable means to satisfy a need for unity, variety, and resolution, but once their appeal was spent, they were quickly discarded.

Complex as their internal structures could be, da-capo and dal-segno forms were based on a simple principle of setting a two-part poem to music with segments for instruments alone ("ritornelli") interspersed among sections for voices accompanied by instruments. The term "aria," in fact, was defined most importantly by text, not by any musical characteristics at all. Properly, an "aria" is an Italian poem of two stanzas. In serious style, vocal pieces set to poems with a smaller or larger number of stanzas were generally not referred to as "arias" in musical scores. Vocal pieces set to poems of one stanza of text, for example, were ordinarily referred to as "cavatinas."

The text of "Non sò, se più t'accendi" is a good example of a two-part poem in serious style whose lines are distributed among the various musical sections according to rigid conventions. The texts of arias were composed in rhymed verse, as opposed to the blank verse utilized in recitative texts. Four or five lines of rhymed verse (occasionally more) were customary in each stanza, and there was usually an accented final syllable considerately added at the end of each stanza by the poet to accommodate an accented note at the end of major structural reference points in the vocal part.

In terms of the drama, arias permitted a character to express his or her emotions at length in reaction to a dramatic situation set up in the recitative section that preceded the aria. Most arias led to a departure from the stage once a character's feelings had been thoroughly vented for the audience. In the aria "Non sò, se più t'accendi," Queen Semiramide relays some advice to the character Tamiri, a princess of Bactria resident in Semiramide's kingdom who must choose a consort from among three suitors. The one she seems to favor is Scitalce, an Indian prince masquerading under the name Idreno. Semiramide recognizes Scitalce as the husband she fled from during her early days as a princess of Egypt. She is anxious to discourage Tamiri from selecting him, handsome as he is, because she wants him for herself:

Non sò, se più t'accendi	I do not know whether you are more aroused
A questa, a quella face;	By this face or that one;
Ma pensaci, ma intendi	But think about it, and try to understand
Forse che più ti piace,	That perhaps the one that pleases you more,
Più traditor sarà.	Will be the greater traitor.
Auria lo stral d'amore	The power of love's dart
Troppo soavi tempre,	Would be too weak,
Se la beltà del core	If the beauty of the heart
Corrispondesce sempre	Is always matched to
Del volto beltà.	The beauty of the face.

In Mysliveček's day, key words or phrases served to project an overall mood or "affect" in the musical setting of Italian arias. In the first stanza, the key word is "pensaci" ("think about it"), as can be seen from the opening in example 7.1. The hesitant, wandering motive at the start, the moderate tempo, the even flow of quarter notes, and the use of small melodic intervals all contribute to an atmosphere of calmness. The impression Semiramide would like to convey in her advice to Tamiri is that she is disinterested.

An accompanimental ensemble of four-part string orchestra plus oboes and horns was the standard grouping used by Mysliveček throughout his career. In fact, the vast majority of serious operatic arias composed in Italy during the 1760s and 1770s were scored either for this combination of instruments or for voice and strings alone; an ensemble of strings and flutes was the most common alternative. Bassoons, clarinets, trumpets, and tympani were also utilized in some arias, but the size of the accompanying ensemble was constrained by custom and the format of operatic scores: one way or another, all of the music had to fit on the ten-stave scores that were used to disseminate Italian operatic music. In the 1760s, wind instruments were rarely employed for any purpose except to add harmonic support and tonal brilliance to selected musical passages. As a rule, it was unusual to encounter anything more imaginative than the occasional doubling of the violin parts by the oboes and long-note harmonic support in the horns, unless an aria was specially designed to feature a wind soloist in dialogue with the vocalist.

The distribution of the text of "Non sò, se più t'accendi" was determined by conventions for da-capo arias that were already well established in the early eighteenth century. In da-capo and dal-segno forms alike, the entire first stanza of text is given out in each of the two main vocal sections of the A portion. These vocal sections are framed by three sections for instruments (the "ritornellos"), one before, one between, and one after the two vocal sections. The first vocal section customarily includes a modulation to the dominant (or its substitute in minor key) and ends with a cadence in the new key. The second vocal section generally begins in the dominant or a closely-related non-tonic key and returns to the tonic key. The obvious resemblance of the first vocal section to the first repeated section of binary form or sonata form (the "exposition") was not lost on composers of the day, nor was the resemblance of the second vocal section to the second repeated section of binary or sonata form (i.e., the "development" and "recapitulation" together).

The B section of a da-capo or dal-segno aria was used to set the second stanza of the poetic text, usually heard twice in its entirety. A word or phrase from the second stanza was chosen to inspire the musical setting of this section, which often contrasted sharply with the A section. In fact, it is not uncommon for the B section to share neither tempo, meter, nor key with the A section to which it is joined. Ritornellos are generally not found in B sections except in the middle portion where a ritornello serves to separate the two statements of text. The key structure of the B section is usually unstable; often it begins in one key and ends in another. Modal contrast is also a common feature of B sections: if the principal key of the A section is in major mode, the B section is typically dominated by minor mode and vice versa.

Because the repeat of the A section in dal-segno arias is only a partial one, some type of abbreviated or condensed version of the opening portion is needed to effect a smooth return. The modulation to the dominant key in the middle of the A section makes it impossible to jump directly from the end of the B section to the interior of the A section and still preserve a "closed" tonal structure for the partial repeat. Without one of the special abbreviated openings that were usually attached to the end of the B section, the repeated portion of the A section would begin

Example 7.1. Mysliveček, Aria "Non sò, se più t'accendi" from *Semiramide*, meas. 1–18 (horns, oboes omitted).

in the dominant and end in the tonic. These abbreviated openings are customarily based on the opening ritornello of the A section so that the listener can easily recognize a musical event that signals a return.

The structure of da-capo form and its adaptation, dal-segno form, can be condensed to a basic plan of keys as follows ("D.C." indicates a repeat starting from the beginning of the A section to its ending, "D.S." a repeat beginning from the decorated "S" sign in the interior of the A section to its ending):

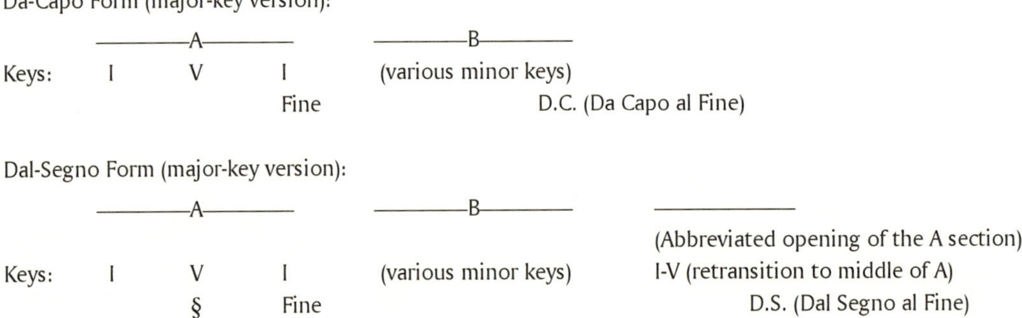

The ritornello structure of the constituent parts of dal-segno form generally conforms to a pattern of this type:

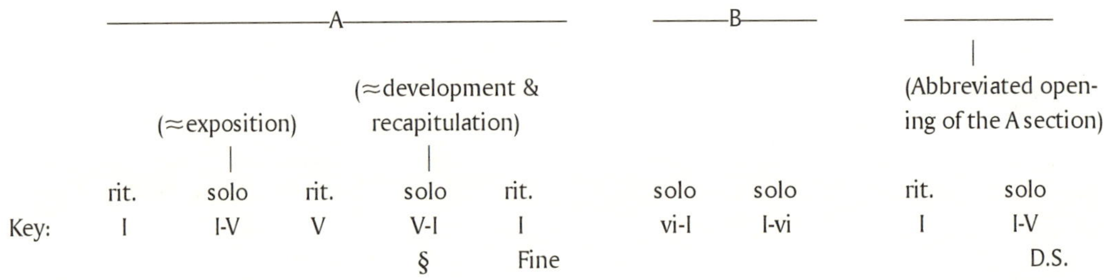

These diagrams are useful to orient the listener in general terms, but so many stylistic conventions had accrued in aria forms by Mysliveček's day that the constituent parts must be broken down further to describe them accurately.

The opening ritornello, often a large section of music for instruments alone, deserves considerable attention in itself, in no small part because of the way that some critics have attempted to equate its structure to sonata-form schemes (in other words, to refer to it as the first of a "double exposition"[13]). Just like the opening ritornellos of concertos, the opening ritornellos of arias had expanded enormously in size since the early eighteenth century,[14] an expansion proportional to the

[13] This interpretation has become somewhat institutionalized through the article "Aria" in *New Grove*.

[14] On expansion of the opening ritornellos of solo concertos and attempts to amalgamate ritornello form and binary form, see Freeman, "The Earliest Italian Keyboard Concertos," 121–45.

increasing size of the arias. This period of enlargement coincided with the transformation of binary form into sonata form, and as the opening ritornellos grew in size, they came more and more to resemble sonata-form "expositions" in terms of melodic organization. The opening ritornellos of arias and concertos, however, begin and end in the same key—they almost always omit the customary modulation of the sonata-form exposition.

There has been speculation about whether these procedures were initiated in concertos and imitated in arias (or vice versa), but the question seems rather beside the point. The adoption of the "thematic function" of sonata form in the opening ritornellos of arias and concertos was most likely nothing more than a practical response to the need in both genres to fill out a substantial musical space with a succession of musical ideas that would offer a pleasing array of textures and melodic styles. There was no better (or more obvious) way to organize the themes in a large section for orchestra alone than according to the standards of the sonata-form exposition as cultivated in symphonies and dramatic overtures. Example 7.1 presents the complete opening ritornello for the aria "Non sò, se più t'accendi," including the customary sonata-form events of "first theme" (meas. 1–8), "transition" or "bridge" (meas. 8–12), and "second theme" and "close" (meas. 13–18). In spite of the presence of melodic events derived from sonata form, it is not appropriate to refer to this musical section as an exposition, since it does not include a modulation to the dominant key.

The vocal sections of da-capo and dal-segno arias from the 1760s exhibit even more complicated conventions that are based directly on formal structures observable in symphonies and sonatas. Indeed, almost all of the experimentation with aria forms in Italy in the 1760s and early 1770s was centered on techniques of amalgamating sonata and binary forms with vocal forms descended from the da-capo aria. It was normal for the first vocal section, which modulates from the tonic to the dominant as in a sonata-form exposition, to feature an opening section in which the tonic key is established with a firm cadence, in other words, something close in conception to a "first theme." The opening melody of the voice part may or may not begin in the same manner as the opening ritornello, depending on factors such as range, melodic style, and textural characteristics. Some opening ritornellos begin with unsingable motivic ideas that are idiomatic for instruments, in which case the voice must begin with something more suitably "cantabile."[15] Since the vocal ranges in serious opera were dominated by alto and soprano singers of both sexes, the melodies typically given out by the first violins in the opening ritornello were usually easy to share, but in the case of bass or tenor soloists, the opening themes were usually not shared. In certain arias, the text invites some type of rhetorical flourish that precludes a repetition of the opening motives given out by the instruments. Words chosen for special emphasis were paused on or drawn out for rhetorical effect. Mysliveček, among others, could rarely resist setting off the words "parto" ("I depart") or "addio" ("goodbye") with fermatas and a suppression of the prevailing tempo and rhythm. In the aria "Non sò, se più t'accendi," the easy, gracious affect presented by the first violins is well suited to a vocal rendering, and the voice takes it up in turn. As seen in Example 7.2, the violins for the most part simply double the vocal part. The two parts diverge only when rests occur in the vocal part to permit the vocalist to breathe (see meas. 21 and 24).

Opening vocal gestures were confined strictly to the first two lines of the first stanza of an aria text, a convention respected almost universally by composers of Italian *opera seria* of Mysliveček's

[15] See ibid. for a discussion of similar phenomena in solo concertos of the mid-eighteenth century.

EXAMPLE 7.2. Mysliveček, Aria "Non sò, se più t'accendi" from *Semiramide*, meas. 18–26 (horns, oboes omitted).

generation, even if the musical interruption created by the cadence at the end of this section made no grammatical or rhetorical sense. This particular aria adheres to a custom of presenting one statement of the first line of text, then two statements of the second line of text. Eric Weimer has designated this an "ABB" opening and claimed it to be dominant type among composers of Italian *opera seria* in this era.[16] In Mysliveček's work, it is more or less equally common to see an "AB" opening that includes only one statement of the second line of text. In this example, the cadence that concludes the section ends with the voice and instruments together. It is also common for the instruments to continue for a time without the voice to create an emphatic cadence that renders the opening gesture even more distinct from the musical section that follows.

In the aria "Non sò, se più t'accendi," none of the text from the first two lines of poetry is heard again until the beginning of the second principal vocal section. In this way, text and music are joined to give the listener a structural reference point identifiable with the beginning of the first vocal section. In some arias, the entire first half of the text is heard again beginning at a point in the first vocal section corresponding to the "second theme" of sonata form. It is a more conservative

[16] Weimer, *Opera Seria*, especially 18–20. "ABB" openings in Mysliveček's work can be seen in examples 7.2 and 7.11.

trait to set the first stanza of text only once in each of the two main vocal sections of the A portion of dal-segno form. The most elaborate arias require two complete statements of the first stanza of text in the first vocal section, otherwise there would be too much musical material to fill up with only two or three lines of text repeated over and over again.

A musical section equivalent to the "transition" of sonata form customarily follows the "ABB" or "AB" opening (ex. 7.3), texted with the remainder of the first stanza of the aria poem (in this case, three lines of text). The exact means by which such sections are worked out is usually unpredictable, but there is often manipulation of thematic material heard earlier, chromatic inflections leading to the establishment of the dominant key, and a busier rhythmic profile. All of these elements are found in Mysliveček's "transition," which is based on the motives given out as the "first theme." In arias written for singers more gifted than Caterina Galli, this section would ordinarily contain the first difficult virtuosic passages. It concludes with a pause on the dominant of the dominant in order to herald the "second theme."

EXAMPLE 7.3. Mysliveček, Aria "Non sò, se più t'accendi" from *Semiramide*, meas. 26–44 (horns, oboes omitted).

continued

EXAMPLE 7.3–*continued*

It can be intriguing to ascertain whether or not the "second theme" of the opening ritornello is shared as the "second theme" of the first principal vocal section. In this aria, the "second theme" of the opening ritornello is repeated in the first main vocal section, but is deemed inappropriate for the voice and confined to the instruments. In its place, the voice is given new material (ex. 7.4, meas. 45-51). The only lines of text used in this section are the last three lines of the first stanza of the aria poem. The "second theme" progresses to a spectacular close that culminates with a strongly-articulated cadence in the new key, another traditional venue for brilliant vocal display.

The cadence used to end the closing gesture (ex. 4, meas. 53–57) is a standard type whose evolution has been documented by Eric Weimer.[17] The salient feature is a bass-line progression from subdominant and dominant to the tonic of the key at hand, always with an octave leap in the bass just before the tonic resolution. This type of bass-line progression has origins far back into the baroque period. As the decades passed, the basic harmonic rhythm increased from eighth notes to quarter notes, then to half notes as the basic unit by the 1760s. In the 1770s, the pattern expanded even to whole notes, pretty much the practical limit. The vocal part at such junctures would almost always conclude with a virtuosic flourish and a trill on the supertonic note. In order to highlight the importance of the cadence, the upper strings typically shift into shimmering tremolos. If horns and oboes are present in the instrumentation, no matter how little they are used elsewhere, they always enter at this point to enhance the brilliance of the cadence. The close of the first principal vocal section is followed by a ritornello in the dominant key that is much shorter than the opening ritornello. The thematic material is often drawn from an earlier obscure passage, a pleasing technique that can leave the listener wondering about where a vaguely familiar motive might have come from. In this case, it is taken from the "transition" of the opening ritornello.

The second ritornello is followed by a vocal section equivalent to the second repeated section of the binary forms that were common in the 1760s. Binary and sonata form offered two alternative means for the structure of the second vocal section at this time. The older type (the "rhyming" scheme) does not include a return of the opening motives of the first vocal section in the tonic key. In this plan, only the second half of the first section is recapitulated in the second section. Another way of describing the practice is to say that only the dominant-key material of the first section returns in the second section in the tonic key. The alternative—rounded binary form—is the equivalent of sonata form: it includes a recapitulation of the entire first section in the tonic key in the second section. If the rounded principle is used as the basis of the aria form, the opening motives from the first section return in the tonic key about half-way through the second section.

The structure of the A sections of da-capo and dal-segno arias of the 1760s lent themselves best to the more old-fashioned rhyming schemes, a characteristic that may have hastened the disappearance of dal-segno aria forms in the 1770s as rhyming schemes fell into disfavor in instrumental music. The presence of a text is what made all the difference. The older traditions of composing da-capo arias mandated that after the first two lines or so of text were heard at the start of each of the two vocal sections within the A portion of the form, they would not be heard again. In the second vocal section, a return of the opening motives in the tonic key at about mid-point in the fashion of rounded binary form would almost automatically demand the return of the first two lines of text along with the music that opened the first vocal section—the music crafted for the opening

[17] Ibid., 25–43.

EXAMPLE 7.4. Mysliveček, Aria "Non sò, se più t'accendi" from *Semiramide*, meas. 44–60.

text could not be used for any other lines of the text. In order to make the A section of the aria conform to the proportions of rounded binary form, the deeply-entrenched tradition not to bring back the first lines of text in the middle of the second vocal section had to be disregarded. Sometimes this was done, but composers who wished to cultivate amalgamations of aria form and rounded binary form generally sought other approaches, as will be described below.

Following the practice of rhyming binary forms that begin the second repeated section with the same motivic material as the opening of the first repeated section, the second vocal section of a typical dal-segno aria usually begins with the opening motive of the first vocal section transposed

EXAMPLE 7.4–*continued*

to the dominant (ex. 7.5). The musical material immediately following the dominant-key statement of the opening motives traditionally reflects the unstable harmonic and melodic characteristics of the "development" section of sonata form. The recapitulatory section enters almost imperceptibly as the text shifts to the subsequent lines. Motives from the transition passage of the first vocal section begin this section, which includes the "second theme" and the final cadential flourishes pretty much without alteration, except that they are now heard in the tonic rather than the dominant. This aria, however, contains an altered version of the final cadence and reserves the customary supertonic trill for the cadenza.

EXAMPLE 7.5. Mysliveček, Aria "Non sò, se più t'accendi" from *Semiramide*, meas. 59–88 (horns, oboes omitted).

Example 7.5–*continued*

The cadenza is the final musical event for the soloist in the A section of dal-segno form. As shown in example 7.6, it is introduced by a short passage for the orchestra, always in *forte* dynamic with string tremolo highlighted with winds. The cadenza is signaled by a stereotypical bass line that rises upward from the leading tone of the dominant to the dominant. This bass-line pattern is usually harmonized with the first inversion of the dominant seventh chord of the dominant key and the second inversion of the tonic chord. The actual vocal cadenza is sung against the second inversion chord. The end of the cadenza is signaled by a supertonic trill in the vocal part and an

EXAMPLE 7.6. Mysliveček, Aria "Non sò, se più t'accendi" from *Semiramide*, meas. 87–102.

EXAMPLE 7.6–*continued*

octave leap downward in the bass. The final ritornello may or may not use motives heard after the first vocal section. Here, the "second theme" and ending of the first ritornello are combined with a suitable flourish.

The B section of a typical dal-segno form aria is usually much shorter and simpler than the A section and shares little or no motivic material. The musical setting for the B section of "Non sò, se più t'accendi" takes as its point of departure the idea of "love's dart" being "too weak" or "too gentle" (ex. 7.7). As in the A section, the B section is divided into two vocal sections, but there are no true ritornellos, only a short passage for orchestra to delineate a break between the two statements of the second stanza of poetry. The internal structure of the B section in this aria is a miniature binary form based on a new tonic key: the first section modulates from the tonic minor to the mediant major and the second portion returns to the tonic. Composers rarely lavished attention on the B sections; usually these sections leave the impression of being mere diversional interludes. Many B sections feature accompanimental patterns that emphasize syncopations and interlocking patterns with downbeats in the bass and off-beats in the upper strings. The last written-out portion of a typical dal-segno aria is an abbreviated version of the opening of the A section in which the voice may or may not participate. The abbreviated opening would always ensure a clear sense of return to the thematic material of the A section and a quick modulation to the dominant key to provide for a smooth connection to the interior of the A section (ex. 7.8; compare with meas. 8–12 of ex. 7.1 and meas. 18–26 of ex. 7.2).

This detailed scrutiny of the structure of Mysliveček's opening aria for *Semiramide* provides an analytical framework for understanding the internal structure in a typical or "normal" aria that could be encountered in any opera, oratorio, or cantata by Mysliveček from the 1760s or early 1770s. Although many of the formal conventions would have been unnoticed by audiences, these "standard operating procedures" were the basis of countless arias written by dozens of composers, and they

EXAMPLE 7.7. Mysliveček, Aria "Non sò, se più t'accendi" from *Semiramide*, meas. 103–18 (horns, oboes tacent).

EXAMPLE 7.8. Mysliveček, Aria "Non sò, se più t'accendi" from *Semiramide*, meas. 133–46 (horns, oboes omitted).

helped shape the structure of the aria forms that came to replace da-capo and dal-segno forms in the 1760s and 1770s. There was always some room for variety and flexibility, however, and certain other arias from *Semiramide* yield alternative procedures, some within the tradition of da-capo or dal-segno forms, some outside them. In fact, Mysliveček's first opera contains examples of all of the common aria forms found in conservative Italian *opere serie* until the widespread introduction in the mid-1770s of vocal numbers based on French *rondeaux* and slow-fast formats.

While opening arias tend to be expansive, with well-developed opening ritornellos, later arias often have rather simple opening ritornellos without the "thematic function" of sonata form. Some, such as "Fuggi degli occhi miei" from act 3, scene 4, of *Semiramide*, have no opening ritornello at all, but otherwise conform to the dal-segno form described above. The absence of an opening ritornello can create a pleasing effect that leaves the impression of a singer impatient for the opportunity to unload his or her feelings without having to wait for a ritornello to end.

AN EXAMPLE OF DAL-SEGNO FORM WITH TEMPO ALTERNATIONS: THE ARIA "SE INTENDE SÌ POCO"

A more significant departure from the usual dal-segno forms is seen in the fifth aria of *Semiramide*, "Se intende sì poco" (act 1, scene 10), originally sung by Carlo Nicolini in the role of Scitalce. Its structure is based on alternations of tempo that the aria text invites (i.e., there are conflicting sentiments within each of the stanzas). The text is of a type in which the character expresses one sentiment for public consumption but also has an aside that provides an outlet for private feelings. In this case, Scitalce realizes that Tamiri favors him as her choice for a husband, but he is still smitten with Semiramide, his long-lost wife. Scitalce observes that Tamiri could not know the painful circumstances of his separation from Semiramide, and he invites Semiramide to perpetuate the charade that he actually does love Tamiri. Semiramide has little choice at this point but to cooperate, since she is trying to rule her kingdom disguised as her own son and cannot reveal her true identity. In the asides, Scitalce recognizes that Semiramide has no desire to see Tamiri happily married to him. The A text reads as follows:

Se intende sì poco	If she [Tamiri] realizes so little
Che ò l'alma piagata	That my soul is wounded
(To Semiramide:)	
Tu dille il mio foco,	Then you express my ardor to her,
Tu parla per me.	You speak for me.
(Aside:)	
(Sospira l'ingrata	(The ungrateful one [Semiramide] sighs,
Contenta non è.)	She is not pleased.)

Whereas the first lines are appropriate for the *Andante* tempo to which they are set (the phrase "l'alma piagata" is clearly the key phrase), the last two lines (with the sentiment "contenta non è") are more appropriate for an agitated *Allegro*. The A section thus follows a pleasing format wherein two changes of tempo from slow to fast create a brilliant close to the entire aria. Each of the two slow sections concludes with a Phrygian cadence that heightens the expectation of a fast section to follow (in this diagram, ritornello structures are not shown):

	(Andante)	Allegro	(Andante) (≈2nd theme area)	Allegro (≈recapitulation of 2nd theme area)
Key:	I	V	ii-I	I
Text:	lines 1–4	lines 5–6, 1–4, 5–6	lines 1-4	lines 5–6, 1–4, 5–6
		§		Fine

The text of the B section is laid out in a parallel structure:

Sai pur che l'adoro	You know that I love her [Tamiri],
Che peno, che moro,	That I am suffering, that I am dying,
(To Semiramide:)	
Che tutta si fida	That all of my soul
Quest'alma di te.	Puts its trust in you.
(Aside:)	
(Si turba l'infida	(The deceitful one [Semiramide] is shocked,
Contenta non è.)	She is not pleased.)

The first part of the B section is set as a *Larghetto* (reflecting the phrase "che peno, che moro"), and there is another *Allegro* for the aside, which ends with the dal-segno indication to return to the interior of the A section. Arias constructed around tempo alternations were a specialty of Mysliveček. He utilized them much more frequently than his contemporaries.[18]

EXAMPLE OF SONATA FORM WITH RITORNELLOS: THE ARIA "VIENI CHE IN POCHI ISTANTI"

Another method of amalgamating aria form and sonata form is exemplified by the aria "Vieni che in pochi istanti" (act 2, scene 7), originally sung by the obscure soprano Rosa Polidora in the role of Sibari. In the 1760s, this type of aria was introduced unobtrusively only here and there, usually in the later portions of operas, but it came to dominate Italian serious opera of the 1770s. Aria forms that were compact, out-of-the-ordinary, or had been introduced only recently were frequently placed near the end of an opera, where they could serve to refresh the audience's interest in the opera. The plain string accompaniment and the compact proportions of this aria are signs of the novelty of its formal layout in the mid-1760s.

The structure of "Vieni che in pochi istanti" (referred to here as "sonata form with ritornellos") has no formal B section, rather it resembles a dal-segno form A section that accommodates the entire text of the two-part poem instead of just the first stanza. The tonal instability and minor-key flavor of the old B sections of da-capo form and dal-segno form are transferred to the equivalent of a development section at the start of the second vocal section. The second stanza of text is shifted to this spot as well. The form of the aria can be diagrammed as follows:

---

[18] A structure very similar to that of "Se intende sì poco" is found in the aria "Vorrei dirti il mio diletto" from part 1 of the oratorio *La passione* of 1773 (available in facsimile), and in one of Mysliveček's most widely disseminated vocal pieces, the aria "Palesar vorrei col pianto" from *Bellerofonte*.

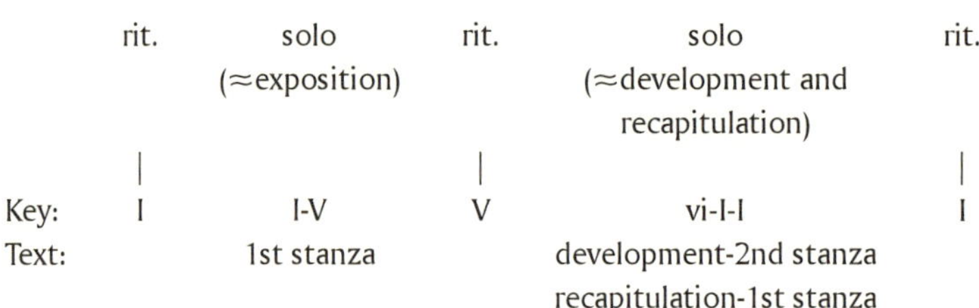

	rit.	solo (≈exposition)	rit.	solo (≈development and recapitulation)	rit.
	|		|		|
Key:	I	I-V	V	vi-I-I	I
Text:		1st stanza		development-2nd stanza recapitulation-1st stanza	

In Mysliveček's first small-scale example of "sonata form with ritornellos" there are two statements each of the first stanza of text in both the exposition and recapitulation sections (the repetition begins at the start of the "second theme"). In traditional da-capo form (which would permit only one statement of the text in each of the two vocal portions of the A section), the first stanza of text is heard in its complete form four times due to the repeat of the A section. In order to offer the listener the same four statements of the first stanza of text in "sonata form with ritornellos," two statements are included in the first vocal section (exposition) and two more in the second half of the second vocal section (recapitulation).[19]

Many traits of dal-segno form are still present in "sonata form with ritornellos"; it was not a large conceptual step from one to the other. In fact, "sonata form with ritornellos" represents the culmination of a logical progression from da-capo form of the early eighteenth century to dal-segno form of the mid-eighteenth century in which the "A" sections start to take on the thematic characteristics of rhyming or rounded binary form, to a complete amalgamation of dal-segno form and sonata form in which the characteristics of the B section of dal-segno form are incorporated into a development section set to the second stanza of the aria text. In "sonata form with ritornellos," one can expect to find the same types of opening ritornellos, the same ABB or AB openings in the vocal part, the same cadential conventions, and the same conventions relating to cadenzas as in dal-segno arias. The superficial resemblance of "sonata form with ritornellos" to concerto first-movement form is probably coincidental. There is no evidence to suggest that operatic composers in Italy in the 1760s suddenly found inspiration for aria forms in solo concertos, when they never had before. The ability to observe gradual stages of amalgamation between da-capo form and sonata form within operatic culture tends to discount the possibility of significant influence from concerto style.

SONATA DA-CAPO FORM: THE ARIA "TU MI DISPREZZI INGRATO"

For aria texts that exhibited sharply contrasting sentiments between the two stanzas, another type of sonata-form amalgamation could also replace dal-segno form. An example in *Semiramide* is "Tu mi disprezzi ingrato" (act 2, scene 2), a rare minor-key aria cast in a ternary scheme. As in "Se intende sì poco," there is no opening ritornello. The key structure can be diagrammed as follows (ritornellos not shown):[20]

---

[19] Three arias in *La passione* offer good examples of this aria form: "Come a vista di pene sì fiere" from part 1, and "Se la pupilla in ferma" and "Se a librarsi in mezzo all'onde" from part 2.

[20] An example by Mysliveček of this form in modern edition is the aria "Sì, ne' tormenti istessi" from the 1777 Munich version of the oratorio *Isacco figura del redentore*, a re-texting of "Lascia, mi adesso in pace" from the opera *Atide* (1774).

	(Allegro) 4/4	Andantino 3/8	(Allegro) 4/4
Key:	i-III	VII	i-i
Text:	1st half	2nd half	1st half

In this plan, an overall ABA form is recognizable in melodic terms, including a B section in contrasting meter and tempo, but the harmonic principles are those of sonata form: there is a first section modulating from tonic to a new key, a middle section dominated by a closely-related key, and a third section that returns to the tonic, remains tonally stable, and features a recapitulation in the tonic key of thematic material heard originally in the first section in the new key. As simple as the form is, a good formal designation is hard to produce. It is referred to here as "sonata da-capo form." There is an exposition and a recapitulation in the manner of sonata form, but instead of a development, there is a contrasting B section in the manner of the old da-capo aria.[21]

RECITATIVES AND ENSEMBLES

While elaborate arias such as those described above lay at the heart of Mysliveček's way of writing operas, there were other elements just as essential. The arias are connected, of course, by the recitative that carries the narration of the plot. The most common type was accompanied only by continuo ("simple recitative"), but a few sections could be accompanied by strings, sometimes with winds added ("accompanied recitative"). Mysliveček was a fluent master of simple recitative, but took no more interest in making it distinctive than most of his conservative contemporaries. A typical *opera seria* of the mid-1760s would include about one section of accompanied recitative per act at points of intense emotion (sometimes one section in each of only two acts). In the 1760s, Mysliveček's accompanied recitatives were not highly developed, nor were those of most of his contemporaries in Italy. Usually the strings would accompany the voice with little more than a few block chords to help highlight emotional expressions or rhetorical gestures. Often the only rhythmic animation would be some dotted rhythms at the end of a character's phrase endings to make the rhetorical gestures more emphatic. *Semiramide* contains only one accompanied recitative, "Di Scitalce il rifiuto," a soliloquy sung by Semiramide before the aria "Il pastor se torna Aprile" in act 2, scene 6. The emotional trauma that invites the accompanied recitative is caused by Scitalce's rejection of her after she reveals herself to him as his long-lost wife. She believes (correctly) that she will be able to win him back.

A love duet is ordinarily encountered at the end of either the first or second act in serious Italian operas of the mid-eighteenth century. In the 1760s, Mysliveček's duets typically reflected the structure of dal-segno arias, and this is true of "Giachè mi sprezzi ingrato," the duet for Scitalce and Semiramide that closes the second act. The underlying principle behind the treatment of the voices in most operatic duets is the idea that each character should first be heard separately, then both of them should join to sing together at the end of major musical sections. When singing together, the voices move in parallel thirds and sixths, a standard technique to evoke agreement or emotional synchronization between characters.

[21] Two arias in the 1777 Munich version of *Isacco figura del redentore* conform to this formal plan, "Madre amico" and "Sì, ne' tormenti istessi," the latter a re-texting of "Lascia mi adesso in pace" from *Atide* (1774). Perhaps the best known example of this form in instrumental music is the overture to Mozart's opera *Die Entführung aus dem Serail*.

Exceptionally, the third act of Mysliveček's *Semiramide* contains a terzetto, "Se sdegni un cor fedele." The structure of this vocal piece is also based on the principle of hearing each character singly, then hearing them sing together at the end of the principal vocal sections, but the structure conforms to "sonata form with ritornellos" (as in the aria "Vieni che in pochi istanti," above): there are two ensemble sections corresponding to the two repeated sections of sonata form, but no separate B section as in dal-segno form.[22]

The only other noteworthy musical items in *Semiramide* are the march that appears in the first act and two short choruses. One might think it strange to encounter so many instrumental marches in *opere serie* of the 1760s and 1770s (generally the only independent instrumental pieces to be found in them), but a serious opera of that era would hardly be complete without one. With so many stories constructed around military struggles, they do seem appropriate at least occasionally. Their format is always very simple: compact binary structures with dotted rhythms in the melody lines and homorhythmic accompaniments.[23] Choruses were never an important element in Mysliveček's operas, and where they are found, they are almost always short and declamatory. The only obligatory chorus was the one that closed the opera. This concluding chorus (actually an ensemble for the principal characters) was intended to intensify the moral lesson learned during the course of the drama or express the joy experienced after the resolution of the dramatic conflicts.

THE OPERAS OF 1767–73

Important new possibilities for musical expression opened up for Mysliveček when he composed his second opera, *Bellerofonte* of 1767, for the Teatro San Carlo in Naples. At the San Carlo, he was able to collaborate with singers as fine as any available, among them the tenor Anton Raaff and the soprano Caterina Gabrielli, both of whom became close professional acquaintances. For the first time, Mysliveček had the chance to present to an audience a full range of aria types intended to showcase the talents of the best singers of Italian serious opera, and the results soon led to his establishment as one of the leading composers in this style. Just as the opening aria of *Semiramide* presages the restrained quality of that opera (dominated by a *cantabile* or *parlante* style), so the opening aria of *Bellerofonte*, "Splende così talora," offers a taste of the brilliance and technical virtuosity of the bravura style so much favored in Naples.

The libretto of *Bellerofonte*, originally written by Giuseppe Bonecchi in 1750 for a production at the court of St. Petersburg with music by Francesco Araya, was chosen for Mysliveček by the Neapolitan *Giunta dal canto*.[24] Although the source of the story in Greek mythology is typical of French opera (and in this respect a significant departure from the usual fare at the San Carlo), it was well suited to Italian taste of the day. The basic pretext of the drama is a tragic separation of the lovers Bellerofonte and Argene due to the hostility of Argene's father, King Ariobate. Bellerofonte is the son of the king of Corinth, but his birthright was usurped by one Clearco. Without a kingdom of his own, Bellerofonte is not deemed an appropriate candidate to marry a royal princess.

---

[22] An ensemble cast in similar format is the duet "Vi sento, oh Dio, vi sento" from part 1 of *La passione*.

[23] The march in part 2 of *Isacco figura del redentore* is a good example of this style.

[24] Appendix 1 reproduces Ulisse Prota-Giurleo's account of the genesis of this opera.

Bellerofonte proves his worthiness by slaying the monster that plagues Ariobate's kingdom with a yearly demand of the sacrifice of a noble virgin. Still, Ariobate accedes to the marriage of Argene and Bellerofonte only after an unexpected turn of events in the third act: news arrives that the usurper Clearco has been overthrown and Bellerofonte may re-claim the kingdom of Corinth. In a sidelight, the virgin Briseide, slated for sacrifice to the monster, is saved from death and finds a lover to marry in the second tier of romantic involvements.

Mysliveček's opera is basically a conservative aria-dominated work such as he specialized in writing throughout his career, but Bonecchi's libretto does contain a few traits typical of French opera, involving supernatural effects and the element of spectacle that necessitated special treatment from the composer. In particular, there is a scene at the end of the second act that depicts a storm and a battle with the monster. The intervention of the goddess Minerva is needed to inspire Bellerofonte's forces to slay it—an event that would have required machinery to showcase her appearance on the stage. This scene includes unusually elaborate accompanied recitative for one of Mysliveček's earlier operas, and even a chorus of demons. The long section of programmatic instrumental music with extensive wind solos is nearly unique among his operas.

Bellerofonte contains many memorable arias that found their way into aria collections copied throughout Europe, beginning with the first aria of the opera, "Splende così talora" from act 1, scene 2, which was composed for the castrato Ferdinando Mazzanti in the title role. This aria, distinguished by lovely chromatic coloring on the words "oscura notte" (dark night) in the opening phrase, was one of the best-known Mysliveček arias in the eighteenth century. Most of the other prominent arias in *Bellerofonte* were intended for the two leading stars of the production, Anton Raaff and Caterina Gabrielli. All three of the arias intended for Gabrielli (one for each act) were frquently copied into aria collections in the late eighteenth century: "Giusti Dei" (act 1, scene 3), "Ch'io mai capace" (act 2, scene 5), and "Palesar vorrei col pianto" (act 2, scene 11). "Ch'io mai capace" is a most affecting *cantabile* aria with *soli* for flutes and horns, but "Palesar vorrei col pianto," with its florid obbligato part for French horn, was the aria clearly designed to make the most memorable impression. Best known of the beautiful tenor arias written for Anton Raaff was "Di due pupille amabili" (act 1, scene 9), which features bassoons and *sordini* strings.

The remaining solo numbers of *Bellerofonte* invite little reason to pause here except to mention the presence of a cavatina, "Riedano gli astri amici" (act 2, scene 14), written for the character of Minerva as sung by the obscure castrato Giuseppe Benigni. Cavatinas, poems of a single stanza, were usually set in a simpler way than two-part aria texts; typically the settings were short in length, plain and direct in melodic style, and incorporated into scenes with accompanied recitative. The most usual formal structures conform to the pattern of "sonata form with ritornellos." This cavatina, like most from the 1760s, is accompanied only by strings, but there is the special attraction of *pizzicato*, doubtless introduced as a special effect appropriate for the appearance of a deity.

The magnificent duet "Vanne pur, ma dimmi pria," sung by Argene and Bellerofonte at the end of act 1, is cast in a formal structure that would soon become standard for duets in Mysliveček's work. The basis of the form is a contrast in tempos and recapitulation of dominant-key thematic material in imitation of sonata form. The concluding fast section ensures an exciting close:

	Andante 3/8	Allegro 4/4	Andante 3/8	Allegro 4/4
Section:	A	B	A	B
Keys:	I-V	V	I	I

In this plan, the voices sing separately in the A sections and together in the fast B sections. Mysliveček followed this basic design in duets throughout his earlier period of writing and sometimes used it in arias. It is also the basis of the terzetto "Barbare stelle," heard near the end of act 3 of *Bellerofonte*.

The eight remaining Mysliveček operas of the late 1760s and early 1770s do not stray significantly from the patterns laid out in *Semiramide* and *Bellerofonte*, except that none offered any opportunity for the sort of programmatic music found in the monster scene in *Bellerofonte*. The first, *Farnace*, commissioned for Naples in 1767 in the wake of the success of *Bellerofonte*, is one of the finest settings of Antonio Maria Lucchini's venerable libretto of 1724, but its music was strangely neglected in aria collections from the second half of the eighteenth century. Much more successful was *Il trionfo di Clelia*, performed in Turin during carnival in 1768. This work featured Caterina Gabrielli in her prime in addition to the aging male star Sebastiano Emiliani. Magnificent set pieces are strategically placed within the body of the work, including the aria "Tempeste il mar" at the end of act 1 for Gabrielli in the title role, with its great variety of textural configurations and imaginative evocations of the sea, and the duet "Si ti fido al tuo gran core" (act 2, scene 3), which initiated a trend in Mysliveček's duets of the late 1760s and early 1770s to introduce spectacular parallel thirds between the singers at the principal cadence points of the fast sections.

Mysliveček's return to Bohemia in 1768 interrupted his production of operas until the next year, when he was presented with fresh commissions from Venice and Florence. As his first offering for the Venetians, Mysliveček's setting of Metastasio's *Demofoonte* permitted him the opportunity to write music for another pair of notable stars, the soprano Anna Lucia de Amicis-Buonsollazzi and the alto castrato Gaetano Guadagni. *Ipermestra*, written for Florence, matched Mysliveček once again with Anton Raaff. As with the other two operas Mysliveček composed for Florence (*Motezuma* and *Adriano in Siria*), arias with wind solos that include difficult passagework in tandem with the vocalists are a specialty of *Ipermestra*. The best examples are Ipermestra's aria "Se pietà da voi non trovo" (act 1, scene 9), with oboe, and Danao's aria "Ah, di calma un solo momento" (act 2, scene 7), with horn.

The spring of 1770 saw a production of Mysliveček's *Nitteti* in Bologna that brought him into contact with Tommaso Guarducci, a distinguished castrato who soon became a close associate (see chapter 8). The quality of the music for this work is not particularly remarkable for Mysliveček, except for the terzetto "Guardami padre amato" (act 2, scene 13), which is striking for its delineation of the individual characters. The true significance of this production was its interest to the fourteen-year-old Mozart, who used it as a partial model for the first opera he composed in Italy, *Mitridate re di Ponto* (see chapter 11).

A pinnacle in Mysliveček's first period of operatic writing was reached with his operas *Motezuma* and *Il gran Tamerlano*, performed in Florence and Milan, respectively, during the carnival seasons of 1771 and 1772. Perhaps because they are preserved in copies in the Österreichische Nationalbibliothek in Vienna (that is, a major collection in close proximity to the Bohemian lands), they have been revived more frequently in modern times than any other Mysliveček operas. It is also possible that the exotic setting of *Motezuma* in sixteenth-century Mexico contributed to its attractiveness for revival.

The libretto for *Motezuma*, written by Vittorio Amedeo Cigna-Santi, was first set to music by Francesco de Majo for Turin in 1765. Set as it was around an epochal struggle between Spanish and Native American cultures, it is notable for the savage behavior of its principal characters in comparison to the usual Metastasian standards. The original production contained stunning scenic effects that were probably not realized so lavishly in Florence.[25] Still, the libretto invited opportunities for more elaborate accompanied recitative than any Mysliveček had set since *Bellerofonte*, and he rose to the occasion. *Motezuma* exemplifies a new approach to setting accompanied recitative that involved adding elaborate evocative introductions and expanding the orchestral material presented between the phrases of text. Whereas in earlier works, the vocal phrases were typically accompanied by block chords with a few dotted rhythms interspersed here and there between phrases, the short interludes inserted between phrases of text in *Motezuma* are much more sophisticated and intended to be programmatic or interpretative. The sections were planned carefully enough to create a sense of motivic unity in the accompaniment, with recurring motives cropping up throughout each segment of accompanied recitative. The lyric sweetness of several arias is striking, among them "Scherza il nocchier" (act 2, scene 11), sung by Marcello Pompili in the role of Teutile (Cortes's Indian general), and another of Teutile's arias, "Non lasci le sponde" (act 3, scene 3).

Agostino Piovene's libretto for *Il gran Tamerlano*, first produced in Milan in 1746, exploits an incident from the life of the famous Mongol khan Timur the Lame (Tamberlaine) to concoct a standardized scenario of a love match fostered by capture in battle. At the battle of Ankara in 1402, Timur succeeded in defeating and capturing the Ottoman sultan Bayazid (Baiazette), an occurrence that was considered amazing at the time. Without historical foundation, Baiazette is portrayed as being captured along with a daughter (Asteria), who falls in love with Tamerlano. The opera ends with the customary two marriages, but the love intrigues take a surprising turn. Asteria is repulsed by Tamerlano after her father's humiliating capture leads him to commit suicide. Instead of the principals marrying each other, two subsidiary characters are used to bring the element of love intrigue to its proper resolution. Outstanding musical numbers include the superb duet for Asteria and Tamerlano at the end of act 1, "Di quel amabil ciglio."

The close of Mysliveček's first period of operatic activity was marked by his first setting of *Demetrio*, one of the most popular of Metastasio's librettos, written for the inauguration of a new theater in Pavia in 1773. Many arias now preserved in eighteenth-century aria collections were composed for *Demetrio*, even though the management could afford only one outstanding singer to grace the production, Lucrezia Aguiari.[26] Finely crafted as they are, however, the *Demetrio* arias represent no great innovations in Mysliveček's approach to setting dramatic texts.

THE OPERAS OF 1773–77

Romolo ed Ersilia of 1773, produced only a few months after *Demetrio*, signaled a whole new period of dramatic writing for Mysliveček—his return to Naples in 1773 seems to have been as inspiring as his first visit there in 1766–67. Now in touch with the latest styles favored at the San Carlo, he had the opportunity to collaborate with younger star singers such as Gasparo Pacchierotti,

---

[25] A new resource for information about the Florence production of Mysliveček's *Motezuma* is Marita P. McClymonds, "The Role of Innovation and Reform in the Florentine Opera Seria Repertory 1760 to 1800," in *Music Observed: Studies in Honor of William C. Holmes*, ed. Colleen Reardon and Susan Parisi (Warren, MI: Harmonie Park Press, 2004), 282–83. New insights concerning the original production in Turin are found in Margaret Butler, "Exoticism in 18th-Century Turinese Opera: *Motezuma* in Context," in *Music in Eighteenth-Century Life: Cities, Courts, Churches*, ed. Mara E. Parker (Ann Arbor: Steglein, 2006), 105–24.

[26] For more information about this production, see Anelide Nascimbene, "Le due versioni di 'Il Demetrio' di Josef Mysliveček: Drammaturgia e prassi musicali," Thesis, University of Pavia, 1987, and "'Il Demetrio' di Josef Mysliveček" in *Gli affetti convenienti all'idee: Studi sulla musica vocale italiana*, ed. Maria Caraci Vela, et al. (Naples: Edizioni Scientifiche Italiane, 1993), 103–39.

Giusto Ferdinando Tenducci, and Antonia Bernasconi. Mysliveček's second period of operatic activity was dominated by works composed for Naples, all of them set to Metastasian texts (*Romolo ed Ersilia* of 1773, *Artaserse* of 1774, *Demofoonte* of 1775, and *Ezio* of 1775), but there was also *Atide* for Padua (1774), *Antigona* for Turin (1774), *La clemenza di Tito* for Venice (1774), *Adriano in Siria* for Florence (1776), and a second *Ezio* for Munich (1777).[27]

The music for these operas hardly represents a radical new approach, but there were some new emphases and innovations. In terms of aria form, this period is completely dominated by "sonata form with ritornellos." Dal-segno arias had been declining in numbers in Mysliveček's works for some time. The near complete dominance of dal-segno arias in *Bellerofonte* and *Semiramide* contrasts with their position of near equality with sonata-form arias in *Nitteti* (1770) and their clear minority status in *Demetrio* (1773). In the early 1770s, as they were going out of fashion, dal-segno arias came to be more and more concentrated at the start of dramas. It was the newer, more innovative forms that were generally reserved for the second and third acts of serious operas. In *Nitteti*, there are six dal-segno arias (and no sonata-form arias) in the first act, three of each type in the second act and three sonata-form arias (but no dal-segno arias) in the third act. In *Demetrio* of 1773, the dal-segno arias are concentrated almost entirely in the first act: only two appear in the second act and none in the third act. From the time of *Romolo ed Ersilia* onward, one expects no more than one dal-segno aria in a Mysliveček opera, if any at all. Once a composer began to start his operas with sonata-form amalgamations, dal-segno arias tended not to be plentiful anywhere in his work.

The abandonment of dal-segno form brought to a halt the ever-increasing length of Italian operatic arias that had been going on since the late seventeenth century. The effect of amalgamating sonata form and dal-segno form was to eliminate a formalized B section, transfer many stylistic characteristics of the B sections of dal-segno arias into development sections within the structure of a single unified movement, and abandon the repeat of all or a portion of a formalized A section. The musical region found earlier at the beginning of the second vocal section of the A section was lengthened somewhat, but in compensation the much longer B section of dal-segno form was eliminated entirely along with repeats of the later portions of the A section.

An important change in the approach to melodic style arose in this second period of operatic writing, an aspect of operatic "reform" that was clearly a response to complaints voiced in the 1760s and early 1770s about the artificial or unnatural vocal lines heard in dal-segno arias with coloratura passagework. It is true that Mysliveček's earlier *opere serie* always included arias of modest proportions with a melodic style suitable for less skilled singers, but in the mid-1770s his move towards "naturalness" and simplicity extended to a larger proportion of the arias, even those intended for the leading singers. Beginning with *Romolo ed Ersilia*, it became common for arias in Mysliveček's works to feature themes dominated by eighth notes or quarter notes with a smooth step-wise melodic contour (ex. 7.9). This newer melodic style can be contrasted to the older type of aria theme excerpted in example 7.10, which begins with a long-note triadic figure in the voice and a rhythmically animated accompaniment. Bravura arias of this type could still be found in later periods, but they were not as common.[28] The new, gracious melodies could even be incorporated into arias with extensive virtuoso passagework (ex. 7.11). As long as the principal thematic material was

[27] On the musical style of the *Ezio* of 1777, see Karl Böhmer, *W. A. Mozarts Idomeneo und die Tradition der Karnevalsopern in München*, Mainzer Studien zur Musikwissenschaft, 39 (Tutzing: Hans Schneider, 1999).

[28] Other excellent examples of this older type of bravura theme by various composers are found in Böhmer, 386.

dominated by simpler themes and the virtuosity was reserved for cadential areas, the goal to project naturalness was accomplished.

With the exception of *La clemenza di Tito*, the weakest of all of Mysliveček's operas, there is hardly an opera from his second period that does not contain at least a few outstanding set pieces. Even in *Romolo ed Ersilia* (1773), which Mysliveček had to compose in such haste that he found it necessary to fill out the work with many arias accompanied by strings only,[29] it is possible to find an exceptional ensemble such as the quartet "Deh, invitati serba" (act 2, scene 9). Compared to the operas from Mysliveček's first period, there are many more arias from the second period that comprise interesting combinations of instruments or special instrumental effects, for example arias with trumpets and clarinets in the orchestral accompaniment. Some of the most richly orchestrated arias of 1774 and 1775 include "Affanni di quest'alma" from act 1, scene 11, of *Atide* (1774), with its *soli* for cello and oboe besides the usual accompaniment of strings, two horns, and two oboes, and "Rende il mar" from act 1, scene 6, of *Antigona* (1774), with trumpets, horns, and oboes.

EXAMPLE 7.9. Mysliveček, Aria "Ah, non son io che parlo" from *Ezio* (1775), meas. 112–24 (horns, oboes tacent meas. 1–9, omitted meas. 10–11).

[29] See chapter 3 above for an explanation of the difficulties surrounding this production.

EXAMPLE 7.10. Mysliveček, Aria "A morir se mi condanna" from *Motezuma*, meas. 26–37.

EXAMPLE 7.11. Mysliveček, Aria "Ah, non son io che parlo" from *Ezio* (1775), meas. 112–24.

Mysliveček's *Demofoonte* (1775) deserves special mention as the true standout among the Neapolitan operas of the years 1773–75, including as it does an unusually large number of well-crafted arias with attractive instrumental combinations. Perhaps the most interesting one is Dircea's aria "Padre perdona, oh pene," which features *pizzicato* in the strings and an obbligato part for bassoon. Another aria of Dircea's, "Se tutti i mali miei" (act 2, scene 6), contains charming *soli* for clarinets, whereas Timante's "Prendente mi chiedo" has similar *soli* for oboes. Antonia Bernasconi, who sang Dircea in the 1775 production, obviously valued the arias Mysliveček composed for her immensely, since she brought them with her to London to use in a *Demofoonte* pastiche in 1778 (see Catalog 2).

THE OPERAS OF 1778–80

Mysliveček's last return to Naples in 1778 marks the beginning of his final period of operatic activity and a fresh absorption on his part of styles popular at the Teatro San Carlo. This last period of composition before his death encompassed only three years of activity that nonetheless saw the composition of seven new works: *Calliroe*, *L'olimpiade*, and *Demetrio* for Naples in 1778 and 1779, *La Circe* for Venice in 1779, *Armida* for Milan in 1780, and *Medonte* and *Antigono* for Rome in 1780. As a whole, the works of this last period are the most varied in musical and dramatic format and exhibit a melodic style closest to that of the mature Mozart.

In this last period of operatic writing, the dominance of Metastasio's librettos finally ended. Only three of Mysliveček's last seven operas are settings of Metastasian librettos (*L'olimpiade*, *Demetrio*, and *Antigono*). The other four (*Calliroe*, *La Circe*, *Armida*, and *Medonte*) form an interesting collection of dramas drawn from various literary sources. Two are based on Greek myths, one about the sorceress Circe, the other about a princess of Lycia named Callirrhoë. *Medonte* is a pseudo-historical tale, the title character a king of ancient Epirus. *Armida* belongs to a long tradition of operas based on Torquato Tasso's *Gerusalemme liberata*, set at the time of the Crusades. All of these exhibit traits that are atypical of Metastasian librettos, in particular, non-conventional sex roles (the sorceress Circe, the warrior female Armida) and violence. Nonetheless, all of Mysliveček's settings are essentially conservative aria-dominated works based on the usual story types about lovers destined for marriage who are kept apart until near the end of the opera. The libretto for *Armida*, a revision by Gianambrogio Migliavacca of his own libretto written for the court of Vienna in 1760, is closest in conception of all Mysliveček's operas to a Franco-Italian fusion. Alongside the usual elaborate arias, its main concession to the musical characteristics of French-influenced "reform" opera is the inclusion of many short choruses woven into the fabric of the drama, the use of minor allegorical characters, and lavish amounts of evocative accompanied recitative.

The most striking new feature of the later Mysliveček operas in terms of musical style is the prominence given to slow-fast arias and slow-fast rondò, types of vocal pieces that became very popular in Italy in the 1770s. The fundamental musical characteristic that distinguishes rondò from most vocal set pieces is an overall structure in two parts, slow-fast. As mentioned earlier, any vocal piece in serious style set to a poem of two stanzas should ordinarily be referred to as an "aria," regardless of musical structure. Slow-fast vocal pieces with texts of two stanzas may still be called "arias," but when three stanzas are present, the designation "rondò" is proper.[30]

Slow-fast vocal pieces entered Mysliveček's operas slowly and unobtrusively in the 1770s, just the way that sonata-form amalgamations had entered in the 1760s. The first one was "Figlia, ti lascio" from *Atide* (1774), but it was not until *Calliroe* (1778) that several could be expected as a

[30] For a further explanation of these distinctions and an overview of research, see Daniel E. Freeman, "Music for the Noble Amateur: Mozart's Scene and Aria 'Misera, dove son?/Ah, non son io che parlo,' K. 369," in *Mozart-Jahrbuch 2000* (Kassel: Bärenreiter, 2002), 47–71.

matter of course in every opera. Slow-fast rondò could not dominate the vocal forms of an opera in the way that dal-segno arias or sonata-form arias had done at various stages, since they could not be used to enhance any and all emotional situations. Rather, their structure demanded a text with an emotional transformation suited to the slow-fast format. Additionally, they were a specialty of male sopranos. But even though less numerous than other types, they were still the most memorable. The effect of beginning a vocal piece with tenderness or pathos and finishing it with emotional excitement can still be thrilling for audiences.

Vocal rondò, apparently the ancestors of the cavatina-cabaletta pairs in nineteenth-century Italian opera, represent a remarkable phenomenon in late eighteenth-century music in that they appeared in the 1770s as a major new category of vocal composition whose structures owed virtually nothing to sonata form. In an era when sonata form permeated almost all styles of vocal and instrumental music in Europe, the vocal rondò stands out as a major outpost of resistance. In rondò, the traditional ritornello structures of dal-segno and sonata-form arias were ignored entirely; all that was obligatory for the orchestra alone was a short introduction before the slow section and a rousing postlude after the fast vocal section. The tonal range of rondò tended to be narrower than in dal-segno arias or sonata-form arias. Expressive chromaticism could certainly be found, but the only keys that were well established with cadences were the tonic and the dominant. The melodies of rondò were generally simple and tuneful, the fast section in particular marked by short, catchy phrases incoporated into antecedent-consequent designs. Repeated deceptive cadences and a rhythmically-active accompaniment with tremolos and rushing scales helped to round out their profile for listeners. Vocal virtuosity was not essential—if the effect of technical brilliance was desired, it could come from the orchestral accompaniment. Gavotte rhythms were especially common in the fast sections, to the point where rondò were often referred to as "gavotte-rondò." The combination of accessible melodic content and stirring orchestral effects in the closing sections offers a ready explanation for the enormous appeal of these vocal numbers to contemporary audiences.

AN EXAMPLE OF A VOCAL RONDÒ: "HO PERDUTO IL MIO TESORO" FROM ANTIGONO (1780)

A good illustration of the way rondò were put together can be seen in the vocal piece "Ho perduto il mio tesoro" from *Antigono* of 1780 (act 2, scene 3), one of Mysliveček's most widely-disseminated compositions. This piece was written for the character Demetrio, a prince of Macedonia who has just had a wrenching exchange with his beloved Berenice, a princess of Egypt. Both Berenice and Demetrio find themselves captives of King Alessandro of Epirus. Alessandro, also in love with Berenice, realizes that his capture of Demetrio's father Antigono, king of Macedonia, provides a perfect means to apply pressure on Berenice to obtain her consent to marry him instead of Demetrio. Alessandro has the idea of freeing Antigono in exchange for Berenice's hand in marriage. In return for the release of his father Antigono, Demetrio abandons his attempts to marry Berenice. This means (for the time being) that Demetrio and Berenice must part. Demetrio's rondò was sung in the original production by the castrato Pietro Benedetti, a reminder that rondò started out as a high-profile vocal form written for the highest-profile voice type. According to custom, the text of three stanzas is divided so that the first two stanzas are given to the slow section, and the last stanza is given to the fast section. The intense sentiment of the first line of the third stanza ("Quante smanie, quante pene") invites the change of tempo:

Ho perduto il mio tesoro, Altra speme, oh Dio, non v'è. Di dolor, d'affanno io moro; Più non splende sol per mè.	I have lost my treasure Oh God, there is no more hope. I am dying from grief and anxiety; The sun no longer shines for me.
Bella fiamma, amato oggetto Saria dolce il nostro ardor, Ma nemico a tant'affetto, Non ci vuol contenti amor.	Bright flame, beloved one, Our love would be so sweet, But the enemy of our great affection Does not wish us to be happy.
Quante smanie, quante pene, Tu mi costi, o genitor. Nel lasciarti, o caro bene, Sento, oh Dio, mancarmi il cor.	What torment, what pain, You cause me, oh father. In leaving you, my beloved, My heart, oh God, feels faint.

A number of options were possible for the form of the slow section of slow-fast vocal pieces. In the rondò "Ho perduto il mio tesoro," it is a simple three-part ABA′ form typical when the slow section sets two stanzas of text. There is no modulation in either section; the A section and its modified repeat are entirely in the tonic, whereas the B section is entirely in the dominant. The resemblance of this structure to the French *rondeau* (a refrain alternating with a contrasting section) is probably the reason for the Italian transliteration "rondò" that came to be applied to such compositions. In the slow section of the slow-fast aria from act 2, scene 11, of *Calliroe* ("Tergi, o caro, il pianto amaro"), where only one stanza of a two-stanza text is set, the form is cast as sonata form without a development section. In this case, the entire stanza is heard first in the exposition, then heard again in its entirety in the recapitulation. When only one stanza of text is set in the slow section, there is no sense of a recurring refrain that appears after a contrasting section, thus the connection with the French *rondeau* is missing and there would be no reason to designate the piece a "rondò."

The fast section of "Ho perduto il mio tesoro" opens with a characteristic gavotte-style rhythm (ex. 7.12) that begins on beat 3 of the first measure. No key except the tonic is established with a full cadence in the fast section, although there is some chromatic coloring on words from the second stanza. The third stanza of text is always what provides the musical inspiration for the fast section, but it is common to bring back at least some of the text from the slow section in the interest of unity of expression. The simplicity of texture and charming motivic materials (especially the cadence patterns) all help to sustain musical interest. No recognized formal plan is at work. Instead, there is merely a succession of repeated phrases.

Slow-fast vocal pieces were not the only type used by Mysliveček to lend variety to the operas of his final period. Among lighter vocal fare, there are cavatinas sprinkled throughout and sometimes also French *rondeaux*, which first entered his work in *Demetrio* (1773).[31] Mysliveček showed little interest in French *rondeaux* in any genre until the late 1770s, and he generally adhered to structures

[31] See the vocal piece "Dal suo gentil sembiante" (act 2, scene 2).

Example 7.12. Mysliveček, Rondò "Ho perduto il mio tesoro" from *Antigono.* After an arrangement for voice and piano published by Filippo Trisobio in Philadelphia ca. 1796–98, meas. 83–150.

continued

Example 7.12–*continued*

EXAMPLE 7.12–*continued*

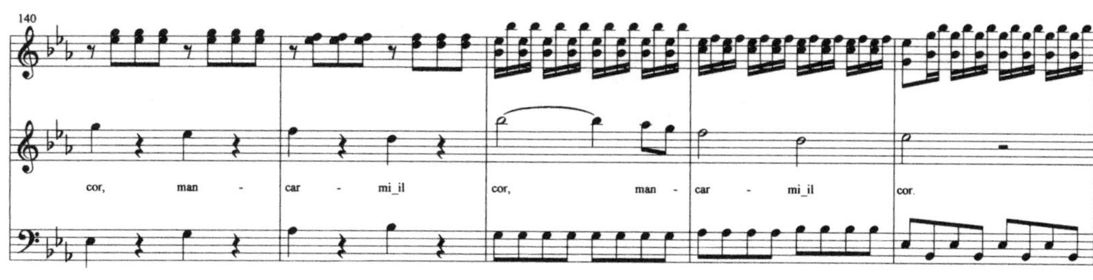

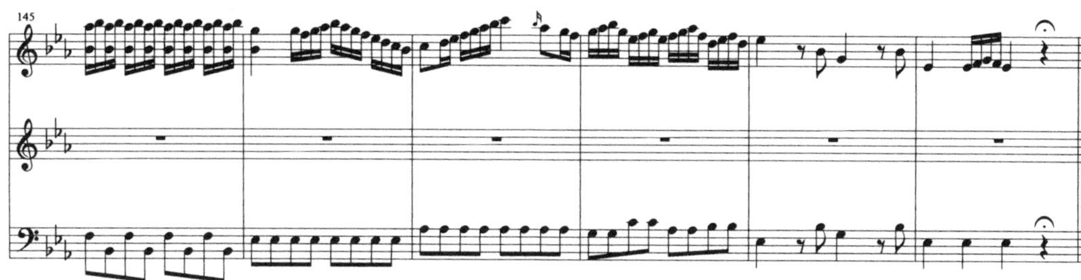

uncomplicated by the subtleties of sonata-rondo. Thus Mysliveček's *rondeaux* (and those of virtually all his contemporaries in Italy) stay close to the conception of the simple refrain form so common in eighteenth-century French vocal and instrumental music. An important part of this conception includes tuneful vocal melodies built around rigid successions of four- or eight-bar phrases (depending on the meter and tempo). The texts of *rondeaux* often consist only of two stanzas, just like arias, and may have only one contrasting section set to the second stanza of text to counter the main *rondeau* section set to the first stanza. *Rondeaux* were the only vocal set pieces in Italian with two stanzas that are not customarily designated "arias" (even though one can sometimes find the designation *aria en rondeau*). Italians could be rather careless about respecting the meanings attached to the French spelling "rondeau" and the Italian spelling "rondò." Some vocal pieces in the style of French *rondeaux* were designated "rondò" in Italy, but two-part "rondò" were never referred to as "rondeaux."

One last innovation to be mentioned in Mysliveček's later operas is a habit of inserting recitative within arias, an effective device that Mysliveček used in only a few high-profile set pieces of the late 1770s. The best example is the aria "Se cerca, se dice" from *L'olimpiade* (1778), but the aria "Tergi, o cara, il pianto amaro" and the duet "Serena quei rai" from *Calliroe* also provide excellent illustrations of the technique. The suspension of musical flow created when recitative segments are inserted into arias and duets heightens a sense of emotional intensity when the main thematic material resumes.

What direction Mysliveček may have taken had he lived even a few years longer is an interesting avenue of speculation. Considering trends in operatic culture in the 1780s, he might have found it increasingly difficult to sustain his career from serious works alone. It is questionable whether Mysliveček would have had the inclination to approach comic styles after so many years of cultivating serious works, but his proven adaptability might well have made it possible for him to renew his reputation once again along different lines. As it is, he left an impressive body of operatic vocal music that could still move listeners if only the will and means were available to revive more of it.

8

IN THE SHADOW OF *OPERA SERIA*: MYSLIVEČEK'S ORATORIOS, CANTATAS, AND MISCELLANEOUS VOCAL WORKS

In most cases, Mysliveček's non-operatic vocal compositions belong to some category of oratorio, cantata, or independent aria; in Italy of the second half of the eighteenth century there were not any other well-established vocal genres available to composers who were not involved in the production of liturgical music. Mysliveček's contributions to the repertory of serious vocal genres that flourished in the shadow of *opera seria* will form the principal focus of this chapter, but mention will be made as well of a number of vocal works outside the usual traditions of Italian serious style that are of interest for one reason or another.

ORATORIOS

The most substantial non-operatic vocal genre composed to texts in Italian was oratorio, the quintessential vehicle for sacred musical drama. Although oratorios were usually not staged, the best composers of oratorios frequently produced works that could compete with any of the finest *opere serie* for musical inspiration and dramatic power. In the hierarchy of musical genres, however, the prestige of oratorio was far lower. Stated simply, oratorio was a "weak" genre that was heavily dependent on *opera seria* for stylistic direction. Virtually every stylistic trait that can be found in Italian oratorios of the second half of the eighteenth century can be traced to secular vocal music, especially opera, whereas it is difficult to think of anything pioneered in oratorio that was commonly imitated in opera. One of the most important reasons for the low prestige of the genre was the modesty of its productions, a factor that can be attributed partly to the relative poverty of the organizations that sponsored them, principally ecclesiastical institutions and lay religious confraternities. Without the spectacle provided by sets and costumes, the same excitement that greeted new operatic works could hardly be expected. There was never an appetite in Italy for new oratorios in the way that there was always an intense appetite for new operas, and sponsoring institutions were content to rely on revivals to a much greater extent than opera theaters. As a dramatic entertainment offered to the public, oratorio was often nothing more than a substitute for opera during Lent, the performers opera singers who happened to be stranded in a town after the end of the local carnival season. Even such details as the usual number of characters (four or five instead of six) and arias (about a dozen instead of a dozen and a half) bespeak a smaller scale and lower prestige in comparison to *opera seria*.

Since successful composers of Italian opera had little incentive to compose new oratorios, either from the standpoint of income or prestige, they typically produced small numbers of them. In all, Mysliveček is known to have written just eight works over a timespan of seven years: *Tobia* (1769), *I pellegrini al sepolcro* (1770), *Giuseppe riconosciuto* (ca. 1770?), *Betulia liberata* (1771), *Adamo ed Eva* (1771), *La passione* (1773), *La liberazione d'Israel* (ca. 1773–74?), and *Isacco figura del redentore* (1776). Interestingly enough, this is exactly the same number of oratorios that survive by Mysliveček's rival Antonio Sacchini, whose talents as a composer of vocal music were so similar to his own. Among the leading operatic composers in Italy of Mysliveček's day, the only one who did write an unusually large number of oratorios was Ferdinando Bertoni, author of nearly fifty. But Bertoni was really only a "local" composer of opera whose output was confined mainly to Venice and its satellite theaters in the Venetian Republic. For his principal employment, he was associated with a sponsoring organization (the Ospedale dei Mendicanti) that would have provided him with a steady demand for new works.

All but one of Mysliveček's oratorios were originally written for performance in Padua (*Tobia*, *I pellegrini al sepolcro*, *Giuseppe riconosciuto*, and *Betulia liberata*) or Florence (*Adamo ed Eva*, *La passione*, and *Isacco*). The exception is *La liberazione d'Israel*, whose first known performance took place in Prague in 1775. As attractive as the notion of a Prague premiere would be, it is impossible to accept. The appearance of one of the arias from *La liberazione d'Israel* in a list of works copied for the household of Lord Cowper in Florence in 1774 is a strong indication that *La liberazione d'Israel* was actually written with an Italian premiere in mind.[1] The librettist specified in the Prague libretto, Giambattista Basso Bassi, is known only from a small number of dramatic works associated with Naples,[2] thus it is likely that the oratorio was first performed there. A good guess for the date of composition would be 1773 or 1774, a period when Mysliveček was mainly resident in Naples.

The preservation of music for Mysliveček's oratorios is much less complete than for the composer's operas, another reflection of the low prestige of the genre. Complete scores survive for only four of the eight oratorios (*Tobia*, *Adamo ed Eva*, *La passione*, and *Isacco*), and unlike his operatic arias, there are very few oratorio arias preserved in aria collections (see Catalog 2). A score of *Giuseppe riconosciuto* in the Cappella Antoniana in Padua is attributed to Mysliveček in a card catalog on the premises (and cited as a genuine work by Mysliveček in many secondary sources), but in actuality the music in the score is by Johann Adolph Hasse. The lack of surviving music for *Betulia liberata* is particularly regrettable, since there is a good possibility that it served as a model for Mozart's setting of the same text.

Josef Mysliveček has been widely recognized as one of the most gifted composers of Italian oratorio in the late eighteenth century, yet no detailed study of the music for his oratorios presently exists in any language. Howard Smithers's monumental study of the classic-era oratorio notes Mysliveček's importance as a composer of oratorios, but in a volume of several hundred pages, the total amount of space allotted to a discussion of his contributions amounts to five lines of text.[3]

---

[1] See the Hertfordshire Record Office, Panshanger archives, ms. D/EP AF221 for a list of music copied for Lord Cowper in 1774. The Mysliveček arias are listed in Catalog II. Among them is one with incipit "Nò, non s'annida in selva," a parody of an aria text, "Nò, non s'annida in sebra" found in the libretto for *La liberazione d'Israel* printed in Prague in 1775.

[2] See Sartori, *I libretti italiani*, appendix volume 1, 235.

[3] See Howard Smithers, *A History of the Oratorio*, vol. 3 (Chapel Hill: University of North Carolina Press, 1987), 77. A facsimile of the title page of a libretto printed for a performance of *Isacco figura del redentore* in Prague in 1778 is on page 46.

Arnold Schering's much older (and much shorter) study actually contains more.[4] At present, the best discussion of the style of Mysliveček's oratorios is found in Joyce L. Johnson's study of late eighteenth-century oratorios performed in Rome, which by necessity includes mention only of the two oratorios by Mysliveček that were actually performed there (*La passione* and *Isacco figura del redentore*).[5]

Just as it is possible to get a good idea of what to expect from a Mysliveček opera by sampling the arias from Mysliveček's first opera *Semiramide*, so it is possible to get a good idea of what to expect from a Mysliveček oratorio from his *Tobia* of 1769. The anonymous libretto of *Tobia*, set in the city of Nineveh, is based on the book of Tobit (Tobias) from the Apocrypha. Two characters in the oratorio face seemingly insoluble personal problems: Tobit (here called "Tobia padre"), who has been blinded by God, and a woman named Sara, who finds herself cursed by a demon who has successively killed all seven of her bridegrooms on their wedding day. Remedies for these afflictions are sought and prayed for by Tobit's wife, Anna, a character who is featured much more prominently in the oratorio than in the original Biblical tale. With the intervention of the angel Raphael (who appears in this work as "Azaria"), Anna is able to see her husband cured of his blindness and her son Tobias (here called "Tobia figlio") married to Sara without fear of death after the wedding ceremony. The custom of ending a dramatic work with a happy marriage thus finds an appropriate outlet in this work just as it usually does in *opera seria*.

Old Testament stories such as the one on which *Tobia* is based had been favored in oratorios since their first appearance in Italy in the seventeenth century. Whatever the original reason for this preference, it is easy to see why they fit so comfortably into a late eighteenth-century notion of oratorio as a sacred imitation of *opera seria*. Within this conception, the Christ-centered tales of the New Testament are somewhat anomalous, since the idea of there being a special divine entity among mortals is incompatible with the usual *opera seria* stories built around networks of family relationships and amorous intrigues. In *opera seria*, there is rarely a place for a deity among mortals. Sometimes a deity does appear briefly to provide a quick solution to the difficulties faced by the mortal characters (a good example is the intervention of the goddess Minerva in *Bellerofonte*), but this sort of scenario is generally found only in librettos that have French-style mythological subject matter. One would not like to see a treatment of Christ so fleeting or insignificant, yet portraying him as just another dramatic character would not seem quite appropriate either. Expressions of carnal love or conjugal love, a staple of Italian *opera seria* of the eighteenth century, would not be proper for Christ, who was viewed as celibate and ineligible for marriage. It is difficult to imagine just how family members as unusual as those in the Holy Family would interact with each other at all. Moreover, it could not have been easy to incorporate a major character who is impervious to sin or error and cannot be morally rehabilitated, since he is holy. In eighteenth-century Germany, means were found to portray Christ effectively in oratorios, but not in Italy.

Italian librettists usually found the most suitable subject matter for their oratorios in the Old Testament, which contains many stories about families whose problems could be treated in a way that is very similar to those of the anguished aristocratic families of conventional *opere serie*. The Old Testament also offered a better means to evoke the aura of "long ago and far away" that was so integral to the setting of operatic dramas. Besides *Tobia*, the stories of Mysliveček's oratorios *Giuseppe riconosciuto*, *Adamo ed Eva*, and *Isacco* are also built around family relationships drawn from Old

[4] See Arnold Schering, *Geschichte des Oratoriums* (Leipzig: Breitkopf & Härtel, 1911), 237–38.

[5] See Johnson, *Roman Oratorio, 1770–1800*, 152–55.

Testament sources, whereas *Betulia liberata* and *La liberazione d'Israel* adapt military scenarios from the Old Testament that are reminiscent of the Armida operas derived from Tasso's *Gerusalemme liberata* and other stories centered around military conquest. Significantly, the New Testament settings found in the two other Mysliveček oratorios (*La passione* and *I pellegrini al sepolcro*) entirely avoid portrayals of Christ.

The music for *Tobia* fits quite comfortably into what was described in the previous chapter as Mysliveček's first period of operatic production (lasting until 1773). The arias are completely dominated by dal-segno forms, and there is great prominence given to arias with elaborate obbligato solos for instrumentalists, just as in a number of Mysliveček operas written in the late 1760s and early 1770s. In all, there are three of them, one with obbligato cello ("Qual fumo in faccia al vento"), one with obbligato oboe ("Fra i perigli dal lungo viaggio"), and one with obbligato violin ("Ah, se ti costa tanto"). Overall the vocal virtuosity is modest and the melodies tend to be rather simple in comparison to the high-profile arias written for serious opera. This may be attributed partially to the availability of less-talented singers. None of the librettos for Mysliveček's Paduan oratorios that survive include the names of singers, a practice that was not at all unusual. Many oratorio librettos from the late eighteenth century suppress the names of the singers (whereas it had been customary to specify the names of singers in operatic librettos since about the turn of the eighteenth century). It is possible that the aura of religious worship discouraged the vanity expressed in the singer's need to have his or her efforts recorded in print, but it may also reflect a simple lack of interest in who the performers were (due to their obscurity).

Dignity, solemnity, and restraint were obviously more appropriate for sacred drama, and one notices immediately in an oratorio the prominence of arias in moderately slow or moderately fast tempos. The opening of the aria excerpted in example 1 perfectly evokes musical qualities conducive to religious expression—it is not easy to find operatic arias that include large-note suspensions such as the one found at the beginning of this aria. There is no lack of attention given to textural subtleties in *Tobia*, however, and nothing lacking from Mysliveček's fertile melodic invention. The magnificent accompanied recitative at the start of Part 2 is as expressive and responsive to the unfolding dramatic action as any he was capable of writing in the 1760s.

A few special generic features found in *Tobia* deserve mention, even aside from the lack of staging and general subject matter that are the most important defining features of oratorios. One is the overall division of the dramatic presentation into two "parts" (as opposed to the customary three "acts" of an opera) with a mechanical symmetry about the number of arias per part (usually six). Another concerns the presence of choruses—rare in the Italian operas of conservative composers such as Mysliveček, but obligatory in oratorios, especially at the end of each of the two parts. The choruses that conclude the two parts of *Tobia* are each cast in two sections (slow-fast) with contrasting meters, a model for Mysliveček's later oratorios. There are a few hints of imitation and counterpoint, but no elaborate fugues. A unique feature among all of Mysliveček's dramatic works is the substitution of a slow-fast *introduzione* for the usual three-part *sinfonia* as the overture to *Tobia*. Whether out of admiration or expediency, Mysliveček re-used this *introduzione* as the overture for his oratorio *La passione*. It is a pity that Mysliveček chose not to repeat this formal experiment in other works; the overture to *Tobia* is unquestionably one of the composer's most effective dramatic overtures.

No music survives from any of the three other oratorios Mysliveček is known to have written for Padua, and there is little reason to pause on them, except to mention some peculiarities of the

EXAMPLE 8.1. Mysliveček, Aria "Quanto vado in colmo è pieno" from *Il Tobia*, meas. 27–34.

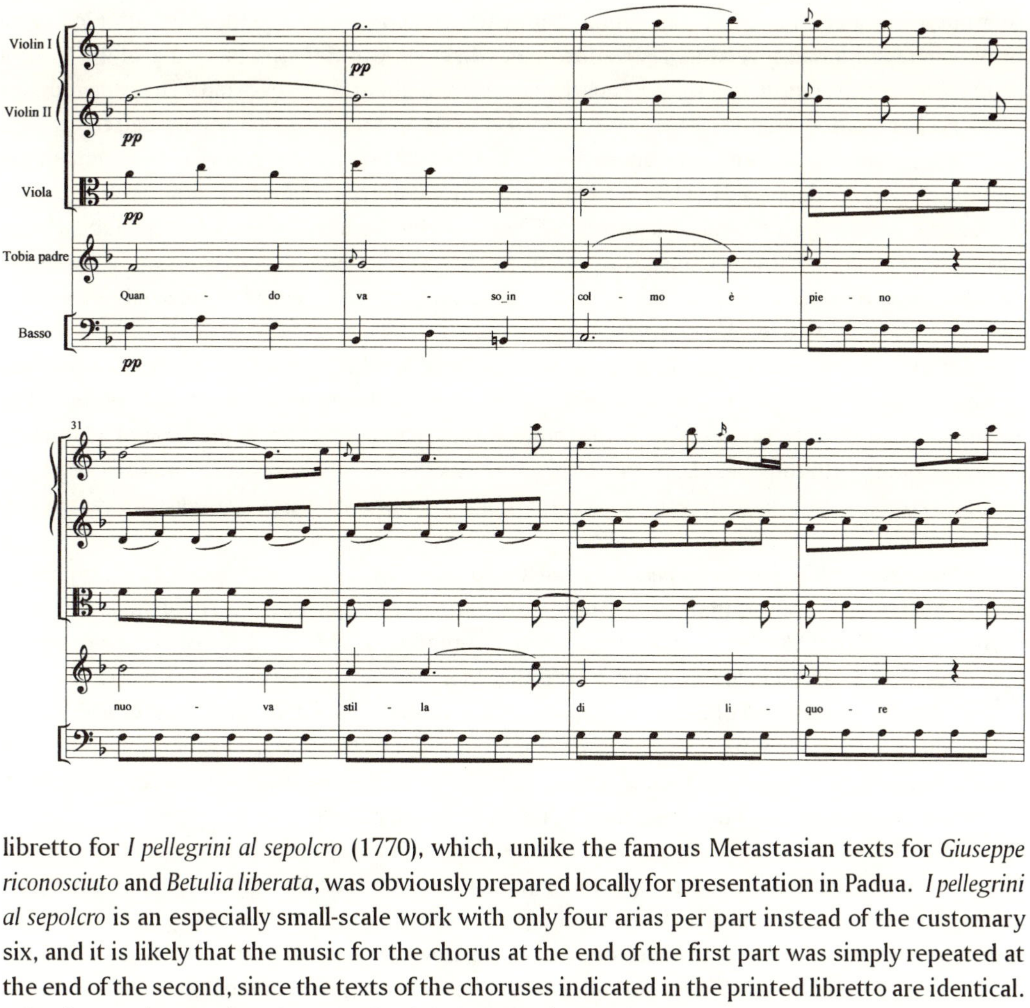

libretto for *I pellegrini al sepolcro* (1770), which, unlike the famous Metastasian texts for *Giuseppe riconosciuto* and *Betulia liberata*, was obviously prepared locally for presentation in Padua. *I pellegrini al sepolcro* is an especially small-scale work with only four arias per part instead of the customary six, and it is likely that the music for the chorus at the end of the first part was simply repeated at the end of the second, since the texts of the choruses indicated in the printed libretto are identical. What is most interesting about *I pellegrini al sepolcro* is the complete absence of female characters. In late eighteenth-century Italy, oratorios were generally the only type of sacred art music in which women were able to perform publicly, an opportunity made possible by the fact that oratorios were non-liturgical compositions often performed outside of churches (for example in theaters and oratories). Considering the preponderance of librettos based on the trials of Biblical families, female characters usually could not be excluded, but the cast of *I pellegrini al sepolcro* consists only of four male "pilgrims" who have come to Jerusalem to contemplate the passion of Christ and the "guide" who escorts them to Gethsemane. This type of scenario strongly hints that the anonymous librettist took as his point of departure Metastasio's libretto for *La passione* (see below).

Mysliveček's three Florentine oratorios (*Adamo*, *La passione*, and *Isacco*) represent a fresh era of oratorio production made possible by the availability of vocal and instrumental performers far superior to those in Padua. In Florence, Mysliveček had the opportunity to write for one of the great eighteenth-century castratos, Tommaso Guarducci, besides other distinguished singers. Guarducci was one of two prominent male sopranos (the other was Luigi Marchesi) who enjoyed decisive support from Josef Mysliveček at a vulnerable time in his career. According to Charles Burney, Guarducci intended to retire at some point, but he was forced to return to the stage after losing all of his money in a bad investment.[6] He first met Mysliveček in Bologna in spring of 1770 for a production of the composer's *Nitteti*; Guarducci was then about fifty years old. The remainder of Guarducci's recorded singing career was centered entirely around roles that Mysliveček created for him. He appeared in all three of Mysliveček's Florentine oratorios of the years 1771–76, and in the autumn of 1776, he appeared in Florence as Farnaspe in Mysliveček's *Adriano in Siria*, a role repeated in Perugia during the carnival season of 1777 as Guarducci's last known operatic appearance. Mysliveček's ability to showcase the talents of singers such as Guarducci in each of his three Florentine oratorios was rewarded with immediate and wide-ranging success; each was revived many more times than any of Mysliveček's operas.

The Florentine oratorios that survive with music from the "first period" of Mysliveček's operatic writing, *Adamo ed Eva* and *La passione*, do not exhibit a radical departure from the style of *Tobia*, but *La passione* of 1773 invites special attention since it is available for study in the form of a facsimile edition.[7] Along with the opera *Demetrio*, *La passione* was the last of Mysliveček's dramatic works to feature dal-segno arias prominently. In all, seven of the twelve arias in *La passione* are cast in dal-segno form.

Metastasio's libretto for *La passione*, first set to music by Antonio Caldara in 1730, is famous for not being a "passion" as that term is understood by most musicians (i.e., a depiction of the last sufferings of Christ). Rather, it concentrates on the reactions of four of Jesus' followers to the spectacle of his execution. In Part 1, the central character is the apostle Peter (Pietro), who is wracked with guilt over his betrayal of Jesus and reveals to the audience the details of Jesus' crucifixion by asking questions about it from three witnesses: Maddalena (=Mary Magdalene), Giovanni (=the apostle John), and Giuseppe (=Joseph of Arimethea?). In Part 2, the emphasis shifts to the expectation of Christ's resurrection and the hope this should bring for mankind.

The music for *La passione* is comparable to the best operatic music written by Mysliveček near the end of his first period of operatic composition and must be counted among the finest settings of Metastasio's libretto. Joyce L. Johnson is probably correct in assuming that Jommelli's setting of *La passione* served as a model for Mysliveček,[8] however his compositional skill far surpassed that of the older composer. The most prominent role is Giuseppe, undoubtedly sung by Guarducci,[9] who was given the most ambitious arias, "Torbido mar che freme" and "All'idea de' tuoi perigli," as well as a magnificent accompanied recitative, "Qual terribil vendetta," at the beginning of Part 2. The role of Pietro, probably sung by Giacomo Veroli (a singer employed by the grand ducal court), is also treated specially. Both of Pietro's arias, "Tu nel duol felice" and "Se la pupilla inferna," are scored with flute solo, and he was accorded his own fascinating accompanied recitative at the

[6] See *Dr. Burney's Musical Tours in Europe*, vol. 1, 198.

[7] Joyce L. Johnson, ed., *Josef Mysliveček: La passione, Italian Oratorio, 1650-1800*, vol. 23 (New York and London: Garland, 1986). The manuscript used as the basis of this edition is the one preserved in Frankfurt-am-Main, Stadt- und Universitätsbibliothek, Musik- und Theaterabteilung, Manskopfisches Museum, which Robert Münster has determined was copied in Munich by the court copyist Sixtus Hirsvogel. It is possible that a performance was intended in Munich when Mysliveček visited there in the years 1777–78. See Münster, "Die hiesige ongenierte Lebensarth gefallet allen," 247 (f. 54).

[8] See Johnson, *Italian Oratorio, 1770–1800*, 55.

[9] For the casts of Mysliveček operas and oratorios performed in Florence, see Weaver and Weaver, *A Chronology*.

beginning of Part 1, "Dove son? Dove corro?," in which the composer took every opportunity to exploit the possibilities presented in the libretto for text painting. In general, the harmonic vocabulary, orchestration, and vocal virtuosity are much more sophisticated than in *Tobia*. Still, there are rather restrained arias with suspensions and touches of imitation in the instrumental accompaniment, such as Giovanni's "Come a vista di pene si fere."

Besides the usual complement of twelve arias (six per part), *La passione* includes a duet, "Vi sento, oh Dio, vi sento," before the chorus that concludes Part 1. In secular dramatic music of this period, love duets were common at the end of the first or second acts, but they could not always be accommodated comfortably into oratorios. In *La passione*, the two characters Pietro and Maddalena are no more than casual acquaintances, but they do have something in common that makes it suitable for them to sing together: profound remorse for past mistakes (specifically Pietro's denial of Christ and Maddalena's life of prostitution). Just as in Mysliveček's operatic duets, the two first express their sentiments separately, then signal their emotional synchronization by concluding in brilliant parallel thirds.

The careful attention paid to the choral writing in *La passione* exceeds that of any other Mysliveček composition. The centerpiece is the chorus at the end of Part 1, "Di qual sangue o mortale," whose slow section is a *cantus firmus* setting with five real parts (SSATB) that represents Mysliveček's most sophisticated cultivation of the archaic *alla breve* style. There are string parts corresponding to each vocal range (including three violin parts), but the upper parts generally do not double the vocal lines. Instead, they are given their own contrapuntal lines that serve to enliven the rhythmic profile and support the harmonic structure. For a composer of Mysliveček's training and experience, it is very much a *tour de force* that makes one wonder how exceptional a composer of liturgical music he might have been if he had only had more opportunity or inclination. The chorus at the end of Part 2, "Santa speme tu sei," is in *alla breve* time throughout and calls for six parts (SSAATB). Although it is also full of interesting contrapuntal experiments, the lack of a more conventional concluding fast section leaves the overall effect somewhat less appealing than in the earlier chorus.

Mysliveček's last oratorio, *Isacco figura del redentore*, is indisputably the composer's finest, and it is possible to make the case that it was his greatest composition of all. The large number of surviving manuscripts (twelve) attests to the high regard with which it was held in the eighteenth century. Its fame has endured over the centuries in large part due to the strong endorsement it received in Mozart's account of his visit to Mysliveček's sickbed in Munich in 1777. Mozart, who referred to the work as *Abramo ed Isacco*, reported to his father that "all Munich" was talking about it.[10] *Isacco* was indeed something of a phenomenon in the late eighteenth century. It was revived at least twenty times after its first performance in Florence, and the music was considered so superior that several of the surviving manuscripts bear attribution to Haydn and Mozart, as if catalogers or copyists could not believe that music so fine could have been written by anyone else. In the 1920s, a researcher who happened to come across a copy of it even announced it as a newly-discovered masterpiece of Mozart.[11]

---

[10] See Anderson, 302–06; Bauer and Deutsch, 2, 43–46.

[11] See Felice Boghen, "Mozarts 'Isacco figura del redentore': ein unbekanntes und noch nicht herausgegebenes Oratorium," *Die Musik* 20 (1928): 491–94. At long last, a complete modern edition has appeared, although it includes music only from the corrupted Munich production of 1777: *Isacco figura del redentore*, ed. James Ackerman. See also James A. Ackerman, "*Abramo ed Isacco* by Josef

The libretto for *Isacco figura del redentore*, one of the most popular Metastasian oratorio texts, was first set to music by Luca Antonio Predieri in 1740. The story, drawn from Genesis 22, is one of the best-known parables from the Old Testament, a lesson in obedience, trust, and filial piety. The plot of the libretto is constructed around a test of faith demanded of the patriarch Abraham by God, who orders Abraham to murder his only son Isaac as a sacrifice. Abraham feels that he has no choice but to obey this heart-breaking command, but just as Abraham is about to thrust a dagger into Isaac's heart, an angel sent from God stops the sacrifice. Abraham's intent to carry out the divine command is deemed sufficient to satisfy the trial of faith. Isaac is spared, but in demonstrating his willingness to die at the behest of his father, he fulfills the epithet "figure" or "presager" of the redeemer Jesus alluded to in the title of the drama.

The appropriateness of the story of Abraham and Isaac for Metastasian dramaturgy is obvious. The moral dilemmas could not have been more attractive: love of one's son versus obedience to God, filial piety versus self-preservation. In order to make the libretto conform even more closely to *opera seria* conventions, the participation of Abraham's wife, Sarah, in the emotional conflicts was added without Biblical authority to form a customary family network. Her feelings about the impending sacrifice of her son, born to her as a miracle after decades of barrenness, are if anything even more intense than Abraham's. In imitation of the confidants attached to many characters in *opera seria*, a completely new character, Gamari, was concocted to offer Abraham emotional comfort.

Mysliveček was fortunate to have at his disposal an unusually gifted pair of singers to perform the two most prominent roles. Besides Guarducci for the title role, the tenor Valentin Adamberger, most famous for his creation of the role of Belmonte in the original production of Mozart's *Die Entführung aus dem Serail* in 1782, was available in Florence for the role of Abramo. Mysliveček took full advantage of the possibilities for incorporating instrumental soloists into individual arias made possible by the use of Lord Cowper's orchestra for the original production.[12] The results are as rich as in Mysliveček's Florentine operas; there is even an aria featuring a pair of obbligato bassoons ("Entra l'uomo, allor che nasce" for Abramo). Consistent with a date of composition during Mysliveček's "second period," most of the arias are constructed as sonata-form amalgamations.

The most beautiful and highly-developed arias in *Isacco* were written for Tommaso Guarducci: "Ah, se macchiar quest'anima," "Madre, amico, ah non piangete," and 'Sperai le sue ritorte." All three were carefully tailored to showcase the elegantly simply vocal style for which Guarducci was famed, and each one has special features intended to make it more memorable. In "Ah, se macchiar quest'anima," there is exquisitely delicate motivic material in the upper strings, whereas "Sperai le sue ritorte" features *sordini* strings. The aria "Madre, amico, ah non piangete" demonstrates a keen ability to compose an aria whose musical and emotional flow is sustained largely without a reliance on ritornellos, its tenderness enhanced by some interesting passages scored with pairs of flutes in combination with divided violas. Another outstanding vocal piece is the accompanied recitative for Abramo, "Eterno Deo," which creates enough dramatic excitement to make one regret that the oratorio would not customarily be staged.

Mysliveček (1737–81): An Italian Oratorio for the Electoral Court at Munich (1777)" (M.A. Thesis, West Chester University, 1996). A rival edition corresponding to the original Florentine production may still be in preparation: Josef Mysliveček, *Isacco figura del redentore*, ed. Giuliana Zaccagnini.

[12] The circumstances are documented in Weaver and Weaver, *A Chronollogy*, 352.

The first part of *Isacco* concludes with the brilliant terzetto "Lascia che un bacio imprima," which is constructed in a clever manner intended to highlight the conflicting loyalties of the character Sara. Sara's vocal line is the only one that is heard almost constantly throughout, sometimes alone, sometimes in combination with her husband, Abramo, sometimes in combination with her son, Isacco, sometimes singing with the both of them. In order to depict the emotional conflicts surrounding Abramo's relationship with his son, Isacco, the two never sing in pairs. Instead, Sara acts as a sort of musical intermediary by singing in tandem with her son and husband in turn to demonstrate her sympathy with both. The listener of course desires to hear the effect of all three singing simultaneously, and at certain points they do express common sentiments that make this appropriate. The impression left by the setting is intensified by the inclusion of an extra section of recitative that has the effect of helping to create a new emotional and musical momentum when the music for the terzetto resumes.

It would be reasonable to expect Mysliveček to continue to refine the sophistication of his choruses after the advances made in *La passione*, but the choruses in *Isacco* are distinguished only for the beauty of their melodic materials, not the ingenuity of their compositional technique. The lack of importance attached to them can be gauged by the way that the terzetto usurps the place of a shepherds' chorus as a means to conclude Part 1. The chorus at the end of Part 2 is a standard slow-fast chorus with beautiful motivic profiles that leaves the listener somewhat disappointed by its short-windedness, just as with so many of Mysliveček's symphonic movements.

Of the many revivals that took place of Mysliveček's *Isacco*, the most significant one was given in Munich during Lent of 1777. This production, sponsored by the electoral court of Bavaria, took place in the Salvatortheater within the grounds of the electoral palace and featured the castrato Luigi Marchesi in the title role. Judging from the account of the performance found in the Seinsheim correspondence, the role of Isacco was as well-suited for Luigi Marchesi as it had been for Tommaso Guarducci. His singing was described as "incomparable," and the subscription for the production was sold out.[13] The dominance of the role was expanded even more with the insertion of an extra aria in Part 2, "Veggo, o Dio, nel cenno espresso," a particularly affecting *rondeau* with clarinets that is a re-texting of an aria from Mysliveček's *Artaserse*, "Cara, o Dio, nel volto espresso." Both of the arias for the character Sara were substituted with re-texted arias borrowed from earlier operas.[14] There is a good possibility that the Munich version of *Isacco* was staged. The oratorio was performed in a theater, of course, and the omission of the shepherds' chorus in the original provides another clue. The final chorus, "Tanti secoli innanzi," could have been sung as an ensemble by the cast members in imitation of the choruses that conclude serious operas. This means that a separate chorus would not need to have been engaged for the production if the shepherds' chorus were omitted.

As documented by Joyce L. Johnson, Mysliveček's *Isacco* was a favorite oratorio at the church of Santa Maria in Vallicella in Rome during the 1780s and early 1790s, particulary on St. Cecilia's Day (22 November). A manuscript preserved in the archive of the oratorio of San Filippo Neri in Rome contains further additions to the work that may well have been made by Mysliveček during the last months of his life. According to Johnson, these additions include an extra quintet and

[13] See chapter 4 above.

[14] The new version of "Che ne' tormenti istessi" is a re-texting of the aria "Lascia mi adesso in pace" from act 1, scene 6, of *Atide* of 1774; the new version of "Sian are i nostri petti" is a re-texting of the aria "Nel mar di tanti affanni" from act 1, scene 4, of *Motezuma*.

chorus and a recitative and aria in rondò style. The introduction of the latter was obviously intended to modernize the work and bring it into closer alignment with the style of the operas of Mysliveček's last period of writing.

CANTATAS

Mysliveček was the author of many secular cantatas in Italian for voices and instruments, but almost no music survives for them (see Catalog 2). The quintessential vehicle for chamber vocal music, cantatas were characterized by a limited cast size (sometimes only a single singer), limited orchestral resources, and modest length. Cantatas in Mysliveček's day tended to be laudatory and "occasional," made to order for special court or civic events. The basic musical building blocks were the same as in opera or oratorio—series of sections in recitative alternating with arias—and there would generally be only a handful of each at most. Allegorical or pastoral themes were favored if the cantata was large-scale enough to admit some semblance of a dramatic scenario. In the hierarchy of musical genres, cantatas ranked even lower than oratorios. Their occasional nature meant that there was little potential for revival and little incentive to save their music, a partial explanation for the scanty preservation of cantata music in Mysliveček's case.

The only substantial cantatas by Josef Mysliveček that still survive with all of their music are two preserved in manuscripts in the České Muzeum Hudby in Prague: the "dramatic" cantata *Il Parnaso confuso* and an untitled work with the characters Alceste and Fileno. The manuscripts for both originate from the eighteenth-century music collection of the Cistercian abbey of Osek in northwest Bohemia. In these sources, *Il Parnaso confuso* is identified as a *Cantata a quattro*, the cantata of Alceste and Fileno as a *Cantata a due*.

The cantata of Alceste and Fileno is dedicated on its title page of the single surviving score to Desiderius Andres, abbot of Osek from 1757 until his death in 1770, "da rappresentarsi festeggiandosi il glorioso giorno della sua Elezzione" ("to be performed in celebration of the glorious day of his election"). Unfortunately, this phrase was interpreted by the Czech scholar Vít Zdrálek to mean that it was performed for Andres's installation in 1757.[15] Clearly the phrase is meant to indicate that it was performed for an anniversary of Andres's election (probably in 1768) in the same way that the phrase "per festeggiare il felicissimo giorno natalizio" ("to celebrate the most happy birthday") was used in librettos for cantatas composed in honor of the birthdays of the rulers of Naples, not their actual births.

Zdrálek thought that the cantata of Alceste and Fileno might be Mysliveček's earliest composition, since he believed it was written in 1757. If the cantata were written in 1757, this would mean that the abbey of Osek went to the trouble and expense of performing a new secular work in Italian written by a twenty-year-old apprentice miller who had no training in composition, a scenario that is impossible to fathom. There can be little question that the cantata of Alceste and Fileno was composed in Italy and brought to Bohemia by Mysliveček at the end of the year 1767 or early in 1768 at the same time as the cantata *Il Parnaso confuso* and the operas *Semiramide*, *Bellerofonte*,

[15] See Vít Zdrálek, "Kantata *Alceste e Fileno*. Nejstarší známé dílo Josefa Myslivečka?" (The Cantata *Alceste e Fileno*: The Earliest Known Composition of Josef Mysliveček?), *Hudební věda* 42 (2005): 137–52.

Farnace, and *Il trionfo di Clelia*. The music for *Il Parnaso confuso* and the cantata of Alceste and Fileno then made its way to Osek, probably as a means to curry favor with the abbot. The overture, arias, and a cavatina all contain sonata-form structures and melodic types that did not exist anywhere in Europe in 1757.

The true occasions for which *Il Parnaso confuso* and the cantata of Alceste and Fileno were originally written are entirely unknown, and it is possible that they were merely intended to offer Mysliveček some experience in operatic style before trying to tackle a full-length staged work. Since its text was written by Pietro Metastasio in Vienna late in 1764, *Il Parnaso confuso* was almost certainly composed between 1765 and 1767. It consists of nothing more than six arias, a duet, and a concluding chorus with recitatives interspersed. Since half of the arias are cast in strict da-capo form (which Mysliveček gradually abandoned before rejecting it completely after 1767), it was probably written closer to 1765. The use of dal-segno arias and a cavatina in the cantata of Alceste and Fileno is an indication that it was composed a bit later than *Il Parnaso confuso*, perhaps in 1767. The arias in general are rather flat and conventional, even though they do show some experimentation with chromatisicm that was typical of eighteenth-century vocal chamber music. In a performance context in which listeners had the opportunity to savor the music at their leisure and discuss the compositional techniques they had just heard (as was frequent in the Italian "academies"), composers could exploit the possibilities for small-scale subtleties.

The cantatas written for the royal family of Naples were sung by some of the greatest singers of the 1760s and 1770s, in fact the same stars engaged by the Teatro San Carlo to perform in the operas that were presented to celebrate the birthdays of the same individuals. With the exception of a single scene from a birthday cantata of 1775 (see Catalog 2), no music survives to judge their merits. They probably did contain at least some excellent music in serious operatic style, thus their loss is as regrettable as the loss of music for the operas *Circe* and *Antigono* and the oratorios *Giuseppe riconosciuto* and *Betulia liberata*.

MISCELLANEOUS VOCAL COMPOSITIONS

The remaining vocal works attributed to Josef Mysliveček form a bewildering miscellany of dramatic works, secular arias, and liturgical compositions. Many are difficult to accept as authentic, but some examples are of interest from the standpoint of genre history or musical quality. In the case of dramatic music, for example, it has recently come to light that Mysliveček was one of the earliest composers of German melodrama. A manuscript preserved in the Fürstlich Fürstenburgische Hofbibliothek in Donaueschingen contains excerpts arranged for keyboard of a melodrama entitled *Theodorich und Elisa*. In this case, there exists an excellent study by Manfred Schuler demonstrating the likely origins of the work in Munich in the years 1777–78 and its relationship to melodramas by other composers of Mysliveček's day.[16] The remaining dramatic works attributed to Mysliveček are curiosities, and in the absence of any surviving music, it is difficult to imagine what the style of the music was like. Specifically, there was a play *Elfrida* performed in Florence in 1774 with Mysliveček

[16] See Manfred Schuler, "Theodorich und Elisa: ein bislang unbekanntes Melodrama von Mysliveček," in *Untersuchungen zu Muzikbeziehungen*, 233–43.

duets inserted, and even more strangely, a "children's operetta" performed in Prague in 1777 under the title *Das ausgerechnete Glück* (see Catalog 2). The authenticity of the latter is obviously highly dubious.

The vast majority of the arias and vocal pieces with sacred words attributed to Josef Mysliveček take the form of re-textings of operatic arias. Those that bear conflicting attributions to composers such as Antonio Boroni or Jan Antonín Koželuh are probably not authentic, but firm conclusions about the other vocal compositions with no known origins in dramatic works are not easy to make. It is tantalizing to imagine Mysliveček the author of four masses, two Requiems, and a great number of sacred arias and ensembles,[17] but only a few liturgical compositions may be considered indisputably genuine works. Most are preserved in locations that Mysliveček never visited.

The most securely attributable liturgical work is the only one preserved in any Italian archive: the antiphon "Veni sponsa Christi," written as a test composition for admission to the Accademia Filarmonica di Bologna. Two other works preserved in Bavarian archives are also likely to be authentic. One is the *Litaniae Laurentanae* found in the Bayerische Staatsbibliothek in Munich, a multi-partite composition for chorus with soloists that is very similar in conception to the settings of the same texts by Wolfgang and Leopold Mozart. The other, a *Laudate Dominum* setting for chorus and orchestra, is preserved among manuscripts from the parish church in the Bavarian town of Weyarn in a collection that contains many works of Mysliveček.[18] In form, the *Laudate Dominum* is cast in a manner very similar to arias set as "sonata form with ritornellos," the most usual format found in Mysliveček's opera *Ezio*, which was performed in Munich in 1777. The melodic style of this composition is compatible with what is seen in Mysliveček's operatic music of the same period.

The remaining liturgical compositions attributed to Mysliveček are preserved only in central European archives. It is easily imaginable that Mysliveček wrote compositions in sacred style during the years of his training in Prague, but it is not possible to assert that any of the sacred compositions now preserved in Bohemia are products of this earlier period of composition. One that has recently found its way into a modern edition is a *Salve Regina* preserved in the University Library of the National Library of the Czech Republic in Prague.[19] This work is scored with an unusual three-part chorus (SAB) plus soloists. The setting is small-scale, consisting mainly of a series of musical phrases arranged as responsorial exchanges. It is certainly a composition worthy of Mysliveček, but its format is so unusual that there is nothing securely attributable to help authenticate it.

Only a few secular vocal pieces attributed to Mysliveček cannot be traced to dramatic works, the ones most frequently performed his three *duetti notturni*. The *notturni* were the first Mysliveček compositions to be published in modern edition, and they are still well known in the Czech Republic. In the unique source in the České Muzeum Hudby in Prague, the three *duetti* are numbered 2, 3 and 5, an indication that they were once part of an original group of six; the preservation of groups of *duetti notturni* in multiples of six is a characteristic documented by Harrison Wignall in his recent

[17] See Catalog 2 for listings of sacred arias and ensembles without any known origins in dramatic music that are preserved in various archives in Austria, Switzerland, the Czech Republic, Germany, and Hungary. Masses attributed to Mysliveček are preserved in the Matica Slovenská in Martin (Slovak Republic) and the library of the Franziskanerkloster in Miltenberg-am-Main. There is also a Sanctus/Benedictus/Agnus Dei setting in the Vlastivědné Muzeum in Jindřichův Hradec (Czech Republic) and requiems attributed to Mysliveček in the Okresní Archiv in Cheb (Czech Republic) and the Herzogliches Archiv in Tegernsee.

[18] A modern edition is available: Josef Mysliveček, *Laudate Dominum: Offertorium pro omni tempore*, ed. Friedrich Hägele (St. Augustin: J. Butz, 1997).

[19] Josef Mysliveček, *Salve Regina*, ed. Friedrich Hägele (St. Augustin: J. Butz, 2000).

study of this genre.[20] Mysliveček's *notturni*, scored with strings and winds, are more grandly conceived than those by most composers known to have written them. Customarily, *duetti notturni* were accompanied only by an instrumental bass. Otherwise, his contributions are rather conventional. The two vocalists sing in parallel thirds in moderate tempo, and there is an easy grace about them perfectly suited to the "nocturnal" nature of the genre.

Examples of Italian arias untraceable to dramatic works are preserved in archives both in Italy and the north,[21] but it is not possible at present to confirm the authenticity of any of these vocal pieces with much certainty. A more fruitful avenue of inquiry can be pursued concerning the origins of the aria "Il caro mio bene," the best-known of all Mysliveček's compositions in the form of the arrangement for voice and piano possibly prepared by Mozart with the text "Ridente la calma," K152/210a, which earlier research assumed was originally composed as an independent aria with orchestral accompaniment, but actually appears to have originated from the opera *Armida* of 1780.

The aria "Il caro mio bene" survives in five manuscript sources as an independent vocal piece.[22] None of these manuscripts identifies it an an excerpt from *Armida*, but it does appear as an aria for act 3, scene 1, in the score of the opera preserved in the Ajuda Palace in Lisbon, the only complete score presently known to exist. The only other score is an incomplete collection of vocal numbers preserved in the music department of the Bibliothèque Nationale de France. The aria "Il caro mio bene" is nowhere to be found in the Paris score, nor is any other aria specified for the place it occupies in act 3. Oddly enough, the surviving librettos from the Milan production of *Armida* in 1780 do not yield the same reading for the text of the aria as that found in the Lisbon manuscript. Rather, they contain two versions of a text with the incipit "Per me, lontano dal caro oggetto" in the corresponding scene.[23] The poetic structure of the text "Per me, lontano dal caro oggetto" would be suitable for use with the music found in the Lisbon score for "Il caro mio bene."

Speculation that "Il caro mio bene" was written earlier than the opera *Armida* was fueled by Georges de Saint-Foix's discovery of its placement in a manuscript in the Bibliothèque Nationale in Paris among Mysliveček arias written in the early and mid-1770s.[24] Saint-Foix failed to emphasize, however, that "Il caro mio bene" is not interspersed among the earlier arias. Rather, it appears last, and it is copied on a paper type and in a different hand from the arias that precede it. There is no particular reason to believe that its presence in this manuscript constitutes evidence of a date of

[20] See Harrison James Wignall, "Mozart and the 'Duetto Notturno' Tradition," in *Mozart-Jahrbuch 1993* (Salzburg: Internationale Stiftung Mozarteum, 1993), 145–61.

[21] As documented in Catalog II, northern archives that preserve secular arias and ensembles without known origins in dramatic music includ the music archive of the Zisterzienserstift in Stams, the music department of the Österreichische Nationalbibliothek in Vienna, the music library of Kloster Einsiedeln, the music department of the Bayerische Staatsbibliothek in Munich, and the Sibelius Museum in Turku (Åbo). In Italy, there are unidentified arias in the Seminario Arcivescovile in Lucca and the Naples Conservatory.

[22] Copies are preserved in the České Muzeum Hudby in Prague, the music library of the Bibliothek der Hansestadt Lübeck, the music department of the Bibliothèque Nationale de France in Paris, the Monumento Nazionale di Montecassino and the library of the Conservatorio di Musica Benedetto Marcello in Venice.

[23] In one version of the text (preserved in the exemplar in the music department of the Library of Congress, among other archives), the text reads "Per me, lontano dal caro oggetto, il colle, il piano piacer non ha. Non dà diletto la verde sponda: ogn'aura, ogn'onda penar mi fa." In another version (preserved in the exemplar in the Fondazione Giorgio Cini in Venice, among other archives), the first lines of the second half of the aria read "Di quella sponda l'ameno aspetto."

[24] See Georges de Saint-Foix, "Mozart, d'après Mysliweczek," *Musique* 2 (1929): 840–43. The manuscript is D. 8205 of the music department of the Bibliothèque Nationale in Paris. It also includes arias from *Motezuma* (1771), *Demetrio* (1773), *Romolo ed Ersilia* (1773), *Artaserse* (1774), and *Atide* (1774). For further discussion of this question, see Marius Flothuis, "Ridente la calma – Mozart oder Mysliveček?," in *Mozart-Jahrbuch 1971/72* (Salzburg: Internationale Stiftung Mozarteum, 1973), 241–43.

composition consistent with the other arias. It is true that the aria is cast in an archaic dal-segno structure not ordinary in Italian opera since the early 1760s, but it would have been as old-fashioned in the mid-1770s as it was in 1780. As an independent aria unassociated with any dramatic work, it is difficult to see how it could have been so widely disseminated. No Mysliveček aria unattached to a dramatic work is known to be preserved in any more than one manuscript source.

The precise nature of Mozart's association with the arrangement "Ridente la calma" is unclear. All that is known is that his wife Constanze inherited the manuscript at the time of his death and included it with a group of manuscripts sold in 1799 to the Leipzig publisher Breitkopf & Härtel.[25] It is not even certain that Constanze herself believed it to be an arrangement that originated from her husband—it is possible that she merely tried to pass it off as such. The origins of the new text is utterly obscure. If the arrangement really is by Mozart, a clue to its dating has been suggested to the present author by Christian Moritz-Bauer. There are two songs in German written by Mozart in Munich during the winter of 1780–81 that match the structure and performing resources of the "Ridente la calma" arrangement remarkably well: "Die Zufriedenheit," K349/367a, and "Komm, liebe Zither, komm," K351/367b. Each is cast in dal-segno form in the manner of "Ridente la calma" with the same type of ritornello structure. The only important difference in conception is the use in these songs of mandolin as accompanying instrument instead of piano (although the first one is also preserved in a version with piano). The theory that "Ridente la calma" also originated in the winter of 1780–81 has much in its favor. The time frame falls after the *Armida* performance and before the time when Mozart began to catalog his musical compositions himself in 1784 (the arrangement appears nowhere in his catalog). The original aria would have been fresh and attractive in Munich during the winter of 1780–81, and there is evidence that Mozart was interested in Mysliveček's work at the time.[26] The surreptitious means by which the music for "Il caro mio bene" has come to the attention of music lovers seems apt for the elusive Mysliveček.

---

[25] See Hermann Abert, "Konstanze Mozarts Briefe an Breitkopf und Härtel in Leipzig," in *Mozart-Jahrbuch* 3 (Würzburg: Arnulf Liebing, 1929), 163.

[26] See Freeman, "Music for the Noble Amateur."

9

THE GRAND INSTRUMENTAL STYLE: SYMPHONIES, OVERTURES, AND CONCERTOS

The approximate counterpart of Italian *opera seria* in instrumental music of the 1760s and 1770s was the symphony, identified as it was with the grandest public settings and largest performing ensembles of any genre of instrumental music. For a composer of Mysliveček's outlook and ambitions, it was only natural to concentrate heavily on symphonic works, and the results are impressive. He was undoubtedly one of the finest symphonists of his day, and among his contemporaries in Italy, he was unsurpassed. Mysliveček's symphonies are full of drama, lyricism, and inventive musical ideas, their only major drawback a certain short-windedness in comparison to better-known repertory by Haydn and Mozart. As representatives of the late eighteenth-century symphony, they tend to come off as charming miniatures—not a single Mysliveček symphony takes longer than about ten minutes to perform.

The precise number of Mysliveček symphonies cannot be tabulated definitively due to difficulties related to attribution and genre definition. The conflicting attributions that plague sources of eighteenth-century symphonies are not as troublesome for Mysliveček as they are for some composers, but they do make for a few vexing problems, particularly in cases where a work is ascribed both to Mysliveček and Carl Ditters von Dittersdorf (see Catalog 1). Also frustrating is the question of whether some pieces for string ensemble are best considered symphonies or chamber music, an issue that arises for about two dozen works in three parts, four parts, and five parts. The flexibility in performance practice that was the delight of musicians and audiences in the eighteenth century makes many compositions difficult to categorize for the modern bibliographer. Additionally, a distinction between symphonies and dramatic overtures could be rather artificial in the 1760s and 1770s. In Italy, symphonies and dramatic overtures were usually more or less the same thing: orchestral works in three movements (fast-slow-fast) with all movements generally cast in binary form or sonata form, the last one a rollicking finale in 3/8 or 2/4 time.[1] Mysliveček shared his fondness for three-movement symphonies with J. C. Bach.[2] Together with Boccherini and Mozart, they wrote the finest three-movement symphonies in Europe during the 1770s.

---

[1] One Italian composer of Mysliveček's day (albeit an expatriate working in Spain) who made a careful distinction between three-movement "overtures" and four-movement "symphonies" was Gaetano Brunetti. See Barry S. Brook, ed., *The Symphony, 1720–1840*, Series A (Italy), 5 (New York and London: Garland, 1979).

[2] Unlike J. C. Bach and Josef Mysliveček, the Bohemian composer Florian Leopold Gassmann, who studied in northern Italy just as they did, abandoned three-movement symphonies when he returned north. After moving to Vienna in 1763 he gradually switched over to four-movement formats consistent with the prevailing tastes there.

As can be seen from Catalog 1, there are in all sixty-two symphonies without any verifiable origins in dramatic music that bear attribution to Mysliveček in eighteenth-century and later sources. Of the ten symphonies given conflicting attributions in manuscript sources, four are clearly spurious. Nine additional symphonies are lost.[3] One Mysliveček symphony cited in a late nineteenth-century catalog may or may not be concordant with one of the symphonies or overtures that is extant.[4] Five Mysliveček symphonies for strings in four parts are preserved in sources that identify them as string quartets, whereas one print of string quintets and two prints of string trios indicate that their contents could be performed as string symphonies.[5] Discounting music written for string ensembles without winds, Mysliveček was the author of nearly fifty symphonies written over a period of eighteen years and must be acknowledged as one of the most prolific symphonists of the eighteenth century. The core repertory is formed by three sets of six symphonies distributed over the length of his musical career: an Op. 1 set published by Haffner in Nuremberg ca. 1763, a set without opus number published by Napier in London ca. 1772, and a group of six preserved along with four dramatic overtures in a Bavarian manuscript collection bearing the date 1778. All but two of the Mysliveček symphonies preserved without conflicting attributions are cast in three movements (fast-slow-fast).[6]

As concerns Mysliveček's dramatic overtures, manuscripts survive for twenty-nine overtures that provided introductions for thirty different dramatic works. The discrepancy in number derives from the existence of two different overtures for the opera *Armida*, the re-use of the overture for the opera *Antigona* in the opera *Atide*, and the re-use of the overture for the oratorio *Tobia* in the oratorio *La passione*. No scores with overtures survive for the operas *Circe* (1779) and *Antigono* (1780), however there is a good possibility that their overtures are extant among the symphony manuscripts at hand, one of them perhaps a symphony now in the Biblioteca Comunale in Rovereto.[7] Almost all of Mysliveček's dramatic overtures were disseminated in manuscript or printed sources as independent symphonies.

EARLY SYMPHONIES TO 1763

Symphonies are the earliest compositions by Mysliveček known to survive. A specific reference to his early activity as a symphonist comes from Pelcl, who asserted that Mysliveček completed a set of six symphonies within six months of study with Josef Seger (see Appendix 1). Presumably

---

[3] The lost symphonies are three listed in a 1771 catalog from the Vorau Monastery in Austria (Symphonies 23–25) and six listed in the Breitkopf catalog of 1776/77 (Symphonies 36–41).

[4] Georg Thouret, *Katalog der Musiksammlung der königlichen Hausbibliothek im Schlosse zu Berlin* (Leipzig, 1895), no. 3200.

[5] Those for four-part string orchestra are Symphonies 14 and 32–35. The print of six string quintets brought out by Venier in Paris and Castaud in Lyon ca. 1767 specifies performance either as symphonies or chamber works, as does the print of six string trios issued by Chevardière in Paris ca. 1768. A set of six string trios published by Welcker in London in 1772 does not leave open the option of chamber performance; they are referred to only as "orchestra trios." Unlike Symphonies 14 and 32–35, Symphony 54 is scored for strings only, but does not survive in any sources that specify the possibility of chamber performance.

[6] Symphonies 50–51 conform to the standard northern format of four movements with a third-movement minuet, Symphony 50 with solo passages in the manner of a *sinfonie concertante*. The exceptional character of these symphonies invites doubts about their authenticity, but they have been listed among Mysliveček's authentic symphonies in Catalog 1 since they are included among manuscripts from the Waldstein estate of Doksy, the largest single source of Mysliveček's symphonies, and no existing sources attribute their music to any other composer.

[7] See Rovereto, Bibliotea Comunale, Ms. S M 1550, dated 1780 (Symphony 48). It is paired with a copy of the overture to *Antigona*, Ms. S M 1551, also dated 1780.

they were written in the early 1760s, perhaps in 1762, as explained in chapter 1. According to Pelcl, the symphonies were published anonymously in Prague, and each was supposed to evoke one of the first six months of the year. No Mysliveček symphonies that bear indications of months have ever been located, but the symphonies in question might actually be identical to the set of six published ca. 1763 by Haffner in Nuremberg as Mysliveček's Op. 1.[8]

Seven symphonies can be dated securely to Mysliveček's early period of activity in Prague, six of them in the Haffner set, the remaining one a symphony in C major dated 1762 from the Waldstein estate of Doksy (Symphony 1). The question of what sorts of symphonies provided models for these early works is not easy to answer. In the early 1760s, Prague was not an important center for the composition or performance of symphonies. Neither of Mysliveček's teachers, Josef Seger and Franz Habermann, is known to have written any at all, but some evidence of the syles then favored in Prague can be gleaned from an examination of symphonies by the Prague composers Antonín Laube, Antonín Kammel, František Xaver Brixi, and Josef Bárta,[9] all of whom cultivated the same type of three-movement Italianate symphony that Mysliveček did.

The most important stylistic models for these composers were probably the Italian *sinfonie* heard as part of the revival of Italian *opera seria* in Prague in the 1760s and independent symphonies by Italians and northerners with an affinity for Italian style. Strangely enough, the works of the Bohemian émigrés active in Mannheim, chief among them Johann Stamitz (Stamic), seem not to have been greatly influential for Mysliveček or his contemporaries in Prague.[10] The one truly momentous Mannheim stylistic trait—a standardization of the four-movement format with a third-movement minuet—was almost completely ignored by this group of composers, and there are only hints of the extravagant Mannheim orchestral effects ("rockets," crescendos, etc.) in the construction of certain passages. A more restrained and more gracious Italianate style was favored in Prague in the 1760s and 1770s, a style probably better suited to the calibre of the performers available there at that time. Mysliveček's particular contribution to a "Prague school" of symphonic writing was the attention he paid to slow movements, which are far more developed and emotionally powerful than those by his contemporaries in Bohemia. It seems likely that Mysliveček became a model for composers in Prague after he established himself in Italy. A symphony by Josef Bárta, for example, is based on Mysliveček's overture to *Bellerofonte*, which was performed in Prague in 1768.[11]

In comparison to the Mysliveček's later symphonies, the symphonies published by Johann Ulrich Haffner as Mysliveček's Op. 1 can be disappointing, since they lack melodic materials as distinctive

---

[8] The original print bears no date, but is unequivocally dated 1763 in a list of Mysliveček works published in Johann Nicolaus Forkel, *Musikalischer Almanach für Deutschland auf das Jahr 1783* (Hamburg, 1782; reprint, Hildesheim and New York: Georg Olms, 1974), 53.

[9] See Barry S. Brook, ed., *The Symphony, 1720-1840*, Series B (Austria, Bohemia, Slokavia, & Hungary), vols. 12 and 13 (New York and London: Garland, 1984). The symphonies of Antonín Kammel are closest in conception to those of Mysliveček, who likely knew Kammel as a student at Charles-Ferdinand University in the early 1750s. Kammel was also associated with Count Vincenz von Waldstein, who offered him financial support to study in Italy and live in England. According to the title page of the *Six Overtures in Eight Parts* published in London by Welcker in 1773, Kammel chose the selections, one of them a symphony by Mysliveček (see Catalog 1). Compositions by Kammel are advertised for sale on the title pages of this and two other Welcker publications of Mysliveček's music: the six "orchestra trios" ca. 1772 and a reprint of the Op. 3 string quartets ca. 1780.

[10] This conclusion is shared in Rudolf Pečman, "Die Mannheimer Schule und Josef Mysliveček," in *Untersuchungen zu Muzikbeziehungen zwischen Mannheim, Böhmen und Mähren im späten 18. und frühen 19. Jahrhundert*, ed. Christine Heyter-Rauland and Christoph-Hellmut Mahling (Mainz: Schott, 1993), 75–83.

[11] See the catalog of Bárta's symphonies on p. xxxvii of vol. 13 of the Brook collection cited in note 9 and example 9.10.

as those he was able to produce after his move to Italy. Most of the principal themes in the Haffner set are "figural"—i.e., based on the elaboration of simple arpeggiations or scale patterns. The only exceptional work is the G minor symphony (Symphony 6), Mysliveček's only minor-key symphony, which may be counted among the finest symphonies written by any composer during the 1760s. Listeners familiar with Haydn's minor-key symphonies of the 1760s will recognize a stylistic affinity.

The Haffner symphonies leave the impression of being crafted carefully to demonstrate a comprehensive mastery of symphonic technique as it existed in the early 1760s. Indeed, they exhibit something of a compendium of the stock gestures employed by composers of that era to delight and startle audiences, among them sweeping scales or arpeggiations over several octaves (ex. 9.1), driving syncopations (ex. 9.2), figures in staccato eighth notes (ex. 9.3), and shimmering tremolos in the upper strings that could appear either in the melody line (ex. 9.4) or as the accompaniment for a melody in the lower parts (ex. 9.5). Mysliveček repeatedly used variations on these sorts of figures to help spin out material for his symphonic works. It is scarcely an exaggeration to view most symphonic composition of the 1760s in the same terms; few composers other than Haydn had the imagination to produce anything truly unique or profound.

The treatment of winds in Mysliveček's early symphonies is generally conventional for its time. The standard instrumentation of the 1760s was strings plus horns and oboes, just as for operatic arias. The oboes and horns were mainly present to augment the orchestral sonorities, not to present important thematic material on their own. Horns typically added harmonic support at key structural points and reinforced *forte* dynamics. Oboes could do the same, but in addition they could double the violins at certain places where greater tonal brilliance was desired. In slow movements, with their emphasis on lyricism, wind instruments were often omitted, especially the horns. The title page of the Haffner print curiously labels the horn and oboe parts *ad libitum*, even though a number of movements, in particular the fast movements of Op. 1, nos. 3 and 5, contain wind *soli* far more interesting and extensive than those usually encountered in symphonies from this period.

In terms of form, what one would expect from the work of almost any symphonist of the early 1760s is a haphazard mix of rounded and rhyming binary schemes. In the Op. 1 symphonies, rounded and rhyming forms are encountered both with and without repeat signs in roughly equal numbers. Alongside the rather archaic forms found in Op. 1, no. 1, which exhibit no strongly articulated sense of thematic function, there are movements such as the first movement of Op. 1, no. 3, which could provide a textbook example of sonata form. Techniques of recapitulation are flexible, including the way in which themes are reordered in the second repeated sections of various movements. As mentioned in chapter 6, it was the exposition (i.e., the first repeated section) that was the first portion of sonata form to take on the standard shape now recognized in "high" classic style; the arrangement of themes in the second repeated section was never completely regularized. Expositions with a fully-developed sense of thematic function could be accommodated both in the rhyming and rounded binary schemes. The last movement of the 1762 symphony from the Doksy collection (Symphony 1) offers a good example of how a conventional sonata-form exposition could be incorporated into a rhyming binary scheme. No matter what choice of form was settled on in a given work, Mysliveček was careful to incorporate unifying motivic elements to ensure that the various parts of his binary forms were never mere successions of unrelated themes, however lovely or ingeniously conceived.

The construction of the "second theme" of the 1762 Doksy symphony is important to highlight as a prototype for many later symphonies by Mysliveček. A typical "second theme" in Mysliveček's work is presented at first only by the violins, the second violin part often with accompanimental patterns that resemble a keyboard texture. It is then answered by the winds, usually with some sort of motivic work in parallel thirds or sixths (ex. 9.6). This technique of featuring wind instruments in the second theme, common in Italian symphonies and overtures of Mysliveček's day, was the basis of procedures that endured even to the era of Rossini. The same symphony of 1762 opens with a type of loud-soft-loud-soft construction that Einstein believed was especially distinctive of Mysliveček (ex. 9.7).[12] It is true that themes of this type are common in Mysliveček's work, but no more so than in the works of many contemporaries.

EXAMPLE 9.1. Mysliveček, Symphony in C Major, op. 1, no. 3 (Symphony 4), third movement, meas. 1–13. Edited from Ms. V B 56 of the České Muzeum Hudby with permission.

[12] Alfred Einstein, *Mozart: His Character, His Work*, trans. Arthur Mendel and Nathan Broder (London: Granada, 1971), 229.

EXAMPLE 9.2. Mysliveček, Symphony in F Major, op. 1, no. 4 (Symphony 5), first movement, meas. 54–66. Edited from Ms. V B 56 of the České Muzeum Hudby with permission.

EXAMPLE 9.3. Mysliveček, Symphony in F Major, op. 1, no. 4 (Symphony no. 5), first movement, meas. 15–24. Edited from Ms. V B 56 of the České Muzeum Hudby with permission.

EXAMPLE 9.4. Mysliveček, Symphony in C Major, op. 1, no. 3 (Symphony 4), first movement, meas. 1–10. Edited from Ms. V B 56 of the České Muzeum Hudby with permission.

continued

EXAMPLE 9.4–*continued*

6

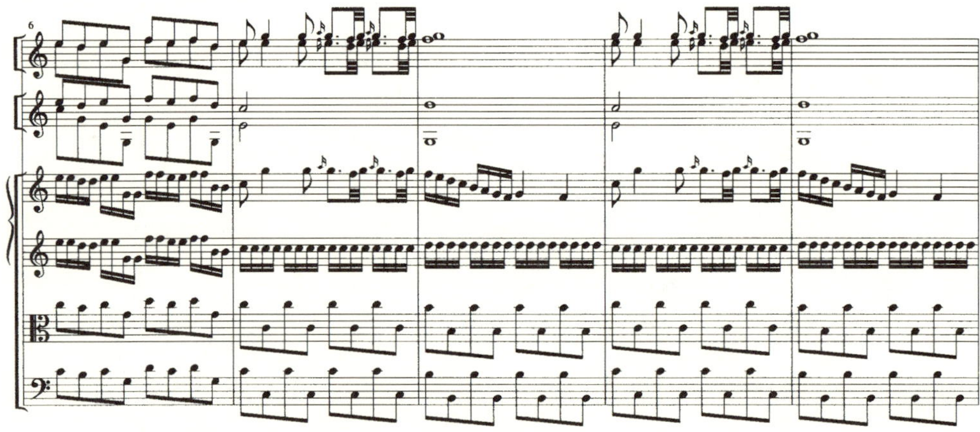

EXAMPLE 9.5. Mysliveček, Symphony in G Minor, op. 1, no. 5 (Symphony 6), first movement, meas. 12–19. Edited from Ms. V B 56 of the České Muzeum Hudby with permission.

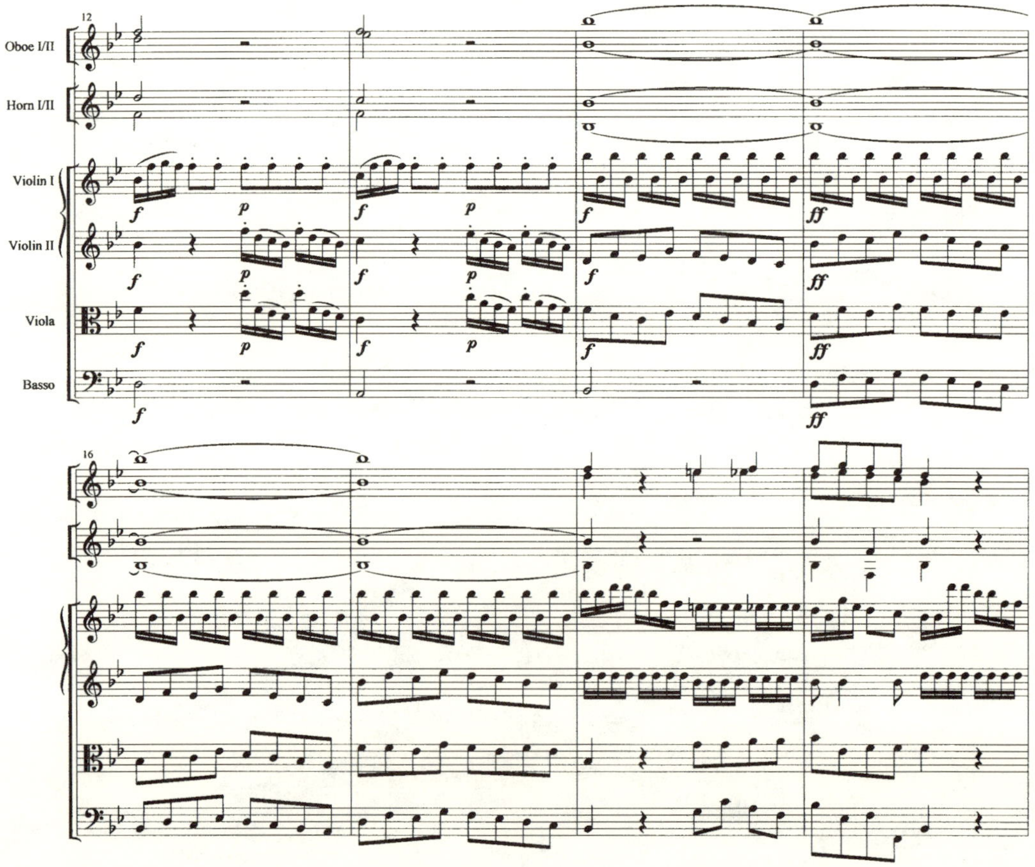
12
Oboe I/II
Horn I/II
Violin I
Violin II
Viola
Basso
16

EXAMPLE 9.6. Mysliveček, Symphony in C Major (Symphony 1), first movement, meas. 16–25.

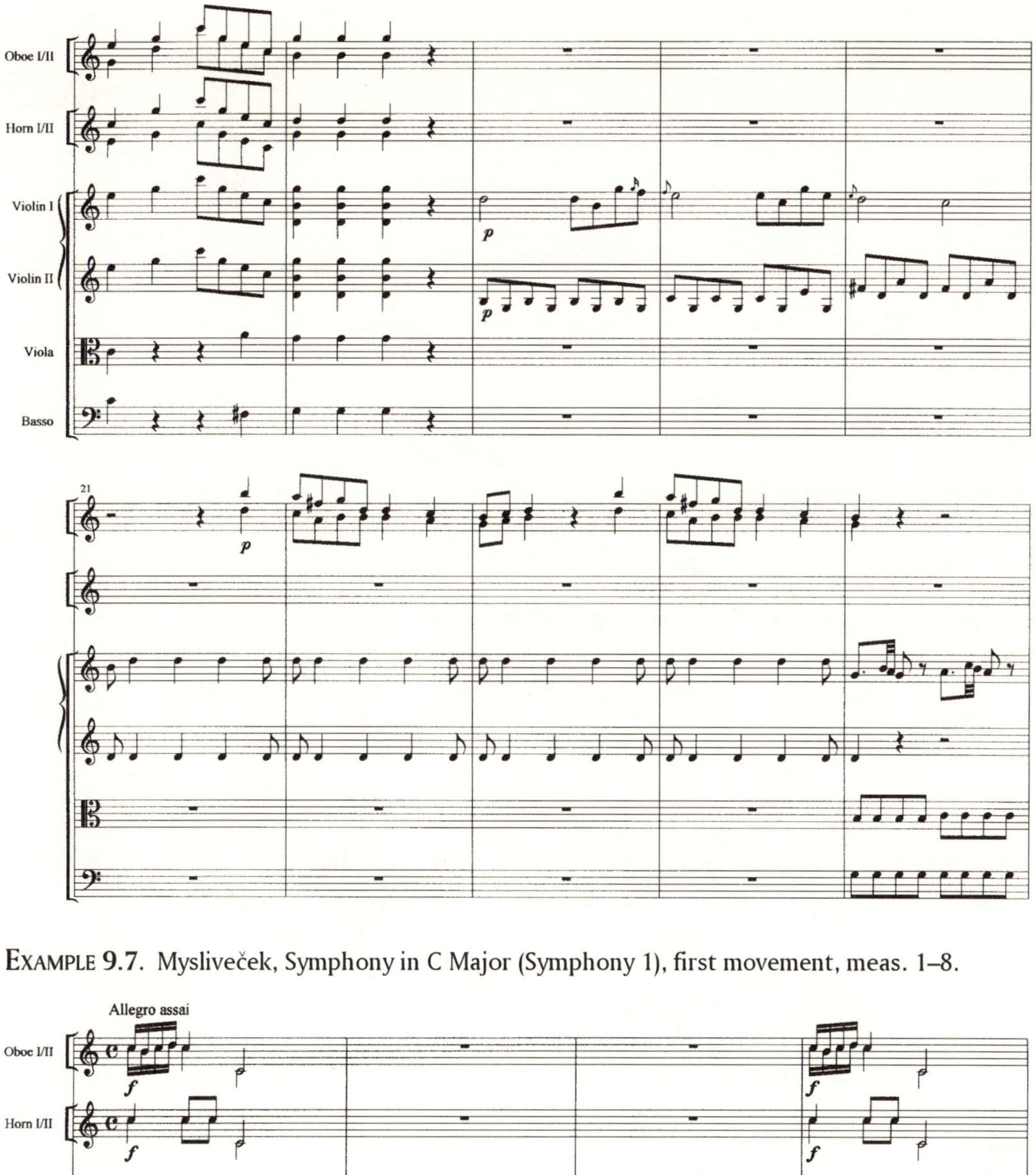
Oboe I/II
Horn I/II
Violin I
Violin II
Viola
Basso
21

EXAMPLE 9.7. Mysliveček, Symphony in C Major (Symphony 1), first movement, meas. 1–8.

Allegro assai
Oboe I/II
Horn I/II
Violin I
Violin II
Viola
Basso

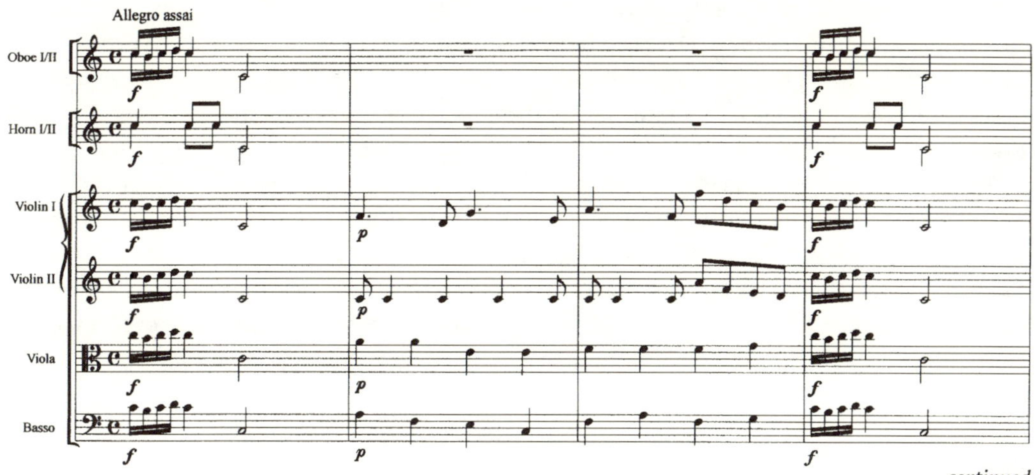

continued

EXAMPLE 9.7–*continued*

SYMPHONIES AND OVERTURES OF THE MID-1760S TO CA. 1770

Mysliveček's move to Italy brought quick advances in his skills as a symphonist. Almost from the moment he set foot in Italy, he could have been considered the most talented symphonist resident there.[13] Once in Italy, it would be accurate to describe Mysliveček's general orientation as geared more toward overture style in the manner of Sacchini or Anfossi than toward the concerted symphonic style favored by most composers outside of Italy, including the expatriate Boccherini. Since he had already adopted an Italianate approach while still in Bohemia, the basic format of Mysliveček's symphonies did not change, but the opportunity to compose opera overtures led to experimentation with certain stylistic procedures specific to overture style. Movements of opera overtures more characteristically lack repeat signs, for example, as a means to ensure that the introduction to a dramatic work would not be overly-long or detract attention from the principal musical event at hand, and there was also the possibility in overtures of incorporating transitional material between the movements of overtures, especially the first two, instead of ending each movement with a final cadence. Overall, Mysliveček's overtures tend to be a bit more extravagant and harmonically adventuresome than his independent symphonies. The festive instrumental resources available at the major operatic houses made possible a richer instrumentation than was customary in his independent symphonies, which were scored almost exclusively for strings, oboes, and horns with flutes occasionally substituting for oboes in the slow movements after about 1767.

One might never imagine that the choice of keys for slow movements would have been more flexible in overture style than in symphonic style, but it was. In most of Mysliveček's three-movement works, no matter what the genre, the key of the slow movement relates to the principal key of the outer movements either as subdominant or parallel minor. In contrast, Italian opera overture style

[13] This is apparent by comparing his symphonies and overtures with works written by composers such as Sacchini, Anfossi, and Sammartini: see series A (Italy) of *The Symphony, 1720–1840*. The expatriate Boccherini, however, was also far more talented than these composers.

in Mysliveček's day permitted third relationships with the keys of the outer movements, virtually the only place where third relationships of this type are found in his work.[14]

A new assurance in orchestral writing is evident in Mysliveček's overture to *Semiramide* (1766), one of the earliest symphonic works he composed in Italy.[15] An important sign of this is the broader layout of thematic material. The opening theme, clearly articulated with a cadence in the tonic, is fourteen measures long (compared to the seven measures or so common in the earlier symphonies) and its motivic ideas are much more distinctive than those generally encountered in the Haffner set (see ex. 9.8). The exposition is well-articulated in terms of sonata-form models, and the "second theme" area is noticeably spacious and well-developed. In 1766 Mysliveček still had not consistently adopted rounded binary forms, however. Rounded binary form is found in the second and third movements, but not in the first. The last movement is more developed than those in his earlier symphonies, and it introduces for the first time in Mysliveček's music another typical method of constructing "second themes" in which an accompanimental figure is heard first, then the main thematic material (ex. 9.9). This device, common in symphonies of the 1760s, lends a degree of drama or surprise by withholding slightly the entrance of the "second theme." Filler in the middle voices provides a means to restore musical momentum after the sudden cessation of activity caused by the grand pause that precedes it.

For several years, each new overture introduced some sort of innovation in orchestration that added to the options available. The overture to *Bellerofonte* (1767) was the first to expand the ensemble beyond strings, horns, and oboes by adding trumpets to achieve an added measure of brightness. The *Bellerofonte* overture is not commensurate in quality with the opera as a whole, but it does present a quirky, whimsical theme punctuated with rests that lends a sense of surprise and unpredictability (ex. 9.10). A similar type of theme was later used in the overture to *Motezuma* (see chapter 6, ex. 6.4).

The overture to *Farnace*, written later in 1767, features a richer orchestration still: trumpets, flutes, and bassoons in addition to the usual strings, horns, and oboes. Unlike the overture to *Bellerofonte*, brilliant use is made of the extra instruments, including some imaginative passages in the third movement for bassoons in dialogue with the first violin. The overture to *Farnace* was also the first to suppress oboes in favor of flutes in the slow movement, a common procedure in later works. Rhyming binary schemes were completely discarded in favor of sonata-form structures. Fully-developed sonata form could now be expected as a matter of course in all symphonic movements not cast in rondo form or minuet and trio form. The only subsequent overture to employ a rhyming form in its first movement is the overture to *Nitteti* (1770).

---

[14] In eight of Mysliveček's opera overtures, the key of the slow movement exhibits a third relationship with the key of the outer movements: *Farnace* (1767), *Il gran Tamerlano* (1772), *Romolo ed Ersilia* (1773), *Adriano in Siria* (1776), *Calliroe* (1778), *L'olimpiade* (1778), and *Medonte* (1780). The only other pieces in which similar third relationships are found are his wind quintet in E-flat major, probably composed in 1780, and four of his late strings quartets (nos. 17, 18, 21, and 23 of Catalog 1).

[15] It is improbable that Mysliveček would wait over two years in Italy to resume symphonic composition, but the chronology and authenticity of Mysliveček's symphonies from the mid-1760s are not secure enough to make firm conclusions about which ones may have been written in Italy earlier than the overture to *Semiramide*. If authentic, Symphony 8 would almost certainly have to predate the overture to *Semiramide*, but it may even predate Mysliveček's move to Italy, considering how early it is known to have circulated in the North (it appears in the Sigmaringen catalog of 1766). Any of the symphonies 9–13 may also predate the overture to *Semiramide* (and the overture to the "dramatic cantata" *Il Parnaso confuso* likely does).

EXAMPLE 9.8. Mysliveček, Overture to *Semiramide* (Overture 2), first movement, meas. 1–14. Edited from Ms. V B 69 of the České Muzeum Hudby with permission.

EXAMPLE 9.9. Mysliveček, Overture to *Semiramide* (Overture), third movement, meas. 28–43. Edited from Ms. V B 96 of the České Muzeum Hudby with permission.

EXAMPLE 9.10. Mysliveček, Overture to *Il Bellerofonte* (Overture 3), first movement, meas. 1–4 (Violin 1 only).

The basic conception of Mysliveček's symphonies and overtures did not change in any significant way after the composition of the overture to *Farnace*, nor did they ever increase substantially in length, but a few stylistic developments that appeared from time to time are worth discussing a bit more in detail. The idea of expanding orchestral sonorities, for example, did continue in the later overtures, albeit haphazardly. For his overture to *Il trionfo di Clelia* (1768), Mysliveček was fortunate in being able to take advantage of the large and accomplished orchestra available at the royal theater in Turin. He added tympani for the first time in addition to oboes, flutes, horns, and trumpets, and he used tympani as well in the overtures to *Demofoonte* and *Ipermestra* of 1769 and *Nitteti* of 1770. A few other innovations in texture and orchestration introduced in later symphonies and overtures will be discussed below.

SYMPHONIES AND OVERTURES OF THE 1770S

A set of six symphonies published by William Napier in London with dedication to Lord Cowper (Symphonies 26–31) were likely composed during Mysliveček's stay in Florence in 1770–71 at the time of the preparations for performances of the opera *Motezuma* and the oratorio *Adamo ed Eva*. No date appears in the original print. Dates between 1771 and 1773 are all possible, based on the low plate number (15) printed on each of the parts. Napier started his music publishing firm about 1772, certainly sometime before 1773.[16] The Napier symphonies represent something of a culmination of Mysliveček's abilities as a symphonist up to the early 1770s. For their energy, passion, and distinctive melodic materials, it would not be unreasonable to consider them the finest symphonies ever composed in Italy up to the early 1770s. The only symphonist who had ever emerged in Europe by that time who was consistently capable of surpassing them in quality was Joseph Haydn.

Judging from the surviving manuscript sources, the Napier set does not appear to have been widely known outside of England, but the large number of exemplars preserved in England attests to its popularity there. Certain stylistic features seem to indicate that the Napier set was specially crafted to appeal to English taste. There is a dignity and solidity about the symphonies that is more in touch with J. C. Bach's style than most of the other symphonies Mysliveček composed while in Italy. The opening movements have more moderate tempos than is typical in his other Italian works, and there are more opening themes with long-note motives. *Rondeaux* are rare in Mysliveček's independent symphonies, but there is one in Symphony 27 that much resembles the style of an English country dance. As with the Haffner set, the Napier symphonies leave the impression of a composer

[16] Frank Kidson, *British Music Publishers, Printers and Engravers* (London: W. E. Hill & Sons, [1900]), 80; and Charles Humphries and William C. Smith, *Music Publishing in the British Isles from the Beginnings until the Middle of the Nineteenth Century* (Oxford: Basil Blackwell, 1970), 241.

seeking to demonstrate a comprehensive mastery of contemporary symphonic technique. At times some of the famous Mannheim devices are introduced, for example the "crescendo" in the opening movement of Symphony 30 and the "rocket" in the opening movement of Symphony 31. There are also experiments with *sordini* violins and *pizzicato*, as in the slow movement of Symphony 30.

The orchestration of the Napier symphonies reflects a vogue for divided violas that reigned in Italy both in symphonic music and in operatic music during the late 1760s and early 1770s.[17] Other composers who introduced divided violas in symphonies in Italy at this time include Giovanni Battista Sammartini and W. A. Mozart,[18] whereas the expatriate Boccherini used them in Spain. The necessity of publishing separate parts for first and second viola, a very rare procedure in a symphonic print, is a strong indication of how prominently the device figures in the Napier set. Due to the cost involved, no eighteenth-century publisher would have produced separate parts for *divise* violas unless it was absolutely necessary for clarity in reading. Perhaps the most characteristic treatment of divided violas in the Napier set is in the opening movement of the first symphony (Symphony 26), where the sonority of divided violas in parallel thirds combined with oboes in parallel thirds is used to present the "second theme." Divided violas with winds add another dimension to Mysliveček's habit of introducing wind *soli* in his "second themes." Their use in the first movement of the overture to *Motezuma* is reproduced in example 9.11. *Soli* for violas in parallel thirds appear intermittently throughout the Napier set, and in the slow movement of Symphony 30 they create a particularly sonorous accompaniment for the upper strings.[19]

EXAMPLE 9.11. Mysliveček, Overture to *Motezuma* (Overture 11), first movement, meas. 28–46.

continued

[17] See David J. Rhodes, "The Origins and Utilisation of Divided Viola Writing in the Symphony at Mannheim and Various Other European Centres in the Second Half of the 18th Century," in *Mannheim – Ein Paradies der Tonkünster?*, ed. Ludwig Finscher et al., Quellen und Studien zur Geschichte der Mannheimer Hofkapelle (Frankfurt-am-Main: Peter Lang, 2002), 8:67–170. The Napier set of Mysliveček symphonies is discussed briefly on p. 76 with excerpts reproduced on pp. 130–31.

[18] See Rhodes, ibid.; and Ada Beate Gehann, "Merkmale der Konzertsatzform in der späten Kompositionsphase G. B. Sammartinis," in *Giovanni Battista Sammartini*, 137–201.

[19] An excerpt of this movement is reproduced in Rhodes, "Origins," 130.

EXAMPLE 9.11–*continued*

There is no reason to believe that Mysliveček wrote any more symphonies with winds for about five years after the completion of the Napier symphonies. None are apparent in the source record until the appearance of a set of six offered for sale in the Breitkopf catalog of 1776/1777 (all of them lost). This set was soon followed by another important grouping of independent symphonies from the 1770s, a set of six preserved in the collection of the Pfarrkirche in Weyarn, Bavaria (Symphonies 42–47). These six symphonies, all dated 1778, were probably part of a shipment of twelve sent by Mysliveček to the archbishop of Salzburg according to a letter of Leopold Mozart of 15 October 1777 (see above chapter 4) and were likely composed in Munich. The F major symphony from the Weyarn set (Symphony 45) substitutes a minuet and trio for the customary 2/4 or 3/8 finale. This is the only such minuet paired with a trio as a finale in a Mysliveček symphony,[20] and it has a recognizable German flavor.

The most distinctive feature of the Weyarn symphonies is the beautiful solo writing for violin and winds sprinkled throughout. The slow movement of the symphony in B-flat (Symphony 47) was actually conceived as a concerto movement for violin solo with ritornellos. Even more moving are the oboe solos written for the slow movement of the symphony in G major (Symphony 46). The treatment of wind soloists in the slow movements of the Weyarn set represents a continuation of experiments found in two recent opera overtures: *Artaserse* (1774), which features two clarinets in its slow movement, and *Adriano in Siria* (1776), which includes a slow movement with oboe solo very similar to the one that appears in Symphony 46.

The excellence of Mysliveček's surviving symphonies from the 1770s is concentrated in the two sets of six just described, thus it is best to turn to his opera overtures for mention of a few other innovations in his symphonic writing of the 1770s. The only remaining instrument to be added to Mysliveček's orchestra after the 1760s was the clarinet, which first appeared in the overtures to *Antigona* (1774), then was used in the overtures to *Artaserse* (1774), and his second setting of *Demetrio* (1779). This last use, in which the clarinets help to mark off a beautiful *rondeau* theme in the slow movement, is particularly affecting. Expanded ensembles were not maintained consistently in the later Mysliveček overtures. After *Nitteti*, there were only a few that employ wind or brass instruments other than oboes and horns. Besides the three overtures with clarinets, there were also the overtures to *Demetrio* (1773), *Demofoonte* (1775), *Isacco figura del redentore* (1776), *Ezio* (1777), and *L'olimpiade* (1778). Their use can be correlated partially to the availability of excellent wind players in Turin, Florence, and Munich, where *Antigona*, *Isacco*, and the 1777 *Ezio* were first performed.

Certain stock rhythmic and melodic figures continued to be introduced in the late 1760s and 1770s, for example a habit of expanding melodic ideas by piling up thirds (ex. 9.11, meas. 39–42). The textual innovation of presenting second theme groups with passages for oboes and divided violas in parallel thirds appeared for the first time in the overtures to *Nitteti* (1770) and *Motezuma* (1771) (ex. 9.11). As mentioned above, this trait was imported into the Napier symphonies written at about the same time. Mysliveček never completely gave up divided violas, but they were less common in his overtures from the mid- and late 1770s consistent with the diminished interest in this procedure generally noticeable in Italy after the early 1770s.

A special topic of interest concerning Mysliveček's orchestral works is their place in the history of music publishing in Italy. In fact, Mysliveček's residence in Italy coincided with the appearance of

[20] A number of other independent symphonies have finales marked "tempo di minuetto," but they are not attached to trios. The overture to *Ezio* of 1775 features a minuet and trio with all of the repeats written out. For incipits, see Evans and Dearling, 127–85.

the earliest symphonic prints in that country. During Mysliveček's stay in Florence in 1775–76, an announcement in the *Gazzetta universale* of Florence on 12 October 1776 actually claimed that one of his symphonies was to be included in a series of three that would constitute the first symphonies ever published in Italy.[21] Although this claim appears not to be true,[22] Mysliveček's reputation as a symphonist in Italy is obviously well attested by his inclusion in this series. His name even appears in the announcement before the Italians who were also to be represented. The most important symphonic publication devoted to Mysliveček at this time was a set of six overtures brought out by Ranieri Del Vivo in Florence with dedication to Lord Cowper, but three other prints of individual overtures also survive (see Catalog 1). How long he could have continued composing the same sort of brief three-movement symphonies is an open question, and for operatic overtures, it can be pondered whether he would have made the switch to the single-movement sonata form that started to be popularized by Paisiello after the late 1760s. The answer is probably that once he would have felt enough pressure from contemporary composers in Italy, he would have learned to adopt newer practices. At the time of his death in 1781, this was not necessary—and perhaps this is a pity. Had Mysliveček lived to increase the proportions of his symphonic works to lengths commensurate with most symphonic writing of the 1780s, his talents likely would have been recognized long ago.

CONCERTOS FOR VIOLIN

In the late eighteenth-century hierarchy of musical genres, solo concertos occupied a special place below symphonies, yet still above genres that did not involve the participation of orchestral ensembles. One of the most important indications of the concerto's lower status was its close dependence on symphonic gestures as a stylistic resource. The evolution of symphonic style can be traced almost as reliably in the opening ritornellos of concerto first movements as it can be traced in symphonies themselves. The dazzling virtuosity of professional instrumentalists had the potential to lend a certain amount of prestige to the genre, but not all concertos were intended as vehicles for virtuoso performers. Many keyboard concertos in particular were written essentially for amateur female performers, with a chamber accompaniment rather than a true orchestral accompaniment.

On the subject of keyboard concertos, it is another great pity for Mysliveček's posthumous reputation that he wrote only two rather mediocre examples, since keyboard concertos of the 1760s and 1770s have been accorded much more attention in modern scholarship than concertos for other solo instruments. For Mysliveček, who was himself a talented violinist, it was only natural that concertos for violin solo would form the centerpiece of his output, and the ones he produced constitute some of his most successful pieces. Indeed, his best violin concertos, for example the E major concerto, may even be regarded as the finest of all his instrumental compositions. Mysliveček rose to the challenge consistently by demonstrating skill in balancing all of the elements that contribute to successful concerto writing, including melodic invention, ingenuity in devising virtuoso

[21] The announcement is transcribed in Bohadlo, 100. One symphony each by Mysliveček, Paisiello, and Bertoni are advertised for sale. The only publisher possible seems to be Ranieri del Vivo.

[22] There is, for example, a print of Luigi Marescalchi's "Sinfonia no. 2 con oboe, e corni ad libitum nel Tutore ingannato, eseguita in Venezia nel Teatro di S. Samuele il carnovale dell'anno 1774" [the overture to the opera *Il tutore ingannato*] published by Innocente Alessandri in Venice in 1774: see RISM A/I.

passagework, and a sure sense of how to connect the various events of ritornello form in a pleasing and logical way.[23]

The repertory of violin concertos by Josef Mysliveček consists of ten works, nine of which survive in complete form. It would not be unreasonable to regard some of them as the best violin concertos composed between the time of Vivaldi and the Mozart violin concertos of 1775. The key collection is a cycle of six (Violin Concertos 4–9) preserved in a manuscript in the Gesellschaft der Musikfreunde in Vienna[24] that contains two outstanding examples of Mysliveček's abilities as a composer of violin concertos: the E major concerto (Violin Concerto 4), an exceptional composition by any standard of comparison, and the G major concerto (Violin Concerto 9) sometimes referred to as a "pastoral" concerto, but which could be described more accurately as a "peasant" concerto—regardless, no other of Mysliveček's surviving instrumental compositions exhibits such obvious evocative effects. Also in the Gesellschaft der Musikfreunde is a concerto in C major (Violin Concerto 3) and a fragment of a concerto in B-flat major (Violin Concerto 10). Manuscript copies of a concerto in D major listed in the Breitkopf catalog of 1769 (Violin Concerto 1) are preserved in Prague and Stockholm.

A complete copy of one other violin concerto long known only from an incipit in the Breitkopf catalog of 1770 (Violin Concerto 2) is preserved in the collection of the Thüringisches Hauptstaatsarchiv in Weimar. In the form of an adaptation for cello that appears to originate from Mysliveček himself, it has been recorded several times. The versions for violin and cello hardly differ except for the range of the solo part and the choice of figural passagework in a few spots. There can be no question that the violin concerto is the original, since some passages are slightly clumsy for cello, whereas there is nothing at all awkward for violin. The cello version may have been prepared for a particular performer or musical occasion. Since cello concertos were much rarer than violin concertos and had limited potential for wide dissemination, one would think that if Mysliveček had needed to provide a performer with a cello concerto, an arrangement would have satisfied the requirement with minimal expenditure of effort. The cellist Antonio Vandini, a resident of Padua at the time of Mysliveček's association with the city between 1768 and 1774, is at present the best possibility to suggest as original recipient of the cello concerto.

Chappell White has argued persuasively that all of the Mysliveček violin concertos were composed during the late 1760s or early 1770s. In the case of two, there is approximate confirmation of this dating from entries in the Breitkopf catalogs of 1769 (Violin Concerto 1) and 1770 (Violin Concerto 2). The close stylistic resemblance of Violin Concerto 1 to Violin Concerto 3 seems to indicate that the latter also belongs to the late 1760s. Telltale signs of composition in Italy include the short length of the slow movements and the presence of long sections for the soloist accompanied only by two violins. The latter trait in slow movements is one of the hallmarks of what might be described as a Tartinian age of violin concerto writing in Italy in the mid-eighteenth century. Mysliveček was involved extensively with music-making in Padua in the late 1760s, and there can be little doubt that he met Giuseppe Tartini before the older composer died there in 1770. His exposure to Tartini provides a plausible explanation for the genesis of all three of the earlier violin concertos.

---

[23] On the style and reception of the Mysliveček violin concertos, see Chappell White, *From Vivaldi to Viotti: A History of the Early Classical Violin Concerto* (Philadelphia: Gordon and Breach, 1992), especially 182–87.

[24] Four of these are available in modern edition: see Catalog 1.

Mysliveček may have composed the set of six concertos preserved in Vienna in preparation for his own use as a traveling virtuoso while in northern Europe in 1772, a trip that included an extended stay in Vienna.[25] Chappell White has noticed a number of stylistic traits that make the Vienna concertos much more compatible with an Austrian or South German taste than the three earlier violin concertos, for example slow movements that are more highly developed and orchestral accompaniments that are much more symphonic in character. Only the concerto in A major (Violin Concerto 5), the weakest of the Vienna set, is still dominated by the accompaniment of two violins. There is no doubt that at least one Mysliveček violin concerto was available in Vienna in this period, since Mozart transcribed the title page of its bass part in his letter from Vienna of 8 September 1773.[26] It seem sensible to assume that the six concertos were composed before the mid-1770s, as Chappell White has pointed out, because they contain no rondo finales or other alternatives to ritornello form in the final movements.

There are many interesting topics to be explored concerning concerto composition, beginning with the customary three-movement format (fast-slow-fast) that was used throughout Europe in the late eighteenth century. In concerto writing, certain traditions of the Vivaldi/Tartini decades of the 1720s–50s endured much longer than those of other genres cultivated by Italian composers of instrumental music. Italian symphonies and string quartets, for example, did not exercise sufficient influence to induce northern composers to employ three-movement cycles consistently, but solo concertos were a different matter. Generally only the simplest keyboard concertos intended for amateur use had less than three movements, whereas concertos in four movements like a northern symphony or string quartet were almost unheard of in the eighteenth century. For Mysliveček and virtually all other composers of solo concertos of his day, anything but the traditional Vivaldian three-movement format was unthinkable.

The orchestral ritornellos used to energize and support the soloist were the foundation of formal plans that perpetually fascinate style critics. First movements yield some of the most complicated amalgamations of forms that can be found in all eighteenth-century instrumental music; probably no other instrumental genre offered so many stereotypical musical events that the informed listener would be waiting for in the course of a musical performance. Modern theorizing about the best ways to analyze concerto first-movement form has been extensive, but its basis is really quite simple, as explained by the German theorist Heinrich Christoph Koch. At the most fundamental level, the late eighteenth-century first movement form consists of three sections featuring the soloist that are interspersed among four sections for the orchestra (i.e., the ritornellos). The form is based on traditional Vivaldian models in which three or four solo sections would be interspersed among four or five ritornellos, respectively. The great formal innovation of the early classic period was to limit the number of solo sections strictly to no more than three and cast them as equivalents to the three main sections of sonata form (exposition, development, and recapitulation). Sometimes the proportions were more compact, with the number of ritornellos reduced to three and the number of solo sections reduced to two. In cases like this, the second solo section would combine development and recapitulation functions into one solo section much longer than the first.

---

[25] White (*From Vivaldi*, 183) believed them to have been written in 1772, perhaps in Munich, unaware that Fétis's indication of a visit by Mysliveček to Munich in 1773 was almost undoubtedly a fabrication (see above chapter 3). White believed mistakenly that the putative trip to Munich took place in 1772, not 1773.

[26] Anderson, 243; Bauer and Deutsch, 1:497.

Mysliveček adopted a trademark formal plan that is found in nearly all of the fast movements of his violin concertos. It can be diagrammed in this fashion:

	rit.	solo	rit.	solo	rit.	solo	rit.
		(=exposition)		(=development)	(=recapitulation)		
Keys:	I	I-V	V	V-vi	vi-I	I-I	I

In Mysliveček's scheme, each of the sections ends with a firm cadence in the key at hand. What makes his practice so distinctive is the consistent handling of the return to the tonic key in the middle of the structure. In Mysliveček's day, the region at the end of the second solo section was the one open to the greatest variation. The third ritornello seen in this diagram could be omitted entirely, and if it was present, it might or might not effect a re-transition to the tonic (in other words, it might or might not begin in the tonic key). Mysliveček, however, consistently fashioned second solo sections that end with a cadence in the submediant key and used the third ritornello to bring back the tonic key.

The basic principle of ritornello form in concerto style may be simple, but conventions associated with the constituent parts can be complicated. A number of them do deserve closer scrutiny as an illustration of how Mysliveček's concertos can be compared to those of other eighteenth-century composers. The opening ritornellos of solo concertos can be as interesting and complicated as any other portion of a concerto movement, and they usually offer a reliable portent of the composer's skill. Even in Vivaldi's time, the opening ritornello was always the longest (or at least no shorter than any other ritornello), and its length as a proportion of the overall dimensions of the first movement continued to grow in the course of the century as the number of ritornellos was reduced. I have argued that this was done in order to bring the proportional length of the opening ritornello and first solo section together into alignment with the proportional length of the exposition of sonata form.[27] It is clear that composers in the mid-eighteenth century reckoned the beginning of the second ritornello to be the equivalent of the place where internal repeat signs were added in sonata form. In the works of conservative composers such as C. P. E. Bach, who retained schemes with five ritornellos and four solos long past the time when most composers gave them up, this meant that the opening ritornellos had to be quite long in order to balance the amount of musical material that came after the second ritornello.

For much of the mid-eighteenth century, several alternatives existed for the form of the opening ritornello,[28] but by Mysliveček's day the usual means of organizing the thematic structure of the long opening ritornellos was roughly the same as in symphonic sonata form expositions. The only element that distinctly separates the two plans is the customary absence of a modulation. Otherwise, the opening ritornellos frequently exhibit "first themes," "transitions," "second themes," etc., just like a sonata form exposition. One special practice associated with the closing themes of the opening ritornello is the habit of reserving them just for two spots in the entire first-movement scheme: once heard at the end of the opening ritornello, they are usually not heard again until the end of the movement. This is a procedure inherited from Vivaldian traditions, and it constitutes one of the most durable formal habits that Vivaldi passed on to the later eighteenth century.

---

[27] Freeman, "The Earliest Italian Keyboard Concertos," 129–36.

[28] Ibid., 132–37.

There has been much discussion in the musicological literature about the best way to analyze the structure of the opening ritornello of late eighteenth-century concertos, in particular whether to consider it the first statement of a "double exposition" (the second "exposition" being the first solo section). Since the appearance of research on concerto form published by Jane Stevens in the 1970s, this terminology has sensibly been discarded by many style critics.[29] In the eighteenth century, the opening ritornello was not regarded by music theorists as an exposition nor was it considered to be part of one; rather, it was simply a "ritornello," i.e., a portion of the concerto to be played by the orchestra before the entrance of the soloist. It is true that thematic events similar to what is seen in sonata form expositions are found in the opening ritornello, but their presence may be best explained by the convenience of using tried and true techniques borrowed from symphonic style. The genre traditions of concerto style demanded a long opening ritornello, just as in the dal-segno aria. For a composer of the 1760s or 1770s, there simply was no better or more familiar means to organize the internal melodic structure of a musical space as long as that of an extended opening ritornello than along the lines of the sonata-form exposition. One has only to compare the rambling, disjointed opening ritornellos of C. P. E. Bach with those of composers such as J. C. Bach and Mysliveček to see the sense of this approach.

For the connoisseur, it can be an enjoyable challenge to ascertain how much of the thematic material from the opening ritornello is incorporated into the solo exposition during a concerto performance. During the era of Tartini's preeminence in the mid-eighteenth century, it was almost an automatic and mechanical procedure to begin the solo with the same theme as the opening ritornello. One observer, Quantz, tried to put his finger on the question of whether the soloist would likely carry the opening theme by recommending that the first theme of the opening ritornello should reappear in the first solo section only if it were "singing" enough.[30] Using this criterion, it can be easy to predict whether or not the soloist will start off by playing the first theme of the opening ritornello. The principle has force even in the mature works of Mozart, as can be seen by comparing the solo exposition of the piano concerto K488 (with an opening theme in "singing" style) and K503 (with an opening theme in "symphonic" style). Concerto style of the Tartinian generation generally mandated a "singing" style of melodic invention, consistent with an early classic ideal in Italy of "naturalness" in music, and that is why his first themes are shared between the orchestra and the soloist. As symphonic style evolved and was imitated in concerto ritornellos, many effects were developed that were incompatible with the capabilities of soloists. By the 1770s, composers drew away more and more from the practice of beginning the opening solo section with the same theme as the opening ritornello. For Mysliveček, it became an option to begin the first solo section in a surprising, unpredictable way that would introduce or replace the first theme of the opening ritornello. In his earlier violin concertos (Violin Concertos 1-3), Mysliveček used the more conservative procedure. The concertos from the Vienna manuscript are more apt to employ the newer procedure.

Regardless of how the first solo begins, it was expected to unfold as a solo exposition with the same principal events as a symphonic exposition, albeit with a few special features. In particular,

---

[29] See especially Jane Stevens, "An Eighteenth-Century Description of Concerto First-Movement Form," *Journal of the American Musicological Society* 24 (1971): 85–95.

[30] Johann Joachim Quantz, *Versuch einer Anweisung die Flöte traversière zu spielen*, trans. Edward R. Reilly, *On Playing the Flute* (London, 1966), 312.

the ending is the element most specific to concerto style. Generally, there would be some sort of virtuosic flourish or a series of virtuosic excursions followed by a trill on the supertonic note of the new key that signals the end of the first solo section. In keyboard concertos, the figuration typically continues up until the start of the trill, but in violin concertos the convention is to play the dominant note of the new key, then play the supertonic trill (ex. 9.12). The distinctive gesture of virtuosic flourish plus supertonic trill was widely imitated in other instrumental genres. As a signal of finality or structural articulation, it was unmatched in effectiveness even if in other genres a bit of extra closing material might be needed at times to mitigate its starkness or abruptness. In concertos there would be no fear of abruptness, because the musical continuity was immediately taken up by the subsequent ritornello.

EXAMPLE 9.12. Mysliveček, Violin Concerto in B-flat Major (Violin Concerto 7), first movement, meas. 43–47 (horns, oboes tacent meas. 43–46, omitted meas. 47).

Just as judgments can be made about a composer's conservatism when considering whether the second ritornello begins with the same thematic material as the first ritornello, so judgments can be made about the way that the thematic material is used at the start of the second ritornello. The Tartinian generation almost always began the second ritornello exactly the same way as the first ritornello, except transposed to the dominant key.[31] By Mysliveček's time, composers had grown weary of such mechanical procedures and were more likely to begin the second ritornello with a theme selected from the interior of the opening ritornello. This practice leaves the listener more surprised than when the opening theme is simply repeated. Once again, Mysliveček's earlier concertos tend to use the more conservative strategy, whereas the concertos in the Vienna manuscript tend to adopt the more modern formula.

From the beginning of the second ritornello nearly to the end of the first movement of the concerto, conventions were less rigid. The most important principle to be respected was the

[31] I have argued that this is similar to a procedure in binary form in which the first and second repeated sections begin with the same thematic material, the first in the tonic key, the second in the dominant key: see Freeman, "The Earliest Italian Keyboard Concertos," 129–33.

construction of the solo portions in imitation of the second repeated section of binary or sonata forms, but this could conform either to the rounded or rhyming schemes. A third ritornello might or might not be present between the development and recapitulation sections of the solo part, and if present, could either begin in the tonic key to signal the start of the recapitulation, or effect a re-transition that brings back the tonic only with the appearance of the soloist. There was no requirement that the recapitulation be as literal as it usually was in symphonies or sonatas, but at least some of the virtuosity heard at the end of the exposition would be expected to appear again at the end of the concluding solo section. The supertonic trill heard at the end of the first solo could also be counted on to make its appearance to signal the end of the last solo section and with it the end of the soloist's participation in the movement—at least that is how it is meant to seem. The informed listener would know that the finality of the ending of the last solo section is a deception as formalized as any other portion of the scheme.

In concertos written for professional virtuosos, the ritornello that follows the last solo section is almost invariably interrupted by a solo cadenza introduced with a stereotyped chord progression over a bass line ascending by a half-step to the dominant note of the key (the same chord progression used to introduce cadenzas in operatic arias). For the third time in the movement, there would be a series of virtuosic excursions ending with a supertonic trill. At that point, the final ritornello would resume to finish out the movement.

The formal options for the second and third movements of solo concertos were not as restricted in Mysliveček's day as they were for the first movements. In slow movements, there may be ritornellos only at the start and ending, schemes with three ritornellos and two solos, schemes with no ritornellos at all, binary forms with repeats, etc. An affectation of Tartini was accompaniment of slow movements entirely by two violins only. But no matter how ritornellos were incorporated or rejected in the formal scheme, one could be sure in Mysliveček's day that the influence of binary or sonata form would be evident in some way in the melodic and harmonic structure of a slow movement. One might not expect the events of sonata form to be as strongly-articulated as in first movements, but they would be present nonetheless.

The slow movements of Mysliveček's earlier violin concertos (Violin Concertos 1–3) are all cast in rhyming binary form with no repeat signs and no ritornellos, whereas the Vienna concertos are consistently laid out with three ritornellos and two solo sections in which the solo sections are equivalent to the two repeated sections of binary form. The only exception among the Vienna concertos is the A major concerto, which omits ritornellos in the manner of the earlier concertos. The slow movements of Mysliveček's violin concertos contain many passages of arresting beauty as well as some of the most archaic stylistic gestures to be found in any of his works, for example Vivaldi-style unison passages in minor key.

In the middle decades of the eighteenth century, the third movements of Italian concertos would usually exhibit the same ritornello forms as the first movements (the most common substitutes were variations and minuets). In the middle and late 1770s, however, the ritornello-form third movements tended to be replaced with rondos. All the Mysliveček violin concertos except Violin Concerto 2 (with its minuet and trio) yield ritornello-form third movements, one of the most important reasons to believe that they were all written before the mid-1770s. The treatment of ritornello form in third movements differs little from that seen in first movements, but in general terms the proportions are smaller, tempos are quicker, the textures are lighter, the melodic materials are livelier, and the sonata-form events are less strongly articulated.

One of the most important stylistic elements to be imported into concerto style from symphonic style during the mid-eighteenth century was the possibility of including wind instruments in the orchestral accompaniment. Nearly as soon as oboes and horns became common in symphonies, they became common in the orchestral accompaniments for concertos. Modern taste, which so much seems to favor nineteenth-century preferences for rich tonal colors, tends to desire wind instruments to be used to their fullest capabilities, but audiences of the 1760s and 1770s were content with more restrained treatment. The wind instruments in Mysliveček's concertos for the most part are used only for harmonic support and enhanced tonal brilliance. Insertions of orchestral material within the solo sections in the manner of Mozart is also appreciated by modern critics, but Mysliveček and most of his contemporaries included few such passages in their orchestral accompaniments.

In another respect Mysliveček fares much better with modern taste, that is, with regard to concerns about the "emptiness" of virtuoso passagework. The imagination of most concerto composers was not up to the task of devising difficult virtuosity that was also musically interesting. Various patterns of scales and arpeggios remained the basis of the virtuosity in the majority of eighteenth-century concertos. One of Mysliveček's undisputed talents was an ability to create new variations on these established patterns, and to do so with what strikes one as inexhaustible inspiration.

CONCERTOS FOR MISCELLANEOUS INSTRUMENTS

Mysliveček composed a few solo concertos for non-string instruments (one for flute, two for keyboard), but the results are disappointing. Without exhibiting incompetence, they are all quite unmemorable. There is evidence in a letter to Padre Martini written from Naples on 12 May 1775 that Mysliveček was close to the flautist Johann Baptist Wendling.[32] Without this connection, Mysliveček's authorship of the flute concerto in D major might be questioned, since its unique source is in a library in Wrocław, Poland, that holds no other Mysliveček manuscripts. The general style of the flute concerto is similar to the Vienna violin concertos, and it could well date from about the same time as the letter that mentions Wendling.

Mysliveček's two keyboard concertos are preserved together in a manuscript in Paris (see Catalog 1) and are probably the latest of his solo concertos. Each contains an alternative to ritornello form in the third movement: a rondo in the B-flat major concerto and a minuet with multiple trios in the F major concerto. For this reason, it is probable that they were written in the late 1770s, the only question to be asked, whether they were composed in Munich or Italy. There are good reasons to consider Munich the more likely place of origin. There was little demand for keyboard concertos in Italy in the 1770s as part of a general decline in the composition of keyboard music after a last flowering in the mid-eighteenth century. In contrast, the keyboard concerto flourished in the German lands, and the names of specific virtuosos present in Munich at the time of Mozart's visit in 1777 are known, among them Ignaz Beecke. It is also known from the Mozart correspondence that Mysliveček was disseminating keyboard sonatas in Munich at this time (see above chapter 4). One of the keyboard

[32] The original is housed in the Civico Museo Bibliografico Musicale in Bologna, sign. I.4.60; see Schnoebelen, no. 3332; letter transcribed with facsimile in Bohadlo, 102–04.

concertos is preserved in the catalog of the collection of the Bavarian Baron Dürniz along with examples of keyboard sonatas and accompanied sonata for keyboard and violin by Mysliveček.[33]

While both the title page of the Paris manuscript and the listing of the Mysliveček keyboard concertos in the Dürniz catalog bear the designation "cembalo," even without dynamic markings it is clear that these concertos are better suited for performance on early piano. In Italian usage, "cembalo" can refer to any wing-shaped keyboard instrument.[34] Passages with quick octave-work in the bass, such as those in the Mysliveček keyboard concertos, simply do not lend themselves well to performance on harpsichord. In general, keyboard composition was not Mysliveček's strong suit, and there is no reason to pause further on these concertos, except to note the uncommon pastoral character of the slow movement in the F major concerto, whose opening became a motivic resource for the slow movement of one of Mysliveček's wind octets (see below chapter 10).

Mysliveček's importance as a composer of concertos for multiple soloists has come to light only recently with the identification of Mysliveček sources in the Monumento Nazionale in Montecassino. His particular contribution was the composition of six works for a solo grouping of two clarinets, two horns, and bassoon with accompaniment of strings. These works are almost certainly identical to the six *concertoni* written for the archbishop of Salzburg in 1777–78 (see above chapter 4). Only three of the original set of six survive,[35] one in a manuscript with designation "concertone," the others in manuscripts with the designation "concerti" (see Catalog 1). The scoring may seem unusual, but it actually does conform closely to common scorings of South German serenades.[36] The use of the term *concertone* to mean a concerto with multiple soloists has been discussed by Hellmut-Christoph Mahling.[37] In Italian, the word "concertone" thus would have a meaning similar to "grand concerto" (concerto grosso). It can also have a meaning similar to the French term *sinfonie concertante* when it is used to denote a concerto for multiple soloists such as Mozart's *Sinfonia concertante* for violin, viola, and orchestra, K364/320d of 1779. Only a single composition of Mozart is designated with the term "concertone": the concerto for two violins and orchestra, K190/186E of 1774, which also includes obbligato parts for oboe and cello. Mysliveček's conception is similar to the latter piece: the surviving *concertoni* are all cast in three movements with ritornellos just like solo concertos. A recent recording by the Concerto Köln confirms their potential interest to music lovers; the Mysliveček *concertoni* are well worth hearing when the unusual solo combination can be assembled.

---

[33] *Freiherr Thaddäus von Dürniz und seine Musikaliensammlung*, ed. August Scharnagl (Tutzing: Hans Schneider, 1992), 35, 38, 45. The catalog was probably compiled in the first decade of the nineteenth century. Baron Dürniz's collection contained twelve of Mysliveček's keyboard sonatas, two sets of accompanied sonatas, and the keyboard concerto in F major.

[34] David Sutherland, "Bartolomeo Cristofori's Paired Cembalos of 1726," *Journal of the American Musical Instrument Society* 26 (2000): 28–29.

[35] The set of six was advertised for sale in the Traeg catalog of 1799; see Alexander Weinmann, ed., *Johann Traeg: Die Musikalien-verzeichnisse von 1799 und 1804 (Handschriften und Sortiment)*, Beiträge zur Geschichte des Alt-Wiener Musikverlages, series 2, no. 17, vol. 1 (Vienna: Universal Edition, 1973), 53, 303. I am grateful to Christian Moritz-Bauer for bringing these citations to my attention.

[36] For a discussion of this repertory, see Andrew Kay Kearns, "The Eighteenth-Century Orchestral Serenade in South Germany" (Ph.D. diss., University of Illinois, 1993), especially 78–91 for wind and string serenades in Munich.

[37] See his introduction to *Wolfgang Amadeus Mozart: Neue Ausgabe sämtlicher Werke*, series 5, Werkgruppe 14, vol. 2 (Kassel: Bärenreiter, 1975).

10

MUSICAL MORSELS: MYSLIVEČEK'S CHAMBER AND KEYBOARD WORKS

The largest body of instrumental compositions by Josef Mysliveček falls into various categories of chamber music for string, wind, and keyboard instruments. Most of it belongs to well-established genres such as string quartet and violin sonata, but some of the instrumental combinations Mysliveček cultivated were innovative indeed. In a few cases, for example string quintet and wind octet, Mysliveček may be considered a true pioneer in the composition of a major species of chamber music. Nonetheless, chamber works do not form a central or defining repertory for Mysliveček. Instrumental chamber music ranked low in the hierarchy of musical genres in the eighteenth century; very little was expected of it other than that the music be pleasing to the ear and enjoyable to play. The intended performers were generally amateurs or professional musicians playing informally. Technical demands tended to be modest, and experimentation with the most sophisticated compositional techniques would generally not be expected. Mysliveček was content to respect these limitations.

Although they may have wished to be remembered for writing other types of music, composers like Mysliveček who turned out chamber compositions by the dozens (or perhaps more accurately, the half-dozens) could accrue significant benefits from cultivating the most popular varieties. One benefit was income. What eighteeenth-century publishers mainly produced and advertised for sale was chamber music aimed at the amateur market, and Mysliveček was hardly alone in having the greater part of his published works represented in this form. The demand for fresh examples of chamber music was always present, and their composition scarcely required the application required to produce a symphony or opera, either from the standpoint of musical invention or the practical burden of copying out all of the music. Another benefit was the potential to advertise one's skill to a wider audience of music lovers than those few who had the opportunity to attend performances of operas and symphonies on a regular basis.

A number of distinctions can be made about the relative prestige of the various types of chamber music in Mysliveček's day. There was much more status associated with the composition of music for string ensembles, for example, than there was for ensembles including wind or keyboard instruments. The presence of even a single wind instrument in combination with strings could send a signal to expect less ambitious artistic goals than what could be encountered in a string quartet. This is a phenomenon that extended even to the works of the greatest masters. One need only compare Mozart's string quartets to his flute and oboe quartets (fine as they are) to gain some appreciation of this. The same lowered expectations were usually associated with chamber ensembles including keyboard instruments, and solo keyboard music had even less standing. In Italy, one of the most revealing signs of this was the lower number of movements customary for keyboard sonatas (one or two, in comparison to three or four for symphonies and other types of instrumental works). Published keyboard music was mainly intended for female amateurs with limited technical capabilities, a circumstance that often yielded music of inferior quality.

The most important element that helps to understand the style of Mysliveček's chamber music for strings is its close kinship to symphonic music. Many eighteenth-century chamber works for strings could double as string symphonies, and for Italianate composers such as Mysliveček this led to the production of string trios, string quartets, and string quintets similar to three-movement symphonies. In Mysliveček's work, almost all instrumental music without keyboard was cast in three movements, but there was more flexibility in the arrangement of chamber movements than there was with symphonic movements. Besides the customary fast-slow-fast disposition standard in symphonies, it is not unusual to find chamber works that begin with slow movements. Minuets especially, but also rondos and variations, are much more common in Mysliveček's chamber music than in his symphonies.

STRING QUINTETS

Some of the best illustrations of the symphonic character of Mysliveček's chamber music for strings can be found in his string quintets for two violins, two violas, and cello. In all there are twelve of them, six published by Venier in Paris ca. 1767 as the composer's Op. 2[1] and another six intended for publication in London in 1773 or 1774 with dedication to Count Vincenz von Waldstein.[2] No eighteenth-century print of the latter quintets has ever been uncovered, but they have garnered much more attention than the earlier quintets ever since they became available in modern edition in the twentieth century.[3] Judging from the large number of surviving sources of the earlier quintets (see Catalog 1), it is clear that the Op. 2 set was better known in the eighteenth century, thus its near total neglect in modern times is much to be regretted.

The more usual type of string quintet in Europe of the 1760s and 1770s was scored for two cellos instead of two violas. The most important composers who cultivated this instrumentation were Luigi Boccherini, an Italian cellist resident in Madrid after 1769, and Giuseppe Maria Cambini, a long-time fixture of musical life in eighteenth-century Paris. It cannot be established whether or not Mysliveček's Op. 2 string quintets were the earliest ones ever composed for two violas, but there can be little doubt that they were the first such quintets ever published.[4] Gaetano Brunetti, another prolific Italian composer of string quintets active in Madrid, also composed early examples with two violas, but his first print did not appear until 1771. As far as is known, the Venier print of

---

[1] Forkel specifies 1768 as the publication date in his *Musikalischer Almanach für Deutschland auf das Jahr 1782*, 53; Evans and Dearling, 105, indicate 1767 without comment. The original print offers no date.

[2] In a letter to Count Waldstein from Naples, 14 September 1773, Mysliveček mentioned a set of string quintets that he intended to dedicate to the count and publish in London. For discussion of the letter, see above, chapter 3.

[3] Vratislav Bělský edited them in two series of three in 1957 and 1988 (see Catalog 1).

[4] Cliff Eisen, in his edition of *Four Viennese String Quintets*, Recent Researches in the Music of the Classical Era, 53 (Madison, WI: A-R Editions, 1998), vii, asserts unequivocally that the "earliest [string] quintets were cultivated in Austria during the 1750s and 1760s, primarily at monastic institutions." Eisen claims that composers such as Johann Nikolaus Tischer, Johann Michael Malzat, and Franz Josef Aumann composed divertimentos at this time scored for two violins, two violas, and bass, but offers no documentation for the dating of the manuscripts involved. He appears not to have noticed that Malzat was not born until 1749. Early string quintets by the Bohemians Mysliveček, Vaňhal, and Gassmann were not evaluated for their possible chronological priority.

Mysliveček's quintets might well have been the catalyst for Brunetti's interest in the genre, not to mention that of the Bohemians Jan Křtitel Vaňhal and Florian Leopold Gassmann. Exactly what it was that prompted Mysliveček to compose quintets with two violas can only be guessed at, but it is possible that it was related to the common practice in Italy of dividing viola parts in symphonic music and operatic music. By the 1760s, this procedure can be found at least occasionally almost everywhere that symphonies were composed.[5]

Mysliveček's Op. 2 quintets were published as *VI Sinfonie concertanti o sia quintetti per due violini, due viole, e basso*. The use of the rather vague term *sinfonia concertante*, so beloved of eighteenth-century Parisian music publishers, raises some questions about stylistic orientation and the best way to perform the pieces. The term could have several meanings, but it usually denoted some sort of amalgamation of symphonic music and soloistic music. It could mean a chamber piece in symphonic style to be realized by only one player per part; a symphony enlivened with solo passages; or, in the case of the most famous *sinfonia concertante* of all, Mozart's K364/320d of 1779, a concerto with two or more soloists. Christian Cannabich's set of *VI Sinfonie concertanti o sia quintetti* for two flutes, violin, viola, and cello, brought out by the same publisher only a year or two later than Mysliveček's Op. 2, conforms to the first meaning: they are clearly "symphonies for soloists." The meaning for Mysliveček's Op. 2 is more flexible. When performed with one player per part, the quintets can also be "symphonies *for* soloists," but when performed with multiple players per part they become "symphonies *with* soloists"—the soloists being the violists, who are given special *soli* sections to permit the sonority of the viola to stand out specially to the listeners.

The title page of the Venier print leaves open the possibility of performance with one player per part (as "quintetti"), but performance with multiple players per part (as "sinfonie") seems optimum, due in particular to the presence of tremolo effects that do not come off as well when executed by single players. One manuscript copy of this set takes the symphonic option one step further by including horn parts.[6] Another important sign that Mysliveček was thinking more in terms of symphonic style in the Op. 2 quintets is the absence of counterpoint. Mysliveček generally introduced a good deal of counterpoint into his chamber music, probably out of respect for Italian traditions descended from the baroque period and the basic desire of individual chamber players to share the most interesting motives heard in the other parts. Mysliveček's first set of quintets concentrates more on the grand gestures typical of symphonic style rather than textural complexities, whereas the second set is more varied in its treatment of texture and includes a number of memorable contrapuntal excursions, for example in the third movement of String Quintet 9 and the first movement of String Quintet 11. The "second theme" of the latter provides one of the best examples of how engaging *galant* counterpoint can be in Mysliveček's hands.

The dichotomy between a symphonic conception for the first set and a chamber conception for the later set is nonetheless hardly set into stone. Some of the parts in the principal source of the later set of quintets (Modena, Biblioteca Estense e Universitaria, Mus. F.803) include occasional indications of solo passages, obviously a hint that performance as string symphonies was possible with alternations of doubled parts and solo parts. On the other hand, the quintets of the first set

[5] Rhodes, "The Origins and Utilisation of Divided Viola Writing," 67–170.

[6] The manuscript is in the library of the Conservatorio di Musica Giuseppe Verdi, Milan; see Catalog 1 below. These quintets are cataloged in error as septets for strings and horns in Evans and Dearling, 105–09.

are clearly designated chamber compositions in the *Quartbuch* catalog[7] and in a number of surviving manuscripts, including the exemplars in the Conservatorio di Musica Nicolò Paganini in Genoa.

It is possible to cultivate many interesting textural configurations in string quintets, but Mysliveček usually restricted himself to a narrow range. The basic strategy in the first set especially is to treat the violin and viola sections something like "choirs": they generally move in tandem with similar rhythms and motivic figures, whereas the bass part moves independently. The typical textures are layered, each type of instrument given its own rhythmic/melodic profile, although there can be surprises: sometimes the violas will follow the second violin part or cello independently of each other. When the violas do stand out from the other parts, they are often employed in the same way that wind instruments are used in Mysliveček's symphonies, i.e., to fill out dormant stretches of the melodic flow in the violin parts, usually with short motives in parallel thirds. When heard in an ensemble of stringed instruments only, it is remarkable how stark the tonal contrast between violins and violas can be; the effect of introducing *soli* passages for violas in a sense does resemble the sound of wind instruments alternating with strings.

The flexibility permitted in chamber style for the format of movements led Mysliveček to include slow-fast-fast and fast-slow-minuet arrangements in each set of quintets alongside the standard fast-slow-fast schemes. String Quintet 6 from the first set offers a particularly successful demonstration of how an opening slow movement could be used to set up an intense anticipation for the livelier and technically more brilliant section that follows. An outstanding work from the second set is String Quintet 8, which features a wonderfully energetic finale. In general, the Mysliveček string quintets are well-crafted chamber compositions with a wealth of distinctive motivic ideas, certainly some of the most interesting examples of the genre written during the 1760s and 1770s.

STRING QUARTETS

Probably due to a much greater demand for string quartets in late eighteenth-century Europe, there are about twice as many string quartets by Mysliveček as there are string quintets. The core repertory is comprised of three sets of six quartets each, one set published in Paris by La Chevardière in 1768 or 1769 as Op. 3, another by André in Offenbach in 1777 as Op. 1, and a posthumous set published in Berlin and Amsterdam by Hummel in 1781 without opus number. In addition, there are five works preserved only in manuscripts whose sources differ in their recommendation for performance either as quartets or string symphonies. One is the delightful quartet in E-flat major (String Quartet 9/Symphony 32), heretofore the most recorded of the Mysliveček quartets (see Catalog 1). Some prospective performers may be disappointed by the modest virtuosity of Mysliveček's string writing, even in the last set, which is by far the most challenging. Still, there is the usual abundance of textural ingenuity, melodic invention, and emotional expressiveness that can be expected from almost any of Mysliveček's compositions.

---

[7] The fragmentary *Quartbuch (2 Thematischer Cathalog verschiedener Compositionen von verschiedener Meistern)*, compiled by Johann Nepomuk Weigl ca. 1775, catalogs an Austrian collection of unverifiable origin that was once in the possession of the Esterházy family. The collection was formerly housed in the Országos Széchényi Könyvtár in Budapest and is believed to have been destroyed during World War II. Haydn knew the catalog and made corrections in it. The original comprised a volume of chamber works as Part 1 and a volume of symphonies as Part 2.

The presence or absence of a second viola part can have all sorts of stylistic implications in string chamber music. With only one part for viola, Mysliveček's string quartets lack the antiphonal writing and contrasts in timbre that enrich his string quintets, but the quartets are better suited to the four-part imitative writing favored by so many composers of late eighteenth-century chamber music as a means to vary the pervasive homophonic textures. Consistent with the practice of his contemporaries, Mysliveček's earlier quartets are very much dominated by the first violin part, whereas his later quartets, especially the Hummel set, conform more to the "conversational" ideal exemplified by the quartets of Joseph Haydn. But even in the Hummel set, only the upper three parts participate in the "conversation"; the bass line in all sets is intended mainly as a harmonic support. The symphonic character of the first set of quartets is obvious,[8] but the later sets downplay this orientation. The part-writing in the Hummel quartets in particular is too intricate and the first violin part too virtuosic even to entertain the idea of playing them with multiple players per part.

All of Mysliveček's quartets are cast in three movements, all but one in the fast-slow-fast arrangement familiar from his symphonies. Only the fourth quartet of Op. 3 uses the alternative slow-fast-fast scheme, unfortunately not with the singular effect seen in String Quintet 6. Rondos and increasingly sophisticated rondo structures were introduced into Mysliveček's quartets in stages. In the Hummel set, rondos can be found both among the slow movements and the finales in contrast to the the predictably-consistent binary forms of Op. 3. The last movement of String Quartet 19 and the slow movement of String Quartet 23 are early examples of sonata-rondo, the former cast in the ABACBA form typical of Mozart's rondos.

The Op. 3 quartets, full of charm, energy, and grace, constitute one of the finest sets of string quartets published in the 1760s, but it is the later Hummel quartets that are the most varied and interesting of Mysliveček's output. The keys of four of the six slow movements exhibit third relationships with the outer movements instead of the customary subdominant, an effect as arresting in Mysliveček's work as when it is found in the music of Haydn and Beethoven. There is a good possibility that the Hummel quartets were among the impressive series of works produced during Mysliveček's stay in Munich in 1777–78. Their virtuosity and "conversational" quality may have originated from an attempt to adapt to northern norms of string quartet writing, and there is also a notable thematic connection between one quartet and a work more securely datable to Mysliveček's stay in Munich, the divertimento in F major, published in 1777.[9] The start of the second movement of String Quartet 19 matches the opening motive of this divertimento almost exactly. The striking resemblance between the opening motive of Mysliveček's String Quartet 18 and Mozart's Piano Sonata in C Major, K309, which Mozart composed in 1777 while Mysliveček was in Munich, may be of importance, as may the complete lack of Italian manuscript sources for these quartets. Regardless, the Hummel quartets present a pleasing mixture of Italian and northern stylistic traits that professional string quartets would be well advised to sample.

---

[8] One manuscript source of the Op. 3 quartets, Ms. Noseda M.33.7–12 of the library of the Conservatorio di Musica Giuseppe Verdi, actually bears the indication "sinfonie o quartetti" (see Catalog 1).

[9] It is the first piece in *Six Easy Divertimentos for the Harpsichord or Piano-Forte* (London: Longman & Broderip, 1777). Examples of these pieces are mentioned in the Mozart correspondence from 1777; see chapter 4.

MUSIC FOR STRINGS AND WINDS IN THREE PARTS

The largest number of chamber works by Mysliveček are compositions scored for two treble instruments plus bass, the majority of them string trios for two violins and bass. Although modern editions tend to be quite specific about performing resources for chamber trios, simple compositions of this sort could be realized by any instruments of appropriate range. The bass line could be played by a single solo instrument (cello in particular), doubled by extra bass instruments, or made the basis of a keyboard realization with or without the participation of a solo bass instrument. Flute, oboe, and violin were the most common instruments used for the treble parts. It is possible to categorize most of Mysliveček's trios into pieces for two violins plus bass (string trios), two flutes plus bass (flute duets), and flute and violin plus bass (flute trios) just from an evaluation of the treble ranges: those that dip below middle C mandate performance on violin, whereas any of the wind parts could be substituted by violins. The trios designated for flute, violin, and bass in eighteenth-century sources are the ones that have proved most attractive to modern editors (see Catalog 1).

The most interesting and substantial of Mysliveček's trios are those that are idiomatic for performance by multiple players per part—orchestral trios. During their brief heyday between the 1750s and the 1770s, compositions for three-part string orchestra were among the most favored items brought out by the leading music publishers in London and Paris. Mysliveček composed eight in all. Six were first published by La Chevardière in Paris in 1768 as *Six sonates en trio qui sont faits pour exécuter à trois ou avec tous l'orchestre* (six trio sonatas intended for performance either by three players or by full orchestra), op. 1. In this set, four trios are cast in four movements (fast-minuet-slow-fast) and two in two movements (fast-minuet). All four of the four-movement trios issued by La Chevardière plus two new four-movement trios were advertised for sale in the Breitkopf catalog of 1769. The identical six trios in four movements were then published without opus number by Peter Welcker in London in 1772 as *Six Orchestra Trios for Two Violins and a Violoncello*. The trios in the latter print are Mysliveček's only four-movement works in any genre of instrumental music except for Symphonies 50 and 51. His cultivation of such works is something of a puzzle, since there was no significant precedent for four-movement trios in Italy. In Mysliveček's day the three other major composers of string trios in Italy—Carlo Antonio Campioni, Pietro Nardini, and Gaetano Pugnani—all employed three-movement formats.

Most likely, Mysliveček found inspiration for his orchestral trios in works of composers active at the electoral court in Mannheim. The prototypical orchestral trios were a set of six published in Paris ca. 1755 by Johann Stamitz, works that were considered as successful as orchestral music as any of his symphonies scored for four-part string orchestra plus winds. Other Mannheimers who subsequently wrote orchestral trios include Anton Filtz and Christian Cannabich. The Mannheim orchestral trios were always cast in four movements, fast-slow-minuet-fast, just like the Mannheim symphonies. As explained in chapter 9, there is little reason to believe that Mysliveček took much interest in Mannheim symphonies as models for his own symphonies, even though many of the musicians active at the court of Mannheim were of Bohemian origin. The hope of having music published by La Chevardière in Paris offers the most probable explanation for Mysliveček's unusual break with Italian traditions. La Chevardière was the leading publisher of orchestral trios in Europe in the 1760s, and one can easily imagine Mysliveček carefully tailoring a set of trios just for him as a means of generating income and acclaim. If this was Mysliveček's plan, his efforts clearly paid off, as attested by the existence of two reprints of his trios (Welcker of 1772 and André of 1777) as well as the publication of a subsequent set of his chamber music in Paris by La Chevardière (the Op. 3 string quartets).

Besides the four-movement plan, a few other traits of Mannheim style were imported into Mysliveček's orchestral trios, including the prominent use of tremolo, counterpoint, and intimations of the famous Mannheim crescendos. A good example of one of Mysliveček's miniature crescendos appears in the first movement of String Trio 8 (see ex. 6.12 in chapter 6). The presence of string tremolo is one of the most important characteristics that make the orchestral trios idiomatic for performance by multiple players on a part, rather than by soloists. The frequent use of counterpoint, on the other hand, points to a basic conception of these trios as something of a fusion of symphonic style and the older baroque trio-sonata style for two violins and basso continuo. In the baroque period, there were two basic techniques that guided the interaction of the violin parts: imitation and doubling at the third. Both techniques are found in abundance in the violin parts of mid-eighteenth-century orchestral trios, including those of Mysliveček. Bass lines would frequently participate fully in the contrapuntal interplay in trios from the baroque period, but in early classic style the bass line tended to lose melodic and rhythmic interest. Often it served only to supply harmonic support in the form of repeated notes ("drum bass"). The counterpoint in Mysliveček's orchestral trios, which does not exclude the bass, is a delight to hear, the epitome of the classical counterpoint with layered textures described in chapter 6. Some of the most interesting movements that exploit counterpoint are the third movement of his String Trio 7, both outer movements of String Trio 8, and the first movement of String Trio 14.

One sign of Mysliveček's independence from the Mannheim composers is his reversal of the order of the internal movements: in his four-movement orchestral trios, the minuet is placed before the slow movement with a consistency that defies explanation. It is a pity that Mysliveček chose not to adopt the four-movement plan with minuets more frequently in his symphonic writing: for their grace, his minuets would not suffer in comparison to any composed by northern symphonists of the 1760s, and their inclusion would mitigate the brevity that modern listeners often perceive.

Mysliveček's chamber trios constitute one repertory in which modern expectations coincide quite well with eighteenth-century ones. Their small-scale proportions, lack of technical virtuosity, and accessible compositional style make them perfectly suited to performance by students and amateurs today, just as they were in Mysliveček's time. The six string trios listed in the Breitkopf catalog of 1767 were likely some of the earliest instrumental compositions composed by Mysliveček in Italy. Since only one of these trios survives in manuscript sources, it would appear that they did not make nearly as much of an impression as his widely-disseminated string trios published in 1772 by Le Menu in Paris as Op. 1. After the composition of the latter set, Mysliveček abandoned string trios entirely, whether orchestral or chamber. In the mid- and late 1770s, he concentrated instead on trios with one or two flutes. The key collection of trios with one flute is a cycle of six published without opus number by Ranieri Del Vivo in the late 1770s. The most important source of trios with two flutes is a manuscript in the private collection of Antonio Venturi in Montecatini-Terme. Identified as "Op. 5," the Venturi set may have been copied from a lost Parisian print (see Catalog 1).

In his chamber music for three parts, Mysliveček carefully differentiated between solo and accompanimental voices. When the treble parts are scored for like instruments (two violins or two flutes), both are treated as soloists accompanied by a bass line with little independent melodic or rhythmic interest. In these trios, the treble parts are largely made up of successions of motives employing imitation or doubling. In flute and violin trios, there are no passages that are particularly idiomatic for flute, but there is a tendency to make the violin part much more accompanimental in character than the flute part. Typically, the violin is given arpeggiated filler over a slow-moving bass, whereas the flute is treated as a soloist.

Unusual contributions that Mysliveček made to the literature of chamber music in three parts include a trio for violin, cello, and string bass and a cycle of six sonatas for two cellos and bass. All are cast in three movements, as usual for Mysliveček, but the set of cello sonatas is noteworthy for the high proportion of movements in slow-fast-fast tempo arrangement instead of fast-slow-fast (three of the six). The combination of violin, cello, and string bass may seem odd, but it was certainly not unprecedented (there are also examples by Leopold Mozart, Leopold Hofmann, and Karl Friedrich Abel). The treatment of the instruments resembles the handling of the parts in Mysliveček's trios for flute, violin, and bass. The treble instrument (violin) is crafted in a manner similar to the flute part of this type of trio, whereas the middle instrument (cello) is given rhythmic filler typical of the violin part. The bottom part (string bass) essentially offers little more than harmonic support, just like the cello part of more conventional trios for flute, violin, and bass.

Mysliveček's sonatas for two cellos and bass, another rare combination of instruments also treated by Leopold Mozart and Leopold Hofmann, are known only from a manuscript of ca. 1780 now preserved in the České Muzeum Hudby in Prague (Ms. XLIX C 247). Both the reason for their composition and the identity of the performers for whom they were intended are completely obscure. The known cultivation of this rare instrumentation in the North and the lack of Italian sources may or may not be a sign that they were written in Munich. The handling of the instruments conforms to a standard trio-sonata conception: the musical material for the cellos is dominated by imitation and passagework in parallel thirds, whereas the bass provides little more than a simple harmonic support. Even a brief sampling of these pieces will dispel any fear that compositions for three bass instruments need sound dark or "muddy." They are as gracious and charming as any of Mysliveček's other chamber compositions.

VIOLIN SONATAS

Mysliveček wrote no music for chamber ensembles with keyboard and multiple string instruments, but the number of his sonatas for keyboard and violin is rather large: eighteen works in three sets of six sonatas. The most important of these collections was published by Thompson in London in 1775; two other sets are preserved only in manuscript in the České Muzeum Hudby in Prague (see Catalog 1). The three-movement sonatas in the Thompson collection are more substantial than the modest two-movement cycles preserved in the Czech manuscripts, which are interesting nonetheless for their large number of rondos (an indication that they may have been composed in the late 1770s). In addition to these sonatas with a fully-realized keyboard part, there are also a few sonatas for violin and bass extant in the Genoa Conservatory (Violin Sonatas 1–5, the last three likely remnants of a set of six). The archaic instrumentation with basso continuo invites speculation that they were composed for Mysliveček's own use not long after his arrival in Italy.[10]

[10] An excellent orientation to the violin sonatas is in Zdeňka Pilková, "Houslové sonáty Českých skladatelo z let 1730–1810" [Violin Sonatas by Czech Composers from the Years 1730–1810], *Hudební věda* 23 (1986): 291–311. Newman, 227–29, is outdated and inaccurate with respect to sources.

Modern violinists and music critics tend to evaluate the merit of sonatas for violin and keyboard on the basis of a latter-day notion of partnership between the two instruments (or even a subservient keyboard part). The eighteenth century, however, was not so anxious to favor the violin when it was paired with a keyboard instrument, and there are many examples of "accompanied" keyboard sonatas published in Paris and London in the 1760s and 1770s in which the violin parts are nearly superfluous. Sonatas of this type often were written by opera composers like Mysliveček who sought to capitalize on the market for amateur music-making and saw no need to make much more of them.[11] In England especially this combination of instruments was popular among married amateurs (violin for the husband, keyboard for the wife). Mysliveček's accompanied sonatas will only partially please those who subscribe to the more modern ideal of partnership between players. The violin parts are elegantly woven into the changing textures, but do not exhibit much virtuosity or independence. The greater independence of the violin in two works of questionable authenticity reinforces doubts about their genuineness.[12]

KEYBOARD MUSIC

Mysliveček's music for solo keyboard does not reveal the composer's talents at their best, although it appears to have made enough of an impression on Wolfgang Mozart for him to have borrowed certain musical ideas for two piano sonatas he composed shortly after visiting Mysliveček in Munich during the autumn of 1777.[13] Mysliveček's contribution to the repertory of solo keyboard music derives mainly from two collections published in Britain: the *Six Easy Divertimentos* (London, 1777) and the *Six Easy Lessons* (Edinburgh, 1784). The latter is a posthumous collection whose attribution to Mysliveček is confirmed by the presence of the pieces in earlier manuscripts (see Catalog 1).

Mysliveček's keyboard sonatas respect Italian traditions quite faithfully. The *Easy Divertimentos*, in fact, are some of the more interesting contributions to the repertory of Italianate single-movement sonatas from the mid- and late eighteenth century. Modest as they are, most examples by composers other than Domenico Scarlatti are inferior in quality. None of the Mysliveček "divertimentos" conform to the usual binary structure seen in most single-movement Italian sonatas; five are rondos, whereas the remaining one is a minuet and trio.

The *Easy Lessons* are all cast in two movements and are more substantial than the *Easy Divertimentos*, even accounting for the greater length created by the additional movement.[14] The "lessons" carefully follow principles of arranging movements that underlie an untold number of Italian keyboard sonatas of the eighteenth century. In the most normal plan, there would be a progression of slow-fast in a two-movement work, but Mysliveček's two movement sonatas generally follow the alternative plan in which a fast movement is followed by one of the three lightest and most popular-oriented types of movements: minuets, variations, or rondos. The results are pleasing,

---

[11] On the style of Italianate solo and accompanied sonatas of the mid-eighteenth century, see Daniel E. Freeman, "Johann Christian Bach and the Early Classical Italian Masters," in *Studies in Musical Genres and Repertories: Eighteenth-Century Keyboard Music*, 2nd ed., ed. Robert L. Marshall (New York and London: Routledge, 2003), 230–69.

[12] See questionable works nos. 2 and 3 in Part 12 of Catalog 1.

[13] Daniel E. Freeman, "Josef Mysliveček and the Piano Sonatas K. 309 (284b) and K. 311 (284c)," in *Mozart-Jahrbuch 1995* (Salzburg: Internationale Stiftung Mozarteum, 1995), 95–109.

[14] See Freeman, "Johann Christian Bach and the Early Classical Italian Masters."

if unremarkable. At least three sonatas (Keyboard Sonatas 7, 11, and 12) take advantage of the keyboard's abilities as an instrument of transcription to evoke symphonic style in their opening movements. Occasionally there are somewhat difficult passages with octaves in the left hand or passagework in the right hand, but Mysliveček never demonstrates a true mastery of keyboard idioms. Simple two-part textures with the melody in the right hand and the accompaniment in the left hand are about all that he offers, but one must keep in mind the intended market for these collections and the appellation "easy" attached to both.

CHAMBER MUSIC FOR WINDS

Considering Mysliveček's Italian training, his vast output of chamber music for strings, and the relative unimportance of music for wind instruments among eighteenth-century composers, the attention he lavished on chamber music for winds, especially the octets for two oboes, two clarinets, two horns, and two bassoons, is one of the most notable phenomena surrounding his production of instrumental music. The octets in fact have been recorded more frequently than any other examples of Mysliveček's music.[15] The wind quintets for two oboes, two horns, and bassoon preserved in the Bischöfliche Priesterseminar in Münster are also attractive works, but they do not exhibit the scope and majesty of the octets. Dedicated to Prince Abbondio Rezzonico, nephew of Pope Clement XIII (r. 1758–69), they were almost certainly composed in Rome during the last few months of Mysliveček's life. The remaining wind compositions listed in Catalog 1 are mainly novelties or curiosities.[16]

Many puzzling circumstances surround the preservation of manuscripts for the wind octets—to the extent that doubts about their authenticity might be entertained. The genre of wind octet was virtually non-existent at the time of Mysliveček's death in 1781, and no sources date from his lifetime, only some copies from the late eighteenth- and early nineteenth centuries in Donaueshingen and St. Petersburg, cities with which Mysliveček was never associated. Nonetheless, the octets are thoroughly Myslivečkian in style and further evidence of Mysliveček's authorship lies in the fact that the slow movement of the third octet clearly shares motives from the opening of Mysliveček's keyboard concerto in F major.[17] The resemblance is too close to leave any doubt that the thematic material was borrowed from one work to another (which came first is not possible to establish).

The two manuscripts in St. Petersburg are part of an early nineteenth-century collection of wind music that was once in the possession of the Princes Yusupov.[18] While the St. Petersburg manuscripts are very distant from Mysliveček both geographically and chronologically, the manuscripts in Donaueschingen that survive from the court of Prince Karl Egon von Fürstenberg seem to offer clues about the origins of the octets. The Donaueschingen manuscripts are certainly earlier than

[15] A useful modern edition has facilitated their accessibility: *Tre ottetti*, ed. Camillo Schoenbaum, Musica antiqua bohemica, 55 (Prague: Státní hudební vydavatelství, 1962; reprint, 1964; reprint as 2nd ed., Editio Supraphon, 1973).

[16] For further information on these works see Daniel E. Freeman, "The Wind Music of Josef Mysliveček," in *Schloss Engers Colloquia zur Kammermusik*, 2: *Zur Harmoniemusik und ihrer Geschichte*, ed. Christoph-Hellmut Mahling et al. (Mainz: Villa Musica, 1999), 83–99.

[17] Camillo Schoenbaum came to his conclusion after seeing a musical example from the F major concerto quoted in Jan Racek, "Příspěvek," 94. The two motives are displayed side-by-side in Pečman, 166–67.

[18] I am grateful to L. I. Buchina of the Rossiĭskaja Nazional'naja Biblioteka im. M. E. Saltykova-Ščedrina for providing this information to me.

the Russian ones, since they appear in the *Copia Verzeichniss* of 1804, a copy of an older catalog of holdings prepared under the supervision of the virtuoso oboist Josef Fiala, who was Kapellmeister to the Prince in Donaueschingen from 1792 until Fiala's death in 1816. As it happens, Fiala, Mysliveček, and Mozart were all present in Munich in the autumn of 1777. Fiala, who was born in western Bohemia and studied music in Prague as a young man, had come there in the spring of 1777 to enter the service of Elector Maximilian III Joseph. That autumn, Fiala met Mozart in Munich. The Mozarts made it possible for Fiala to join the orchestra of the archbishop of Salzburg in October 1778, and it is also known that Fiala visited Mozart in Vienna in 1785.[19]

According to Wolfgang Mozart's letter to his father of 3 October 1777, Fiala coached wind players who performed at the tavern of Franz Albert in Munich.[20] Mozart mentioned that a band of five wind players (two clarinets, two horns, and a bassoon) played music in Mozart's honor in front of the house of a certain Frau von Tosson and that the performers were the same ones who played in Albert's dining hall during meals. The social context of the public tavern is of course just where one would imagine Mysliveček to be perfectly at home, but even if he never set foot in Albert's tavern, it seems probable that Fiala either commissioned the Mysliveček octets or made sure that he had copies to take with him, and that he brought the octets to Donaueschingen. It is also likely that Fiala was responsible for transporting them to St. Petersburg, where he served in the households of Empress Catherine the Great and her lover Prince Orlov between 1786 and 1790. It is known that wind music was widely cultivated in Munich, often in the context of the serenading described in the Mozart letter.[21] In sum, there seems little reason to doubt that the Mysliveček wind octets were written for Munich.

Mysliveček's wind octets are distinguished compositions, perhaps most importantly for their unusually early date of composition. Whether or not they were composed in Munich in 1777–78, the octets were obviously completed before Mysliveček's death in 1781. But even if they were composed close to that time, they would be among the earliest wind octets ever to appear for two oboes, two clarinets, two horns, and two bassoons. The only other octets for this grouping known to have been written before the early 1780s are by Ernst Eichner, a composer and bassoonist active at courts in Zweibrücken and Potsdam, who died in 1777.[22] The two composers almost certainly arrived at this combination of instruments independently, since they lived far distant from one another and their respective octets were drawn from two distinct stylistic heritages. Whereas Eichner's octets are based on the tradition of military wind music, Mysliveček's are based on symphonic style. The significance of these early precedents is difficult to gauge. After 1782, when permanent wind bands were established in Vienna, octets for two oboes, two clarinets, two horns, and two bassoons became the quintessential type of wind chamber music.[23] With so many different configurations of

---

[19] I am grateful to James Hepokoski for sharing with me his hypothesis that Beethoven in his Septet Op. 21 used motives from Mysliveček's third wind octet. The theory is bolstered by the presence of Fiala in Vienna in the 1780s and the sponsorship of the first performance of the Septet in the household of the Bohemian Prince Schwarzenberg. Prince Schwarzenberg maintained one of the leading *Harmoniemusik* ensembles in Vienna at the time and assembled a large library of wind repertory.

[20] Anderson, 293; Bauer and Deutsch, 2:31.

[21] Kearns, "The Eighteenth-Century Orchestral Serenade."

[22] Roger Hellyer, "Harmoniemusik: Music for Small Wind Band in the Late Eighteenth and Early Nineteenth Centuries" (Ph.D. diss., Oxford University, 1973), 104–10.

[23] Ibid., 95–145.

instruments in circulation during the 1770s, it is probably mere coincidence that these two composers came up with the same combination that was soon to find so much favor in Vienna.

Although not influential models for later composers, Mysliveček's octets are some of the finest examples of wind ensemble music (*Harmoniemusik*) ever composed in the eighteenth century. It is remarkable that Mysliveček could have produced such excellent wind pieces without any known period of experimentation, though he did draw heavily on his mastery of symphony and overture style for inspiration.[24] The octets are essentially "wind symphonies," a conception shared among many composers of the era. Usually, *Harmoniemusik* was composed in four-movement cycles like symphonies or in multi-movement cycles akin to suites or serenades. The atypical aspect of Mysliveček's practice is the Italianate arrangement in three movements. Ordinarily wind music in symphonic style was organized into four movements with a third-movement minuet, just as in northern symphonies. Prominent composers who cultivated the latter style include Josef Fiala, Paul Winneberger, Anton Rossetti, Josef Rejcha, and Friedrich Witt.

Unlike some other categories of chamber music, Mysliveček treated all participants in his octets as soloists and took great care to provide everyone with something interesting to play—even the bassoonists, who are given a prominence unusual for the day.[25] It may be accurate to describe the wind octets as the finest of all Mysliveček's chamber music, in particular the most difficult to perform and the most idiomatic for the participating instruments. They provide perfect demonstrations of Mysliveček's versatility and ingenuity as a composer in almost any genre he chose to cultivate.

---

[24] Further discussion of their musical style see Freeman, "The Wind Music of Josef Mysliveček," 83–99.

[25] See Hellyer, 108–10, for a discussion of the lavish use of bassoons in the octets and a general description of their musical style.

Part 3

MYSLIVEČEK AND MOZART

11

A SPECIAL RELATIONSHIP

Mozart's friendship with Mysliveček was unlike any relationship he had with any other composer, with implications for both his personal and professional life. For the most part, composers with whom Mozart had the most contact during his youth were his father and various colleagues at the court of Salzburg, such as Anton Adlgasser and Michael Haydn, both of whom father and son spoke of with an affectionate contempt. All these composers were limited in outlook and ability, but they did transmit and reinforce regional traditions of composition in various genres. There were also composers such as J. C. Bach, Padre Martini, and Thomas Linley, whom Mozart met briefly and spoke of fondly, but they seem not to have provided him with models of musical expertise over long periods of time, and not in a wide range of compositional styles. Josef Mysliveček, on the other hand, was a frequent visitor to the Mozart household during all three of Wolfgang's trips to Italy during the early 1770s, and, as was seen in chapter 4, there is no question that correspondence between Mysliveček and the Mozart family continued until 1778. In addition, Mysliveček was a composer of unusual skill who possessed the rare distinction of being equally talented as a composer of vocal music and instrumental music. After Mozart's move to Vienna in 1781, it would not be accurate to describe any of the relationships he formed with professional composers as intimate. The high regard he held for composers such as Gluck and Joseph Haydn was not reinforced by close personal contacts. Most other composers known to him, for example, Pavel Vranický and Antonio Salieri, are properly classed either as casual acquaintances or as rivals. There is no parallel in all of the Mozart correspondence for the concern for Mysliveček that Wolfgang revealed to his father during the autumn of 1777. No person outside of Mozart's family was ever the cause for such an outpouring of emotion.

Leopold Mozart's strong early attraction for Mysliveček might be attributed in large part to their similar backgrounds. Both spoke German fluently, professed the Catholic faith, and had roots among the artisan classes (bookbinders in Leopold's case, millers in Mysliveček's). Both were brought up in households with incomes equivalent to the modern middle class and were educated to a level of some university training. It would appear that the Mozarts and Mysliveček even had mutual acquaintances in Salzburg (see chapter 3). The social compatibility of the two was reinforced by Mysliveček's personal charm. Except for Padre Martini, it is impossible to name another composer whom Leopold Mozart found so agreeable during his son's formative years. Leopold is never known to have expressed fondness for J. C. Bach, nor is there any evidence that he or his son ever exchanged correspondence with him.

As regards Wolfgang, Mysliveček's potential as a role model was likely one of the most important attractions for him. Mysliveček, as a foreigner, had achieved what the Mozart family wanted for

Wolfgang in Italy: a solid reputation as a composer of opera with a reliable stream of new operatic commissions. He would surely have been seen as a source of advice and connections. It must have struck Wolfgang as enviable that Mysliveček could pursue a successful career without institutional employment and could indulge his love of travel at any time he wished. Mozart also loved to travel and shared Mysliveček's extravagant spending habits. For an adolescent boy from a strict middle-class Catholic household, the sort of sexual liberation represented by Mysliveček's way of living probably could not have failed to intrigue Mozart, even if it was instinctively condemned by both his father and him.

Had Mysliveček not betrayed their trust, the hold he exercised over Leopold and Wolfgang Mozart could have continued well beyond 1778. There were few people inside or outside the profession of music who succeeded in deceiving the shrewd Leopold Mozart. However, as was seen in chapter 4, Mysliveček skillfully used him in the years 1777–78 to obtain patronage from the archbishop of Salzburg while stringing him along with the promise of an opera commission for Wolfgang in Naples, which then never materialized. Considering the way that Wolfgang described Mysliveček's behavior towards him in Munich during the autumn of 1777, it is probable that Leopold had Mysliveček principally in mind in a passage of his oft-quoted letter of 16 February 1778 in which he criticized his son for failing to see through the faults of flatterers:[1]

> . . . it is just your good heart that prevents you from detecting any shortcomings in a person who showers praises on you, has a great opinion of you and flatters you to the skies, and who makes you give him all your confidence and affection. . . .

Leopold had been irritated with Mysliveček for some time about the stalled opera commission for Naples, but at this point Wolfgang still remained loyal to his friend, hence Leopold's admonition.

In Leopold's letter of 13 August 1778 to Wolfgang in Paris (quoted in chapter 4), Mysliveček also figures in some of the most eloquent fatherly advice that Leopold ever offered to his son. He ends by making it clear that, despite his considerable help, Mysliveček, had not been heard from.[2] Frequently, when this letter is excerpted and discussed (Leopold writes, ". . . there is no true friend—using the word *in its fullest sense*—but a father"), the remarks about Mysliveček are simply ignored. But what this letter actually does is identify Mysliveček as a personal friend at one time so close to Wolfgang Mozart that he could have rivaled Leopold for the expectation of loyalty that Leopold felt could only be found in a parent.

There can be no question that Mysliveček helped shape Mozart's compositional style at certain times in his life. The similarity in their styles has been frequently commented on by music critics, and there has even been the offhand observation that "Mysliveček's music is almost too Mozartean before the fact to have an identity of its own."[3] There are specimens of Mysliveček's earlier music, for example, the slow movement of String Quartet, op. 3, no. 2 (String Quartet 2), published in the late 1760s, that sound like mature compositions of Mozart of years later—in this case, particularly like the slow movement of Symphony no. 34, K338—but it is usually only individual movements

---

[1] Anderson, 483; Bauer and Deutsch, 2:283–84.

[2] Ibid., 598; ibid., 2:443–44.

[3] Newman, 228.

that sound so much like Mozart. The one large-scale work that consistently does sound like a masterpiece of Mozart is Mysliveček's oratorio *Isacco figura del redentore*, which is attributed to Mozart in two surviving manuscripts and was once advertised as a newly-discovered Mozart masterpiece.[4]

It is easy to overestimate the importance of various kinds of resemblances of Mozart's style to passages in the work of many late eighteenth-century composers. To a large extent, the music of all major European composers of the 1770s and 1780s is reasonably similar to Mozart's. The composers of that era subscribed to a "common practice" of shared techniques and stock melodic gestures that makes it difficult to evaluate the true significance of passages here and there that sound similar to passages by Mozart or other composers. Style criticism is not precise enough to measure quantitatively the overall similarity of one composer's work with that of another, and historians are fortunate when they are able to produce evidence that similarity in style can be correlated to personal contacts or the availability of specific models.

One example of how difficult it can be to judge whether a passage is a quotation from another composer's works can be found in Mysliveček's String Quintet in C major (no. 9), meas. 23–27. These measures are audibly very similar to measures 11–15, in the same key, of Mozart's Violin Concerto no. 3, K216 of 1775 (exx. 11.1–11.2). That the composition of the quintet preceded the composition of the violin concerto is clear since the quintet comes from a set of six mentioned by Mysliveček in his letter to Count Waldstein from Naples, 14 September 1773.[5] Mysliveček claimed that his quintets were already well known in Italy by that time. There is thus a good possibility that Mozart could have heard them during his last trip to Italy. He may have taken one or more quintets back to Salzburg with him. It is also plausible that Mozart came into contact with them for the first time after his return to Salzburg but before he composed K216. Still, whether the similarity between these two short passages can accurately be attributed to Mysliveček's precedent remains a matter very much open to question.[6] Even if the presence of these motives in Mozart's concerto can be attributed to Mysliveček's example, there could still be a question about his estimation of the way they were used originally. Mozart picked up musical ideas continuously and from a bewildering variety of sources, sometimes leaving the impression that his goal was to demonstrate how brilliantly he—and he alone—could enrich them. In a case such as the one just detailed, the borrowing of a snatch of motivic material to be incorporated into a large-scale work need not be taken as an indication of admiration for another composer's skill, since it would have no impact on basic compositional technique.

It is reasonable nonetheless to interpret Mysliveček's contact with Mozart overall as an opportunity to acquire expertise in the composition of certain musical genres that were cultivated with particular success by his older friend. Mozart's first contacts with Mysliveček coincided with a critical stage in his development as a composer: the period immediately preceding and accompanying the composition of his first true masterpieces. Surely the earliest compositions by Mozart that

[4] Boghen, 491–94.

[5] The original letter is in the castle library at Mnichovo Hradiště, collection Rodinný Archiv Valdštejnů, dokeská manipulace, sign. III–21/28 (see chapter 3 for a translation and discussion of its contents).

[6] Much the same can be said for the resemblance between the opening motives of Mozart's Piano Sonata in C Major, K309, and Mysliveček's String Quartet 18 in C Major, which work out the same chord with exactly the same rhythms. Warnings about thematic affinities can be drawn from the examples in Böhmer, *W. A. Mozart's Idomeneo*. His example 11a (p. 395) shows what seems a remarkable resemblance between the opening vocal phrases from "Vi fida lo sposo" in Mysliveček's *Ezio* of 1777 and "Se il padre perdei" in Mozart's *Idomeneo*. When compared with the opening phrase of the aria "A torto spergiuro" from Sales's *Antigono*, however, it is clear that Mozart could well have arrived at the similar opening with knowledge of common melodic types.

EXAMPLE 11.1. Mysliveček, String Quintet in C Major (String Quintet 9), first movement, meas. 23–27.

EXAMPLE 11.2. Mozart, Violin Concerto, no. 3, K213, first movement, meas. 11–15.

have achieved widespread exposure and approval among ordinary music lovers are the Divertimenti for Strings, K136–138 (125a–c), a series of three-movement string symphonies in Italian style composed in Salzburg in 1772. These works pre-date a significant advance in Mozart's abilities as a composer that can be traced rather precisely to the year 1773, when he turned seventeen years of age. At the beginning of the year, while resident in Italy, he completed his renowned motet "Exultate jubilate," K165 (158a), and later that year composed his Symphony no. 25, K183 (173dB), the "Little G Minor," a landmark in symphonic composition, besides a series of brilliant chamber and symphonic works that are not as familiar today. The year 1774 saw the composition of the well-known Symphony no. 29, K201 (186a), and in 1775 he produced the great series of four violin concertos K211, 216, 218, and 219.[7] As we will see, there is little reason to doubt that Mozart found useful models in the work of Josef Mysliveček that assisted him in the process of developing his own techniques of composing

[7] All of these works pre-date the Piano Concerto no. 9, K271 (1777). Charles Rosen (*op. cit.*, 59, 198) has posited that K271 "may be considered Mozart's first large-scale masterpiece in any form" (it features an interesting treatment of ritornello form in its first movement), but Symphonies nos. 25 and 29 and the Violin Concertos nos. 2–5, all written earlier than it, are of course large-scale masterpieces.

symphonic works, violin concertos, and vocal music in Italian style—in sum, all of the genres to which his earliest masterpieces belong.

Mozart's use of Mysliveček's music for stylistic models began almost as soon as the two came into contact with each other in the early 1770s. Indeed Josef Mysliveček was the only composer whom the Mozarts were truly close to during all three of their trips to Italy between 1770 and 1773. As was discussed in chapter 3, Wolfgang and Leopold Mozart first encountered Mysliveček in Bologna in March 1770 at the time of the preparations underway for a production of Mysliveček's opera *La Nitteti*. The Mozarts probably did not see a performance of it, since they soon left Bologna for their tour of central and southern Italy, but when they returned in July Mysliveček was still in the city, and he probably remained there with the Mozarts until they left in October.

In the summer of 1770, the fourteen-year-old Mozart was preoccupied with the composition of his opera *Mitridate re di Ponto*, a work that had been commissioned by Count Karl von Firmian for presentation at the Regio-Ducal Teatro in Milan at the end of the year. Interestingly enough, the libretto originally intended for the commission had been Metastasio's *La Nitteti*, and it was a surprise when the libretto for *Mitridate* was delivered to the Mozarts instead. In his mid-teens, a project as large as a three-act Italian serious opera was quite daunting for Mozart, and Harrison Wignall has meticulously documented the long period it took Mozart to complete the work and the difficulties he had preparing music to suit the singers engaged for the production. In light of this, it is hard to over-emphasize the importance of Mysliveček's acquaintance with the Mozarts at this time. The goal of their trip to Italy was to establish Wolfgang sufficiently so that he could gain permanent musical employment. The opportunity presented by Count Firmian to compose an opera for one of the greatest opera theaters in Europe could not be squandered. There were a number of talented composers who might have been able to acquaint the young Mozart with the latest trends in operatic composition in Italy, either directly or indirectly, but only one—Mysliveček—was a daily visitor to the Mozart household and an intimate friend of Leopold Mozart at the time Wolfgang composed his *Mitridate*.[8]

Mozart's *Mitridate* could certainly be described as a Myslivečkian work. Although Mozart's use of musical motives from the 1767 *Mitridate* of Mysliveček's friend Quirino Gasparini should not be discounted,[9] there is no mistaking the orientation of Mozart's opera towards Mysliveček's compositional procedures. The arias Mozart composed for *Mitridate* represent a significant stylistic shift from the arias in such works as *Die Schuldigkeit des ersten Gebots* (1767), *Apollo et Hyacinthus* (1767), and *La finta semplice* (1769), and the concert arias he composed in Italy in 1770 before he began work on *Mitridate* (K77/73e, K82/73o, K83/73p, and K88/73c). The *Mitridate* arias are laid out on much broader lines than his earlier arias, even those written earlier the same year, and sonata-form events are much better articulated within the dal-segno structures, especially the opening

[8] It is known from Leopold Mozart's letters of 5 August and 27 October 1770 that Mysliveček visited the Mozarts frequently while they stayed in Bologna, and that Leopold regarded him as a friend. Wignall and Christoph-Hellmut Mahling have commented on Mozart's interest in Mysliveček's operatic music: see Harrison James Wignall, "Mozart, Guglielmo d'Ettore, and the Composition of *Mitridate* (K. 87/74a)" (Ph.D. diss., Brandeis University, 1995), and Christoph-Hellmut Mahling, "Mysliveček und Grétry - Vorbilder Mozarts?," in *Die frühdeutsche Oper und ihre Beziehungen zu Italien, England und Frankreich: Mozart und die Oper seiner Zeit*, ed. Martin Ruhnke, *Hamburger Jahrbuch für Musikwissenschaft* 5 (Laaber: Laaber-Verlag, 1981), 203–09.

[9] For Gasparini's impact on the composition of Mozart's *Mitridate*, see Tagliavini, "Quirino Gasparini and Mozart," 151–71. There is no mention of Mysliveček, nor is there in Carolyn Gianturco, *Mozart's Early Operas* (London: Batsford, 1981). In Philipp Adlung, *Mozarts Opera seria "Mitridate, re di Ponto,"* Hamburger Beiträge zur Musikwissenschaft no. 46 (Eisenach: Karl Dieter Wagner, 1996), Mysliveček's name figures only (p. 15) as one of several composers who set Cigna-Santi's libretto *Motezuma*.

ritornellos. The sudden prominence of syncopation so typical of Mysliveček is also noteworthy. Syncopated melodies and accompanimental patterns are found only in modest proportions in Mozart's earlier arias; in comparison, *Mitridate* provides a feast of syncopation.

Some corroboration for these points is found in a survey of opera arias from the late 1760s and early 1770s prepared by Martha Feldman.[10] Although *Nitteti* was not examined for this study, Mysliveček's name comes up repeatedly as a composer whose arias share important defining characteristics with the young Mozart. In fact, the arias of Mysliveček and Gassmann are deemed the ones most similar in style. The clear articulation of sonata-form events within aria forms appears to be one of the most enduring legacies of Mozart's contacts with Mysliveček's operatic music. The finding that J. C. Bach's arias are not as similar should not be surprising. When Mozart began his career as an operatic composer in Italy, he maintained no contacts with J. C. Bach whatsoever; in distant London, J. C. Bach was not even active as a composer of opera during the period between his *Carattaco* (1767) and his later *Temistocle* (1772), and the operas he had composed for Italy in the early 1760s would have been old-fashioned for a young composer trying to master the styles current in the early 1770s.

A full evaluation of all the ways that Mozart might have used both Mysliveček and Gasparini as models for the vocal selections in *Mitridate* would require a separate study, but a few examples from Mozart's first aria, "Al destin, che la minaccia," will suffice to demonstrate his interest in Mysliveček's music. The stylistic signals set by the opening aria is a phenomenon discussed in chapter 7, and in this case the first aria of *Mitridate* portends an opera dominated by elaborate dal-segno arias with strongly-articulated amalgamations of sonata form, just like the arias in Mysliveček's operas of the same period. There is no question that Mozart made use of the opening aria of Mysliveček's *Nitteti*, "Sono in mar," as a model for his own opening aria; the similarities at the start of each are so close that further commentary is unnecessary (see exx. 11.3–11.4). The clearest use of Mysliveček's music elsewhere in the vocal portions of *Mitridate* has been documented by Harrison James Wignall in versions of the aria "Lungi da te" that are based on motives from Mysliveček's "Se la cagion saprete."[11]

Mozart's interest in *Nitteti* extended not only to its vocal selections, but also to its overture. A number of significant similarities between the two overtures can be observed by comparing the excerpts in examples 11.5–11.7. The opening motive of the *Mitridate* overture strikes one as a simplification of Mysliveček's opening: the unisons in the first two measures of the *Nitteti* overture are condensed into a single unison half note in all the parts; the staccato eighth notes of meas. 3–4 and 7–8 of the Mysliveček overture are similarly condensed to one measure. Additionally, the phrase structure of the two openings is exactly the same. Mozart's "second theme" in the first movement (ex. 11.6, meas. 15–24) appears to be an adaptation of the "second theme" of the third movement of Mysliveček's overture (ex. 11.7), a type in which the textural complex begins with an accompanimental figure; Mozart even used the same repeated note in the violas. The second movements of both overtures begin with another kind of textural complex that features a *cantabile* melody accompanied by a characteristic figure in the second violins. The form of both is sonata form without development (whereas Gasparini chose rhyming binary form for his *Mitridate* overture). Similarities in the third movements include a shared sonata-form structure (Gasparini's third movement is a

---

[10] Martha Feldman, "Mozart and His Elders: Opera-seria Arias, 1766–1775," *Mozart-Jahrbuch 1991* (Kassel: Bärenreiter, 1992), 564–75.

[11] Wignall, 173–210.

rondeau), and "second themes" in both that begin with an accompanimental figure followed by a leading-tone motive.

As Mozart matured as a composer of opera, the influence of Mysliveček's operatic style weakened, as is evident in the operas *Ascanio in Alba* (1771) and *Lucio Silla* (1773), both composed for the Regio-Ducal Teatro in Milan. This is only to be expected, since Mysliveček was not in close contact with Wolfgang during the composition of these works, as he had been during preparations for the opera *Mitridate* (he only met up with the Mozarts in Italy after the two works had been completed). Both operas exhibit characteristics of the Viennese *festa teatrale* that were foreign to Mysliveček's way of writing. *Ascanio in Alba*, for example, features choruses and ballet integrated into the fabric of the drama. The characters are drawn from classical mythology and the overture is cast in one movement instead of three. Additionally, Mozart made sonata form with ritornellos the dominant aria form in his operas at an earlier stage than Mysliveček. In 1773 Mysliveček was still writing many arias in dal-segno form, whereas they were already nearly banished in Mozart's *Ascanio in Alba*.

EXAMPLE 11.3. Mysliveček, Aria 1, "Son in mar non veggo sponde" from *La Nitteti*, meas. 23–30 (horns, oboes tacent meas. 23–29, omitted meas. 30).

EXAMPLE 11.4. Mozart, Aria 1, "Al destin, che la minaccia" from *Mitridate, re di Ponto*, meas. 19–26 (horns, oboes tacent meas. 19–21, omitted meas. 22–26).

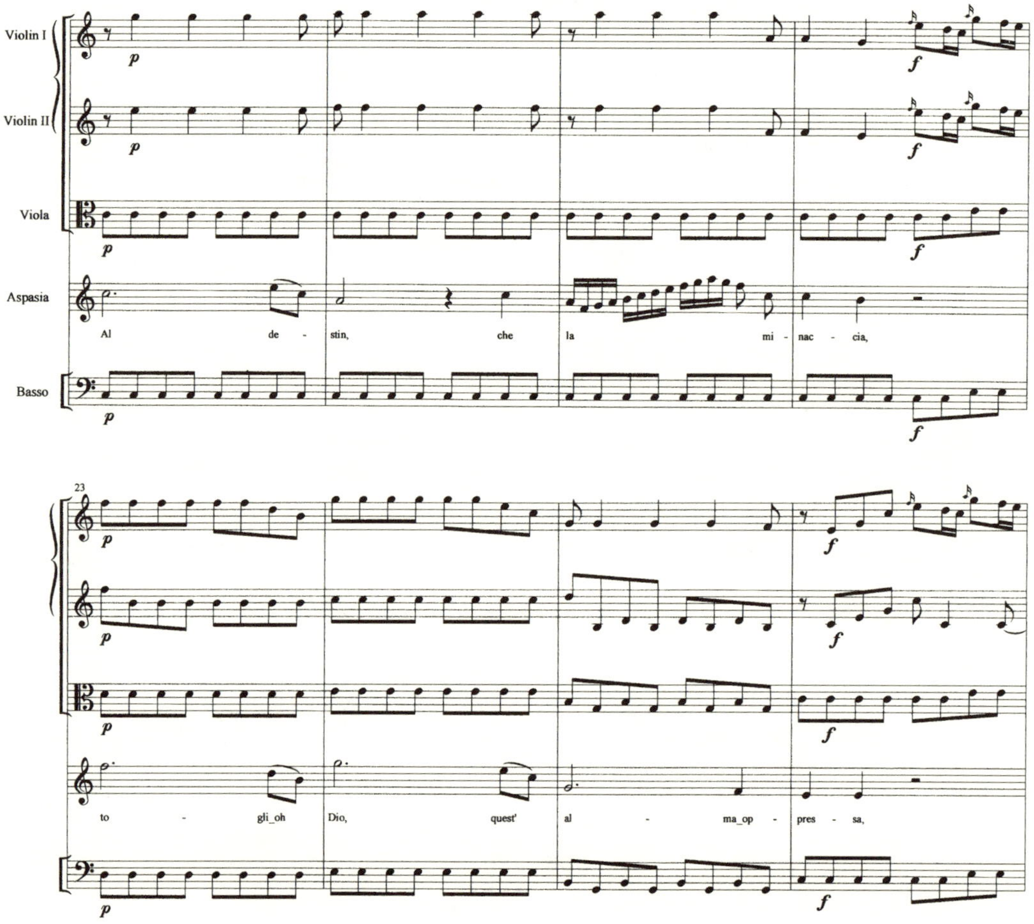
Violin I
Violin II
Viola
Aspasia
Basso
Al de - stin, che la mi - nac - cia,
23
to - gli_oh Dio, quest' al - ma_op - pres - sa,

EXAMPLE 11.5. Mysliveček, Overture to *La Nitteti*, first movement, meas. 1–18 (horns, oboes omitted).

Allegro con spirito
Violin I
Violin II
Viola
Basso

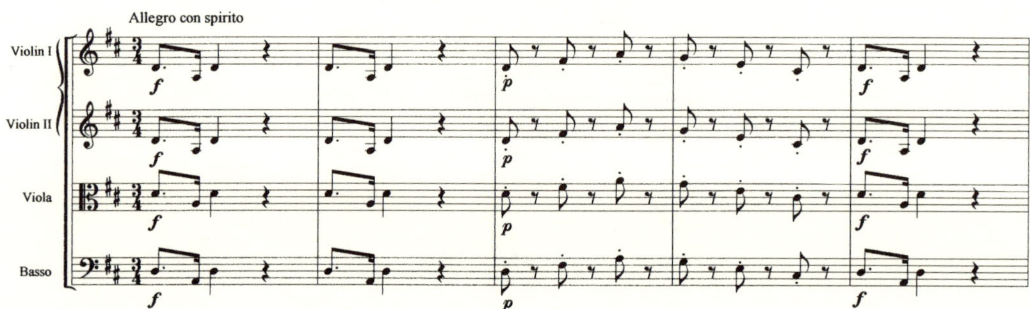

EXAMPLE 11.5–*continued*

EXAMPLE 11.6. Mozart, Overture to *Mitridate, re di Ponto*, first movement, meas. 1–19 (horns, oboes omitted).

continued

Example 11.6–*continued*

Example 11.7. Mysliveček, Overture to *La Nitteti*, third movement, meas. 17–30 (horns, oboes omitted).

EXAMPLE 11.7–*continued*

Mysliveček's dramatic vocal style still asserts itself strongly in Mozart's oratorio *La Betulia liberata* (1771), however. The latter was one of three settings of Metastasio's oratorio text that were prepared for Padua in 1771 (the others were by Mysliveček and Antonio Calegari). Mysliveček's setting may well be the oratorio mentioned by Leopold Mozart as being readied for Padua in a letter to his wife from Milan dated 27 October 1770.[12] The Mozart version is dominated by elaborate dal-segno arias and, just as in *Mitridate*, the opening aria, "D'ogni colpa la colpa maggiore," is particularly close to Mysliveček's style. Unfortunately, no music survives from Mysliveček's setting to evaluate the possibility of direct motivic borrowings.

Mysliveček's symphonic music had an impact on Mozart at least as great as his vocal music, and his interest is confirmed by the fact that Mysliveček was the only composer whose symphonies were singled out for praise in Mozart's Italian correspondence. Since Mysliveček was the finest symphonist resident in Italy during all three of Mozart's trips there in the early 1770s, this should not be wondered at. The comment Mozart made to his sister in December 1770, about trying to make sure that a specific Mysliveček symphony would be available for him in Salzburg, is really quite extraordinary: The incipit he included to help identify it constitutes the only attributable music in the entire Mozart correspondence that is not by Mozart himself.[13] The work in question came to light as the overture to Mysliveček's opera *Demofoonte* (1769) only in the 1980s.[14] In spite of Mozart's stated admiration for Mysliveček, no symphonies by Mysliveček are discussed as possible stylistic models in Neal Zaslaw's substantive study of the Mozart symphonies.[15] And while Wolfgang Gersthofer drew attention to Mysliveček as a prominent symphonist of the 1760s and 1770s, it would have been more fruitful to seek models for Mozart's development as a symphonist during

---

[12] Anderson, 167; Bauer and Deutsch, 1:398–99. Other possibilities are *I pellegrini al sepolcro* and *Giuseppe riconosciuto*.

[13] Ibid., 176; ibid., 1:411 (see chapter 3 for further discussion).

[14] Manuscript copies were identified by several persons independently in the 1980s, among them Stanislav Bohadlo and Angela Evans. The modern premiere took place in Stuttgart in 1991. I am grateful to Wolf-Dieter Seiffert for bringing this performance to my attention.

[15] Neal Zaslaw, *Mozart's Symphonies: Context, Performance Practice, Reception* (Oxford: Clarendon Press, 1989), 162. Two earlier scholars who published studies suggesting that Mozart may have found direct inspiration in Mysliveček's symphonic music were Paul Nettl (*Mozart in Böhmen*, 65 and 225) and Jan Racek, "Příspěvek k otázce 'mozartského' stylu v české hudbě předklasické" (A Contribution to the Question of "Mozartean" Style in Czech Pre-Classic Music), *Musikologie* 5 (1958): 71–101, especially 94–97; also in German translation in *Internationale Konferenz über das Leben und Werk W. A. Mozarts*, ed. Pavel Eckstein (Prague: Verband Tschechoslowakischer Komponisten, 1958), 34–43, but without the musical examples.

the early 1770s by concentrating on works by Mysliveček that Mozart certainly knew (such as the overtures to the operas *Nitteti* and *Demofoonte*) rather than a work such as Sacchini's overture to *La contadina in corte*, which Mozart may never have known.[16]

The question of just how Mozart used Mysliveček's symphonies as models is complicated by problems concerning the chronology and authenticity of Mozart's early symphonies, but it may be possible to recognize a whole body of Mozart symphonies that exhibit Mysliveček's influence in one way or another. In broad terms, works such as Mysliveček's overtures to *Demofoonte* (1769) and *Nitteti* (1770) would have provided Mozart with precedents for a number of important traits that he associated with Italian symphonic style for years to come, the principal large-scale features being three-movement format, the presence of transitional material between internal movements, and the absence of repeat signs in sonata-form structures. On the smaller scale, there was much greater experimentation with syncopation and the sudden prominence of a sprightly figure made up of two thirty-second notes followed by a dotted quarter (ex. 11.5, meas. 10–14). This simple figure is very distinctive of Italian overture style and it was very effective in evoking Italian style for northern audiences. It is almost never found in Mozart's symphonies before his first trip to Italy, and, while J. C. Bach used it frequently when he resided in Italy in the early 1760s, he largely abandoned it after he moved to London—hence, a plausible explanation why Mozart did not pick it up for his Symphonies nos. 1, K16, and 4, K19, when he knew J. C. Bach at the age of eight and nine. Another important general trait that may result from contact with Mysliveček is Mozart's firming up of sonata form along the lines of Mysliveček's highly systematic procedures, for example, "first themes" articulated with a clear cadence in the tonic key.

Among Mozart's Italianate symphonies of the early 1770s, some of the clearest traces of Mysliveček's influence are found in Symphony no. 10, K74, a companion work to the overture to *Mitridate*. Symphony no. 10 is so close in style that the autograph manuscript of it even includes an inscription (not by Mozart) identifying it as the overture to *Mitridate*.[17] There can be no question that it was also prepared with reference to Mysliveček's *Nitteti* overture (see exx. 11.8 and 11.5–11.7): the opening theme is constructed in a similar way, and later in the movement Mozart borrowed motives from Mysliveček's *Nitteti* more directly (see ex. 11.5, meas. 10–15 and ex. 11.8, meas. 18–26). It is true that similar motives appear in the works of many composers, but the specific shapes seen in these two movements are far too analogous to be coincidental: the same notes are used even though the two movements are in a different key. The motives also appear in the same sonata-form event ("transition" to the "second theme"). The "second theme" fashioned by Mozart is another variant of the "second theme" of the third movement of Mysliveček's *Nitteti* overture, now with syncopation added. The development section of the first movement, actually more like a re-transition to the "first theme," is also constructed in a similar manner to the overture to *Mitridate*, with repeated notes in the viola eventually growing into a rush to the principal theme.

The use of Mysliveček's motives in Mozart's Symphony no. 10 is an important factor that may help refine the dating of the work. Wolfgang Plath established that the paper of the autograph is a rare type that is shared with the autograph of the concert aria "Se ardire, e speranza," K82/73o, which

[16] Wolfgang Gersthofer, "Orchestrale Satzbilder in Sinfonien des jungen Mozart und seiner Zeit,"*Mozart-Jahrbuch 1991* (Kassel: Bärenreiter, 1992), 824–43; *Mozarts frühe Sinfonien (bis 1772): Aspekte frühklassischen Sinfonik* (Salzburg: Internationale Stiftung Mozarteum, 1993); and "Mozarts italienische Sinfonien und die italienische Opernsinfonien der Zeit," *Mozart-Studien* 5 (1995): 183–211.

[17] Zaslaw, 178.

Example 11.8. Mozart, Symphony no. 10 in G Major, K74, first movement, meas. 1–31 (horns, oboes omitted).

continued

Example 11.8–*continued*

Mozart composed in Rome in April 1770.[18] It is possible that Mozart composed Symphony no. 10 in Rome about that time, after having encountered Mysliveček and his overture to *Nitteti* in Bologna the previous month. It is also possible that Mozart composed Symphony no. 10 only after renewing contacts with Mysliveček in Bologna during the summer of 1770. Mozart could have purchased a supply of paper in Rome, then carried some of it with him to Bologna. It does not seem possible, however, that the Symphony no. 10 could pre-date Mozart's acquaintance with Mysliveček in Bologna in March of 1770.

Also tricky to evaluate is the apparent use of Mysliveček's motives in two symphonies that are attributed to Mozart, but whose authenticity and chronology are by no means settled. In the case of the Symphony no."45," K95/73n, perhaps composed in the year 1770, Paul Nettl and Jan Racek both suggested that the opening of the second movement was based on the opening motive of the second movement of Mysliveček's *Nitteti* overture (see exx. 11.9–11.10).[19] They may well have been correct in spite of the later speculation that the symphony might pre-date Mozart's acquaintance with Mysliveček. No eighteenth-century source survives for this symphony, which is known only from a manuscript once housed in the archives of the publisher Breitkopf and Härtel.[20] As Neal Zaslaw has pointed out, there is no explanation for the year 1770 given in various editions of the Köchel catalog, and it exhibits certain stylistic traits that might relate it to some of Mozart's earliest symphonies. Zaslaw was dubious about the Italian origins of this work and did not include discussion of it along with the other Mozart symphonies that are believed to have been composed in the early 1770s. Rather, he included it among works written in the late 1760s.

---

[18] Ibid.

[19] Nettl, *Mozart in Böhmen*, 65 and 225; and Racek, "Příspěvek," 95.

[20] Zaslaw, 95–98.

Example 11.9. Mysliveček, Overture to *La Nitteti*, second movement, meas. 1–5 (violin 1 part only).

Example 11.10. Mozart, Symphony in D Major, no. "45," K95/73n, second movement, meas. 1–6 (violin 1 part only).

The present author is of the opinion that Symphony K95/73n is more likely an Italian work from the early 1770s rather than a northern work from the late 1760s, a view also held by Wolfgang Gersthofer.[21] Zaslaw believed that K95/73n had been included among the Italian symphonies in the Köchel catalog because it opens with motives similar to Symphony no. 10, K74 and Symphony no. "47," K97/73m, which is securely datable to Rome, April 1770. There is much to be said for this reasoning. Mozart's overture to *Mitridate* and Mysliveček's overture to *Nitteti* have similar openings that make it possible to recognize a group of works from the year 1770 constructed using common techniques. All of these symphonic compositions share a common way of beginning the first movement with block chords followed by eighth-note figures and eighth-note rests, plus a repetition of the opening phrase member (in the case of K95/73n, the repeated portion is unusually long). The first movement of Symphony K95/73n shares two important rhythmic motives with Symphony no. 10, K74: an anapestic figure with two eighth notes and a quarter note and the typically Italian thirty-second-note figure with a dotted quarter note (ex. 11.11, meas. 13–23 and ex. 11.8, meas. 17–23). Interestingly, the two figures appear inverted in K74. The use of transitional material to connect the first and second movements, as seen in K95/73n, is not found in any of the Mozart symphonies dating before his first trip to Italy. Zaslaw has theorized that the minuet may have been added at a later time. Without it, the symphony would be cast in the style of a standard three-movement Italian *sinfonia*.

Another motive from Mysliveček's overture to *Nitteti* is found in the third movement of Mozart's Symphony no. "44," K81/73l. Indeed, the opening of its third movement actually begins with the same notes that are found in the first violin part of Mysliveček's third movement (exx. 11.12–11.13). The manuscript parts for this symphony in the Gesellschaft der Musikfreunde in Vienna identify it as a work by Wolfgang Mozart that was copied in Rome on 25 April 1770. But it has also been attributed to Leopold Mozart, and some scholars at various times have been convinced of Leopold's authorship.[22] The use of one of Mysliveček's motives in the symphony need not disqualify Leopold as its author since Leopold knew Mysliveček as well as his son did, if not better. However, there is nothing about this symphony that would make it stylistically incompatible with the other symphonies attributed to Wolfgang from 1770.

[21] See Gersthofer, "Mozarts italienische Sinfonien," 189.

[22] Zaslaw, 170.

EXAMPLE 11.11. Mozart, Symphony in D Major, no. "45," K95/73n, first movement, meas. 13–28 (horns, oboes omitted).

EXAMPLE 11.12. Mysliveček, Overture to *La Nitteti*, third movement, meas. 1–8 (horns, oboes omitted).

EXAMPLE 11.13. Mozart, Symphony in D Major, no. "44," K81/73l, third movement, meas. 1–12 (horns, oboes omitted).

Definitive conclusions about the resemblances between the *Nitteti* overture and various symphonies attributed to Wolfgang Mozart of course cannot be made. It may be just too tidy to recognize three Mozart symphonies written in Italy in 1770 that borrow motives from one movement each of the three movements of the *Nitteti* overture: K74, with material perhaps also borrowed from the first movement of the *Nitteti* overture; K95/73n, with material from the second movement; and K81/73l, with material from third movement. The authenticity of two of these works (K81/73l and 95/73n) has been questioned with good reason. If one or all of them were actually written in Rome in the spring of 1770, any influence from Mysliveček's *Nitteti* overture would presuppose that his overture had been written by the end of March 1770 (about one month before the opera received its premiere) and was picked up by Mozart the week he and Mysliveček stayed at the same inn in Bologna. Mysliveček could have written the overture before the arias, and used the time available to him in Bologna strictly to work with the singers engaged for the production. Regrettably, there is no information concerning his working habits in this regard. Nonetheless, the idea that Mozart met Mysliveček in Bologna and snatched up a fresh example of symphonic style that became a model for his own works is a logical one. It does provide an explanation for all of the thematic resemblances detailed above.

The evidence of possible borrowings from Mysliveček's *Nitteti* overture strengthens speculation that the two newly-composed symphonies mentioned in Mozart's letter to his sister from Rome of April 1770 were his Symphony no. 10, K74 (which was copied on the same kind of paper as the aria, K82/73o, also mentioned in this letter), and Symphony no. "44," K81/73l (which survives in the form of parts that identify the symphony as being composed by Wolfgang Mozart in Rome in April 1770). The recent composition of four symphonies announced to his sister in a letter from Bologna of 4 August 1770 could refer to the same two symphonies plus the symphonies K95/73n and 97/73m that were perhaps composed during the summer. Symphony no. 11, K84/73q, which is attributed to other composers in various sources, could be a spurious work or could belong to a slightly earlier period of composition (January or February of 1770).[23]

Stylistic traits that Mozart picked up in Italy appear frequently in the symphonies he composed through the year 1773. The important innovation of his Symphony no. 13, K112, which was written in Milan in November of 1771, is the use of divided violas with winds, a technique that had entered Mysliveček's music the previous year (see chapter 9). The first movement of Mozart's Symphony no. 13 contains in its "second theme" a figure little found in the earlier Mozart symphonies that is quite prominent in the first movement of Mysliveček's *Demofoonte* overture (1769), also from the "second theme" (exx. 11.14–11.15),[24] but the most obvious use of a phrase from the *Demofoonte* overture comes not from this symphony, but rather from the third movement of Mozart's Piano Concerto no. 9, K271 of 1777 (exx. 11.16–11.17).[25] Something like it also appears in the opening ritornello of the first movement of Mozart's Violin Concerto no. 5, K219 (1775), and in the opening of Monostatos' aria "Alles fühlt der Liebe Freuden" from *Die Zauberflöte* (1791). Those who imagine this motive to be a stock figure will be hard-pressed to find other examples. Its use in multiple compositions likely indicates that Mozart did take pains to ensure that Mysliveček's *Demofoonte* overture would be available to him in Salzburg, just as he told his sister.

EXAMPLE 11.14. Mysliveček, Overture to *Demofoonte*, first movement, meas. 22–29 (horns, oboes omitted).

[23] These possibilities are discussed in Zaslaw, 175–76.

[24] This motive is not unique to Mysliveček; it also appears prominently in the first movement of J. C. Bach's Symphony op. 6, no. 6.

[25] I am grateful to Wolf-Dieter Seiffert for pointing out this quotation to me.

EXAMPLE 11.15. Mozart, Symphony no. 13 in F Major, K112, first movement, meas. 24–32 (horns tacent).

EXAMPLE 11.16. Mysliveček, Overture to *Demofoonte*, first movement, meas. 1–6 (Violin 1 part only).

EXAMPLE 11.17. Mozart, Piano Concerto in E-flat Major, K271, third movement, meas. 35–42 (Violin 1 part only).

Symphony no. 14, K114, which Mozart composed in Salzburg at the end of December 1771, once again exhibits experiments with syncopation in a period immediately after contacts with Mysliveček were renewed in Italy during November and December of 1771. It is likely that Mozart would have come into contact with the overture to Mysliveček's opera *Il gran Tamerlano* near the end of the year 1771, since it is mentioned in Leopold Mozart's letter of 23 or 24 November 1771 as being prepared for production in Milan during carnival season of 1772. Interestingly, Mozart's Symphony no. 9, K73, exhibits the same type of opening motive as in the overture to *Il gran Tamerlano* (exx. 11.18–11.19), including the same scale degrees at the start and the same loud-soft-loud-soft phrase structure. A possible date of composition for Mozart's Symphony no. 9 early in 1772 has been proposed, and the resemblance of the opening with Mysliveček's overture could lend support to a date of 1772 in preference to the earlier dates that have been suggested for it.[26]

EXAMPLE 11.18. Mysliveček, Overture to *Il gran Tamerlano*, first movement, meas. 1–15 (horns, oboes omitted).

[26] For a discussion of theories about the dating of this work, see Zaslaw, 167.

EXAMPLE 11.19. Mozart, Symphony no. 9 in C Major, K73, first movement, meas. 1–11 (horns, oboes, trumpets, tympani omitted).

It is quite possible that four symphonies Mozart composed in the wake of his last visits with Mysliveček in Italy early in 1773 also owe some of their character to Mysliveček's example. In Symphony no. 22, K162 (April 1773), there is a return to the thirty-second-note figures so prominent in Mysliveček's *Demofoonte* overture (ex. 11.20), now more highly developed. Syncopation and thirty-second-note figures are also prominent in Mozart's three-movement Symphonies nos. 26, K184/161a (March 1773), 23, K181/162b (May 1773), and 24, K182/173dA (October 1773), but his experiments with these elements reach a culmination in his four-movement Symphony no. 25, K183/173dB (the "Little G Minor"), which he completed in October 1773. Its opening theme with syncopated unisons is extraordinarily powerful, and Mozart's manipulation of that same thirty-second-note motive shared with Mysliveček's *Demofoonte* overture is highly effective as well (ex. 11.21). Mysliveček himself composed a symphony in G minor which has a much less distinctive kind of syncopated opening, his Symphony op. 1, no. 5 (exx. 11.22–11.23). There is no question that Mysliveček's Op. 1 set was still then circulating in the German lands, since it was offered for sale in the Breitkopf catalog of 1774. This symphony, one of the finest composed anywhere in Europe in the 1760s, was perhaps known to Mozart.

Whether Mysliveček provided symphonic models for Mozart after the two composers ceased to have personal contacts and Mozart became more experienced as a symphonist is much less certain. Still, a few speculative observations about Mysliveček's possible impact on Mozart's compositional output can be made. In the case of the brilliant Symphony no. 29, K201/186a, written in April 1774, the opening motive bears a remarkable resemblance in rhythm and melodic shape to the opening of a section of accompanied recitative from Mysliveček's opera *Motezuma*, which Mozart may have become acquainted with in Italy (see exx. 11.24–11.25). It is difficult to be sure what to make of the similarity between these two particular passages, but it is clear that Mozart did associate the typically Myslivečkian traits of syncopation, thirty-second-note figures, and compound-meter finales with Italian three-movement symphonies for years after his last trip to Italy. The next time they are featured prominently is in the three-movement Symphony no. 31, K297/300a (the "Paris" Symphony) of 1778, then once more (albeit more faintly) in the three-movement Symphony no. 34, K338, of 1780.

Example 11.20. Mozart, Symphony no. 22 in C Major, K162, first movement, meas. 13–21 (horns, oboes, trumpets omitted).

Example 11.21. Mozart, Symphony no. 25 in G Minor, K183/173dB, first movement, meas. 29–48 (horns, oboes omitted).

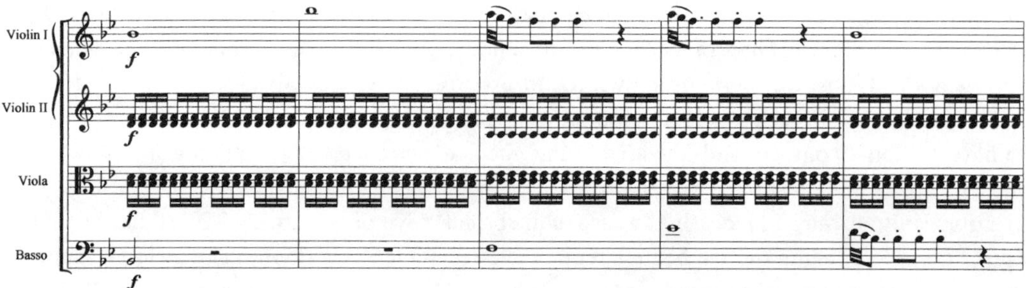

EXAMPLE 11.21–*continued*

EXAMPLE 11.22. Mozart, Symphony no. 25 in G Minor, K183/173dB, first movement, meas. 1–5 (horns, oboes omitted).

Example 11.23. Mysliveček, Symphony in G Minor, op. 1, no. 5, first movement, meas. 1–5 (horns, oboes omitted). Edited from Ms. V B 56 of the České Muzeum Hudby with permission.

Example 11.24. Mysliveček, Accompanied recitative "Dov'è son? Che m'avvene?" from opening of *Motezuma*, meas. 1–9.

EXAMPLE 11.25. Mozart, Symphony no. 29 in A Major, K201/186a, first movement, meas. 1–19 (oboes, horns tacent meas. 1–12, omitted meas. 13–19).

Mozart completed only three new symphonies between 1775 and 1781, all of them in the period 1778–80. These three, Symphonies nos. 31, 33, and 34, were all cast in three movements (the minuet of the Symphony no. 33, K319, of 1779 was a later addition). Although it may be only a coincidence, it should be pointed out that Mysliveček sent no less than a dozen symphonies to the court of Salzburg in the year 1777 and his three-movement *concertoni* followed the next year. A body of unspecified music by Mysliveček had been sent there a few years earlier.[27] It seems unlikely that the archbishop of Salzburg would have had these works brought to his court without expecting that they would be performed. Their high quality is not in doubt. Thus this sudden infusion of Mysliveček repertory into the Salzburg musical establishment could provide part of the explanation for Mozart's attraction to three-movement symphonies for a short period in the late 1770s. In particular, Mozart's Symphony no. 34 can be interpreted as something of an apotheosis of the basic Myslivečkian model of a three-movement symphony with a rollicking compound-meter finale.

A little-known repertory of small-scale orchestral pieces that Mozart composed in Salzburg appears to yield further evidence of his enduring interest in Mysliveček's music. It is formed by seventeen "church sonatas" that Mozart composed between 1772 and 1780 for performance in masses presided over by the archbishop of Salzburg. Mozart himself referred to these works as "epistle" sonatas,[28] meaning that they were to be performed before, during, or after the epistle reading of the mass. Famously, since the masses officiated at Salzburg Cathedral by Count Colloredo were to last no longer than forty-five minutes,[29] the sonatas in the mass had to be quite short. All are cast in single-movement formats that take no longer than about three minutes to perform.

The largest grouping of church sonatas by Mozart are thirteen works scored for two violins and bass that constitute his only known contribution to the repertory of orchestral trios: K67/41h, K68/41i, K69/41k, K144/124a, and K145/124b of ca. 1772; K212 of 1775; K224/241a, K225/241b, K241, K244, and K245 of 1776; K274/271d of 1777; and K328/317c, perhaps written in 1779. In addition, the Sonata in C major, K263 of 1776, conforms to the same conception with the addition of two trumpets. All of the church sonatas are single-movement compositions in binary form; all but the first one, K67/41h, include repeats of the brief binary sections. The five sonatas believed to date from ca. 1772 bear traits of Mysliveček's style, in particular the Sonata in B-flat major, K68/41i, and the Sonata in D major, K144/124a. In the early 1770s it would have made sense for Mozart to turn to Mysliveček as a resource for works scored for strings in three parts, since his older friend was one of the most gifted composers of orchestral trios at that time. The characteristic syncopations of Italian overture style and the thirty-second-note figure described above are prominent in several of these sonatas, which would have been composed close in time to Mozart's visits with Mysliveček in Italy.

It is clear that Mozart found inspiration in Italian overture style to help craft two church sonatas that originated in the late 1770s: the Sonata in C major, K278, written in the spring of 1777, and the Sonata in C major, K329/317a, that is believed to have been written sometime in the late 1770s (his last church sonata, K336 of 1780, in contrast, is shaped as an organ concerto movement in ritornello form). The sonatas K278 and K329 are scored with oboes, horns, and tympani besides the three-part string ensemble used in his earlier sonatas. For this expanded orchestration,

---

[27] This can be established from Leopold Mozart's letter to his son, 15 October 1777 (see chapter 4).

[28] See Mozart's letter to Padre Martini in Bologna, 4 September 1776, in Anderson, 266; Bauer and Deutsch 1:532.

[29] Mozart complained about this in the same letter.

the compact proportions of the binary segments as utilized in the earlier sonatas would not offer the best means to exploit the instruments to best advantage. Italian overture style, with its more spacious exposition and recapitulation sections—but no repeat signs—offered a solution to ensure a short length with sufficient opportunity to showcase the tonal colors of the ensemble at hand. The sonata K329/317a, probably composed after the influx of Mysliveček repertory that reached Salzburg in the years 1777–78, is virtually an imitation of Mysliveček's style. One of the clearest traces of his influence is the way Mozart's "second theme" is constructed with a passage for oboes in parallel thirds after the principal thematic material is given out in the strings.

Although Mozart's memories of Mysliveček may have been rather distant by the mid-1780s, certain stylistic features of his three-movement Symphony no. 38, K504 (the "Prague" Symphony), perhaps echo in some measure his acquaintance with Mysliveček's symphonies. Mozart's Prague Symphony, consistent with its nickname, was first performed in Prague in January of 1787 by members of the opera orchestra of the National Theater. But while it has been speculated that the symphony may not have been originally intended for Prague, but rather for performance in Vienna or London, such speculation fails to take into account evidence that the work was carefully crafted to please the musical public of Prague.[30] One of the most important clues comes from the lavish use of wind instruments. The number of wind *soli* and the attention given to imaginative treatments of wind sonorities in combination with strings far exceed what can be found in any of Mozart's earlier symphonies. Mozart may well have introduced these elements deliberately to exploit the capabilities of the Bohemian wind players who were famed throughout Europe for their skill. Few other symphonies from the eighteenth century are scored with so many passages in which no stringed instruments play at all. A similarly lavish use of winds was actually singled out in the Prague press as contributing to the success, in the winter of 1786, of *Le nozze di Figaro*.[31] Such writing seems a reason to believe that the Prague Symphony was tailored to suit the capabilities of the orchestra players of the National Theater in Prague, who, according to Leopold Mozart, having had the experience of playing *Le nozze di Figaro*, were among the ones responsible for inviting Mozart to Prague.[32]

The unprecedented technical difficulty of the Prague Symphony might be attributable to Mozart's realization that he would be composing for musicians supportive of his talents and willing to rehearse unusually intricate music in order to achieve performance standards pleasing to him. The same could be said about his opera *Don Giovanni*, also first performed in Prague by the same ensemble of musicians, also unprecedented for its technical challenges. The excellence of the opera orchestra of the National Theater has not been generally recognized; but according to the memoirs of the Prague pianist Wilhelm Kuhe, this orchestra, first built up by the conductor Johann Joseph Strobach in the 1780s, had the reputation of being the finest in Germany until about 1830.[33]

The chronology of the Prague Symphony is certainly problematic. The first extant mention of Mozart's invitation to Prague is an announcement in the *Prager Oberpostamtzeitung*, 12 December 1786 (report dated 11 December).[34] Mozart had completed the symphony on 6 December. On such

---

[30] For a summary of the speculation, see Elaine R. Sisman, "Genre, Gesture, and Meaning in Mozart's *Prague* Symphony," in *Mozart Studies 2*, ed. Cliff Eisen (Oxford: Clarendon Press, 1997), 29–33.

[31] Otto Erich Deutsch, *Mozart: A Documentary Biography*, trans. Eric Blom et al., 2nd ed. (London: Adam & Charles Black, 1966), 281.

[32] See Leopold Mozart's letter to his daughter, 12 January 1787 in Anderson, 902, and Bauer and Deutsch, 4:7.

[33] Wilhelm Kuhe, *My Musical Recollections* (London, 1896), 7. Kuhe was born in Bohemia but lived most of his adult life in England.

[34] Deutsch, *Mozart*, 282–83.

short notice it might appear that he had not had the time to compose a work specifically for Prague. But the assumption in much Mozart literature that *Le nozze di Figaro* was not performed in Prague until December 1786 is almost certainly incorrect. The National Theater was open in November and the English traveler Hester Lynch Piozzi reported seeing a performance there then.[35] Surviving librettos indicate that *Le nozze di Figaro* shared the winter season that year with Stephen Storace's *Gli sposi malcontenti*. In Prague the winter season could begin surprisingly early. According to the diary of August Gottlieb Meissner, a resident of Prague in the late eighteenth century, *Don Giovanni* was first performed in Prague on 29 October 1787, as the first production of that year's winter season.[36] Thus if *Le nozze di Figaro* had seen its first performances by early November of the previous year, it is reasonable to believe that Mozart could have completed a new symphony with the Prague instrumentalists in mind by early December.

Proponents of theories that Mozart composed the Prague Symphony for Vienna have offered no explanation for the lack of performances there; theories that Mozart intended it for London have failed to take into account how tentative Mozart's plans to travel to London actually were.[37] As far as is known, he had not received an invitation from anyone in England, and he had planned no musical compositions in advance (his young student Thomas Attwood was to try to find commissions for him). Thus Mozart would have had no idea whether or not he would have use for a new symphony in London or, if he did, what type of ensemble he would be writing for. The whole project died in the spring of 1787, when Mozart finally realized that he did not have sufficient cash on hand to travel to England without an invitation. In the case of the first performance of the Prague Symphony in January 1787, Mozart had an ensemble waiting for him to play a new symphony, and he would have known precisely what instruments were available.

Another point to be made about the Prague Symphony is that when it was composed late in 1786, the only Prague symphonist whom Mozart had ever been close to was Josef Mysliveček (his friend František Dušek at that time was probably known to him only as a keyboard player and keyboard composer). Keeping this in mind, the three-movement Italianate format of the Prague Symphony makes perfect sense as a means to please the musical public of Prague, but just as noteworthy is the affinity of Mozart's famous opening to the fast section of the first movement to a style of Italian symphonic writing that was closely associated with Mysliveček. This passage represents a sophisticated juxtaposition of a Myslivečkian syncopated accompanimental figure with a typical kind of Myslivečkian syncopated melodic construction (ex. 11.26). Neither figure had been prominent in Mozart's own symphonies since the early 1770s, when his interest in Italianate symphonies was at its height. The slow introduction also contains striking syncopations of a type seen nowhere else in Mozart's symphonies. Thus the Prague Symphony may have been deliberately crafted to evoke the style of a symphonist that Mozart knew had appealed to Prague audiences in the past, naturally with a sense of one-upmanship—a demonstration of how earlier modes of expression could be transformed by Mozart's surpassing skill. As for the theories concerning a planned performance of the symphony in Vienna, there is no reason to believe that Mozart would think that the Viennese

[35] Hester Lynch Piozzi, *Observations and Reflections Made in the Course of a Journey Through France, Italy, and Germany*, ed. Herbert Barrows (Ann Arbor: University of Michigan Press, 1967), 382–83. Regrettably, Piozzi did not name the opera she witnessed.

[36] Alfred Meissner, *Rococo-Bilder: Nach Aufzeichungen meines Grossvaters*, 2nd ed. (Lindau and Leipzig, 1876), 113.

[37] For Mozart's plans to travel to London, see Leopold Mozart's letters to his daughter, 17 November 1786 and 2 March 1787, in Anderson, 901–02 and 906, and Bauer and Deutsch, 3:606 and 4:28–29.

EXAMPLE 11.26. Mozart, Symphony no. 38 in D Major ("Prague"), K504, first movement, meas. 37–45 (winds, brass, tympani tacent meas. 37–42).

would find favor with an old-fashioned three-movement Italian-style symphony when four-movement symphonies were the norm in that city. Mozart never composed any three-movement symphonies for Vienna, not even in the 1760s, when they were common in many parts of Europe.

Returning to the period when Mozart's acquaintance with Mysliveček's works was fresher, it seems appropriate to mention another group of compositions that reflects the spirit of Mysliveček's way of writing, namely the three-movement Divertimenti for Strings of 1772, K136–138, which exhibit very much the same kind of grace, energy, and wit that is so striking in Mysliveček's String Quartets op. 3. Giovanni Battista Sammartini's works have been proposed for models for the quartets Mozart created in Milan in 1773,[38] but Mysliveček is also a likely model, considering his closeness to the Mozart family at that time. One might think that Mozart in his first string quintet, K174, composed in Salzburg in 1773, would have gained some inspiration from Mysliveček's pioneering string quintets, but in this case the conventional wisdom that Mozart's immediate stylistic model for the work was a string quintet by Michael Haydn seems correct. Mozart's first string quintet does not at all evoke the symphonic conception seen in Mysliveček's quintets, even though Mozart could well have come to know them before leaving Milan in 1773.

Violin concertos form the last major repertory in which Mysliveček is likely to have provided models that shaped Mozart's stylistic development in a decisive way. In 1773 and 1775, when Mozart wrote his magnificent series of five violin concertos in Salzburg, it appears likely that he turned

[38] See in particular Bathia Churgin, "Did Sammartini Influence Mozart's Earliest String Quartets?," *Mozart-Jahrbuch 1991* (Salzburg: Internationale Stiftung Mozarteum, 1992), 529–39.

to Mysliveček as a source of inspiration. In the genre of violin concerto, with which Mozart had no prior experience, Mysliveček was clearly the most gifted composer known to him personally. There is no question that Mozart knew Mysliveček's concertos: he copied out the title page of the bass part of one them in a letter to his mother from Vienna of 8 September 1773.[39] Mozart's concertos exhibit the same kind of pacing and virtuosic figuration as Mysliveček's concertos, and the possibility that Mozart's Violin Concerto no. 4, K218 used the beginning of a Mysliveček Violin Concerto in D major (Violin Concerto 8) as the basis for the opening theme has been recognized since the 1920s.[40]

The greatest influence of Mysliveček in the Mozart violin concertos is evident in the earliest one, K207 in B-flat major, a work barely known to modern audiences that does strike one as the product of an individual trying out the genre for the first time. Mozart composed it in Salzburg in the spring of 1773 just after he had personal contact with Mysliveček in Italy. The opening is very typical of Mysliveček, based on a syncopated motive, and it is similar to the opening theme of Mozart's Bassoon Concerto, K191/186e of 1774. But the feature that sticks out most as a telltale sign of Mysliveček's influence is the formal plan used in both of the fast movements, precisely the one described in chapter 9 as standard for the fast movements of Mysliveček's concertos. In Mozart's first violin concerto, techniques of orchestration and the use of *tutti* insertions are conservative, also in the manner of Mysliveček, but in Mozart's second violin concerto of two years later immense advances in melodic invention and ingenuity in orchestration are evident. Mysliveček's formal models were abandoned, but one wonders whether Mozart may have found inspiration in some of Mysliveček's rhythmic patterns, for instance, syncopation in the first movement of no. 2 and thirty-second-note figures in the first movement of no. 3, as well as in Mysliveček's inventive technique of opening the first solo sections of his first movements in a surprising way with material unrelated to the opening ritornello. The impression left by the whole series of five concertos is that Mozart found Mysliveček's models helpful in getting started, but that Mozart soon transcended the abilities of his principal model and all contemporary composers of violin concertos.

Other evidence of Mozart's interest in Mysliveček's music can be dealt with here rather quickly, since there is already a body of musicological literature that describes it. At the time that Mozart visited Mysliveček in Munich in 1777, he came into contact with Mysliveček's *Easy Divertimentos* for keyboard solo. Rondos from this set are mentioned in several Mozart letters from the autumn of 1777, and recently it was recognized that motives from Mysliveček's keyboard music were adapted in Mozart's Piano Sonatas K309 and 311.[41] On a subsequent visit to Munich in the winter of 1780–81 for a production of his opera *Idomeneo*, Mozart was called upon to compose a setting of Metastasio's scene and aria "Misera, dove son?/ Ah, non sò io che parlo," K369, apparently as a replacement for Mysliveček's setting of the same text that had been sung by the recipient of the Mozart setting, Countess Maria Josepha von Paumgarten.[42] The Mysliveček aria had originally been performed in his opera *Ezio* for Munich in 1777. In this case, only a few of Mysliveček's motives (if any) were actually used to help create the new setting. It has been suggested that another piece for the Munich *Ezio*, the vocal quartet at the end of act 2, was a model for a similar quartet that appears in

---

[39] Anderson, 243; Bauer and Deutsch, 1:497.

[40] Pincherle, 108.

[41] Freeman, "Josef Mysliveček and the Piano Sonatas K. 309 (284b) and K. 311 (284c)."

[42] Ibid., "Music for the Noble Amateur."

Mozart's opera *Idomeneo*.[43] Additionally, an instrumental march that was heard in the Munich production of *Isacco figura del redentore* (1777) may have provided some inspiration for a march that also appears in *Idomeneo*.[44] The possibility that Mozart arranged Mysliveček's aria "Il caro mio bene" for voice and keyboard with the text "Ridente la calma" in Munich during the winter of 1780–81 was discussed in chapter 8.

One of the most intriguing suggestions about Mozart's use of Mysliveček's music has been proposed by Christoph-Hellmut Mahling,[45] who noticed a resemblance between the opening of an accompanied recitative from Mysliveček's oratorio *Isacco figura del redentore* ("Eterno Dio" from part 1) and the opening of a scene from *Die Zauberflöte* ("Zu Hülfe, zu Hülfe" from act 1). The passages do indeed sound very much alike. It is not known whether Mozart actually attended a production of *Isacco* in Munich in 1777 when he reported that "all Munich" was talking of it (chapter 4), but it is quite possible that he could have encountered the score at that time or later. *Isacco* was widely disseminated in many parts of Europe in the 1770s and 1780s. Furthermore, Emanuel Schikaneder, the librettist for *Die Zauberflöte*, lived in Munich in the late 1770s and, according to Rudolf Pečman, produced *Isacco* in Buda in 1785 as one of his projects as an impresario.[46]

Whether or not Mozart's interest in Mysliveček's music did last until the composition of the Singspiel *Die Zauberflöte* just a few months before his death, there can be no doubt that Josef Mysliveček stimulated his musical imagination for years after their first meeting, apparently even after the disintegration of their friendship. Mysliveček should never again require a "resurrection from the dead" to be brought back into the consciousness of Mozart scholarship. And no consideration of Mozart's compositional models or personal development after the year 1770 should be considered complete without taking into account the impact of his contacts with him.

---

[43] Böhmer, 325–29.

[44] Ibid., 315–16.

[45] Mahling, 205–6; Pečman, 157–58.

[46] Pečman, 155.

Part 4

CATALOGS OF MYSLIVEČEK'S INSTRUMENTAL AND VOCAL MUSIC

ORGANIZATION OF CATALOGS

Two catalogs of Mysliveček's works have been prepared for this volume: one for his instrumental music and one for his vocal music.

CATALOG OF INSTRUMENTAL MUSIC

The catalog for instrumental music has been designed to complement and update the existing catalog of Mysliveček's instrumental music by Angela Evans and Robert Dearling: *Josef Mysliveček, 1737–1781: A Thematic Catalogue of His Instrumental and Orchestral Music* (Munich: Katzbichler, 1999). The basic format of the entries is similar in order to facilitate consultation in both catalogs and make it easier to identify corrections and additions. The numbering system of the Evans and Dearling catalog has not been adopted, however; rather, the organization of the present catalog preserves the groupings of pieces that are found in the original collections whenever possible. The arrangement of compositions progresses from those with the fullest instrumentation to those with the sparest instrumentation. There are fifteen categories, each headed "Part," as follows:

Part 1: Symphonies
Part 2: Dramatic Overtures
Part 3: Solo Concertos
Part 4: Concertos for Multiple Soloists
Part 5: Music for Wind Ensemble
Part 6: Miscellaneous Chamber Works for Strings and Winds
Part 7: Music for Strings in Five Parts
Part 8: Music for Strings in Four Parts
Part 9: Music for Strings in Three Parts
Part 10: Trios for Flute, Violin, and Bass (Flute Trios)
Part 11: Duets for Two Flutes and Bass (Flute Duets)
Part 12: Sonatas for Violin and Bass or Violin and Keyboard (Violin Sonatas)
Part 13: Sonata for Cello and Bass
Part 14: Keyboard Sonatas
Part 15: Miscellaneous Works for Solo Instruments.

Within each category, the compositions are arranged in chronological order; where dating is not certain, the placement is based on the best information available. Each entry lists the title of the composition; a numbering if it is a work within a grouping of several works; the principal key; the dating; a cross reference, within square brackets, to the composition's listing in the Evans/Dearling catalog (for example, [10:C1],[1]); the instrumental scoring; the manuscript sources and their present location, listed by RISM sigla; references in earlier inventories; existing editions; and recordings. Additional remarks follow, for example, information about the dating and provenance of specific sources or notes about misattributions. Musical incipits are not supplied, but can be located in the Evans/Dearling catalog by means of the cross references.

Particular information related to provenance is furnished for manuscripts preserved in the Czech and Slovak Republics. The manuscripts specified from a "collection" are generally twentieth-century copies prepared by scholars such as Jan Pohl, Josef Šrogl, Václav Král, and Alois Altrichter. Manuscripts once in the possession of Roman Nejedlý (1844–1920), a school teacher in the town of Mnichovo Hradiště, are late eighteenth-century sources originating from the Waldstein estate of Doksy. Other specifications within parentheses indicate the place of origins or the name of a former noble collection. All modern editions published in Prague are available in *CZ-Pnm* and/or *CZ-Pu*.

CATALOG OF VOCAL MUSIC

The catalog of vocal music is also broadly organized by musical genres, the most substantial ones laid out first. In all there are eleven categories, each headed "Part," as follows:

Part 1: Operas
Part 2: Operatic Pastiches with Music of Mysliveček
Part 3: German Melodrama
Part 4: Plays with Music
Part 5: Oratorios
Part 6: Cantatas
Part 7: Larger Liturgical Vocal Works
Part 8: *Duetti notturni*
Part 9: Arias, Ensembles, and Other Shorter Vocal Works
Part 10: Vocal Works Listed in Inventories of Lost or Dispersed Eighteenth-Century Collections
Part 11: Questionable Mysliveček Vocal Works in Earlier Editions.

The entries for dramatic works are the most detailed. They include the city, theater, or other venue of the first performance and the date, if known; the name of the librettist; printed sources of the libretto and their present locations; sources of the scores and their present locations, listed by RISM sigla; cross references to borrowings of individual arias in other dramatic works; the names of

[1] In this thematic catalog, 10.C1 refers to section 10, "Symphonies and Overtures," the first of the C major works; see Evans and Dearling, p. 128.

the original cast members; editions; and recordings. The listings of shorter vocal works identify the text incipit; the composition's origins in dramatic music (if known); and information about sources, editions, and recordings. In the same fashion as in the catalog of instrumental music, places of origin and the names of former noble collections are designated. There are cross references to individual works' listings in the unpublished catalog of Mysliveček vocal music by Stanislav Bohadlo.[2]

ABBREVIATIONS

The following abbreviations for musical instruments are employed in the catalogs:

b	bass/basso continuo	pf	pianoforte
bsn	bassoon	pr	principale (i.e., soloist)
cl	clarinet	str	strings
fl	flute	timp	timpani
hpd	harpsichord	trp	trumpet
hrn	horn	vla	viola(s)
kbd	keyboard	vlc	violoncello(s)
ob	oboe	vln	violin(s)
obl	obbligato/i	vlone	violone

The following general abbreviations are used:

acc.	accompaniment/ according to	f(f).	folio(s)
acc. rec.	accompanied recitative	inc.	incomplete
ad lib.	ad libitum	lib.	libretto/ librettist
anon.	anonymous	LP	long-playing record
arr.	arrangement/ arranged for	meas.	measure(s)
attr.	attribution/ attributed to	ms(s).	manuscript(s)
ca.	circa	p(p).	page(s)
cat.	catalog	pub.	publisher/ published by
CD	compact disc	ref(s).	reference(s)
cond.	conductor/ conducted by	repr.	reprint
dir.	director/ directed by	sign.	signature
ed.	edition	s.s.	senza segnatura (no shelf number)

[2] The catalog can be accessed at the website www.jmc.cz/stan/myslivecek/.

LIBRARY SIGLA

The abbreviations for libraries are, whenever possible, the sigla established by RISM (Répertoire International des Sources Musicales):

A (Austria)

A-GÖ	Göttweig, Benediktinerstift, Musikarchiv
A-HE	Heiligenkreuz, Musikarchiv
A-KN	Klosterneuberg, Augustiner-Chorherrenstift, Bibliothek
A-LA	Lambach, Benediktiner-Stift, Bibliothek
A-M	Melk an der Donau, Benediktiner-Stift, Bibliothek
A-SB	Schlierbach, Stift
A-Sca	Salzburg, Archiv der Stadt Salzburg mit Archiv des Salzburger Museums Carolino-Augusteum
A-ST	Stams, Zisterzienserstift, Bibliothek und Musikarchiv
A-VOR	Vorau, Stift
A-Wgm	Vienna, Gesellschaft der Musikfreunde in Wien, Bibliothek
A-Wmi	Vienna, Musikwissenschaftliches Institut der Universität Wien
A-Wn	Vienna, Österreichische Nationalbibliothek, Musiksammlung

B (Belgium)

B-Bc	Brussels, Conservatoire Royal de Musique, Bibliothèque
B-Br	Brussels, Bibliothèque Royale Albert 1.er
B-Lc	Liège, Conservatoire Royal de Musique, Bibliothèque

CDN (Canada)

CDN-Lu	London, University of Western Ontario Library System, Music Library
CDN-Tu	Toronto, University of Toronto, Edward Johnson Music Library

CH (Switzerland)

CH-BM	Beromünster, Musikbibliothek des Stifts
CH-Bu	Basel, Öffentliche Bibliothek der Universität Basel, Musiksammlung
CH-E	Einsiedeln, Kloster Einsiedeln, Musikbibliothek
CH-EN	Engelberg, Kloster, Musikbibliothek
CH-Fcu	Fribourg, Bibliothèque Cantonale et Universitaire
CH-FF	Frauenfeld, Thurgauische Kantonsbibliothek
CH-Gc	Geneva, Conservatoire de Musique, Bibliothèque
CH-MÜ	Müstair, Frauenkloster St. Johann
CH-Zz	Zürich, Zentralbibliothek

CZ (Czech Republic)

CZ-BER	Beroun, Okresní Archiv
CZ-Bm	Brno, Moravské Zemské Muzeum, Oddělení Dějin Hudby

CZ-BRE	Brežnice, Kostel sv. Ignáce
CZ-BRO	Broumov, Děkanský Úřad, Chrám sv. Petra a Pavla
CZ-Bu	Brno, Universita Jan Evangelista Purkyně, Universitní Knihovna
CZ-CBj	České Budějovice, Jihočeské Muzeum, Hudební Oddělení
CZ-CH	Cheb, Okresní Archiv
CZ-CT	Česká Třebová, Městské Muzeum
CZ-JIa	Jindřichův Hradec, Státní Oblastní Archiv v Třeboni—Pracoviště v Jindřichově Hradci, Zámek
CZ-JIm	Jindřichův Hradec, Vlastivědné Muzeum
CZ-K	Český Krumlov, Státní Oblastní Archiv v Třeboni—Pracoviště v Českém Krumlově, hudební sbírka
CZ-KL	Klatovy, Okresní Muzeum
CZ-KRa	Kroměříž, Arcibiskupský Zámek a Zahrady, hudební archiv
CZ-KRI[3]	Křimice, Zámek
CZ-KU	Kutná Hora, Oblastní Muzeum
CZ-LIa	Česká Lípa, Okresní Archiv
CZ-LIT	Litoměřice, Státní Oblastní Archiv
CZ-LO	Loukov, Farní Kostel
CZ-LUa	Louny, Okresní Archiv
CZ-MB	Mladá Boleslav, Okresní Archiv
CZ-MHz	Mnichovo Hradiště, Zámecká Knihovna
CZ-Nlobkowicz	Nelahozeves, Roudnická Lobkowiczká sbírka, Zámek
CZ-NR	Nová Říše na Moravě, Klášter Premonstrátů, knihovna a hudební sbírka
CZ-NYd	Nymburk, Děkanský Úřad, Kostel sv. Jiljí
CZ-OP	Opava, Slezské Muzeum
CZ-Pa	Prague, Národní Archiv (formerly Státní Ústřední Archiv)
CZ-Pak	Prague, Archiv Pražského Hradu, Knihovna Metropolitní Kapituly u Sv. Víta, hudební sbírka
CZ-PEL	Pelhřimov, Okresní Archiv
CZ-Ph	Prague, Česká Církev Holešovice (in CZ-Pu)
CZ-PI	Písek, Okresní Archiv
CZ-Pk	Prague, Konservatoř v Praze, hudební archiv
CZ-Pkříž	Prague, Rytířský Řád Křižovníků s Červenou Hvězdou, hudební sbírka
CZ-PLa	Plzeň, Archiv Města Plzně
CZ-PLm	Plzeň, Západočeské Muzeum, Národopisné Oddělení
CZ-Pnm	Prague, České Muzeum Hudby (formerly Muzeum České Hudby; formerly Národní Muzeum, Hudební Oddělení), hudební archiv
CZ-Pnmk (Radenín)	Prague, Národní Muzeum, Knihovna, sbírka Radenín
CZ-Pr	Prague, Český Rozhlas, Ústřední Notový Archiv

[3] Claudio Sartori, *I libretti italiani a stampa dalle origini al 1800* (Cuneo: Bertola & Locatelli, 1990–94), consistently misidentifies the Křimice castle collection with the siglum CS-KRE. At the time that Sartori's work was published, CS-KRE referred to a collection in the Slovak Republic of the former Czechoslovakia: Krémnica, Mestský Archív. This archive is now recognized by RISM as SK-KRE: Krémnica, Štátny Okresný Archív v Žiari nad Hronom. RISM has not established a siglum for the Křimice castle collection.

CZ-Ps	Prague, Literární Archiv Památníku Národního Písemnictví (Strahov)
CZ-Psj	Prague, Farní Úřad, Chrám sv. Jakuba
CZ-Pu	Prague, Národní Knihovna České Republiky, Universitní Knihovna, Hudební Oddělení
CZ-Puh	Prague (Uhříněves), Kostel Všech Svatých
CZ-ROk	Rokycany, Děkanský Úřad, Kostel
CZ-RU	Rumburk, Městské Muzeum
CZ-RY	Rychnov nad Kněžnou, Muzeum Orlických Hor
CZ-TEb	Teplice nad Bečvou, Brixiho Komorní Soubor
CZ-TEP	Teplice nad Metují, Chrám sv. Vavřince
CZ-TREd	Třeboň, Děkanský Úřad, Kostel sv. Jiljí
CZ-TU	Turnov, Městské Muzeum, hudební sbírka
CZ-VM	Vysoké Myto, Okresní Muzeum A. V. Šembery

D (Germany)

D-AB	Amorbach, Fürstlich Leiningensche Bibliothek
D-Au	Augsburg, Universitätsbibliothek
D-B	Berlin, Staatsbibliothek zu Berlin Preussischer Kulturbesitz, Musikabteilung
D-BAR	Bartenstein, Fürst zu Hohenlohe-Bartensteinsches Archiv
D-BAs	Bamberg, Staatsbibliothek
D-BFb	Burgsteinfurt, Fürst zu Bentheimische Musikaliensammlung (in D-MÜu)
D-Dl	Dresden, Sächsische Landesbibliothek, Staats- und Universitätsbibliothek Dresden, Musikabteilung
D-DO	Donaueschingen, Fürstlich Fürstenburgische Hofbibliothek (in D-KA)
D-DS	Darmstadt, Hessische Landes- und Hochschulbibliothek, Musikabteilung
D-EB	Ebrach, Katholisches Pfarramt, Bibliothek
D-F	Frankfurt-am-Main, Universitätsbibliothek Johann Christian Senckenberg
D-FS	Freising, Dombibliothek
D-HL	Haltenbergstetten, Schloss (über Niederstetten, Baden-Württemberg), Fürst zu Hohenlohe-Jastberg'sche Bibliothek (in D-Mbs)
D-HR	Harburg über Donauwörth, Fürstlich Oettingen-Wallerstein'sche Bibliothek, Schloss Harburg (in D-Au)
D-Hs	Hamburg, Staats- und Universitätsbibliothek Carl von Ossietzky, Musikabteilung
D-KA	Karlsruhe, Badische Landesbibliothek, Musikabteilung
D-KNh	Cologne, Staatliche Hochschule für Musik, Bibliothek
D-LEmi	Leipzig, Universität, Zweigbibliothek Musikwissenschaft und Musikpädagogik (in D-LEu)
D-LEu	Leipzig, Universitätsbibliothek, "Bibliotheca Albertina"
D-LÜh	Lübeck, Bibliothek der Hansestadt Lübeck, Musikabteilung
D-MBG	Miltenberg-am-Main, Franziskanerkloster, Bibliothek
D-Mbs	Munich, Bayerische Staatsbibliothek, Musikabteilung
D-Mh	Munich, Staatliche Hochschule für Musik, Bibliothek
D-MÜp	Münster, Diözesanbibliothek

D-MÜs	Münster, Santini-Bibliothek (in D-MÜp)
D-MÜu	Münster, Universitäts- und Landesbibliothek
D-RH	Rheda, Fürst zu Bentheim-Tecklenburgische Musikbibliothek Rheda (in D-MÜu)
D-Rp	Regensburg, Bischöfliche Zentralbibliothek, Proske-Musikbibliothek
D-Rtt	Regensburg, Fürstlich Thurn und Taxis Hofbibliothek
D-SI	Sigmaringen, Fürstlich Hohenzollernsche Hofbibliothek
D-SWl	Schwerin, Landesbibliothek Mecklenburg-Vorpommern, Musiksammlung
D-TEGha	Tegernsee, Herzogliches Archiv
D-Tl	Tübingen, Schwäbisches Landesmusikarchiv
D-TRb	Trier, Bistumsarchiv
D-W	Wolfenbüttel, Herzog-August-Bibliothek, Musikabteilung
D-WEY	Weyarn, Pfarrkirche, Bibliothek (in D-FS)
D-WRl	Weimar, Thüringisches Hauptstaatsarchiv, Musiksammlung
D-Z	Zwickau, Ratsschulbibliothek
D-ZL	Leutkirch-Zeil, Fürstlich Waldburg-Zeil'sches Archiv, Schloss Zeil, private collection

DK (Denmark)

DK-Kk	Copenhagen, Det Kongelige Bibliotek Slotsholmen
DK-Ou	Odense, Universitetsbibliotek, Musikafdelingen
DK-Sa	Sorø, Sorø Akademi, Biblioteket

E (Spain)

E-Mba	Madrid, Archivo de Música, Real Academia de Bellas Artes de San Fernando
E-Mn	Madrid, Biblioteca Nacional
E-Mp	Madrid, Palacio Real, Biblioteca y Archivo

F (France)

F-Lm	Lille, Bibliothèque Municipale
F-Pa	Paris, Bibliothèque de l'Arsenal
F-Pn	Paris, Bibliothèque Nationale de France, Département de la Musique
F-Po	Paris, Bibliothèque-Musée de l'Opéra
F-Sgs	Strasbourg, Grand Séminaire, Bibliothèque Musicale

FIN (Finland)

FIN-As	Turku (Åbo), Sibelius Museum Musikventenskapliga Institutionen vid Åbo Akademi

GB (Great Britain)

GB-CDp	Cardiff, Public Libraries, Central Library
GB-Ckc	Cambridge, Rowe Music Library, King's College
GB-Cumc	Cambridge, University Musical Club
GB-Er	Edinburgh, Reid Music Library of the University of Edinburgh

GB-Gu	Glasgow, Glasgow University Library
GB-Lam	London, Royal Academy of Music, Library
GB-Lbl	London, The British Library
GB-Lcm	London, Royal College of Music, Library
GB-Lgc	London, Gresham College
GB-Mp	Manchester, Central Public Library
GB-Ob	Oxford, Bodleian Library
GB-SMleatham	Stamford, Burghley House, Lady Victoria Leatham, private collection
H (Hungary)	
H-Bn	Budapest, Országos Széchényi Könyvtár
H-P	Pécs, Székesgyházi Kottatár
H-VEs	Veszprém, Székesegyházi Kottatár
HR (Croatia)	
HR-Dsmb	Dubrovnik, Samostan Male Braće
HR-Sk	Split, Glazebni Archiv Katedrale
HR-Zha	Zagreb, Zbirka Don Nikole Udina Algarotti
I (Italy)	
I-Af	Assisi, Centro di Documentazione Francescana, Biblioteca
I-Baf	Bologna, Accademia Filarmonica, Biblioteca
I-Bam	Bologna, Collezioni d'Arte e di Storia della Casa di Risparmio (Biblioteca Ambrosini)
I-Bas	Bologna, Archivio di Stato, Biblioteca
I-Bc	Bologna, Civico Museo Bibliografico Musicale
I-BGc	Bergamo, Biblioteca Civica Angelo Mai
I-BRq	Brescia, Biblioteca Civica Queriniana
I-Bsf	Bologna, Biblioteca San Francesco (Convento dei Frati Minori Conventuali)
I-CMbc	Casale Monferrato, Biblioteca Civica Giovanni Canna
I-CRE	Crema, Biblioteca Comunale
I-FAsn	Fabriano, S. Nicolò, Archivio Parrocchiale
I-Fc	Florence, Conservatorio di Musica Luigi Cherubini, Biblioteca
I-FEwalker	Ferrara, Biblioteca privata Thomas Walker
I-Fm	Florence, Biblioteca Marucelliana
I-FZc	Faenza, Biblioteca Comunale Manfrediana
I-Gl	Genoa, Conservatorio di Musica Niccolò Paganini, Biblioteca
I-IBborromeo	Isola Bella, Biblioteca privata Borromeo
I-La	Lucca, Archivio di Stato
I-LDEsormani	Lurago d'Erba, Biblioteca privata Sormani Verri di Lurago
I-Lg	Lucca, Biblioteca Statale
I-Ls	Lucca, Seminario Arcivescovile, Biblioteca
I-Ma	Milan, Biblioteca Ambrosiana

I-MAav	Mantua, Accademia Virgiliana di Scienza Lettere ed Arti, Biblioteca
I-MAC	Macerata, Biblioteca Comunale Mozzi-Borgetti
I-Mb	Milan, Biblioteca Nazionale Braidense
I-Mc	Milan, Conservatorio di Musica Giuseppe Verdi, Biblioteca
I-MC	Montecassino, Monumento Nazionale di Montecassino, Biblioteca
I-Mcom	Milan, Biblioteca Comunale Sormani
I-MEs	Messina, Biblioteca Painiana del Seminario Arcivescovile San Pio X
I-MOe	Modena, Biblioteca Estense
I-Ms	Milan, Biblioteca Teatrale Livia Simoni, Museo Teatrale alla Scala
I-MTventuri	Montecatini-Terme, Biblioteca privata Antonio Venturi
I-Nc	Naples, Conservatorio di Musica San Pietro a Majella, Biblioteca
I-Nn	Naples, Biblioteca Nazionale Vittorio Emanuele III
I-OS	Ostiglia, Opera Pia Greggiati, Biblioteca
I-PAc	Parma, Biblioteca Nazionale Palatina, Sezione Musicale presso il Conservatorio di Musica Arrigo Boïto
I-PAVbc	Pavia, Biblioteca Civica Carlo Bonetta
I-Pca	Padua, Biblioteca Antoniana con Archivio Musicale
I-Pci	Padua, Museo Civico, Biblioteca Civica e Archivio Comunale
I-PEc	Perugia, Biblioteca Comunale Augusta
I-PESo	Pesaro, Biblioteca Comunale Oliveriana
I-PEsp	Perugia, Basilica Benedettina di San Pietro, Archivio e Museo della Badia
I-Pl	Padua, Conservatorio di Musica Cesare Pollini, Biblioteca
I-Pmc	Padua, Museo Civico, Biblioteca
I-Ra	Rome, Biblioteca Angelica
I-Rc	Rome, Biblioteca Casanatense
I-Rcagli	Rome, Biblioteca privata Bruno Cagli
I-Rdp	Rome, Archivio Doria-Pamphilj
I-Rf	Rome, Padri dell'Oratorio della Chiesa Nuovo (Filippini), Archivio
I-Rig	Rome, Istituto Storico Germanico di Roma, Sezione Storia della Musica, Biblioteca
I-Rmassimo	Rome, Biblioteca privata dei Principi Massimo
I-Rn	Rome, Biblioteca Nazionale Centrale Vittorio Emanuele III
I-Rrostirolla	Rome, Biblioteca privata Giancarlo Rostirolla
I-Rsc	Rome, Conservatorio di Musica Santa Cecilia, Biblioteca Musicale Governativa
I-Rsg	Rome, Basilica di San Giovanni in Laterano, Archivio Musicale
I-Rvat	Vatican City, Biblioteca Apostolica Vaticana
I-RVE	Rovereto, Biblioteca Civica Girolamo Tartarotti
I-SML	Santa Margherita Ligure, Biblioteca Comunale Francesco Domenico Costa, Biblioteca Comunale Moderna Achille e Amalia Vago
I-Tac	Turin, Archivio Storico Civico
I-Tci	Turin, Biblioteca Civica Musicale Andrea della Corte
I-Tf	Turin, Accademia Filarmonica, Archivio
I-Tfanan	Turin, Bibiloteca privata Giorgio Fanan

I-Tlegger	Turin, Biblioteca privata Legger (in I-Tfanan)
I-Tn	Turin, Biblioteca Nazionale Universitaria
I-Tp	Turin, Biblioteca Storica della Provincia
I-Tstrona	Turin, Biblioteca privata Strona
I-TVco	Treviso, Biblioteca Comunale
I-Vc	Venice, Conservatorio di Musica Benedetto Marcello, Biblioteca
I-VCa	Vercelli, Biblioteca Agnesiana e Diocesana
I-Vcg	Venice, Casa di Goldoni, Biblioteca
I-VEas	Verona, Archivio di Stato
I-Vgc	Venice, Istituto di Lettere, Musica e Teatro della Fondazione Giorgio Cini, Biblioteca
I-Vnm	Venice, Biblioteca Nazionale Marciana
I-Vsm	Venice, Procuratoria di San Marco, Archivio
I-Vsmc	Venice, Santa Maria della Consolazione (Della Fava), Archivio

NL (The Netherlands)

NL-At	Amsterdam, Toonkunst-Bibliotheek, Openbare Bibliotheek Amsterdam

P (Portugal)

P-La	Lisbon, Biblioteca do Palácio Nacional da Ajuda

PL (Poland)

PL-CZ	Czestochowa, Archiwum OO. Paulinów na Jasnej Górze
PL-Kd	Cracow, Biblioteka Studium OO. Dominikanów, Archiwum Prowincji OO. Dominikanów
PL-MO	Mogiła, Opactwo Cystersów, Archiwum i Biblioteka
PL-SA	Sandomierz, Biblioteka Wyzego Seminarium Duchownego
PL-WRu	Wrocław, Biblioteka Uniwersytecka
PL-Wu	Warsaw, Biblioteka Uniwersytecka, Zbiory Specjalne

RUS (Russia)

RUS-SPit	St. Petersburg, Rossijskij Institut Istorii Iskusstv
RUS-SPsc	St. Petersburg, Rossijskaja Nacional'naja Biblioteka

S (Sweden)

S-HÄ	Härnösand, Länsmuseet-Murberget
S-L	Lund, Universitetsbiblioteket
S-LI	Linköping, Stiftsbiblioteket i Stadsbiblioteket
S-Sdt	Stockholm, Drottningholms Teatermuseum
S-SK	Skara, Stifts- och Landesbiblioteket
S-Sk	Stockholm, Kungliga Biblioteket
S-Skma	Stockholm, Statens Musikbiblioteket (formerly Kungliga Musikaliska Akademiens Bibliotek)

S-Sm	Stockholm, Musikmuseet
S-Uu	Uppsala, Universitetsbiblioteket
S-V	Västeras, Stadsbiblioteket
SK (Slovakia)	
SK-BRsav	Bratislava, Ústav Hudobnej Vedy, Slovenská Akadémia Vied
SK-J	Svätý Jur, Okresný Archív, Bratislava - Vidiek (in SK-MO)
SK-Mms	Martin, Matica Slovenská
SK-MO	Modra, Štátny Okresný Archív Pezinok
SK-TR	Trnava, Štátny Okresný Archív
UA (Ukraine)	
UA-Kan	Kiev, Central'naja Naučnaja Biblioteka im. V. I. Vernads'kogo, Nacional'noj Akademii Nauk Ukrainy
US (United States)	
US-AAu	Ann Arbor, University of Michigan, Music Library
US-AUS	Austin, University of Texas at Austin, The Harry Ransom Humanities Research Center
US-BAu	Baltimore, Johns Hopkins University Libraries
US-BEm	Berkeley, University of California, Music Library
US-BLl	Bloomington, Indiana University, Lilly Library
US-I	Ithaca, Cornell University Music Library
US-LAuc	Los Angeles, University of California, William Andrews Clark Memorial Library
US-LAum	Los Angeles, University of California, Music Library
US-LOu	Louisville, University of Louisville, School of Music Library
US-NYp	New York, Public Library at Lincoln Center, Music Division
US-PHchs	Philadelphia, American Catholic Historical Society Library
US-R	Rochester, Sibley Music Library, Eastman School of Music, University of Rochester
US-SFsc	San Francisco, San Francisco State University, Col. Frank V. DeBellis Collection
US-SY	Syracuse, Syracuse University Music Library
US-Wc	Washington, D.C., Library of Congress, Music Division

SIGLA FOR EARLY AND MODERN EDITIONS

André 1777a — *Sei quartetti a due violini, viola e violoncello . . . opera I.* Offenbach: Johann André, [1777]. (= RISM A/I M 2886; exemplar in S-L)
(String Quartets 12–17)

André 1777b — *Sei sonate a due violini, e violoncello . . . opera II.* Offenbach: Johann André, [1777]. (= RISM A/I M 2890; exemplar in US-Wc)
No. 1 = String Trio 8 — No. 4 = String Trio 7

	No. 2 = String Trio 9	No. 5 = String Trio 11
	No. 3 = String Trio 12	No. 6 = String Trio 10

Bělský 1957 — *Tři smyčcové kvintéty* (= *Tre quintetti d'archi*). Ed. Vratislav Bělský. Musica antiqua bohemica, No. 31. Prague: Státní nakladatelství krásné literatury, hudby a umění, 1957/reprint, Prague: Editio Supraphon; Artia, 1973.
(String Quintets 7–9)

Bělský 1988 — *Tre quintetti d'archi, IV–VI*. Ed. Vratislav Bělský. Musica antiqua bohemia, No. 83. Prague: Editio Supraphon, 1988; reprint, 1993.
(String Quintets 10–12)

Bland 1790 — *Six Trios, Three for a German Flute, Violin, Bassoon or Violoncello and Three for Two German Flutes or Violins, Bassoon or Violoncello by Misliwecek, Venturini and Leo*. London: John Bland, [ca. 1790]. (not listed in RISM; exemplar in GB-Gu; cat. ref. BUC indicates a date of publication about 1795, however it is known that the publisher either died or went out of business by 1794)
(Mysliveček selections: Flute Trios 3 and 6)

Branberger & Růžková 1938 — *Šest sonát pro klavír*. Ed. Jan Branberger and Vilma Růžková. Prague: Urbánek, 1938.
(Keyboard Sonatas 7–12)

Corri & Sutherland 1784 — *Six Easy Lessons for the Harpsichord*. Edinburgh: Corri & Sutherland, [1784]. (= RISM A/I M2896; exemplars in GB-CDp, GB-Lbl, I-Vc)
(Keyboard Sonatas 7–12)

Del Vivo 1 — *Sinfonia da orchestra con oboe e corni obbligati*. Florence: Ranieri del Vivo, [late 1770s?]. (=RISM A/I M2884; examplars in D-W, E-Mba)
= Overture 20 (*Ezio* of 1775)

Del Vivo 2 — *Sei sinfonie da orchestra dedicate a Sua Eccelenza Lord de Nassau Conte di Cowper*. Florence: Ranieri del Vivo, [late 1770s?]. (not listed in RISM; exemplar in I-MEs; see cat. ref. I-MEs; parts for vln I, vla lacking)
No. 1 = Overture 16 (*Antigona* of 1774)
No. 2 = Overture 20 (*Ezio* of 1775)
No. 3 = Overture 19 (*Demofoonte* of 1775)
No. 4 = Overture 18 (*Artaserse* of 1774)
No. 5 = Overture 14 (*Demetrio* of 1773)
No. 6 = Overture 22 (*Adriano in Siria* of 1776)

Del Vivo 3 — *Sinfonia da orchestra con oboe e corni obbligati*. Florence: Ranieri del Vivo, [late 1770s?]. (not listed in RISM; exemplar in CZ-K)
= Overture 22 (*Adriano in Siria* of 1776)

Del Vivo 4 — *Sinfonia del Sig. Misliwecek*. Florence: Ranieri del Vivo, [late 1770s?]. (not listed in RISM; exemplar in I-Mc)
= Overture 24 (*Calliroe* of 1778)

Del Vivo 5 — *Sei trii per flauto, violino, e violoncello*. Florence: Ranieri del Vivo, [1778?]. (not listed in RISM; exemplar in I-OS; see cat. ref. I-OS)

(Flute Trios 1–6)

Note: In a confusing citation, Evans/Dearling, 152, appears to specify the existence of a Del Vivo print in E-Mn with the title *Sinfonia sesta eseguita nell'Adriano in Siria nel Teatro di Via del Cocomero di Firenze*, which would correspond to the last selection in the Del Vivo 2 print. In fact, the archive E-Mn preserves no Del Vivo prints of Mysliveček symphonies, either the complete collection Del Vivo 2 or any *separatum*. A Del Vivo print of Mysliveček trios advertised for sale in Florence on 14 March 1778 may be identical to Del Vivo 5; prints of individual symphonies advertised for sale on 6 February and 1 May 1779 are impossible to match definitively with any surviving prints. See Bianca Maria Antolini, "Editori, copisti, commercio della musica in Italia: 1770–1800," *Studi musicali* 18 (1989): 326–27.

Divertimenta 1930 — *Šest klavírních divertimentů* (= *Sei divertimenti per il cembalo*). Kutná Hora: Česká hudba, 1930.

(Keyboard Sonatas 1–6)

Emingerová 1919 — *České sonatiny pro klavír na 2 ruce* (= *Divertimenta pro klavicembalo*). Ed. Kateřina Emingerová. Prague: Barvitius, 1919/six reprints to 1943.

(Myslivecek selections):
No. 1 = Keyboard Sonata 5
No. 2 = Keyboard Sonata 2
No. 3 = Keyboard Sonata 3
No. 4 = Keyboard Sonata 8 (2nd movement only)
No. 5 = Keyboard Sonata 9 (2nd movement only)
No. 6 = Keyboard Sonata 1

Emingerová & Kredba 1954 — *České sonatiny*. Ed. Kateřina Emingerová and Oldřich Kredba. Musica antiqua bohemica, No. 17. Prague: Státní nakladatelství krásné literatury, hudby a umění, 1954/2nd ed., 1958.

(Mysliveček selections):
No. 1 = Keyboard Sonata 8 (2nd movement only)
No. 2 = Keyboard Sonata 2
No. 3 = Keyboard Sonata 1
No. 4 = Keyboard Sonata 3
No. 5 = Keyboard Sonata 5
No. 6 = Keyboard Sonata 9
No. 7 = Keyboard Sonata 12

Emingerová & Kredba 1961 — *České sonatiny* (= *Sonatinen alter böhmischen Meister*). Selected by Kateřina Emingerová, ed. Oldřich Kredba. Musica viva historica, No. 5. Prague: Státní hudební vydavatelství, 1961/reprint 1965, 1966/reprint, Editio Supraphon, 5 edns., 1976–88.

(Mysliveček contents same as Emingerová & Kredba 1954)

Freeman 2001 — *Six Trios for Flute, Violin, and Violoncello*. Ed. Daniel E. Freeman. Fish Creek, WI: Alliance Publications, 2001.

(Flute Trios 1–6)

Freeman Del Vivo — *Six Symphonies by Josef Mysliveček from the Printing by Ranieri del Vivo*. Ed. Daniel E. Freeman. Monuments of Tuscan Music, Series I: Orchestral Music. Symphonies, vol. 1. Louisville, KY: Musica Toscana, in preparation.

No. 1 = Overture 16 (*Antigona* of 1774)
No. 2 = Overture 20 (*Ezio* of 1775)
No. 3 = Overture 19 (*Demofoonte* of 1775)
No. 4 = Overture 18 (*Artaserse* of 1774)
No. 5 = Overture 14 (*Demetrio* of 1773)
No. 6 = Overture 22 (*Adriano in Siria* of 1776)

Freeman n.d. — *Six String Quartets*. Ed. Daniel E. Freeman. The Early String Quartet, No. 7. Ann Arbor: Steglein, in preparation.

(String Quartets 18–23)

Freeman & Ackerman n.d. — *Chamber Music for Strings*. Ed. Daniel E. Freeman and James A. Ackerman (in preparation)

(String Quintets 1–6 and String Trios 7–10, 13–14)

Haffner 1763 — *VI Sinfonie a quattro cioè II. violini, alto viola, e violoncello, con II. corni da caccia e II oboe ad lib. dedicate a sua eccellenza illustrissima Signora Antonia contessa di Wratislaw nata contessa di Kinsky, etc. etc., . . . opera Ima*. Nuremberg: Johann Ulrich Haffner, [ca. 1763]. (= RISM A/I M2882; exemplars in CH-E, CH-FF, UA-Kan)

(Symphonies 2–7)

Hummel 1781 — *Six quatuors à deux violons, taille et basse*. Berlin: Johann Julius Hummel; Amsterdam: Grand Magazin de Musique, [ca. 1781]. (= RISM A/I M 2887; exemplars in B-Bc, CZ-Bm, CZ-Jla, CZ-Pnm, CZ-Pl, I-Vc, S-L, UA-Kan; an exemplar reported in RISM in FIN-A has been declared lost by archival staff as of 1987)

(String Quartets 18–23)

Jícha 1981 — *Skladby českých mistrů: housle (flétna) a kytara*. Ed. Bohumil Jícha. Edicije hrajeme doma, No. 13. Prague: Supraphon, 1981.

(Mysliveček selections):
No. 1 = Keyboard Sonata 2 (arr. fl or vl, guitar)
No. 2 = Keyboard Sonata 3 (arr. fl or vl, guitar)

Klement 1978 — *Čtyři sonáty pro flétnu, housle a violoncello*. Ed. Miloslav Klement. Musica viva historica, No. 42. Prague: Editio Supraphon, 1978/2nd ed., 1983.

No. 1 = Flute Trio 3
No. 2 = Flute Trio 1
No. 3 = Flute Trio 2
No. 4 = Flute Trio 6

Kölbel 1991	*2 Trios Op. 1 für Flöte, Violine und Violoncello*. Ed. Wilhelm Kölbel. Wilhelmshaven: Heinrichshofen, 1991. No. 1 = Flute Trio 3 No. 2 = Flute Trio 1
La Chevardière 1768	*Six sonates en trio qui sont faits pour exécuter à trois ou avec tous l'orchestre . . . oeuvre Ier*. Paris: La Chevardière, [ca. 1768]. (= RISM A/I M 2889; exemplars in B-Bc, S-Skma) (String Trios 7–12)
La Chevardière/ Castaud 1768/69	*Sei quartetti a due violini alto e basso . . . opera III*. Paris: La Chevardière; Lyon: Castaud, [ca. 1768/69]. (not listed in RISM; exemplar in S-Skma) (String Quartets 1–6)
Le Menu 1772	*Six sonates pour deux violons & basse . . . oeuvre Ive*. Paris: Le Menu, [1772]. (= RISM A/I M 2891; exemplars in F-Pn, UA-Kan) (String Trios 15–20)
Longman & Broderip 1777	*Six Easy Divertimentos for the Harpsichord or Piano-Forte*. London: Longman & Broderip, [1777]. (= RISM A/I M2895; exemplars in GB-Lbl, US-Wc) (Keyboard Sonatas 1–6)
Napier 1772	*Six Overtures for Two Violins, Two Hoboys, Two French Horns, Two Tenors, with a Thorough Bass for the Harpsichord or Violoncello* ("most humbly dedicated to the Right Honourable the Earl Cowper by Giuseppe Misliwecek"). London: William Napier, [ca. 1772]. (= RISM A/I M2885; exemplars in E-Mn, GB-Lam, GB-Lbl, GB-Lcm, GB-Mp, GB-Ob, GB-SMleatham) (Symphonies 26–31)
Němec & Zuckerová 1988	*Šest sonát/Sei sonate*. Ed. Věroslav Němec and Olga Zuckerová. Prague: Editio Supraphon, 1988; 2nd ed., 1999. (contains Keyboard Sonatas 7–12)
Pilková 1984	*The Symphony, 1720–1840*, Series B, Vol. XIII, Nos. 4–6. Ed. by Zdeňka Pilková. New York and London: Garland, 1984. No. 4 = Overture 5 (*Il trionfo di Clelia* of 1768) No. 5 = Symphony 43 No. 6 = Symphony 45
Salter 1983	*Six Easy Divertimentos*. Ed. Lionel Salter. London: The Associated Board of The Royal Schools of Music, 1983. (Keyboard Sonatas 1–6)
Schmitt	*IV trios pour la flûte, violon, e violoncello, oeuvre I*. Amsterdam: J. Schmitt, [late 1770s?] (not listed in RISM; exemplars in CZ-Pnm, I-Mc) No. 1 = Flute Trio 3 No. 2 = Flute Trio 1 No. 3 = Flute Trio 2 No. 4 = Flute Trio 6

Schoenbaum 1962 — *Tre ottetti*. Ed. Camillo Schoenbaum. Musica antiqua bohemica, No. 55. Prague: Státní hudební vydavatelství, 1962/reprint 1964/reprint as "2nd ed.," Editio Supraphon, 1973.

(Wind Octets 1–3)

Thompson 1775 — *Six Sonatas for the Piano Forte or Harpsichord with an Accompaniment for a Violin*. London: Charles & Samuel Thompson, [ca. 1775]. (= RISM A/I M 2894; exemplar in GB-Lbl)

(Violin Sonatas 6–11)

Thompson 1790 — *Six Overtures in Eight Parts* [by Stamitz, Vaňhal, Mysliveček, Maria Antonia Walpurgis of Saxony, and Haydn]. London: Thompson, [1790]. (see RISM B/v.2, p. 278; exemplars in GB-Ckc and US-Wc; contents = Welcker 1773)

No. 3 = Symphony 16

Venier/Castaud 1767 — *VI Sinfonie concertanti o sia quintetti per due violini, due viole, e basso . . . opera IIa . . . les parties des altos pourront s'exécuter avec des bassons ou violoncelles*. Paris: Venier; Lyon: Castaud, [ca. 1767]. (= RISM A/I M2883; exemplars in F-Pa, F-Pn; RISM A/I incorrectly indicates the lack of a part for vla 1 in the exemplar in F-Pn; the exemplar in F-Pa lacks a part for vlc)

(String Quintets 1–6)

Welcker 1772 — *Six Orchestra Trios for Two Violins and a Violoncello*. London: Welcker, [ca. 1772]. (= RISM A/I M 2892; exemplars in GB-Lbl, S-Skma, US-BEm, US-R; RISM A/I M 2893 is the same edition as Welcker 1772 without indication of publisher; exemplars in B-Bc, GB-CDp)

No. 1 = String Trio 9	No. 4 = String Trio 10
No. 2 = String Trio 8	No. 5 = String Trio 13
No. 3 = String Trio 7	No. 6 = String Trio 14

Welcker 1773 — *Six Overtures in Eight Parts* [by Stamitz, Vaňhal, Mysliveček, Maria Antonia Walpurgis of Saxony, and Haydn]. London: Welcker, [ca. 1773]. (see RISM B/v.2, p. 278; exemplars in GB-Lbl, GB-Lcm, GB-Ob, and US-BEm, those in GB-Lcm and US-BEm incomplete; additional exemplar in E-Mn unreported in RISM)

No. 3 = Symphony 16

Welcker 1780 — *Six Quartettos for Two Violins, a Tenor and Violoncello*. London: Welcker, [ca. 1780]. (= RISM A/I M 2888; exemplars in E-Mn, GB-SMleatham, US-Wc)

No. 1 = String Quartet 2	No. 4 = String Quartet 5
No. 2 = String Quartet 3	No. 5 = String Quartet 4
No. 3 = String Quartet 6	No. 6 = String Quartet 1

White 1994 — *Three Violin Concertos*. Ed. Chappell White. Recent Researches in the Music of the Classical Era, Vol. 41. Madison, WI: A-R Editions, 1994.

(Violin Concertos 1, 7, and 8)

SIGLA FOR EARLIER CATALOGS

The following is a list of sigla for earlier catalogs, most of which are described more fully in Barry S. Brook and Richard Viano, eds., *Thematic Catalogues in Music: An Annotated Bibliography*, 2nd ed. (Stuyvesant, NY: Pendragon Press, 1997). Only the most relevant of the older catalogs are included here. In the case of the more modern catalogs, only the most recent edition or reprint is cited. The numbering or pagination of catalog entries is specified only occasionally for the sake of clarity; typically, the Mysliveček compositions can be located from the alphabetical arrangement of most catalogs (bearing in mind that Mysliveček's name frequently appears with the second letter "i" in alternate spellings such as "Misliweczek" or "Mislivecek"). In the body of Catalog 1, modern catalog references for early editions of music are included only for prints not listed in RISM A/I or RISM B.

A-GÖ 1830 — Göttweig Benediktinerstift, Austria, *Katalogus operum musicalium in choro musicali monasterii O. S. P. B. Gottwicensis* (a manuscript catalog in A-GÖ comp. R. D. Heinrich Wondratsch and dated 1830).

A-LA 1768 — *Catalogus Musicalium et Instrumentorum ad Chorum Lambacensum pertinentium conscriptge* (a manuscript catalog of the holdings of the Benediktinerstift in Lambach prepared in 1768).

A-VOR 1771 — Stift Vorau, Musikarchiv, *Musikalienkatalog* (a manuscript catalog compiled in 1771; the symphonies of this catalog are divided into three informal groupings referred to as "classes")

Benton/Pleyel — Benton, Rita. *Ignace Pleyel: A Thematic Catalogue of His Compositions*. Thematic Catalogues, 2. New York: Pendragon Press, 1977.

Brook — Brook, Barry S., ed. *The Breitkopf Thematic Catalogue: The Six Parts and Sixteen Supplements, 1762–1787*. New York: Dover, 1966. (This publication constitutes a facsimile edition with new consecutive pagination)

BUC — Schapper, Edith, ed. *British Union-Catalogue of Early Music Printed before the Year 1801*. London: Butterworths Scientific Publications, 1957.

CZ-Pnm Doksy — Rutová, Milada. "Valdštejnská hudební sbírka v Doksech." Doctoral dissertation, Charles University, Prague, 1971. (lists sources in CZ-Pnm from the Waldstein estate of Doksy, including those once in the possession of Roman Nejedlý)

D-B Thouret — Thouret, Georg. *Katalog der Musiksammlung der königlichen Hausbibliothek im Schlosse zu Berlin*. Leipzig, 1895.

D-DO Copia Verzeichnis 1804 — *Copia Verzeichniss Nr. 12 der fürstlichen Musikalien, Pulte Instrumente . . . im Monat Junij 1804* (a manuscript catalog in D-DO of the holdings of the Fürstlich Fürstenbergische Hofbibliothek in 1804, with further entries up to 1816).

D-SI 1766 — *Catalogus über die sämtliche musicalische Werck, und derselben Authorn, nach alphabetischer Ordnung: Welche von Ihro Hochfürstl. Durchlaucht dem . . . Fürsten Herrn Herrn Carl Friedrich Erbprinz zu Hohenzollern angeschafft worden seynd* (a manuscript catalog in D-SI compiled in 1766 by Johann Michael Schindele, music director at the court of Sigmaringen, with later additions).

EitnerQ — Eitner, Robert. *Biographisch-bibliographisches Quellen-Lexikon der Musiker und Musikgelehrter*. Graz: Akademische Druck- und Verlagsanstalt, 1959.

Evans/Dearling — Evans, Angela, and Robert Dearling. *Josef Mysliveček (1737–1781): A Thematic Catalogue of His Instrumental and Orchestral Works*. Musikwissenschaftliche Schriften, 35. Munich: Katzbichler, 1999.

Fugger — Haberkamp, Gertraut, and Barbara Zuber. *Die Musikhandschriften Herzog Wilhelms in Bayern, der Grafen zu Toerring-Jettenbach und der Fürsten Fugger von Babenhausen*. Kataloge bayerischer Musiksammlungen, No. 13. Munich: Henle, 1988.

GraveF — Grave, Margaret H. "First-Movement Form as a Measure of Dittersdorf's Symphonic Development." Ph.D. dissertation, New York University, 1977.

Grave/Dittersdorf — Margaret H. Grave's thematic index for the symphonies by Carl Ditters von Dittersdorf (1739–99) in *Dittersdorf: Six Symphonies*, The Symphony, 1720–1840, Series B, Vol. 1 (New York and London: Garland, 1985), xli–lxviii.

Haberkamp and Münster — Haberkamp, Gertraut, and Robert Münster. *Die ehemaligen Musikhandschriftsammlungen der Königlichen Hofkapelle und der Kurfürstin Maria Anna in München*. Kataloge bayerischer Musiksammlungen, No. 9. Munich, Henle, 1982.

Haberkamp and Zuber — Haberkamp, Gertraut, and Barbara Zuber. *Die Musikhandschriften Herzog Wilhelms in Bayern, der Grafen Toerring-Jettenbach und der Fürsten Fugger von Babenhausen*. Kataloge bayerischer Musiksammlungen, No. 13. Munich: Henle, 1988.

Hickman/Hoffmeister — Roger Hickman's thematic index for the symphonies by Franz Anton Hoffmeister (1754–1812) in *Hoffmeister: Two Symphonies*, The Symphony, 1720–1840, Series B, Vol. 5 (New York and London: Garland, 1984), xix–xxv.

Hoboken/Haydn — Hoboken, Anthony van. *Joseph Haydn: Thematisches-bibliographisches Werkverzeichnis*. Mainz: Schott, 1957–71.

Hofmeister 1817 — [Whistling, Carl Friedrich, and] Friedrich Hofmeister. *Handbuch der Musikalische Litteratur*. Leipzig, 1817; supplements, 1–10, 1818–27/reprint, New York: Garland, 1975.

I-MAav — Bernardi, Gian Giuseppe. *Catalogo dell'archivio musicale della Reale Accademia Virgiliana di Mantova*. Mantua: G. Mondovi, 1923.

I-MEs — Chirico, Teresa. *Il fondo musicale della Biblioteca Painiana di Messina*. Cataloghi di fondi musicali italiani, 14. Rome: Edizioni Torre d'Orfeo, 1992.

I-MTventuri — Kishimoto, Hiroko. *Il fondo musicale Venturi nella Biblioteca Comunale di Montecatini Terme*. Inventari e cataloghi toscani, 28. Milan: Giunta Regionale Toscana, 1989.

I-OS — Sartori, Claudio, ed. *Ostiglia, Biblioteca dell'Opera Pia Greggiati: Catalogo del fondo musicale*, Vol. 1: *Le edizioni*. Bibliotheca musicae, 7. Milan: Nuovo Istituto Editoriale Italiano, 1983.

I-Pca — Tebaldini, Giovanni. *L'Archivio muscale della Capella Antoniana in Padova*. Padua, 1895.

Köchel/Mozart — Köchel, Ludwig Ritter von. *Chronologisch-thematisches Verzeichnis sämtlicher Tonwerke Wolfgang Amadé Mozart*. 6th ed. Wiesbaden: Breitkopf & Härtel, 1964.

Kroyer	(Theodor Kroyer's manuscript catalog in D-Mbs of musical sources compiled in 1918–19 for the series *Denkmäler der Tonkunst in Bayern*)
Mennicke/Hasse	Mennicke, Carl H. *Hasse und die Brüder Graun als Symphoniker*. Leipzig: Breitkopf & Härtel, 1906.
Qb 1775	Quartbuch (or "kleines Quartbuch"): *2 Thematischer Cathalog verschiedener Compositionen von verschiedener Meistern*, 2 vols., comp. Johann Nepomuk Weigl, ca. 1775. This is a fragmentary catalog of an Austrian collection of unverifiable origins once in the possession of the Esterházy family and formerly housed in H-Bn. It is believed to have been destroyed during World War II. The catalog was known to Haydn, who made corrections in it. The original catalog comprised a volume of chamber works as Part I and a volume of symphonies as Part II. A list of contents is preserved in A-Wn. The Mysliveček listings here append the suffixes "Ch" and "Sym" to "Qb" in order to distinguish between the various parts of the catalog.
RISM A/I	Répertoire International des Sources Musicales. *Einzeldrucke vor 1800*. Ed. Karlheinz Schlager. Kassel: Bärenreiter, 1971–81 (+ supplements).
RISM A/II	Répertoire International des Sources Musicales. *Musikhandschriften 1600–1800: Datenbank-Index*. Unpublished database edited at RISM Zentralredaktion, Frankfurt-am-Main.
RISM B/v.2	Répertoire International des Sources Musicales. *Recueils imprimés XVIIIe siècle*. Ed. François Lesure. Munich-Duisburg: Henle, 1964.
RISM-US	RISM-US (Répertoire International des Sources Musicales, US Center for Musical Sources at Harvard University). *Music Manuscripts 1600–1800*. (unpublished database)
Rompaey/Maldere	Rompaey, Willy van. *Pieter van Maldere, 1729–1768: Thematische Katalog van de Instrumental Werken*. Aartselaar: Willy van Rompaey, 1990.
Santos	Santos, Marianna Amélia. *Biblioteca da Ajuda: catálogo de música manuscritta*. Lisbon: Biblioteca da Ajuda, 1959.
Sartori	Sartori, Claudio. *I libretti italiani a stampa dalla origine al 1800*. Cuneo: Bertola & Locatelli, 1990–94.
Traeg	Traeg, Johann. *Verzeichniss alter und neuer sowohl geschriebener als gestochener Musikalien, welche in der Kunst- und Musikalienhandlung des Johann Traeg, zu Wien, in der Singerstrasse Nr. 957 zu haben sind*. Vienna, 1799. This catalog is reprinted in full in Alexander Weinmann, ed., *Johann Traeg: Die Musikalienverzeichnisse von 1799 und 1804 (Handschriften und Sortiment)*, Beiträge zur Geschichte des Alt-Wiener Musikverlages, Reihe 2, Folge 17, Vol. 1 (Vienna: Universal Edition, 1973).
Vester	Vester, Frans. *Flute Music of the Eighteenth Century: An Annotated Bibliography*. 2nd ed. Monteux: Musica Rara, 1985.
Warburton/Bach	Warburton, Ernest. *The Collected Works of Johann Christian Bach, 1735–1782*, Vol. 48, part 1: *Thematic Catalogue*. New York: Garland, 1999.

CONCORDANCES FOR BREITKOPF CATALOG ENTRIES

Note: references to page numbers correspond to those found in cat. ref. Brook (see siglum in previous section)

1. Breitkopf 1767 (p. 266)—"VI. Sinfonie di van Maldere"
   No. 2 = Spurious Symphony No. 1
2. Breitkopf 1767 (p. 275)—"VI. Trii di Mislewecek"
   = String Trios 1–6
3. Breitkopf 1768 (p. 316)—"VI. Quintetti di Gius. Mislewecek"
   = Venier/Castaud 1767, String Quintets 1–6
4. Breitkopf 1769 (p. 339)—"III. Sinfonie di Gius. Mislewecek"
   No. 1 = Symphony 11
   No. 2 = Symphony 12
   No. 3 = Overture 5 (*Il trionfo di Clelia* of 1768)
5. Breitkopf 1769 (p. 349)—"VI. Trii di Gius. Mislewecek"
   No. 1 = String Trio 9
   No. 2 = String Trio 7
   No. 3 = String Trio 10
   No. 4 = String Trio 13
   No. 5 = String Trio 14
   No. 6 = String Trio 8
6. Breitkopf 1769 (p. 354)—"I. Conc. Gius. Mislewecek"
   = Violin Concerto 1
7. Breitkopf 1770 (p. 390)—"I. Conc. Gius. Mislewecek"
   = Violin Concerto 2
8. Breitkopf 1770 (p. 391)—"Solo di Misliwezek "
   = Sonata for Cello and Bass
9. Breitkopf 1772 (p. 443)—"I. Sinf. di Gius. Mislwecek"
   = Overture 10 (*La Nitteti* of 1770)
10. Breitkopf 1773 (p. 483)—"I. Sinf. da Mislewezeck"
    = Overture 6 (*Demofoonte* of 1769)
11. Breitkopf 1773 (p. 492)—"III. Trii di Giorgio Lang"
    No. 2= String Trio 19
12. Breitkopf 1774 (p. 526)—"VI. Sinf. da Gius. Misleweczek"
    = Haffner 1763, Symphonies 2–7
13. Breitkopf 1774 (p. 532)—"II. Sinfonie da Gius. Misleweczek"
    No. 1 = Questionable Symphony 1
    No. 2 = Overture 7 (*L'Ipermestra* of 1769)

14. Breitkopf 1775 (p. 562)—"I Sinf. da Boemo"
    = Symphony 19

15. Breitkopf 1775 (p. 563)—"II. Sinf. da Gius. Misleweczek"
    No. 1 = Symphony 16
    No. 2 = Symphony 18

16. Breitkopf 1776/77 (p. 592)—"VI. Sinf. da Gius. Misleweczeck"
    = Symphonies 36–41

17. Breitkopf 1778 (p. 651)—"Trio da Punto"
    (see Part 6, Questional Work No. 2)

18. Breitkopf 1778 (p. 639)—"VI. Quattri da Misliwezek"
    = André 1777a, String Quartets 12–17

19. Breitkopf 1779/80 (p. 679)—"VI. Trii da Misliwececk"
    = André 1777b, String Trios 7–12

20. Breitkopf 1781 (p. 731)—"I. Trio da Misliwezeck"
    (see Part 6, Questionable Work No. 2)

21. Breitkopf 1782/84 (p. 783)—"VI. Quintetti da Gius. Misliwececk"
    = Oboe Quintets 1–6

SIGLA FOR SCHOLARLY WORKS OTHER THAN EDITIONS AND EARLIER CATALOGS

The following list comprises sigla for items *not* included in the Select Bibliography at the end of the volume.

Bereths	Bereths, Gustav. *Die Musikpflege am kurtrierischen Hofe zu Koblenz-Ehrenbreitstein*. Beiträge zur mittelrheinischen Musikgeschichte, No. 5. Mainz: Schott, 1964.
Bernsdorf	Bernsdorf, Eduard. *Neues Universal-Lexikon der Tonkunst*. Dresden, 1857–61. [see Vol. 2, 1082–83]
BohadloCat	Bohadlo, Stanislav. *Josef Mysliveček: Thematic Catalogue of Vocal Works* [in preparation].
Böhmer	Böhmer, Karl. "Das Oratorium *Gioas, re di Giuda* in den Vertonungen von Johannes Ritschel (Mannheim 1763) und Pompeo Sales (Koblenz 1781)." In *Mannheim – Ein Paradies der Tonkünstler?: Kongressbericht Mannheim 1999*, 227–51. Ed. Ludwig Fischer et al. Frankfurt-am-Main: Peter Lang, 2002.
Brunelli	Brunelli Bonetti, Bruno. *I teatri di Padova dalle origini alla fine del secolo XIX*. Padua: A. Draghi, 1921.

Čeleda — Čeleda, Jaroslav. *Josef Mysliveček, tvůrce pražského nářečí hudebního rokoka tereziánského* (Josef Mysliveček, Founder of the Prague Dialect of Theresian Musical Rococo). Prague: J. Svoboda, 1946.

CSHS — *Československý hudební slovník* (The Czechoslovak Music Dictionary). Prague: Státní hudební vydavatelství, 1963–65. [see Vol. 2, 140–41]

De Angelis — De Angelis, Marcello. *Melodramma spettacolo e musica nella Firenze dei Lorena*. Inventari e cataloghi toscani, Vols. 37–38. Milan: Giunta Regionale Toscana & Editrice Bibliografica, 1991.

ES — *Enciclopedia dello spettacolo*, Vol. 7. Rome: Le Maschere, 1960. [see cols. 989–90]

Fétis — Fétis, François-Joseph. *Biographie universelle des musiciens*. 2nd ed. Paris, 1866–70.

Grove6 — *The New Grove Dictionary of Music and Musicians*. 6th ed. London: Macmillan, 1980. [see Vol. 13, 6–8]

Grove Online — (Online version of various *Grove* music dictionaries maintained by Oxford University Press as *Oxford Music Online* at www.oxfordmusiconline.com)

Hansell — Hansell, Kathleen Kuzmick. "Opera and Ballet at the Regio Ducal Teatro of Milan, 1771–1776: A Musical and Social History." Ph.D. diss., University of California-Berkeley, 1980.

Kneidl — Kneidl, Pravoslav. "Pražské činoherní a operní texty z doby působení Divadla v Kotcích" (Prague Plays and Opera Texts from the Time of the Operation of the Divadlo v Kotcích). In *Divadlo v Kotcích, 1739–1783*, 266–85. Ed. František Černý. Prague: Panorama, 1992. [see p. 276]

Legband — Legband, Paul. *Münchener Bühne und Litteratur im achtzehnten Jahrhundert*. Oberbayerishces Archiv für vaterländische Geschichte, Vol. 51. Munich: G. Franz, 1904.

MGG 1961 — *Die Musik in Geschichte und Gegenwart*, Vol. 9. Kassel: Bärenreiter, 1961. [see cols. 1238–42]

Piperno — Piperno, Franco. "Drammi sacri in teatro (1750–1820)." In *Mozart, Padova e la Betulia liberata: liberata: Committenza, interpretazione e fortuna delle azioni sacre metastasian nel '700*, ed. Pado Pinamonti, 289–316. Florence: Olschki, 1991.

Schmidl — Schmidl, Carlo. *Dizionario universale dei musicisti*. Milan: Sonzogno, 1938.

Weaver & Weaver — Weaver, Robert Lamar, and Norma Wright Weaver. *A Chronology of Music in the Florentine Theater, 1751–1800*. Warren, MI: Harmonie Park Press, 1993.

Catalog 1

SOURCES OF MYSLIVEČEK'S INSTRUMENTAL MUSIC

Part 1

SYMPHONIES

Symphony 1: C major, 1762 [10:C1]

Scoring: 2 vln, vla, b, 2 ob, 2 hrn

Ms. sources: A-Wn Mus.Hs. 36.206; CZ-Pnm XXXIV E 177 (Doksy): ms. dated 1762; D-Rtt Mysliveček 6: ms. ca. 1770

Edition: *Sinfonia*, ed. H. H. Stuckenschmidt (Vienna: Universal Edition, 1940)

Recordings: Orchestra of the Kroměříž Conservatory, cond. Jaroslav Hýl, Panton 8110 0106, 1980 [LP]; Prague Chamber Orchestra, Supraphon 1110 2836, 1981 [LP]

Symphonies 2–7:

6 symphonies in Haffner 1763 (probably composed 1762–63).

No. 1 = Symphony 2 (D major) [10:D1]
No. 2 = Symphony 3 (G major) [10:G1]
No. 3 = Symphony 4 (C major) [10:C2]
No. 4 = Symphony 5 (F major) [10:F1]
No. 5 = Symphony 6 (G minor) [10:g1]
No. 6 = Symphony 7 (D major) [10:D2]

Scoring: 2 vln, vla, b, 2 ob, 2 hrn

Ms. source: CZ-Pnm V B 56 (Jan Pohl collection)

Cat ref.: Breitkopf 1774 (p. 526)

Additional editions: *Sinfonia I in D-dur aus: VI Sinfonie a quattro, op. 1*, ed. Michi Gaigg and Christian Moritz-Bauer (Passau: Musikverlag Peter Lechl, 2003): Symphony 2; *Sinfonia II in G-dur aus: VI Sinfonie a quattro, op. 1*, ed. Michi Gaigg and Christian Moritz-Bauer (Passau: Musikverlag Peter Lechl, 2003): Symphony 3; *Sinfonia III in C-dur aus: VI Sinfonie a quattro, op. 1*, ed. Michi Gaigg and Christian Moritz-Bauer (Passau: Musikverlag Peter Lechl, 2003): Symphony 4; *Sinfonia IV in F-dur aus: VI Sinfonie a quattro, op. 1*, ed. Michi Gaigg and Christian Moritz-Bauer (Passau: Musikverlag Peter Lechl, 2003): Symphony 5; *Sinfonia V in g-moll aus: VI Sinfonie a quattro, op. 1*, ed. Michi Gaigg and Christian Moritz-Bauer (Passau:

Musikverlag Peter Lechl, 2003): Symphony 6; *Sinfonia VI in D-dur aus: VI Sinfonie a quattro, op. 1*, ed. Michi Gaigg and Christian Moritz-Bauer (Passau: Musikverlag Peter Lechl, 2003): Symphony 7

Recordings: Prague Chamber Orchestra, Supraphon 1110 3036, 1981 [LP]: Symphonies 2–7; Prague Chamber Orchestra, Supraphon 11 0304–2, 1988 [CD]: Symphonies 3 and 5; L'Orfeo Barockorchester, cond. Michi Gaigg, CPO 777 050–2, 2004 [CD]: Symphony 6; Czech Chamber Philharmonic Orchestra, cond. Vojtěch Spurný, Musical Concepts ALC1014, 2007 [CD]: Symphonies 4 and 7

Symphony 8: D major, 1766 or before [10:D4]

Scoring: 2 vln, vla, b, 2 ob, 2 hrn

Ms. sources: CZ-Pnm II E 133 (Roman Nejedlý collection); CZ-Pnm V B 65 (Jan Pohl collection): attr. "Ditters"'; CZ-Pnm XXXIV E 187 (Doksy): ms. ca. 1770; I-Gl T.C.7.2. (Sc. 100), No. 6: lacks vln 1 part

Cat. refs.: A-VOR 1771: "sinf. primae classis Nr. 16"; D-SI 1766: attr. "Diters"; Grave/Dittersdorf (symphony Q:D7); GraveF (symphony D-21)

Note: The attributions to Carl Ditters von Dittersdorf are considered questionable in Grave/Dittersdorf and GraveF.

Symphony 9: G major, 1768 or before [10:G3]

Scoring: 2 vln, vla, b, 2 ob, 2 hrn

Ms. sources: A-LA Ms. M III: adds a Minuet and Trio as 3rd movement to form a four-movement work; D-Rtt Mysliveček 5: ms. ca. 1770

Cat. refs.: A-LA 1768, No. 107; A-VOR 1771: "sinf. tertiae classis Nr. 36"

Symphony 10: D major, 1768 or before [10:D6]

Scoring: 2 vln, vla, b, 2 ob, 2 hrn

Ms. sources: CZ-Pnm XXXIV E 174 (Doksy): ms. ca. 1780; I-Gl T.C.7.2. (Sc. 100), No. 1: lacks vln 1 part

Cat. refs.: A-LA 1768, No. 108; A-VOR 1771: "sinf. secundae classis Nr. 21" (same designation in Vorau catalog as Symphony 25)

Symphony 11: D major, 1769 or before [10:D7]

Scoring: 2 vln, vla, b, 2 ob, 2 hrn

Ms. source: CZ-Pnm XXXIV E 180 (Doksy): ms. dated 1771

Cat. ref.: Breitkopf 1769 (p. 339): "III. Sinfonie," No. 1

Symphony 12: E-flat major, 1769 or before [10:E flat 1]

Scoring: 2 vln, vla, b, 2 ob, 2 hrn

Ms. sources: CZ-Pnm XXXIV E 167 (Doksy); US-Wc M1004.A1M3 Case (No. 6 of 4th series of symphonies by various composers): ms. from early 1770s?, 1st and 2nd movements only

Cat. ref.: Breitkopf 1769 (p. 339): "III. Sinfonie," No. 2

Edition: *Sinfonia in Mi bemolle maggiore*, ed. Emil Hradecký (Prague: Český hudební fond, 1957)

Recording: Prague Chamber Orchestra, Supraphon 1110 2836, 1980 [LP]

Symphony 13: D major, 1769 or before [10:D8]

Scoring: 2 vln, vla, b, 2 ob, 2 hrn

Ms. sources: CZ-Bm A 12.215 (Rajhrad): attr. "Ditters," ms. dated 1769; D-Rtt Mysliveček 3: ms. ca. 1770; SK-J Ms. H-623 (Podolínec): ms. dated 1775

Cat. refs.: Grave/Dittersdorf (symphony Q:D15); GraveF (symphony D-33)

Note: The attribution to Carl Ditters von Dittersdorf in CZ-Bm A 12.215 is considered doubtful in Grave/Dittersdorf and GraveF.

Symphony 14: G major, 1770 or before [10:G7]

Scoring: 2 vln, vla, b

Ms. source: CZ-Pnm II E 136 (Roman Nejedlý collection)

Cat. ref.: A-GÖ 1830 2905: "symphonia, 1770"

Note: Also disseminated in sources as a string quartet (see String Quartet 7).

Symphony 15: F major, ca. 1770 or before [10:F2]

Scoring: 2 vln, vla, b, 2 ob, 2 hrn

Ms. source: CZ-Pnm XLII C 315: attr. J. C. Bach; D-Rtt Mysliveček 1: ms. ca. 1770

Cat. ref.: Warburton/Bach YC 66: believed to be more likely a work of Mysliveček

Symphony 16: B-flat major, ca. 1770 or before [10:B-flat 2]

Scoring: 2 vln, vla, b, 2 ob, 2 hrn

Ms. sources: CZ-Pnm II E 127 (Roman Nejedlý collection); CZ-Pnm V B 59 (Jan Pohl collection); CZ-Pnm XXXII A 10 (Osek); CZ-Pnm XXXIV E 186 (Doksy): ms. ca. 1770; US-Wc M1004.A1M3 Case (No. 5 of 4th series of symphonies by various composers): ms. from early 1770s?, 1st and 2nd movements only

Cat. refs.: Breitkopf 1775 (p. 563): "II Sinfonie," No. 1; RISM B/v.2, p. 278: Welcker print below; Thompson print below

Editions: Welcker 1773, No. 3; Thompson 1790, No. 3

Recordings: Prague Chamber Orchestra, Supraphon 1110 2836, 1980 [LP]; Prague Chamber Orchestra, Supraphon 11 0304–2, 1988 [CD]; Vogtland Philharmonie Greiz/Reichenbach, cond. Stefan Fraas, Ton Studio Lengenfeld s.s. [1998?] [CD]; Moscow Radio Symphony Orchestra, cond. Karl Eliasberg, Levné Knihy LK 3022–2, 2005 [CD]; 2nd and 3rd movements only

Symphony 17: G major, early 1770s or before [10:G12]

Scoring: 2 vln, vla, b, 2 ob, 2 hrn

Ms. source: US-Wc M1004.A1M3 (No. 2 of 4th series of symphonies by various composers): ms. from early 1770s?

Symphony 18: F major, 1771 or before [10:F5]

Scoring: 2 vln, vla, b, 2 ob, 2 hrn

Ms. sources: CZ-Pnm XXXIV E 179 (Doksy): ms. dated 1771; US-Wc M1004.A1M3 Case (No. 4 of 4th series of symphonies by various composers): ms. from early 1770s?

Cat. ref.: Breitkopf 1775 (p. 563): "II. Sinfonie," No. 2

Symphony 19: C major, 1771 or before [10:C6]

Scoring: 2 vln, vla, b, 2 ob, 2 hrn

Ms. sources: CZ-Pnm II E 134 (Roman Nejedlý collection); CZ-Pnm V B 66 (Jan Pohl collection); CZ-Pnm XXXII A 560 (Osek): attr. "Ditters," key = D major; CZ-Pnm XXXIV E 185 (Doksy): ms. ca. 1775; D-AB C8: ms. before 1793; I-Gl T.C.7.2. (Sc. 100), No. 4: lacks vln 1 part; US-Wc M1004.A1M3 Case (No. 3 of 4th series of symphonies by various composers); ms. from early 1770s?

Cat. refs.: A-VOR 1771: "sinf. secundae classis Nr. 23"; Breitkopf 1775 (p. 562): attr. "Boemo"; Grave/Dittersdorf (symphony Q:D16); GraveF (symphony D-35)

Note: The attribution to Carl Ditters von Dittersdorf in CZ-Pnm XXXII A 560 is considered doubtful in GraveF and Grave/Dittersdorf.

Symphony 20: D major, 1771 or before [10:D10]

Scoring: 2 vln, vla, b, 2 ob, 2 hrn

Ms. source: DK-Kk mu 7504.2212 (Camillo Schoenbaum); ms. ca. 1800

Cat. ref.: A-VOR 1771: "sinf. tertiae classis Nr. 15"

Note: Falsely designated lost in Evans/Dearling.

Symphony 21: D major, 1771 or before [10:D12]

Scoring: 2 vln, vla, b, 2 ob, 2 hrn

Ms. source: A-VOR 937

Cat. ref.: A-VOR 1771: "sinf. primae classis Nr. 30"

Symphony 22: F major, 1771 or before [10:F3]

Scoring: 2 vln, vla, b, 2 ob, 2 hrn

Ms. sources: CZ-Pnm II E 131 (Roman Nejedlý collection); CZ-Pnm V B 63 (Jan Pohl collection); CZ-Pnm XXXIV E 183 (Doksy): ms. ca. 1776; I-Gl T.C.7.2. (Sc. 100), No. 2: lacks vln 1 part

Cat. ref: A-VOR 1771: "sinf. primae classis Nr. 34"

Symphony 23: C major, 1771 or before [Lost; 10:C5]

Scoring: ?

Cat. ref.: A-VOR 1771: "sinf. tertiae classis Nr. 27"

Symphony 24: D major, 1771 or before [Lost; 10:D11]

Scoring: ?

Cat. ref.: A-VOR 1771: "sinf. tertiae classis Nr. 22"

Symphony 25: F major, 1771 or before [Lost; 10:F4]

Scoring: ?

Cat. ref.: A-VOR 1771: "sinf. secundae classis Nr. 21" (same designation in Vorau catalog as Symphony 9)

Symphonies 26–31:

6 symphonies in Napier 1772 (almost certainly composed 1770–71 during Mysliveček's stay in Florence).

No. 1 = Symphony 26 (C major) [10:C7]
No. 2 = Symphony 27 (A major) [10:A2]
No. 3 = Symphony 28 (F major) [10:F6]
No. 4 = Symphony 29 (D major) [10:D14]
No. 5 = Symphony 30 (B-flat major) [10:B-flat 3]
No. 6 = Symphony 31 (G major) [10:G5]

Scoring: 2 vln, 2 vla, b, 2 ob (2 fl in 2nd movements of Symphony 26 and Symphony 29), 2 hrn

Ms. sources: E-Mp Leg. 1.630 (Cat. 2.058): Symphony 30; E-Mp Leg. 1.630 (Cat. 2.060): Symphony 29; I-MAav Cart. 2 n. 14: Symphony 29; I-MOe Mus. F.804, No. 1: Symphony 29; I-MOe Mus. F.804, No. 2: Symphony 27; I-MOe Mus. F.804, No. 3: Symphony 30; I-MOe Mus. F.804, No. 4: Symphony 26

Additional editions: *Overture I aus: Six Overtures (1772)*, ed. Michi Gaigg and Christian Moritz-Bauer (Passau: Musikverlag Peter Lechl, 2003): Symphony 26; *Overture II aus: Six Overtures (1772)*, ed. Michi Gaigg and Christian Moritz-Bauer (Passau: Musikverlag Peter Lechl, 2003): Symphony 27; *Overture III aus: Six Overtures (1772)*, ed. Michi Gaigg and Christian Moritz-Bauer (Passau: Musikverlag Peter Lechl, 2003): Symphony 28; *Overture IV aus: Six Overtures (1772)*, ed. Michi Gaigg and Christian Moritz-Bauer (Passau: Musikverlag Peter Lechl, 2003): Symphony 29; *Overture V aus: Six Overtures (1772)*, ed. Michi Gaigg and Christian Moritz-Bauer (Passau: Musikverlag Peter Lechl, 2003): Symphony 30; *Overture VI aus: Six Overtures (1772)*, ed. Michi Gaigg and Christian Moritz-Bauer (Passau: Musikverlag Peter Lechl, 2003): Symphony 31

Recordings: London Mozart Players, cond. Matthias Bamert, Chandos CHAN 10203, 2004 [CD]: Symphonies 26-31; L'Orfeo Barockorchester, cond. Michi Gaigg, CPO 777 050–2, 2004 [CD]: Symphonies 26–31; Concerto Köln, cond. Werner Eberhardt, Archiv Produktion 477 6418, 2006 [CD]: Symphony 27

Symphony 32: D major, ca. 1775 or before [10:D17]

Scoring: 2 vln, vla, b

Ms. source: CZ-Pnm II E 138 (Roman Nejedlý collection)

Notes: Also preserved in one source as a string quartet (see String Quartet 8). The dating here is based on the appearance of the 2nd movement as an incipit in Qb Ch D 21.

Symphony 33: E-flat major, ca. 1775 or before [10:E-flat 4]

Scoring: 2 vln, vla, b

Ms. sources: CZ-Pnm XXXVII E 157 (Alois Altrichter collection); CZ-Pr 14540; unidentified ms., of which microfilm #M128 in CZ-Pnm is a copy (mistakenly cited as a ms. by Evans/

Dearling). The film is listed as no. 746 in the catalog of the CZ-Pnm Doksy collection, compiled by Milada Rutova.

Cat. ref.: CZ-Pnm Doksy

Edition: *Sinfonia in Es a quattro voci*, ed. Emil Hradecký (Prague: Český hudební fond, 1957)

Recordings: Musici Pragenses Chamber Orchestra, Schwann Musica Mundi VMS 2024,1968 [LP]; Musici di Praga, cond. Milan Výměr, Disques Pierre Verany PV.788053, 1988 [CD]; Suk Chamber Orchestra, cond. Josef Vlach, Dabringhaus und Grimm L 3316, 1989 [CD]; Suk Chamber Orchestra, cond. Josef Vlach, Panton 81 0953, 1990 [CD]; Musici di Praga, cond. Milan Výměr, Disques Pierre Verany PV.730013, 1994 [CD]; Pro Arte Antiqua Praha, Arta F1 0071–2, 1997 [CD]; Suk Chamber Orchestra, cond. Josef Vlach, Dabringhaus und Grimm MDG 601 0316–2, 1997 [CD]

Notes: Also preserved in one source as a string quartet (see String Quartet 9). The dating here is based on the appearance of the work as a quartet in Qb 1775 Ch E 25 and E 55.

Symphony 34: A major, ca. 1775 or before [10:A3]

Scoring: 2 vln, vla, b

Ms. source: CZ-Pnm II E 126 (Roman Nejedlý collection)

Recording: Brno Chamber Orchestra, cond. Jiří Mottl, Klavier K 11116, 2001 [CD]

Notes: Also preserved in sources as a string quartet (see String Quartet 10). The dating here is based on the appearance of the work as a quartet in Qb 1775 Ch A 15. In the notes to his recording, Jiří Mottl claims to have identified a ms. source in CZ-KRa among uncataloged holdings; this claim is unsupported from a search by archival staff.

Symphony 35: B-flat major, ca. 1775 or before [10:B-flat 6]

Scoring: 2 vln, vla, b

Ms. source: CZ-Pnm II E 137 (Roman Nejedlý collection)

Notes: Also preserved in one source as a string quartet (see String Quartet 11). The dating here is based on the appearance of the work as a quartet in Qb 1775 Ch B 18.

Symphonies 36–41:

"VI. Sinf. da Gius. Misleweczeck" in Breitkopf 1776/77 (p. 592) [all Lost].

No. 1 = Symphony 36 (D major) [10:D19]
No. 2 = Symphony 37 (B-flat major) [10:B-flat 7]
No. 3 = Symphony 38 (G major) [10:G9]
No. 4 = Symphony 39 (E-flat major) [10:E-flat 5]
No. 5 = Symphony 40 (C major) [10:C9]
No. 6 = Symphony 41 (F major) [10:F7]

Scoring: 2 vln, vla, b, 2 ob, 2 hrn

Symphonies 42–47:

A series of six symphonies found in mss. in D-WEY, all of them dated 1778. There is good reason to believe that they were part of a set of twelve symphonies sent to the archbishop of Salzburg, according to a letter of Leopold Mozart of 15 October 1777 (see chapter 4).

D-WEY 627 = Symphony 42 (C major) [10:C11]
D-WEY 628 = Symphony 43 (D major) [10:D21]
D-WEY 630 = Symphony 44 (E-flat major) [10:E-flat 6]
D-WEY 631 = Symphony 45 (F major) [10:F8]
D-WEY 632 = Symphony 46 (G major) [10:G10]
D-WEY 634 = Symphony 47 (B-flat major) [10:B-flat 8]

Scoring: 2 vln, vla, b, 2 ob, 2 hrn

Additional ms. source: CZ-Pu 59 R 243 (Nesselrode): ms. copied in the 1780s (Symphonies 42–47, ordered 43, 45, 47, 44, 46, 42)

Editions: Pilková 1984, No. 5: Symphony 43; Pilková 1984, No. 6: Symphony 45

Recordings: Prague Chamber Orchestra, Supraphon 1110 3215, 1982 [LP]: Symphonies 43 and 44; Prague Chamber Orchestra, Supraphon 1110 3216, 1982 [LP]: Symphonies 42, 45, 46, and 47; Prague Chamber Orchestra, Supraphon 11 0304–2, 1988 [CD]: Symphonies 45–47; Virtuosi di Praga, cond. Oldřich Vlček, Multisonic 31 0399–02, 1997 [CD]: Symphony 47; Virtuosi di Praga, cond. Oldřich Vlček, Multisonic 31 0509–02, 2000 [CD]: Symphony 47; Concerto Köln, cond. Werner Eberhardt, Archiv Produktion 477 6418, 2006 [CD]: Symphonies 44–46

Symphony 48: D major, 1780 or before [missing from Evans/Dearling]

Scoring: 2 vln, vla, b, 2 ob, 2 hrn

Ms. source: I-RVE S M 1550: ms. dated 1780

Symphony 49: C major, date? [10:C14]

Scoring: 2 vln, vla, b, 2 fl, 2 ob, 2 hrn

Ms. sources: A-SB 855; CZ-Pnm II E 132 (Roman Nejedlý collection); CZ-Pnm V B 64 (Jan Pohl collection); CZ-Pnm XXXIV E 171 (Doksy): ms. ca. 1780; D-Rtt Mysliveček 2: ms. ca. 1780; PL-CZ AJG Muz. III-400: ms. 1784–87

Recording: Concerto Köln, cond. Werner Eberhardt, Archiv Produktion 477 6418, 2006 [CD]

Symphony 50: D major, date? [10:D23]

Scoring: 2 vln, vla, b, 2 ob, 2 hrn

Ms. source: CZ-Pnm XXXIV E 173 (Doksy): ms. ca. 1780

Symphony 51: F major, date? [10:F9]

Scoring: 2 vln, vla, b, 2 ob, 2 hrn

Ms. source: CZ-Pnm XXXIV E 172 (Doksy): ms. ca. 1780

Edition: *Ouvertura, F dur*, ed. Emil Hradecký (Prague: Český hudební fond, 1956)

Recording: Musici Pragenses Chamber Orchestra, Schwann Musica Mundi VMS 2024, 1968 [LP]

Symphony 52: F major, date? [10:F10]

Scoring: 2 vln, vla, b, 2 ob, 2 hrn

Ms. source: CZ-Pnm XXXIV E 176 (Doksy): ms. ca. 1780

Symphony 53: G major, date? [10:G11]

Scoring: 2 vln, vla, b, 2 ob, 2 hrn

Ms. sources: CZ-Pnm XXXIV E 178 (Doksy): ms. ca. 1780; D-W Ms Cod. Guelf. 163: "Cembalokonzert" (includes a reduction of the orchestral parts for kbd), adds a Minuet as 3rd movement to form a four-movement work

Recording: Prague Chamber Orchestra, Supraphon 1110 2836, 1981 [without minuet] [LP]

Note: The Mysliveček works' list in *Grove6* mistakenly indicates four kbd concertos in D-W based on an incorrect reading of EitnerQ (the four "Sätze" of the ms. in D-W were taken to indicate the presence of four concertos, not four movements in a single ms.); the mistake was corrected for *New Grove* (2001) and *Grove Music Online*.

Symphony 54: E major, date? [10:E2]

Scoring: 2 vln, vla, b

Ms. source: CZ-Pnm XLI C 183 (Kačina)

Symphony 55 ("sinfonia-serenade"): G major, date? [6:G1]

Scoring: 2 vln, vla, b, 2 hrn

Ms. source: I-MOe Mus. F.808

Note: This work is cataloged mistakenly in Evans/Dearling as a sextet for chamber ensemble.

SYMPHONIES OF QUESTIONABLE AUTHENTICITY

1. D major, 1774 or before [10:DQ1]

   Scoring: 2 vln, vla, b, 2 ob, 2 hrn

   Ms. source: F-Pn Rés. 2571: attr. "sigr. Bach"

   Cat. refs.: Breitkopf 1774 (p. 532): "II. Sinfonie," No. 1, attr. Mysliveček; Warburton/Bach YC 37: attr. to J. C. Bach considered doubtful

2. F major, date? [10:F11]

   Scoring: 2 vln, vla, b, 2 ob, 2 hrn

   Ms. sources: CZ-Pnm XXXII A 564 (Osek): attr. "Dietters"; D-B Mus. ms. 14527 (Otto Jahn): ms. ca. 1840–50;D-B Mus. ms. 14527/1 (parts for above); D-Z Mus. G1.5

   Cat. refs.: Grave/Dittersdorf (symphony Q:F3); GraveF (symphony F-6)

   Note: The attribution to Carl Ditters von Dittersdorf in CZ-Pnm XXXII A 564 is considered questionable in GraveF and Grave/Dittersdorf.

3. E-flat major, 1771 or before [10:E-flat 2]

   Scoring: 2 vln, vla, b, 2 ob, 2 cl, 2 hrn

   Ms. source: PL-CZ Ms. 1-15 (230/226): attr. "Ditters"

   Cat. refs.: A-VOR 1771: "sinf. tertiae classis Nr. 19," attr. Mysliveček; Grave/Dittersdorf (symphony Q:Eb8); GraveF (symphony Eb-16)

Note: The attribution to Carl Ditters von Dittersdorf in PL-CZ Ms. 1-15 (230/226) is considered doubtful in GraveF and Grave/Dittersdorf.

UNTRACEABLE SYMPHONY

C major, date? lost? [10:C15]

Scoring: ?

Ms. source: D-B: destroyed in World War II

Cat. refs.: D-B Thouret, No. 3200; EitnerQ (ms. in D-B)

Note: This work may have been a copy of one of the known C-major symphonies.

SPURIOUS SYMPHONIES

1. C major, 1764 or before [10:CS1]: work of Pieter van Maldere

Scoring: 2 vln, vla, b, 2 ob, 2 hrn

Ms. sources: CZ-Pnm II E 128 (Roman Nejedlý collection): attr. Mysliveček; CZ-Pnm V B 60 (Jan Pohl collection): attr. Mysliveček; CZ-Pnm XXXII A 323: attr. Maldere; CZ-Pnm XXXIV B 84: attr. Maldere; CZ-Pnm XLII B 310: attr. Maldere; D-HR III 4 1/2 2 750: ms. dated 1765, attr. Maldere; I-BGc Antologia N.C.13.2, No. 2: attr. Maldere; US-Wc M1004.A2M25, No. 2: attr. Maldere

Cat. refs.: Breitkopf 1767 (p. 266): Venier print of Maldere Op. 4; Rompaey/Maldere VR 54 (Symphony No. 20)

Editions: Pieter van Maldere, *Sei sinfonie a più strumenti*, Op. 4 (Paris: Venier, 1764), No. 2; Pieter van Maldere, *Six Favourite Overtures in Eight Parts*, Op. 4 (London: John Johnston, 1768), No. 2; Pieter van Maldere, *Six Favourite Overtures in Eight Parts*, Op. 4 (London: Longman & Broderip, n.d.), No. 2; Pieter van Maldere, *Six Favourite Overtures in Eight Parts*, Op. 4 (London: Longman, Lukey & Co.; John Johnston, n.d.), No. 2; Pieter van Maldere, *A Select Overture in 8 Parts* (London: John Johnston, n.d.)

2. D major, ca. 1763–66 [10:DS1]: work of Carl Ditters von Dittersdorf

Scoring: 2 vln, vla, b, 2 ob, 2 hrn

Ms. sources: A-ST M II 20: attr. "Ditters"; CZ-KRa Ms. A 4982 (Hamilton): ms. ca. 1770, attr. Mysliveček; CZ-Pnm II E 135 (Roman Nejedlý collection): attr. Mysliveček; CZ-Pnm V B 67 (Jan Pohl collection): attr. anonymous; CZ-Pnm XXII C 19 (Pachta): attr. "Ditters"; CZ-Pnm XXXII A 453 (Osek): attr. "Ditters"; D-DO 338: attr. "Ditters"; D-Rtt Dittersdorf 24: ms. ca. 1770; I-Gl 35.B.3.133: attr. Dittersdorf; PL-CZ I-12 225/221: attr. "Ditters"; PL-MO 942: ms. dated 1777, attr. "Ditters"; SK-BRsav s.s. (Fíntice): attr. anonymous

Cat. refs.: D-SI 1766, No. 24: attr. "Diters"; Grave/Dittersdorf (symphony D26); GraveF (symphony D-41); Qb 1775 Sym D 23: attr. "Ditters"

Note: Dating of work from GraveF and Grave/Dittersdorf.

3. D major, date? [10:DS2]: work of Domenico Cimarosa
   Scoring: 2 vln, vla, b, 2 ob, 2 hrn
   Ms. source: US-AAu M1001.C57 S8 17—: original attr. to Cimarosa crossed out, replaced with attr. to Mysliveček
   Note: The attribution to Cimarosa in US-AAu M1001.C57 S8 17—is obviously mistaken, transposed with the attribution in the ms. in US-AAu for Overture 20.

4. E-flat major, before 1793 [10:E-flatS1]: work of Franz Anton Hoffmeister
   Scoring: 2 vln, vla, b, fl, 2 ob, 2 hrn
   Ms. sources: D-Dl Mus 3944-N-9: attr. Hoffmeister; I-MAav Cart. 13 n. 2: attr. Hoffmeister
   Cat. refs.: D-DO Copia Verzeichnis 1804, Nr. 12: attr. Hoffmeister; Hickman/Hoffmeister (symphony Eb7); I-MAav 219: attr. Mysliveček; RISM A/II 28373 (ms. in I-MAav): attr. Mysliveček
   Editions: Franz Anton Hoffmeister, *Sinfonie pour deux violons, 2 obois, 2 cors, flûte-traversière, fagotte, violoncelle, alto et basse* (Vienna: Hoffmeister, n.d.); Franz Anton Hoffmeister, *Simphonie à plusieurs instruments* . . . no. II (Vienna: Artaria, n.d.); Franz Anton Hoffmeister, *Sinfonie pour deux violons, 2 obois, 2 cors, flûte traversière, fagotte, violoncelle, alto et basse* (Amsterdam: Schmitt, n.d.)
   Notes: Attributions to Mysliveček are found only in cat. refs. I-MAav and RISM A/II (which describes the same ms. in I-MAav). Ms. I-MAav Cart. 13 n. 2 bears an attribution to Hoffmeister and this inscription: "l'attribuzione dell'autore è fatta dal Bernardi, senza spiegazioni" ("the attribution [to Mysliveček] was made by Bernardi without explanation"). The dating for this work given above is taken from Hickman/Hoffmeister.

Part 2

DRAMATIC OVERTURES

1. Overture in G major, "dramatic cantata" *Il Parnaso confuso*, 1765–67 (unknown location) [10:G2]
   Scoring: 2 vln, vla, b, 2 ob, 2 hrn
   Ms. sources: CZ-Pnm XXXII A 61 (Osek): complete cantata (score) dated 1782; CZ-Pnm XXXII A 64 (Osek): complete cantata (parts) dated 1782; CZ-Pnm XXXIV E 184 (Doksy): ms. ca. 1775; D-AB C7: ms. before 1793; I-Gl T.C.7.2. (Sc. 100), No. 5: lacks vln 1 part; I-Rsc A. Mss. 3800: complete cantata
   Cat. ref.: A-VOR 1771: "sinf. primae classis Nr. 27"
   Notes: See chapter 8 for a discussion of the dating of this work. Evans/Dearling mistakenly lists CZ-PNM II E 128 and XXXIV B 84 as sources.

2. Overture in D major, *Semiramide*, summer fair 1766 (Bergamo) [10:D3]
   Scoring: 2 vln, vla, b, 2 ob, 2 hrn

Ms. sources: CZ-Pnm II E 140 (Roman Nejedlý collection); CZ-Pnm V B 69 (Jan Pohl collection); CZ-Pnm XXXVIII D 343: incomplete opera dated Prague, 1769; P-La 45-II-6 a 8: complete opera; US-Wc M1004.A1M3 Case (No. 1 of 4th series of symphonies by various composers): ms. from early 1770s?

3. Overture in C major, *Il Bellerofonte*, 20 January 1767 (Naples) [10:C3]

Scoring: 2 vln, vla, b, 2 ob, 2 hrn, 2 trp

Ms. sources: CZ-Pnm II E 139 (Roman Nejedlý collection); CZ-Pnm V B 68 (Jan Pohl collection); CZ-Pnm XXXIV E 175 (Doksy): ms. ca. 1780; D-Dl Mus. 3405: complete opera; D-SWl 4736/9: scored for str, 2 hrn, 2 trp; F-Pn D. 8199–8200: complete opera dated 1769, overture lacks 3rd movement; I-Fc D.I.391-393: complete opera; I-Rdp 102–103: Act 1 only of complete opera, vln, vla parts only; P-La 45-I-27 a 29: complete opera; P-La 54-II-49 a 51: complete opera

Recordings: Prague Chamber Orchestra, cond. Zoltán Peskó, Supraphon SUP 0006–2, 1987 [CD]: complete opera; Prague Chamber Orchestra, cond. Zoltán Peskó, Koch 3–4036–2, 1994 [CD]

4. Overture in D major, *Il Farnace*, 4 November 1767 (Naples) [10:D5]

Scoring: 2 vln, vla, b, 2 ob (2 fl in 2nd movement), 2 bsn, 2 hrn, 2 trp

Ms. sources: CZ-Pnm XXXIV E 166 (Doksy); D-Mbs Mus. ms. 12603: complete opera; H-Bn OE-73: complete opera; I-Gl SS.A.1.2.(G.7); I-Nc 29.3.13–14: complete opera; P-La 45-I-46 a 48: complete opera; P-La 54-I015035 a 37: complete opera

5. Overture in A major, *Cantata a due: Alceste e Fileno*, ca. 1767 (unknown location) [10:A1]

Scoring: 2 vln, vla, b, 2 ob, 2 hrn

Ms. sources: CZ-Pnm II E 130 (Roman Nejedlý collection); CZ-Pnm V B 62 (Jan Pohl collection); CZ-Pnm XXXII A 62 (Osek): *Cantata a due*, complete cantata; CZ-Pnm XXXIV E 182 (Doksy): ms. ca. 1780; D-AB C3: ms. before 1793; I-Gl T.C.7.2. (Sc. 100), No. 3: lacks vln 1 part

Cat. ref.: A-VOR 1771: "sinf. tertiae classis Nr. 36"

Note: See chapter 8 for a discussion of the dating of this work.

6. Overture in B-flat major, *Il trionfo di Clelia*, 26 December 1767 (Turin) [10:B-flat1]

Scoring: 2 vln, vla, b, 2 ob (2 fl in 2nd movement), 2 hrn, 2 trp, timp

Ms. sources: CH-E Ms. Th. 6,6 (Ms. 1719); CH-EN Ms A 490 (Ms. 5862): scored for str, trp; CZ-KRa A 4802 (Hamilton): ms. ca. 1770; CZ-Pnm II E 125 (Roman Nejedlý collection); CZ-Pnm II E 141 (Roman Nejedlý collection); CZ-Pnm V B 58 (Jan Pohl collection); CZ-Pnm XXXIV E 181 (Doksy): ms. ca. 1780; D-W Ms. Cod. Guelf. 165; I-Fc D.I.397–399: complete opera; I-Tf 10 II 4–40: complete opera; P-La 45-II-9 a 11: complete opera; S-Skma Alströmer-saml. s.s.

Cat. ref.: Breitkopf 1769 (p. 339): "III. Sinfonie," No. 3

Edition: Pilková 1984, No. 4

7. Overture in C major, *Demofoonte* [1st setting], 17 January 1769 (Venice) [10:C4]

Scoring: 2 vln, vla, b, 2 ob (2 fl in 2nd movement), 2 hrn, 2 trp, timp

Ms. sources: CZ-Pnm XXXIV E 169 (Doksy); D-Rtt Mysliveček 4; E-Mp Leg. 1.539 (Cat. 830); I-Vnm Cod. It. IV 260 = 9831: Act 1 only of complete opera; P-La 45-I-41 e 42: complete opera; P-La 54-I-42 a 44: complete opera; US-Wc M1004.A1M3 Case (No. 3 of 3rd series of symphonies by various composers): ms. from early 1770s?

Cat. ref.: Breitkopf 1773 (p. 483): scored for 2 ob or fl, 2 hrn, str

Edition: *Ouvertüre zur Oper: Il Demofoonte (1769)*, ed. Michi Gaigg and Christian Moritz-Bauer (Passau: Musikverlag Peter Lechl, 2003)

Recording: L'Orfeo Barockorchester, cond. Michi Gaigg, CPO 777 050–2, 2004 [CD]

Notes: This is the symphony mentioned in a postscript attached by Wolfgang Mozart to a letter written by his father to his mother from Milan on 22 December 1770. The source for this work in E-Mp indicates its use as the overture for an unknown production of *Gli tre amanti ridicoli*. Evans/Dearling indicates a source in D-AB; according to the library staff (communication, 7 June 1996), there is no such source in this library.

8. Overture in E major, *L'Ipermestra*, 27 March 1769 (Florence) [10:E1]

Scoring: 2 vln, vla, 2 ob (2 fl in 2nd movement), 2 bsn, 2 hrn, 2 trp, timp

Ms. sources: A-Wn Mus.Hs. 17.796: complete opera; CZ-Pnm II E 129 (Roman Nejedlý collection); CZ-Pnm V B 61 (Jan Pohl collection); CZ-Pnm XIX E 125 (Jan Pohl collection): complete opera; CZ-Pnm XXXIV E 168 (Doksy); D-W Ms. Cod. Guelf. 164; I-Fc D.I.388-90: complete opera; P-La 47-III-43: Act 1 only of complete opera (Act 3 is 47-V-37)

Cat. ref.: Breitkopf 1774 (p. 532): "II. Sinfonie," No. 2

Recording: Prague Chamber Orchestra, Supraphon 1110 2836, 1980 [LP]

9. Introduction, C minor, *Tobia*, 1769 (Padua)/*La passione di Nostro Signore Gesù Cristo*, 24 March 1773 (Florence) [10:c1]

Scoring: 2 vln, vla, b, 2 ob, 2 hrn

Ms. sources: D-F Mus. Hs. 193: *La passione*, complete oratorio; D-Mbs Mus. ms. 2364: *La passione* (part 1 only); D-Mbs Mus. ms. 2365: *Il Tobia*, complete oratorio, ms. ca. 1780; D-Rp C 137: *Il Tobia*, complete oratorio, ms. ca. 1770; D-Rp C 137: *La morte di Giesù* (= *La passione*), complete oratorio, ms. ca. 1780; I-Pca D-V-1808: *Il Tobia*, complete oratorio

Edition: *La passione*, ed. Joyce L. Johnson, The Italian Oratorio, 1650–1800, 23 (New York: Garland, 1986): facsimile of ms. in D-F

10. Overture in D major, *La Nitteti*, 29 April 1770 (Bologna) [10:D9]

Scoring: 2 vln, vla, b, 2 ob (2 fl in 2nd movement), 2 hrn, 2 trp, timp

Ms. sources: CZ-Pnm II E 124 (Roman Nejedlý collection); CZ-Pnm V B 57 (Jan Pohl collection); CZ-Pnm XXXIV E 170 (Doksy); D-Rtt Mysliveček 7: ms. ca. 1770; I-Fc D.I.376-378: complete opera; P-La 45–I–49 a 51: complete opera; RUS-SPit No. 752-753: Acts 1 and 2 only of complete opera

Cat. ref.: Breitkopf 1772 (p. 443)

Edition: *Sinfonia in re maggiore*, ed. Emil Hradecký (Prague: Český hudební fond, 1957)

Recordings: Prague Chamber Orchestra, cond. Martin Turnovský, Supraphon LPV 423 [195-] [LP]; Czech Philharmonic Orchestra, cond. Martin Turnovský, Supraphon SUA 19 040, [1961?] [LP]; Prague Chamber Orchestra, Supraphon 1110 2836, 1980 [LP]; Prague Chamber Orchestra, cond. Ulf Björlin, EMI C 065-03 659, 1980 [LP]

11. Overture in G major, *Motezuma*, 23 January 1771 (Florence) [10:G4]

Scoring: 2 vln, vla, b, 2 ob, 2 hrn

Ms. sources: A-Wgm IV 15271: complete opera; CZ-Pnm V B 45 (Jan Pohl collection): complete opera; D-WEY 633: ms. dated 1778; I-Fc D.I.379-381: complete opera; US-Wc 1500.M658 M5: complete opera

Recording: L'Orfeo Barockorchester, cond. Michi Gaigg, CPO 777 050–2, 2004 [CD]

Note: The score of *Motezuma* in P-La (47-V-63 e 64) consists only of Acts 2 and 3, thus includes no overture.

12. Overture in E-flat major, *Adamo ed Eva*, 24 March 1771 (Florence) [10:E-flat 3]

Scoring: 2 vln, vla, b, 2 ob, 2 hrn

Ms. sources: I-Gl SS.A.1.2.(G.7); I-Rf F.I.9: complete oratorio

13. Overture in D major, *Il gran Tamerlano*, 26 December 1771 (Milan) [10:D13]

Scoring: 2 vln, vla, b, 2 ob, 2 hrn

Ms. sources: A-Wn Mus.Hs. 17.797: complete opera; CH-Zz AMG 7000 & a-i (Ms. 919); F-Pn D. 8202-8204: complete opera; I-Fc D.I.373-375: complete opera; I-Mc 1117; I-Mc Noseda O.25.7; P-La 47–III–45: Act 1 only of complete opera (Act 3 is 47-V-53)

Edition: *Sinfonia D-dur*, ed. Hermann Müller (Zürich: Edition Eulenburg, 1975; reprint 1978): now published by Edition Kunzelmann, Adliswil

Recording: Camerata Amsterdam, cond. Jeroen Weierink, Ars Produktion Schumacher F 368 414, 2002 [CD]

14. Overture in D major, *Il Demetrio* [1st setting], 24 May 1773 (Pavia) [10:D15]

Scoring: 2 vln, vla, b (+ 2 bsn in 2nd movement), 2 ob (+ 2 fl in 2nd movement), 2 hrn, 2 trp, timp

Ms. sources: D-B Mus. ms. autogr. Misliweczek 1: complete opera; CH-EN Ms. A 485 (Ms. 5857); I-Fc D.I.382-384: complete opera; I-Mc Noseda O.25.5; I-Mcom T Mus. Var. 699: ms. dated 1939 copied by Giusto Zampieri from ms. in I-MAav, basis of Zampieri edition below; I-MAav Cart. 2 n. 2: scored for str, 2 ob, 2 hrn

Editions: Del Vivo 2, No. 5; "Una sinfonia del Venatorini," ed. Giusto Zampieri, in *Bollettino storico pavese* 2 (1939): 1–32, omits meas. 1, scored for str, 2 ob, 2 hrn, with pf reduction; *Ouvertüre zur Oper: Il Demetrio (1773)*, ed. Michi Gaigg and Christian Moritz-Bauer (Passau: Musikverlag Peter Lechl, 2003); Freeman Del Vivo, No. 5

Recording: L'Orfeo Barockorchester, cond. Michi Gaigg, CPO 777 050–2, 2004 [CD]

15. Overture in G major, *Romolo ed Ersilia*, 13 August 1773 (Naples) [10:G6]
    Scoring: 2 vln, vla, b, 2 ob (2 fl in 2nd movement), 2 hrn
    Ms. sources: F-Pn Rés. 2568; I-Fc D.I.391–393: complete opera; I-Nc 29.3.18–20: complete opera; P-La 45-II-3 a 5: complete opera
    Edition: *Ouvertüre zur Opera: Romolo ed Ersilia (1773)*, ed. Michi Gaigg and Christian Moritz-Bauer (Passau: Musikverlag Peter Lechl, 2003)
    Recording: L'Orfeo Barockorchester, cond. Michi Gaigg, CPO 777 050–2, 2004 [CD]
    Note: A report in EitnerQ of a source in A-Wgm appears to be false.

16. Overture in D major, *Antigona*, 26 December 1773 (Turin)/*Atide*, June 1774, perhaps 13 June, the feast day of St. Anthony (Padua) [10:D16]
    Scoring: 2 vln, vla, b, 2 ob (+ 2 cl in 2nd movement), 2 hrn, 2 trp, timp
    Ms. sources: A-Wn Mus.Hs. 16.418: *Atide*, complete opera; A-Wn Mus.Hs. 16.420: *Antigona*, complete opera; I-MAav Cart. 3 n. 18: scored for str, 2 ob, 2 hrn; I-Pl ATVa 2/I–II: *Atide*, complete opera; I-Rdp 182/2; I-RVE S M 1551: ms. dated 27 March 1780, scored with 2 fl instead of 2 ob, no cl; P-La 45-II-1: Act 1 only of *Antigona*
    Editions: Del Vivo 2, No. 1; Freeman Del Vivo, No. 1

17. Overture in B-flat major, *La clemenza di Tito*, by 5 February 1774 (Venice) [10:B-flat 4]
    Scoring: 2 vln, vla, b, 2 ob (2 fl in 2nd movement), 2 hrn
    Ms. source: P-La 45-I-30 a 32: complete opera

18. Overture in B-flat major, *Artaserse*, 13 August 1774 (Naples) [10:B-flat 5]
    Scoring: 2 vln, vla, b, 2 ob (2 cl in 2nd movement), 2 hrn, 2 trp
    Ms. sources: CH-EN Ms. A 487 (Ms. 5859); D-DS Ms. 3238: destroyed during World War II; I-Fc D.I.370–372: complete opera; I-MAav Cart. 2 n. 11; I-Nc 29.3.32–34: complete opera
    Editions: Del Vivo 2, No. 4; *Artaserse: Overtura*, ed. Jiří Sehnal (Prague: Český hudební fond, 1973); Freeman Del Vivo, No. 4

19. Overture in D major, *Demofoonte* [2nd setting], 20 January 1775 (Naples) [10:D18]
    Scoring: 2 vln, vla, b, 2 ob (2 fl in 2nd movement), 2 hrn, 2 trp, timp
    Ms. sources: A-Wn Mus.Hs. 16.421: complete opera; D-WEY 626: ms. dated December 1778; I-Fc D.I.394–396: complete opera; I-MAav Cart. 3 n. 24; I-Nc 29.3.7–9: complete opera; P-La 45–I–38 a 40: complete opera; US-Wc M1500.M658D3 Case: complete opera
    Editions: Del Vivo 2, No. 3; Freeman Del Vivo, No. 3

20. Overture in G major, *Ezio* [1st setting], 30 May 1775 (Naples) [10:G8]
    Scoring: 2 vln, vla, b, 2 ob, 2 hrn
    Ms. sources: A-Wn Mus.Hs. 16.419: complete opera; CH-EN Ms A 486 (ms. 5858): 2 cl, 2 trp added later; D-W 74, 1-8 Mus. div. 2°: incomplete ms. ca. 1780; F-Pn D.119: Acts 1 and

2 only of complete opera, attr. Anfossi; F-Pn D.20272; I-MAav Cart. 2 n. 13; I-Nc 29.3.10–12: complete opera; P-La 45-I-43 a 45: complete opera
Editions: Del Vivo 1; Del Vivo 2, No. 2; Freeman Del Vivo, No. 2

21. Overture in C major, *Isacco figura del redentore*, 10 March 1776 (Florence) [10:C10]
Scoring: 2 vln, vla, b, 2 ob (2 bsn in 2nd mvt), 2 hrn, 2 trp
Ms. sources: CZ-Nlobkowicz X B c 2: complete oratorio; CZ-Pnm V B 81 (Jan Pohl collection): complete oratorio; CZ-Pu 59 R 649: complete oratorio; D-B Mus. ms. 14517: *Abramo ed Isacco*, complete oratorio, attr. J. Haydn; D-Dl Mus. 3356–D–545: *Abramo ed Isacco*, complete oratorio, attr. J. Haydn; D-Mbs Mus. ms. 246: complete oratorio, D-MÜs SANT Hs 2726; D-Rp C 138: complete oratorio, ms. ca. 1780; D-WEY 625; F-Pn Vma.ms.268(-5): complete oratorio, 20th-century ms.; H-Bn Ms. mus. IV 664: complete oratorio; I-Fc A 11.175: complete oratorio, attr. W. A. Mozart; I-MOe Mus. F.809: complete oratorio; I-Rf F.III.3: complete oratorio
Cat. refs.: Köchel/Mozart (Anhang C 3.11); Hoboken/Haydn (Werkgrupe XXXI:A)
Edition: *Isacco figura del redentore*, ed. James A. Ackerman (Madison, WI: A-R Editions, 2000): based on D-Mbs Mus. ms. 246
Recordings: Prague Chamber Orchestra, cond. Peter Maag, Supraphon 112 1021, 1972 (complete oratorio) [LP]; Prague Sinfonietta, cond. Ivan Pařík, Bonton Classics 71 0049–2 632, 1991 (complete oratorio) [CD]; Prague Sinfonietta, cond. Ivan Pařík, Bonton Baltic GD 125, 1992 (complete oratorio) [CD]; Prague Sinfonietta, cond. Ivan Pařík, Supraphon 3209, 1995 (complete oratorio) [CD]
Note: A report in Köchel/Mozart of a source for this work in Würzburg, "Bibliothek der Musikschule," cannot be confirmed.

22. Overture in D major, *Adriano in Siria*, 8 September 1776 (Florence) [10:D20]
Scoring: 2 vln, vla, b, 2 ob, 2 hrn
Ms. sources: D-WEY 629: ms. dated December 1778; I-MAav Cart. 13 n. 1
Editions: Del Vivo 2, No. 6: identified as overture to *Adriano in* Siria; Del Vivo 3; Freeman Del Vivo, No. 6
Note: The only known complete score for the opera *Adriano in Siria* (I-Fc D.I.385–387) lacks the overture.

23. Overture in C major, *Ezio* [2nd setting], 10 January 1777 (Munich) [10:C8]
Scoring: 2 vln, vla, b, 2 ob, 2 bsn, 2 hrn, 2 trp, timp
Ms. sources: CH-EN Ms. A 488 (Ms. 5860); CZ-Pnm XIX C 39; D-Mbs Mus. mss. 160 and 203: complete opera
Edition: *Ouverture zur Oper Ezio*, ed. Robert Münster (Milan: Ricordi, 1962)
Recording: Prague Opera Orchestra, cond. František Škvor, Supraphon MBA 13028, ca. 1949 [78 rpm]

24. Overture in D major, *La Calliroe*, 30 May 1778 (Naples) [10:D22]
Scoring: 2 vln, vla, b, 2 ob, 2 hrn

Ms. sources: CH-E Ms. 1718 Th. 6, 5: ms. dated 1783, scored for str, 2 ob, 2 cl, 2 hrn, with trp added later; CH-EN Ms. A 489 (Ms 5861): ms. dated 1788, scored for str and organ, with 2 cl, 2 hrn added later; CZ-NR A 148/17798: ms. ca. 1800; CZ-Pnm V B 70 (Jan Pohl collection); D-DS Ms. 3963: destroyed during World War II; F-Pn D 8208 (3–6): complete opera; I-Mc Noseda O.25.6.; I-MOe Mus. F.805; I-Nc 29.3.1–3: complete opera; P-La 45-I-33 e 34: Acts 1 and 2 of complete opera only; S-Skma O-R s.s.

Editions: Del Vivo 4; *Sinfonia Nr. 1 D-dur*, ed. Hermann Müller (Zürich: Edition Eulenburg, 1979): now published by Edition Kunzelmann, Adliswil

Recording: Camerata Amsterdam, cond. Jeroen Weierink, Ars Produktion Schumacher F 368 414, 2002 [CD]

25. Overture in C, *L'olimpiade*, 4 November 1778 (Naples) [10:C12]

Scoring: 2 vln, vla, b, 2 ob, 2 hrn, 2 trp, timp

Ms. sources: I-Nc 29.3.15–17: complete opera; P-La 45-I-52 a 54: complete opera; S-Skma O-R s.s.

Edition: *Ouvertüre zur Oper: Olimpiade (1778)*, ed. Michi Gaigg and Christian Moritz-Bauer (Passau: Musikverlag Peter Lechl, 2003)

Recording: L'Orfeo Barockorchester, cond. Michi Gaigg, CPO 777 050–2, 2004 [CD]

26. Overture in B-flat major, *Demetrio* [2nd setting], 13 August 1779 (Naples) [10:B-flat 9]

Scoring: 2 vln, vla, b, 2 ob (2 cl in 2nd movement), 2 hrn, 2 trp, timp

Ms. sources: I-Nc 29.3.4–6: complete opera; P-La 45-I-35 a 37: complete opera

27. Overture in C major, *Armida*, 26 December 1779 (Milan) [10:C13]

Scoring: 2 vln, vla, b, 2 ob, 2 hrn

Ms. sources: CZ-Bm A 306 (Lipník); F-Pn D. 8196–8: fragmentary score of complete opera; I-MOe Mus. F.806: "sinfonia . . . Milano, Teatro Nobile del Carnevale 1780"; I-Rc Mss. 5961

Edition: *Symfonie C dur*, ed. Emil Hradecký (Prague: Český hudební fond, 1957)

Recordings: Musici di Praga, cond. František Vajner, Panton 11 0229, 1970 [LP]; Leningrad Chamber Orchestra, cond. Lazar Gozman, Melodiya CM 03441-2, 1972 [LP]; Virtuosi di Praga, cond. Oldřich Vlček, Lupulus Clara 57 010, 1992 [CD]; Virtuosi di Praga, cond. Oldřich Vlček, Cantus-Lin 5.00004, 1998 [CD]; Virtuosi di Praga, cond. Oldřich Vlček, Cantus-Lin 5.00126, 2001 [CD]

Note: Evans/Dearling assumes incorrectly that the complete score of the opera in P-La (see below) begins with this overture, not Overture 28.

28. Overture in D major, *Armida*, 26 December 1779 (Milan) [missing from Evans/Dearling]

Scoring: 2 vln, vla, b, 2 ob, 2 hrn

Ms. sources: P-La 45-I-25 e 26: complete opera

Note: Evans/Dearling mistakenly groups the source for this work together with those for Overture 27.

29. Overture in D major, *Il Medonte*, 26 January 1780 (Rome) [10:D24]

Scoring: 2 vln, vla, b, 2 ob, 2 hrn, 2 trp

Ms. sources: CZ-KRa Ms. A 4914 (Hamilton); F-Pn D.8201: Act 1 only of complete opera; I-MOe Mus. F.807; I-PEsp M CXXXIII/5; I-Rc Ms. 2775: Act 1 only of complete opera; I-Rsg Ms. Mus. C.122: arr. kbd and b, b part missing; RUS-SPsc 891157–8: overture, arias, and acc. recit. only of complete opera; US-AAu M1001.M98 S9 17—: original attr. to Mysliveček crossed out, replaced with attr. to Domenico Cimarosa

Cat. ref.: EitnerQ (unknown ms. in collection of O. Lindner, Berlin)

Note: The attribution to Cimarosa in US-AAu M1001.M98 S 17 is obviously mistaken, transposed with the attribution in the ms. for Spurious Symphony 3.

SPURIOUS OVERTURE

Overture in F major, *Giuseppe riconosciuto*, 1741 (Vienna) [10:FS 1]: work of Johann Adolf Hasse

Scoring: 2 vln, vla, b, 2 fl, 2 ob, 2 bsn

Ms. sources: D-B Mus. ms. 9470: complete oratorio, attr. Hasse; D-Dl Mus. 2477-D-13 (and 2477-D-13a): complete oratorio, attr. Hasse, dated 1741; D-Hs ND VI 2459: complete oratorio, attr. Hasse; D-LEmi N.I. 103/8: complete oratorio, attr. Hasse; GB-Er D13: complete oratorio, attr. Hasse; I-Mc M.S. Ms. 136.1: complete oratorio, attr. Hasse; I-Pca D-V-1809: complete oratorio, attr. Hasse; I-Vnm Cod. It. IV-249: complete oratorio, attr. Hasse; I-Vsmc s.s.: complete oratorio, attr. Hasse

Cat. refs.: I-Pca: attr. Mysliveček; Mennicke/Hasse 82: attr. Hasse

Notes: The attribution to Mysliveček in cat. ref. I-Pca appears to be based on information from the card catalog in I-Pca, which identifies the ms. as a work of Mysliveček. The actual ms. in I-Pca attributes the work to Hasse, and all of the music, including the overture, matches the music of the other Hasse mss.

Part 3

SOLO CONCERTOS

Violin Concerto 1: D major, ca. 1768–70? [9a:D1]

Scoring: vln pr, 2 vln, vln III or vla, vla, vlone (b)

Ms. sources: CZ-Pnm XXXVIII F 158 (Úterý): ms. before 1800; S-Sm s.s.: late 18th-century ms.

Cat. ref.: Breitkopf 1769 (p. 354)

Edition: White 1994, No. 1

Recording: Shizuka Ishikawa, Dvořák Chamber Orchestra, cond. Libor Pešek, Supraphon SU 3259-2 031 (Vol. 2), 1996 [CD]

Violin Concerto 2: C major, ca. 1768–70? [missing from Evans/Dearling]

Scoring: vln pr, 2 vln, vla, b, 2 ob, 2 hrn

Ms. source: D-WRl HMA 3842: ms. ca. 1775; parts added for 2 trp, timp

Cat. ref.: Breitkopf 1770 (p. 390)

Notes: The incipit found in Breitkopf 1770 corresponds exactly to the 1st movement of the cello concerto listed below except for its range and indication of solo instrument. There is no question that the violin version represents the original.

Violin Concerto 3: C major, ca. 1768–70? [9a:C1]

Scoring: vln pr, 2 vln, vla, b, 2 ob, 2 trp

Ms. sources: A-Wgm IX 16992 (Q 16694); CZ-Pnm V B 51 (Jan Pohl collection); CZ-Pnm XIV G 156: arr. vln, pf; CZ-Pnm XV D 354: arr. vln, pf; CZ-Pnm XL C 369 and C 370 (Bertramka): XL C 369 arr. vln, pf by Jaroslav Čeleda; XL C 370 is full score copied by Čeleda; I-Gl M.4.29.16.

Editions: *Houslový koncert C-dur*, ed. Jaroslav Čeleda (Kutná Hora: Česká hudba, 1928): arr. vln, pf; *Concerto in Do magg. per violino e orchestra*, ed. Emil Hradecký (Prague: Český hudební fond, 1957); *Concerto in Do maggiore per violino e piano*, ed. Jaroslav Čeleda, rev. Jan Faust (Prague: Státní nakladatelství krásné literatury, hudby a umění, 1958/reprint Státní hudební vydavatelství, 1966)

Recordings: Ernö Sebestyén, Berlin Radio Symphony Orchestra, cond. Ernö Sebestyén, Schwann Musica Mundi VMS 1610, 1981 [LP] and Schwann Musica Mundi/Koch 3–1614–2, [1983] [CD]; Shizuka Ishikawa, Dvořák Chamber Orchestra, cond. Libor Pešek, Supraphon 1110 4031/2, 1983 [LP]; 38 C 37–7285, [198-] [CD]; Ivan Ženatý, Virtuosi di Praga, cond. Oldřich Vlček, Discover International 920265, 1995 [CD]; Shizuka Ishikawa, Dvořák Chamber Orchestra, cond. Libor Pešek, Supraphon 0016, [198-] [CD]; Shizuka Ishikawa, Dvořák Chamber Orchestra, cond. Libor Pešek, Supraphon SU 0016–2 011 (Vol. 1), 1995 [CD]; Valentin Zhuk, Camerata Amsterdam, cond. Jeroen Weierink, Ars Produktion Schumacher F 368 414, 2002 [CD]

Violin Concertos 4–9:

6 concertos in A-Wgm IX 16992 (Q 16467), copied 1772 or before? (perhaps composed for Mysliveček's trip to Vienna in 1772).

No. 1 = Violin Concerto 4 (E major) [9a:E1]
No. 2 = Violin Concerto 5 (A major) [9a:A1]
No. 3 = Violin Concerto 6 (F major) [9a:F1]
No. 4 = Violin Concerto 7 (B-flat major) [9a:B-flat 1]
No. 5 = Violin Concerto 8 (D major) [9a:D2]
No. 6 = Violin Concerto 9 (G major) [9a:G1]

Scoring: vln pr, 2 vln, vla, b, 2 ob, 2 hrn (Violin Concerto 9 omits ob)

Additional ms. sources: CZ-Pnm II D 22 (Roman Nejedlý collection): Violin Concerto 4; CZ-Pnm V B 46–50 (Jan Pohl collection): Violin Concertos 4–6, 8–9, ordered 9, 5, 4, 6, 8; CZ-Pnm V B 52 (Jan Pohl collection): Violin Concerto 7; CZ-Pnm XX D 429: Violin Concerto 6, arr. vln, pf; CZ-Pnm XL C 371 (Bertramka): Violin Concerto 7, ed. Jaroslav Čeleda; CZ-Pnm XL C 372

(Bertramka): Violin Concerto 8, arr. vln, pf by Jaroslav Čeleda; CZ-Pnm XL C 373 (Bertramka): Violin Concerto 5, ed. Jaroslav Čeleda; CZ-Pu Roz Arch 0-2923: Violin Concerto 6; CZ-Pu Roz Arch 0-5181: Violin Concerto 8; CZ-Pu Roz Arch 0-5182: Violin Concerto 4

Editions: *Concerto per violino con orchestra*, ed. Karel Moor and Ladislav Láska (Prague: Zdeněk Vlk, 1948): Violin Concerto 6, arr. vln, pf; *Konzert F dur pro housle a orchestr* (Prague: Český hudební fond, 1955): Violin Concerto 6, no editor specified; *Concerto in Re maggiore per violino e orchestra*, ed. Emil Hradecký (Prague: Česky hudební fond, 1956): Violin Concerto 8; *Concerto in Mi maggiore per violino e orchestra*, ed. Emil Hradecký (Prague: Český hudební fond, 1957; reprint 1965 with vln, pf arr.): Violin Concerto 4; White 1994, No. 2: Violin Concerto 7; White 1994, No. 3: Violin Concerto 8

Recordings: Karel Šneberger, Orebo Chamber Orchestra, cond. František Vajnar, Bluebell BELL 149, n.d. [LP]: Violin Concerto 6; Eugen Prokop, Prague Chamber Orchestra, cond. Milan Sádlo, Supraphon 1110 1060, 1971 [LP] and Supraphon CO-2054, n.d. [CD]: Violin Concerto 8; Ernö Sebestyén, Berlin Radio Symphony Orchestra, cond. Ernö Sebestyén, Schwann Musica Mundi VMS 1610, 1981 [LP] and Schwann Musica Mundi/Koch 3–1614–2, [1983] [CD]: Violin Concertos 6 and 8; Shizuka Ishikawa, Dvořák Chamber Orchestra, cond. Libor Pešek, Supraphon 1110 4031–2, 1983 [LP] and 38 C 37–7285, [198-] [CD]: Violin Concertos 4, 5, 6, and 8; Shizuka Ishikawa, Dvořák Chamber Orchestra, cond. Libor Pešek, Supraphon 0016, [198-] [CD]: Violin Concertos 4, 5, 6, and 8; Shizuka Ishikawa, Dvořák Chamber Orchestra, cond. Libor Pešek, Supraphon SU 0016–2 011 (Vol. 1), 1995 [CD]: Violin Concertos 4–6; Shizuka Ishikawa, Dvořák Chamber Orchestra, cond. Libor Pešek, Supraphon SU 3259–2 031 (Vol. 2), 1996 [CD]: Violin Concertos 7–9; Elizabeth Wallfisch, Brandenburg Orchestra, cond. Roy Goodman, Hyperion 66840, 1996 [CD]: Violin Concerto 7; Oldřich Vlček, Virtuosi di Praga, cond. Oldřich Vlček, Multisonic 310399, 2000 [CD]: Violin Concerto 7; Elliott Golub, Music of the Baroque Orchestra, cond. Thomas Wikman, Music of the Baroque Orchestra s.s., [2002?] [CD]: Violin Concerto 8; Valentin Zhuk, Camerata Amsterdam, cond. Jeroen Weierink, Ars Produktion Schumacher F 368 414, 2002 [CD]: Violin Concerto 6; Elizabeth Wallfisch, Brandenburg Orchestra, cond. Roy Goodman, Helios CDA66840, 2003 [CD]: Violin Concerto 7

Violin Concerto 10: B-flat major, date? [missing from Evans/Dearling]

Scoring: ?

Ms. source: A-Wgm IX 19802 (Q 16695): vln pr, fragment of b part only

Concerto for Cello: C major, 1770 or before? [9b:C1]

Scoring: vlc pr, 2 vln, vla, b, 2 ob, 2 hrn

Ms. sources: A-Wgm IX 16993; CZ-Pnm V B 53 (Jan Pohl collection); CZ-Pu Roz Arch 59 R 625 (Alois Hnilička collection)

Edition: *Konsert dlia violoncheli s orkestrom do mazhor*, ed. Oldřich Pulkert (Leningrad: Muzyka, 1973): arr. vlc, pf

Recordings: Boris Pergamensikov, Leningrad Chamber Orchestra, cond. Lazar Gozman, Melodiya CM 0344–2, 1972 [LP]; Bohuslav Pavlas, Prague Chamber Orchestra, cond. Hubert Soudant,

Supraphon 1110 4120, 1972 [LP]; Michaela Fukačová, Virtuosi di Praga, cond. Oldřich Vlček, Lupulus Clara 57 010, 1992 [CD]; Ofra Harnoy, I soloisti veneti, cond. Claudio Scimone, RCA 09026 61228, 1993 [CD]; Bohuslav Pavlas, Prague Chamber Orchestra, cond. Hubert Soudant, MusicVars VA0090–2, 1998 [CD]; Michaela Fukačová, Virtuosi di Praga, cond. Oldřich Vlček, Cantus-Lin 5.00004, 1998 [CD]: 3rd movement only; Michaela Fukačová, Virtuosi di Praga, cond. Oldřich Vlček, Cantus-Lin 5.00126, 2001 [CD]; Arturo Muruzubal, Camerata Amsterdam, cond. Jeroen Weierink, Ars Produktion Schumacher FCD 368 414, 2002 [CD]; Jan Škrdlík, Brno Chamber Soloists, Gnosis Brno GMUSIC027–2, 2004 [CD]

Note: For dating, see notes for Violin Concerto 2.

Concerto for Flute: D major, date? [9c:D1]

Scoring: fl pr, 2 vln, vla, b, 2 ob, 2 hrn

Ms. source: PL-WRu 60049 Muz. (*olim* Mus. Ha 15)

Edition: *Koncert D dur pro flétnu a orchestr*, ed. Milan Munclinger, Musica viva historica, 23 (Prague: Editio Supraphon, 1969; reprint 1975, 1989)

Recordings: Jan Hecl, Musici di Praga, cond. Miloš Konvalinka, Supraphon 1110 2625, 1979 [LP]; Bruno Meier, Prague Chamber Orchestra, cond. Oldřich Vlček, Koch-Schwann Musica Mundi 311 104, 1989 [CD]; Václav Kunt, Prague Chamber Orchestra, cond. Ondřej Kukal, MusicVars VA0074–2, 1997 [CD]

Note: Reports of the existence of flute concertos in D-KA and CZ-Pnm (see Vester M 840a and M 841, respectively) are false.

Keyboard Concerto 1: B-flat major, late 1770s, perhaps Munich [9d:B-flat 1]

Scoring: kbd, 2 vln, vla, b, 2 ob, 2 hrn

Ms. sources: F-Pn Ms. 1128, No. 1; F-Pn Vma.ms.266: 20th-century ms. copied by Georges de Saint-Foix

Edition: *Concerto per Cembalo con più stromenti*, ed. Michi Gaigg and Christian Moritz-Bauer (Passau: Musikverlag Peter Lechl, 2003)

Note: See notes for Keyboard Concerto 2 and Symphony 53.

Keyboard Concerto 2: F major, late 1770s, perhaps Munich [9d:F1]

Scoring: kbd, 2 vln, vla, b, 2 ob, 2 hrn

Ms. sources: CZ-Pnm XIII F 382: omits hrn; D-MÜs SANT Hs 2724: date of ca.1765 attached to ms. by library staff seems impossibly early on stylistic grounds; F-Pn Ms. 1128, No. 2; I-Rc Ms. 2517,2: omits ob, hrn; I-Rsg Ms. Mus. C.123: kbd part only; S-Skma PO-R s.s.: 2 copies, score and parts

Edition: *Concerto No. 2 for Harpsichord (or Piano) and Orchestra*, ed. Edvard Fendler, cadenza by Martin Hall (London: Boosey & Hawkes, 1958; reprint 1963 & 1964)

Notes: The Fendler edition designates this concerto "No. 2" on the basis of its position within the ms. in F-Pn; no edition corresponding to "No. 1" (Keyboard Concerto 1) was ever prepared. See also note for Symphony 53 concerning a mistaken report of kbd concertos in D-W.

Part 4

CONCERTOS FOR MULTIPLE SOLOISTS

All of the surviving concertos for 2 clarinets, 2 horns and bassoon with string accompaniment were likely part of a set of six "concertoni" composed by Mysliveček for the archbishop of Salzburg, according to a letter of Leopold Mozart dated 13 April 1778 (see chapter 4). The entire set, in manuscript, was offered for sale in 1799 in Traeg (see pp. 53 and 303), but three of the selections are now lost.

1. "Concertino" [or "Concertone"] in E-flat major, 1777–78? [9e:E-flat 1]
   Scoring: 2 cl obl, 2 hrn obl, bsn obl, 2 vln, vla, b
   Ms. sources: D-BFb Ms. M-is 55; D-Rtt Mysliveček 9: ms. ca. 1780
   Editions: *Concertone in Es für 2 Klarinetten, 2 Hörner, Fagott und Streicher*, ed. Michi Gaigg and Christian Moritz-Bauer (Passau: Musikverlag Peter Lechl, 2003); *Concerto in Es*, ed. Miloslav Richter (Prague: Český rozhlas, 2003)
   Recording: Concerto Köln, cond. Werner Eberhardt, Archiv Produktion 477 6418, 2006 [CD]

2. "Concerto" in E-flat major, 1777–78? [missing from Evans/Dearling]
   Scoring: 2 cl obl, 2 hrn obl, bsn obl, 2 vln, vla, b
   Ms. source: I-MC 4-A-15a ("Concerto Secundo")

3. "Concerto" in E-flat major, 1777–78? [missing from Evans/Dearling]
   Scoring: 2 cl obl, 2 hrn obl, bsn obl, 2 vln, vla, b
   Ms. source: I-MC 4-A-12a ("Concerto IV")

Part 5

MUSIC FOR WIND ENSEMBLE

Wind Octet 1: E-flat major, probably written in Munich, 1777–78 [8:E-flat 1]
   Scoring: 2 ob, 2 cl, 2 hrn, 2 bsn
   Ms. sources: D-DO Mus. Ms. 1290, No. "2": ms. ca. 1790, arr. kbd by J. Mašek; D-DO Mus. Ms. 1597: ms. ca. 1800; RUS-SPsc 167/85 – MK, No. 18
   Edition: Schoenbaum 1962, No. 1
   Recordings: Prague Chamber Ensemble, Supraphon SUA 19763, 1967 [LP]; SUA ST 59763; Banda Classica, Ex Libris EL 16971, 1985 [LP]; Virtuosi di Praga, cond. Oldřich Vlček, Lupulus Clara 57 010, 1992 [CD]; Schweitzer Oktett, CPO 999 314-2, 1995 [CD]; Meyer Wind Ensemble, EMI/Angel EMIA 55512, 1996 [CD]; Academia Wind Quintet Prague, Rotag

RG0022–2, 1996 [CD]; Budapest Wind Ensemble, Hungaroton Classic HCD 31676, 1997 [CD]; Cracow Wind Ensemble, Column Classics COLM 555005, 1997 [CD]; Harmoniemusik of London, Virgin VM 561368–2, 1997 [CD]; Virtuosi di Praga, cond. Oldřich Vlček, Cantus-Lin 5.00126, 2001 [CD]; Meyer Wind Ensemble, EMI Classics 567644–2, 2001 [CD]

Wind Octet 2: E-flat major, probably written in Munich, 1777–78 [8:E-flat 2]

Scoring: 2 ob, 2 cl, 2 hrn, 2 bsn

Ms. sources: D-DO Mus. Ms. 1290, No. "3": ms. ca. 1790, arr. kbd by J. Mašek; D-DO Mus. Ms. 1597: ms. ca. 1800; RUS-SPsc 167/85 – MK, No. 21

Edition: Schoenbaum 1962, No. 2

Recordings: Prague Chamber Ensemble, Supraphon SUA 19763, 1967 [LP]; SUA ST 59763; Musica Viva Ensemble, cond. James Bolle, Monitor MCS 2126, n.d. [LP]; Banda Classica, Ex Libris EL 16971, 1985 [LP]; Harmonie Ensemble, New York, cond. Steven Richman, Music and Arts 691, 1991 [CD]; Queensland Wind Ensemble, Vox Australis VAST 008–2, 1992 [CD]; Ottetto Amsterdam, Erasmus WVH 089, 1994 [CD]; Schweitzer Oktett, CPO 999 314–2, 1995 [CD]; Meyer Wind Ensemble, EMI/Angel EMIA 555 12, 1996 [CD]; Academia Wind Quintet Prague, Rotag RG0022–2, 1996 [CD]: 3rd movement only, appended to Wind Octet 1; Budapest Wind Ensemble, Hungaroton Classic HCD 31676, 1997 [CD]; Cracow Wind Ensemble, Column Classics COLM 555005, 1997 [CD]; Harmoniemusik of London, Virgin VM 561368–2, 1997 [CD]; Meyer Wind Ensemble, EMI Classics 567644–2, 2001 [CD]; V. Madatov, cond., unspecified soloists, Levné Knihy LK 0322–2, 2005 [CD]

Wind Octet 3: B-flat major, probably written in Munich, 1777–78 [8:B flat 1]

Scoring: 2 ob, 2 cl, 2 hrn, 2 bsn

Ms. source: D-DO Mus. Ms. 1597: ms. ca. 1800

Edition: Schoenbaum 1962, No. 3

Recordings: Musica Viva Ensemble, cond. James Bolle, Monitor MCS 2126, n.d. [LP]; Collegium Musicum Pragense, cond. František Vajnar, Panton 01 0229, 1970 [LP]; Banda Classica, Ex Libris EL 16971, 1985 [LP]; Collegium Musicum Pragense, Supraphon 11 0097, 1990 [CD]; Schweitzer Oktett, CPO 999 314–2, 1995 [CD]; Meyer Wind Ensemble, EMI/Angel EMIA 55512, 1996 [CD]; Budapest Wind Ensemble, Hungaroton Classic HCD 31676, 1997 [CD]; Cracow Wind Ensemble, Column Classics COLM 555005, 1997 [CD]; Harmoniemusik of London, Virgin VM 561368–2, 1997 [CD]; Westdeutsche Bläsersolisten, Ars Produktion Schumacher 368 357, 1998 [CD]; Meyer Wind Ensemble, EMI Classics 567644–2, 2001 [CD]

Wind Quintets 1–6:

6 wind quintets in D-MÜs SANT Hs 2725a (score) and D-MÜs SANT Hs 2725b (parts). The quintets bear dedication to "sua Eccellenza il Sig. Principe Rezzonico Senatore di Roma" and were undoubtedly written in 1780–81 at the time of Mysliveček's residence in Rome. The dedicatee can be identified as Prince Abbondio Rezzonico (d. 1810), nephew of Pope Clement XIII (r. 1758–69).

No. 1 = Wind Quintet 1 (D major) [5:D2]

No. 2 = Wind Quintet 2 (G major) [5:G2]

No. 3 = Wind Quintet 3 (E-flat major) [5:E-flat 3]
No. 4 = Wind Quintet 4 (B-flat major) [5:B-flat 3]
No. 5 = Wind Quintet 5 (F major) [5:F3]
No. 6 = Wind Quintet 6 (C major) [5:C3]
Scoring: 2 ob, 2 hrn, bsn

"Cassation" in B-flat major, date? [3:B flat 7]
Scoring: cl, 2 hrn
Ms. source: RUS-SPsc 162/85 – MK, No. 19

ARRANGEMENT

Minuet in D major, date? [missing from Evans/Dearling]
Scoring: 2 fl (or 2 ob or 2 vln)
Cat. ref.: RISM B/v.2, p. 389
Edition: In *Thompson's Miscellaneous Collection of Elegant Duettinos*, Vol. 1 (London, [ca. 1790]), No. 61: called a "favourite minuet"; exemplar in S-L; arrangement of the 2nd movement of Keyboard Sonata 7, transposed to D major

QUESTIONABLE WORK

"Kasace" (Cassation) in B-flat major, the "Hunting Partita," date? [5:B flat 4]
Scoring: 2 cl, 2 hrn, bsn
Ms. source: CZ-Bm A 19416
Recording: Collegium Musicum Pragense, Panton 01 0229, 1970 [LP]

Part 6

MISCELLANEOUS CHAMBER WORKS FOR STRINGS AND WINDS

Oboe Quintets (Flute Quintets) 1–6:

6 oboe quintets listed in Breitkopf 1782/84 (p. 783). A *terminus ante quem* for the dating of these works may be established in a letter of Leopold Mozart to his son of 15 October 1777. Here, Leopold mentioned that Mysliveček intended to send the archbishop of Salzburg six oboe quintets along with twelve symphonies. These quintets are the only surviving Mysliveček quintets that could fit this description.

No. 1 = Oboe Quintet 1 (B-flat major) [5:B flat 2]

No. 2 = Oboe Quintet 2 (D major) [5:D1]
No. 3 = Oboe Quintet 3 (F major) [5:F2]
No. 4 = Oboe Quintet 4 (C major) [5:C2]
No. 5 = Oboe Quintet 5 (A major [5:A2]
No. 6 = Oboe Quintet 6 (E-flat major) [5:E-flat 2]

Scoring: ob or fl, 2 vln, vla, b

Ms. sources: E-Mp Leg. 1630 (Cat. 2.059): Oboe Quintet 1; I-Rc Mss. 5963: Oboe Quintet 3; I-Rcagli 11: Oboe Quintet 2; I-TVco Ms 4893: Oboe Quintets 1–6, lacks parts for fl/ob

Notes: The Oboe Quintets 2, 4, 5 and 6 are mistakenly declared lost in Evans/Dearling. The mss. in I-Rc and I-Rcagli are both from the collection of the Compagnoni Marefoschi di Macerata.

QUESTIONABLE WORKS

1. "Kvartet" in B-flat major, date? [11:B-flat 1]
   Scoring: 4 hrn, 2 vln, vla, (b), 2 ob, 2 cl
   Ms. source: CZ-Pnm XXXI D 130

2. Trio in E-flat major, 1778 or before [Lost; 3:E-flat 4]
   Scoring: hrn, vln, b
   Cat. refs.: Breitkopf 1778 (p. 651): attr. Giovanni Punto; Breitkopf 1781 (p. 731): attr. Mysliveček
   Note: More likely the work of Giovanni Punto rather than Mysliveček in view of the scoring, which is otherwise unknown among Mysliveček's chamber works.

Part 7

MUSIC FOR STRINGS IN FIVE PARTS

(all scored for 2 vln, 2 vla, vlc/b)

String Quintets (String Symphonies) 1–6:

6 string quintets (or string symphonies) in Venier/Castaud 1767.

No. 1 = String Quintet 1 (B-flat major) [7:B-flat 1]
No. 2 = String Quintet 2 (E major) [7:E1]
No. 3 = String Quintet 3 (G major) [7:G1]
No. 4 = String Quintet 4 (A major) [7:A1]
No. 5 = String Quintet 5 (D major) [7:D1]
No. 6 = String Quintet 6 (C major) [7:C1]

Ms. sources: CZ-JIa Krt. 24, No. 126: String Quintet 3; CZ-JIa Krt. 24, No. 127: String Quintet 1; CZ-Pnm V B 75 (Jan Pohl collection): String Quintet 4; CZ-Pnm XXVII B 7 (Horšovský Týn): String Quintet 6; CZ-Pnm XXVII B 8 (Horšovský Týn): String Quintet 3; CZ-Pnm XXVII B 9 (Horšovský Týn): String Quintet 2; CZ-Pnm XXXII A 13 (Osek): String Quintet 3; CZ-Pnm XLI C 246 (Kačina): String Quintet 3; CZ-Pnm XLI C 247 (Kačina): String Quintet 2; CZ-Pnm XLII F 204: String Quintet 1; CZ-Pnm XLIX C 246 (Radenín): String Quintet 4; I-Gl N.1.7.3. (Sc. 19): String Quintets 1–6, ordered 6, 1, 2, 5, 3, 4; I-Gl M.4.29.11/15.: String Quintets 1–6, ordered 6, 1, 2, 5, 3, 4; I-Gl M.4.29.20/25.: String Quintets 1–6, ordered 6, 1, 2, 5, 3, 4; I-Mc Noseda s.s.: String Quintets 1–6, includes parts for 2 hrn; I-TVco Ms 4894: String Quintets 1–6, ordered 6, 4, 3, 2, 1, 5, lacks part for vla 2

Cat. refs.: Breitkopf 1768 (p. 316): String Quintets 1–6; Qb 1775 Ch C 18: String Quintet 6; Qb 1775 Ch D 20: String Quintet 5; Qb 1775 Ch E 31 & E 57: String Quintet 2; Qb 1775 Ch G 17: String Quintet 3; Qb 1775 Ch A 16: String Quintet 4; Qb 1775 Ch B 17: String Quintet 1; all entries in QB 1775 attr. "Venatorino"

Additional edition: Freeman & Ackerman n.d.

Recordings: Uralsk Philharmonic Orchestra, Gary Brain, cond., Toccata Classics TOCC 0023, 2006 [CD]: String Quintets 1–6; Concerto Köln, cond. Werner Eberhardt, Archiv Produktion 477 6418, 2006 [CD]: String Quintet 6

Notes: Evans/Dearling cites "F-Pa, ms" and "F-Pc Ac.e4.44" as ms. sources for these six quintets; however, both library references correspond to the print Venier/Castaud 1767. Evans/Dearling catalogs this set as chamber septets on the basis of the existence of a single ms. with added horn parts.

String Quintets (String Symphonies) 7–12:

6 string quintets (or string symphonies) in I-MOe Mus. F.803, probably composed by 1773. They are likely the quintets mentioned in a letter written by Mysliveček from Naples to his patron Count Vincenz von Waldstein on 14 September 1773 that is reproduced in transcription and facsimile in Bohadlo, 92–96. Here, Mysliveček mentioned a set of quintets to be published in London with dedication to the count. No such print is known to have been issued.

No. 1 = String Quintet 7 (G major) [5:C1]
No. 2 = String Quintet 8 (E-flat major) [5:E-flat 1]
No. 3 = String Quintet 9 (C major) [5:C1]
No. 4 = String Quintet 10 (A major) [5:A1]
No. 5 = String Quintet 11 (F major) [5:F1]
No. 6 = String Quintet 12 (B-flat major) [5:B-flat 1]

Additional ms. source: I-Mc Noseda M.33.1–6: String Quintets 7–12

Editions: Bělský 1957: String Quintets 7–9; Bělský 1988: String Quintets 10–12

Recordings: Czech Chamber Soloists, dir. Miroslav Matyáš, Supraphon 110 1880, 1976 [LP]: String Quintets 7–10, 12; Czech Chamber Soloists, dir. Miroslav Matyáš, Supraphon SUPD 003, [197-] [LP]: String Quintets 7–10, 12; Czech Chamber Soloists, dir. Leoš Svárovský, Panton 811399–2, 1995 [CD]: String Quintets 7–12; Pro Arte Antiqua Praha, Arta F1 0071–2, 1997 [CD]: String Quintets 7–12; Münchner Streichquintett, AudioMax 7030266–2, 2004 [CD]: String Quintets 7-9

SPURIOUS WORK

Quintet in E-flat major, 1785 or before [5:E-flatS1]: work of Ignace Pleyel

Scoring: 2 vln, 2 vla, vlc/b

Ms. sources: A-Sca Hs 1723, No. 1: attr. Pleyel, ms. ca. 1800; A-Wn S.m. 11486: attr. Pleyel, ms. 1788; CZ-Pnm XLII D 558 (Alois Altrichter collection): attr. Mysliveček; D-BAR s.s., No. 1: attr. Pleyel, ms. ca. 1800; D-HL 9.10.11, No. 1: attr. Pleyel, ms. ca. 1815; D-Rtt Pleyel 29: ms. ca. 1790; S-V s.s.: attr. Pleyel

Editions: numerous editions with attribution to Pleyel detailed in Benton/Pleyel, 83–87, including arrangements

Note: Modern copy in ms., prepared by Alois Altrichter in 1950 (in CZ-Pnm), is drawn from an unknown source with attribution to Mysliveček.

Part 8

MUSIC FOR STRINGS IN FOUR PARTS

(all scored for 2 vln, vla, vlc/b)

String Quartets 1–6:

6 string quartets in La Chevardière/Castaud 1768/69.

No. 1 = String Quartet 1 (A major) [4:A1]

No. 2 = String Quartet 2 (F major) [4:F1]

No. 3 = String Quartet 3 (B-flat major) [4:B-flat 1]

No. 4 = String Quartet 4 (G major) [4:G1]

No. 5 = String Quartet 5 (E-flat major) [4:E-flat 1]

No. 6 = String Quartet 6 (C major) [4:C1]

Ms. sources: A-Wn Mus.Hs. 12.118–123: String Quartets 1–6, ordered 1–2, 4, 3, 5–6; CZ-Bm A 26.308 (Kvašice): String Quartet 3; CZ-Pnm V B 72, No. 2 (Jan Pohl collection): String Quartet 2; CZ-Pnm V B 72, No. 5 (Jan Pohl collection): String Quartet 5; CZ-Pnm V B 72, No. 6 (Jan Pohl collection): String Quartet 3; CZ-Pnm V B 72, No. 7 (designated as "No. 6") (Jan Pohl collection): String Quartet 6; CZ-Pnm XX C 39: String Quartet 6; CZ-Pnm XXVII B 10 (Horšovský Týn): String Quartet 2; CZ-Pnm XXVII B 11 (Horšovský Týn): String Quartet 1; CZ-Pnm XXVII B 12 (Horšovský Týn): String Quartet 4; CZ-Pnm XXXIV E 188 (Doksy): String Quartet 3; CZ-Pnm XXXVII E 553 (Alois Altrichter collection): String Quartet 5; CZ-Pnm XLI C 177 (Kačina): String Quartet 5, vla and vlc/b parts only; CZ-Pnm XLI C 178–182 (Kačina): String Quartets 1–4, 6, ordered 3, 2, 4, 1, 6; CZ-Pnm XLII E 201–206 (Frýdlant/Clam-Gallas): String Quartets 1–6, ordered 6, 5, 4, 3, 2, 1; CZ-Pnm XLIX C 242–245 (Radenín): String Quartets 2–3, 5–6, mss. ca. 1780; D-ZL HR 85: String Quartet 2, ms. ca. 1780; I-Mc Noseda M.33.7–12: String Quartets 1–6, ordered 6, 4, 2, 1, 3, 5, designated "sinfonie o quartetti"; I-Mc Polo 40/3: String Quartets 1–6; SK-BRsav s.s.: String Quartet 2; US-Wc M451.M3 Case: String Quartets 1–6

Cat. refs.: Qb 1775 Ch C 20: String Quartet 6; Qb 1775 Ch E 56: String Quartet 5; Qb 1775 Ch F 34: String Quartet 2; Qb 1775 Ch G 18: String Quartet 4; Qb 1775 Ch A 17: String Quartet 1; Qb 1775 Ch B 19: String Quartet 3: all attr. "Venatorino"

Additional editions: Welcker 1780: String Quartets 1–6, ordered 2, 3, 6, 5, 4, 1; *Streichquartett, C-dur*, ed. Walter Höckner (Leipzig: Pro MusicaVerlag, 1947): String Quartet 6; *Divertimento in F*, ed. Alena Martínková, Edice symfonické a komorní hudby, 9 (Prague: Ústřední dům lidové umělecké a komorní tvořivosti, 1971): String Quartet 2; *Quartet C major for Two Violins, Viola and Violoncello*, ed. František Xaver Thuri, Czech Classics Collection (Prague: Metronome Edition, 1992): String Quartet 6

Recordings: Slovak String Quartet, Schwann Musica Mundi VMS 4041, 1966 [LP] and Charlin CL 27 [LP]: String Quartet 6; Suk Chamber Orchestra, cond. Josef Vlach, Dabringhaus und Grimm L 3316, 1989 [CD]: String Quartet 2 performed as a "divertimento" for string orchestra; Suk Chamber Orchestra, cond. Josef Vlach, Panton 81 0953–2, 1990 [CD]: String Quartet 2 performed as a "divertimento" for string orchestra; Martino Quartet, Panton 71 0487–2, 1992 [CD]: String Quartet 6; Martino Quartet, Panton 81 1001–2, 1992 [CD]: String Quartet 6; Archi Boemi, cond. Hynek Farkač, Start Classics 501, 1995 [CD]: String Quartet 2 performed as a "divertimento" for string orchestra); Pro Arte Antiqua Praha, Arta F10074–2, 1996 [CD]: String Quartet 6; Ensemble Vox Aurae, cond. Giancarlo De Lorenzo, Agorà AG 133, 1997 [CD]: String Quartets 1–6, ordered 6, 4, 2, 1, 3, 5 as in ms. I-Mc Noseda M.33, all performed as string symphonies; Nezavislý Komorní Orchestr, Gz Classic 136, 1997 [CD]: String Quartet 2 performed as a "divertimento" for string orchestra; Suk Chamber Orchestra, cond. Josef Vlach, Dabringhaus und Grimm MDG 601 0316–2, 1997 [CD]: String Quartet 2 performed as a "divertimento" for string orchestra; String Quartet of the Moscow Radio Orchestra, Levné Knihy LK 3022–2, 2005 [CD]: String Quartet 2, 1st movement only

Notes: Evans/Dearling cites "E-Mn M680–683–10," "US-Wc M452.M65.Q9," and S-Skma Nordins Samling" as ms. sources for these six quartets. The first two shelf numbers, however, correspond to the print Welcker 1780, and the third shelf number corresponds to the print La Chevardière/Castaud 1768/69 (communications, US-Wc, 6 March 1995; S-Skma, 25 January 1995).

String Quartet (String Symphony) 7: G major, 1770 or before [4:G2]

Ms. sources: CZ-Pnm V B 72, No. 1 (Jan Pohl collection); CZ-Pnm XXXVI D 534 (Alois Altrichter collection); CZ-Pnm XLIX C 240 (Radenín)

Cat. ref.: Qb 1775 Ch G 19: attr. "Venatorino"

Notes: Also preserved in one source as a symphony for string orchestra (see Symphony 14). The dating given above is based on that given for this symphony in cat. ref. A-GÖ 1830 2905.

String Quartet (String Symphony) 8: D major, ca. 1775 or before [4:D1]

Ms. source: CZ-Pnm V B 73 (Jan Pohl collection)

Cat. ref.: Qb 1775 Ch D 21 (2nd movement): attr. "Venatorino"

Note: Also preserved in one source as a symphony for string orchestra (see Symphony 32).

String Quartet (String Symphony) 9: E-flat major, ca. 1775 or before [4:E-flat 2]

Ms. source: CZ-Pnm V B 72, No. 3 (designated as "No. 2") (Jan Pohl collection)

Cat. ref.: Qb 1775 Ch E 25 & E 55: attr. "Venatorino"

Note: Also disseminated in sources as a symphony for string orchestra (see Symphony 33).

String Quartet (String Symphony) 10: A major, ca. 1775 or before [4:A2]

Ms. sources: CZ-Pnm V B 72, No. 4 (designated as "No. 3") (Jan Pohl collection); CZ-Pnm XLIX C 241 (Radenín); CZ-Pu 59 R 3536 (Panenský Týnec)

Cat. ref.: Qb 1775 Ch A 15: attr. "Venatorino"

Recording: Pro Arte Antiqua Praha, Harmonia Mundi HM 30 601, 1957 [LP]

Note: Also disseminated in one source as a symphony for string orchestra (see Symphony 34).

String Quartet (String Symphony) 11: B-flat major, ca. 1775 or before [4:B-flat 2]

Ms. source: CZ-Pnm V B 74 (Jan Pohl collection)

Cat. ref.: Qb 1775 Ch B 18: attr. "Venatorino"

Note: Also disseminated in sources as a symphony for string orchestra (see Symphony 35).

String Quartets 12–17:

6 string quartets in André 1777a.

No. 1 = String Quartet 12 (E-flat major) [4:E-flat 3]

No. 2 = String Quartet 13 (C major) [4:C2]

No. 3 = String Quartet 14 (D major) [4:D2]

No. 4 = String Quartet 15 (F major) [4:F2]

No. 5 = String Quartet 16 (B-flat major) [4:B-flat 3]

No. 6 = String Quartet 17 (G major) [4:G3]

Ms. sources: D-ZL HR 85: String Quartet 15; I-FAsn s.s. (in Cartella 2 F5): String Quartets 12–17, ordered 17, 16, 14, 15, 13, 12; I-Gl 4.29.10: String Quartets 12–17, ordered 17, 16, 14, 15, 13, 12; I-Rdp 203: String Quartets 14, 16–17, ordered 17, 16, 14, No. 3 (String Quartet 14) is incomplete; I-Rdp 204: String Quartets 12–13, 15, ordered 15, 13, 12, as continuation of I-Rdp 203 (numbered 4–6); PL-WRu 60050 Muz.: String Quartet 12 (ms. also contains vln 2 part for 3rd movement of String Quartet 16); PL-WRu 60051 Muz.: String Quartet 13

Cat. refs.: Breitkopf 1778 (p. 639); Hofmeister 1817, p. 65

Note: Evans/Dearling lists "S-L Barnekow No. 38" as a ms. source for these six quartets, however, this library shelf number corresponds to the print Andre 1777a.

String Quartets 18–23:

6 string quartets in Hummel 1781.

No. 1 = String Quartet 18 (C major) [4:C3]

No. 2 = String Quartet 19 (F major) [4:F3]

No. 3 = String Quartet 20 (B-flat major) [4:B-flat 4]
No. 4 = String Quartet 21 (E-flat major) [4:E-flat 4]
No. 5 = String Quartet 22 (G major) [4:G4]
No. 6 = String Quartet 23 (A major) [4:A3]

Cat ref.: Hofmeister 1817, p. 65

Ms. sources: CZ-Bm HAM A 2426: String Quartets 18–23; CZ-CBj H 424: String Quartets 18–23; CZ-Pnm V B 80 (Jan Pohl collection): String Quartets 18–23; CZ-Pnm XIII E 351 (Josef Šrogl collection): String Quartet 22, 2nd movement only, arr. vln, pf; CZ-Pnm XIII F 385: String Quartets 18–23; CZ-Pnm XVI A 191 (Josef Šrogl collection): String Quartet 22, 2nd movement only, arr. vln, pf; CZ-Pnm XXXVI F 449: String Quartet 19; CZ-Pnm XLII A 495 (Alois Altrichter collection): String Quartet 22; CZ-Pnm XLIX C 503 (Radenín): String Quartets 18–23, vlc/b part only

Additional edition: Freeman n.d.

Notes: Evans/Dearling cites "B-Bc, ms" and "S-L Barnekow, No. 43" as ms. sources for these six quartets, and "Fin-As, ms" for the first five. However, all three of these references correspond to the print Hummel 1781 (communications, B-Bc, 22 January 2001; Fin-As, 13 December 1994).

SPURIOUS WORK

Quartet (Serenade) in F, 1790 or before [4:FS1]: work of Ignace Pleyel

Scoring: vln, 2 vla, b

Ms. sources: A-Wgm XI 35276: attr. Pleyel, scored for str, ob, 2 hrn; CZ-Pu 59 R 185: attr. Mysliveček; S-V Molér 94 (61): attr. Pleyel, scored for str, ob, 2 hrn

Cat. ref.: Benton/Pleyel No. 216 (pp. 75–76)

Edition: Ignace Pleyel, *Serenate à deux violons, hautbois, deux cors, viola et basse*, Op. 6 (Offenbach: André, 1790)

Note: See Benton/Pleyel, 76, for alternate and fragmentary versions of this work.

LOST WORK

Quartet (?) in C, ca. 1775 or before [3:C4]

Scoring: 2 vl, vla, vlc/b?

Cat. ref.: Qb 1775 Ch C 19: attr. "Venatorino"

Notes: Qb 1775 provides no indication of instrumentation for its chamber music entries. It has been assumed here that this work is a quartet, because it appears between two others, thus forming a grouping of three (the other pieces in the grouping survive in mss. that confirm them as quartets). Evans/Dearling includes it among trios without explanation.

Part 9

MUSIC FOR STRINGS IN THREE PARTS

(all scored for 2 vln, vlc/b except String Trio 21 and Cello Sonatas)

String Trios 1–6:

6 string trios in Breitkopf 1767 (p. 275).

No. 1 = String Trio 1 (A major) [Lost; 3:A1]
No. 2 = String Trio 2 (G minor) [Lost; 3:g1]
No. 3 = String Trio 3 (F major) [Lost; 3:F1]
No. 4 = String Trio 4 (E-flat major) [3:E-flat 1]
No. 5 = String Trio 5 (B-flat major) [Lost; 3:B-flat 1]
No. 6 = String Trio 6 (C minor) [Lost; 3:c1]

Ms. source: US-BEm It. 297: String Trio 4

Cat. ref.: D-SI 1766 12: String Trio 5, attr. Pokorný (undoubtedly spurious)

String Trios (Orchestral Trios) 7–12:

6 string trios in La Chevardière 1768.

No. 1 = String Trio 7 (C major) [3:C1]
No. 2 = String Trio 8 (A major) [3:A2]
No. 3 = String Trio 9 (D major) [3:D1]
No. 4 = String Trio 10 (F major) [3:F2]
No. 5 = String Trio 11 (A major) [3:A3]
No. 6 = String Trio 12 (E-flat major) [3:E-flat 2]

Ms. sources: A-Wgm IX 23414 ("a"): String Trio 7; A-Wgm IX 23414 ("b"): String Trio 9; A-Wgm IX 23414 ("d"): String Trio 10; A-Wgm IX 23414 ("e"): String Trio 8; CZ-Jla Krt. 24, No. 124: String Trio 10; CZ-LUa B 117: String Trio 7; CZ-Pk 5223 (Schönborn-Lobkovic): String Trio 9, lacks vln 1; CZ-Pnm V B 71 (Jan Pohl collection): String Trios 7-9, two copies, one arr. vln, pf; CZ-Pnm XVI A 190 (Josef Šrogl collection): String Trio 9, arr. vln, pf; CZ-Pnm XLIX C 229 (Radenín): String Trio 9, ms. ca. 1780; CZ-Pnm XLIX C 230 (Radenín): String Trio 8; CZ-Pnm XLIX C 231 (Radenín): String Trio 7; CZ-Pu 59 R 3597 (Panenský Týnec): String Trio 7; CZ-VM 451: String Trio 7; S-HÄ I1E1, 48, No. 1: String Trios 7–12, ordered 7, 9, 12, 10, 8, 11, parts for vln 1, b only; US-Wc M350.M28 Case, Nos. 1–4: String Trios 7–10, ordered 9, 8, 7, 10

Additional editions: Welcker 1772, Nos. 1–4: String Trios 7-10, ordered 9, 8, 7, 10; André 1777b: String Trios 7–12, ordered 8, 9, 12, 7, 11, 10; Freeman & Ackerman n.d.: String Trios 7-10

Cat. refs.: Breitkopf 1769 (p. 349): "VI. Trii," Nos. 1, 2, 3, 6: String Trios 9, 7, 10, and 8, respectively; Breitkopf 1779/80 (p. 679): André 1777b; Hofmeister 1817, p. 79: André 1777b

Notes: Evans/Dearling cites "US-Wc M351.M66" and "S-Skma, ms" as ms. sources for these six trios. According to library staff, the first shelf number appears to be an incomplete reference to M351.M66 Op. 2 Case, which is, however, not a ms. but the print André 1777b. The second library reference corresponds to the print La Chevardière 1768 (communications, US-Wc, 6 March 1995; S-Skma, 25 January 1995).

String Trio (Orchestral Trio) 13: G major, 1769 or before [3:G1]

Ms. sources: A-Wgm IX 23414 ("c"); CZ-Pnm V B 71 (Jan Pohl collection); CZ-Pnm XLIX C 232 (Radenín); I-Mc Da Camera Ms. 17/1; US-Wc M350.M28 Case, No. 5; US-Wc M351.M975 Case: ms. dated 1775

Cat. ref.: Breitkopf 1769 (p. 349): "VI. Trii," No. 4

Editions: Welcker 1772, No. 5; Freeman & Ackerman n.d.

Notes: Evans/Dearling cites "S-Skma Od-R" as a ms. source for String Trios 13–14. According to the staff, the library has no Mysliveček mss. for trios; however, that reference does correspond to the print Welcker 1772 (communication, 1 February 1995).

String Trio (Orchestral Trio) 14: B-flat major, 1769 or before [3:B-flat 2]

Ms. sources: A-Wgm IX 23414 ("f"); CZ-Pnm V B 71 (Jan Pohl collection): two copies, one arr. vln, pf; CZ-Pnm XLIX C 233 (Radenín); US-Wc M350.M28 Case, No. 6; US-Wc M351.M975P Case: ms. dated 1775

Cat. ref.: Breitkopf 1769 (p. 349): "VI Trii," No. 5

Editions: Welcker 1772, No. 6; Freeman & Ackerma n.d.

Note: See the note under the previous entry.

String Trios 15–20:

6 string trios in Le Menu 1772.

No. 1 = String Trio 15 (C major) [3:C2]
No. 2 = String Trio 16 (G major) [3:G2]
No. 3 = String Trio 17 (E-flat major) [3:E-flat 3]
No. 4 = String Trio 18 (A major) [3:A4]
No. 5 = String Trio 19 (B-flat major) [3:B-flat 3]
No. 6 = String Trio 20 (F major) [3:F3]

Ms. sources: A-M V 91 ("No. 1"): String Trio 16; A-M V 92 ("No. 3"): String Trio 18; A-M V 93 ("No. 4"): String Trio 17; A-M V 94 ("No. 5"): String Trio 15; A-M V 95 ("No. 6"): String Trio 20; A-M V 96 ("No. 2"): String Trio 19; A-Wgm IX 2174 ("g"): String Trio 18; CZ-Pnm V B 71 (Jan Pohl collection): String Trio 18, two copies, one arr. vln, pf; CZ-Pnm XIII C 130 (Josef Šrogl collection): String Trio 16, arr. vln, pf; CZ-Pnm XIII E 353 (Josef Šrogl collection): String Trio 16, 2nd and 3rd movements only, arr. vln, pf; CZ-Pnm XXVII B 6 (Horšovský Týn): String Trio 18; CZ-Pnm XXVII B 143 (Horšovský Týn): String Trio 17; CZ-Pnm XXXVII F 388: String Trio 16; CZ-Pnm XXXVII F 394 (Břevnov): String Trio 16, 2nd movement only; ms. dated 1847; CZ-Pnm XXXVII F 397 (Břevnov): String Trio 16, 3rd movement only; I-Mc Da Camera Ms. 17/2: String Trio 20; I-Rdp 205, Nos. 1–6: String Trios 15-20, ordered 19, 20, 18, 15, 16, 17; US-Wc M350.M3 Case: Nos. 1–6: String Trios 15–20, ordered 19, 20, 18, 15, 16, 17

Cat. refs.: Breitkopf 1773 (p. 492): String Trio 19, attr. Lang; Qb 1775 Ch C 52: String Trio 15; Qb 1775 Ch E 54: String Trio 17; Qb 1775 Ch F 35: String Trio 20; Qb 1775 Ch G 48: String Trio 16; Qb 1775; Ch A 41: String Trio 18; Qb 1775 Ch B 42: String Trio 19: all entries in Qb 1775 attr. "Venatorino"

Notes: Evans/Dearling cites "F-Pn Vm^7 1219, Ac e3 133" as a ms. source for these six trios. That library shelf number, however, corresponds to the print Le Menu 1772.

String Trio 21: G major, date? [3:G4]

Scoring: vln, vlc, b

Ms. sources: CZ-Pnm V B 78 (Jan Pohl collection); CZ-Pnm XLIL C 234; 235 (Radenín): ms. ca. 1780

Edition: *Trio, housle, violoncello, kontrabass*, ed. Bohumil Malotín, Edice hrajeme doma, 9 (Prague: Editio Supraphon, 1975)

Recording: M. Chernyakhovsky, vln, Fedor Luzanov, vlc, V. Gataullin, cb, Levné Knihy LK 0322–2, 2005 [CD]

String Trio 22: D major, date? [3:D5]

Ms. source: CZ-Pnm XLIX C 238 (Radenín)

String Trio 23: E major, date? [3:E1]

Ms. source: I-Pca D-V-1806: 3rd movement fragmentary

Note: According to the ms., the first trio of a set of six (the rest perhaps concordant with other sources listed here).

String Trio 24: F major, date? [3:F5]

Ms. sources: CZ-Pnm V B 76 (Jan Pohl collection); CZ-Pnm XLIX C 237 (Radenín)

String Trio 25: F major, date? [3:F7]

Ms. source: CZ-Pu 59 R 3463 (Panenský Týnec)

String Trio 26: G major, date? [3:G7]

Ms. source: CZ-Pnm XLIX C 239 (Radenín)

String Trio 27: A major, date? [3:A6]

Ms. sources: CZ-Pnm V B 77 (Jan Pohl collection); CZ-Pnm XLIX C 236 (Radenín)

Sonatas for Two Cellos and Bass (Cello Duets) 1–6:

6 sonatas for two cellos and bass in CZ-Pnm XLIX C 247 (Radenín), a ms. of ca. 1780, and CZ-Pnm V B 79 (Jan Pohl collection), a modern copy of the Radenín ms. The sonatas are undatable, but perhaps composed in Munich, 1777–78.

No. 1 = Cello Duet 1 (A major) [3:A5]
No. 2 = Cello Duet 2 (D major) [3:D3]
No. 3 = Cello Duet 3 (G major) [3:G5]
No. 4 = Cello Duet 4 (F major) [3:F4]
No. 5 = Cello Duet 5 (C major) [3:C5]
No. 6 = Cello Duet 6 (B-flat major) [3:B-flat 5]

Edition: *Sonata sol' mazhor dlia dvuch violoncheli s basom*, ed. Lev Ginzburg, arr. vlc, pf by Bohuš Heran (Moscow: Muzgiz, 1960): Cello Duet 3

Recordings: Pro Arte Antiqua Praha, Harmonia Mundi HMO 30.509, [195-] [LP]: Cello Duet 3; Radomír Širc and Jan Širc, vlc, Václav Hoskovec, string bass, and Robert Hugo, hpd, Matouš MK 0019-2131, 1994 [CD]: Cello Duets 1-6; Radomír Širc and Jan Širc, vlc, Václav Hoskovec, string bass, and Robert Hugo, hpd, Matouš MK 704–2131, 1999 [CD]: 3rd movement of Cello 3, 2nd movement of Cello Duet 1, and 3rd movement of Cello Duet 5 only; Michal Kaňka and František Host, vlc, Jiří Hůdec and Jaroslav Tůma, continuo, Praga PRD 250 132, 1999 [CD]: Cello Duets 1–6; Fedor Luzanov, vlc, J. Cheglakova, pf, Levné Knihy LK 0322–2, 2005 [CD]: Cello Duet 3, arr. vlc, pf, after Ginzburg ed. of 1960

Part 10

TRIOS FOR FLUTE, VIOLIN, AND BASS (FLUTE TRIOS)

Flute Trios 1–6:

6 trios for flute, violin, and bass in Del Vivo 5, probably from the late 1770s.

No. 1 = Flute Trio 1 (D major) [3:D4]
No. 2 = Flute Trio 2 (G major) [3:G6]
No. 3 = Flute Trio 3 (C major) [3:C6]
No. 4 = Flute Trio 4 (A major) [3:A7]
No. 5 = Flute Trio 5 (F major) [3:F6]
No. 6 = Flute Trio 6 (B-flat major) [3:B-flat 6]

Ms. sources: A-HE VI a 5, No. "I": Flute Trio 2; A-HE VI a 5, No. "IV": Flute Trio 4; A-HE VI a 5, No. "V": Flute Trio 5; CZ-Bm A 7520: 2nd movement only of Flute Trio 2, arr. vln, pf; CZ-Pnm II C 58 (Roman Nejedlý collection): Flute Trios 1–3 and 6, ordered 3, 1, 2, 6; CZ-Pnm V B 55 (Jan Pohl collection): Flute Trios 1–3 and 6, ordered 3, 1, 2, 6; CZ-Pnm XIII E 263 (Josef Šrogl collection): 2nd movement only of Flute Trio 2, arr. vln, pf; CZ-Pnm XIII F 378 (Josef Šrogl collection): 2nd movement only of Flute Trio 2, arr. vln, pf; CZ-Pnm XXXVIII C 496 (Alois Altrichter collection): Flute Trio 6; CZ-Pnm XLIV E 520 (Václav Král collection): Flute Trio 6, arr. as string quartet; CZ-Pnm XLIV E 532 (Václav Král collection): Flute Trio 6, arr. as string quartet; I-Mc Da Camera 86/5, nos. 1–4: Flute Trios 1–3 and 6, ordered 3, 2, 1, 6; I-MTventuri A19: Flute Trios 1–6

Additional editions: Schmitt: Flute Trios 1–3 and 6, ordered 3, 1, 2, 6; Bland 1790: Flute Trios 3 and 6; *Trio für Flöte, Violine und Violoncello*, ed. Hugo Riemann, Collegium Musicum, 20 (Leipzig: Breitkopf & Härtel, 1904) and reprint as *Trio in B-flat Major, Opus 1, No. 4* (New York: International Music Co., 1948): Flute Trio 6; *Sonata Op. 1, c. III* (Kutná Hora: Česká hudba, 1914): Flute Trio 2, no editor specified; *Trio in B-flat Major for Flute, Violin and Cello*, Kalmus Chamber Music Series (Melville, NY: Belwin Mills, 19—): Flute Trio 6; *Sonate in B-dur, für Flöte (Oboe), Violine und Violoncello*, ed. Hans Steinbeck (Zürich: Edition Eulenburg, 1972): Flute Trio 6; now published by Edition Kunzelmann, Adliswil; Klement 1978: Flute Trios 1–3 and 6, ordered 3, 1, 2, 6; *Trio in G á flauto traverso, violino con basso*, ed. T. Donley

Thomas (Bellingham, WA: Medici Music Press, 1983): Flute Trio 2; *Trio in A á flauto traverso, violino con basso*, ed. T. Donley Thomas (Bellingham, WA: Medici Music Press, 1983): Flute Trio 4; Kölbel 1991: Flute Trios 1 and 3; Freeman 2001: Flute Trios 1–6

Recordings: Genser-Winkler Trio, Musical Heritage Society MHS 524, [1963?] [LP]: Flute Trio 6, performed with fl, vln, vlc, pf; Ars Rediviva Ensemble, Supraphon 111 3376, 1984 [LP]: Flute Trios 2 and 6; Adamus Wind Trio (arr. Jan Adamus for ob, cl, bsn), Supraphon 111 3596, 1986 [LP]: Flute Trio 2; Reicha Trio, Arta Records F10051–2, 1996 [CD]: Flute Trio 1; Accademia Farnese, Mondo Musica MM 96022, 1996 [CD]: Flute Trios 1–6; Václav Kunt, fl, Petr Maceček, vln, Karel Fiala, vlc, Jaroslav Tůma, hpd, EZ Gramofonové Závody Z1 0336–2131, 1998 [CD]: Flute Trios 1–6; Trio Spektrum, North Pacific Music LD005, 1999 [CD]: Flute Trio 6, arr. Tomáš Svoboda for fl, cl, and pf

Notes: Evans/Dearling cites "GB-Gu, ms" as a ms. source for trios nos. 3 and 6. According to library staff, GB-Gu has no Mysliveček mss., but holds the only exemplar of the print Bland 1790 (communication, 31 March 1995).

Part 11

DUETS FOR TWO FLUTES AND BASS (FLUTE DUETS)

Flute Duets 1–6:

6 duets in ms. I-MTventuri A20, all perhaps written in the mid-1770s.

No. 1 = Flute Duet 1 (G major) [3:G3]
No. 2 = Flute Duet 2 (C major) [3:C3]
No. 3 = Flute Duet 3 (A minor) [3:a1]
No. 4 = Flute Duet 4 (E minor) [3:e1]
No. 5 = Flute Duet 5 (D major) [3:D2]
No. 6 = Flute Duet 6 (B-flat major) [3:B-flat 4]

Cat. ref.: I-MTventuri ("Op. 5")

Additional ms. sources: A-HE VI a 5, No. "3": Flute Duet 3; A-HE VI a 5, No. "4": Flute Duet 4; A-HE VI a 5, No. "5": Flute Duet 1; A-HE VI a 5, No. "6": Flute Duet 6; HR-Dsmb 27/862: Flute Duet 1; PL-SA A VII 29: Flute Duet 1 scored for fl, fl or vln, vlc

Editions: *Trio in G*, ed. T. Donley Thomas (Bellingham, WA: Medici Music Press, 1985): Flute Duet 1; *Trio in A minor*, ed. T. Donley Thomas (Bellingham, WA: Medici Music Press, 1985): Flute Duet 3; *Trio in E minor*, ed. T. Donley Thomas (Bellingham, WA: Medici Music Press, 1985): Flute Duet 4; *Trio in B-flat major*, ed. T. Donley Thomas (Bellingham, WA: Medici Music Press, 1985): Flute Duet 6

Notes: Cat. ref. Vester M 850 identified an edition of trios published in Paris by Bérault ca. 1775–77 as Mysliveček's Op. 5. No exemplar of this print was cited by Vester, and none has ever been identified, thus its contents cannot be matched definitively with any incipits. It is possible, however, that the works in the print are the trios designated

"Op. 5" in the ms. I-MTventuri (Flute Duets 1–6). Evans/Dearling lists the match unequivocally. It is possible to verify the offer of Mysliveček trios for sale in a Bérault catalog of ca. 1775 from a facsimile (plate 9) published in Cari Johansson, *French Music Publishers' Catalogues of the Second Half of the Eighteenth Century* (Stockholm: Musikaliska Akademiens Bibliotek, 1955), but no further information is available about a Bérault print of Mysliveček trios.

Part 12

SONATAS FOR VIOLIN AND BASS OR VIOLIN AND KEYBOARD (VIOLIN SONATAS)

Violin Sonatas 1–2:

2 sonatas for violin and bass in undated ms. I-Gl N.1.7.3. (Sc 19), perhaps from the 1760s.

No. 1 = Violin Sonata 1 (A major) [2:A1]
No. 2 = Violin Sonata 2 (B-flat major) [2:B-flat 3]

Additional ms. source: I-VEas ms.n.44: Violin Sonata 2

Note: The Violin Sonatas 1–5 have been placed here before the Violin Sonatas 6–23 because their archaic instrumentation for violin and bass is probably an indication that they were composed before the violin sonatas with a fully written-out keyboard part.

Violin Sonata 3: G major, 1760s? [2:G3]

Scoring: vln, b
Ms. source: I-Gl M.4.29.17. (No. "I")

Violin Sonata 4: C major, 1760s? [2:C3]

Scoring: vln, b
Ms. source: I-Gl M.4.29.18. (No. "IV")

Violin Sonata 5: F major, 1760s? [2:F3]

Scoring: vln, b
Ms. source: I-Gl M.4.29.19. (No. "V")

Violin Sonatas 6–11:

6 sonatas for violin and keyboard in Thompson 1775.

No. 1 = Violin Sonata 6 (E-flat major) [2:E-flat 1]
No. 2 = Violin Sonata 7 (D major) [2:D1]
No. 3 = Violin Sonata 8 (C major) [2:C2]

No. 4 = Violin Sonata 9 (B-flat major) [2:B-flat 1]
No. 5 = Violin Sonata 10 (G major) [2:G1]
No. 6 = Violin Sonata 11 (F major) [2:F1]

Additional edition: In *Böhmische Klaviermusik im Zeitalter der Klassik*, ed. Sonja Gerlach and Zdeňka Pilková (Munich: Henle, 1985): Violin Sonata 7

Recording: Oldřich Kredba, hpd, Supraphon SUG 20017, [195-]: Violin Sonata 7 arr. for hpd solo

Violin Sonatas 12–17:

6 sonatas for violin and keyboard in CZ-Pnm XIII F 383, a ms. dated 1777.
No. 1 = Violin Sonata 12 (D major) [2:D2]
No. 2 = Violin Sonata 13 (F major) [2:F2]
No. 3 = Violin Sonata 14 (E-flat major) [2:E-flat 2]
No. 4 = Violin Sonata 15 (G major) [2:G2]
No. 5 = Violin Sonata 16 (B-flat major) [2:B-flat 2]
No. 6 = Violin Sonata 17 (E-flat major) [2:E-flat 3]

Additional ms. sources: I-MC 1-C-17/13a–b: Violin Sonatas 12-13; I-MC 1-C-17/13d–f: Violin Sonatas 15–17

Violin Sonatas 18–23:

6 sonatas for violin and keyboard in undated ms. CZ-Pnm XIII F 381.
No. 1 = Violin Sonata 18 (D major) [2:D3]
No. 2 = Violin Sonata 19 (G major) [2:G4]
No. 3 = Violin Sonata 20 (C major) [2:C4]
No. 4 = Violin Sonata 21 (B-flat major) [2:B-flat 4]
No. 5 = Violin Sonata 22 (F major) [2:F4]
No. 6 = Violin Sonata 23 (C major) [2:C5]

Additional ms source: I-MC 1-C-17/13c: Violin Sonata 20

QUESTIONABLE WORKS

1. Minuet in D major, date? [2:D4]

   Scoring: vln, pf

   Ms. source: CZ-Pnm XIII E 351, No. 1 (Josef Šrogl collection)

   Note: Arrangement made from an unknown source by Josef Šrogl in 1914.

2. Minuet in E major, date? [2:EQ1]

   Scoring: vln, pf

   Ms. source: CZ-Pnm XIII E 361 (Josef Šrogl collection): transposed to E-flat major

   Editions: *Menuetto per il violino con accompagnato di cembalo*, ed. Jaroslav Čeleda (Kutná Hora: Česká hudba, 1930); in *Čestí klasíkové: předchůdci Smetanovi*, ed. Jan and Bohumír Št'edron,

Musica antiqua bohemica, 11 (Prague: Státní hudební vydavatelství, 1953; reprint four times to 1989; In *Dawni mistrzowie polscy i czescy*, ed. Franciszek Jamry and Kiejstut Bacewicz, Mała antologia skrzypcowa, 4 (Cracow: Polskie wydawnictwo muzyczne, 1957); in *Dva menuety*, ed. Jan Kratina, Edice lidových škol umění (Prague: Editio Supraphon, 1971)

Note: No pre-20th-century source is known for this work; the Čeleda edition, based on an edition in *Česká hudba* 31 (1928–29), constitutes the earliest record of it.

3. Adagio in B-flat major, date? [2:B-flatQ1]

Scoring: vln, hpd

Edition: *Adagio: housle a cembalo*, ed. Jaroslav Čeleda, Staří mistři, 15 (Kutná Hora: Česká hudba, 1933)

Note: No pre-20th-century source is known for this work; the Čeleda edition constitutes the earliest record of it.

Part 13

SONATA FOR CELLO AND BASS

Cello Sonata in C major, 1770 or before [2:C1; Lost]

Cat. ref.: Breitkopf 1770 (p. 391)

Part 14

KEYBOARD SONATAS

Keyboard Sonatas 1–6:

6 sonatas for keyboard in Longman & Broderip 1777.

No. 1 = Keyboard Sonata 1 (F major) [1:F1]
No. 2 = Keyboard Sonata 2 (A major) [1:A1]
No. 3 = Keyboard Sonata 3 (D major) [1:D1]
No. 4 = Keyboard Sonata 4 (B-flat major) [1:B-flat 1]
No. 5 = Keyboard Sonata 5 (G major) [1:G1]
No. 6 = Keyboard Sonata 6 (C major) [1:C1]

Ms. sources: CZ-Pnm XIII F 384: Keyboard Sonatas 1–6; I-MC 1-C-17/13g–l: Keyboard Sonatas 1–6; I-MC 4-A-16e: Keyboard Sonata 1 only

Additional editions: Emingerová 1919, No. 1: Keyboard Sonata 5; Emingerová 1919, No. 2: Keyboard Sonata 2; Emingerová 1919, No. 3: Keyboard Sonata 3; Emingerová 1919, No. 6: Keyboard Sonata 1; *Divertimenta* 1930: Keyboard Sonatas 1–6; Emingerová & Kredba 1954, No. 2: Keyboard Sonata 2; Emingerová & Kredba 1954, No. 3: Keyboard Sonata 1; Emingerová & Kredba 1954, No. 4: Keyboard Sonata 3; Emingerová & Kredba 1954, No. 5: Keyboard Sonata 5; Emingerová & Kredba 1961, No. 2: Keyboard Sonata 2; Emingerová & Kredba 1961, No. 3: Keyboard Sonata 1; Emingerová & Kredba 1961, No. 4: Keyboard Sonata 3; Emingerová & Kredba 1961, No. 5: Keyboard Sonata 5; in *Klasíkové a jejich současníci*, vol. 2, ed. Alois Saurer and Drahomíra Křížková-Černá (Prague: Editio Supraphon, 1971): Keyboard Sonata 3; Jícha 1981, No. 1: Keyboard Sonata 2, arr. fl or vl and guitar; Jícha 1981, No. 2: Keyboard Sonata 3, arr. vl or fl and guitar; Salter 1983: Keyboard Sonatas 1–6

Recordings: Josef Hála, hpd, Supraphon 111 3728, 1983 [LP]: Keyboard Sonatas 1, 2, and 5; Antonín Kubálek, pf, Dorian DOR-90121, 1989 [CD]: Keyboard Sonata 3

Keyboard Sonatas 7–12:

6 sonatas for keyboard in Corri & Sutherland 1784.

No. 1 = Keyboard Sonata 7 (C major) [1:C2]
No. 2 = Keyboard Sonata 8 (B-flat major) [1:B-flat 2]
No. 3 = Keyboard Sonata 9 (A major) [1:A2]
No. 4 = Keyboard Sonata 10 (G major) [1:G2]
No. 5 = Keyboard Sonata 11 (F major) [1:F2]
No. 6 = Keyboard Sonata 12 (D major) [1:D2]

Ms. sources: A-Wn Mus.Hs. 2413 (ff. 33'–53): Keyboard Sonatas 7–12; CZ-Pnm XVI B 270, No. 1: Keyboard Sonata 12; CZ-Pnm XVI B 270, No. 2: Keyboard Sonata 11; CZ-Pnm XVI B 270, No. 3: Keyboard Sonata 9; CZ-Pnm XVI B 270, No. 8: Keyboard Sonata 8; D-B Mus. ms. autogr. Misliweczek 2: Keyboard Sonata 12; D-B Mus. ms. 14530/1: Keyboard Sonata 12; D-B Mus. ms. 14530/2: Keyboard Sonata 10; D-B Mus. ms. 14530/3: Keyboard Sonata 10; D-B Mus. ms. 14530/4: Keyboard Sonata 11; D-Mbs Mus. ms. 1712/1-6: Keyboard Sonatas 7–12; D-Rtt Mysliveček 8: Keyboard Sonatas 7–12, ms. ca. 1780; I-Bsf Fc. M.V. 14 ("sonata IV"): Keyboard Sonata 11; I-PEsp MCXXXII/32: Keyboard Sonatas 7–12

Additional editions: Emingerová 1919, No. 4: 2nd movement only of Keyboard Sonata 8; Emingerová 1919, No. 5: 2nd movement only of Keyboard Sonata 9; in *Čeští mistři XVIII. století*, ed. Josef Flegl (Prague: Urbánek, 1936): 2nd movement only of Keyboard Sonata 8; Branberger & Rožková 1938: Keyboard Sonatas 7–12; Emingerová & Kredba 1954, No. 1: 2nd movement only of Keyboard Sonata 8; Emingerová & Kredba 1954, No. 6: 2nd movement only of Keyboard Sonata 9; Emingerová & Kredba 1954, No. 7: Keyboard Sonata 12; in *Čeští mistři XVIII. století*, ed. Josef Flegl, revised by Ladislav Láska (Prague: Státní nakladatelství krásné literatury, hudby a umění, 1957): 2nd movement only of Keyboard Sonata 8; Emingerová & Kredba 1961, No. 1: 2nd movement only of Keyboard Sonata 8; Emingerová & Kredba 1961, No. 6: 2nd movement only of Keyboard Sonata 9; Emingerová & Kredba 1961, No. 7: Keyboard Sonata 12; *Sonate en re majeur pour flûte et guitarre*, arr. Jean-Maurice Mourat, Collection Robert Hériché-J. Maurice Mourat (Paris: Girard Billaudot,

1986): Keyboard Sonata 12, arr. fl, guitar; Němec & Zuckerová 1988: Keyboard Sonatas 7-12; in *Böhmische Klaviermusik im Zeitalter der Klassik*, 2, ed. Peter Roggenkamp (Vienna: Universal Edition, 1990): Keyboard Sonata 12

Recordings: János Sebestyén, hpd, Candide CE 31033, [197-] [LP]: Keyboard Sonata 8, 2nd movement only; Josef Hála, hpd, Supraphon 111 3728, 1983 [LP] : Keyboard Sonatas 7–12

Note: The 2nd movement of Keyboard Sonata 7 was arranged as a duet for two flutes and published as a "favourite minuet" ca. 1790 (see Part 5).

Keyboard Sonata 13: C major, date? [1:C3]

Ms. source: I-PEsp MCXXXII/31, c. 14–16

Part 15

MISCELLANEOUS WORKS FOR SOLO INSTRUMENTS

1. "Marchia" for keyboard, E-flat major, date? [Lost; missing from Evans/Dearling]

   Cat. refs.: Fugger, p. 121; Kroyer (Bl. 126)

   Notes: Formerly in the collection of the Princes Fugger von Babenhausen (destroyed during World War II). The work represents an arrangement for keyboard of an orchestral march from the oratorio *Isacco figura del redentore*.

2. "Gesellschafts Sonate" for guitar, E major, date? [probably spurious; missing from Evans/Dearling]

   Ms. source: A-Wn Mus.Hs. 14.375: 19th-century ms.

Catalog 2

SOURCES OF MYSLIVEČEK'S VOCAL MUSIC

Part 1

OPERAS

Asterisks indicate autograph scores; vocal "excerpts" refer to ms. sources listed in Part 9; detailed information on sources of operatic *sinfonie* is found in Catalog 1.

1. *Semiramide* (Bergamo, Teatro di Cittadella, summer fair 1766) [BohadloCat I.1]

   Librettist: Pietro Metastasio

   Libretto: I-BGc

   Score: P-La

   Excerpts: 1 aria in CZ-LIT; 1 terzetto in CZ-Pa; 2 arias in CZ-Pkříž; 5 arias (+ 2 duplicates) and 1 terzetto (+ 1 duplicate) in CZ-Pnm; 1 aria and 1 terzetto in CZ-Psj; 2 arias in CZ-TEP; 1 terzetto in CZ-VM; 1 terzetto in I-MAav; *sinfonia* in CZ-Pnm (2 copies), US-Wc

   Cast: Caterina Galli (Semiramide); Carlo Nicolini (Scitalce); Marianna Bucinelli (Tamiri); Adamo Solzi (Mirteo); Antonio Pini (Ircano); Rosa Polidora (Sibari)

   Note: Sartori incorrectly indicates 1765 as the publication date of the libretto.

   ________ (as *Semiramide riconosciuta*; Alessandria, Teatro Guasco, 7 October 1766)

   Libretto: I-Vnm

   Cast: Caterina Galli (Semiramide); Antonio Perelini (Scitalce); Marianna Bucinelli (Tamiri); Adamo Solzi (Mirteo); Antonio Pini (Ircano); Domenico Bicht (Sibari)

   ________ (Parma?, date?)

   Note: A performance in Parma is suggested by the survival of a score of *Semiramide* copied in Parma in P-La and a claim in Pelcl that Mysliveček's first opera was performed there.

   ________ (Alessandria?, "fiera d'ottobre" 1767)

   Note: A production in Alessandria is indicated in the score of *Semiramide* preserved in CZ-Pnm.

   ________ (as *Semiramide riconosciuta*; Prague, Divadlo v Kotcích, autumn 1768)

   Libretto: CZ-Pu

Score: CZ-Pnm (incomplete, dated 1769)

Cast: Angela Calori (Semiramide); Giovanni Priori (Scitalce); Barbara Girelli (Tamiri); Francesco Bossio (Mirteo); Giovanni Ansani (Ircano); N.N. (Cibari)

________ (Prague?, Divadlo v Kotcích, 1769)

Note: A production in Prague in 1769 is indicated in the score of *Semiramide* preserved in CZ-Pnm.

2. *Bellerofonte* (Naples, Teatro San Carlo, 20 January 1767) [BohadloCat I.2]

Librettist: Giuseppe Bonecchi

Libretto: B-Bc, I-Bc, I-MAC, I-Nc

Score: F-Pn (dated 1769), I-Fc, I-Rdp (Act 1 only; parts for vl, vla only), P-La (2 copies)

Excerpts: 1 aria and 1 duet in A-Wgm; 1 duet in A-Wn; 1 aria in CH-E; 1 aria in CH-FF; 1 aria in CH-MÜ; 3 arias (+ 2 duplicates) and 1 duet in CZ-Bm; 2 arias in CZ-BER; 1 aria in CZ-BRE; 1 aria in CZ-BRO; 1 aria in CZ-CH; 3 arias (+ 1 duplicate) in CZ-Jlm; 1 aria in CZ-K; 3 arias in CZ-KL; 2 arias in CZ-KRa; 2 arias in CZ-KU; 1 aria in CZ-Lla; 1 duet in CZ-LO; 2 arias (+ 1 duplicate) in CZ-MB; 6 arias (+ 1 duplicate) and 1 duet in CZ-Pkříž; 11 arias (+ 27 duplicates), 1 duet (+ 3 duplicates), and 1 terzetto (+ 3 duplicates) in CZ-Pnm; 4 arias and 1 duet in CZ-Psj; 2 arias (+ 2 duplicates) and 1 terzetto in CZ-Pu; 1 aria in CZ-Puh; 4 arias in CZ-PEL; 1 aria in CZ-PLa; 1 aria in CZ-RU; 1 aria in CZ-TEb; 5 arias in CZ-TREd; 1 aria (+ 1 duplicate) and 1 duet (+ 1 duplicate) in D-B; 1 aria in D-LÜh; 1 duet in D-MÜs; 1 aria (+ 1 duplicate) in D-RH; 1 aria in DK-Kk; 1 aria in F-Pn; 1 aria in HR-Zha; 1 aria in I-Bc; 1 aria in I-Gl; 2 arias (+ 1 duplicate) and 1 duet in I-MC; 1 aria (+ 1 duplicate) in I-Nc; 1 aria in I-Rsc; 1 aria in I-Vc; 1 aria in PL-Kd; 3 arias (+ 2 duplicates) in PL-Wu; 1 duet in S-Skma; 1 aria in SK-Mms; 2 arias in US-BEm; 1 duet in US-Wc; *sinfonia* in CZ-Pnm (3 copies), D-SWl

Cast: Anton Raaff (Ariobate); Caterina Gabrielli (Argene); Ferdinando Mazzanti (Bellerofonte); Francesca Gabrielli (Briseide); Angelo Monnani (Diomede); Giuseppe Coppola (Atamante); Giuseppe Benigni (Minerva)

Editions: aria "Palesar vorrei col pianto" as *Aria für Sopran, Horn, und Klavier aus der Oper "Il Bellerofonte,"* arr. Peter Schmalfuss (Koblenz: P. Schmitt, 1994), also as *Triosatz für Klarinette (oder Violine, Flöte, Oboe), Horn (Fagott) und Klavier aus der Oper "Il Bellerofonte*, arr. Peter Schmalfuss (Koblenz: P. Schmitt, 1994) and *Aria aus der Oper "Il Bellerofonte" übertragen für Sopran, Horn ad lib. & Klavier/ Tasteninstrument*, arr. Peter Schmalfuss (Magdeburg: Edition Walhall, 1998)

Recordings: Marta Boháčová, soprano, Musici di Praga, cond. František Vajnar, Panton 11 0229, 1970 [LP]: aria "Palesar vorrei col pianto" with text "Quod est in igne calor"; Prague Chamber Orchestra, cond. Zoltán Peskó, various soloists, Supraphon SUP 0006–2, 1987 [CD]: complete opera; Zdena Kloubová, soprano, Benda Chamber Orchestra, cond. Miroslav Hrdlička, Panton 81 1044–2231, 1992 [CD]: arias "Splende così talora" with text "O coena nuptialis," "Ch'io mai capace" with text "Tibi laus Deus," and "Palesar vorrei col pianto" with text "Ave digna mundi laude"; Věnceslava Hrubá-Freiberger, soprano, Virtuosi di Praga, cond. Oldřich Vlček, Lupulus Clara 57 010–2, 1992 [CD]: aria "Palesar vorrei col pianto" with text "Quod est in igne calor"; Trio Cantabile (Lydie Hartelová, harp, Václav Kunt, flute, Ludmila Vernerová, soprano), MusicVars VA0113–2, 2000 [CD]: aria "Qual ristretto in picciol letto" with text "Cesset umbra tenebrosa"; Věnceslava Hrubá-Freiberger, soprano, Virtuosi di Praga, cond. Oldřich Vlček, Cantus-Lin 5.00126, 2001 [CD]: aria "Palesar vorrei col pianto" with text "Quod est in igne calor"

________ (Siena, Accademia degl'Intronati, spring 1767)

Libretto: I-Rn, I-Rsc, I-Vgc, US-Wc (music attr. Mysliveček "ed altri valenti autori"; libretto bears date 6 May 1767)

Cast: Salvatore Casetti (Ariobate); Maria Piccinelli Vezziani (Argene); Domenico Luciani (Bellerofonte); Margarita Giannelli (Briseide); Angelo Monnani (Diomede); Fedele Rossellini (Atamante); Gaetano Gai (Minerva)

________ (Prague, Divadlo v Kotcích, carnival 1768)

Libretto: CZ-Bu, CZ-KRI, CZ-Pu, CZ-RY (all erroneously dated 1767)

Score: D-Dl

Cast: Antonio Prati (Ariobate); Angela Calori (Argene); Emanuelle Cornacchia (Bellerofonte); Marianna Ottini (Briseide); Stella Lodi (Diomede); Giovanni Delpini (Atamante)

________ (Naples?, Teatro San Carlo, 1769)

Note: A production in Naples is indicated in the score of *Bellerofonte* preserved in F-Pn and an aria in I-Vc.

3. *Farnace* (Naples, Teatro San Carlo, 4 November 1767) [BohadloCat I.4]

Librettist: Antonio Maria Lucchini

Libretto: I-Bc, I-Nc

Score: D-Mbs, H-Bn, I-Nc,* P-La (2 copies)

Excerpts: *sinfonia* in CZ-Pnm, I-Gl

Cast: Carlo Reina (Farnace); Antonia Maria Girelli Aguilar (Tamiri); Clemenza Bardetti (Selinda); Ercole Ciprandi (Atridate); Giuseppe Compagnucci (Pompeo); Girolamo Speciali (Gilade)

________ (Prague, Divadlo v Kotcích, December 1768)

Libretto: CZ-KRI, CZ-MHz, CZ-Pnmk (Radenín), CZ-Pu

Cast: Antonio Priori (Farnace); Angela Calori (Tamiri); Barbara Girelli (Selinda); Giovanni Ansani (Atridate); Francesco Bossio (Pompeo); Franceso Menati (Gilade)

4. *Il trionfo di Clelia* (Turin, Teatro Regio, carnival 1768; 1st performance 26 December 1767) [BohadloCat I.3]

Librettist: Pietro Metastasio

Libretto: D-Mbs, I-Rsc, I-Tac, I-Tci, I-Tfanan, I-Tn, I-Tp, I-Vgc, US-BEm, US-Wc

Score: I-Fc, I-Tf, P-La

Excerpts: 1 aria in CH-BM; 2 arias in CH-E; 2 arias in CH-EN; 1 duet in CZ-BER; 1 aria in CZ-BRE; 3 arias in CZ-Pak; 5 arias in CZ-Pkříž; 9 arias (+ 9 duplicates) in CZ-Pnm; 2 arias in

CZ-Psj; 2 arias in CZ-Pu; 1 aria in CZ-TREd; 1 aria in D-BFb; 1 duet in I-MTventuri; *sinfonia* in CH-E, CH-EN, CZ-KRa, CZ-Pnm (4 copies), D-W, S-Skma

Cast: Gaetano Ottani (Porsenna); Caterina Gabrielli (Clelia); Luca Fabri (Orazio); Francesca Gabrielli (Larissa); Sebastiano Emiliani (Tarquinio); Filippo Lorenzini (Mannio)

5. *Demofoonte* (Venice, Teatro San Benedetto, carnival 1769; 1st performance 17 January 1769) [BohadloCat I.5]

Librettist: Pietro Metastasio

Libretto: A-Wmi, F-Pn, I-Mb, I-Vcg, I-Vnm, US-LAum, US-Wc

Score: I-Vnm (Act 1 only), P-La (2 copies)

Excerpts: 1 scene in CH-Gc; 2 arias in CZ-LIT; 2 arias in CZ-Pak; 1 aria in CZ-Pnm; 1 aria in D-B; 1 aria in D-EB; 1 aria in D-LÜh; 1 aria in DK-Ou; 1 aria in I-Bsf; 1 aria in I-Gl; 3 arias (+ 1 duplicate) in I-MC; 1 aria in I-MOe; 1 aria in I-OS; 1 aria in I-Tci; 6 arias and 1 scene and duet in US-BEm; 1 scene, 3 arias, and 1 duet in US-Wc; *sinfonia* in CZ-Pnm, D-Rtt, E-Mp, US-Wc

Cast: Franceso Zanetti (Demofoonte); Anna Lucia de Amicis-Buonsollazzi (Dircea); Gaetano Guadagni (Timante); Marianna Lombardi (Creusa); Giovanni Ripa (Cherinto); Franceso Sandali (Matusio); Giovanni Caffariello (Adrasto)

6. *Ipermestra* (Florence, Teatro della Pergola, spring 1769; 1st performance 27 March 1769) [BohadloCat I.6]

Librettist: Pietro Metastasio

Libretto: I-Bc, I-Fc

Score: A-Wn,* CZ-Pnm, I-Fc, P-La (Acts 1 and 3 only)

Excerpts: 1 aria in A-Wgm; 1 aria in CH-Gc; 1 aria in D-Dl; 2 arias in F-Pn; 1 aria in S-Skma; 1 aria in US-R; *sinfonia* in CZ-Pnm (3 copies), D-W

Cast: Anton Raaff (Danao); Elisabetta Teuber (Ipermestra); Adamo Solzi (Linceo); Daniella Mienci (Elpinice); Giuseppe Cicognani (Plestene); Filippo Bertocchini (Adrasto)

7. *La Nitteti* (Bologna, Teatro Nuovo Pubblico, spring 1770; 1st performance 29 April 1770) [BohadloCat I.7]

Librettist: Pietro Metastasio

Libretto: I-Bam, I-Bc, I-Lg, I-Tfanan (dedication dated 5 May 1770)

Score: I-Fc, P-La, RUS-SPit* (Acts 1 and 2 only)

Excerpts: 1 aria in CH-Gc; 1 aria in CZ-KU; 1 aria (+ 1 duplicate) in CZ-Pkříž; 1 aria (+ 1 duplicate) in CZ-Pnm; 1 aria in CZ-Psj; 1 aria in D-B; 1 aria in D-HR; 1 aria in D-Mbs; 2 arias in D-MÜs; 1 aria in D-TEGha; 2 arias in DK-Kk; 1 aria (+ 1 duplicate) in I-Bc; 2 arias in I-FZc; 1 scene in I-Gl; 1 aria in I-MAav; 1 aria in I-MC; 2 arias in I-Nc; 1 aria in I-OS; 1 aria in US-R; *sinfonia* in CZ-Pnm (3 copies), D-Rtt

Cast: Salvatore Casetti (Amasi); Tommaso Guarducci (Sammete); Clementina Spagnuoli (Beroe); Daniella Mienci (Nitteti); Marcello Pompili (Amenosi); Giacomo Panato (Bubaste)

Recording: Zdena Kloubová, soprano, Benda Chamber Orchestra, cond. Miroslav Hrdlička, Panton 81 1044–2231, 1992 [CD]: aria "Ah, non temer ben mio"

________ (Pavia, Teatro Nuovo, carnival 1777)

Note: Information about this production comes from Anelide Nascimbene, based on materials in I-PAVcb.

8. *Motezuma* (Florence, Teatro della Pergola, carnival 1771; 1st performance 23 January 1771) [BohadloCat I.8]

Librettist: Vittorio Amedeo Cigna-Santi

Libretto: I-Bc, I-Fc, I-Fm

Score: A-Wgm,* CZ-Pnm, I-Fc, P-La (Acts 2 and 3 only), US-Wc

Excerpts: 2 arias in D-B; 1 aria in D-LÜh; 1 aria in E-Mp; 2 arias (+ 1 duplicate) and 1 scene and cavatina in F-Pn; 1 aria (+ 1 duplicate) in I-Nc; 1 aria in I-MTventuri; *sinfonia* in D-WEY

Borrowing: 1 aria from *Motezuma* borrowed in oratorio *Isacco figura del redentore* ("Nel mar di tanti affanni")

Cast: Carlo Nicolini (Motezuma); Giovanni Carmignani (Guacozinga); Salvatore Casetti (Ferdinando Cortes); Marcello Pompili (Teutile); Maddalena Mori dalla Casa (Lisinga); Francesco Papi (Pilpatoe)

Edition: aria "Scherza il nocchier talora," in *Journal d'ariettes italiennes*, No. 137 (September 1784) (Paris: Bailleux, 1784): exemplars in B-Bc, B-Lc, F-Pa, F-Pn, S-Skma

Recording: Zdena Kloubová, soprano, Benda Chamber Orchestra, cond. Miroslav Hrdlička, Panton 81 1044–2231, 1992 [CD]: aria "Cara, che torna in pace"

9. *Il gran Tamerlano* (Milan, Regio-Ducal Teatro, carnival 1772; 1st performance 26 December 1771) [BohadloCat I.9]

Librettist: Agostino Piovene

Libretto: CDN-Tu, I-Bc, I-LDEsormani, I-Ma, I-Mb, I-Mc, I-Ms, I-Rn, I-Rsc, US-WC

Score: A-Wn,* F-Pn, I-Fc, P-La (Acts 1 and 3 only)

Excerpts: 1 aria in B-Bc; 2 arias (+ 1 duplicate) and 1 duet in CH-E; 1 scene in CZ-Pnm; 1 scene in CZ-Ps; 1 aria and a fragment of an aria in CZ-Pu; 1 aria in D-B; 1 scene formerly in D-DS; 1 duet in D-HR; 1 duet and 2 scenes without arias in F-Pn; 1 aria in I-CMbc; 1 aria in I-Mc; 1 chorus in I-Ms; 1 duet in I-MAav; 3 arias in I-MC; 1 aria in I-Nc; 1 aria in I-Pca; *sinfonia* in CH-Zz, I-Mc (2 copies)

Borrowings: 2 arias from *Il gran Tamerlano* borrowed in *Atide* ("Sento nell'alma mia" and "Tradito ed oppresso")

Cast: Giuseppe Millico (Tamerlano); Giovanni Battista Zonca (Bajazette); Antonia Maria Girelli Aguilar (Asteria); Giuseppe Cicognagni (Andronico); Anna Boselli (Irene); Rosa Polidora (Idaspe)

________ (Pavia, Teatro Nuovo, carnival 1776)

Note: Information about this performance comes from Anelide Nascimbene, based on materials in I-PAVcb.

10. *Demetrio* (Pavia, Teatro Nuovo, spring 1773; 1st performance 24 May 1773) [BohadloCat I.10]

Librettist: Pietro Metastasio

Libretto: I-Bc, I-BRq, I-PAc

Score: D-B,* I-Fc

Excerpts: 1 aria in A-Wgm; 4 arias in CH-E; 1 aria in CZ-CT; 1 aria in CZ-KRa; 1 aria in CZ-OP; 1 aria in CZ-Pnm; 6 arias in CZ-Pu; 6 arias (+ 1 duplicate) in D-B; 2 arias in DK-Ou; 4 arias in F-Pn; 1 aria in GB-Lbl; 1 aria in H-P; 1 aria in I-Gl; 1 scene and 1 aria in I-MC; 1 aria in I-Nc; 2 arias in S-Skma; *sinfonia* in CH-EN, I-Mc, I-Mcom, I-MAav

Cast: Lucrezia Aguiari (Cleonice); Giovanni Rubinelli (Alceste); Giuseppe Afferri (Fenicio); Giuseppe Benedetti (Olinto); Anna Benvenuti (Barsene); Rosa Polidora (Mitrane)

11. *Romolo ed Ersilia* (Naples, Teatro San Carlo, 13 August 1773) [BohadloCat I.11]

Librettist: Pietro Metastasio

Libretto: I-Bc, I-Fm, I-Nc, I-Rig, US-NYp

Score: A-Wgm* (Act 2 only), CZ-Pnm (Act 2 only), I-Fc, I-Nc, P-La

Excerpts: 1 duet in B-Bc; 1 duet in CZ-BER; 2 scenes and 1 aria in CZ-Pnm; 1 aria in CZ-Psj; 1 aria in CZ-Pu; 1 duet in D-B; 1 scene in D-MÜs; 1 aria in D-Tl; 3 arias (+ 1 duplicate) in F-Pn; 1 duet in I-Af; 2 arias in I-Mc; 1 scene (+ 3 duplicates) and 2 arias (+ 4 duplicates) in I-MC; 1 aria and 1 duet in I-Nc; 1 duet in S-Skma; 1 aria in SK-TR; 1 aria in US-LOu; 1 aria and 1 duet in US-Wc; *sinfonia* in F-Pn

Borrowings: 2 arias and final chorus from *Romolo ed Ersilia* borrowed in *Atide* (arias "Prence, che affanno" and "Quel traditore intendo"; chorus "Numi, che intenti siete")

Cast: Gasparo Pacchierotti (Romolo); Anna de Amicis-Buonsollazzi (Ersilia); Giuseppe Tibaldi (Curzio); Pietro Santi (Acronte); Margherita Gibetti (Valeria); Rosaria de Juliis (Ostilio)

12. *Antigona* (Turin, Teatro Regio, carnival 1774; first performance 26 December 1773) [BohadloCat I.12]

Librettist: Gaetano Roccaforte

Libretto: D-Mbs, I-Rsc, I-Tac, I-Tci, I-Tlegger, I-Tn, I-Tp, I-Tstrona, I-Vgc, I-VCa

Score: A-Wn,* P-La (Act 1 only; in spite of an indication in Santos, ms. 45-II-2 of P-La is actually a portion of Giovanni Battista Borghi"s *Ricimero* of 1773, not a continuation of *Antigona*)

Excerpts: 2 arias in CH-E; 1 aria in CZ-Pnm; 1 aria in D-Dl; 1 aria in I-MC; 1 aria in I-Nc; *sinfonia* in I-MAav, I-Rdp, I-RVE

Borrowing: *sinfonia* of *Antigona* shared with *Atide*

Cast: Elisabetta Teuber (Antigona); Giuseppe Afferri (Creonte); Venanzio Rauzzini (Euristeo); Francesca Varrese (Ermione); Lorenzo Piatti (Learco); Teresa Silvani (Alceste)

Recordings: Zdena Kloubová, soprano, Benda Chamber Orchestra, cond. Miroslav Hrdlička, Panton 81 1044-2231, 1992 [CD]: aria "Rendi il mar" with text "Nil me gladius vel parmo"; Magdalena Kožená, soprano, Prague Philharmonia, cond. Michel Swierczewski, Deutsche Grammophon 289 471 334–2, 2001 [CD]: aria "Sarò qual è del torrente"

13. *La clemenza di Tito* (Venice, Teatro San Benedetto, carnival 1774; 1st performance by 5 February 1774) [BohadloCat I.13]

Librettist: Pietro Metastasio

Libretto: I-Mb, I-Vcg, I-Vnm

Score: P-La
Excerpts: 2 scenes formerly in D-DS; 1 aria in HR-Sk; 1 aria in I-MC; 1 aria in I-Pca
Cast: Giovanni Ansani (Tito Vespasiano); Caterina Schindler (Vitellia); Maria Anna Schindler (Servilia); Pietro Benedetti (Sesto); Antonio Solari (Annio); Giacomo Fantoni (Publio)

14. *Atide* (Padua, Teatro Nuovo, June 1774, perhaps 13 June, the feast day of St. Anthony) [BohadloCat I.14]
Librettist: Tomaso Stanzani, after Philippe Quinault
Libretto: I-Mb, I-Pmc, I-Rn
Score: A-Wn,* I-Pl
Excerpts: 3 arias in CZ-Pak; 1 aria in D-LÜh; 1 aria in F-Pn; 1 aria in I-MC; *sinfonia* in I-MAav, I-Rdp
Borrowings: sinfonia of *Atide* shared with *Antigona;* 2 arias borrowed from *Il gran Tamerlano* ("Sento nell'alma mia" and "Tradito ed oppresso" with new text "Da quei vezzosi"); 2 arias ("Prence, che affanno" and "Quel traditore intendo") and final chorus ("Numi, che intenti siete" with new text "Numi, che in ciel regnate") borrowed from *Romolo ed Ersilia;* 1 aria borrowed in oratorio *Isacco figura del redentore* ("Lasciami adesso in pace")
Cast: Michele Neri (Atide); Giovanni Rubinelli (Adrasto); Angela Galliani (Erissena); Antonio Ansani (Licasto); Anna Benvenuti (Esione)
Edition: aria "Figlia ti lascio, addio" with parody text "Cara ti lascio, addio" in *The Favourite Songs in the Opera Alessandro nelle Indie* (London: Napier, London, [1779]): exemplar in US-AUS

15. *Artaserse* (Naples, Teatro San Carlo, 13 August 1774) [BohadloCat I.15]
Librettist: Pietro Metastasio
Libretto: I-Bc, I-Nn, I-Pmc, US-NYp
Score: I-Fc, I-Nc
Excerpts: 1 aria in CH-Bu; 1 aria in CZ-LIT; 1 aria in CZ-Pnm; 5 arias and 1 duet in CZ-Pu; 1 aria in D-B; 1 aria in D-MÜs; 1 scene in E-Mp; 3 arias (+ 2 duplicates) in F-Pn; 1 aria in I-Bsf; 1 aria in I-BGc; 2 arias in I-Mc; 1 aria in I-Mcom; 1 scene (+ 1 duplicate) and 3 arias (+ 3 duplicates) in I-MC; 3 arias in I-Nc; 1 aria in US-Wc; *sinfonia* in CH-EN, D-DS, I-MAav
Borrowing: 1 aria from *Artaserse* borrowed in oratorio *Isacco figura del redentore* ("Cara, o Dio, nel volto espresso")
Cast: Giuseppe Pugnetti (Artaserse); Antonia Bernasconi (Mandane); Giuseppe Tibaldi (Artabano); Giusto Ferdinando Tenducci (Arbace); Elisabetta Fiorentini (Elmira); Celidea Squillace (Megabise)

16. *Demofoonte* (Naples, Teatro San Carlo, 20 January 1775) [BohadloCat I.16]
Librettist: Pietro Metastasio
Libretto: I-Fm, I-Nc, I-Ra, US-NYp
Score: A-Wn,* I-Fc, I-Nc, P-La, US-Wc
Excerpts: 1 aria in CZ-Pu; 2 arias in F-Pn; 1 aria in F-Sgs; 1 aria in I-Gl; 1 aria (+ 3 duplicates) in I-MC; 1 aria in I-Nc; 7 arias and 1 duet in US-BEm; *sinfonia* in D-WEY, I-MAav

Cast: Giuseppe Tibaldi (Demofoonte); Antonia Bernasconi (Dircea); Giusto Ferdinando Tenducci (Timante); Giuseppe Pugnetti (Cherinto); Elisabetta Fiorentini (Creusa); Michele Mazziotti (Matusio); Celidea Squillace (Adrasto); N.N. (Olinto)

Editions: arias "In te spero, o sposo amato" and "Padre, perdona, oh pene" in *The Favourite Songs in the Opera Demofoonte* (London: Napier, [1778]): exemplars in D-Mbs, F-Pn, GB-Lbl, GB-Ob, US-Wc; aria "In te spero, o sposo amato" in *Journal d'ariettes, scènes et duo traduits, imités ou parodiés de l'italien*, No. 27 (Paris: De Roullède de La Chavardière, 1782): exemplars in D-HR, F-Pa, F-Pn

Recording: Trio Cantabile (Lydie Hartelová, harp; Václav Kunt, flute; Ludmila Vernerová, soprano), MusicVars VA0113-2, 2000 [CD]: aria "Quanto mai felici siete"

17. *Ezio* (Naples, Teatro San Carlo, 30 May 1775) [BohadloCat I.17]

Librettist: Pietro Metastasio

Libretto: I-Bf, I-FEwalker, I-Mc, I-Nc, I-Nn, I-Ra, I-Vgc, US-NYp

Score: A-Wn,* CZ-Pnm (Act 2 only), F-Pn (Acts 1 and 2 only, attr. Anfossi), I-Nc, P-La

Excerpts: 1 aria in CZ-Pak; 1 aria in CZ-Pnm; 1 aria in CZ-Pu; 1 scene and 2 arias in D-MÜs; 1 aria in F-Pn; 1 aria in I-Gl; 1 scene and 2 arias (+ 3 duplicates) in I-MC; 1 aria in I-MOe; 2 arias in I-Nc; *sinfonia* in CH-EN, D-W, F-Pn, and I-MAav

Cast: Giuseppe Benedetti (Valentiniano III); Anna de Amicis-Buonsollazzi (Fulvia); Gasparo Pacchierotti (Ezio); Elisabetta Ranieri (Onoria); Arcangelo Cortoni (Massimo); Nicola Lancellotta (Varo)

Edition: arias "Quanto mai felici siete" and "Caro padre, a me non dei" in Jan Branberger, ed., *Album Českého bel canta* (Prague: Orbis, 1949), arr. voice and pf

18. *Adriano in Siria* (Florence, Teatro Cocomero, autumn 1776; 1st performance 8 September 1776) [BohadloCat I.18]

Librettist: Pietro Metastasio

Libretto: I-Bc, I-Fc, I-Tfanan

Score: I-Fc (without *sinfonia*)

Excerpts: 2 arias (+ duplicate) in D-B; 4 arias in D-MÜs; 1 aria in DK-Sa; 1 aria in I-Bc; 1 aria in I-Gl; 1 scene (+ 1 duplicate) in I-MC; 1 aria in I-MTventuri; *sinfonia* in D-WEY, I-MAav

Borrowing: 1 aria from *Adriano in Siria* borrowed in *Demetrio* of 1779 ("Dal labbro che t'accende")

Cast: Michele Neri (Adriano); Giovanni Ansani (Osroa); Clementina Chiavacci (Emirena); Lucia Alberoni (Sabina); Tommaso Guarducci (Farnaspe); Francesco Papi (Aquilio)

________ (Perugia, Teatro dei Nobili del Casino, carnival 1777; libretto is dated 17 January 1777)

Libretto: US-SY

Cast: Giuseppe Pagliardini (Adriano); Giuliano Petti (Osroa); Vitale Damiani (Emirena); Gaspare Manzetti (Sabina); Tommaso Guarducci (Farnaspe); Marco Bittoni (Aquilio)

________ (Pavia, Teatro Nuovo, spring 1777; libretto is dated 13 May 1777)

Libretto: I-LDEsormani, I-PAc, I-Vgc, US-Wc

Cast: Nicola Cecini (Adriano); Ercole Ciprandi (Osroa); Giuseppa Maccherini Ansani (Emirena); Giacomo Veroli (Farnaspe); Clotilde Chiossi (Sabina); Angiola Dassia (Aquilio)

19. *Ezio* (Munich, Hoftheater, carnival 1777; 1st performance 10 January 1777) [BohadloCat I.19]

Librettist: Pietro Metastasio

Libretto: A-Wn (2 copies; printed libretto dated 1778; ms. libretto gives title as *Aetius*), D-Mbs (dated 1778)

Score: D-Mbs (two copies)

Excerpts: 1 scene in D-MÜs; 2 arias in I-MC; *sinfonia* in CH-EN, CZ-Pnm

Cast: Tommaso Consoli (Valentiniano III): Angela Galliani (Fulvia); Luigi Marchesi (Ezio); Rosa Manservisi (Onoria); Domenico de Panzacchi (Massimo); N.N. (=Gaetano Ravanni?) (Varo)

20. *La Calliroe* (Naples, Teatro San Carlo, 30 May 1778) [BohadloCat I.20]

Librettist: Matteo Verazi

Libretto: D-Mbs, I-Nc, I-Nn, US-NYp

Score: I-Nc,* F-Pn, P-La (Acts 1 and 2 only)

Excerpts: 1 aria in B-Br; 1 aria in CH-E; 1 aria in CH-EN; 2 arias in D-B; 1 aria (+ 2 duplicates) in D-Dl; 1 aria in D-Hs; 1 aria in D-W; 1 scene in DK-Sa; 1 cavatina, 3 scenes. and 7 arias (+ 2 duplicates) in F-Pn; 1 scene in HR-Dsmb; 2 arias in I-Gl; 2 arias in I-Mc; 5 scenes (+ 4 duplicates) and 4 arias (+ 3 duplicates) in I-MC; 2 arias (+ 2 duplicates) in I-Nc; 1 aria in I-PAc; 1 scene in I-Rc; 1 scene in S-Skma; 1 scene in US-SFsc; 1 scene in US-Wc; *sinfonia* in CH-E, CH-EN, CZ-NR, CZ-Pnm, D-DS, F-Pn, I-Mc, I-MOe, S-Skma

Cast: Giovanni Ansani (Agricane); Giuseppa Maccherini Ansani (Calliroe); Luigi Marchesi (Tarsile); Pietro Muschietti (Arsace); Gertrude Flavis (Briceste); Antonia Rubinacci (Sidonio)

Edition: aria "Se dal cielo amiche stelle" in *Journal d'ariettes italiennes*, No. 97 (January 1783) (Paris: Bailleux, 1783): exemplars in B-Bc, B-Lc, D-KNh, F-Pa, F-Pn, S-Skma

________ (Pisa, Teatro Prini, spring 1779; 1st performance 5 April 1779)

Libretto: I-Vgc

Cast: Giovanni Ansani (Agricane); Giuseppa Maccherini Ansani (Calliroe); Giuseppe Aprile (Tarsile); Giuseppe Pasqualini (Arsace); Palmira Sassi (Briceste)

Excerpts: 1 aria in F-Pn; 1 aria in I-Bsf

________ (Pontremoli, spring 1779)

Note: See Bohadlo 1989, 152.

________ (Siena, summer 1779)

Libretto: US-BLl

Cast: Carlo Angiolini (Agricane); Giuseppa Maccherini Ansani (Calliroe); Michele Neri (Tarsile); Antonio Petroni (Arsace); Anna Gherardi (Briceste); N.N. (Sidonio)

21. *L'olimpiade* (Naples, Teatro San Carlo, 4 November 1778) [BohadloCat I.22]

Librettist: Pietro Metastasio

Libretto: US-NYp

Score: I-Nc, P-La

Excerpts: 1 aria in A-Wgm; 1 scene and 3 arias in D-MÜs; 1 scene in E-Mp; 4 arias (+ 1 duplicate) in F-Pn; 1 aria in I-BGc; 1 aria in I-Fc; 1 aria in I-Gl; 3 scenes (+1 duplicate) and 5 arias (+ 3 duplicates) in I-MC; 1 duet (+ 1 duplicate) and 3 arias (+ 1 duplicate) in I-Nc; 1 aria in S-Skma; *sinfonia* in S-Skma

Cast: Giovanni Ansani (Clistene); Giuseppa Maccherini Ansani (Aristea); Luigi Marchesi (Megacle); Pietro Muschietti (Licida); Geltrude Flavis (Argene); Giacinto Perroni (Aminta); Antonia Rubinacci (Alcandro)

Recordings: Magdalena Kožená, soprano, Prague Philharmonia, cond. Michel Swierczewski, Deutsche Grammophon 289 471 334-2, 2001 [CD]: arias "Non più si trovano" and "Che non me disse"; Magdalena Kožená, soprano, Prague Philharmonia, cond. Michel Swierczewski, Deutsche Grammophon 0289–4776153–2, 2006 [CD]: aria "Che non mi disse"

22. *La Circe* (Venice, Teatro San Benedetto, Ascension, 1779; 1st performance 12 May 1779) [BohadloCat I.23]

Librettist: Domenico Perelli

Libretto: A-Wmi, F-Pn, I-Bc, I-Mb, I-Pmc, I-Vcg, I-Vgc, I-Vnm

Score: none

Excerpts: 1 scene formerly in D-DS; 1 scene and 1 aria in D-Mh; 3 scenes and 1 aria in D-MÜs; 1 aria in I-MC

Cast: Cecilia Davies (Circe); Luigi Marchesi (Ulisse); Giacinto Perroni (Prisco); Vittoria Moreschi Bolzani (Canente); Gaetano Quistapace (Sabino); Giuseppe Desirò (Clerinto)

23. *Demetrio* (Naples, Teatro San Carlo, 13 August 1779) [BohadloCat I.24]

Librettist: Pietro Metastasio

Libretto: I-Bc, I-Fc, US-NYp

Score: I-Nc, P-La

Excerpts: 1 scene in D-MÜs; 1 aria in DK-Sa; 3 scenes (+ 1 duplicate) and 1 aria in E-Mp

Borrowings: 1 aria in *Demetrio* borrowed from *Adriano in Siria* ("Dal labbro che t'accende"); music for 1 aria from *Demetrio* borrowed in *Armida* ("Non sò frenare il pianto")

Cast: Rosa Agostini (Cleonice); Domenico Bedini (Alceste); Gaetano Scovelli (Fenicio); Gaspare de Filippis (Olinto); Caterina Lusini (Barsene); Antonia Rubinacci (Mitrane)

24. *Armida* (Mila, Teatro alla Scala, carnival 1780; 1st performance 26 December 1779) [BohadloCat I.21]

Librettist: Gianambrogio Migliavacca, after Philippe Quinault

Libretto: CDN-Tu, I-Bam, I-Bc, I-LDEsormani, I-Ma, I-Mc, I-Mcom, I-Ms, I-PAc,I-Rsc, I-Rn (acc. Sartori), I-Vgc, US-Wc

Score: F-Pn (incomplete), P-La

Excerpts: 1 duet in D-B; 1 aria in D-LÜh; 1 scene and 1 aria in D-MÜs; aria "Il caro mio bene" in CZ-Pnm, D-LÜh, F-Pn, I-MC, and I-Vc; 1 cavatina in I-IBborromeo; one version of *sinfonia* in CZ-Bm, F-Pn, I-MOe, and I-Rc; another version of *sinfonia* in P-La (see Catalog 1)

Borrowing: music for 1 aria borrowed from *Demetrio* II of 1779 ("Non sò frenare il pianto")
Cast: Caterina Gabrielli (Armida); Luigi Marchesi (Rinaldo); Caterina Lorenzini (Fenicia and Lucinda); Rosa Franchi (Sidonia and Melissa); Valentin Adamberger (Idraote, Odio e Cavalier danese); Gaetano Quistapace (Aronte, Artemidoro, and Ubaldo)

25. *Medonte* (Rome, Teatro Argentina, carnival 1780; 1st performance 26 January 1780) [BohadloCat I.25]
Librettist: Giovanni De Gamerra
Libretto: F-Pn, I-Bc, I-MAC, I-Rvat (Farraioli), US-AUS
Score: F-Pn* (Act 1 only), I-Rc (Act 1 only), RUS-SPsc (incomplete), private library of O. Lindner, Berlin, acc. EitnerQ (lost?)
Excerpts: 1 aria in A-Wgm; 1 scene in B-Bc; 1 scene in CDN-Lu; 2 arias (+ 1 duplicate) in CZ-Pnm; 1 scene and 2 arias (+ 2 duplicates) in D-B; 1 scene formerly in D-DS; 1 aria in D-Hs; 1 aria in D-LÜh; 1 scene and 1 aria in D-Mh; 2 scenes in D-MÜs; 1 scene in D-RH; 1 aria in D-Tl; 2 scenes in DK-Sa; 1 aria in F-Pn; 1 aria in FIN-A; 1 aria in H-P; 1 aria in I-Bc; 1 aria in I-Bsf; 1 aria in I-Gl; 3 arias in I-Mc; 1 scene (+ 1 duplicate) and 1 aria in I-MC; 1 aria in I-Rc; 1 scene in I-Tf; 1 aria in I-Vc; 1 aria in S-Skma; 1 aria in S-Sm; *sinfonia* in CZ-KRa, I-MOe, I-PEsp, I-Rsg, US-AAu (attr. Cimarosa)
Cast: Giacomo David (Medonte); Michelangelo Bologna (Selene); Tommaso Consoli (Arsace); Silvestro Fiammenchi (Zelinda); Biagio Parca (Evandro); Lorenzo Galeffi (Talete)
Editions: aria "Ah, disponi di mia sorte" in *Journal d'ariettes italiennes*, No. 84 (June 1782) (Paris: Bailleux, 1782): exemplars in B-Bc, B-Lc, F-Pa, F-Pn, GB-Cumc, GB-Lbl, S-Skma; scene and rondò "Cedere è forza, o cara/Luci belle, se piangete," in *Journal d'ariettes italiennes*, No. 112 (August 1783) (Paris: Bailleux, 1783): exemplars in B-Bc, B-Lc, D-KNh, F-Pa, F-Pn, S-Skma; aria "Al caro ben vicina" in *Journal d'ariettes italiennes*, No. 192 (December 1786) (Paris: Bailleux, 1786): exemplars in B-Lc, F-Pn, H-Bn; rondò "Luci belle, se piangete" with text "Ömma maka!" in *Musikaliskt tidsfördrif*, Nos. 8–9 (Stockholm: Kongl. Privilegierade Not Tryckeriet, Stockholm, 1794), arr. voice and pf: exemplars in S-Sdt, S-Sk, S-SK, S-Skma, S-L, S-LI, S-Sm, S-Uu, S-V

26. *Antigono* (Rome, Teatro Alibert, spring 1780; 1st performance 5 April 1780) [BohadloCat I.26]
Librettist: Pietro Metastasio
Libretto: B-Bc, F-Pn, I-Bc, I-MAC, I-PAc, I-Rsc, I-Rvat (Ferraioli)
Score: none
Excerpts: 1 aria in A-Wn; 1 scene in CH-Fcu; 1 aria in D-B; 2 scenes and 1 aria in D-Mh; 1 scene in DK-Sa; 1 duet in E-Mp; 1 scene in F-Lm; 1 scene in I-BGc; 1 scene in I-Rc; 1 aria in I-Rsc; 1 aria in US-LAuc; 1 scene in US-R
Cast: Giovanni Ansani (Antigono); Pietro Benedetti (Demetrio); Giuseppe Benigni (Berenice); Michelangelo Bologna (Alessandro); Silvestro Fiammenchi (Ismene); Lorenzo Galeffi (Clearco)
Editions: scene and rondò "Ubbidisco ti lascio/Ho perduto il mio tesoro" with text "Tu me quittes mais songe à ce cœur qui t'adore" in *Journal d'ariettes italiennes*, No. 98 (January

1783) (Paris: Bailleux, 1783): exemplars in B-Bc, B-Lc, D-KNh, F-Lm, F-Pa, F-Pn, S-Skma; rondò "Ho perduto il mio tesoro: The Favourite Rondò" (London: J. Bland, [1790]), arr. voice and pf: exemplar in GB-Lgc; rondò "Ho perduto il mio tesoro: The Favourite Rondò" (Philadelphia: Trisobio, [ca. 1796–98]), arr. voice and pf: exemplar in US-PHcgs

DOUBTFUL OR SPURIOUS OPERATIC PRODUCTIONS

1. *Medea* (Parma, Teatro Ducale, 1764)

   Notes: An operatic production in Parma was first hinted at by Pelcl (see Appendix 1). Later, an unnamed opera for Parma with a date of 1764 was claimed in Schmidl. The title *Medea* was first indicated in ES by Ulisse Prota-Giurleo, then transferred to MGG 1961 and Grove6. In the absence of any firm documentation that any such production took place, it was omitted from the works' lists for Mysliveček in *New Grove* (2001) and *Grove Music Online*. The same is true for putative productions of *Erifile* and *Merope* (see below).

2. *Erifile* (Munich, 1773)

   Note: First specified in Fétis, then Bernsdorf, Schmidl, ES, MGG 1961, CSHS, and Grove6.

3. *Achille in Sciro* (Naples, 1775)

   Note: First specified in Pečman 1970, then Pečman 1981.

4. *Merope* (Naples, 1775)

   Note: First specified in Bernsdorf (without location), then Schmidl, Čeleda, ES, MGG 1961, Pečman 1970, Pečman 1981, and Grove6.

5. *Armida* (Lucca, Teatro Pubblico, autumn, 15 August 1778)

   Librettist: Gianambrogio Migliavacca

   Libretto: I-Fm, I-La, I-Lg

   Notes: The music for this production was first specified as the work of Mysliveček in ES. No music from the production is known to survive. Since the libretto contains no attribution to Mysliveček and there is no indication from any other source that his music was used, there is no justification to include this production in Mysliveček works' lists. BohadloCat nonetheless accepts the likely mis-attribution.

from CSHS:

"neznamá it. opera z doby *M.* pobytu ve vlasti (v inv. oseckého konventu)" (an unknown Italian opera from the time of Mysliveček's residence in his homeland cited in the inventory of the Osek monastery); this information probably derives from Kamper, 193–94; acc. Mikanová, it is likely meant to be a reference to the "dramatic cantata" *Il Parnaso confuso*.

Part 2

OPERATIC PASTICHES WITH MUSIC OF MYSLIVEČEK

1. *Orfeo ed Euridice* (Naples, Teatro San Carlo, 4 November 1774)

   Principal composers: Christoph Willibald von Gluck, Johann Christian Bach

   Librettist: Ranieri de' Calsabigi

   Libretto: I-Nc, I-PAc, I-Ra, I-Vgc

   Score: I-Nc, P-La

   Mysliveček contributions: uncertain; a great deal of music in the middle of Act 1 and the beginning of Act 2 cannot be traced either to Bach or Gluck; in all, the unidentified passages include the recitative for Act 1, scene 1, and Act 2, scenes 1 and 2; the accompanied recitatives for Act 1, scene 7, and Act 2, scene 3; the arioso "Il silenzio, la pace" (Act 1, scene 7); the choruses "Sciolto ognun dal terreo" (Act 1, scene 6) and "Chiari fonti, ermi ritiri" (Act 2, scene 5); and the arias "La legge accetto, oh Dei" (Act 1, scene 5), "Se quel dolor" (Act 1, scene 7), "Uno sposo così fido" (Act 2, scene 1), and "Spieghi alle belle" (Act 2, scene 2)

   Edition: *The Collected Works of Johann Christian Bach, 1735–1782*, ed. Ernest Warburton, Vol. 11 (New York and London: Garland, 1987): facsimile ed. of score in I-Nc

2. *Creso* (Naples, Teatro San Carlo, 4 November 1776)

   Principal composer: Antonio Sacchini

   Other composers represented: Giovanni Paisiello, Domenico Fischietti, Francesco Zanetti

   Librettist: Gioacchino Pizzi

   Libretto: I-Baf, I-Nc, I-Ra, US-NYp

   Score: I-Nc, P-La

   Mysliveček contribution: cavatina "Ah, mio cor che mai prevedi" attr. Mysliveček in Act 2, scene 3

3. *Adriano in Siria* (Livorno, Teatro di Livorno, carnival 1777)

   Attribution of music: "vari autori"

   Librettist: Pietro Metastasio

   Libretto: I-Fc

   Score: none

   Mysliveček contribution: according to an aria ms. in D-B, the aria "Leon piagato" from Mysliveček's setting of *Adriano in Siria* was sung by Giovanni Ansani in the role of Osroa in this production; Ansani sang the same aria in the original production

4. *Ezio* (Genoa, Teatro Sant'Agostino, spring 1777)

   Principal composer: Michele Mortellari

   Librettist: Pietro Metastasio

   Libretto: F-Pn, I-Tfanan

Score: none

Mysliveček contributions: according to an aria ms. in I-Gl, Lucia Alberoni sang the arias "Agitata in tanti affani" from *Demetrio* I of 1773 and "Caro padre, a me non dei" from *Ezio* I of 1775 in this production

5. *Demofoonte* (London, King's Theater, November 1778)

Composers: Ferdinando Bertoni, Carlo Monza, Josef Mysliveček, Giuseppe Sarti

Librettist: Pietro Metastasio

Libretto: B-Bc, F-Pc, GB-Lbl, US-Wc

Score: printed ed. of "Favourite Songs"

Mysliveček contributions: arias "In te spero, o sposo amato" and "Padre, perdona, oh pene" from *Demofoonte* II of 1775

6. *Alessandro nell'Indie* (London, King's Theater, November 1779)

Composers: Alessandri, Anfossi, Bertoni, Durán, Handel, Molza, Mysliveček, Piccinni, Sarti, Tozzi (+ 4 anonymous arias)

Librettist: Pietro Metastasio

Libretto: F-Pn, GB-Lbl

Score: printed ed. of "Favourite Songs"

Mysliveček contributions: arias "Affretti i passi, o caro" (an aria of unknown origins) and "Cara ti lascio, addio" (a parody of "Figlia ti lascio, addio" from *Atide*)

7. *Il soldano generoso* (London, King's Theater, carnival 1780)

Composers: Ferdinando Bertoni, Tommaso Giordani, Mysliveček, Antonio Salieri, Tommaso Traetta

Librettist: Antonio Andrei

Libretto: US-I

Score: none ("Favourite Songs" collection does not include the Mysliveček aria)

Mysliveček contribution: aria "Agitata in tanti affanni" from *Demetrio* I of 1773

8. *Erifile?* (Genoa, Teatro Sant'Agostino, carnival, 1780)

Composer: Giuseppe Giordani

Librettist: Giovanni De Gamerra

Libretto: I-Fc, I-SML

Score: unknown

Mysliveček contribution: recitative "In questo tanto ingrate" and cavatina "Povero cor tu palpiti" from *La Nitteti* in ms. in I-Gl, if indication of character Erifile in ms. refers to this production; the ms. in I-Gl is dated carnival, 1779, however no *Erifile* is recorded for carnival of 1779 in Genoa, only a *Quinto Fabio* pastiche; an *Erifile* was produced in Genoa in 1780

9. *Il Begliar-Bey di Caramania* (Dresden, Piccolo Teatro Elettorale, 1780)

Principal composer: Giuseppe Amendola

Librettist: unknown
Libretto: I-Rsc, B-Bc, D-Dl, F-Pc, US-Wc
Score: D-Dl
Mysliveček contribution: aria "Son guerriero e sono amante" from *La Calliroe* inserted between scenes 8 and 9 of Act 1; see also D-Dl Mus. 1.F.125, Db. 9, Nr. 4, and F-Pn, ms. D. 81, listed in Part 9

10. *Mitridate a Sinope* (Genoa, Teatro Sant'Agostino, carnival 1781)
Attribution of music: none
Librettist: anon.
Libretto: I-SML, US-NYp
Score: unknown
Mysliveček contribution: duet "Al fiero dolore non regge quest'alma" acc. ms. in I-Gl, which specifies the characters Almira and Farnace

11. *Giunio Bruto* (Genoa, Teatro Sant'Agostino, summer 1782)
Principal composer: Domenico Cimarosa
Librettist: Giovanni Pindemonte
Libretto: US-Wc
Score: H-Bn, I-Fc, I-Nc, I-Rmassimo
Mysliveček contribution: aria "Se fedel mi serba il fato" from *La Calliroe* acc. to a ms. in I-Gl

12. *Giannina e Bernardone* (Vienna, Burgtheater, 24 September 1784)
Principal composer: Domenico Cimarosa
Librettist: Filippo Livigni
Libretto: unknown
Score: A-Wn
Mysliveček contribution: aria "Ah, non temer ben mio" inserted in Act 1, scene 6, from *La Nitetti*

Part 3

GERMAN MELODRAMA

Theodorich und Elisa (Munich?, 1777–78?) [BohadloCat VII.1]
Librettist: anon.
Libretto: none
Score: none
Note: This work is known only from a pf, hpd arr. in D-DO, Mus. ms. 1338 (see Schuler).

Part 4

PLAYS WITH MUSIC

1. *Elfrida* (Florence, Piazza Vecchia, 8 December 1774; performances ended 21 December 1774) [BohadloCat III.9]

   Librettist: "Poema drammatico scritto sopra il modello dall'antica tragedia greca dal Sig. [William] Mason Inglese e tradotto in versi dall'Abate Antonio Pillori fiorentino"

   Libretto: I-Rn

   Score: none

   Note: This is a play with duets inserted (see De Angelis and Weaver & Weaver).

2. *Das ausgerechnete Glück* (Prague, Divadlo v Kotcích, 22 April 1777)

   Librettist: anon.; based on Johann Christian Krüger's play *Herzog Michel*

   Libretto: none

   Score: none

   Mysliveček contribution: uncertain

   Note: This is a "children's operetta" known only from a listing in the *Taschenbuch von der Prager Schaubühne auf das Jahr 1778* (Prague, 1778).

Part 5

ORATORIOS

1. *Tobia* (Padua, 1769) [BohadoCat II.1]

   Librettist: anon. (claim of Apostolo Zeno in Pečman 1981 is unfounded)

   Libretto: I-PAc, I-Pca

   Score: D-Mbs, D-Rp, I-Pca

   Excerpts: 1 aria (+ 1 duplicate) in CZ-Pnm; 1 aria in D-WEY

   Borrowing: *sinfonia* shared with *La passione*

   Recording: Zdena Kloubová, soprano, Benda Chamber Orchestra, cond. Miroslav Hrdlička, Panton 81 1044–2231, 1992 [CD]: aria "Fra i perigli del lungo viaggio"

   ________ (Prague, Church of St. Francis Serafin, Good Friday, 14 April 1770)

   Libretto: CZ-KRI, CZ-Pnm, CZ-Pu

   ________ (Bologna, Oratorio de' Padri della Congregazione di San Filippo Neri, 1775)

   Libretto: I-Bc, I-Vgc

________ (Modena, Accademia de' Signori Filarmonici di Modena, Quaresima, 1783)

Libretto: I-Lg

Note: This oratorio is referred to by some as *La famiglia di Tobia*, however no source records this title for Mysliveček's setting.

2. *I pellegrini al sepolcro* (Padua, 1770) [BohadloCat II.2]

Librettist: Stefano Benedetto Pallavicino?

Libretto: I-Vcg

Score: none

Note: Equated incorrectly in Schmidl and ES with *La passione*.

3. *Adamo ed Eva* (Florence, Sala dell'Accademia degl'Ingegnosi, 24 March 1771) [BohadloCat II.3]

Librettist: anon.

Libretto: I-Fm, I-Rn

Score: I-Rf

Excerpts: 1 aria and duet in D-MÜs; *sinfonia* in I-Gl

Cast: Tommaso Guarducci (Adamo); Elisabetta Melani (Eva); Francesco Campana (Angelo di Giustizia); Antonio Goti (Angelo di Misericordia)

________ (performed anonymously 19 March 1770 in the Ospizio del Melani in Florence, acc. De Angelis and Weaver & Weaver; the latter assert that the music for this production was by Mysliveček)

Libretto: I-Fc, I-Fn, I-Rsc

________ (Prague, Church of St. Francis Serafin, 1771)

Libretto: CZ-KRI, CZ-Pnm

________ (as *Adamo*; Perugia, Oratorio di San Filippo Neri, 1772)

Libretto: I-PEc, CDN-Tu

________ (as *Adamo*; Milan, Regio Ducal Teatro, Lent, 1772 acc. Hansell, 193, and Piperno, 290 and 302)

Libretto: F-Po (acc. Hansell), I-Ma, I-Mb (acc. Piperno), I-Vgc

________ (Bologna, Oratorio della Nobilissima Arciconfraternità e Spedale di Santa Maria della Morte, Good Friday, 1775)

Libretto: I-Bam, I-Bca, I-Rn

________ (Prato, Church of the Monastery of S. Niccolao di Prato, St. Cecilia's Day, 22 November 1775)

Libretto: B-Bc, I-Vgc

________ (as *Adamo*; Rimini, Cathedral, feast of St. Anthony of Padua, 13 June 1776)

Libretto: I-PESo

4. *Betulia liberata* (Padua, 1771) [BohadloCat II.4]
   Librettist: Pietro Metastasio
   Libretto: I-Pca, I-Pci, I-Rsc
   Score: none

5. *Giuseppe riconosciuto* (Padua, 1771?, 1769 acc. CSHS and Grossato) [BohadloCat II.5]
   Librettist: Pietro Metastasio
   Libretto: GB-Lbl, I-Pca (acc. Cattelan 1990), I-Pmc, I-Rsc
   Score: none; score in I-Pca attr. Mysliveček is actually by Hasse

6. *La passione di Nostro Signore Gesù Cristo* (Florence, Porta Rossa, 24 March and 6 April 1773) [BohadloCat II.6]
   Librettist: Pietro Metastasio
   Libretto: none; see De Angelis and Weaver & Weaver
   Score: D-F (copied in Munich acc. Münster 2001, p. 247), D-Mbs (part 1 only), D-Rp (as *La morte di Gesù*)
   Excerpts: 1 aria and 1 duet in D-MÜs
   Cast: Tommaso Guarducci (Giuseppe?); Giacomo Veroli (Pietro?); Elisabetta Melani (Maddalena); Vincenzo Nicolini (Giovanni?)
   Borrowing: *Introduzione* from oratorio *Il Tobia*
   Edition: *La passione*, ed. Joyce L. Johnson, The Italian Oratorio, 1650–1800, Vol. 23 (New York and London: Garland, 1986): facsimile ed. of score in D-F
   Recording: Das Neue Orchester, cond. Christoph Spering, various soloists, Chorus Musicus Köln, Capriccio CC 71 025/26, 2005 [CD]
   Note: There is no basis for indications in CSHS and Pečman 1981 that *La passione* was performed under the title *La morte di Gesù* in Padua in 1770.

________ (*La passione di Jesù Christo Signor Nostro*; Prague, Church of St. Francis Serafin, Good Friday, 9 April 1773)
   Libretto: CZ-Pu

________ (*La passione di Nostro Signore Gesù Cristo*; Florence, Porta Rossa, 2 March 1774)
   Cast: Tommaso Guarducci (Giuseppe?); Elisabetta Melani (Maddalena); Giovanni Battista Gherardi (Pietro?); Vincenzo Nicolini (Giovanni?)
   Note: See De Angelis and Weaver & Weaver.

________ (*La passione di Gesù Cristo Signor Nostro*; Bologna, Oratorio della Nobilissima Arciconfraternità e Spedale di Santa Maria della Morte, Good Friday, 1777)
   Libretto: I-Bas, I-Bc, I-Bca

________ (Munich?, 1777–78?)
   Note: The possibility of a production in Munich is invited by the existence of a copy prepared in Munich by court copyist Sixtus Hirsvogel, now in D-F (see Münster 2001, 247).

________ (Rome, Vallicella, 20 November 1780; see Johnson, 154)

________ (Prague, Church of St. Francis Serafin, 1782)

Libretto: CZ-Ppp

________ (Padua?, 1783; music perhaps not by Mysliveček, since the libretto contains no attribution)

Libretto: I-Pci

________ (Rome, Vallicella, 30 November 1783; see Johnson, 154)

________ (Rome, Vallicella, 12 March and 3 December 1786; see Johnson, 154)

________ (Rome, Vallicella, December 1788; see Johnson, 154)

________ (Rome, Vallicella, 2 January 1791; see Johnson, 154)

________ (Rome, Vallicella, 15 November 1791; see Johnson, 154)

Notes: There is also an undated libretto for this work in D-BAs, published in Bamberg without specification of a performance venue. Mysliveček's *La passione* has been equated incorrectly, especially in Schmidl and ES, with *I pellegrini al sepolcro*.

7. *La liberazione d'Israel* (first known performance Prague, Church of St. Francis Serafin, Good Friday, 1775, but probably composed in Naples, the only known residence of the librettist, ca. 1773–74) [BohadloCat II.7]

   Librettist: Giambattista Basso Bassi

   Libretto: CZ-Pu

   Excerpt: one aria, "Nò, non s'annida in selva" was copied in the household of Lord Cowper in Florence in 1774 with incipit "Nò, non s'annida in sebra" (see Part 9)

   Note: This work is frequently equated incorrectly with *Betulia liberata* in secondary sources.

8. *Isacco figura del redentore* (Florence, Casino dei Nobili, 10 March 1776, 19 March 1776, Accademia degl'Armonici) [BohadloCat II.8]

   Librettist: Pietro Metastasio

   Libretto: I-Fc, I-Fm

   Score: CZ-Nlobkowicz, CZ-Pnm, CZ-Pu, D-B (attr. J. Haydn), D-Dl (attr. J. Haydn), D-Mbs, D-Rp, F-Pn, H-Bn, I-Fc (attr. W. A. Mozart), I-MOe (text in German), I-Rf

   Excerpts: 1 terzetto in D-Mbs; 4 arias in D-MÜs; *sinfonia* in D-MÜs, D-WEY

   Cast: Valentin Adamberger (Abramo); Tommaso Guarducci (Isacco); Giovanni Battista Gherardi (Gamari); Giovanni Gelati (Angelo); Antonio Goti (Sara)

   Recordings: Prague Chamber Orchestra, cond. Peter Maag, various soloists, Supraphon 112 1021, 1972 [LP]; Sinfonietta Praha, cond. Ivan Pařík, various soloists, Bonton Classics 71 0049–2 632, 1991 [CD]; Sinfonietta Praha, cond. Ivan Pařík, various soloists, Bonton Baltic GD 125, 1992 [CD]; Sinfonietta Praha, cond. Ivan Pařík, various soloists, Supraphon 3209, 1995 [CD]; Magdalena Kožená, soprano, Prague Philharmonia, cond. Michel

Swierczewski, Deutsche Grammophon 289 471 334–2, 2001 [CD]: aria "Deh, parlate, che forse tacendo"

________ (as *Isacco*; libretto listed without date or place in Sartori; could be for a possible production in Milan, 1777, based on the presence of the singers)

Libretto: I-Ma, I-Mb

________ (Munich, Salvatorheater, 21 February 1777; referred to by Mozart in a letter of 11 October 1777 as *Abramo ed Isacco*)

Score: D-Mbs

Cast: Luigi Marchesi (Isacco); Giovanni Valesi (Abramo); others, perhaps including Tommaso Consoli and Gaetano Ravanni

Borrowings: 1 aria in *Isacco* borrowed from opera *Motezuma* ("Nel mar di tanti affanni" with new text "Sian are i nostri petti"); 1 aria from opera *Artaserse* ("Cara, o Dio, nel volto espresso" with new text "Veggo, o Dio, nel cenno espresso"); 1 aria from opera *Atide* ("Lasciami adesso in pace" with new text "Sì, ne tormenti istessi")

Edition: *Isacco figura del redentore*, ed. James A. Ackerman, Recent Researches in the Music of the Classical Era, Vol. 60 (Madison, WI: A-R Editions, 2000)

________ (as *Isacco*; Florence, Piazza Vecchia, 30 November 1777, possibly with music of Mysliveček, acc. Weaver & Weaver)

Libretto: none (see Weaver & Weaver)

________ (Prague, Church of St. Francis Serafin, Good Friday, 1778)

Libretto: CZ-Pu

________ (as *Isak ein Sinnbild des Erlösers*, trans. Karl Ignaz Förg; Munich, 1778)

Note: See Legband, 288–93.

________ (Rome, Vallicella, 1779; see Johnson, 152)

Libretto: I-Rsc, I-Vgc, US-BAu

________ (Rome, Vallicella, 22 November 1780, St. Cecilia's Day; see Johnson, 152)

________ (Rome, Vallicella, 4 March 1781; see Johnson, 152) [5 March given in newspaper announcement from the Roman *Diario ordinario* of 10 March 1781 in Bohadlo 1989, 8]

________ (Rome, Vallicella, 22 November 1781, St. Cecilia's Day; see Johnson, 152)

________ (Rome, Vallicella, 9 March 1783; see Johnson, 152)

________ (Buda, October 1785)

Note: See Pečman 1981, 155.

________ (Bratislava, March 1786)

Note: See Pečman 1981, 155.

________ (as *Isak ein Sinnbild des Erlösers*; Munich, National Theater, 28 March and 2 April 1787)

Note: See Legband, 454.

________ (Koblenz, Ehrenbreitstein Castle, 1787)

Note: See Bereths, 197; Böhmer, 251.

________ (Pest, 1787)

Note: See Bohadlo 1989, 153.

________ (Rome, Vallicella, 22 November 1788, St. Cecilia's Day; see Johnson, 152)

________ (Rome, Vallicella, 21 December 1789, St. Cecilia's Day; see Johnson, 152)

________ (Rome, Vallicella, 22 November 1790, St. Cecilia's Day; see Johnson, 152)

________ (Rome, Vallicella, 22 November 1791, Sr. Cecilia's Day; see Johnson, 152)

Notes: A score of *Abramo ed Isacco* was available to Haydn at Eszterháza according to an inventory of 1784, however the work was never performed. See Landon 1978, 483–85.

SPURIOUS ORATORIO

L'ascenza di S. Benedette cited in CSHS and Pečman 1981 as having been performed in Padua in 1768; neither work offers a source; likely the title resulted from confusion with the phrase "fiera d'ascensione" at the Teatro San Benedetto in Venice; Mysliveček's operas *Demofoonte* of 1769, *La clemenza di Tito* of 1774, and *La Circe* of 1779 were all performed in that theater, the last one during the Ascension season.

Part 6

CANTATAS

1. *Il Parnaso confuso* (unknown venue, 1765–67) [BohadloCat III.2]

   Librettist: Pietro Metastasio

   Libretto: ms. libretto in CZ-MHz

   Score: CZ-Pnm (2 copies), I-Rsc

   Excerpts: 2 arias in CZ-Pnm; 1 aria in CZ-Pu; *sinfonia* in CZ-Pnm, D-AB, I-Gl

   ________ (Osek monastery, 1782)

   Note: Date is from mss. in CZ-Pnm.

________ (Osek monastery, 1783)

Note: Date is from mss. in CZ-Pnm.

________ (Osek monastery, 1793)

Notes: Date is from mss. in CZ-Pnm. See chapter 8 for a discussion of the origins of this work.

2. *Cantata a due: Alceste e Fileno* (unknown venue, ca. 1767) [BohadloCat III.1]

   Librettist: anon.

   Libretto: none

   Score: CZ-Pnm

   Excerpts: 1 aria in CZ-Pnm; *sinfonia* in CZ-Pnm (3 copies), D-AB, I-Gl

   ________ (Osek monastery, 1768?)

   Notes: This cantata was performed for an anniversary of the election of Desiderius Andres as abbot of Osek sometime before Andres' death in 1770, perhaps in 1768. See chapter 8 for a discussion of the origins of this work.

3. *Cantata a tre voci* (Naples, Teatro San Carlo, birthday of Charles III, king of Spain, 20 January 1767) [BohadloCat III.3]

   Librettist: anon.

   Libretto: I-Bc, I-Nc

   Score: none

   Cast: Anton Raaff (Giove); Ferdinando Mazzanti (Mercurio); Caterina Gabrielli (Liberia)

4. *Narciso al fonte* (Padua, unknown venue, 1768) [BohadloCat III.4]

   Librettist: Giambattista Zangarini

   Libretto: I-Vgc

   Score: none

   Note: There is no mention of this work in Brunelli or Grossato, although it does appear in Sartori.

5. *Cantata per S[ua] E[ccellenza] Marino Cavalli* (Padua, Accademia dei Ricovrati, 30 August 1768) [BohadloCat III.5]

   Librettist: Nicola Mussato

   Libretto: none

   Score: none

   Cast: included Gaetano Guadagni and Antonio Casati (see Grossato, 194)

   Note: This is the cantata dated 1763 in Grove6 and Brunelli, 353. See Grossato, 193–95.

6. *Cantata a tre voci* (Naples, Teatro San Carlo, birthday of Maria Carolina, queen of Naples, 13 August 1773) [BohadloCat III.7]

   Librettist: anon.

   Libretto: I-Nc

Score: none
Cast: Gasparo Pacchierotti (Giove); Anna de Amicis-Buonsollazzi (Giunone); Giuseppe Tibaldi (Mercurio)

7. *Cantata a tre voci* (Naples, Teatro San Carlo, birthday of Maria Carolina, queen of Naples, 13 August 1774) [BohadloCat III.8]
   Librettist: Saverio Mattei acc. CSHS (without documentation)
   Libretto: I-Nc, I-Rrostirolla
   Score: none
   Cast: Giusto Ferdinando Tenducci (Mitridate); Antonia Bernasconi (Berenice); Giuseppe Tibaldi (Eumene)

8. *Cantata a tre voci* (Naples, Teatro San Carlo, birthday of Ferdinand IV, king of Naples, 12 January 1775) [BohadloCat III.10]
   Librettist: anon.
   Libretto: I-Nn, I-Rrostirolla
   Score: none
   Cast: Giusto Ferdinando Tenducci (Giove); Giuseppe Tibaldi (Marte); Antonia Bernasconi (Partenope)
   Excerpt: 1 scene in I-MC

9. *Cantata a tre voci* (Naples, Teatro San Carlo, birthday of Charles III, king of Spain, 20 January 1775) [BohadloCat III.11]
   Librettist: anon.
   Libretto: I-Rrostirolla
   Score: none
   Cast: Giuseppe Tibaldi (Alcide); Antonia Bernasconi (Diana); Giusto Ferdinando Tenducci (Ispalo)

10. *Enea negl'Elisi/Il tempio dell'eternità* (Munich, 1777) [BohadloCat III.12]
   Librettist: Pietro Metastasio
   Libretto: none
   Score: lost; once housed in the collection of the Electress Maria Anna of Bavaria (see Part 10)
   Notes: This work is mentioned in a letter of Mozart to his father of 13 November 1777 with title *Enea negl'Elisi* as intended for performance along with Carlo Monza's opera *Attilio Regolo* in Munich during carnival of 1778. The death of Elector Maximilian III Joseph on 30 December 1777 led to the cancellation of the Monza opera. The score was formerly housed in the collection of the Electress Maria Anna in Munich under the title *Il tempo* [sic] *d'eternità*.

11. *Cantata a tre voci* (Naples, Teatro San Carlo, birthday of Maria Carolina, queen of Naples, 13 August 1779) [BohadloCat III.13]
   Librettist: anon.

Libretto: I-Nc, I-Rsc

Score: none

Cast: Rosa Agostini (Livia); Domenico Bedini (Quirino); Gaetano Scovelli (Metello)

12. *Ebbi, non ti smarir* (date?) [BohadloCat III.15]

Librettist: Pietro Metastasio

Score: GB-Lbl; probably remnant of original set of twelve cantatas, along with Cantata 13

13. *Non, non turbati, o Nice* (date?) [BohadloCat III.16]

Librettist: Pietro Metastasio

Score: GB-Lbl, I-CRE

14. *Armida* (date?) [BohadloCat III.14]

Librettist: unknown

Score: A-Wn*

Notes: A notation in Pečman 1981, 251, cites the existence of "několik kantát, veňovaných oseckému opatu P. Kaj. Březinovi (do r. 1763)" ("several cantatas dedicated to Father Kajetán Březina, abbot of Osek up to the year 1763"). This remark appears to have originated from Kamper, 194. The citation in Kamper was probably meant to refer to *Il Parnaso confuso* and the *Cantata a due* in CZ-Pnm.

Part 7

LARGER LITURGICAL VOCAL WORKS

1. Mass in D Major (Sanctus/Benedictus/Agnus Dei only) [BohadloCat IV.3]

Source: CZ-Jlm 164, dated 1772

2. Mass in D major [BohadloCat IV.4]

Source: NL-At 303-B-14, ms. of ca. 1772

3. Mass in G major

Source: D-MBG K 6 II 52; attr. "Sig. Bazziatertmeki"; attribution crossed out, replaced with "Mitlisvazek"

4. Mass in F major

Source: SK-Mms D V/195 (Vel'ké Leváre)

5. Requiem in E-flat Major [BohadloCat IV.9]

   Source: D-TEGha Ms 41 (Benediktinerabtei Banz), a ms. copied 1790; attr. Ignaz Holzbauer in D-TRb 104/101 02, a ms. of ca. 1810

   Edition: *Requiem ex Es*, ed. Christian Mortiz-Bauer (Passau: Musikverlag Peter Lechl, 2004)

6. Requiem in E-flat Major

   Source: CZ-CH S-40–52–915 (Chrám sv. Mikuláše), a nineteenth-century ms.

7. "Lytaniae laurentanae" [BohadloCat IV.5]

   Source: D-Mbs Mus. ms. 283, No. 7; probably composed in Munich, 1777–78

LOST?

2 masses, acc. Dlabač, who reported them in 1786 in the "Raudnitzer Kirchenchore."

Note: The 1894 catalog of the holdings of the musical establishment at Roudnice (now in CZ-Nlobkowicz) contains no mention of these works. It is possible that they were concordant with two of the masses still preserved in ms.

Part 8

DUETTI NOTTURNI

The following three are almost certainly remnants of an original set of six.

1. "Dimmi che vaga" [BohadloCat VI.1]

   Source: CZ-Pnm XVII D 185, "Notturno II"

2. "Ad altro laccio, vedere in braccio" [BohadloCat VI.1]

   Source: CZ-Pnm XVII D 186, "Notturno III"

3. "Se il morir fosse mia pena" [BohadloCat VI.1]

   Source: CZ-Pnm XVII D 187, "Notturno V"

   Editions: *Tři nokturna*, ed. Bohumil Vendler (Prague: Urbánek, [ca. 1900]) + 1 undated reprint, arr. voice and pf; Notturno 2 in *Dějiny české hudby v příkladech*, ed. Jaroslav Pohanka (Prague: Státní nakladatelství krásné literatury, hudby, a umění, 1958; *Tre notturni*, ed. Vratislav Bělský, Musica antiqua bohemica, series II, No. 7 (Prague: Editio Supraphon, 1972; reprint 1983)

Recordings: Musici Pragenses, cond. Josef Veselka, Supraphon SUA ST 59665, 1966 [LP]; Musici Pragenses, cond. Josef Veselka, Crossroads 22 16 0065, 1967 [LP]; children's choir Permoník Karviná, cond. Eva Šeinerová, Eden Centrum s.s., 1994 [CD]: Notturno 1; Czech Philharmonic Children's Choir, cond. Jiří Chvala, Studio SM D2435, 1995 [CD]: Notturno 1 with text "Combien plaisant, charmant"; Bambini di Praga, Multisonic 31 0528–2, 2000 [CD]

Part 9

ARIAS, ENSEMBLES, AND OTHER SHORTER VOCAL WORKS

A. Arias, Ensembles, and Shorter Vocal Works in the Czech Republic

CZ-Bm - Brno, Moravské Zemské Muzeum, Oddělení Dějin Hudby

"Duetto in G" (A 524) (Nové Město): music = CZ-Pu 59 R 184; text is "Huc gentes festinate"

"Aria" (A 5694) (Žďár nad Sázavou): music = aria "Splende così talora" from *Bellerofonte* of 1767; text is "Exultabunt sancti"

"Duetto ex B" (A 7024) (Lomnice u Tišnova): music = duet "Vanne pur, ma dimmi pria" from *Bellerofonte* of 1767; text is "Ubi mi amor quiescis"

"Sono in mar, non veggo sponde" (A 7566) (Třeboň): from *La Nitteti* of 1770

"Aria in B" (A 10070) (Bučovice): music = aria "Splende così talora" from *Bellerofonte* of 1767; text is "Gaudete omnes gentes"

"Grata lucente aurora" (A 14276) (Rajhrad cloister): dated 1793; music = aria "Ch'io mai capace" from *Bellerofonte* of 1767

"Aria de Tempore in F" (A 21087) (Dřevohostice): music = aria "Ch'io mai capace" from *Bellerofonte* of 1767; text is "Grata lucente"

"Justus in Domo alma florebit" (A 23970) (Jevišovice u Znojma): music = aria "Parto, ma in quest'istante" from *Bellerofonte* of 1767

"Duetto in A" (A 31176) (Dědice u Vyškova): dated 1843; music = CZ-OP A 316; text is "Maria mater"

CZ-BER - Beroun, Okresní Archiv

"Aria solemnis" (HU 314) (estate of Tekla Podleská-Batková): no text; music = aria "Palesar vorrei col pianto" from *Bellerofonte* of 1767

"Justi Dei" (HU 315) (estate of Tekla Podleská-Batková): music = aria "Giusti Dei" from *Bellerofonte* of 1767

"Duetto" (HU 316): no text; music = duet "Si ti fido al tuo gran core" from *Il trionfo di Clelia* of 1768

"Sidera coeli serenam" (HU 317): music = duet "Vanne pur, ma dimmi pria" from *Bellerofonte* of 1767

"Ah, che vuol dir quel pianto" (HU 318): duet from *Romolo ed Ersilia* of 1773

CZ-BRE - Březnice, Kostel sv. Ignáce

"O mi Deus fons bonitatis/O Maria fons bonitatis" (Sign. 282): dated 4 June 1835; music = aria "Sol del Tebro" from *Il trionfo di Clelia* of 1768

"Sol splendesce" (Sign. 283): "Del Sig. Venatorino"; copied before 1800; music = aria "Giusti Dei" from *Bellerofonte* of 1767

CZ-BRO - Broumov, Děkanský Úřad, Chrám sv. Petra a Pavla

"Cesset umbra tenebrosa" (371): copied ca. 1775; music = aria "Palesar vorrei col pianto" from *Bellerofonte* of 1767

CZ-CBj - České Budějovice, Jihočeské Muzeum, Hudební Oddělení

"Aria Solenis ex F" (H 985): music attr. Antonio Boroni in CZ-Pnm VI C 87; text is "Tubae canora voce"

CZ-CH - Cheb, Okresní Archiv

"Aria solemnis" (S-40–3–35) (Chrám sv. Mikuláše): nineteenthth-century ms.; music = aria "Come potrai, tiranno" from *Bellerofonte* of 1767; text is "O astra quo me vertam terra"

CZ-CT - Česká Třebová, Městské Muzeum

"Motetto in Dis" (H 137): consists of aria "Ave mundi" and solo + chorus "In te confido"; music of aria = "Alme incaute" from *Demetrio* I of 1773; the origin of the music for the chorus is unknown

CZ-JIm - Jindřichův Hradec, Vlastivědné Muzeum

"O Jesu summum bonum" (177): music = aria "Prometti ognor la calma" from *Bellerofonte* of 1767

"Pria ch'io perda" (178): dated 1775; from *Bellerofonte* of 1767

"In hoc die o fideles" (179): music = aria "Pria ch'io perda" from *Bellerofonte* of 1767

"Huc pie mentes" (259): music = aria "Splende così talora" from *Bellerofonte* of 1767

"Post partum virgo inviolata" (284)

CZ-K - Český Krumlov, Státní Oblastní Archiv v Třeboni - Pracoviště v Českém Krumlově, hudební sbírka

"Jesu dulcis memoria" (2826) (Kostel, Hluboká nad Vltavou): music attr. Antonio Boroni in CZ-Pnm VI C 87

"Sol splendesce" (2827) (Kostel, Hluboká nad Vltavou): music = aria "Giusti Dei" from *Bellerofonte* of 1767

CZ-KL - Klatovy, Okresní Muzeum

"Aria in Dis" (XIII/342, D 4997), lost: music = aria "Palesar vorrei col pianto" from *Bellerofonte* of 1767; substitute text is "Salve virgo florens"

"Ariae duae" (I/310, D 4998): music of 1st aria = aria "Prometti ognor la calma" from *Bellerofonte* of 1767 with substitute text "O Jesu spes amata"; music of 2nd aria = aria "Di due pupille amabili" from *Bellerofonte* of 1767 with substitute texts "O Jesu spes amata," "Benedicamus Patrem," and "Affectu vos amabili"

Signatures for 9 Mysliveček arias declared lost by archival staff: I/301, D 4993; I/365, D 4994; I/293, D 4995; I/313, D 4996; I/298, D 4999; I/294, D 5000; I/299, D 5001; I/319, D 5002; I/324, D 5003

CZ-KRa - Kroměříž, Arcibiskupský Zámek a Zahrady, hudební archiv

"Aria ex Eb" (A 2123): music = aria "Alme incaute" from *Demetrio* I of 1773

"Aria ex C" (A 2124): music = aria "Nuove procelle ancora" from *Bellerofonte* of 1767; texts are "Ah d'ascoltar già parmi" and "Veni creator spiritus"

"Aria" (A 2125): textless

"Cantata" (A 4120): music = aria "Palesar vorrei col pianto" from *Bellerofonte* of 1767

CZ-KU - Kutná Hora, Oblastní Muzeum

"Adoro te devote" (Hr 285): music = aria "Di due pupille amabili" from *Bellerofonte* of 1767

"Festinate ad cantus" (Hr 307) (Ursuline cloister): music = aria "Pria ch'io perda" from *Bellerofonte* of 1767

"Festiva resplendet dies fidelis" (Hr 366) (Ursuline cloister): music = CZ-Pnm XXX C 280

"Si consistant contra me" (Hr 635) (Kostel sv. Jakuba in Kutná Hora): copied ca. 1800; music = aria "Sono in mar, non veggo sponde" from *La Nitteti* of 1770

CZ-LIa - Česká Lípa, Okresní Archiv

"8 Rorate coeli" (No. 2115 hud.) (Farní Úřad Velenice): music for No. 3 = aria "Ch'io mai capace" from *Bellerofonte* of 1767

CZ-LIT - Litoměřice, Státní Oblastní Archiv

"Pace e calma in questo seno" (Sign. 699): from *Artaserse* of 1774

"Festinate o mortales" (Sign. 700) (Loretánský Hudební Archiv): music = aria "Fiumiciel che s'ode appena" from *Semiramide* of 1766

"Grata lucente aurora" (Sign. 702) (Loretánský Hudební Archív): music = aria "In te spero, o sposo amato" from *Demofoonte* I of 1769

"Amati quaeso montes" (Sign. 717) (Loretánský Hudební Archív): music = aria "Misero pargoletto" from *Demofoonte* I of 1769

CZ-LO - Loukov, Farní Kostel

"Aria in C" (201/178): dated 1830; music = duet "Di due pupille amabili" from *Bellerofonte* of 1767; text is "Si quaeris me angat"

CZ-MB - Mladá Boleslav, Okresní Archiv

"Ad te sospiro" (138): copied 1st half of nineteenth century; music = aria "Di due pupille amabili" from *Bellerofonte* of 1767

"Justi Dei" (139): dated 7 March 1840; music = aria "Giusti Dei" from *Bellerofonte* of 1767

"Justi Dei" (140): copied 1st half of nineteenth century; music = aria "Giusti Dei" from *Bellerofonte* of 1767

CZ-OP - Opava, Slezské Muzeum

"Tremendum et venerabile" (A 316): early nineteenth-century ms.; duet; music = CZ-Bm A 31176

"Ave mundi spes Maria" (A 317) (Slavkov): early nineteenth-century ms.; music = aria "Alme incaute" from *Demetrio* I of 1773

CZ-Pa - Prague, Národní Archiv (formerly Státní Ústřední Archiv)

"Laudate Deum omnes" (Fond Milosrdní Bratři, carton 190): "Del Sig. Mislivetzek detto il Boemo per la fiera di Bergamo 1766"; music = terzetto "Se sdegni un cor fedele" from *Semiramide* of 1766

CZ-Pak - Prague, Archiv Pražského Hradu, Knihovna Metropolitní Kapituly u Sv. Víta, hudební sbírka

"Aria" (Sign. 902): music = aria "Non speri onusto il pino" from *Il trionfo di Clelia* of 1768; texts are "Alatae coeli stellae" and "O Maria Virgo pia"

"Aria in C" (Sign. 903): music = aria "Pensa, a serbami, o cara" from *Ezio* I of 1775; text is "Ave Virgo singularis"

"Aria in C" (Sign. 904): music = aria "Sperai vicino il lido" from *Demofoonte* I of 1769; text is "Cantemus praeconia Divo"

"Aria in B" (Sign. 905): music = aria "Chi d'un paterno affetto" from *Atide* of 1774; includes original text and additional text "Ah, ardeat cor meum"

"Aria solemnis ex B" (Sign. 906): music = aria "In te spero, o sposo amato" from *Demofoonte* I of 1769; text is "Grata lucente"

"Aria de omni solennitate item de festo B. V. Maria" (Sign. 907): music = aria "Serbo infelice" from *Atide* of 1774; text is "Homo, qui dormis, surge, salutis"

"Aria de dedicatione et Sancto de B. V. Maria" (Sign. 908): text is "O quam metuendus est locus"

"Aria in D" (Sign. 909): music = aria "Alma grande" from *Atide* of 1774; text is "Quis me dicat infelicem"

"Aria in D" (Sign. 910): music = aria "Sol del Tebro" from *Il trionfo di Clelia* of 1768; text is "Si tranquillo in casto amore"

"Aria in B" (Sign. 1697): music = aria "Spesso, se ben l'affetto" from *Il trionfo di Clelia* of 1768; text is "Laudes cantemus, Deo"

CZ-Pkřiž - Prague, Rytířský Řád Křižovníků s Červenou Hvězdou, hudební sbírka

"O Deus consolator" (XXXV B 164a): music = aria "Prometti ognor la calma" from *Bellerofonte* of 1767

"O ter sancta et individua" (XXXV B 164b): music = aria "Pria ch'io perda" from *Bellerofonte* of 1767

"Jesu dulcissime spes suspirantis animae" (XXXV B 164c): music = aria "Splende così talora" from *Bellerofonte* of 1767

"Surrexit Dominus de sepulcro" (XXXV B 164d): music = aria "Già cinto sembrami" from *Bellerofonte* of 1767

"Sancte Spiritus fons bonitatis" (XXXV B 164e): music = aria "Sono in mar, non veggo sponde" from *La Nitteti* of 1770

"Rex gloriose caelitum" (XXXV B 164f): music = aria "Si tacerò se vuoi" from *Il trionfo di Clelia* of 1768

"Ave Regina caelorum" (XXXV C 85): music attr. J. A. Koželuh in CZ-Pnm L C 191

"Huc piae mentes" (XXXV C 86): music = aria "Splende così talora" from *Bellerofonte* of 1767

"Jesu dulcissime fons bonitatis" (XXXV C 87): music = aria "Sono in mar, non veggo sponde" from *La Nitteti* of 1770

(Aria) (XXXV C 88): no text; music = aria "Come potrai, tiranno" from *Bellerofonte* of 1767

"Hac aurora gratiosa" (XXXV C 89): music = aria "Non speri onusto il pino" from *Il trionfo di Clelia* of 1768

"Veni o care Jesu" (XXXV C 90): music = aria "Sai che piegar si vede" from *Il trionfo di Clelia* of 1768

"O mi Deus fons bonitatis" (XXXV C 91): music = aria "Sol del Tebro" from *Il trionfo di Clelia* of 1768

"Exurgit urbis aurora" (XXXV C 93): music = aria "De folgori di Giove" from *Il trionfo di Clelia* of 1768

"Aria solenne à canto solo" (XXXV C 94): no text; music = aria "Palesar vorrei col pianto" from *Bellerofonte* of 1767

"Fuggi dagl'occhi miei" (XXXV C 95): from *Semiramide* of 1766

"Ah, non è vano il pianto" (XXXV C 96): from *Semiramide* of 1766

"Nostra spes in te quiescit" (XXXV D 159): music = duet "Vanne pur, ma dimmi pria" from *Bellerofonte* of 1767

CZ-Pnm - Prague, České Muzeum Hudby (formerly Muzeum České Hudby; formerly Národní Muzeum, Hudební Oddělení), hudební archiv

"Aria sollennis à soprano solo" (IX C 118): music = aria "Giusti Dei" from *Bellerofonte* of 1767

"Aria a alto solo" (X B 200) (Ondřej Horník collection): ms. copied in early 19th century; attr. "Giuseppe Kozeluh"; music = aria "Si tacerò se vuoi" from *Il trionfo di Clelia* of 1768; text is "Exultet dies clara"

"Aria a soprano solo" (XIII C 119) (Kutná Hora; originally from Cítoliby): music = aria "Sono in mar, non veggo sponde" from *La Nitteti* of 1770; text is "Si consistant"

(2 arias) (XIII C 120) (1st aria from Rychnov nad Knežnou; 2nd aria from Jiříkov): 1st aria copied near the end of the eighteenth century; 2nd aria dated 14 January 1817; music of 1st aria = "Che quel cor, quel ciglio altero" from *Semiramide* of 1766; text of 1st aria is "Alma redemptoris mater"; music of 2nd aria = "Ah, non è vano il pianto" from *Semiramide* of 1766; text of 2nd aria is "Adoro te mi Jesu chare"

"Aria à alto solo" (XIII C 121) (Nymburk, originally Potštejn): music = aria "Sperai vicino il lido" from *Demofoonte* I of 1769; includes original text and additional text "Cantemus preconia"

"Aria solemnis de dedicatione ecclesiae et de tempore" (XIII C 122) (Ustí nad Orlicí): early nineteenth-century ms.; music = aria "Si tacerò se vuoi" from *Il trionfo di Clelia* of 1768; text is "Ad festum properate"

"Aria a canto solo" (XIII C 123) (Jiřikov): music = aria "De folgori di Giove" from *Il trionfo di Clelia* of 1768; text is "Ad festum properate"

"Aria à tenore solo" (XIII C 124) (Královský Vyšehrad): music = rondò "Luci belle, se piangete" from *Medonte* of 1780; text is "Ad hoc festum"

"Offertorium" (XII C 125) (Slaný): music = aria "Di due pupille amabili" from *Bellerofonte* of 1767; text is "O salutaris hostia"

"Aria à basso solo" (XIII C 126) (České Budějovice): copied from a ms. in the archive of the church of St. Nicholas in 1906; text is "Lauda Sion"

"Aria à canto solo" (XIII C 127) (Cítoliby): music = aria "Ch'io mai capace" from *Bellerofonte* of 1767; text is "Tibi laus Deus"

"Aria à soprano solo" (XIII C 128) (Heřmanův Městec & Polná): music attr. Antonio Boroni in CZ-Pnm VI C 88; = CZ-Pnm L B 223 and CZ-Pu 59 R 49; text is "Si adversum me"

"Aria à canto solo" (XIII C 129) (Prague, church of St. Nicholas): dated 1802; music attr. J. A. Koželuh in CZ-Pnm XI E 52, XXVII B 164, and XXXII C 262; text is "Spes mea"

"Quartetto" (XIII C 130) (Dačice): text is "Di tua Grazia o Signore"

"Aria a oboe solo e soprano" (XIII C 131): music = aria "Fra i perigli del lungo viaggio" from *Tobia* of 1769; text is "Festinate, o mortales"

"Aria de venerabili" (XIII C 132) (Cítoliby): music = aria "Splende così talora" from *Bellerofonte* of 1767; text is "O coena nuptialis"

"Aria de omni solemnitate" (XIII C 133) (Mladá Boleslav): text is "Amati quaeso montes"; music = CZ-Pnm XXXVII B 131

"Aria de tempore et Sancto et SS. Angelis" (XIII C 134) (Ústí nad Orlicí): early nineteenth-century ms.; music = aria "Qual ristretto in picciol letto" from *Bellerofonte* of 1767; text is "Nil affecto nil expecto"

"Aria a canto solo" (XIII C 135) (Polná): early nineteenth-century ms.; music attr. J. A. Koželuh in CZ-Pnm X B 209; texts are "Adeste huc, fideles" and "Non vincent me catena"

"Pastorella à tenore solo" (XIII C 136) (Ústí nad Orlicí): early nineteenthth-century ms.; music = aria "Il pastore torna Aprile" from *Semiramide* of 1766; text is "Huc pastores"

"Aria a tenore solo" (XIII C 137) (Jiřikov): music = aria "Sai che piegar si vede" from *Il trionfo di Clelia* of 1768; text is "Laudemus coelestis cives"

"II Arie à voce cantante" (XIII C 138) (1st aria from Polná; 2nd aria from Potštejn): music of 1st aria = "Pria ch'io perda" from *Bellerofonte* of 1767; text of 1st aria is "Mente tota semper devota"; music of 2nd aria = "Giusti Dei" from *Bellerofonte* of 1767; text of 2nd aria is "In victe Martyr unicum Patris"

(3 arias) (XIII C 139) (Domažlice): music of 1st aria = "Ch'io mai capace" from *Bellerofonte* of 1767; text of 1st aria is "Grata lucente"; music of 2nd aria = "Di due pupille amabili" from *Bellerofonte* of 1767; text of 2nd aria is "Adoro te devote"; music of 3rd aria = "Talor se il vento fremi" from *Semiramide* of 1766; text of 3rd aria is "Adeste nunc fideles"

"Aria a soprano solo" (XIII C 140) (Cítoliby): text is "Hac aurora"; original text identified with incipit "Quel che il fato"

"Aria à basso solo" (XIII C 141) (Rožálovice): early nineteenth-century ms.; music = CZ-Pnm XV F 332; text is "Hic est locus"

"Ariae duae a canto solo" (XIII C 142): early nineteenth-century mss.; music of 1st aria = "Di quei sassi" from *Bellerofonte* of 1767 with introductory rec.; text of 1st aria is "Letare anima"; text of 2nd aria is "In hac die"

"Aria à canto solo" (XIII C 143) (Polná): music = aria "Sol del Tebro" from *Il trionfo di Clelia* of 1768; text is "Amati quaeso"

"Aria de omni Sancto et de Beata" (XIII C 144) (Plzeň): music = aria "Non speri onusto il pino" from *Il trionfo di Clelia* of 1768; texts are "O, mi Sancte adamate" and "O Maria virgo pia"

"Aria a 2" (XIII C 145) (Cítoliby): early nineteenth-century ms.; music = duet "Vanne pur, ma dimmi pria" from *Bellerofonte* of 1767; text is "Vivere ultra"

"Aria à canto solo" (XIII C 146) (Mladá Boleslav): music = aria "Palesar vorrei col pianto" from *Bellerofonte* of 1767; text is "Salve amor"

"Salve Regina" (XIII C 147) (Cítoliby): music = terzetto "Se sdegni un cor fedele" from *Semiramide* of 1766

"Aria in B a soprano solo" (XV C 242): early nineteenth-century ms.; music = aria "Fra i perigli del lungo viaggio" from *Tobia* of 1769; text is "Tu es Petrus"

"Aria a basso solo" (XV E 238) (Přeštice): early nineteenth-century ms.; also attr. Johann Stamitz in same ms.; texts are "Omni die dic Maria" and "Festinate huc clientes"

"Offertorium de Beata Matre" (XV F 330) (Bakov nad Jizerou): text is "Omni die dic Maria"

"Aria ex B solemnis a canto solo" (XV F 331) (Bakov nad Jizerou): music = aria "Splende così talora" from *Bellerofonte* of 1767; text is "Huc piae mentes"

"Aria de Festivate" (XV F 332): "Del Sig. Benatorino"; music = CZ-Pnm XIII C 141; text is "Hic est locus"

"Barbare stelle" (XVI A 200) (E. E. Homolka collection): ms. copied 1935; terzetto from *Bellerofonte* of 1767

"Barbare stelle" (XVII D 188): terzetto from *Bellerofonte* of 1767

"Aria in C a canto solo" (XIX D 257): early nineteenth-century ms.; music = aria "Pensa, a serbarmi, o cara" from *Ezio* I of 1775; text is "Salve Jesu pie"

"Pria di salir nel trono" (XXVI F 336): ms. dated 1904; scene and aria from *Il gran Tamerlano* of 1772

"Aria ab alto solo" (XXVIII E 38) (Emil Trolda collection): ms. copied by Emil Trolda in 1933; music = aria "Conservati fedele" from *Artaserse* of 1774; text is "Voce mea clamavi"; ms. also includes incipits for five arias with Latin texts from *Il trionfo di Clelia* that are recorded as being preserved in 1933 in the Strahov monastery in Prague

"Aria de Sancto" (XXVII E 39) (Emil Trolda collection): twentieth-century ms. copied from a ms. of 1806; text is "Coelesti voboratus"

"Sol splendesce" (XXVII E 40) (Emil Trolda collection): ms. copied in 1904 from a ms. in Žamberk dated 1824; music = aria "Giusti Dei" from *Bellerofonte* of 1767

"Ave mundi spes Maria" (XXVII E 41) (Emil Trolda collection): twentieth-century ms.; music = aria "Alme incaute" from *Demetrio* I of 1773

"Aria Pastoritia" (XXXII C 243) (Osek): music = aria "Se dall'amato gregge" from Cantata 2; text is "Ad neonati cunas"

"Aria canto solo" (XXXII C 251) (Osek): music = aria "De folgori di Giove" from *Il trionfo di Clelia* of 1768; text is "Ad festum properate"

"Aria De Tempore" (XXXII C 254) (Osek): music = aria "Ah, celar la bella face" from *Il trionfo di Clelia* of 1768; text is "Confitebor tibi, Deus"

"Aria Canto solo" (XXXII C 255) (Osek): music = aria "Resta, o cara" from *Il trionfo di Clelia* of 1768; text is "Gemebunda dies"

"Aria Tenore Solo" (XXXII C 256) (Osek): music = aria "Sai che piegar si vede" from *Il trionfo di Clelia* of 1768; texts are "Laudemus coelestes cives" and "Laudemus coeli Reginam"

"Aria a canto solo" (XXXII C 257) (Osek): music = aria "Nuove procelle ancora" from *Bellerofonte* of 1767; text is "Venite gratae gentes"

"Aria pro omni festivate" (XXXII C 258) (Osek): music = aria "Tempeste il mar" from *Il trionfo di Clelia* of 1768; text is "Hac die tam amoena"

"Aria Vta" (XXXII C 263) (Osek): music = aria "Se intende, sì poco" from *Semiramide* of 1766; text is "O chara dulcedo"

"Aria ex B" (XXXII C 265) (Osek): music = aria "Splende così talora" from *Bellerofonte* of 1767; text is "Canite caeli"

"Aria De Beata" (XXXII C 272) (Osek): music = aria "Palesar vorrei col pianto" from *Bellerofonte* of 1767; texts are "Ave digna mundi laude" and "Dogma datur Christianis"

"Aria ex D" (XXXII C 279) (Osek): music = aria "Talor se il vento fremi" from *Semiramide* of 1766; text is "Adeste nunc fideles"

"Aria solemnis" (XXXII C 280) (Osek): text is "Festiva resplendet dies fideles"

Recording: Helga Spatzek, soprano, Thurgauer Barockensemble, Swiss Pan 510043, 2001 [CD]

"Aria alto solo" (XXXII D 98) (Osek): music = aria "Si tacerò se vuoi" from *Il trionfo di Clelia* of 1768; text is "Canite chori loeta"

"Aria di guosto" (XXXII E 68) (Osek): music = aria "Giusti Dei" from *Bellerofonte* of 1767; includes original text and additional text "Lauda Sion"

"Aria de Sanctissimo Sacramento" (XXXII E 76) (Osek): music = aria "Ah, non è vano il pianto" from *Semiramide* of 1766; text is "Adoro te cui Jesu chare"

"Aria ex C" (XXXII E 77) (Osek): music = aria "Di due pupille amabili" from *Bellerofonte* of 1767; text is "Ach qui sunt hi dolores"

"Aria" (XXXII E 156) (Osek): music attr. Antonio Boroni in CZ-Pnm VI C 88; = CZ-Pnm L B 223 and CZ-Pu 59 R 49; text is "O plena omni dole"

"Duetto" (XXXIII B 66) (Osek): music = duet "Vanne pur, ma dimmi pria" from *Bellerofonte* of 1767; text is "Supra Maria agitata"

"Duetto de Venerabili Sacramento" (XXXIII E 97) (Osek): text is "Amo te corde devoto"

"Duetto in B" (XXXVII B 125) (Břevnov cloister): ms. dated 1783; music = duet "Vanne pur, ma dimmi pria" from *Bellerofonte* of 1767; text is "Coelites semper felices"

"Aria de Communione" (XXXVII B 126) (Břevnov cloister): music = aria "Resta, o cara" from *Il trionfo di Clelia* of 1768; text is "Amo te Deus"

"Aria De SS. Communione" (XXXVII B 127) (Břevnov cloister): music = aria "Ch'io mai capace" from *Bellerofonte* of 1767; text is "Jesu electe sponse dilecte"

"Aria a Tenore solo de communione" (XXXVII B 128) (Břevnov cloister): from *Bellerofonte* of 1767; includes original text "Di due pupille amabili" and new text "Adoro te devote"

"Aria De Communione à Canto Solo" (XXXVII B 129) (Břevnov cloister): music = aria "Parto, ma in quest'istante" from *Bellerofonte* of 1767; text is "Ave Jesu summe"

"Aria a soprano" (XXXVII B 130) (Břevnov cloister): music = aria "Giusti Dei" from *Bellerofonte* of 1767; text is "Justi Dei furorem timete"

"Cantata pro Omni Solenitate" (XXXVII B 131) (Břevnov cloister) [BohadloCat III.6]: ms. dated 1769; text is "Stellae bellae scintillate"; music = CZ-Pnm XIII C 133

"Aria ex A dur" (XXXVII B 132) (Břevnov cloister): ms. dated 1768; music = aria "Pria ch'io perda" from *Bellerofonte* of 1767; text is "Festinate ad cantus ad plausus"

"Aria a soprano" (XXXVII B 133) (Břevnov cloister): ms. ca. 1770; music = aria "Qual ristretto in picciol letto" from *Bellerofonte* of 1767; text is "Cesset umbra tenebrosa"

(2 arias) (XXXVII B 134) (Břevnov cloister): ms. ca. 1770; music of 1st aria = "Palesar vorrei col pianto" from *Bellerofonte* of 1767; text is "Gratiosa hodierna peramoena aurora"; 2nd aria attr. Antonio Sacchini

"Ariae duae" (XXXVII B 135) (Břevnov cloister): ms. ca. 1770; music of 1st aria = aria "Fin la dove l'aurora" from *Il Parnaso confuso*; text is "O dies ter optata"; 2nd aria attr. Václav Pichl

"Aria No. 1 a canto solo" (XXXVII B 166) (Břevnov cloister): ms. ca. 1770; music = aria "In fronte a voi vi splende" from *Il Parnaso confuso*; text is "Huc adeste piae mentes"

"Terzetto" (XXXVIII A 150) (Broumov): music = terzetto "Barbare stelle" from *Bellerofonte* of 1767; text is "Anima quid moraris"

"Cantata a Soprano" (XXXVIII A 294) (Broumov): music = aria "Giusti Dei" from *Bellerofonte* of 1767; text is "Sol resplende"

"Sarete al fin contenti/Ch'io mai capace" (XXXVIII A 295) (Broumov): scene and aria from *Bellerofonte* of 1767; text is "Affectu toto corde"

"Ariae 2" (XXXVIII A 296) (Broumov): music of 1st aria = aria "Parto, ma in quest'istante" from *Bellerofonte* of 1767; text of 1st aria is "Ave maris stella"; music of 2nd aria = "Non è la morte" from *Bellerofonte* of 1767; text of 2nd aria is "Vos piae mentes laudes"

"Aria in C" (XXXVIII F 31) (Úterý): music = aria "Rende il mar" from *Antigona* of 1774; text is "Nil me gladius vel parmo"

"Aria in Dis" (XXXVIII F 111) (Úterý): nineteenth-century ms.; text is "Infelicem ne me dicas"

"Aria solemnis" (XL A 292) (Želiv): music = aria "Ch'io mai capace" from *Bellerofonte* of 1767; text is "Quam suavis amor properate"

"Aria in C" (XL A 293) (Želiv): music = aria "De folgori di Giove" from *Il trionfo di Clelia* of 1768; text is "Huc cito clientes"

"Aria in F" (XL A 294) (Želiv): music = aria "Ch'io mai capace" from *Bellerofonte* of 1767; text is "Grata lucente"

"Aria duplex Theoph." (XL A 295) (Želiv): text of aria is "O michi superi," text of quartet is "Jesu dulcissime"

"Aria solennis in C" (XL A 296) (Želiv): music = aria "Di due pupille amabili" from *Bellerofonte* of 1767; text is "Non solum venerati"

"Aria solemnis ex F" (XL A 297) (Želiv): music = aria "Mille dubbi mi destano in petto" from *Il trionfo di Clelia* of 1768; text is "Tibi cor meum"

"Duetto in B (XL D 348) (Bertramka, originally from Svatá Hora): ms. dated 1805; music = duet "Vanne pur, ma dimmi pria" from *Bellerofonte* of 1767

"Questa è la bella face" (XLII E 61) (Frýdlant): from *Romolo ed Ersilia* of 1773

"Per brevi istanti/Basta così vincesti" (XLII E 64) (Frýdlant): scene and aria from *Romolo ed Ersilia* of 1773

"E tace, Ersilia/Ah, che vuol dir quel pianto" (XLII E 65) (Frýdlant): scene and duet from *Romolo ed Ersilia* of 1773

"Il caro mio bene" (XLII E 66) (Frýdlant): from *Armida* of 1780

"Serba costante il core" (XLII E 67) (Frýdlant): from *Medonte* of 1780

"Luci belle, se piangete" (XLII E 215) (Frýdlant): from *Medonte* of 1780

"Conservati fedele" (XLII E 216) (Frýdlant): from *Artaserse* of 1774

"O aeterna veritas" (XLVI A 466) (Prague, Strahov): ms. copied ca. 1800: music = aria "Non speri onusto il pino" from *Il trionfo di Clelia* of 1768

"O mens exhilerata" (XLVI A 467) (Prague, Strahov): ms. ca. 1800; music = aria "Si tacerò se vuoi" from *Il trionfo di Clelia* of 1768

"Corrus cante caeli face/Ave Maria/Ave maris stella" (XLVII A 6) (Prague, Strahov): music = aria "Palesar vorrei col pianto" from *Bellerofonte* of 1767

"Aria in Dis" (XLVII A 8) (Prague, Strahov): music = aria "Giusti Dei" from *Bellerofonte* of 1767; text is "Ave mundi spes"

"Cantata in C" (XLVII A 9) (Prague, Strahov): music = aria "Di due pupille amabili" from *Bellerofonte* of 1767; text is "Ad te suspiro"

"Terzetto" (XLVII A 22) (Prague, Strahov): music and text is terzetto "Barbare stelle ingrate" from *Bellerofonte* of 1767

"Aria pro omni festo" (XLVII E 103) (Prague, Strahov): music = aria "Giusti Dei" from *Bellerofonte* of 1767; text is "Amati quaeso montes"

"Ariae duae" (XLVII F 20) (Prague, Strahov): music of one aria = aria "Splende così talora" from *Bellerofonte* of 1767; text is "Si nocte coelum"

"Salve Regina" (XLIX D 494) (Kuks): music = terzetto "Se sdegni un cor fedele" from *Semiramide* of 1766

"Aria de Sancto vel Sancta" (XLIX D 506) (Kuks): ms. dated 12 August 1820; text is "Caelis amoenae"

"Aria in C" (L A 65) (Alžbětinky): ms. dated 1781; music = aria "De folgori di Giove" from *Il trionfo di Clelia* of 1768; text is "Accensa clara face"

"Aria ex Fb" (L B 223) (Alžbětinky): music attr. Antonio Boroni in CZ-Pnm VI C 88; music = CZ-Pnm XXXII E 156 and CZ-Pu 59 R 49; text is "Amati quaeso montes"

"Aria in E" (L B 461) (Alžbětinky): nineteenth-century ms.; music = aria "Giusti Dei" from *Bellerofonte* of 1767; text is "Veni creator spiritus"

"Aria in C Guthe Hirt" (L C 30) (Alžbětinky): ms. dated 1779; music = aria "Sono in mar, non veggo sponde" from *La Nitteti* of 1770; text is "Si nocte coelum"

CZ-Ps - Prague, Literární Archiv Památníku Národního Písemnictví (Strahov)

"Pria di salir nel trono" (s.s) (from the Lešehradeum, the former collection of the poet E. Lešetický): scene and aria from *Il gran Tamerlano* of 1772

CZ-Psj - Prague, Farní Úřad, Chrám sv Jakuba

"Amati quaeso montes" (Kat. Pulk. 169): music = aria "Care luci nel mirarvi tal dolcezza" from *La Nitetti* of 1770

"Hostia grata" (Kat. Pulk. 204): music = aria "Questa è la bella face" from *Romolo ed Ersilia* of 1773

"Per montes et per vales" (Kat. Pulk. 281): music = aria "Talor se il vento fremi" from *Semiramide* of 1766

"Amati quaeso montes" (Kat. Pulk. 359)

"Rex gloriose coelitum" (Kat. Pulk. 360): music = aria "Si tacerò se vuoi" from *Il trionfo di Clelia* of 1768

"Vos clientes, huc piae mentes" (Kat. Pulk. 361): music = aria "Di quei sassi" from *Bellerofonte* of 1767

"Vos piae gentes" (Kat. Pulk. 384): music = terzetto "Se sdegni un cor fedele" from *Semiramide* of 1766

"Adeste fideles" (Kat. Pulk. 429): music = aria "Giusti Dei" from *Bellerofonte* of 1767

"Quaeso amati montes" (Kat Pulk. 430): music = aria "Splende così talora" from *Bellerofonte* of 1767

"In Deo speravit cor meum" (Kat. Pulk. 431): music = aria "Già cinto sembrami" from *Bellerofonte* of 1767

"Festinate, o mortales" (Kat. Pulk. 432)

"Vale jam vane munde" (Kat. Pulk. 433): music = duet "Vanne pur, ma dimmi pria" from *Bellerofonte* of 1767

"Maria Gustum" (Kat. Pulk. 434)

"Ave Maria" (Kat. Pulk. 435): music = aria "In questa selva oscura" from *Il trionfo di Clelia* of 1768

"Adeste hunc fideles" (Kat. Pulk. 436): music attr. J. A. Koželuh in CZ-Pnm X B 209

CZ-Pu - Prague, Národní Knihovna České Republiky, Universitní Knihovna, Hudební Oddělení

Collection of 5 arias and 1 duet from *Artaserse* of 1774 and 1 aria from *Romolo ed Ersilia* of 1773 (59 R 31) (from collection of Charles Francis, Count Nesselrode): arias from *Artaserse* are "Per pietà bell'idol mio," "Per quel paterno amplesso," "Và tra le selve Ircane," "Cara, oh Dio nel volto espresso," and "Pace e calma in questo seno," plus duet "Tu vuoi, ch'io viva, o cara"; aria from *Romolo ed Ersilia* is "Questa è la bella face"

Collection of 6 arias from *Demetrio* I of 1773 (59 R 32) (from collection of Charles Francis, Count Nesselrode): includes arias "Fra tanti pensieri," "Se non posso su quel trono," "Scherza il nocchier talora," "Alme incaute," "Non fidi al mar che freme," and "Agitata in tanti affanni"

"Si adversum me venti consurgunt" (59 R 49): music attr. Antonio Boroni in CZ-Pnm VI C 88

"Si martio furore/Non solum venerari/O salutaris hostia/O virgo gloriosa" (59 R 50): music = aria "Di due pupille amabili" from *Bellerofonte* of 1767

"Di due pupille amabili" (59 R 65): from *Bellerofonte* of 1767

"Per lei fra l'armi" (59 R 140): from *Demofoonte* II of 1775

"Di due pupille amabili" (59 R 141): from *Bellerofonte* of 1767

"Dall'amor mio guidate" (59 R 184): duet; music = CZ-Bm A 524; alternate text is "Huc gentes festinate"

"Pria di salir nel trono" (59 R 621): fragment from Act 3, scene 2, of *Il gran Tamerlano* of 1772

"Barbare stelle" (59 R 628): terzetto from *Bellerofonte* of 1767

"M'offende il nemico" (59 R 1157): from *Il gran Tamerlano* of 1772

"Quam bonus Israel" (59 R 1167): music = aria "Ah, celar la bella face" from *Il trionfo di Clelia* of 1768

"Lauda Sion" (59 R 1531): music = aria "Ch'io mai capace" from *Bellerofonte* of 1767

"Ad laudes properate Deum" (59 R 1896): music = aria "Pensa, a serbarmi, o cara" from *Ezio* I of 1775

"Salve Regina" (59 R 3291) (Dlouhý Most) [BohadloCat IV.8]: copied in 1789; purchased from collection of the Česká Církev Holešovice (CZ-Ph) in 1983

Edition: *Salve Regina*, ed. Friedrich Hägele (St. Augustin: J. Butz, 2000)

"Ave decus angelorum" (59 R 3665) (Panenský Týnec)

"Ave virgo singularis" (59 R 4330) (Koleč, Farní Kostel): music = aria "Tempeste il mar" from *Il trionfo di Clelia* of 1768

"Huc adeste piae mentes" (59 R 4331) (Koleč, Farní Kostel): music = aria "In un mar che non ha sponde" from *Il Parnaso confuso*

CZ-Puh - Prague (Uhříněves), Kostel Všech Svatých

"Aria solemnis" (s.s.): no text; music = aria "Giusti Dei" from *Bellerofonte* of 1767

CZ-PEL - Pelhřimov, Okresní Archiv

"Aria ex A a tenore solo" (inv. ca. 147, sign. V/8, kart. 17) (Hořepník): music = aria "Pria ch'io perda" from *Bellerofonte* of 1767; text is "Si quaeris quidem angat"

"Aria ex C a tenore solo" (inv. ca. 147, sign. V/8, kart. 17) (Hořepník): music = aria "Di due pupille amabili" from *Bellerofonte* of 1767; text is "Adoro te devoto"

"Aria ex E a canto solo" (inv. ca. 147, sign. V/8, kart. 17) (Hořepník): music = aria "Giusti Dei" from *Bellerofonte* of 1767; text is "Justi Dei"

"Aria ex F a canto solo" (inv. ca. 147, sign. V/8, kart. 17) (Hořepník): music = aria "Ch'io mai capace" from *Bellerofonte* of 1767; text is "Grata lucente"

CZ-PLa - Plzeň, Archiv Města Plzně

"Ferrenda sunt" (Hu 1635) (František Vaneček collection): ms. ca. 1820; music = CZ-PLm NMP 52896, CZ-TU M 328

"Ave maris stella" (Hu 4329) (Václav Mentberger collection): copied 1784; music = aria "Palesar vorrei col pianto" from *Bellerofonte* of 1767

CZ-PLm - Plzeň, Západočeské Muzeum, Národopisné Oddělení

"Justus ut palma" (NMP 52896): nineteenth-century ms.; music = CZ-PLa Hu 1635, CZ-TU M 328

CZ-ROk - Rokycany, Děkanský Úřad, Kostel

"Duetto di Jesu in A" (M/49): text is "Jesu dulcis amator"

CZ-RU - Rumburk, Městské Muzeum

"Aria solemnis à soprano" (s.s): early nineteenth-century ms.; 2 offertories for SATB chorus; texts of 1st offertory are "Alleluja" and "Festa sanctorum"; text of 2nd offertory is "In te confido"; music of 2nd offertory = chorus attached to aria CZ-Pnm XXVIII E 41 with same text

CZ-TEb - Teplice nad Bečvou, Brixiho Komorní Soubor

"Aria solemis in E" (No. 74): music = aria "Giusti Dei" from *Bellerofonte* of 1767; text is "Justi omnes"

CZ-TEP - Teplice nad Metují, Chrám sv. Vavřince

2 Alma redemptoris mater (B 120 [161]): ms. ca. 1835; music of 1st aria = aria "Che quel cor, quel ciglio altero" from *Semiramide* of 1766; music of 2nd aria = aria "Ah, non è vano il pianto" from *Semiramide* of 1766; same music as for arias in CZ-Pnm XII C 120

CZ-TREd - Třeboň, Děkanský Úřad, Kostel sv. Jiljí

"Aria ex D" (358 - Q/13) (Joseph Rejcha collection): music = aria "Di quei sassi" from *Bellerofonte* of 1767; text is "Astra nubes insurgat horescat"

"Aria in A" (359 - Q/14): ms. dated 19 July 1774; music = aria "Pria ch'io perda" from *Bellerofonte* of 1767; text is "Huc ad festum"

"Aria ex F" (360 - Q/15): ms. dated 1 June 1769; music attr. Antonio Boroni in CZ-Pnm VI C 87; text is "Tubae canora voce"

"Aria ex Es" (361 - Q/16): ms. perhaps copied ca. 1775; music = aria "Palesar vorrei col pianto" from *Bellerofonte* of 1767; text is "Ad hoc festum properate"

"Aria solemnis" (362 - Q/17): ms. copied ca. 1780; music = aria "Giusti Dei" from *Bellerofonte* of 1767; text is "Sol splendesce"

"Aria in C" (403 - Q/58): ms. copied during 1st quarter of nineteenth century; music = aria "Nuove procelle ancora" from *Bellerofonte* of 1767; text is "Laetae ad est dies"

"Aria in A" (404 - Q/59): ms. copied during 1st quarter of nineteenth century; music attr. Antonio Boroni in CZ-Pnm VI C 89 and XXXVII B 170; text is "Plaude coelestis aula"

"Aria solemnis" (444 - R/16): music = aria "Si tacerò se vuoi" from *Il trionfo di Clelia* of 1768; texts are "Spargete gratum maelos" and "Lauda Syon"

CZ-TU - Turnov, Městské Muzeum, hudební sbírka

"Ferrenda sunt" (M 328): music = CZ-PLa Hu 1635, CZ-PLm NMP 52896

CZ-VM - Vysoké Myto, Okresní Muzeum A. V. Šembery

"Laudate Deum omnes" (529): music = terzetto "Se sdegni un cor fedele" from *Semiramide* of 1766

B. Arias, Ensembles, and Shorter Vocal Works in German-speaking Countries

A-ST - Stams, Zisterzienserstift, Bibliothek und Musikarchiv

"Huc piae mentes" (A VI 29): ms. copied ca. 1780

"Bei labbri/Mundus caro blandiatur" (F I 56): ms. copied ca. 1770

"Jesus tu solus/Bei labbri" (F I 56): ms. copied ca. 1780

"Ben potete/Sancte Joannes" (F I 57): ms. copied ca. 1780; from *Antigona* of 1774

A-Wgm - Vienna, Gesellschaft der Musikfreunde in Wien, Bibliothek

"Alme incaute" (VI 252/Q 3123): from *Demetrio* I of 1773

"Di due pupille amabili" (VI 288/Q 3124): from *Bellerofonte* of 1767

"Superbo di me stesso" (VI 295/Q 3125): from *L'olimpiade* of 1778

"Vanne pur, ma dimmi pria" (VI 293/Q 21101): duet from *Bellerofonte* of 1767

"Se pietà da voi non trovo" (VI 313/Q 3126): from *Ipermestra* of 1769

"Bester Freund, so sprach sie freundlich" (VI 17129/Q 3127): re-texting of "Luci belle, se piangete" from *Medonte* of 1780

A-Wn - Vienna, Österreichische Nationalbibliothek, Musiksammlung

"Ho perduto il mio tesoro" (S.m. 4150): from *Antigono* of 1780

"Vanne pur, ma dimmi pria" (S.m. 4151): duet from *Bellerofonte* of 1767

CH-Bu - Basel, Öffentliche Bibliothek der Universität Basel, Musiksammlung

"Pace e calma in questo seno" (Kr IV 185/Ms. 177): from *Artaserse* of 1774

CH-BM - Beromünster, Musikbibliothek des Stifts

"Gaudent in caelis" (Ms. 6623): music = aria "De folgori di Giove" from *Il trionfo di Clelia* of 1768

CH-E - Einsiedeln, Kloster Einsiedeln, Musikbibliothek

"Mille cose in un momento" (Ms. 2416): from *La Calliroe* of 1778

"Poveri affetti miei" (Ms. 2511)

"Il caro e solo oggetto" (Ms. 2512): from *Il gran Tamerlano* of 1772

"Ad festum convolate fideles" (Ms. 3050): music = aria "Nuove procelle ancora" from *Bellerofonte* of 1767

"Laudate pueri" (Ms. 4160)

"O Jesu dilecte" (ms. 4161): music = duet "Di quel amabil ciglio" from *Il gran Tamerlano* of 1772

"Magnae Deus potentiae" (Ms. 4162): music = aria "Il caro e solo oggetto" from *Il gran Tamerlano* of 1772

"Laetatus sum" (Ms. 4163): ms. dated 1791; music = aria "Vanne la sorte mia" from *Il gran Tamerlano* of 1772

"O gloriosa Domina" (Ms. 4165): music = aria "Tempeste il mar" from *Il trionfo di Clelia* of 1768
"Dominus a dextris" (Ms. 4166): a quartet
"Se non posso su quel (trono)" (Ms. 4663): from *Demetrio* I of 1773; includes new text "Omnes gentes plaudite manibus"
"Frema in orrida sembianza" (Ms. 4664): from *Antigona* of 1774; includes additional text "Factus est protector meus"
"Ben potete" (Ms. 4665): from *Antigona* of 1774; includes additional text "Deus meus adiutor meus"
"Agitata in tanti affanni" (Ms. 4666): from *Demetrio* I of 1773; includes additional text "Justus ut palma"
"Fra tanti pensieri" (Ms. 4667): from *Demetrio* I of 1773; includes new additional text "Omni die"
"Scherza il nocchier talora" (Ms. 4668): from *Demetrio* I of 1773; includes additional text "Verbum supernum"
"Laudate pueri" (Ms. 4791): music = aria "Saper ti basta o cara" from *Il trionfo di Clelia* of 1768

CH-EN - Engelberg, Kloster, Musikbibliothek
"O vere digna hostia" (Ms A 482/Ms. 5854): music = aria "Mille cose in un momento" from *La Calliroe* of 1778
"Dei di Roma, ah perdonate" (Ms A 483/Ms. 5855): from *Il trionfo di Clelia* of 1768; includes additional text "Fidelis servus et prudens"
"Saper ti basta o cara" (Ms A 484/Ms. 5856): from *Il trionfo di Clelia* of 1768

CH-Fcu - Fribourg, Bibliothèque Cantionale et Universitaire
"Aria con recitativo" (Ebaz II-90/Ms. 1592): music = scene and rondò "Ubbidisco ti lascio/Ho perduto il mio tesoro" from *Antigono* of 1780; vocal part missing

CH-FF - Frauenfeld, Thurgauische Kantonsbibliothek
"Se ognor fra cento affanni" (UK 349/Ms. 6399): from *Bellerofonte* of 1767

CH-Gc - Geneva, Conservatoire de Musique, Bibliothèque
"Care luci" (Ms. 10642): from *La Nitteti* of 1770
"La destra ti chiedo" (Ms. 10643): duet with preceding recitative from *Demofoonte* I of 1769
"Ah di calma un sol momento" (Ms. 10644): from *Ipermestra* of 1769

CH-MÜ - Müstair, Frauenkloster St. Johann
"Amati quaeso monte" (Ms A 155/Ms. 5221)
"Aria ex C" (Ms A 376/Ms. 5340): music = aria "Giusti Dei" from *Bellerofonte* of 1767; text is "Mater Dei clientes audi"

D-B - Berlin, Staatsbibliothek zu Berlin Preussischer Kulturbesitz, Musikabteilung
"Luci belle, se piangete" (Mus. ms. 7194, no. 2): from *Medonte* of 1780

"Palesar vorrei col pianto" (in Mus. ms. 7793/4): ms. ca. 1870; from *Bellerofonte* of 1767; text is "D'obbliar sospiro"
"Palesar vorrei col pianto" (in Mus. ms. 11251/5): from *Bellerofonte* of 1767; attr. Jommelli
"Ah che vol dir" (Mus. ms. 14517/5): duet from *Romolo ed Ersilia* of 1773
"Per lei fra l'armi" (Mus. ms. 14518/5): from *Demofoonte* I of 1769
"Alme incaute" (Mus. ms. 14519/5): from *Demetrio* I of 1773
"Ah che fugir/Se il ciel mi che rida" (Mus. ms. 14520/5): "Rec. e Aria"
"Leon piagato a morte" (Mus. ms. 14521/5): from *Adriano in Siria* of 1776
"Sono in mar, non veggo sponde" (Mus. ms. 14521/30): from *La Nitteti* of 1770
"Il caro e solo oggetto" (in Mus. ms. 14522): from *Il gran Tamerlano* of 1772
"Và cediamo al destin" (in Mus. ms. 14522): scene from *Demetrio* I of 1773
"Dal suo gentil sembiante" (in Mus. ms. 14522): from *Demetrio* I of 1773
"Fra tanti pensieri" (in Mus. ms. 14522): from *Demetrio* I of 1773
"Agitata in tanti affanni" (in Mus. ms. 14522): from *Demetrio* I of 1773
"Senzo aime nel seno un foco" (in Mus. ms. 14522)
"Per quel paterno amplesso" (in Mus. ms. 14522): from *Artaserse* of 1774
"Quel labbro adorato" (in Mus. ms. 14522): from *Demetrio* I of 1773
"Non sò frenare il pianto" (in Mus. ms. 14522): from *Demetrio* I of 1773
"Rammenta al tuo sovrano" (Mus. ms. 14522/3): from *Motezuma* of 1771
"Luci belle, se piangete" (Mus. ms. 14522/3): from *Medonte* of 1780
"Vanne pur, ma dimmi pria" (Mus. ms. 20494/15): duet from *Bellerofonte* of 1767
"Vanne pur, ma dimmi pria" (Mus. ms. 20497/5): duet from *Bellerofonte* of 1767
"Alme incaute" (Mus. ms. 300128): from *Demetrio* I of 1773
"Leon piagato a morte" (in Mus. ms. 30119): "Livorno carnival 1777"; from *Adriano in Siria* of 1776
"Che della sorte infida" (in Mus. ms. 30119): from *Adriano in Siria* of 1776
"Ho perduto il mio tesoro" (in Mus. ms. 30119): from *Antigono* of 1780
"Dove ahi, dove son io/Adorata mia speranza" (in Mus. ms. 30119): scene and aria from *Medonte* of 1780
"Luci belle, se piangete" (in Mus. ms. 30119): from *Medonte* of 1780
"Cara, deh torna in pace" (in Mus. ms. 30119): "Roma 1780"; originally from *Motezuma* of 1771
"Serba costante il core" (in Mus. ms. 30119): from *Medonte* of 1780
"Son guerriero e sono amante" (Mus. ms. 30124): from *La Calliroe* of 1778
"È felice la mia sorte" (Mus. ms. 30181): from *Armida* of 1780
"Se fedel mi serba il fato" (Mus. ms. 30306): from *La Calliroe* of 1778

D-BFb - Burgsteinfurt, Fürst zu Bentheimische Musikaliensammlung (in D-MÜu)
"Mille dubbi mi destano in petto" (M-is 40): from *Il trionfo di Clelia* of 1768

D-Dl - Dresden, Sächsische Landesbibliothek, Staats- und Universitätsbibliothek Dresden, Musikabteilung
"Ben potete" (Mus. 1-F-49, Bd. 14, Nr. 2): from *Antigona* of 1774

"Rende il mar" (Mus. 1-F-49, Bd. 14, Nr. 3): from *Antigona* of 1774

"Se pietà da voi non trovo" (Mus. 1-F-49, Bd. 9, Nr. 4): from *Ipermestra* of 1769

"Son guerriero e sono amante" (Mus. 1.F.125, Db. 9, Nr. 4): from *La Calliroe* of 1778; also preserved as an insertion in Giuseppe Amendola's opera *Il Beglierbei da Caramania*, part 1, between scene 8 and 9 (Mus. 3419-F-1 and Mus. 3419-F-500)

D-DS - Darmstadt, Hessissche Landes- und Hochschulbibliothek, Musikabteilung (all Mysliveček arias destroyed during World War II)

"Cedere è forza, o cara/Luci belle, se piangete" (Ms. 5866): scene and rondò from *Medonte* of 1780

"Misera che faro/Tremo fra dubbi miei" (Ms. 5873): scene and aria from *La clemenza di Tito* of 1774

"Eccotti giunta al fin/Non mi vedo" (Ms. 5874): scene and aria from *Il gran Tamerlano* of 1772

"Se mai senti spirarti sul volto" (Ms. 5875): from *La clemenza di Tito* of 1774

"Che fù che avenne/Idol mio, pietoso" (No. 3 of a Sacchini aria collection): "gesungen 1785 von Regina Guaito"; scene and aria from *La Circe* of 1779

D-EB - Ebrach, Katholisches Pfarramt, Bibliothek

"Beatus Bernardy" (s.s.) [BohadloCat IV.2]

"Per lei fra l'armi" (s.s.): attr. Mysliveček in ms., however the music matches neither setting of this text from *Demofoonte* I of 1769 or *Demofoonte* II of 1775

"Sperai vicino il lido" (s.s.): from *Demofoonte* I of 1769

D-Hs - Hamburg, Staats- und Universitätsbibliothek Carl von Ossietzky, Musikabteilung

"Se fedel mi serba il fato" (M A/821): from *La Calliroe* of 1778

"Cedere è forza, o cara/Luci belle, se piangete" (M A/830): scene and rondò from *Medonte* of 1780

D-HR - Harburg über Donauwörth, Fürstlich Oettingen-Wallerstein'sche Bibliothek, Schloss Harburg (in D-Au)

"Ave splendens caeli" (02/III 4 1/2 2° 216) [BohadloCat IV.6]: "Offertorium" for four voices and orchestra; ms. ca. 1780

"Magnae Deus potentiae" (02/III 4 1/1 2° 217): "Offertorium" for five voices and orchestra; ms. ca. 1780

"Di quel amabil ciglio" (02/III 4 1/2 4° 217): duet from *Il gran Tamerlano* of 1772

"Ah non temer ben mio" (02III 4 1/2 4° 218): from *La Nitteti* of 1770

D-LÜh - Lübeck, Bibliothek der Hansestadt Lübeck, Musikabteilung

"Se il mio duolo, se il mio fato" (Mus. Q 255): from *Armida* of 1780

"Lasciami adesso in pace" (Mus. Q 256): from *Atide* of 1774

"Scherza il nocchier talora" (Mus. Q 257): dated 1771; from *Motezuma* of 1771; incomplete

"Il caro mio bene" (Mus. Q 258): from *Armida* of 1780

"Sperai vicino il lido" (Mus. Q 259): from *Demofoonte* I of 1769
"Palesar vorrei col pianto" (Mus. Q 260): from *Bellerofonte* of 1767
"Luci belle se piangete" (Mus. Q 261): from *Medonte* of 1780

D-Mbs - Munich, Bayerische Staatsbibliothek, Musikabteilung
"Lascia che un bacio" (Mus. ms. 1681): terzetto from *Isacco* of 1776
"Ave maris stella" (Mus. ms. 5081)
"Care luci" (Mus. ms. 3958/2): from *La Nitteti* of 1770

D-Mh - Munich, Staatliche Hochschule für Musik, Bibliothek (in D-Mbs)
"Prisco t'amai, no, niego/Senti bell'idol mio" (in ms. 28): scene and terzetto from *La Circe* of 1779
"Saprai con tuo rossore" (in ms. 29): from *La Circe* of 1779
"Berenice, che fai/Non partir bell'idol mio" (in ms. 32): scene and cavatina from *Antigono* of 1780
"Ubbidisco ti lascio/Ho perduto il mio tesoro" (in ms. 32): scene and rondò from *Antigono* of 1780
"Cedere è forza, o cara/Luci belle, se piangete" (in ms. 32): scene and rondò from *Medonte* of 1780
"Meglio rifletti al dono" (in ms. 32): from *Antigono* of 1780
"Serba costante il core" (in ms. 32): from *Medonte* of 1780

D-MÜs - Münster, Santini-Bibliothek (in D-MÜp)
"Dove, ah! dove son'io" (Hs. 2690): scene from *Medonte* of 1780
"Cedere è forza, o cara/Luci belle, se piangete" (Hs. 2691): scene and rondò from *Medonte* of 1780
"Lode al cielo con sola" (Hs. 2692): scene from *La Circe* of 1779
"Che fu, che avenne" (Hs. 2693): scene and rondò from *La Circe* of 1779
"Vanne pur, ma pria" (Hs. 2694): scene and duet from *La Circe* of 1779
"Fù questa il primo oggetto/Mia vita se m'ami" (Hs. 2695): scene and duet from *Ezio* I of 1775
"Se cerca, se dice" (Hs. 2696): scene from *L'olimpiade* of 1778
"Per quel paterno amplesso" (Hs. 2697): from *Artaserse* of 1774
"Pensa, a serbarmi, o cara" (Hs. 2698): "1775: Monaco di Baviera / Aria"; scene from *Ezio* II of 1777 in spite of date indicated in the ms.
"Sono in mar, non veggo sponde" (Hs. 2699): from *La Nitteti* of 1770
"Se la cagion saprete" (Hs. 2700): from *La Nitteti* of 1770
"Saprai con tuo rossore" (Hs. 2701): from *La Circe* of 1779
"Dopo un tuo sguardo ingrata" (Hs. 2702): from *Adriano in Siria* of 1776
"A ritrovar mi chiama" (Hs. 2703): from *Adriano in Siria* of 1776
"Prigionera abbandonata" (Hs. 2704): from *Adriano in Siria* of 1776
"Se il mio duolo, se il mio fato" (Hs. 2705): from *Armida* of 1780
"Caro mio bene, addio" (Hs. 2706): from *Ezio* I of 1775
"Se tu la reggi al volo" (Hs. 2707): from *Ezio* I of 1775

"Superbo di me stesso" (Hs. 2708): from *L'olimpiade* of 1778
"Non sò d'onde viene" (Hs. 2709): from *L'olimpiade* of 1778
"Tu di saper procura" (Hs. 2710): from *L'olimpiade* of 1778
"Non sò frenare il pianto" (Hs. 2711): from *Demetrio* II of 1779 acc. ms.; music does not match any arias in the surviving scores for this opera
"Và cediamo al destin/Non sò frenare il pianto" (Hs. 2712): scene and aria from *Demetrio* II of 1779
"Sian are i nostri petti" (Hs. 2713): from *Isacco* of 1776
"Madre, amico" (Hs. 2714): from *Isacco* of 1776
"Datti pace" (Hs. 2715): from *Isacco* of 1776
"Entra l'uom'allor che nasce" (Hs. 2716): from *Isacco* of 1776
"Quell'affanno, e quel dolore" (Hs. 2717): from *Adamo ed Eva* of 1771
"Non è crudel rigore" (Hs. 2718): duet from *Adamo ed Eva* of 1771
"Vorrei dirti il mio dolore" (Hs. 2719): from *La passione* of 1773
"Ad amar tu m'insegni/È felice la mia sorte" (Hs. 2720): scene and duet from *Armida* of 1780
"E tace, Ersilia/Ah, che vuol dir quel pianto" (Hs. 2721): scene and duet from *Romolo ed Ersilia* of 1773
"Vi sento oh Dio" (Hs. 2722): from *La passione* of 1773
"Parto, resto" (Hs. 2723): cavatina from *Adriano in Siria* of 1776

D-RH - Rheda, Fürst zu Bentheim-Tecklenburgische Musikbibliothek Rheda (in D-MÜu)

"Palesar vorrei col pianto" (Ms 254): from *Bellerofonte* of 1767; attr. Gluck
"Palesar vorrei col pianto" (Ms 255): from *Bellerofonte* of 1767
"Cedere è forza, o cara/Luci belle, se piangete" (Ms 526): scene and rondò from *Medonte* of 1780

D-Tl - Tübingen, Schwäbisches Landesmusikarchiv

"Aria" (G 112): music = aria "Questa è la bella face" from *Romolo ed Ersilia* of 1773; new text is "Ad te suspirat"
"Serba costante il core" (G113): from *Medonte* of 1780

D-TEGha - Tegernsee, Herzogliches Archiv

"Ah non temer ben io" (Ms 40) (Benediktinerabtei Banz): ms. copied 1789; from *La Nitteti* of 1770; texts are "Salve Regina," "O ter beatam me dicant," and "Alma redemptoris mater"

D-W - Wolfenbüttel, Herzog-August-Bibliothek, Musikabteilung

"Tergi, o cara, il pianto amaro" (Ms. Cod. Guelf. 309, no. 1): from *La Calliroe* of 1778

D-WEY - Weyarn, Pfarrkirche, Bibliothek (in D-FS)

"Laudate Dominum" (341) [BohadloCat IV.7]

Edition: *Laudate Dominum: Offertorium pro omni tempore*, ed. Friedrich Hägele (St. Augustin: J. Butz, 1997)

Recording: Convivium Musicum München, cond. Erich Keller, Musica Bavarica MB 303, 1976 [LP]

"Palpitante disperato" (342): includes texts "O Domine mi Jesu" and "Palpito et ingemisco"

"Vanitas sunt omnia vana" (343): music = aria "Empi tremate" from *Tobia* of 1769

C. Arias, Ensembles, and Shorter Vocal Works in Italy

I-Af - Assisi, Centro di Documentazione Francescana, Biblioteca

"Ah, che vuol dir quel pianto" (Mss. N. 262/3): duet from *Romolo ed Ersilia* of 1773

I-Baf - Bologna, Accademia Filarmonica, Biblioteca

"Veni sponsa Christi" (Capsa IV, n. 139) [BohadloCat IV.1]: "Bologna a dì 15 Maggio anno 1771"; antiphon composed for entry into the Accademia Filarmonica of Bologna, also preserved in I-Bc

I-Bc - Bologna, Civico Museo Bibliografico Musicale

"Veni sponsa Christi" (Ms. Martini 2.6/82, ca. 76): "15 maggio 1771"

"Veni sponsa Christi" (DD 56)

"Di due pupille amabili" (HH 172): from *Bellerofonte* of 1767

"Sono in mar, non veggo sponde" (HH 173): from *La Nitteti* of 1770, in versions for soprano and tenor

"Luci belle, se piangete" (HH 174): from *Medonte* of 1780

"Cara, se le mie pene" (KK 13): from *Adriano in Siria* of 1776

I-Bsf - Bologna, Biblioteca San Francesco (Convento dei Frati Minori Conventuali)

"Luci belle, se piangete" (FCA. M. V. 13): from *Medonte* of 1780

"Tergi, o caro, almeno il pianto" (M. M II-6): "Del Sig.re G. M. In Pisa la prima vera l'anno 1779."; from *La Calliroe* of 1778

"Per quel paterno amplesso" (M. M II-7): from *Artaserse* of 1774

"Sperai vicino il lido" (M. M II-8): from *Demofoonte* I of 1769

I-BGc - Bergamo, Biblioteca Civica Angelo Mai

"Pace e calma in questo seno" (Sala 32 E. a. 3/9): from *Artaserse* of 1774

"Superbo di me stesso" (Sala 32 E. 1. 2/6): from *L'olimpiade* of 1778

"Ubbidisco, ti lascio/Ho perduto il mio tesoro" (Sala 32 E. 1. 36/3): scene and rondò from *Antigono* of 1780

I-CMbc - Casale Monferrato, Biblioteca Civica Giovanni Canna

"Il caro e solo oggetto" (Leardi, N.58): from *Il gran Tamerlano* of 1772

I-Fc - Florence, Biblioteca del Conservatorio di Musica Luigi Cherubini, Biblioteca
"Non sò donde viene quel tenero affetto" (B. 1894): from *L'olimpiade* of 1778

I-FZc - Faenza, Biblioteca Comunale
"Sono in mar, non veggo sponde" and "Care luci" (A.VI.4): from *La Nitteti* of 1770

I-Gl - Genoa, Conservatorio di Musica Niccolò Paganini, Biblioteca
"In questo tanto ingrate" (M.1.5.): "Recitat. e Cavatina. In Genova, il Carnevale, 1779."; a character Erifile is indicated in the ms., but no *Erifile* opera is recorded for Genoa in 1779, although one was performed in 1780; the aria is originally from *La Nitteti* of 1770
"Son guerriero e sono amante" (M.2.9.): from *La Calliroe* of 1778
"Agitata in tanti affanni" (Sca.4 n.n.): "Aria cantata da Lucia Alberoni nell'Ezio in Genova, 1777."; from *Demetrio* I of 1773
"Al fiero dolore non regge quest'alma" (Sca. 4 n.n.): "Recitat. con strumenti e Duetto, 1781"; ms. indicates characters Almira and Farnace from a *Mitridate a Sinope* performed in Genoa during carnival of 1781; origins of music unknown
"Amati quaeso montes" (Sca. 4 n.n.): "Aria per basso, 1777 in Vienna."; music = aria "Prometti ognor la calma" from *Bellerofonte* of 1767, transposed for bass voice
"Caro padre, a me non dei" (Sca. 4 n.n.): "Aria cantata da Lucia Alberoni nell'Ezio. Genova 1777."; from *Ezio* I of 1775
"Luci belle, se piangete" (Sca. 4 n.n.): from *Medonte* of 1780
"Se fedel mi serba il fato" (Sca. 4 n.n.): "Aria cantata da Sebastiano Fulicaldi nel Giunio Bruto. In Genova 1782."; from *La Calliroe* of 1778
"Tu di saper procura" (Sca. 4 n.n.): "Aria cantata da Marina Serra. In Genova, carnevale 1781."; from *L'olimpiade* of 1778; there is no record of a carnival opera performed in Genoa in 1781
"Tu sai chi son" (Sca. 4 n.n.): "Aria cantata da Lucia Alberoni nell'Artaserse, 1780."; from *Demofoonte* II of 1775; there is no record of Alberoni in an *Artaserse* of 1780
"Leon piagato a morte" (Sca. 5 n.n.): "Aria cantata da Valentino Adamberger, in Firenza 1779."; from *Adriano in Siria*; no librettos record Adamberger in Florence in 1779

I-IBborromeo - Isola Bella, Biblioteca privata Borromeo
"Il piacer tranquillo" (s.s.): cavatina from *Armida* of 1780

I-Ls - Lucca, Seminario Arcivescovile, Biblioteca
"Si vedono oggi giorno" (s.s.): music similar to aria "Vi fida lo sposo" from *Ezio* I of 1775

I-Mc - Milan, Conservatorio di Musica Giuseppe Verdi, Biblioteca
"Il caro e solo oggetto" (Noseda): from *Il gran Tamerlano* of 1772
"Conservati fedele" (Noseda): from *Artaserse* of 1774
"Fra gli affanni, oh Dio, che provo" (Noseda): from *Medonte* of 1780
"Mesti affanni fiere pene" (Noseda): from *Medonte* of 1780

"Mille cose in un momento" (Noseda): from *La Calliroe* of 1778
"Pensa che sol per poco" (Noseda): from *Medonte* of 1780
"Per quel paterno amplesso" (Noseda): from *Artaserse* of 1774
"Quel traditore intendo" (Noseda): from *Romolo ed Ersilia* of 1773
"Questa è la bella face" (Noseda): from *Romolo ed Ersilia* of 1773
"Tergi, o caro, il pianto amaro" (Noseda): from *La Calliroe* of 1778

I-Mcom - Milan, Biblioteca Comunale Sormani
"Per quel paterno amplesso" (T. Mus. Var. 698): from *Artaserse* of 1774

I-Ms - Milan, Biblioteca Teatrale Livia Simoni, Museo Teatrale alla Scala
"Coro" (s.s.): = chorus "Dopo il nembo e la procella" from *Il gran Tamerlano* of 1772

I-MAav - Mantua, Accademia Nazionale Virgiliana di Scienza Lettere ed Arti, Biblioteca
"Sono in mar, non veggo sponde" (Cart. 6 n. 46): from *La Nitteti* of 1770
"(Se) sdegni d'un cor fedele" (Cart. 10 n. 5): terzetto from *Semiramide* of 1766
"Di quell'amabil ciglio" (Cart. 10 n. 8): duet from *Il gran Tamerlano* of 1772

I-MC - Montecassino, Monumento Nazionale di Montecassino, Biblioteca
"Tu di saper procura" (4–A–11a): from *L'olimpiade* of 1778
"Se fedel mi serba il fato" (4–A–11b): from *La Calliroe* of 1778
"Padre, perdona, oh pene" (4–A–11c): from *Demofoonte* I of 1769
"Volgi ridente, o cara" (4–A–11d): from *La Calliroe* of 1778
"Io gelo, io manco/Per quel paterno amplesso" (4–A–11e): scene and aria from *Artaserse* of 1774
"E tace, Ersilia/Ah, che vuol dir quel pianto" (4–A–11f): scene and duet from *Romolo ed Ersilia* of 1773
"Superbo di me stesso" (4–A–11g): from *L'olimpiade* of 1778
"Se fedel mi serba il fato" (4–A–11h): from *La Calliroe* of 1778
"Parto, ma in questo addio" (4–A–11i): from *La Calliroe* of 1778
"Sorprender mi vorresti" (4–A–11j): from *Romolo ed Ersilia* of 1773
"Oh Numi, qual rabbia/Barbaro non comprendo se sei feroce" (4–A–11k): scene and aria from *Adriano in Siria* of 1776
"In van ragioni/Tergi, o cara, il pianto amaro" (4–A–12b): scene and aria from *La Calliroe* of 1778
"Conservati fedele" (4–A–12d): from *Artaserse* of 1774
"Cedere è forza, o cara/Luci belle, se piangete" (4–A–12e): scene and rondò from *Medonte* of 1780
"Caro mio bene, addio" (4–A–12f): from *Ezio* I of 1775
"Lasciami almeno in pace" [= "Lasciami adesso in pace"] (4–A–12g): from *Atide* of 1774
"Caro mio bene, addio" (4–A–12h): from *Ezio* I of 1775
"Superbo di me stesso" (4–A–12i): from *L'olimpiade* of 1778

"Padre, perdona, oh pene" (4–A–12j): from *Demofoonte* II of 1775
"Che risolve Tarsile/Mille cose in un momento" (4–A–12k): scene and aria from *La Calliroe* of 1778
"Questa è la bella face" (4–A–12l): from *Romolo ed Ersilia* of 1773
"Sorprender mi vorresti" (4–A–12m): from *Romolo ed Ersilia* of 1773
"E tace, Ersilia/Ah, che vuol dir quel pianto" (4–A–12n): scene and duet from *Romolo ed Ersilia* of 1773
"Per quel paterno amplesso" (4–A–13a): from *Artaserse* of 1774
"Conservati fedele" (4–A–13b): from *Artaserse* of 1774
"Se fedel mi serba il fato" (4–A–13c): from *La Calliroe* of 1778
"Palesar vorrei col pianto" (4–A–13d): from *Bellerofonte* of 1767
"Che intesi eterni Dei/Cara, non dubitar" (4–A–13e): scene and cavatina from *L'olimpiade* of 1778
"Il caro mio bene" (4–A–13f): from *Armida* of 1780
"Fu questo il primo oggetto/Mia vita se m'ami" (4–A–13g): scene and duet from *Ezio* I of 1775
"Signor, facil arcano già tutto si svelò/Voi m'inspiraste in seno" (4–A–13h): scene and aria from the *Cantata a tre voci* written for the birthday of the king of Naples in 1775
"Se frà gelosi sdegni" (4–A–13i): from *La Nitteti* of 1770
"Tu di saper procura" (4–A–13j): from *L'olimpiade* of 1778
"Del destin non vi lagnate" (4–A–13k): from *L'olimpiade* of 1778
"Se mai senti spirarti sul volto" (4–A–13l): from *La clemenza di Tito* of 1774
"Quell'empio cor instabile" (4–A–13m): from *Il gran Tamerlano* of 1772
"Vedrai con tuo rossore" [= "Saprai con tuo rossore"] (4–A–13n): from *La Circe* of 1779
"Che risolve Tarsile/Mille cose in un momento" (4–A–13o): scene and aria from *La Calliroe* of 1778
"Misero me che veggo/Se cerca, se dice" (4–A–13p): scene and aria from *L'olimpiade* of 1778
"Oh Numi, qual rabbia/Barbaro non comprendo se sei feroce" (4–A–13q): scene and aria from *Adriano in Siria* of 1776
"E mi lascia così/Nè giorni tuoi felici" (4–A–14a): scene and duet from *L'olimpiade* of 1778
"Padre, perdona, oh pene" (4–A–14b): from *Demofoonte* II of 1775
"Ma il mio tenero affetto/Care pupille, belle pupille" (4–A–14c): scene and cavatina from *La Calliroe* of 1778
"Palesar vorrei col pianto" (4–A–14d): from *Bellerofonte* of 1767
"Intanto almeno tu, Briceste/Parto, ma in questo addio" (4–A–14e): scene and aria from *La Calliroe* of 1778
"Caro padre, a me non dei" (4–A–14f): from *Ezio* II of 1777
"Sarete alfin contenti/Agitata in tanti affanni" (4–A–14g): scene and aria from *Demetrio* I of 1773
"Volgi ridente, o cara" (4–A–14h): from *La Calliroe* of 1778
"E tace, Ersilia/Ah, che vuol dir quel pianto" (4–A–14i): scene and duet from *Romolo ed Ersilia* of 1773
"Ogni procella infida" (4–A–14j): from *Demetrio* I of 1773
"Sorprender mi vorresti" (4–A–14k): from *Romolo ed Ersilia* of 1773
"Superbo di me stesso" (4–A–14l): from *L'olimpiade* of 1778

"Se cerca, se dice" (4–A–15b): from *L'olimpiade* of 1778

"In van ragioni/Tergi, o cara, il pianto amaro" (4–A–15c): scene and aria from *La Calliroe* of 1778

"Pace e calma in questo seno" (4–A–15d): from *Artaserse* of 1774

"Vanne pur, ma dimmi pria" (4–A–15e): duet from *Bellerofonte* of 1767

"In van ragioni/Tergi, o cara, il pianto amaro" (4–A–15f): scene and aria from *La Calliroe* of 1778

"Pensa, a serbarmi, o cara" (4–A–15g): from *Ezio* I of 1775

"Padre, perdona, oh pene" (4–A–15h): from *Demofoonte* II of 1775

"Io gelo, io manco/Per quel paterno amplesso" (4–A–15i): scene and aria from *Artaserse* of 1774

"Caro mio bene, addio" (4–A–15j): from *Ezio* I of 1775

"Che mai risponderti" (4–A–16a): from *Demofoonte* I of 1769

"Se mai turbo il tuo riposo" (4–A–16b): music = "In te spero, o sposo amato" from *Demofoonte* I of 1769

"Pace e calma in questo seno" (4–A–16c): from *Artaserse* of 1774

"E tace, Ersilia/Ah, che vuol dir quel pianto" (4–A–16d): scene and duet from *Romolo ed Ersilia* of 1773

"Misero me che veggo/Se cerca, se dice" (4–A–16f): scene and aria from *L'olimpiade* of 1778

"Padre, perdona, oh pene" (4–A–16g): from *Demofoonte* II of 1775

"Questa è la bella face" (4–A–16h): from *Romolo ed Ersilia* of 1773

"Caro son tua così" (4–A–16j): from *L'olimpiade* of 1778

"Non sò donde viene quel tenero affetto" (4–A–16k): from *L'olimpiade* of 1778

"Caro mio bene, addio" (4–A–16l): from *Ezio* I of 1775

"Ah no, Tarsile, oh Dio!/Serena, quei rai" (4–A–16m): scene and duet from *La Calliroe* of 1778

"Sì, ti credo amato bene" (4–A–16n): duet

"Luci belle, se piangete" (4–A–16o): from *Medonte* of 1780

"Mi dona, mi rende" (4–A–16p): from *Ezio* II of 1777

"Rende il mar" (4–A–16q): from *Antigona* of 1774

"Se dal cielo amiche stelle" (4–A–16r): from *La Calliroe* of 1778

"Questa è la bella face" (4–A–16s): from *Romolo ed Ersilia* of 1773

"In te spero, o sposo amato" (4–A–16t): from *Demofoonte* I of 1769

"Che per voi sospiro" (4–A–16u): from *Il gran Tamerlano* of 1772

"Vanne la sorte mia" (4–A–16v): from *Il gran Tamerlano* of 1772

"Cedere è forza, o cara/Luci belle, se piangete" (4–E–1l): scene and rondò from *Medonte* of 1780

"Giusti Dei" (5–A–8p): from *Bellerofonte* of 1767

"Conservati fedele" (6–A–1/10): from *Artaserse* of 1774

"Che risolve Tarsile/Mille cose in un momento" (6–D–7/10): scene and aria from *La Calliroe* of 1778

I-MOe - Modena, Biblioteca Estense

"Caro mio bene, addio" (in GAMMA. L. 10. 2., Campori App. 2246): from *Ezio* I of 1775

"Sperai vicino il lido" (Mus. F. 2012 1–9): from *Demofoonte* I of 1769

I-MTventuri - Montecatini-Terme, Biblioteca privata Antonio Venturi

"Leon piagato a morte" (A 233): from *Adriano in Siria* of 1776
"Se mi fido al tuo gran core" (A 235): duet from *Il trionfo di Clelia* of 1768; incomplete
"Rammenta al tuo sovrano" (A 236): from *Motezuma* of 1771; incomplete

I-Nc - Naples, Biblioteca del Conservatorio di Musica San Pietro a Majella, Biblioteca

"Per quel paterno amplesso" (in 34.6.4.): from *Artaserse* of 1774
"Tu di saper procura" (in 34.6.4.): from *L'olimpiade* of 1778
"Superbo di me stesso" (in 34.6.4.): from *L'olimpiade* of 1778
"Caro mio bene, addio" (in 34.6.4.): from *Ezio* I of 1775
"Nè giorni tuoi felici" (in 34.6.4.): duet from *L'olimpiade* of 1778
"Pensa, a serbarmi, o cara" (in 34.6.4.): from *Ezio* I of 1775
"Di due pupille amabili" (in 34.6.4.): from *Bellerofonte* of 1767
"Ben potete" (in 34.6.4.): from *Antigona* of 1774
"Questa è la bella face" (in 34.6.4.): from *Romolo ed Ersilia* of 1773
"Se cerca, se dice" (in 34.6.5.): from *L'olimpiade* of 1778
"Sono in mar, non veggo sponde" (in 34.6.5.): from *La Nitteti* of 1770
"Palesar vorrei col pianto" (in 34.6.5.): from *Bellerofonte* of 1767
"Tergi, o caro, il pianto amaro" (in 34.6.5.): from *La Calliroe* of 1778
"Se fedel mi serba il fato" (in 34.6.5.): from *La Calliroe* of 1778
"Pace e calma in questo seno" (in 34.6.5.): from *Artaserse* of 1774
"Conservati fedele" (in 34.6.5.): from *Artaserse* of 1774
"Ah, che vuol dir quel pianto" (in 34.6.5.): duet from *Romolo ed Ersilia* of 1773
"Dal suo gentil sembiante" (in 57.2.8.): from *Demetrio* I of 1773
"Care luci nel mirarvi" (in 57.2.8.): from *La Nitteti* of 1770
"Padre, perdona, oh pene" (in 57.2.8.): from *Demofoonte* II of 1775
"Volgi ridente, o cara" (in 57.2.34.): from *La Calliroe* of 1778
"Rammenta al tuo sovrano" (in Od.3.7.): "1774"; from *Motezuma* of 1771
"Tergi, o caro, il pianto amaro" (in Scaff. 64, N. 29): from *La Calliroe* of 1778
"Se fedel mi serba il fato" (in Scaff. 64, N. 29): from *La Calliroe* of 1778
"Superbo di me stesso" (in Scaff. 64, N. 29): from *L'olimpiade* of 1778
"Nè giorni tuoi felici" (in Scaff. 64, N. 29): duet from *L'olimpiade* of 1778
"Non mi vedo" (in Scaff. 64, N. 29): from *Il gran Tamerlano* of 1772
"Rammenta al tuo sovrano" (X.2856.): from *Motezuma* of 1771

I-OS - Ostiglia, Opera Pia Greggiati, Biblioteca

"Sono in mar, non veggo sponde" (Mss. MUSICE B. 1639): from *La Nitteti* of 1770
"Misero pargoletto" (Mss. MUSICE B. 2402): from *Demofoonte* I of 1769

I-PAc - Parma, Biblioteca Nazionale Palatina, Sezione Musicale presso il Conservatorio di Musica Arrigo Boïto

"Tergi, o cara, almeno il pianto": from *La Calliroe* of 1778

I-Pca - Padua, Biblioteca Antoniana con Archivio Musicale

"Sento nell'alma mia" (D. 7): from *Il gran Tamerlano* of 1772

"Se mai senti spirarti sul volto" (D. 25): from *La clemenza di Tito* of 1774

I-Rc - Rome, Biblioteca Casanatense

"Luci belle, se piangete" (2280): from *Medonte* of 1780

"Ubbidisco ti lascio/Ho perduto il mio tesoro" (Mss. 5962): scene and rondò from *Antigono* of 1780

"In van ragioni/Tergi, o cara, il pianto amaro" (Mss. 6218): scene and aria from *La Calliroe* of 1778

I-Rsc - Rome, Conservatorio di Musica Santa Cecilia, Biblioteca Musicale Governativa

"Giusti Dei" (A.Ms.2604): from *Bellerofonte* of 1767

"Frà tanti affanni" (G.Mss.201, no. 8): from *Antigono* of 1780

I-Tci - Turin, Biblioteca Civica Musicale Andrea della Corte

"Sperai vicino il lido" (Mus.Ms. 94): from *Demofoonte* I of 1769

I-Tf - Turin, Accademia Filarmonica, Archivio

"Cedere è forza, o cara/Luci belle, se piangete" (2 IV 4): scene and rondò from *Medonte* of 1780

I-Vc - Venice, Conservatorio di Musica Benedetto Marcello, Biblioteca

"Il caro mio bene" (Correr 71–96, No. 85): from *Armida* of 1780

"Splende così talora" (Correr 124–149, No. 138): "Del Sig, Giuseppe Misliwicek. In Napoli 1769."; from *Bellerofonte* of 1767

"Luci belle, se piangete" (Correr 150–160, No. 151): from *Medonte* of 1780

D. Arias, Ensembles, and Shorter Vocal Works in Miscellaneous Locations

B-Bc - Brussels, Conservatoire Royal de Musique, Bibliothèque

"Ah, che vuol dir quel pianto" (4421): duet from *Romolo ed Ersilia* of 1773

"Sento nell'alma mia" (4422): from *Il gran Tamerlano* of 1772

"Cedere è forza, o cara/Luci belle, se piangete" (26326): scene and rondò from *Medonte* of 1780

B-Br - Brussels, Bibliothèque Royale Albert 1.er

"Se fedel mi serba il fato" (Ms II 4043 Mus Fétis 2622): from *La Calliroe* of 1778

CDN-Lu - London, University of Western Ontario Library System, Music Library

"Cedere è forza, o cara/Luci belle, se piangete" (GM/AR 231, no. 16): scene and rondò from *Medonte* of 1780

DK-Kk - Copenhagen, Det Kongelige Bibliotek Slotsholmen

"Care luci" (mu 7501.1836): from *La Nitteti* of 1770

"Se la cagion saprete" (mu 7501.1837): from *La Nitteti* of 1770

"(Aria) de Sancte Joan. de Deo" (mu 7504.2210, no. 1) (Camillo Schoenbaum collection): music = aria "Palesar vorrei col pianto" from *Bellerofonte* of 1767; text is "O Joannes, o vir Dei"

"(Aria) de Resurrectione" (mu 7504.2210, no. 2) (Camillo Schoenbaum collection): text is "Surrexit Christus"

DK-Ou - Odense, Universitetsbibliotek, Musikafdelingen

"Fra tanti pensieri" (R314): from *Demetrio* I of 1773

"Agitata in tanti affanni" (R315): from *Demetrio* I of 1773

DK-Sa - Sorø, Sorø Akademi, Bibliotheket

"Padre ti lascio addio" (R165): from *Adriano in Siria* of 1776

"Cedere è forza, o cara/Luci belle, se piangete" (R166): scene and rondò from *Medonte* of 1780

"In van ragioni/Tergi, o caro, il pianto amaro" (R167): scene and aria from *La Calliroe* of 1778

"Dove ahi, dove son io/Adorata mia speranza" (R168): scene and cavatina from *Medonte* of 1780

"Ubbidisco ti lascio/Ho perduto il mio tesoro" (R169): scene and rondò from *Antigono* of 1780

"Alme incaute" (R170): from *Demetrio* II of 1779

E-Mp - Madrid, Palacio Real, Biblioteca y Archivo

"Cara, che torna in pace" (Leg. 1.630): from *Motezuma* of 1771

"Obliar l'amato sposo" (Leg. 1.630): from *Demetrio* II of 1779

"Io gelo io moro/Per quel paterno amplesso" (Leg. 1.630): scene and aria from *Artaserse* of 1774

"Va, cediamo al destin/Non sò frenare il pianto" (Leg. 1.630): scene and aria from *Demetrio* II of 1779

"Intendo, intendo/Ah, se dite mi privi" (Leg. 1.630): scene and duet from *Demetrio* II of 1779

"Non temer non son più amante" (Leg. 1.630): duet from *Antigono* of 1780

"Intendo, intendo/Ah, se dite mi privi" (Leg. 1.630): scene and duet from *Demetrio* II of 1779

"Misero me che veggo/Se cerca se dice" (Leg. 1.630): scene and aria from *L'olimpiade* of 1778

F-Lm - Lille, Bibliothèque Municipale

"Tu me quittes mais songe" (M 5569): music = scene and rondò "Ubbidisco ti lascio/Ho perduto il mio tesoro" from *Antigono* of 1780

F-Pn - Paris, Bibliothèque Nationale de France, Département de la Musique

"Di quell'amabil ciglio" (Ms. 2367, a-e): from fragment of *Il gran Tamerlano*, including this duet from Act 1, scene 15, and scenes 3 and 6 from Act 2, which contain no arias

"Son guerriero e sono amante" (D. 81): from *La Calliroe* of 1778; inserted in the opera *Il Beglierbei di Caramania* by Giuseppe Amendola; see Part 2
"Ah se mi sei fedele" (D. 8205, No. 1): duet from *Motezuma* of 1771
"Cara, deh torna in pace" (D. 8205, No. 2): from *Motezuma* of 1771
"Sorprender mi vorresti" (D. 8205, No. 3): from *Romolo ed Ersilia* of 1773
"Non sò frenare il pianto" (D. 8205, No. 4): from *Demetrio* I of 1773
"Quel labbro adorato" (D. 8205, No. 5): from *Demetrio* I of 1773
"Cara, oh Dio" (D. 8205, No. 6): from *Artaserse* of 1774
"Figlia ti lascio addio" (D. 8205, No. 7): from *Atide* of 1774
"Dove son/Numi tiranni" (D. 8205, No. 8): scene and cavatina from *Motezuma* of 1771
"Pace e calma in questo seno" (D. 8205, No. 9): from *Artaserse* of 1774
"Agitata in tanti affanni" (D. 8205, No. 10): from *Demetrio* I of 1773
"Alme incaute" (D. 8205, No. 11): from *Demetrio* I of 1773
"Il caro mio bene" (D. 8205, No. 12): from *Armida* of 1780
"Ah, che vuol dir quel pianto" (D. 8206, No. 1): duet from *Romolo ed Ersilia* of 1773
"Cara, non dubitar" (D. 8206, No. 2): cavatina from *L'olimpiade* of 1778
"Care pupille, belle pupille" (D. 8206, No. 3): cavatina from *La Calliroe* of 1778
"Caro mio bene, addio" (D. 8206, No. 4): from *Ezio* I of 1775
"Conservati fedele" (D. 8206, No. 5): from *Artaserse* of 1774
"Del destin non vi lagnate" (D. 8206, No. 6): from *L'olimpiade* of 1778
"Mille cose in un momento" (D. 8206, No. 7): from *La Calliroe* of 1778
"Misero pargoletto" (D. 8206, No. 8): from *Demofoonte* II of 1775
"Tu di saper procura" (D. 8207, No. 1): from *L'olimpiade* of 1778
"Volgi ridente, o cara" (D. 8027, No. 2): from *La Calliroe* of 1778
"Che risolve Tarsile/Mille cose in un momento" (D. 8207, No. 3): scene and aria from *La Calliroe* of 1778
"Luci belle, se piangete" (D. 8207, No. 4): from *Medonte* of 1780
"Ah non parlar d"amore" (D. 8207, No. 5): from *Ipermestra* of 1769
"Cara, deh torna in pace" (D. 8207, No. 6): from *Motezuma* of 1771
"Di due pupille amabili" (D. 8207, No. 7): from *Bellerofonte* of 1767
"Tergi, o cara, il pianto amaro" (D. 8207, No. 8): "In Pisa in prima vera l'anno 1779."; from *La Calliroe* of 1778, which was also performed in Pisa in 1779
"Conservati fedele" (D. 8208, No. 1): from *Artaserse* of 1774
"Pace e calma in questo seno" (D. 8208, No. 2): from *Artaserse* of 1774
"Se fedel mi serba il fato" (D. 8208, No. 3): from *La Calliroe* of 1778
"Tergi, o cara, il pianto amaro" (D. 8208, No. 4): from *La Calliroe* of 1778
"Parto, ma in questo addio" (D. 8208, No. 5): from *La Calliroe* of 1778
"Se dal cielo amiche stelle" (D. 8208, No. 6): from *La Calliroe* of 1778
"Per sei fra l'armi" (D. 8208, No. 7): from *Demofoonte* II of 1775
"Sorprender mi vorresti" (D. 8208, No. 8): from *Romolo ed Ersilia* of 1773
"Questa è la bella face" (D. 8208, No. 9): from *Romolo ed Ersilia* of 1773
"Se dal cielo amiche stelle" (Rés. Vmca.ms.8, No. 1): from *La Calliroe* of 1778
"Se fedel mi serba il fato" (Rés. Vmca.ms.8, No. 2): from *La Calliroe* of 1778

"Se il mio duol, se i mali miei" (Rés. Vmca.ms.8, No. 3): from *Ipermestra* of 1769, although indicated as an aria from *Demofoonte*

"Ah no, Tarsile, oh Dio!/Serena, quei rai" (Rés. Vmca.ms.8, No. 4): scene and duet from *La Calliroe* of 1778

"Superba di me stesso" (Rés. Vmca.ms.8, No. 5): from *L'olimpiade* of 1778

"In van ragioni/Tergi, o cara, il pianto amaro" (Rés. Vmca.ms.8, No. 6): scene and aria from *La Calliroe* of 1778

"Tu di saper procura" (Rés. Vmca.ms.8, No. 7): from *L'olimpiade* of 1778

F-Sgs - Strasbourg, Grand Séminaire, Bibliothèque Musicale

"Ave maris stella" (M 422): dated 1789; music = aria "No, non chiedo amate" from *Demofoonte* II of 1775

FIN-A - Turku (Åbo), Sibelius Museum Musikventenskapliga Institutionen vid Åbo Akademi

"Öma maka, se hvad smärta" (s.s): music = rondò "Luci belle, se piangete" from *Medonte* of 1780

"Cara sposa, quel dolor" (s.s)

GB-Lbl - London, The British Library

"Di quell'ingiusto sdegno" (Ms. Add. 14208/No. 14): from *Demetrio* I of 1773

H-P - Pécs, Székesgyházi Kottatár

"In omnem terram" (M 16): music = aria "Alme incaute" from *Demetrio* I of 1773

"Lauda Sion" (M 17): music = rondò "Luci belle, se piangete" from *Medonte* of 1780

H-VEs - Veszprém, Székesegyházi Kottatár

"Festinate o mortales" (Grad.301)

HR-Dsmb - Dubrovnik, Samostan Male Braće

"In van ragioni/Tergi, o caro, il pianto amaro" (174/4771): scene and aria from *La Calliroe* of 1778

HR-Sk - Split, Glazebni Archiv Katedrale

"Se mai senti spirarti sul volto" (LX/731): from *La clemenza di Tito* of 1774

HR-Zha - Zagreb, Zbirka Don Nikole Udina Algarotti

"Giusti Dei" (XLVI.W): from *Bellerofonte* of 1767

Pl-Kd - Cracow, Biblioteka Studium OO.Dominikanów, Archiwum Prowincji OO. Dominikanów

"Aria ex C de omni Festo Sanctorum resortita" (212, No. 1): music = aria "Nuove procelle ancora" from *Bellerofonte* of 1767; text is "Laeta adeste dies pacis optata quies"

PL-Wu - Warsaw, Biblioteka Uniwersytecka, Zbiory Specjalne

"Aria a Canto Solo" (RM 4687) (Wrocław/Breslau): music = aria "Palesar vorrei col pianto" from *Bellerofonte* of 1767; text is "Omni die dic Mariae"

"Aria" (RM 4688) (Wrocław/Breslau): ms. dated 1782; text is "Solemne melos adorate"

"Aria pro omni festivitate" (RM 4689) (Wrocław/Breslau): ms. dated 1784: music = aria "Giusti Dei" from *Bellerofonte* of 1767; text is "Sol resplende"

"Aria in Dis a soprano" (RM 4690) (Wrocław/Breslau): ms. dated 1783; music = aria "Giusti Dei" from *Bellerofonte* of 1767; no text

"(Aria) de SS. Angelus" (RM 4742, No. 2) (Wrocław/Breslau): music = aria "Giusti Dei" from *Bellerofonte* of 1767; texts are "Sol resplende" and "Alma redemptoris mater"

"Aria(e) â canto solo" (RM 9768) (Wrocław/Breslau): text of 1st aria is "Beatae caeli mentes"; origins of music of 1st aria unknown; music of 2nd aria = aria "Splende così talora" from *Bellerofonte* of 1767; text of 2nd aria is "Plausus parate Deo"

S-Skma - Stockholm, Statens Musikbiblioteket (formerly Kungliga Musikaliska Akademiens Bibliotek)

"Luci belle, se piangete" (T-SE-R): from *Medonte* of 1780

"Che risolve Tarsile/Mille cose in un momento" (T-SE-R): scene and aria from *La Calliroe* of 1778

"Vanne pur, ma dimmi pria" (T-SE-R): duet from *Bellerofonte* of 1767

"Alme incaute" (T-SE-R): from *Demetrio* I of 1773

"Dal suo gentil sembiante" (T-SE-R): from *Demetrio* I of 1773

"Se pietà da voi non trovo" (T-SE-R): from *Ipermestra* of 1769

"Lo seguitai felice" (T-SE-R): from *L'olimpiade* of 1778

"Ah, che vuol dir quel pianto" (T-SE-R): duet from *Romolo ed Ersilia* of 1773

S-Sm - Stockholm, Musikmuseet

"Luci belle, se piangete" (s.s.): from *Medonte* of 1780

SK-Mms - Martin, Matica Slovenská

"Aria in Dis" (D III/I-51) (Kostol sv. Trojice in Košice): ms. of ca. 1770; music = aria "Palesar vorrei col pianto" from *Bellerofonte* of 1767; includes original text and additional text "Ah quis me separabit"

SK-TR - Trnava, Štátny Okresný Archív

"Justus ut palma florebit" (inv. ca. 981): music = aria "Quel traditore intendo" from *Romolo ed Ersilia* of 1773

US-BEm - Berkeley, University of California, Music Library

7 arias and 1 duet from *Demofoonte* II of 1775 (MS 453): "In te spero, o sposo amato"; "Sperai vicino il lido"; "Padre, perdona, oh pene"; "Se tutti i mali miei"; duet "La destra ti chiedo"; "Se ti bramasti estinto"; "Misero pargoletto"; and "Che mai rispondesti"

Collection of 10 arias and 4 duets by various composers (MS 86): includes aria "Misero pargoletto" from *Demofoonte* I of 1769; possibly also "Poveri affetti miei" is by Mysliveček (the aria is also preserved in CH-E without any known origins in dramatic music)

Collection of 13 arias and 1 duet by various composers (MS 89): includes 4 arias and 1 duet from *Demofoonte* I of 1769 ("Padre, perdona, oh pene"; "Prudente mi chiedi"; "In te spero, o sposo amato"; scene and duet "Timante, oh Dio/La destra ti chiedo"; and "Se tutti i mali miei")

Collection of 4 arias, 2 duets, and 1 rec. by various composers (MS 90): includes aria "Sperai vicino il lido" from *Demofoonte* I of 1769

Collection of 13 arias and 1 duet by various composers (MS 91): includes aria "Se il mio duol, se i mali miei" from *Ipermestra* of 1769

Collection of arias and duets by various composers (MS 1159): includes aria "Parto, ma in quest'istante" from *Bellerofonte* of 1767

Collection of 3 arias and 4 duets by various composers (MS 1160): includes aria "Palesar vorrei col pianto" from *Bellerofonte* of 1767

US-LAuc - Los Angeles, University of California, William Andrews Clark Memorial Library

"Ho perduto il mio tesoro" (FA6964M4, No. 13): from *Antigono* of 1780

US-LOu - Louisville, University of Louisville, School of Music Library

"Questa è la bella face" (Profana 132): from *Romolo ed Ersilia* of 1773

US-R - Rochester, Sibley Music Library, Eastman School of Music, University of Rochester

"Ah, non temer ben mio" (s.s./accession No. 1066982): from *La Nitteti* of 1770

"Se il mio duol, se i mali miei" (s.s./accession No. 1067217 in a ms. of 15 arias by various composers): from *Ipermestra* of 1769

"Ubbidisco ti lascio/Ho perduto il mio tesoro" (s.s./accession No. 1067217 in a ms. of 15 arias by various composers): scene and rondò from *Antigono* of 1780

US-SFsc - San Francisco, San Francisco State University, Col. Frank V. DeBellis Collection

"In van ragioni/Tergi, o caro, il pianto amaro" (*M2.5 v.39, entry No. 34): scene and aria from *La Calliroe* of 1778

US-Wc - Washington, D.C., Library of Congress, Music Division

"Conservati fedele" (M1505.A1 Case, Vol. 129, entry No. 4): from *Artaserse* of 1774

"In van ragioni/Tergi, o caro, il pianto amaro" (M1505.A1 Case, Vol. 129, entry No. 5): scene and aria from *La Calliroe* of 1778

"Vanne pur, ma dimmi pria" (M1505.A1 Case, Vol. 238, entry No. 1): duet from *Bellerofonte* of 1767

"Ah, che vuol dir quel pianto" (M1505.A1 Case, Vol. 239, entry No. 2): duet from *Romolo ed Ersilia* of 1773

"Questa è la bella face" (M1505.A1 Case, Vol. 245 B, entry No. 12): from *Romolo ed Ersilia* of 1773

"In te spero, o sposo amato" (M1505.M263 Case, Vol. 1): from *Demofoonte* I of 1769

"Sposa, Timante, oh Dei/La destra ti chiedo" (M1505.M263 Case, Vol. 1): scene and aria from *Demofoonte* I of 1769

"Per lei fra l'armi" (M1505.M263 Case, Vol. 2): from *Demofoonte* I of 1769

"Misero pargoletto" (M1505.M263 Case, Vol. 2): from *Demofoonte* I of 1769

"Sperai vicino il lido" (M1505.M263 Case, Vol. 3): from *Demfoonte* I of 1769

Part 10

VOCAL WORKS LISTED IN INVENTORIES OF LOST OR DISPERSED EIGHTEENTH-CENTURY COLLECTIONS

Arias copied for the household of Lord Cowper in Florence:

from Hertfordshire Record Office, Panshanger archives, D/EP AF221, a list of music copied for Lord Cowper, signed by Giovanni Schmied, and dated 6 September 1774:

"Alme incaute": from *Demetrio* I of 1773

"No, non s'annida in selva": parody of this text found in oratorio *La liberazione d'Israel*

"Palesar vorrei col pianto": from *Bellerofonte* of 1767

"Per quel paterno amplesso": from *Artaserse* of 1774

from Hertfordshire Record Office, Panshanger archives, D/EP AF210. a list of music copied for Lord Cowper, signed by Giorgio Giuseppe Korbmann, and dated 31 March 1779:

"Rammenta al tuo sovrano": from *Motezuma* of 1771

Lost works from the Bavarian Fugger von Babenhausen collection (see Haberkamp and Zuber):

"Bell'innocente figlio" (Fugger-Slg. F.33): parody text of "Quell'innocente figlio" from *Isacco* of 1776

"Deh parlate che forse" (Fugger-Slg. F.32): from *Isacco* of 1776

"Aria in G" (Fugger-Slg. F.31): = aria "Finche per te mi palpita" from *Ezio* II of 1777

"Finche per te mi palpita" (Fugger-Slg. F.34): from *Ezio* II of 1777

"Ubbidisco ti lascio/Ho perduto il mio tesoro" (Fugger-Slg. F.29): scene and rondò from *Antigono* of 1780

"Si non ne tormenti istessi" (Fugger-Slg. F.30): from *Isacco* of 1776

Lost works listed in the catalog of the Electress Maria Anna of Bavaria (some arias perhaps surviving in D-Mh; see Haberkamp and Münster):

(*Ezio*, *La passione*, and *Tobia*, for which sources exist in D-Mbs)

"Oratorio Abrahamo": probably = *Isacco figura del redentore*, for which sources exist in D-Mbs
"Berenice, che fai/Non partir bell'idol mio" (Bl.52v): scene and cavatina from *Antigono* of 1780
"Ho perduto il mio tesoro" (Bl.52v): aria from *Antigono* of 1780
"Duetto a 2 soprani . . ." (Bl.55r): impossible to match with preserved music
"Mille cose" (Bl.52v): from *La Calliroe* of 1778
"Cantata a sette personaci.il Tempo d'Eternita." (Bl.35r)
"Berenice, che fai/Non partir bell'idol mio" (Bl.40r, No. 2): scene and cavatina from *Antigono* of 1780
"Ubbidisco ti lascio/Ho perduto il mio tesoro" (Bl.40r, No. 3): scene and rondò from *Antigono* of 1780
"Cedere è forza, o cara/Luci belle, se piangete" (Bl.40r, No. 5): scene and rondò from *Medonte* of 1780
"Meglio rifletti al dono" (Bl.40r, No. 6): from *Antigono* of 1780
"Serba costante il core" (Bl.40r, No. 9): from *Medonte* of 1780
"Saprai con tuo rossore" (Bl.40r): from *La Circe* of 1779
"Prisco t'amai, no, niego/Senti bell'idol mio": scene and terzetto from *La Circe* of 1779

Arias listed in Carl Friedrich Cramer, *Magazin der Musik*, Vol. 1 (Hamburg, 1783), 290–91, as part of the Westphal collection:
"Dove, ahi dove son io/Adorata mia speranza": from *Medonte* of 1780
"Luci belle se piangete": from *Medonte* of 1780
"Alme incaute": from *Demetrio* I of 1773
"Parmi a dire il poverino"
"Ah, disponi di mia sorte": from *Medonte* of 1780

Lost work listed in the Breitkopf catalog, supplement 15 of 1782/84 (see Brook):
"Parmi a dire il poverino"

From a catalog of the collection of the Comte d'Ogny, ca. 1785, in GB-Lbl:
"Ah, non temer ben io": from *La Nitteti* of 1770
"Scherza il nocchier talora": from *Motezuma* of 1771

Works listed in the *Catalogue de la musique vocale de M. le Comte d'Ogny*, ca. 1785, in US-Wc:
"Cedere è forza, o cara/Luci belle, se piangete": scene and rondò from *Medonte* of 1780
"Ah, disponi di mia sorte": from *Armida* of 1780
"Se dal cielo amiche stelle": from *La Calliroe* of 1778
"Ubbidisco ti lascio/Ho perduto il mio tesoro": scene and rondò from *Antigono* of 1780
"Eccomi sola al fine": parody text of "Eccotti giunta al fin," a scene from *Il gran Tamerlano* of 1772

Part 11

QUESTIONABLE VOCAL WORKS ATTRIBUTED TO MYSLIVEČEK IN EARLIER EDITIONS

1. Aria "Affretti i passi, o caro" attr. Mysliveček in *The Favourite Songs in the Opera Alessandro nelle Indie* (London: Napier, [1779]): exemplar in US-AUS

2. Aria "Son tradito e sono amante" *Zpěvy XVII. a XVIII. století*, ed. Jan Němeček (Prague: Státní nakladatelství krásné literatury, hudby, a umění, 1956), arr. voice with vln cues without pf acc.; purportedly from an *Ezio* by Mysliveček, however the music matches no arias from either surviving version

Appendices

Appendix 1

TWO SEMINAL BIOGRAPHICAL SKETCHES

1. František Martin Pelcl. *Abbildungen böhmischer und mährischer Gelehrten und Künstler nebst kurzen Nachrichten von ihren Leben und Werken*. Prague: Wolfgang Gerle, 1782. Vol. 4, pp. 189–92.

Joseph Misliweczek: ein Tonkünstler

Der Vater dieses berühmten Tonkünstlers war *Matthias Misliweczek*, oberältester geschworner Müller im Königreich Böhmen, und der auch zugleich die Direction über die Wasserleitungen in demselben hatte. Sein Sohn *Joseph*, den wir hier aufstellen, kam zu Prag, im Jahr 1737 den 9 März, und mit ihm in der nehmlichen Stunde, ein Bruder, *Franz*, auf die Welt. Diese Zwillinge wuchsen nun mit einander auf, giengen zusammen in die Schule, und studierten auch die Philosophie miteinander bey den Jesuiten; zu gleicher Zeit liess sie ihr Vater die Musik lernen. Beyde hatten den nehmlichen Wuchs, gleiche Haare, und die Gesichtszüge einer wie der andere. Weil sie gleiche Kleider trugen, so konnte man sie kaum unterscheiden, ja die Aehnlichkeit dieser zwey Brüder war so gross, dass sich der Vater selbst oft zu irren pflegte. Es geschah nicht einmal, dass er zum *Joseph* sagte "geh, hole mir den *Joseph*," weil er ihn für den *Franz* gehalten, bis ihm *Joseph*, hier bin ich, geantwortet.

Nach geendigter Philosophie liess der Vater beyde seine Söhne die Müllerprofession lernen. Zugleich schickte er sie aber zu dem ständischen Professor die Mathematik, *Ferdinand Schorr*, wo sie sich in Hydraulik, und anderen Theilen der Mathematik geschickt machten. Hierauf verfertigte *Joseph* ein hydraulisches Model, als das erfoderliche Meisterstück, und wurde in das Buch der Müllermeister von Prag eingeschrieben. Allein unser junge Müller fühlte bey sich einen edlern Trieb. Er spielte die Violine mit grosser Geschicklichkeit. Da eben sein Vater mit Tod abgegangen war, liess er die Mühle seinem um eine Stunde jüngeren Bruder, der sie noch besitzt, und legte sich ganz auf die Tonkunst. Um sich in den Stand zu setzen musikalische Stücke zu verfertigen, nahm er anfangs bey *Franz Habermann* in Contrapuncte Unterricht. Da aber dieser mit ihm zu langsam fortzuschreiten schien, denn Genieen machen gerne grosse Schritte, so wandte er sich an H. *Joseph Segert*, Organisten bey der Teynkirche, welcher schon so viele berühmte Componisten gebildet hat. Bey diesem geschickten Meister machte er so schnellen Fortgang, dass er schon nach einem halben Jahre im Stande war, Symphonien aufzusetzen. Er schrieb derselben sechste hintereinander, und gab sie unter den Namen, *Januarius*, *Februarius* etc. heraus, ohne seinen Namen darauf zu setzen, weil er sehen wollte, ob seine Arbeit bey Kennern Beyfall finden würde. Sie wurden im Theater öffentlich produciret, und mit mehr Beyfall, als er gehofft hatte, aufgenommen.

Wie nun unser *Misliweczek* überzeugt war, dass seine Kunst sowohl, als der Geschmack von den geschicktesten Tonverständigen zu Prag, deren es hier gar viel giebt, gutgeheissen wurde, beschloss er nach Italien zu reisen, um sich daselbst in der Musik noch fester zu setzen. Er verliess also seine Vaterstadt im Jahr 1763 am 5. Nov. und reiste nach Venedig. Hier nahm er von dem berühmten Kapellmeister *Pescetti* Unterricht in Recitativen. Er hatte sich zu gleicher Zeit eine grosse Fertigkeit in der italienischen Sprache beygeleget, dazu ihm sowohl seine Muttersprache, nämlich die böhmische, als auch das Latein viel Leichtigkeit verschafte.

Hierauf verliess er Venedig und gieng nach Parma. Hier schrieb er seine erste Opera. Dieser Versuch war ihm sowohl gerathen, und hat so viel Beyfall gefunden, dass ihm der Neapolitanische Gesandte den Vorschlag that, mit ihm nach Neapel zu reisen, und daselbst eine Opera für das Namensfest des Königs zu schreiben. *Misliweczek* folgte dem Rufe. Man führte Bellerofonte, dazu er die Musik componirt hatte, am erwähnten Tage auf. Der Hof, der Adel, und über zweyhundert italienische Musikmeister wohnten derselben bey, und erstaunten über die vortrefliche Composition dieses Böhmen. Zur folgenden Fassnacht rief man ihn nach Venedig. Hier ward seine Opera mit so grossem Beyfall aufgenommen, dass man ihn zu Ehren Sonnete warf; ja der Adel stellte sich in Reihen, als *Misliweczek* vom Theater gieng, und erwies ihm öffentliche Ehrenbezeugungen.

Von dieser Zeit an wurde sein Name in ganz Italien bekannt. Man nannte ihn insgemein, *il Boemo*, weil man *Misliweczek* nicht recht aussprechen konnte. Die Italiener erstaunten, und wurden zum erstenmal überzeugt, dass ihre grossen Maestri von einen dieseits der Alpen gebohrnen Tonkünstler übertroffen werden können. Man hatte an seiner ausserordentlichen Art des Ausdrucks ein so grosses Vergnügen, dass man sie überall zu hören wünschte. Er schrieb also in den folgenden Jahren zu Turin, zu Mayland, zu Florenz, und wie der Bau des prächtigen Theaters zu Pavia vollendet worden, so musste *Misliweczek* dahin reisen, und die Musik zur ersten Opera, die daselbst gespielt wurde, verfertigen.

Sein Ruhm breitete sich immer mehr und mehr aus. Der Kurfürst, *Joseph Maximilian* von *Bayern*, ein grosser Kenner der Tonkunst, wünschte gleichfalls Opern mit des *Misliweczek* Musik zu hören. Er rief ihn also im J. 1777 nach München, und beehrte ihn mit seinem hohen Beyfalle. Nach dessen Tode kehrte *Misliweczek* nach Italien wieder zurück. Er gieng nach Neapel, welcher Aufenthalt ihm vor allen andern am angenehmsten war. Man liess ihn aber nicht lange daselbst. Der Erzherzog *Ferdinand* rief ihn zu sich. Nachdem er hier einige Opern geschrieben, und mit dem gewöhnlichen Beyfall aufgeführet, begab er sich nach Rom. Hier überfiel ihn eine Krankheit, welche ihn nach kurzer Zeit ins Grab legte. Er starb am 4 Febr. des 1781 Jahrs. Ein englischer Edelmann, Mr. *Barri*, sein Scholar, liess ihn in der Kirche St. Lorenzo in Lucina auf das prächtigste begraben, und ihm daselbst ein Monument von Marmor aufrichten.

Misliweczek hat in Italien keinen Reichthum gesammelt. Ungeachtet der grossen Geschenke und Belohnungen, die er von Königen und Fürsten erhielt, hat er doch sein Erbtheil noch zusetzen müssen. Er war überaus grossmüthig gegen diejenigen, die seine Gedanken in der Composition, so wie es seyn sollte, zu exequiren gewusst. Er befand sich oft in so misslichen Umständen, dass er Geld borgen musste. Ruhm und Ehre zog er allem Reichthum vor. Er hat über dreyssig Opern geschrieben und eine Menge Oratorien, Concerte, Symphonien und einzelne Arien verfertiget. Zu Amsterdam werden itzt sechs Quarteti von seiner Arbeit in Kupfer gestochen.

English translation:

Josef Mysliveček: A Musician

The father of this famous musician was Matěj Mysliveček, a duly sworn senior miller in the kingdom of Bohemia who also directed the regulation of water supplies. His son Josef, whom we are considering here, was born in Prague on the 9th of March in the year 1737 within an hour of his brother František. The twins grew up with each other, went to elementary school together, and studied philosophy together under the Jesuits; at the same time their father had them study music. Each had the same build, the same hair, and the same features as the other. Because they wore identical clothing, it was scarcely possible to tell them apart; indeed, the similarity between these brothers was so great that their own father often mistook them. It happened more than once that he would say to Josef, "Go and fetch Josef for me" (because he thought he was František), and Josef would answer, "Here I am."

After the completion of their philosophy studies, their father had both of his sons learn the millers' trade. At the same time he sent them to Ferdinand Schorr, Professor of Mathematics of the Estates of Bohemia, who instructed them in hydraulics and other mathematical subjects. Upon completion of these studies, Josef constructed a hydraulic model as a stipulated project [for admission into the millers' guild] and was registered in the roll of master millers in Prague. Our young miller however felt in himself a noble impulse. He played the violin with great skill. Upon the death of his father, he turned over the family mill to his brother (younger by one hour), who still owns it, and devoted himself entirely to music. In order to acquire the ability to compose music, he first took up the study of counterpoint with Franz Habermann. But because he felt that Habermann's pace of instruction was too slow (geniuses like to make swift progress), he turned to Josef Seger, organist at the Týn Church, who had already trained so many famous composers. Under this eminent master he made such rapid progress that he was able to compose symphonies within half a year. He wrote six such works one after the other and circulated them under the titles January, February, etc., without putting his name to them, because he wanted to see whether his work would find favor among connoisseurs. They were performed publicly in a theater and garnered greater esteem than he had hoped for.

As our Mysliveček was now convinced that his art was approved of greatly (as a result of the opinions of the most eminent musical figures in Prague), he decided to travel to Italy in order to establish himself even more securely as a musician. Thus he left his native city on 5 November 1763 and traveled to Venice. There he took instruction in recitative from the famous *maestro di capella* Pescetti. At the same time he acquired great facility in the Italian language in addition to his mother tongue (Czech) and the great ease he had in Latin.

From Venice he went to Parma. Here he wrote his first opera. This attempt turned out so well, and met with so much approval, that the Neapolitan ambassador proposed that Mysliveček travel with him to Naples in order to write an opera for the nameday of the king. Mysliveček obeyed the summons. This led to the composition of *Bellerofonte* for the appointed day. The court, the nobility, and over two hundred Italian musicians attended the performance, and they were astonished at the excellent composition of this Czech. In the following carnival season, he was called to Venice. Here his opera was received with such approbation that sonnets were written in his honor; indeed the nobles stood in line as Mysliveček left the theater and rendered him public expressions of esteem.

From this time onward his name was known in all Italy. He was commonly called "il Boemo," because the Italians could not pronounce "Mysliveček" correctly. The Italians were amazed and convinced for the first time that their own great *maestri* could be surpassed by a musician from this side of the Alps. So much pleasure was taken in his extraordinary style of expression that all of Italy wished to hear it. Thus in the following years he wrote for Turin, Milan, and Florence, and when construction was completed on a splendid theater in Pavia, Mysliveček had to be asked to travel there to compose the first opera to be performed in it.

His fame spread more and more. The elector [Maximilian III Joseph] of Bavaria, a great connoisseur of music, also wished to hear operas with music by Mysliveček. He thus summoned him to Munich in 1777 and favored him with his high approval. After the elector's death, Mysliveček returned to Italy. He traveled to Naples, and his stay there was the most agreeable of all. He was not long permitted to stay, however, since the archduke Ferdinand summoned him [to Milan]. After he wrote some operas there, performed with the usual success, he removed himself to Rome. Here an illness befell him that shortly carried him to the grave. He died on 4 February 1781. An English nobleman, Mr. Barry, his student, had him buried magnificently in the church of San Lorenzo in Lucina, and had a marble monument erected in his memory.

Mysliveček did not accumulate a fortune in Italy. Despite the many presents and gratuities that he received from kings and princes, he came to lose his inheritance. He was particularly generous to those who, as it should be, performed his compositions according to his ideals. He so often found himself in unfortunate circumstances that he had to borrow money. He preferred fame and honors to any amount of wealth. He wrote over thirty operas and a great number of oratorios, concertos, symphonies, and individual arias. Six of his quartets are now to be published in Amsterdam.

2. Ulisse Prota-Giurleo. "L'Abate Galiani messo in imbarazzo da un musicista boemo," *Nostro tempo* (December 1957): 1–5. Reprinted with permission.

Fra i compositori stranieri che, nella seconda metà del '700 vennero a dare le loro opere nei teatri d'Italia, uno dei più applauditi fu certamente Joseph Mysliweczek, detto il Boemo, perché nato a Praga il 9 marzo 1737, e a Praga aveva studiato con Habermann e Seger organo e composizione, pubblicandovi, nel 1760, le sue prime opere, cioè 6 Sinfonie, portanti per titolo i primi sei mesi dell'anno (da Gennaio a Giugno). Dunque fino a quell'epoca, nulla che preannunziasse il futuro compositore teatrale. Ma, trasferitosi a Venezia nel 1763, ivi completò la sua educazione musicale col Pescetti, e il clima squisitamente teatrale di quella città destò in lui il vivo desiderio di dedicarsi tutto alla carriera operistica.

Il suo primo melodramma, *Medea*, fu rappresentato a Parma nel 1764, e gli procurò subito fama di eccellente compositore, tanto che il 23 dic. 1766 l'Impresario del nostro San Carlo, Amadori, come ultima opera della sue gestione da rappresentarsi il prossimo 20 gennaio, proponeva a S. M. il *Bellerofonte*, dramma che era stato rappresentato in altre Reali Corti con applauso, e come maestro per musicarlo Giuseppe Misliwecek (questa era la grafia del suo cognome corrente in Italia, e accettata anche da lui), di nazione boema, che aveva già dato in Italia cospicui saggi del suo valore. La Giunta dal canto suo assicurava che il libretto di detta opera, scritto dal Console di Toscana D. Giuseppe Bonechi, era stato altrove ricevuto con sommo applauso "non meno per lo metro che per lo spettacolo." Del Maestro di Cappella, la Giunta assicurava di aver favorevolissimi riscontri per le notizie ricevute "e per le composizioni di lui qui capitate, così istrumentali come vocali."

Venuto a Napoli il Misliwecek, in meno d'un mese scrisse la musica non solo del *Bellerofonte*, ma anche della cantata, detta Prologo, perché di solito precedeva la rappresentazione del dramma. L'Opera andò regolarmente in iscena nel R. Teatro S. Carlo la sera del 20 gennaio 1767, e riportò un successo meraviglioso, anche perché vi cantarono il celebre tenore Raaff, e la non meno celebre Caterina Gabrielli.

"Per l'incontro felice del *Bellerofonte*," il Misliwecek ebbe l'incarico di mettere in musica anche il *Farnace*, su libretto di Apost. Zeno, pel 4 novembre dello stesso anno, e pure quest'opera riportò un lieto successo.

Furono appunto questi successi napoletani ad aprirgli le porte dei principali teatri d'Italia. Compose infatti *Il Trionfo di Clelia* (Torino, 1768), l'*Ipermestra* (Roma, 1769), il *Demofoonte* (Venezia, 1769), la *Nitteti* (Bologna, 1770), *Montezuma* (Firenze, 23 genn. 1771) e l'Oratorio *Adamo ed Eva* (ivi, 24 magg. 1771) e *Il Gran Tamerlano* (Milano, 1772).

Poi venne chiamato nuovamente a Napoli per porre in musica "il dramma del celebre Metastasio, intitolato *Romolo ed Ersilia*, il quale aveva sempre incontrato felice riuscita in tutti i teatri dove s'era rappresentato."

Anche quest'opera, col relativo Prologo, fu posta in musica dal Maestro boemo in un tempo incredibilmente breve. Pensate che l'Opera doveva andare in iscena il 13 agosto 1773, per festiggiare il genetliaco della Regina, e fino al 21 luglio il Misliwecek non era ancora giunto a Napoli, malgrado l'obbligo di trovarvisi pel 15 giugno. L'Impresario, preoccupato per tale ritardo, già pensava di far musicare il dramma, un atto per ciascuno, ai tre migliori "soggetti" che allora erano a Napoli, cioè Piccinni, Paisiello e Insanguine, naturalmente a danno a spese del Misliwecek. Ma, interrogato in proposito il Maestro Cafaro, "questi disse di aspettare ancora qualche altro giorno l'arrivo del Boemo, al quale sarebbe bastata una settimana di tempo per mettere in piedi qualsiasi Opera." E infatti il 23 luglio si apprese che il Misliwecek si trovava a Capua, ivi trattenuto per mancanza di passaporto.

Il *Romolo ed Ersilia* ed il Prologo furono pronti per la data prescritta, "incontrando l'universale aggradimento," perché il Boemo era riuscito a mettere in bella luce le eccelse qualità dei cantanti, che erano il Pacchierotti, il Tibaldi, e la napoletana Anna De Amicis-Buonsollazzi. Una conferma della buona riuscita dell'Opera l'abbiamo della seguente notizia: "Avendo l'Opera presente, posta in musica dal Maestro di Cappella Misliwecek, fatto notabile incontro presso la Corte e presso il Pubblico, L'Impresario chiede il Real Permesso, e il Re glielo accorda, di poter scritturare detto Maestro anche pel venturo anno, e propriamente per l'Opera dei 13 agosto, per non fargli prendere altri impegni per li molti teatri d'Italia, e forse d'Europa, essendo dovunque ritenuto uno dei migliori."

Tornato a Napoli l'anno seguente, proveniente da Padova, ove aveva composto l'*Atide* per la Fiera del Santo, e già nel Carnev. 1774 aveva dato l'*Antigona* al Regio di Torino, mise in musica, con la solita celerità e bravura, l'*Artaserse* col relativo Prologo, che andò in iscena la sera del 13 agosto 1774, e fu cantato dal Tenducci, dal Tibaldi e dalla Bernasconi.

Sempre più soddisfatti di lui, gli fu dato l'incarico di porre in musica il *Demofonte* col Prologo, che fu rappresentato al S. Carlo il 20 genn. 1775, (con gli stessi cantanti dell'*Artaserse*), e l'*Ezio*, metastasiano, rappresentato il 5 giugno dello stesso anno, con grande sfarzo, festeggiandosi la nascita del Real Primogenito, coi cantanti Pacchierotti, Cortoni e la De Amicis.

A questo punto qualche Lettore potrebbe giustamente chiedermi: "Ma nel titolo del presente scritto avete promesso di dirci qualcosa anche dell'abate Galiani. Finora non ci avete parlato che del Misliwecek, e l'abate quando vi deciderete a trarlo fuori?" Chiedo scusa al Lettore: ciò dipende dal fatto che del maestro boemo finora si sa ben poco, anche nella sua patria, e queste notiziole intorno a lui, che possono sembrarvi noiose, mi son costate anni di fatica, e servono a darvi un panorama preciso dell'attività felicemente svolta in Italia, e particolarmente a Napoli, da quel simpatico compositore straniero, a cui anche il piccolo Mozart deve qualcosa.

Per l'abate Galiani, invece, si sa tutto, sotto tutti i punti di vista, specialmente per merito dell'illustre Fausto Nicolini, che, dal lontano 1904 (vedi in Nap. Nob. XIII: *L'Abate Galiani epigrafista*), fino a oggi, col grazioso scherzo drammatico *Galiani adversus illuministas*, non ha lasciato un sol cantuccio inesplorato nella vita dell'arguto e dotto abate. Sarei dunque felicissimo, se quanto sto per narrare non fosse a sua conscenza, così gli farei una piacevola sorpresa. Ma veniamo al fatto.

Il Misliwecek era uno vero *enfant de Bohême*, che si prendeva la vita con la stessa facilità e spensieratezza con cui componeva la sua musica, e poiché spendeva più di quanto guadagnava (e i suoi guadagni non erano lauti!) era costretto a far debiti.

Quando venne a Napoli nel luglio del 1773 per mettere in musica il *Romolo ed Ersilia*, era andato a prendere alloggio nella locanda dell'Alabardiere Claudio Arnold. Dopo qualche tempo, avendo bisogno di danaro, pregò il detto Arnold di trovargli qualcuno che gliene prestasse. Questi gli fece conoscere il Sig. Giuseppe Berti, con negozio di galanterie in via Chiaia, il quale, con un ripiego molto comune in quell'epoca per mascherare un prestito usuario con un'operazione commerciale, giacché, come giustamente ha scritto testè il Nicolini, "in quei tempi il mutuo con interesse era considerato dalla Chiesa peccaminoso," invece di prestargli in contanti la somma richiesta, gli consegnò una ripetizione d'oro con catenina d'oro per donna, ed una scatola similmente d'oro con smalto. Ma è bene farci raccontare il fatto dallo stesso Misliwecek: ". . . e sebbene io avessi ricusato ricevermele per non aver persona che se l'avesse comperato, lo stesso Monzù Berti si esibì procurarne la vendita, e poiché necessitavami positivamente il denaro, a ciò condiscesi, ed avendo lo stesso Berti fatto il prezzo di detta robba, ascendente a zecchini romani 184, che in moneta di regno compongono la somma di duc. 460, ed avendone cautelato il Berti con tre cambiali mentre detto pagamento si doveva fare in tre rate, e con istromento ancora in solidum col locandiere suddetto per maggior cautela, finse il Berti di far comperare dette robbe da altre persone sue dipendenti, e poi egli stessi se le ripigliò per ducati trecento."

Il Misliwecek scontò al Berti 100 zecchini e avrebbe voluto pagare fino al compimento dei duc. 300 effettivamente ricevuti, non già dei 460, usurariamente pretesi, ma poiché il Berti minacciava di mandarlo in galera, il Boemo ricorse per protezione all'Ambasciatore Imperiale, Conte di Wilzeck. Questi, convintosi della verità dei fatti, si mandò a chiamare il Berti per accomodar con le buone l'affare, ma il mercante, sebbene gliene desse speranza, ricorse al Magistrato del Commercio ed ottene un'ordinanza, purtroppo firmata dal nostro caro abate Galiani, "per eseguire realmente e personalmente D. Giuseppe Misliwecek a pagare al negoziante D. Giuseppe Berti la valuta di zecchini romani 84, debiti in forza di lettera di Cambio protestata, e, preso, di persona, condurlo a scure carceri . . ."

La mattina del 12 settembre 1774, una squadra di sbirri si presentò alla locanda dell'Alabardiere Arnold, sita in via Nardones, per procedere all'arresto del nominato D. Giuseppe Misliwecek, Maestro di Capella forestiero, in forza delle suddette lettere esecutoriali. Gli sbirri rimasero fuori; nella camera del Maestro entrò soltanto il Portiere del Tribunale di Commercio, scortato dal Capitano di Giustizia. Il Misliwecek li accolse con la sue solita bonomìa e stette a sentire senza scomporsi la lettura del mandato di arresto:

> "Ferdinando IV, per Grazia di Dio Re delle Due Sicilie, etc. Portiere e Capitano del Supremo Magistrato di Commercio ed altri Serventi, ad ogni istanza e richiesta di D. Giuseppe Berti di Nazione estera, etc. eseguirete realmente e personalmente D. Giuseppe Misliwecek etc. etc., stante Decreto dell'Ill.mo Regio Consigliere Sig. D. Ferdinando Galiani, Commissario. Così é stato ordinato e così eseguirete."

Dopo di che, il Misliwecek, trattosi dalla tasca della giamberga un altro foglio, munito d'un enorme sigillo di ceralacca rossa, e ornato in alto d'un'aquila bicipite, lo porse dignitosamente al Portiere. Era una Patente di protetezione rilasciatagli dal Ministro Imperiale allo scopo di salvarlo dalla procedura criminale in corso. Il Portiere lesse:

> "Giovanni Giuseppe del S. R. I. Conte di Wilzek, Barone di Hultschin e Guttenland, etc. etc. Gentiluomo di Camera, Consigliere attuale aulico nel Supremo Dipartimento di Giustizia, Inviato straordinario e Ministro Plenipotenziario delle LL. MM. II. RR. appresso S. M. Il Re delle Due Sicilie, etc. etc. Attestiamo d'aver ricevuto il Latore del presente D. Giuseppe Misliwecek, Maestro di Cappella, e Suddito delle Loro Maestà Imperiale e Reale apostolica, sotto la nostra protezione, essendo a Noi nota la sua pendenza col Negoziante Berti, e fino a tanto che l'avrà condotta a fine. Ed acciocché detto D. Giuseppe Misliwecek goder possa la nostra protezione con tutte le prerogative e privilegi, abbiamo spedito la presente per la nostra Segretaria in forma solita e firmata da noi stesso anche coll'impronta delle nostre Armi. - Napoli, 30 agosto 1774 – Wilzech - Per ordine del suddetto Sig. Ministro - Ferdinando Haumpria Ufficiale delle Segretaria."

Il Portiere, che non s'aspettava questo colpo di scena e non aveva ordini o istruzioni al riguardo, chiese garbatamente di poter trarre una copia fedele di quella Patente. Il Maestro gli offrì della carta da musica, e curvo sul clavicembalo, il Messo del Supremo Magistrato trascrisse il documento Imperiale, poi, abbozzata una riverenza, se ne andò, sempre scortato dal Capitano di Giustizia, a dar conto dell'accaduto al Consigliere Commissario D. Ferdinando Galiani, il quale, non sapendo neppure lui che pesci pigliare, informò della cosa il Ministro Tanucci, mettendo in rilievo che quella Patente o Salvacondotto, rilasciata dal Ministro Imperiale in favore del Misliwecek, "era d'un tenore e d'uno stile ignoto affatto, e tutto nuovo in questi Regni." Il Tanucci gli rispose secco secco che "quel Magistrato avesse fatto liberamente la giustizia, senza imbarazzarsi di altro che delle Leggi ed ordini del Re," ed intanto scrisse a Vienna al Marchese della Sambuca, nostro Ministro presso quella corte, perché avesse fatto sapere alla Corte di Vienna questa novità. La questione divenne diplomatica e sa la sbrigarono Sambuca e Kaunitz.

Da parte sua il Misliwecek non se ne stette. Consigliato da un esimio *paglietta* napoletano, denunziò il Berti per delitto di usura *moecha* (?) presso il Giudice Delegato della Pravità usuraria, e così facendo, il Misliwecek passò, come suol dirsi, da carcerato a cerceriere. Dopo una rapida istruttoria fatta da quel Giudice, D. Gennaro Pallante, col quale c'era poco da scherzare, accertata la colpabilità del Berti, questi venne arrestato e tradotto al carcere di San Felice. E "stando il Berti in carcere, tornato in sé stesso, fece delle forti premure per esserne liberato, al debitore Misliwecek, porse le più umili suppliche al Ministro Imperiale, e, confessando con una dichiarazione il proprio delitto, pentito dell'errore commesso, domandò mercé. Il Ministro Imperiale, pago di vedere con i mezzi che prescrivevano la giustizia e gli ordini Reali, tenuta lontana quella violenza che dal Magistrato del Commercio sovrastava al Misliwecek (questa botta va al Galiani in persona), ordinò che questi avesse pagato Berti duc. 55 a completamento dei duc. 300 che solo ricevuti avea, e volle che discolpato l'avesse del resto che, querelandolo, gli aveva addossato e con cui, a norma delle Reali Prammatiche, incorso era nella pena della galera. Ricevè il Berti li duc. 55 di propria volontà, escì dalle carceri, se fece istromento di soddisfazione e quietenza in beneficio del Misliwecek, il quale passò atto di contentamento ed escolpazione a favore del Berti."

Con tale "contentamento" fu conclusa la vertenza Misliwecek-Berti, nella quale il Galiani non fece una bella figura, stando per mandare in galera un galantuomo, capitato nelle grinfie d'un usuario camuffato da mercante.

Il Maestro Boemo, felicemente liberatosi da quel guaio, potette con tranquillità dedicarsi a concertare l'*Orfeo ed Euridice*, dramma in 3 atti di Gluck e G. C. Bach, che fu rappresentato al S. Carlo la sera del 4 no. '74, sotto la sua direzione. Dopo le rappresentazioni dell'*Ezio* che, come abbiamo detto, andò in iscena il 5 giugno 1775, il Misliwecek partì da Napoli, lasciando della sua arte un eccellente ricordo.

Passano così tre anni. Nel settembre '77 è a Monaco e lì s'incontra con giovane Mozart, che tanto lo ammira e lo stima. Il Salisburghese, questa volta occompagnato dalla madre, aveva ripreso il suo pellegrinaggio artistico attraverso i centri europei, e la prima delusione l'ha proprio a Monaco. Lo consola l'amico Misliwecek, che gli dice: "La prego, vada in Italia; là si è tenuto in considerazione." E Wolfgango che aveva conosciuto la generosità dei successi conseguiti nel nostro Paese, commenta: "Egli ha perfettamente ragione; se ben ci penso, in verità, io non ho mai avuto tanti onori, non sono mai stato così stimato, come in Italia; e uno acquista credito, sol se ha scritto opere in Italia, specialmente a Napoli!" (Barblan, *Mozart in Italia*, Ricordi, 1956, p. 194).

Proprio in quel settembre '77 l'Impresario del S. Carlo, D. Gaetano Santoro (col quale il Mozart, per consiglio del Misliwecek, avrebbe voluto accordarsi, per venire e comporre un'opera a Napoli) scriveva al Misliwecek a Monaco, invitandolo a Napoli l'anno seguente per una sola opera.

Da una relazione della Giunta apprendiamo la risposta del Misliwecek: "L'Impresario Santori ci ha fatto presente che avendo invitato il Maestro di Cappella Misliwecek a venir qui a scrivere un'Opera per l'anno venturo teatrale 1778, dal medesimo se gli è risposto che non gli conveniva intraprendere un viaggio così disastroso e lungo, quanto è quello da Monaco di Baviera fin qua, per scrivere una sola Opera, l'onorario della quale lo consumerebbe per spese di viaggio, onde ha detto di volerne scrivere due. La Giunta riflettendo che questo Maestro di Capella ha sempre incontrato quante volte ha scritto pel Real Teatro, crede che possa invitarsi il Misliwecek per scrivere due Opere nel venturo anno teatrale. Il Re approvò la proposta, e il Maestro Boemo tornò a Napoli, e col più grande entusiasmo compose la musica della metastasiana *Olimpiade*, che andò in iscena al Teatro S. Carlo la sera del 4 novembre 1778. Il successo di quest'Opera fu memorabile. Riferisce la Gazzetta di Napoli: "10 nov. 1778 – Nel dì 4 stante di solenizzò con la più sfarzosa gala il nome di S. M. Cattolica. Nella sera le LL. MM. si portarono al Regio Teatro, ove si rappresentò il celebre Dramma l'*Olimpiade*, musica nuova del Sig. Giuseppe Misliwecek, detto il Boemo, a cui il pubblico ha fatto straordinario applauso, per aver superato sé stesso nel comporre quest'Opera."

L'altra Opera da lui data al S. Carlo il 13 agosto '79 fu il *Demetrio* del Metastasio, completamente rinovato. Ricaviamo dalla medesima fonte: "17 agosto 1779 – Venerdì, ricorrendo il giorno della nascita di S. M. la Regina, nella sera andò in iscena al R. Teatro di S. Carlo il Dramma il *Demetrio*, posto in musica dal celebre Maestro Sig. Misliwicek, detto il Boemo, il quale non ostante che abbia scritto consecutivamente più opere, ha sempre riportato un generale incontro ed applauso."

Questa fu l'ultima opera scritta per Napoli da quel valoroso compositore che nella sua lunga carriera non conobbe mai sconfitte, e il cui stile chiaro, brillante, armonioso, faceva andare in visibilo tutti i teatri d'Italia.

Nel dicembre di quell'anno il Misliwecek era a Milano ad allestire l'*Armida*, opera che nell'estate precedente aveva scritta nel Teatro Pubblico di Lucca. Da Milano passò a Roma, ove dette nella primavera nel 1780 al Tr. Alibert, col solito immancabile successo, l'*Antigono*. A Roma, ammalatosi gravemente, morì solo come un cane, nella più nera miseria, il 4 febbraio 1781. Fétis riferisce che un inglese suo allievo, Sir Barry, gli avesse fatto erigere un monumento in marmo in S. Lorenzo in Lucina. Certo è che di tal monumento non esiste la minima traccia.

Questo compositore straniero, che aveva così bene assimilato lo stile teatrale italiano, merita d'essere studiato con competenza ed amore, perché egli non fu soltanto il predecessore di Mozart, ma ne fu il modello, tanto è vero che l'Oratorio *Isacco*, che il Misliwecek fece eseguire a Monaco nel 1777, e che tanta impressione aveva suscitato nel giovane Mozart, era già stato composto dal Boemo per Firenze, e dato in quel Casino dalla Nobiltà, nella Quaresima del 1776, col titolo originale *Isacco Figura del Redentore*. Questa fu una mia felice scoperta. Intanto la partitura ms. di quest'*Isacco Figura del Redentore*, che fu dato a Firenze nel 1776 dal Misliwecek, si trova nella Bibl. dell'Istituto di Musica di Firenze, sotto il nome di . . . Wolfgang Mozart. Infatti fino a pochi anni fa si sostenava che il Misliwecek avesse ispirato il suo stile a quello di Mozart, mentre è precisamente il contrario. E mi meraviglio come nel trascorso anno mozartiano, nessuno ci abbia chiarito questa importante questione.

Qui mi fermo, perché m'avvendo che sto uscendo fuori tèma. Io voleva soltanto raccontarvi la curiosa disavventura capitata a Napoli al Maestro Boemo, che stava per finire in galera dietro ordine dell'abate Galiani. Ho il dovere di dirvi donde ho tratto quella ed altre notizie: dai Fasci Teatrali (sub anno), che si conservano in questo Archivio di Stato. Non so spiegarmi come esse siano sfuggite all'accortissimo Croce, che studiò attentamente quelle carte pei suoi pregevoli *Teatri di Napoli*. Se le avesse viste, almeno qualche noterella doveva apparire nella sua prima edizione del 1891, che è una miniera inesauribile di notizie.

English translation with annotations:

Among the foreign composers who came to have their operas performed in the theaters of Italy during the second half of the eighteenth century, one of the most successful was certainly Josef Mysliveček, known as Il Boemo because he was born in Prague on 9 March 1737. He studied organ and composition in Prague with Habermann and Seger, and in 1760 published his first works, six symphonies bearing titles corresponding to the first six months of the year (from January to June). Until this time, there was no reason to believe that he would one day become a composer of theater music, but in 1763 he moved to Venice, where he completed his musical education with Pescetti, and the exquisite theatrical climate of this city wakened in him the keen desire to devote himself entirely to an operatic career.

His first opera, *Medea*, was performed in Parma in 1764, and it procured for him immediate fame as an excellent composer, so much so that on 23 December 1766 the impresario of our Teatro di San Carlo, Amadori, proposed *Bellerofonte* to his majesty [Ferdinand IV] to produce as the last work of the operatic season at hand for 20 January next. The drama had been performed with success in other royal courts and to set the text to music he proposed the Czech composer "Giuseppe Misliwecek" (this is how his name was spelled in Italy), who had already produced conspicuous examples of his talents in Italy. The *Giunta dal canto* assured his majesty that the libretto, written by the Tuscan consul Giuseppe Bonecchi, had been received elsewhere with great applause "not only for its poetry, but also for its spectacle." Concerning Mysliveček, the *Giunta dal canto* offered assurance of having received the most favorable verification of his abilities from reports that had come its way "and from compositions, both instrumental and vocal, that he brought here with him."

Upon his arrival in Naples, Mysliveček in less than a month wrote the music not only for *Bellerofonte*, but also for the cantata (or prologue) that usually preceded the performance of an opera [at the Teatro San Carlo].[1] The opera went into production at the San Carlo on the evening of 20 January 1767. It was proclaimed a magnificent success, enhanced as it was by the singing of the famous tenor Raaff and the no-less famous Caterina Gabrielli.[2]

"Due to the positive reception of *Bellerofonte*," Mysliveček was also given the task of setting *Farnace*, a libretto of Apostolo Zeno,[3] for 4 November of the same year. This opera was successful as well.

These Neapolitan successes opened up for him the doors of the prinicpal theaters of Italy. He subsequently composed *Il trionfo di Clelia* (Turin, 1768), *Ipermestra* (Rome, 1769),[4] *Demofoonte* (Venice, 1769), *La Nitteti* (Bologna, 1770), *Motezuma* (Florence, 23 January 1771), the oratorio *Adamo ed Eva* (Florence, 24 May 1771),[5] and *Il gran Tamerlano* (Milan, 1772).

Then he was called to Naples once again to set "the drama *Romolo ed Ersilia* by the celebrated Metastasio, which has been received favorably in every theater in which it has been performed."

This opera also, along with its introductory prologue,[6] was set to music by the Czech maestro in an incredibly short amount of time. Consider that the opera was to be produced on 13 August 1773 in order to celebrate the birthday of the queen [Maria Carolina], and as late as 21 July Mysliveček had not yet arrived in Naples in spite of his contractual obligation to present himself by 15 June. The impresario, greatly concerned by this delay, had already considered having the music set (one act each) by the three best composers then available in Naples, namely Piccinni, Paisiello, and Insanguine, naturally at Mysliveček's expense. When Maestro Cafaro was asked for his opinion, "he advised waiting a few days more for Il Boemo to come, as he required only a week to set the opera to music."[7] And indeed, it was learned on 23 July that Mysliveček could be found in Capua, where he had been detained for lack of a passport.

Romolo ed Ersilia and its prologue were ready in time for the appointed date. They found "universal approbation," because Il Boemo succeeded so well in setting off the talents of the singers Pacchierotti, Tibaldi, and the Neapolitan Anna de Amicis-Buonsollazzi. We have confirmation of the success of the opera from the following report: "Since the present opera, set to music by Maestro di Capella Mysliveček, has found notable success with the court and the public, the impresario requested the king's permission (which has been granted) to contract said Maestro for next year as

---

[1] The "prologue" was the *Cantata a tre voci* now preserved only in the form of librettos housed in the Civico Museo Bibliografico Musicale in Bologna and the library of the Conservatorio di Musica San Pietro a Majella in Naples (see Catalog 2).

[2] See Catalog 2 for the cast lists preserved from Mysliveček opera productions.

[3] The libretto for *Farnace* was written by Antonio Maria Lucchini, not Apostolo Zeno.

[4] *Ipermestra* was given in Florence, not Rome.

[5] The correct date should be 24 March 1771.

[6] This "prologue" was the *Cantata a tre voci* now preserved only in the form of a libretto housed in the library of the Conservatorio di Musica San Pietro a Majella in Naples (see Catalog 2).

[7] The composer Pasquale Cafaro held the post of *primo maestro* of the Neapolitan royal chapel and would have been responsible for supervising the production.

well, specifically for the opera to be given on 13 August, lest he take on other commitments from other theaters in Italy, or perhaps all of Europe, he being one of the best composers."

Mysliveček returned to Naples the next year, coming from Padua, where he had composed *Atide* for the feast of St. Anthony [13 June].[8] Earlier, during carnival of 1774, he had *Antigona* given at the royal theater of Turin. With the usual speed and skill, he set *Artaserse* to music with an introductory prologue,[9] and it went into production on the evening of 13 August 1774 sung by Tenducci, Tibaldi, and Bernasconi.

Ever more pleased with him, [the *Giunta dal canto*] gave him the task of setting Metastasio's *Demofoonte* to music with a prologue[10] (which was presented at the San Carlo on 20 January 1775 with the same singers as *Artaserse*) and Metastasio's *Ezio*, which was given on 5 June of the same year with great pomp to celebrate the birth of the heir apparent[11] with the singers Pacchierotti, Cortoni, and De Amicis.

At this point the reader could justifiably ask me: "In the title of the this article you promised to tell us something about the Abbé Galiani. Up until now you have spoken only about Mysliveček; when are you going to decide to talk about the abbé?" I apologize to the reader; it was necessary to do this due to the fact that Mysliveček has up to now been very little known even in his native country. The information about him collected here, which may seem tedious to you, required years of effort to make possible for you a precise overview of the activity happily spent in Italy, particularly Naples, by this fine foreign composer, one to whom the young Mozart was indebted.

For the Abbé Galiani, on the other hand, it would seem that everything is known from every point of view, due in particular to the efforts of the illustrious Fausto Nicolini [1879–1965], who from 1904 until the present day[12] has not left a single nook or cranny about this witty and learned abbé unexplored. Thus it would be most delightful to present [Nicolini] with a pleasant surprise by relating something not known to him. So let us come to the point.

Mysliveček was a true *enfant de Bohème*.[13] He approached life with the same ease and nonchalance that he did musical composition, and because he spent more than he earned (and his earnings were not large!), he ran up debts.

When he came to Naples in July of 1773 in order to set *Romolo ed Ersilia*, he took lodgings at the inn of Claudio Arnold.[14] After a while, he found himself in need of money, and so he asked

---

[8] The libretto for this production indicates that it was performed for the "fiera" of 1774 (which must mean in the month of June during commemorations for St. Anthony), but there is no documentary confirmation of the specific date of the first performance.

[9] This "prologue" was the *Cantata a tre voci* now preserved only in the form of librettos housed in the library of the Conservatorio di Musica San Pietro a Majella in Naples and the private library of Giancarlo Rostirolla in Rome (see Catalog 2).

[10] This "prologue" was the *Cantata a tre voci* now preserved only in the form of librettos housed in the library of the Biblioteca Nazionale Vittorio Emanuele III in Naples and the private library of Giancarlo Rostirolla in Rome (see Catalog 2).

[11] Prince Charles of Naples, born 4 January 1775, died 17 December 1778.

[12] The bibliographic references provided here by Prota-Giurleo as examples of Nicolini's long commitment to Galiani scholarship are an article "L'abbate Galiani epigrafista" in the journal *Napoli nobilissima* 13 (1904) and the play *Galiani adversus illuministas*, undated, but apparently a recent work in 1957.

[13] Apparently this is an allusion to Bizet's opera *Carmen*. In the famous "Habanera" from act 1 ("L'amour est un oiseau rebelle"), one of the strophes sung by Carmen begins with the line "L'amour est enfant de Bohème." Prota-Giurleo seems to have introduced this reference in order to draw attention to Mysliveček's reputation for sexual promiscuity.

[14] Documents concerning Mysliveček's finances recently discovered by Lucio Tufano in the Archivio Storico del Banco di Napoli confirm that Claudio Arnold was also Mysliveček's landlord during his last stay in Naples during the years 1778 and 1779. See Lucio Tufano, "Josef Mysliveček e l'esecuzione dell'*Orfeo* di Gluck (1774)," *Hudební věda* 43 (2006): 271–74.

Arnold to find him somebody who could make him a loan. Arnold introduced him to Signor Giuseppe Berti, owner of a jewelry shop in Via Chiaia. The shop was run as a front for lending money at usurious rates, a common arrangement at that time, since, as Nicolini has observed, "in those days lending money with interest was considered by the church to be sinful." Instead of lending Mysliveček the sum he requested in cash, Berti gave him a woman's gold watch with a gold chain and an enameled gold [snuff?] box. But it is better to have the facts of the case related by Mysliveček himself: ". . . and even though I refused to accept these items, because I did not have anyone willing to buy them, Monzù Berti put them up for sale on his own. Because I had urgent need of the money, I acquiesced. Berti set the price for these goods at 184 Roman zecchini, equivalent to the sum of 460 ducats in the currency of this realm.[15] The loan was secured with three bills of exchange that required repayment in three installments, the terms set down in a promissory note left with my innkeeper. Berti pretended to have the goods bought back by one of his retainers and received 300 ducats for them [the amount that was given to me]."

Mysliveček owed Berti 100 zecchini and would have wanted to pay back only the 300 ducats he actually received, not the 460 ducats lent usuriously, but because Berti threatened to have him imprisoned, Il Boemo turned for protection to the imperial ambassador, Count Vlček. The latter, convinced of the truth of the facts of the case [as related by Mysliveček], summoned Berti to settle the matter, but the merchant, hoping for a better result, turned to the Magistrate of Commerce and obtained an order (indeed one signed by our dear Abbé Galiani), "to compel Josef Mysliveček to pay the merchant Giuseppe Berti at once and in person the amount of 84 Roman zecchini owed to him by the force of a dishonored letter of credit on pain of imprisonment . . ."

On the morning of 12 September 1774, a squadron of policemen presented themselves at Claudio Arnold's inn located in Via Nardones in order to arrest the foreign Maestro di Capella on the authority of the warrant [from the Magistrate of Commerce]. The police remained outside; only the bailiff from the Tribunal of Commerce entered Mysliveček's room, escorted by the chief constable. Mysliveček received them with his usual affability and listened to the order for his arrest without a qualm:

> "[On the authority of] Ferdinand IV, by the grace of God King of the Two Sicilies, etc, the bailiff, the chief constable of the Supreme Magistrate of Commerce, and other officers, at the insitigation and request of Giuseppe Berti, a foreign national, are to carry out at once and in person [the arrest] of Josef Mysliveček, etc. etc. pursuant to a decree of the most illustrious royal consul and commissioner Signor Ferdinando Galiani. So it has been decreed and so it will be carried out."

After this, Mysliveček took out of his pocket another document, this one decorated with an enormous seal of red wax and ornamented on the top with a double eagle. He presented it solemnly to the bailiff. It was a patent of protection issued to him by the imperial embassy for the purpose of rescuing him from the criminal action then in progress. The bailiff read:

[15] There are irreconcilable problems with the monetary values presented by Prota-Giurleo, however the exchange rate presumed here (2.5 Neapolitan ducats to one Roman zecchino, or "sequin") should probably be taken as a basic reference point.

> "Jan Josef, Count Vlček of the Holy Roman Empire, Baron of Hlučín and Guttenland, etc., etc., chamberlain and court counselor in the Supreme Bureau of Justice, Ambassador Extraordinary and Minister Plenipotentiary of their Royal and Imperial Majesties to His Majesty the King of the Two Sicilies, etc., etc., attests to the bearer of having taken the present Josef Mysliveček, Maestro di Capella and subject of Their Imperial and Royal Apostolic Majesties, who has explained to us his pending dispute with the merchant Berti, under our protection until such time as the matter is settled. And in order that said Josef Mysliveček will be able to enjoy our protection with all due prerogatives and privileges, we have sent the present document on behalf of our Secretariat in the usual form signed by us and stamped with our arms - Naples, 30 August 1774 – Vlček - by order of said Lord Minister - Ferdinand Haumpria, officer of the Secretariat."

The bailiff, who did not expect this *coup de théâtre* and had no orders or instructions on how to deal with the situation, politely asked to be able to have a copy of the patent. The Maestro offered him some music paper, and on the curve of the harpsichord the bailiff of the Supreme Magistrate transcribed the imperial document, then bowed and left escorted by the chief constable. The bailiff gave an account of this event to consul and commissioner Ferdinando Galiani, who was at wit's end about how to proceed. He apprised Minister [Bernardo] Tanucci of the situation, stressing that the patent of safe conduct issued by the imperial ambassador for the benefit of Mysliveček, "was of a tone and a style that is quite strange and completely new in our realm." Tanucci responded to him dryly saying, "the magistrate has made justice freely, without being encumbered by the laws and decrees of the king." He wrote to Vienna to [Giuseppe Bologna] the Marchese della Sambuca, our ambassador to that court, in order to make this innovation known to the court of Vienna. The question became a diplomatic one and Sambuca discussed it with [Count Wenzel Anton von] Kaunitz [the imperial foreign minister].

For his part, Mysliveček was not satisfied. Advised by an excellent Neapolitan attorney, he denounced Berti for the crime of usury before the Magistrate for Criminal Usury, and by doing so, Mysliveček passed, so to speak, from jailed to jailer. After a rapid judicial inquiry conducted by the judge, Gennaro Pallande, someone not to be trifled with, Berti's culpability was ascertained, and he was arrested and conducted to the prison of San Felice. "Berti, finding himself in prison, came to his senses, and became very anxious to be freed by his debtor Mysliveček. He submitted the most humble entreaties before the imperial ambassador, confessed his guilt in a formal declaration, repented of his crime, and asked for mercy. The imperial ambassador, satisfied that a means could be found to uphold both justice and the royal decrees, had the sentence imposed on Mysliveček stayed by the Magistrate of Commerce and decreed that Mysliveček pay Berti 55 ducats in addition to the 300 that he had received, if Berti were willing to forego the rest (which was, after all, the cause of his imprisonment, according to royal custom). Berti accepted the 55 ducats of his own volition, left prison, and drew up an instrument of settlement to end his dispute with Mysliveček, who drew up an act of contentment and esculpation in favor of Berti."

With this "settlement," the Mysliveček-Berti dispute concluded, one in which Galiani did not figure well, since he was content to send to prison an honest man who had fallen into the clutches of a usurer disguised as a merchant.

Il Maestro Boemo, happily freed from this scrape, could now dedicate himself with tranquility to putting on *Orfeo ed Euridice*, a drama in three acts by Gluck and J. C. Bach, which was performed at the San Carlo on the evening of 4 November 1774 under his direction. After the performances of *Ezio* went into production on 5 June 1775, as we have already mentioned, Mysliveček quit Naples, having left an excellent record of his art.

Three years passed. In September 1777 he was in Munich and encountered the young Mozart, who admired and valued him so much. The Salzburger, this time accompanied by his mother, had taken up his artistic pilgrimage throughout Europe once more, and the first disappointment that came to him was in Munich. His friend Mysliveček consoled him, and said to him: "I implore you to go to Italy. There you are held in esteem." And Wolfgang, who had known the generosity of admirers in our country, commented [to his father], "I have to admit that in no country have I received so many honors, nowhere have I been so esteemed as in Italy; and certainly is it a real distinction to have written operas in Italy, especially for Naples."[16]

Just at this time, in September of 1777, the impresario of the San Carlo, Gaetano Santoro (with whom Mozart, at the advice of Mysliveček, would have wanted to negotiate about coming to Naples to compose an opera), wrote to Mysliveček in Munich, inviting him to Naples the following year to write just one opera.

From a report of the *Giunta* we learn of Mysliveček's response: "The impresario Santoro has brought it to our attention that he has invited Maestro di Capella Mysliveček to come to write an opera for the upcoming theatrical season of 1778. Mysliveček has responded that he could not undertake such a long and dangerous journey, which would be all the way from Munich, just to write only one opera; the honorarium would be consumed by the travel expenses. Since he has composed several times for the royal theater, he believes that he could be invited to write two operas for the upcoming season." The king approved the proposal, and Il Maestro Boemo returned to Naples. With the greatest enthusiasm he composed the music for Metastasio's *Olimpiade*, which went into production at the San Carlo on the evening of 4 November 1778. The success of the opera was memorable. The *Gazzetta di Napoli* reported: "10 November 1778—due to the solemnity of the most sumptuous gala to celebrate the nameday of His Catholic Majesty [King Charles III of Spain], Their Majesties on the evening of the 4th were conveyed to the royal theater, where the famous drama *Olimpiade* was presented, newly set to music by Signor Josef Mysliveček, called Il Boemo. The audience accorded it extraordinary applause; the composer surpassed himself in the composition of this opera."

The other opera given by him at the San Carlo on 13 August 1779 was Metastasio's *Demetrio*, set completely anew. We learn from the same source: "17 August—Friday, in the evening, to commemorate the birthday of her majesty the queen, *Demetrio* went into production at the royal San Carlo theater set to music by the famous Maestro Signor Mysliveček, called Il Boemo, who, not hesitating to write several operas consecutively [for the San Carlo], has always received a general good reception."

This was the last opera written for Naples by this talented composer who never knew defeat during his long career, and whose clear, brilliant, and harmonious style made him known in all of the theaters of Italy.

---

[16] Prota-Giurleo used as his reference for these quotations Guglielmo Barblan, *Mozart in Italia* (Milan: Ricordi, 1956), 194, however the translations used here are drawn from Anderson, 302–06 (they come from Mozart's long letter to his father of 11 October 1777, which is transcribed in full in chapter 4). The original texts are found in Bauer and Deutsch, 2:43–46.

In December of the same year Mysliveček was in Milan to prepare *Armida*, an opera he had written for the Teatro Pubblico in Lucca the preceding summer.[17] From Milan he traveled to Rome, where in the spring of 1780 at the Teatro Alibert he encountered his usual inevitable success with *Antigono*. In Rome he fell gravely ill and died alone like a dog in the blackest misery on 4 February 1781. Fétis reported that an English student, Sir Barry,[18] had a marble monument erected in the church of San Lorenzo in Lucina. It is certain that not the slightest trace of such a monument exists today.

This foreign composer, who so well assimilated Italian theatrical style, deserves to be studied with competence and love, because he was not just Mozart's predecessor, but his model. Indeed, the oratorio *Isacco*, which Mysliveček had performed in Munich in 1777, and had excited so much interest from the young Mozart, had already been composed by Il Boemo for Florence. It was performed in the Casino della Nobiltà during Lent of 1776 under its original title *Isacco figura del Redentore*. This was one of the happy discoveries of my research. Meanwhile the manuscript score of this *Isacco figura del Redentore*, given in Florence in 1776 by Mysliveček, is found in the library of the Istituto di Musica in Florence [now the Conservatorio di Musica Luigi Cherubini], under the name of . . . Wolfgang Mozart. In fact until a few years ago it was believed that it was Mysliveček who had inspired Mozart's style, but exactly the opposite is the case. It is astonishing to me in the course of the Mozart year [1956] that nobody tried to clarify this important question.

I stop here, because I have nothing further to say about this subject. I only wanted to relate the curious misadventure that befell Il Maestro Boemo in Naples and should have ended with his imprisonment at the order of the Abbé Galiani. I was able to tell you what happened from accounts in the Fasci Teatrali (arranged by year) preserved in the Archivio di Stato [in Naples].[19] I cannot explain how these escaped the attention of the meticulous [Benedetto] Croce [1866–1952], who attentively studied these sources for his valuable *Teatri di Napoli*. If he saw them, at least some mention would have appeared in the first edition of 1891, which is an inexhaustible mine of information.

---

[17] In fact, there is no reason whatever to believe that any music for the Lucca *Armida* of 1778 was composed by Mysliveček.

[18] This is the first known instance in which Mysliveček's student "Barry" (now known to be James Hugh Smith Barry) was identified incorrectly with the title "Sir."

[19] These documents are now believed to be lost.

Appendix 2

DOCUMENTS

Documents translated into English in the chapters are given here in the original language. The present library location of the documents and the prior studies that reproduce and discuss them are identified in the chapter footnotes referred to below.

Chapter 1, fn. 102

L[audetur] J[esus] Ch[ristus]/Wohledel Gebohrner Hochgeehrtheste Herrn Herrn. Dero von 3 hujus an mich gnädigst überreichtes Schreiben habe richtig erhalten, darauf versichere, dass ich mir allemahl ein Vergnügen gemacht hätte ihnen mit meiner wenigen Kunst eine gefälligkeit zu erzeigen, sofern ich schon (wie die Zuschrift lautet) ein Landesgeschworner Müller wäre; weilen aber dieser Streitt unvormüthlig einen solchen erfordert, dahero ich mich darzu nicht entschlüssen kan und mich ferner in dero Wohlgewogenheit recommendire und verharre euer wohledlen dienstwilliger/ Josephe Misliwetzek.

Chapter 2, fn. 12

L.J.Ch./Euer Excellentz Reichs-Hoch Gräffliche Gnaden!/Aus ein Schreiben meines Bruders habe vernohmen, wie das sie gern den Joseph Obermair zu Hauß hätten, dahero thue nicht ermanglen, denselben zu Ende oder noch Ehender des Maij mit gehorsambster dancksagung zuruckstellen, was ihme anlanget, so versichere das der selbe braw Violin spielet, wie auch ich mir den möglichsten fleiß genohmen, demselben in der Composition zu informiren, er hatte mich gebetten indeme er so nahend bey Rom ist, damit ich ihme die Reisenkosten dahin möchte machen, welche ich ihm auch gegeben aus ursachen etwas zu thun und mehreres zu hören, ich gehe baldigstens nacher Wenedig, und alda kommen wir zu samen, Euer Excellentz möchten mir eine Grosse Gnad erweisen so fern sie mir die Reis Unkosten nacher Wenedig addressirend ersetzen möchten indeme wohl bewust das die Italienische luft starck dem beutel zehren thut und man in Italien mit lauter Complimenten um das Geld komt. In übrigens seind sie versichert das ich an ihme allen fleiß angewendet habe um Euer Eccellentz recht zu bedienen, und freud zu machen, der selbe wird schon etwas seiner Composition mitbringen, und ge weiter ist immer mehr zu hoffen mich in dero unzehlbahre Gnaden und Affection recomendirend Verharre Euer Excellentz und Gnaden unwürdiger diener/ Joseph Misliwecek.

Chapter 2, fn. 13

L. J. Ch./Euer Excellentz Reichs-Hoch Gräfliche Gnaden!/Werden Allergnädigst pardonniren, das ich mir die Freiheit nehme mit gegenwärtigen zu molestiren, dieweilen ich aber um meiner schuldigsten pflicht ein gnügen zu leisten darzu angetrieben, kan also onmöglicher weiß unterlassen in gehorsamster dancksagung, demselben der mir von Euer Eccellentz anvertrauet zu praesentiren; welcher auch eine grosse begierde traget immer Euer Eccellentz zu bedienen, imfall sie vor Gutt erkennen, damit derselbe bey dero Hoche Gnaden seine Vocation zu der Musik weiter fortpflanzen könte; ich meiner seyts, wegen seiner gutten Aufführung durch die gantze zeit recommendire ihm unter der Gnädigste protection, er hat sich, sie werden selber distinguiren in der Violin qualificiret, wie auch in der Composition profitiret, und ge weiter ist immer mehr zu hoffen; hiemit mich in dero unzehlbahre Gnaden und fernere hoche Affection recommendire und verharre Eurer Eccelentz und Gnaden unwürdigster diener/Joseph Misliwecek.

Chapter 2, fn. 14

Euer Excellentz undt Gnaden!/Werden mir nicht ungnädig deuten, das ich mich untergepfange mit gegenwärtigen überlästig zu erscheinen, die ursach ist dieweilen ich von meinen Bruder aus Italien von 1. April einen bitt brieffe empfangen habe (wo ich auch nicht zweiffle das Euer Excellentz undt Gnaden einen bekomen haben) in welchem er mir zu wissen thuet das er den Joseph Obermayer auf seine Reise 100 f vorgestrecket, undt er sich auf der Reise nacher Böhmen würcklich befindet, bittet um solches an wieder Gnädigst an mich zu assigniren, er thuet mir auch zu wissen das er sehr vieles in der Violin profitiret, wie auch in der Composition indeme er ihme instruiret, undt seyn talente nicht genug beloben kann, wollen aber Euer Excellenz undt Gnaden so Gnädig seyn undt vor meinen Bruder noch etwas mehreres assigniren, indeme er gesinnet ist seine Reise noch weiter forzusetzen, vor welche grosse Gnadt, er nicht ermanglen wirdt bey seyner ankunfft der gebührenden Schuldigkeit ein gnügen zu leisten den unterthänigsten danck abzustatten wessent tröstend verharre jezt undt zu allen zeiten Eure Excellenz und Gnaden unwürdigster diener/Joachim Myslyweczek.

Chapter 2, fn. 15

Euer Excellentz undt Gnaden!/Werden mir nicht ungnädig deuten das ich mit gegenwärtigen überlästig erscheinendt genöthiget bin, in deme ich in zweiffel stehe ob Eure Excellenz undt Gnaden, den von meiner unwürdigen Persohn überschückten Brieff empfangen haben, dieweillen annoch keine resolution beckommen habe wegen den Biett Brieff aus Italien von meinen Bruder, also noch einmahl Gnädigst Bitte um das (von meinen Bruder den Joseph gegebene) Reißgeldt, es betraget ja nicht viel in rerum natura hat er ihme 100 f auf die Reiße vorgestrecket, undt auf die kleine unkosten in kleydern 50 f, also bitte Gnädigst es allhier zu assigniren dieweillen ich ihme solches alsogleich übermachen muß den in der Frembde ist schwer wan man sich des Gelds erlediget wessent tröstendt verharre Euer Excellenz undt Gnaden unwürdigster diener/Joachim Myslyweczek.

Chapter 2, fn. 16

Euer Excellentz Reichs-Hoch Gräffliche Gnaden!/Hoffe, das gegenwärtige unwürdige bey gutten Wohlstand antreffen werden, wie auch das Joseph Obrmeir zu dero vergnügen glücklich alda angetrofen, es ist hier ein vexel per 30 ducaten um seine reiß zu beförderen eingehendiget worden, da aber ich jenen das Reiß-Geld mehr als ein Monath vorhin anticipiret, so bitte ich gantz gehorsambst Ordre zu ertheilen, damit mir die 30 ducaten ausgezahlet würden, wolten sie aber über dieses vor mich die hoche Gnad haben, und um meine gehabte Spessen zu vermindern, etwas mehr anweisen, möchte ich mich vor glücklich schätzen, in deme mein Bruder recht schlecht mich anjetzo mit Geldt versehen thut, ich küsse in tiefester dermuth dero und der Eccelentz Gräffin schoß und ersterbe Euer Eccelentz und Gnaden unwürdiger diener/Joseph Misliwecek.

Chapter 2, fn. 17

Euer Excellentz, Reichs-Hoch Gräffliche Gnaden!/Ich hoffe das der Mr. Josef Obrmeir zu dero Consolation glücklich werde angelanget sein, in übrigens avisire, wie das der hiesige Banquier mir zu verstehen geben das die angeweiste 30 Czechin wiederum zuruckgestellet, welches mir onmöglich scheinet. Dahero bitte in unterthänigkeit mir es zu avisiren, dann der Obrmeir werdet schon können sagen ob ich ihme das geld in bahren vorgestrecket. Ich lebe erwartend eine fröliche nachricht küssend den Schoss und ernenne mich Euer Eccellentz und Gnaden unwürdiger diener/Joseph Misliwecek.

Chapter 2, fn. 18

Euer Eccelentz Reichs-Hoch Gräffliche Gnaden!/Mit gegenwärtigen avisire, wie ich das von dem 29 9bris aus dero hochen anordnung überschicktes Schreiben richtig erhalten, und daraus die Rechnung des Obrmeirs richtig befunden, weiter aber der obgenandte mir ein grosses hertzensleid verursachet, das er Euer Eccelentz solche falsche sachen zu verstehen geben (welche ich niemahlen um ihme nicht zu prejudiciren an dem tag gegeben hätte) so fern derselbe seiner üblen misethat (weis nicht aus was ursach) mich zu beschuldigen suchte; die historie aber in kurtzen zu beschreiben, so diene, das der Obrmeir, da ich ihme in Florentz bey dem Marquis Riccardi aufgeführet, mir unter der hand ein schlechten streich gespielet, und wolte als husar auf dem wagen zu sitzen in des Marquis dienste gehen, da ich jenes erfahren habe keines wegs zugelassen, damit eine Person die mir von dero Gnaden an vertrauet eine solchen undanckbahren actum exequiren könte, und habe mein möglichstes daran gewendet alles zu verhindern, inzwischen dachte ich, es seyn am besten baldigstens jenen zuruckstellen dann da ich von seinen treuen gemuth die erste Probe gehabt, wolte ich nicht die andere mit gegebener gelegenheit erleben; ich aber um zu beweisen, das ich imer ein Getreuer diener von dem Hoch-löblichen Waldsteinischen Hause bin, so habe zur grösseren bekräftigung grösseren bekräftigung über dieses ein Attestat von unsern haus-hern zu Florentz komen lassen, und allhier beygeleget, das er aber saget ich habe ihme als ein bedienten tractiret über dieses mus ich mich billiger weiß aufhalten, indeme er selber mit gutten gewissen gestehen muß, das er mit mir gespeiset, und geschlaffen, mit Wäsch und Kleidung die gantze Zeit wohl versehen, und ihme niemahlen auch auf seine Divertissement kein Geldt (wan ich eins gehabt) abgehen lassen. Jetzt habe ich gar wohl sein Caracter abgenohmen, und da ich hier in Venedig die historie erzehlet, so habe ich auch müssen erfahren, das er allhier in unterschiedlichen Örtern dienst gesuchet, um nicht müssen mehr zur Euer Eccelentz zuruckzukehren, was mir aber am leidsten wäret so fern er sich gegen Euer Gnaden solte undanckbar erzeigen, wie er es mir bis dato gethan, im übrigens habe auch aus dem überschickten vernohmen, das ich allen petitis bis zu meiner zuruckkunft superdotiren solte, ich habe ja keine praetension gemacht, als über das gegebene Reißgeldt, indeme ich wohl weyß das die jenigen die es um Euer Gnaden meritiren nicht unbelohnt davonkommen leztlich bitte mich in dero Hochen, und unzehlbahren Gnaden zu erhalten, und ersterbe Euer Eccellentz, und Gnaden unwürdiger getreuer diener/Joseph Misliwecek.

Chapter 2, fn. 20

Alla richiesta del Signore Giuseppe Mislivecek faccio io infrascritto giusto testimonio che Giuseppe Obomeir contro la volonta di detto Signore Mislivecek voleva andare al Servizio del Marchese Carlo Ricchardi, e detto Mislivecek non volle mai accordare un tal fatto, perche disse che non voleva che fosse un ingrato al Suo benefattore, ed attesto che se non avesse operato il detto Signore Mislivecek con l'ultimo calore acciò non avesse esito un tal fatto il conte di Obomeir mai lo averebbe riveduto in fede di ciò/Tommaso Mancini.

Chapter 2, fn. 21

Hoch und Wohl Gebohrner Reichs-Graf! Es ist Euer Excell Camerdiener H. Obermeyer Vermög anschlüsslgen zweyen Schuld-Scheinen, wo von die Originalien in Händen des glaubigers befündlich sind, dem Seelen Herrn Joseph Misliweczek 12. und 24 somit in Suma 36 [Dukaten] schuldig geblieben, welche lezterer einen gewiesen Schneidermeister Huttner aus Venedig, wegen einer ihme zubezahlen Ruckständig gebliebenen Schuld adgedretten. Wie nun diesen Mann, der sich seith geraumer Zeit hier in Prag aufhaltet, auf seine umständige Bitt, versprochen, diesfalls an Euer Excellenz schreiben zu wollen, womit derselbe durch dero Einschreittung die Richtigkeit obiger 36 (Dukaten) erlangen möchte, um wieder den Schuldner nicht erst eine gerichtliche Klage zuerhöben./So binn ich so frey Euer Excellenz anmit zu bitten, diese Schuld-Sache dahin zu Vermitteln, womit dermahlige Creditor klagloos gestellt, somit die Richtigkeit von Euer Excell: H. Cammerdiener in der Gütte erlangen möchte: die Entschuldigung, welche H. Obermeyer dem Huttner, dem Vernehmen nach, bereits gemacht haben solle, dass derselbe den Seelen Misliveczek bezahlt habe kann ohnmöglich angenohmen werden, da sich H. Obermeyer über die diesfällige Richtigkeith weder durch eine Quittung, weithmünder durch die ihme zugestelte zwey Schuldt-Scheine ausweißen kann, da die Urkunden deren letzteren in Händen des H. Huttners befündlich sind: Ich gewärtige über die gegenwärtiges eine ohnbeschwehrte Andtworth, und erharre in schuldigster Ehrfurcht./Euer Excellenz gehorsamster Gnümitz.

Chapter 2, fn. 53

Qui di nuovo non c'è nulla, l'opera prima del Teatro Real di S. Carlo era già finita il mese passato, la ventura scritta dal Signor Maestro Piccini, anderà in scena ai 4. novembre e l'ultima di questo Carneval, come si crede, scriverà un certo Signor Misliwecek di natione boemo, quest'è tutto, che posso dire intorno alle cose teatrali . . .

Chapter 3, fn. 15

. . . Il Signor Giuseppe Myslivecech detto il Boemo, che deve venire a Bologna a compor l'opera per questa primavera mi scrive da Venezia con calda istanza di presentarlo alla Paternita Vostro Molto Reverenda, il che ardirò di fare per esser questo un onesto sogetto assaissimo sospriando di conoscere la pregiatissima di Lei Persona. Qui in Torino (2 anni sono) lodevolmente compose la prim'opera . . .

Chapter 3, fn. 16

Molto Reverendo Padre Maestro Padron Collendissimo/ Il Sig. Giuseppe Mislivecechi detto il Boemo, che qui in Torino lodevolmente hà composto un opera nel Real Teatro due anni sono, e che hà l'impegno di compor una a Bologna in questa primavera, desiderando per sua gran stima di conoscere la insigne di Lei Persona, mi faccio animoso di presentarglielo con questa. È sogetto onestissimo, e di merito ne suoi impegni, e perció non dispero dalla di Lei Protezzione il ricevimento. In quest'incontro mi dó il nuovo contento di umilmente ossequirla, e con pieno preggio di prottestarmi di Vostra Paternita Molto Reverenda umillissimo divotissimo ed obligatissimo servitore vero/ Quirino Gasparini.

Chapter 3, fn. 17

Molto Reverendo Padre Maestro Venerissimo/ Egli è ormai quasi un'anno che vado pensando e facendo proponimento di scrivere al Padre Maestro di rinovargli la mia antica vera servitù, ma li proponimenti sin'adesso sono stati inefficaci. Il Padre Maestro ne sa il motivo, perciò non occorre scrive altro. Il lupo cangia il pelo ma non la natura, io vado invecchiando, ma sarò sempre poltrone nello scrivere. Il mio caro amico Misliwecek mi scrisse tempo fa, che andava a Bologna per comporre un'opera pregandomi di scrivere al Padre Maestro e di raccomandarlo come pure al Signor Cavagliere Don Carlo. Io ero portatissimo di farlo, ma non m'è riuscito di vincere quella carogna della poltroneria. Ho fatto proponimenti d'un giorno all'altro, ma senza effetto. Ora finalmente mi viene fatto uno sforzo e benché tardi, penso però che è meglio che mai; suppongo che questo mio amico avrà avuto il piacere di fare conoscenza con Padre Maestro senza la mia raccomandazione, e che egli sia conosciuto per valente nel mestiere e, quel che stimo più tutto, per vero onorato Tedesco come egli è, la sua opera a quest'ora sarà decisa, spero in suo vantaggio, ma sto sempre con timore finché non lo sento assicurato, perché il fenomeni teatrali sono tali e tanti che nessuno, credo io, si sia potuto o potrà mai compromettersi del buon esito . . .

Chapter 3, fn. 32

Venerabilis, ac Eximie Domine Pater Magister!/La supplico di perdonarmi se non adempii prima il mio dovere nell'augurarle un felicissimo Capo d'anno colmo d'ogni prosperità, e secondato dai propri voti. La cagione fù le mie fattiche teatrali, le qualli grazie a dio furono competite a segno che ho mottivo d'essere grato a questo benigno publico. Fin'ora non potei esquire i suoi stimmatissimi cenni circa il Signor Marchese di Ligneville. E Maestro Ruttini, ma quanto prima mi porterò da loro portando gli distintissimi saluti. Alla più lunga verso gli primi della Quaresima spero d'aver l'alto onore d'inchinarla in Bologna. Intanto la suplico di conservarmi la Sua Validissima Prottetione, e bacciandole mani mi dò l'onore di chiamarmi per sempre dell'virtuosissimo Padre Maestro umilissimo divotissimo osequissimo servo/Giuseppe Misliwecek.

Chapter 3, fn. 33

Mi trovo inaspettamente favorito da Vostra Paternita Reverendissima de duei primi tomi della sua opera famosa sopra la musica. Dalla naturale inchinazione che io ho per le produzioni di quest'arte, come le è stato accenato per quanto veggo dal Maestro Mislivecech, potrà ella arguire i sentimenti di gratitudine che io nutro per la di lei gentilezza ad i vivi desideri di poterle corrispondere: frattanto ella mene presenti un'occasione con qualche suo comando e mi tenga in circostanze di aquistar un diritto di dichiararmi di Vostra Paternita Reverendissima devotissimo et obligatissimo servitore/De Nassau Cowper.

Chapter 3, fn. 46

Venerabilis ac Eximie domine, Domine Pater Magister!/Per adempir all'mio umilissimo dovere mi dò l'onore d'augurare un felicissimo capo d'anno colmo d'ogni prosperità, e secondato da i propri voti desideri. L'opera mia grazia a dio ebbe un compatimento universale a segno ch'io non potrei desiderar di più. Giacchè non ebbi la grazia d'ottener nell'arrivo di Cicognani la musica lasciata a Vostra Signoria molto reverenda, così la supplico di conseguar all' Signor don Marchi il libro delle 6 sinfonie. E gli 2. spartiti prego di ritenere, sino all mio ritorno. Intanto suplicandola di voler continuarmi il di lei pregiatissimi favori mi dò l'alto onore di dirmi per sempre di Vostra Signoria Molto Reverenda umilissimo divotissimo servo/Giuseppe Misliwecek.

Chapter 3, fn. 49

Venerabilis ac Eximie Pater Magister/Spero, che Vostra Signoria Molto Reverenda averà ottenuta un'altra mia ove pregai di consegnare all'Signor Don Marchi le 6. sinfonie, e tener gli Spartiti della Nitteti, e Motezuma. Adesso dunque per le gran premure che mi vengono fate costì, avrà la bontà di consegnar all'Signor Don Marchi le 6. sinfonie e gli detti Spartitti, il qualle già tiene ordine di spedirmeli sollecitamente. La supplico di conservarmi la di lei validissima protettione, e mi protesto per sempre di Vostra Signoria Reverenda umilissimo divotissimo servo/Giuseppe Misliwecek.

Chapter 3, fn. 67

Eccelenza!/ So, che la di lei innata bontà eccederà il mio demerito nell'ardire ch'io mi prendo d'indagar lo stato della di lei preziosa salute con tutta l'eccellentissima famiglia: E memore pur troppo delle innumere grazie ricevute da Vostra Eccelenza contro mio nesunissimo merito spero ch'ella mi farà la grazia di permettere ch'io possa metter a piedi suoi 6. quintetti qualli avendo avuto per tutta l'Italia un benignissimo compatimento sono intentionato di far stampar a Londra e per render cotesti più grati al publico: E più illesi dell critica, permetterà l'Eccelenza Vostra ch'io con profondissimo rispetto le umili la dedica che così con quel Gran Nome in fronte spero di conseguir tutta la perfezione che pur troppo manca all'opera della mia debol penna. Nella lusinga di conseguir tal, da me molto sospirata, grazia, supplico d'inviarmi i titoli quai sopra la dedica verranno stampati. In attenzione di quelli fratanto prego di continuarmi la di lei validissima protettione. E sono a piedi d'Eccelenza Vostra umilissimo divotissimo osequissimo servitore/Giuseppe Misliwecek/ P. S. questo carnivale scriverò la prima opera a Torino la seconda in Venezia. Il mio recapito più sicuro e a Milano: appresso il Signor Francesco Weiskopf, taxateur de la poste a Milan.

Chapter 3, fn. 77

In adempimento dei veneratissimi comandi ho esaminato il *Demofoonte* del celeberrimo maestro signor Hasse detto il Sassone ed il dramma del signor cavaliere Kluck, e trovai che il *Demofoonte*, non ostante la sua gran maestria, non conviene di mettersi in scena non essendo in veruna parte adatto a la presente compagnia; l'*Orfeo*, poi, essendo un spettacolo nuovo cavato dell'ordinario, ben inteso anche delle loro maestà reali, trovo più a proposito da rappresentarsi, ed è quasi sicura la riuscita per questo intelligente pubblico.

Chapter 3, fn. 81

Molto illustre, e Reverendo Padre!/Il lattore della presente è il rinommato Monsieur Wendling virtuossimo professore di flauto all'servizio di Sua Altezza Elettorale Palatina, quale in compagnia d'un Signor Cavaliere anche di detta corte, vorrebbe aver il contento, ed il piacer d'inchinarla, così scuserà, se con questa sono a pregarla d'accogliere il sudetto colla sua solita innata bontà. Toccante la mia persona le dirò che messo ch'avrò in scena l'opera partirò ed'avrò anch'io l'onore di presto inchinarla, intanto bacciandole le mani prego di conservarmi la di lei validissima padronanza. E mi dò l'onore di dichiararmi per sempre di Vostra Signoria Molto Reverenda divotissimo osequissimo servitore/Giuseppe Misliwecek.

Chapter 3, fn. 89

Venerabilis ac Eximie Domine Domine, Pater Magister!/ Sono stato molto sensibile all'onore che Vostra Signoria si è degnata compartirmi nell'raccommandarmi la Signora Giuseppa Maccherini. E certamente non averei mancato all mio dovere nell servir detta Signora con le mie debolezze atteso una raccommandazione così forte che mi sarà sempre legge ma l'indisposizione di detta Signora ed il poco buon contegno dei impresari a fatto sì, che cotesta assolutamente non volse impegnarsi di cantare. E per conseguenza resto privo per questa volta di esguir gli veneratissimi commandi, e con gran mio dispiacere veramente. Intanto suplicandola di continuarmi la di lei validissima padronanza mi dò l'invidiabil onore di dichiararmi per sempre di Vostra Signoria Reverendissima umilissimo divotissimo osequissimo servitore/Giuseppe Misliwecek.

Chapter 4, fn. 3

Die heuerige grosse Opera solle sehr schön werden, der famose böhmische Compositore Wickelseck, oder wie er heisset, hat die Musique gemacht, das Dramma ist Ezio von Metastasio, es sollen auch sehr artige Ballets und Decorationes dabey zu sehen seyn: Der Compositore is würklich hier, und haltet sich meistens sonsten in Welschland besonders zu Florenz auf . . .

Chapter 4, fn. 4

Die Hauptprob der neuen Opera gehet heut vor sich, und Montag wird selbe das erstemahl producieret werden, die Musique wollen viele loben, die Tänze oder Ballets sollen aber besonders schön und magnifiques sowohl wegen denen verschiedenen Kleidungen als artigen Decorationen ausfallen welche viel mehr als die Opera selbst kosten . . .

Chapter 4, fn. 5

Gestern is die Opera vor das erstemahl repraesentieret worden, die Musique solle künstlich seyn, viele aber glauben bessere gehört zu haben, die das Ohr mehr flatieren, indessen ist der Compositore, so ein Böhme ist, einer der famosesten in Welschland, die Singerin hat einen starken Carthar, und hat einem grossen Theil ihrer Stimme verlohren, man glaubet sie arbeite an der Lungensucht, dass sie ihre vorige Stimme nit mehr zu bekommen Hoffnung hat: Die 2 Castraten sind aber vortrefflich, und der alte Panzachi hat auch das seinige besonders als ein guter Actore gethan . . .

Chapter 4, fn. 14

Gestern ist ein schönes Oratorium auf dem alten Theatro gehalten werden, die Musique von dem Misslowez oder wie er heisset, einem Böhmen, der die Opera componieret, und die Singer sind die meiste, so auf der Opera gesungen, ausser den Bassisten, so sehr gut, den bekannten Valesi Tenoristen, und eine Singerin von Weilheim, so eine sehr schöne Stimme hat. Das Thema ist "Isacco figura del redentore" gewesen: es sind sehr viele darinne gewesen, und es ist anbey Abonnement suspendieret worden, welches dem Grafen von Seeau vieles eingetragen hat. Die Singer besonders Marchesi, so Isacco, und Valesi, so Abraam vorgestellet, haben onvergleichlich wohl gesungen, dieses Oratorium hat besser dan die lezte Opera gefallen . . .

Chapter 4, fn. 19

Veneratissimo, e stimatissimo Padre Maestro!/Per adempir all'mio umilissimo dovere, mi dò l'onore d'augurar a Vostra Signoria Reverendissima un'felicissimo capo d'anno, colmo d'ogni prosperità, e scondato da i propri voti, e desideri. Inoltre le partecipò l'infausta nuova che ai 30 dicembre scaduto morì in età di 51. anno del male di vajuolo Sua Altezza l'Elettor di Baviera. Il suo successore è l'Elettor Palatino il qualle di già si ritrova costi, e si dice che soggiornerà sempre in questa dominante. Provai sommo piacere che Monsieur Ottanni riscosse univeral applauso colla sua opera in Napoli. Solito effetto di chi se può vantar scolare d'un si gran-celebre maestro, com'è Vostra Signoria Reverendissima. Sono scritturato per 2. opera in Napoli per l'anno venturo questo anno. Se la mia mal poco buona salute mi permetterà d'andarci, anvrò la bella sorte questa prima-vera d'inchinar Vostra Signoria molto Reverenda in Bologna. Frattanto supplicandola di continuarmi la di lei validissima protettione sono con profondissimo rispetto di Vostra Signoria Reverenda umilissimo divotissimo osequessimo servitore/Giuseppe Misliwecek.

Chapter 5, fn. 6

Dieses vortefliche Drama ward vom berühmten Capellmeister Misliwicek auch in Music gesetzt, und auf dem Königl. Theater St. Carlo zu Neapel 1778 aufgeführt. In der berühmten Arie: *Se cerca, se dice* &c. und vornehmlich im zweyten Theile: *Che abisso di pene, Lasciare il suo bene!* erregte Marchesi Bewunderung bis zum Unsinn. Die Composition davon ist auch wirklich ein Meisterstück von Misliwicek vom schönsten, bedeutendstem Gesange, und einem ganz neuen sehr verwebten Accompagnement. Die Composition übertrift an sehr vielen Stellen die von Sacchini und Pergolesi. Was würde Rousseau, der in seinem Dictionaire sich in so lebhaften Ausdrücken über Pergolesi's Composition dieser auslässt, dazu gesagt haben, wenn er sie von Misliwicek gesetzt, und von Marchesi gesungen gehört hätte?

Chapter 5, fn. 13

Milano 29. dicembre . . . Domenica andò in scena in questo Regio-Ducal Teatro della Scala, l'Armida, drama tradotto dal francese di Quinault, musica del Signor Maestro Giuseppe Misliwecek detto il

Boemo, e i balli dal Sig. Angiolini rappresentato l'uno Achille in Sciro, l'altro Annetta, e Lubino. I primi personaggi dell'opera la Sig. Caterina Gabrielli, e l'incomparabile soprano Sig. Luigi Marchesi si disimpegnano colla maggior bravura, ma lo spettacolo tutto insieme non ha avuto quell'applauso, che si sperava, e per il quale i nobili interessanti non han risparmiato denaro. Nel lunedì susseguente andò in scena nel Teatro della Canobiana il dramma buffo intitolato lo Sposo Disperato, musica del Sig. Anfossi, ma anche questo ebbe la stessa sorte del dramma serio.

Chapter 5, fn. 14

[Milano] 5 gennaio 1780. La celebre virtuosa Gabrielli si sgravò negli scorsi giorni felicemente di una bambina, e domenica nella Parrocchia dei Santi Nazzario e Celso, tutta apparate e illuminata, le furono administrate le acque battesimali. Ebbe per compare S. E. il Sig. Conte Ferdinando Gardines della Cerra, Grande di Spagna, di prima classe e per compare la Signora Principessa di Buttera di Napoli, e in loro vece il negoziante Sig. Carlo Castelli e la Signora Butteroni. Oltre i regali soliti farsi in tali occasioni, fu fatta un'elemosina di lire cento ai poveri.

Chapter 5, fn. 17

Milano 19. Gennajo. Risquote ora gli universali applausi la grand'opera dell'Armida, che attualmente si rappresenta in questo Nuovo Teatro. Comparsa domenica sera in scene la celebre Sig. Caterina Gabbrielli con altre tre arie nuove, come si disse, le cantò con tal voce e maestria, che fecero sentire la somma abilità della medesima. Anche l'incomparabile Sig. Marchesi, e il Sig. Adembergh aumentano il pregio di questo spettacolo.

Chapter 5, fn. 31

Zweymal hat er auf dem mayländischen theatre die Hauptrolle gespielt, and beyde mal im Carneval. Die erste Oper ward 1780 gegeben, und die zweyte 1782. In jenem Jahre erweckte er eine halb unsinnige Freude (*fece fanatismo*); das zweyte Jahr gefiel er nicht in der ersten Oper, vielleicht seines Eigensinns halber; aber wohl in der zweyten. Jenes erste Jahr ward, wegen der Kürze des Carnevals, nur eine einzige Oper, nämlich die Armida gegeben, von dem böhmischen Componisten, Herrn Misliwicek componirt. Die Music fiel durch, und die Sänger wurden genöthigt, nach ihrem Gutdünken Arien andrer Componisten unterzuschieben. Marchesi schaltete in den zweyten Acte ein Rondo ein: *Mia speranza, io pur vorrei &c.* das er von vorhergehenden Herbst in einer andern Oper zu Florenz von dem jetzigen unvergleichen Dohmcapellmeister Sarti, gesetzt bekommen hatte, nebst einer Minuett im dritten Acte: *Se piangi, e peni*, vom Capellmeister Bianchi aus Cremona componirt. In diesen Stücke erregte er einen ausserordentlichen Enthusiasmus, vorzüglich durch das Rondo; setzte aber doch auch nicht minder durch die Bravourarie in Erstaunen, die nach Misliwiceks Composition blieb.

Chapter 5, fn. 39

Der berühmte Misliwizech, ein Böhme, hätte in diesem Jahre beynahe ein ähnliches Schicksal gehabt, wenn man ihn nicht aus Achtung für den anwesenden Erzherzog Ferdinand verschont hätte. Dieser Mann hatte sich in Neapel durch neun verfertigte Opern Beyfall erworben, and erhielt den Auftrag die Music für ein hiesiges Operntheater zu componiren, weil man dem ihn beschützenden Herzog durch diese Wahl ein Vergnügen mehr zu machen hofte; allein es fiel schlecht aus, und ganz Rom war der Meynung, dass man nie ein elendere Music gehabt hätte.

Chapter 5, fn. 45

Rome 8. Aprile. Mercoledì sera apertosi il Teatro di Aliberti colla maggior magnificenza fu recitato l'Antigono con musica del tutto nuova del Signor Maestro Giuseppe Misliwecek, che ha avuto molto incontro, e specialmente l'Overtura, il Rondò di Santorini, un'Aria d'Ansani, e la scena di Berenice. I balli sono del Sig. Onorato Viganò, che pensa di rimettere in scena uno di quelli che fese nel passato Carnevale. A questo spettacolo intervennero le LL. AA. RR. tutta la nobiltà nazionale, con gran concorso di ogni ceto di persone. In tale occasione Monsignor Spinelli governatore di Roma fece servire di copiosi rinfreschi, dolci, ecc . . .

Chapter 5, fn. 57

Roma 10. Febbrajo. Doppo lunga, e penosa malattia Domenica scorsa 4. del corrente cesso di vivere il celebre Maestro di Capella Sig. Giuseppe Misliwecek detto il Boemo perchè nato in Praga. Questo eccellente Professore è stato quasi a tutte le Corti d'Europa, dove la sua abilità ha ricevuti i maggiori applausi, e si è conciliata l'amicizia dei più gran personaggi amanti della musica. Un suo scolare Gentiluomo Inglese ha voluto farli a sue spese i funerali, e questi sono eseguiti nella Chiesa di S. Lorenzo in Lucina dove ha avuto onorevole sepoltura.

Chapter 5, fn. 64

Rom, den 10. Hornung. Nach einer langen und schmerzhaften Krankheit, ist Sonntags, 4. dieses der berühmte Kapellmeister, Joseph Misliwecek, aus Prag in Böheim gebürtig, gestorben. Dieser vortrefflicher Meister in der Tonkunst was fast bey allen Höfen Europens, allwo er immer den bleb-hatesten Beyfall einerudtete, und sich die Hochachtung und Freundschaft der vornehmsten Liebhaber der Musik erwarb. Ein seiniger hiesiger Schüler, ein engländischer Edelmann, hat ihn auf seine Kosten in der Kirche bey San Lorenzo in Lucina sehr prächtig begraben lassen.

Chapter 5, fn. 74

Myslivecek, ein Böhme und sehr berühmter Komponist. Er hielt sich meistens in Italien auf und setzte daselbst grosse *Operen*, welche zu Florenz, Turin und Genua viel Beifall erhielten. Sein Gesang ist einfach und eindringend, seine Arien und Kavatinen sind reich an neuen Motiven, seine Rezitative gründlich und seine Chöre stark und himmelhebend. Er versteht die Kunst, die Instrumente so zu bearbeiten, dass sie dem Gesang keinen Eintrag tun—in einem hohen Grade. Auch seine *Kammerstücke* werden in allen europäischen orchestern als Meisterstücke gesucht und exekutiert. Dieser vortreffliche Künstler starb 1722 zu Florenz in achtunddreisigsten Jahre seines Alters. Da er sehr fleissig war, so besitzt die Welt von ihm einen reichen Vorrat von Geistesprodukten.

Select Bibliography

Ackerman, James A. "*Abramo ed Isacco* by Josef Mysliveček (1737–81): An Italian Oratorio for the Electoral Court at Munich (1777)." M.A. Thesis, West Chester University, 1996.

Balatka, Antonín. "Mozart a Mysliveček." *Divadelní listy* 8 (1932–33): 605–11.

Barblan, Guglielmo. *Mozart in Italia*. Milan: Ricordi, 1956.

Bellina, Anna Laura. "Appunti sul repertorio padovano (1738–1797)." In *Mozart, Padova e la Betulia liberata: Commitenza, interpretazione e fortuna delle azioni sacre metastasiani nel '700*, ed. Paolo Pinamonti, 173–90. Florence: Olschki, 1991.

Böhmer, Karl. *W. A. Mozart's Idomeneo und die Tradition der Karnevalsopern in München*. Mainzer Studien zur Musikwissenschaft, 39. Tutzing: Hans Schneider, 1999.

Boghen, Felice. "Mozarts *Isacco figura del redentore*: ein unbekanntes und noch nicht herausgegebenes Oratorium." *Die Musik* 20 (1928): 491–94.

Bohadlo, Stanislav. "Die deutsch-tschechischen Aspeckte, dargestellt an Josef Myslivečeks Biographie." In *Aktuelle lexikographische Fragen, Bericht: 1. Sudetendeutsch-Tschechisches Musiksymposium, 30. September–3. Oktober 1991, Regensburg*, ed. Peter Brömse, 80–85. Regensburg: Sudetendeutsch-Tschechisches Institut, 1994.

_______. "Josef Mysliveček, Called il Boemo, in the Light of New Sources." *Music News from Prague* 2/3 (1988): 4–6.

_______. "Josef Mysliveček v dopisech" (Josef Mysliveček in Letters). *Opus musicum* 19/1 (1987): 24–32; 19/3 (1987): 93–96, IX–XI; 19/4 (1987): 122–28, IX–XII; 19/5 (1987): 158–60, IX–XVI; 19/6 (1987): 178–92; 19/7 (1987): 223–24, IX–XVI; 19/8 (1987): 251–56, IX; 19/9 (1987): 281–88, IX–XI; 19/10 (1987), 312–20; 20/1 (1988): 26–38, XXIII–XXIX.

_______. *Josef Mysliveček v dopisech*. Brno: Opus musicum, [1989].

_______. "Mysliveček a Mozartové—nedokončené přátelství" (Mysliveček and the Mozarts—An Incomplete Friendship). *Hudební věda* 28 (1991): 305–08.

Burney, Charles. *A General History of Music*. 4 Vols. London, 1776–89.

_______. *The Present State of Music in France and Italy*. London, 1773; reprint, New York: Broude Bros., 1969.

_______. *The Present State of Music in Germany, The Netherlands and United Provinces*. 2 vols. London, 1773–75.

_______. *Tagebuch einer musikalischen Reise*. 3 vols. Hamburg, 1772–73; reprint, Kassel: Bärenreiter, 1959.

Cattelan, Paolo. "L' 'Accademia' nei dintorni del Santo (1768–1785)." In *Storia della musica al Santo di Padova*, ed. Sergio Durante and Pierluigi Petrobelli, 223–64. Vicenza: Neri Pozza, 1990.

_______. "La musica 'omnigena religio': Accademie musicali a padova nel secondo Settecento." *Acta musicologica* 59 (1987): 153–86.

Čeleda, Jaroslav. *Josef Mysliveček, tvůrce pražského nářečí hudebního rokoka tereziánského* (Josef Mysliveček, Founder of the Prague Dialect of Theresian Musical Rococo). Prague: J. Svoboda, 1946.

_______. "Il Boemo divino Venatorini." *Hudba a Škola* 4 (1931–32): 65–67, 96–97, 118–21, 151–54.

_______. "Houslové skladby Josefa Myslivečka" (The Violin Compositions of Josef Mysliveček). *Česká hudba* 36 (1932–33): 238–40.

Della Porta, Dario. *Josef Mysliveček: profilo biografico-critico.* Rome: Il Bagatto, 1981.

Dlabač, Jan Bohumír (Johann Gottfried Dlabacž). *Allgemeines historisches Künstler-Lexikon für Böhmen und zum Theil auch für Mähren und Schlesien.* 3 vols. Prague, 1815; reprint, Hildesheim and New York: Georg Olms, 1973.

Durante, Sergio, and Pierluigi Petrobelli, eds. *Storia della musica al Santo di Padova.* Vicenza: Neri Pozza, 1990.

Emingerová, Kateřina. "Český skladatel—příznivec Mozartův" (A Czech Composer—Well-Wisher of Mozart). *Zvon* 8 (1908): 598–99.

_______. "Klavírní skladby Jos. Myslivečka" (The Keyboard Compositions of Josef Mysliveček). *Česká hudba* 34 (1930–31): 102–04.

Evans, Angela, and Robert Dearling. *Josef Mysliveček (1737–1781): A Thematic Catalogue of His Instrumental and Orchestral Works.* Musikwissenschaftliche Schriften, 35. Munich: Katzbichler, 1999.

Feldman, Martha. "Mozart and His Elders: Opera-seria Arias, 1766–1775." In *Mozart-Jahrbuch 1991*, 564–75. Kassel: Bärenreiter, 1992.

Flothuis, Marius. "Ridente la calma—Mozart oder Mysliveček?" In *Mozart-Jahrbuch 1971/72*, 241–43. Salzburg: Internationale Stiftung Mozarteum, 1973.

Freeman, Daniel E. "Josef Mysliveček and the Piano Sonatas K. 309 (284b) and K. 311 (284c)." In *Mozart-Jahrbuch 1995*, 95–109. Salzburg: Internationale Stiftung Mozarteum, 1995.

_______. "Music for the Noble Amateur: Mozart's Scene and Aria 'Misera, dove son?/Ah, non son io che parlo,' K. 369." In *Mozart-Jahrbuch 2000*, 47–71. Kassel: Bärenreiter, 2002.

_______. *The Opera Theater of Count Franz Anton von Sporck in Prague.* Studies in Czech Music, 2. Stuyvesant, NY: Pendragon Press, 1992.

_______. "The Wind Music of Josef Mysliveček." In *Schloss Engers Colloquia zur Kammermusik, 2: Zur Harmoniemusik und ihrer Geschichte*, ed. Christoph-Hellmut Mahling, et al., 83–99. Mainz: Villa Musica, 1999.

Gambassi, Osvaldo. *L'Accademia Filarmonica di Bologna: Fondazione, statuti, e aggregazioni.* Historiae musicae cultores biblioteca, 63. Florence: Olschki, 1992.

Gersthofer, Wolfgang. *Mozarts frühe Sinfonien (bis 1772): Aspekte frühklassischen Sinfonik.* Salzburg: Internationale Stiftung Mozarteum, 1993.

_______. "Mozarts italienische Sinfonien und die italienischen Opernsinfonie der Zeit." *Mozart-Studien* 5 (1995): 183–211.

_______. "Orchestrale Satzbilder in Sinfonien des jungen Mozart und seiner Zeit." In *Mozart-Jahrbuch 1991*, 824–43. Kassel: Bärenreiter, 1992.

Griesinger, Georg August. *Biographische Notizen über Joseph Haydn.* Leipzig, 1810; reprint, Leipzig: VEB Deutscher Verlag für Musik, 1979.

Grossato, Elisa. "Le accademie musicali a Padova (1766–1790)." In *Mozart, Padova e la Betulia liberata: Committenza, interpretazione e fortuna delle azioni sacre metastasiane nel '700*, ed. Paolo Pinamonti, 191–207. Florence: Olschki, 1991.

Heyter-Rauland, Christine, and Christoph-Hellmut Mahling, eds. *Untersuchungen zu Muzikbeziehungen zwischen Mannheim, Böhmen und Mähren im späten 18. und frühen 19. Jahrhundert.* Beiträge zur Mittelrheinischen Musikgeschichte, 31. Mainz: Schott, 1993.

Hnilička, Alois. "Josef Mysliveček." *Zvon* 9 (1909): 260–63, 279–81, 291–95.

_______. *Portréty starých českých mistrů hudebních* (Portraits of the Early Masters of Czech Music). Prague: Fr. Borový, 1922.

Hudba v českých dějinách: od středověku do nové doby (Music in Czech History: From the Middle Ages to Modern Times). Ed. Jaromír Černý et al. 2nd ed. Prague: Supraphon, 1989.

Johnson, Joyce L. *Roman Oratorio, 1770–1800: The Repertory at Santa Maria Vallicella*. Ann Arbor: UMI Research Press, 1987.

Joss, Viktor. "Mysliweczek." *Der Auftakt* 7 (1927): 94–95.

Kamper, Otakar. *Hudební Praha v XVIII. věku* (Musical Prague in the Eighteenth Century). Prague: Melantrich, 1936.

Kneidl, Pravoslav. "Libreta italské opery v Praze v 18. století" (Librettos of Italian Operas in Prague in the Eighteenth Century). *Strahovská knihovna* 2 (1967): 115–88.

Komma, Karl Michael. *Das Böhmische Musikantentum*. Kassel: Johann Philipp Hinnenthal-Verlag, 1960.

Kratochvílová, Jaromíra. *Josef Mysliveček: vyběrová bibliografie* (Select Bibliography). Brno: Státní Vedecká Knihovna, 1978.

Krones, Hartmut. "Musikalische Symbolsphären in der *Zauberflöte*." In *W. A. Mozart in Wien und Prag: Die grossen Opern*, 206–21. Wege zu Mozart, 2. Vienna: Hölder-Pichler-Tempsky, 1993.

Landon, H. C. Robbins. *Haydn: Chronicle and Works*, 1: *The Early Years, 1732–1765*. Bloomington and London: Indiana University Press, 1980.

_______. *Haydn: Chronicle and Works*, 2: *Haydn at Eszterháza, 1766–1790*. Bloomington and London: Indiana University Press, 1978.

Mahling, Christoph-Hellmut. "Mysliveček und Grétry—Vorbilder Mozarts?" In *Die frühdeutsche Oper und ihre Beziehungen zu Italien, England und Frankreich: Mozart und die Oper seiner Zeit*, ed. Martin Ruhnke, 203–09. Hamburger Jahrbuch für Musikwissenschaft, 5. Laaber: Laaber-Verlag, 1981.

Maione, Paologiovanni, and Francesco Seller. "Mutamenti della drammaturgia metastasiana a Napoli nella seconda metà del Settecento: il caso *Artaserse*. Problemi formali e strutturali." *Musica/Realtà* 19 (1998): 57–89.

Massaro, Maria Nevilla. "La capella musicale del Santo della seconda metà del Settecento: Musicisti e repertorio." In *Mozart, Padova e la Betulia liberata: Committenza, interpretazione e fortuna delle azioni sacre metastasiane nel '700*, ed. Paolo Pinamonti, 209–26. Florence: Olschki, 1991.

Mikanová, Eva. "Neznamá mozartská bohemika" (Unknown Bohemian Mozartiana). *Hudební rozhledy* 41 (1988): 181–85.

Morelli, Giovanni, and Elvidio Suran. "Contagi d'Erminia." In *Tasso, la musica, i musicisti*, ed. Maria Antonella Balsano and Thomas Walker, 165–205. Florence: Olschki, 1988.

Moritz-Bauer, Christian. "Die Bläseroktette von Josef Mysliveček (1737–1781)." M.A. Thesis, University of Heidelberg, 2001.

Münster, Robert. "'Die hiesige ongenierte Lebensarth gefallet allen . . .': Nachrichten zum Münchner Musikleben der Jahre 1772 bis 1779 aus den Briefen Joseph Franz von Seinsheims an seinem Bruder Adam Friedrich von Seinsheim." In *Mozarts Idomeneo und die Musik in München zur Zeit Karl Theodors*, ed. Theodor Göllner and Stephan Hörner, 237–51. Munich: Bayerische Akademie der Wissenschaften, 2001.

_______. "'Ich bin hier sehr beliebt': eine Chronik von Mozarts Münchener Aufenthalt 1777." *Acta Mozartiana* 24 (1978): 3–18.

Nascimbene, Anelide. "L'avventura italiana del boemo amico di Mozart." In *Viaggio in Italia*, ed. C De Incontrera, 235–54. Trieste: Stella Arti, 1989.

_______. "'Il Demetrio' di Josef Mysliveček." In *Gli affetti convenienti all'idee: Studi sulla musica vocale italiana*, ed. Maria Caraci Vela, et al., 103–39. Archivio del teatro e dello spettacolo, 3. Naples: Edizioni Scientifiche Italiane, 1993.

_______. "Le due versioni di 'Il Demetrio' di Josef Mysliveček: Drammaturgia e prassi musicale." Thesis, University of Pavia, 1987.

_______. "Mysliveček e i Mozart a Bologna: documenti, cronaca e critica." In *Mozart: gli orientamenti della critica moderna*, ed. Giacomo Fornari. Lucca: Libreria Musicale Italiana, 1994.

Němeček, Jan. *Nástin české hudby XVIII. století* (Outline of Czech Music of the Eighteenth Century). Prague: Státní nakladatelství krásné literatury, hudby a umění, 1955.

Nettl, Paul. "Mozart and the Czechs." *The Musical Quarterly* 27 (1941): 329–42.

_______. *Mozart in Böhmen*. Prague: Karlin, Neumann, 1938.

_______. "Mozart und Mysliveček." *Prager Rundschau* 7 (1937): 114–24.

Newman, William S. *The Sonata in the Classic Era*. 3rd ed. New York: W. W. Norton, 1983.

Nosek, Václav. "Tamerlan, opéra de Mysliveček (Remarques sur la réalisation scénique)." Trans. Alena Krutová. In *Musica antiqua: Colloquium Brno 1967*, ed. Rudolf Pečman, 183–87. Brno: Mezinárodní Hudební Festival, 1968.

Pala, František. "Mozartův 'Idomeneo.'" *Národní Divadlo* 9 (1931–32): 3–5.

Pasquatti, Guido. *L'oratorio musicale in Italia*. Florence: Successori Le Monnier, 19—.

Pečman, Rudolf. "De Gamerrovo libreto k poslední opeře Josefa Myslivečka" (The De Gamerra Libretto for the Last Opera of Josef Mysliveček). *Sborník práce Filosofické Faculty Brněnské University* 14/F9 (1965): 183–94.

_______. "Händel a Mysliveček." *Opus Musicum* 10/3 (1978): 67–70.

_______. "Johann Christian Bach a Joseph Mysliveček." *Hudební věda* 31/4 (1994): 393–98.

_______. *Josef Mysliveček*. Hudební profily, 24. Prague: Supraphon, 1981.

_______. Josef Mysliveček als Reformator der Neapolitanischen Oper seria." In *Der Einfluss der italienischen Musik in der ersten Hälfte des 18. Jahrhunderts*, ed. Eitelfriedrich Thom and Frieder Zschoch, 18–22. Michaelstein/Blankenburg: Kultur- und Forschungsstätte Michaelstein, 1988.

_______. *Josef Mysliveček und sein Opernepilog*. Brno: Universita J. E. Purkyně, 1970. [includes extensive bibliography of minor literature, including fiction about Mysliveček]

_______. "K Myslivečkov opeře Medon, král epirský" (On Mysliveček's Opera Medonte, king of Epirus). *Sborník práce filosofické fakulty brněnské University* F6 (1962): 141–43.

_______. "Die Klarinette in der Neapolitanischen Schule und bei Josef Mysliveček." In *Die Blaseninstrumente und ihre Verwendung sowie zu Fragen des Tempos in der ersten Hälfte des 18. Jahrhunderts: Konferenzbericht der 4. Wissenschaftlichen Arbeitstagung, Blankenburg/Harz 26./27. Juni 1976*, ed. Eitelfriedrich Thom and Renate Bormann, 42–45. Blankenburg/Harz: Kultur- und Forschungsstätte Michaelstein, 1977.

_______. "Die Mannheimer Schule und Josef Mysliveček." In *Untersuchungen zu Muzikbeziehungen zwischen Mannheim, Böhmen und Mähren im späten 18. und frühen 19. Jahrhundert*, ed. Christine Heyter-Rauland and Christoph-Hellmut Mahling, 75–83. Mainz: Schott, 1993.

_______. "Neznámá Myslivečkova opera" (An Unknown Mysliveček Opera). *Hudební rozhledy* 14/9 (1961): 391–92.

_______. "Il Parnaso confuso—první Myslivečkova opera" (Il Parnaso confuso—The First Mysliveček Opera). *Opus musicum* 7 (1975): 136–43.

_______. "Pietro Metastasio jako libretista Myslivečkových oper" (Pietro Metastasio as Librettist of Mysliveček's Operas). In *Otázky divadla a filmu: theatralia et cinematographica*, 2, ed. A. Závodský, 82–100. Brno: Universita J. E. Purkyně, 1971.

_______. "Rakušan Mysliveček?" (Mysliveček the Austrian?). *Hudební věda* 35 (1998): 68–71.

_______. "Zum oratorischen Schaffen Joseph Haydn und Josef Myslivečeks." In *Joseph Haydn: Bericht über den Internationalen Joseph Haydn Kongress*, ed. Eva Badura-Skoda, 101–04. Munich: Henle, 1986.

_______. "Zur Leningrader Handschrift der letzten Oper Josef Myslivečeks." *Sborník práci Filosofické Fakulty Brněnské University* H1 (1966): 121–34.

Pelcl, František Martin. "Joseph Misliweczek: ein Tonkunstler." In *Abbildungen böhmischer und mährischer Gelehrter und Künstler*, 4, 189–92. Prague, 1782.

Pfannhauser, Karl. "Mozart hat kopiert." *Acta Mozartiana* 3 (1954): 38–41.

Pilková, Zdeňka. "Houslové sonáty českych skladatelo z let 1730–1810" (Violin Sonatas by Czech Composers from the Years 1730–1810). *Hudební věda* 23 (1986): 291–311.

Pinamonti, Paolo, ed. *Mozart, Padova e la Betulia liberata: Committenza, interpretazione e fortuna delle azioni sacre metastasiani nel '700*. Florence: Olschki, 1991.

Pincherle, Marc. "Un oublié: Il divino Boemo." In *Feuillets d'histoire du violon*, 103–09. Paris: Leguoix, 1927.

Pražák, Richard. "K působení českých hudebních a divadelních umělců v Uhrách na přelomu 18. a 19. století" (On the Activity of Czech Musical and Theatrical Artists in Hungary at the Turn of the Nineteenth Century). In *Otázky dějin střední a východní Evropy*, 75–94. Brno: Univerzita J. E. Purkyně, 1975.

Prota-Giurleo, Ulisse. "L'Abate Galiani messo in imbarazzo da un musicista Boemo." *Nostro tempo* (December 1957): 1–5.

Racek, Jan. "Beitrag zur Frage des 'Mozartschen' Stils in der tschechischen vorklassischen Musik." In *Internationale Konferenz über das Leben und Werk W. A. Mozarts*, ed. Pavel Eckstein, 34–43. Prague: Verband Tschechoslowakischer Komponisten, 1958.

_______. *Česká hudba: od nejstarších dob do počátku 19. století* (Czech Music: From the Earliest Times until the Beginning of the Nineteenth Century). Prague: Státní nakladatelství krásné literatury, hudby a umění, Prague, 1958.

_______. "Příspěvek k otázce 'mozartského' stylu v české hudbě předklasické" (A Contribution to the Question of "Mozartean" Style in Czech Pre-Classic Music). *Musikologie* 5 (1958): 71–101.

Rhodes, David J. "The Origins and Utilisation of Divided Viola Writing in the Symphony at Mannheim and Various Other European Centres in the Second Half of the 18th Century." In *Mannheim – Ein Paradies der Tonkünstler?: Kongressbericht Mannheim 1999*, ed. Ludwig Finscher, et al., 67–170. Quellen und Studien zur Geshichte der Mannheimer Hofkapelle, 8. Frankfurt-am-Main: Peter Lang, 2002.

Ross, Mark Alan. "A Comparative Study of String Quartets and Quintets of Four Classical Viennese Composers: Dittersdorf, Mysliveček, Haydn, and Mozart." M.Mus. Thesis, University of Cincinnati, 1974.

Saint-Foix, Georges de. "Un ami de Mozart: Joseph Mysliweczek." *Revue Musicale* 9/5 (March 1928): 124–28.

_______. "Mozart, d'après Mysliweczek." *Musique* 2 (1929): 840–43.

Schering, Arnold. *Geschichte des Oratoriums*. Leipzig: Breitkopf & Härtel, 1911.

Scholes, Percy, ed. *Dr. Burney's Musical Tours*. London: Oxford University Press, 1959.

Schubart, Christian David. *Ideen zu einer Ästhetik der Tonkunst*. Vienna, 1806/reprint, Hildesheim: Georg Olms, 1969; modern ed., ed. Jürgen Maika, Leipzig: Verlag Philipp Reclam, 1977.

Schuler, Manfred. "*Theodorich und Elisa*: ein bislang unbekanntes Melodrama von Mysliveček." In *Untersuchungen zu Muzikbeziehungen zwischen Mannheim, Böhmen und Mähren im späten 18. und frühen 19. Jahrhundert*, ed. Christine Heyter-Rauland and Christoph Hellmut Mahling, 233–43. Mainz: Schott, 1993.

Shaginian, Marietta. *Voskreshenie iz mertvykh: povest' ob odnom issledovanin* (Resurrection from the Dead: The Story of an Investigation). Moscow: Khudozhestvennaya literatura, 1964.

_______ (Šagiňanová, Marietta). *Zapomenutá historie* (Forgotten History). Trans. Anna Nováková. Prague: Mladá Fronta, 1965.

Schwartz, Boris. "Geiger um Mozart." In *Mozart-Jahrbuch 1978/79*, 228–35. Salzburg: Internationale Stiftung Mozarteum, 1979.

_______. Violinists around Mozart." In *Music in the Classic Period: Essays in Honor of Barry S. Brook*, ed. Allan W. Atlas, 233–40. Festschrift series, 5. New York: Pendragon Press, 1985.

Slavický, Tomáš. "Die Arien aus der Oper *Il Bellerofonte* von Josef Mysliveček in böhmischen Chören." In *Musicologicum I: Hudobné žánre evropskej hudibnej kultúry v minulosti a súčastnosti*, 9–13. Bratislava: Universitas Comeniana Institutum Artis Musicae, 1995.

Srb-Debrnov, Josef. *Dějiny hudby v Čechách a na Moravě* (The History of Music in Bohemia and Moravia). Prague, 1891.

Stolařík, Ivo. *Leningradský rukopis opery Josefa Myslivečka "Nitteti"* (The Leningrad Manuscript of Josef Mysliveček's Opera *Nitteti*). Opava: Slezský Ústav ČSAV, 1963.

Stolz, Richard. "Genie und Geschick Josef Mysliweczeks, genannt Giuseppe Venatorini." *Der Auftakt* 17 (1937): 136–40.

Sýkora, Josef. "Nález dopisu Josefa Myslivečka" (The Discovery of a Letter of Josef Mysliveček). *Bertramka* 3 (1951): 7–8.

Tagliavini, Luigi Ferdinando. "Quirino Gasparini and Mozart." In *New Looks at Italian Opera: Essays in Honor of Donald J. Grout*, ed. William W Austin, 151–71. Ithaca: Cornell University Press, 1968.

Thom, Eitelfriedrich, ed. *Die Entwicklung des Solokonzertes im 18. Jahrhunderts*. Studien zur Aufführungspraxis und Interpretation von Instrumentalmusik des 18. Jahrhunderts, 20. Blankenburg: Die Kultur- und Forschungsstätte, 1983.

Tufano, Lucio. "Josef Mysliveček e l'esecuzione dell'*Orfeo* di Gluck (1774)." *Hudební věda* 43 (2006): 257–79.

Vysloužil, Jiří. "Das Musikland Böhmens im Zeitalter der Klassik." In *Untersuchungen zu Muzikbeziehungen zwischen Mannheim, Böhmen und Mähren im späten 18. und frühen 19. Jahrhundert*, ed. Christine Heyter-Rauland and Christoph-Hellmut Mahling, 11–21. Mainz: Schott, 1993.

Webster, James. "Violoncello and Double Bass Parts in the Chamber Music of Haydn and His Viennese Contemporaries." *Journal of the American Musicological Society* 29 (1976): 413–38.

White, Chappell. *From Vivaldi to Viotti: A History of the Early Classical Violin Concerto*. Philadelphia: Gordon and Breach, 1992.

Wignall, Harrison James. "Mozart and the 'Duetto Notturno' Tradition." In *Mozart Jahrbuch 1993*, 145–61. Salzburg: Internationale Stiftung Mozarteum, 1993.

_______. "Mozart and the First 'Mitridate,' Guglielmo d'Ettore." Ph.D. diss., Brandeis University, 1995.

Winkelmann, Hans. "Joseph Mysliweczek als Opernkomponist." Ph.D. diss., University of Vienna, 1905.

Zampieri, Giusto. "Una sinfonia del Venatorini." *Bollettino storico pavese* 2 (1939): 59–107.

Zdrálek, Vít. "Kantata *Alceste e Fileno*: Nejstarší známé dílo Josefa Myslivečka?" (The Cantata *Alceste e Fileno*: The Earliest Known Composition of Josef Mysliveček?). *Hudební věda* 42 (2005): 137–52.

Index

About the Author

Daniel E. Freeman gives lectures on music at the University of Minnesota and at the Smithsonian Institution in Washington, D.C., where he is a regular Resident Associate. He formerly taught music history at the University of Illinois at Urbana-Champaign and at the University of Southern California. A specialist in the eighteenth century, his published research includes studies on music in Bohemia in that century, eighteenth-century keyboard music, baroque opera, and the composers Antonio Vivaldi, J. S. Bach, and W. A. Mozart, as well as the music of the Renaissance composer Josquin des Prez. His book, *The Opera Theater of Count Franz Anton von Sporck in Prague* (Pendragon Press, 1992), was the first monograph devoted to eighteenth-century musical culture in the Czech lands to have been written originally in English. Dr. Freeman holds the Ph.D. degree from the University of Illinois at Urbana-Champaign.